Lecture Notes in Computer Science   12859

More information about this subseries at http://www.springer.com/series/7409

Leong Hou U · Marc Spaniol ·
Yasushi Sakurai · Junying Chen (Eds.)

Web and Big Data

5th International Joint Conference, APWeb-WAIM 2021
Guangzhou, China, August 23–25, 2021
Proceedings, Part II

 Springer

Editors
Leong Hou U (ID)
University of Macau
Macau, China

Yasushi Sakurai
Osaka University
Osaka, Japan

Marc Spaniol (ID)
University of Caen Normandie
Caen, France

Junying Chen (ID)
South China University of Technology
Guangzhou, China

ISSN 0302-9743   ISSN 1611-3349   (electronic)
Lecture Notes in Computer Science
ISBN 978-3-030-85898-8   ISBN 978-3-030-85899-5   (eBook)
https://doi.org/10.1007/978-3-030-85899-5

LNCS Sublibrary: SL3 – Information Systems and Applications, incl. Internet/Web, and HCI

This Springer imprint is published by the registered company Springer Nature Switzerland AG
The registered company address is: Gewerbestrasse 11, 6330 Cham, Switzerland

Preface

This volume (LNCS 12858) and its companion volume (LNCS 12859) contain the proceedings of the fifth Asia-Pacific Web (APWeb) and Web-Age Information Management (WAIM) Joint Conference on Web and Big Data, called APWeb-WAIM. With the increased focus on big data, the new joint conference is expected to attract more professionals from different industrial and academic communities, not only from the Asia-Pacific countries but also from other continents. The objective is to enable the sharing and exchange of ideas, experiences, and results in the areas of the World Wide Web and big data, thus covering web technologies, database systems, information management, software engineering, and big data.

The fifth APWeb-WAIM conference was held in Guangzhou during August 23–25, 2021. As an Asia-Pacific flagship conference focusing on research, development, and applications in relation to Web information management, APWeb-WAIM builds on the successes of APWeb and WAIM: APWeb was previously held in Beijing (1998), Hong Kong (1999), Xi'an (2000), Changsha (2001), Xi'an (2003), Hangzhou (2004), Shanghai (2005), Harbin (2006), Huangshan (2007), Shenyang (2008), Suzhou (2009), Busan (2010), Beijing (2011), Kunming (2012), Sydney (2013), Changsha (2014), Guangzhou (2015), and Suzhou (2016); and WAIM was held in Shanghai (2000), Xi'an (2001), Beijing (2002), Chengdu (2003), Dalian (2004), Hangzhou (2005), Hong Kong (2006), Huangshan (2007), Zhangjiajie (2008), Suzhou (2009), Jiuzhaigou (2010), Wuhan (2011), Harbin (2012), Beidaihe (2013), Macau (2014), Qingdao (2015), and Nanchang (2016). The APWeb-WAIM conferences were held in Beijing (2017), Macau (2018), Chengdu (2019), and Tianjin (2020). With the fast development of web-related technologies, we expect that APWeb-WAIM will become an increasingly popular forum that brings together outstanding researchers and developers in the fields of the Web and big data from around the world.

The high-quality program documented in these proceedings would not have been possible without the authors who chose APWeb-WAIM for disseminating their findings. A total of 184 submissions were received and, after the double-blind review process (each paper received at least three review reports), the conference accepted 44 regular papers (23.91%), 24 short research papers, and 6 demonstrations. The contributed papers address a wide range of topics, such as graph mining, data mining, data management, topic model and language model learning, text analysis, text classification, machine learning, knowledge graphs, emerging data processing techniques, information extraction and retrieval, recommender systems, and spatial and spatio-temporal databases. The technical program also included keynotes by M. Tamer Özsu (University of Waterloo, USA), Huan Liu (Arizona State University, Tempe, USA), X. Sean Wang (Fudan University, China), and Xiaokui Xiao (National University of Singapore, Singapore). We are grateful to these distinguished scientists for their invaluable contributions to the conference program. As a joint conference, teamwork is particularly important for the success of APWeb-WAIM. We are deeply thankful to the Program Committee members and the external reviewers for lending their time and expertise to the conference. Special thanks go to the local Organizing Committee led by Yi Cai. Thanks also go to the workshop chairs (Yunjun Gao, An Liu, and Xiaohui Tao), demo chair (Yanghui Rao), industry chair (Jianming Lv), tutorial chair (Raymond Chi-Wing Wong), publication chair (Junying Chen), local arrangement chairs (Guohua Wang and Junying Chen), and publicity chairs (Xin Wang and Jianxin Li). Their efforts were essential to the success of the conference. Last but not least, we wish to express our gratitude to the Webmaster (Jianwei Lu), for all the hard work, and to our sponsors who generously supported the smooth running of the conference.

We hope you enjoy the exciting program of APWeb-WAIM 2021 as documented in these proceedings.

July 2021

Yi Cai
Tom Gedeon
Qing Li
Baltasar Fernández Manjón
Leong Hou U
Marc Spaniol
Yasushi Sakurai

Organization

Organizing Committee

General Chairs

Yi Cai	South China University of Technology, China
Tom Gedeon	Australia National University, Australia
Qing Li	Hong Kong Polytechnic University, China
Baltasar Fernández Manjón	UCM, Spain

Program Committee Chairs

Leong Hou U	University of Macau, China
Marc Spaniol	Université de Caen Normandie, France
Yasushi Sakurai	Osaka University, Japan

Workshop Chairs

Yunjun Gao	Zhejiang University, China
An Liu	Soochow University, China
Xiaohui Tao	University of Southern Queensland, Australia

Demo Chair

Yanghui Rao	Sun Yat-sen University, China

Tutorial Chair

Raymond Chi-Wing Wong	Hong Kong University of Science and Technology, China

Industry Chair

Jianming Lv	South China University of Technology, China

Publication Chair

Junying Chen	South China University of Technology, China

Publicity Chairs

Xin Wang   Tianjin University, China
Jianxin Li   Deakin University, Australia

Local Arrangement Chairs

Guohua Wang   South China University of Technology, China
Junying Chen   South China University of Technology, China

Webmaster

Jianwei Lu   South China University of Technology, China

APWeb-WAIM Steering Committee Representative

Yanchun Zhang   Victoria University, Australia

Senior Program Committee Members

Feida Zhu   Singapore Management University, Singapore
Lei Chen   Hong Kong University of Science and Technology,
                        China
Mizuho Iwaihara   Waseda University, Japan
Peer Kroger   Christian-Albrechst-University Kiel, Germany
Reynold Cheng   The University of Hong Kong, China
Wolf-Tilo Balke   TU Braunschweig, Germany
Xiang Zhao   National University of Defence Technology, China
Yunjun Gao   Zhejiang University, China
Zhiguo Gong   University of Macau, China

Program Committee Members

Alex Delis   University of Athens, Greece
An Liu   Soochow University, China
Aviv Segev   KAIST, Korea
Baoning Niu   Taiyuan University of Technology, China
Bin Cui   Peking University, China
Bo Tang   Southern University of Science and Technology, China
Bohan Li   Nanjing University of Aeronautics and Astronautics,
                        China
Bolong Zheng   Huazhong University of Science and Technology,
                        China
Carson K. Leung   University of Manitoba, Canada
Cheqing Jin   East China Normal University, China
Chih-Hua Tai   National Taipei University, China

Defu Lian	University of Electronic Science and Technology of China, China
Dhaval Patel	IBM TJ Watson Research Center, USA
Dimitris Sacharidis	ULB, Belgium
Giovanna Guerrini	University of Genoa, Italy
Guoqiong Liao	Jiangxi University of Finance and Economics, China
Haibo Hu	Hong Kong Polytechnic University, China
Hailong Sun	Beihang University, China
Haiwei Zhang	Nankai University, China
Han Su	University of Southern California, USA
Hao Wang	Nanjing University of Information Science and Technology, China
Hiroaki Ohshima	University of Hyogo, Japan
Hongzhi Wang	Harbin Institute of Technology, China
Hua Wang	Victoria University, Australia
Hui Li	Xiamen University, China
Hui Luo	RMIT University, Australia
Ilaria Bartolini	University of Bologna, Italy
Jian Yin	Sun Yat-sen University, China
Jianbin Huang	Xidian University, China
Jianbin Huang	XDU, China
Jianming Lv	South China University of Technology, China
Jianxin Li	Beihang University, China
Jianzhong Qi	The University of Melbourne, Australia
Jieming Shi	The Hong Kong Polytechnic University, China
Ju Fan	Renmin University of China, China
Jun Gao	Peking University, China
Junhu Wang	Griffith University, Australia
Junjie Yao	East China Normal University, China
Junying Chen	South China University of Technology, China
Kai Yang	City University of Hong Kong, China
Kai Zeng	Microsoft, USA
Kai Zheng	University of Electronic Science and Technology of China, China
Krishna Reddy P.	International Institute of Information Technology, India
Kyuseok Shim	Seoul National University, Korea
Lei Duan	Sichuan University, China
Leong Hou U	University of Macau, China
Liang Hong	Wuhan University, China
Lianghuai Yang	Zhejiang University of Technology, China
Lu Chen	Zhejiang University, China
Man Lung Yiu	Hong Kong Polytechnic University, China
Maria Luisa Damiani	University of Milan, Italy
Markus Endres	University of Augsburg, Germany
Meng Wang	Southeast University, China
Mirco Nanni	ISTI-CNR, Italy

Panagiotis Karras	Aarhus University, Denmark
Peiquan Jin	University of Science and Technology of China, China
Peng Wang	Fudan University, China
Qingbao Huang	Guangxi University, China
Raymond Chi-Wing Wong	Hong Kong University of Science and Technology, China
Rong-Hua Li	Beijing Institute of Technology, China
Sanghyun Park	Yonsei University, Korea
Sangkeun Lee	Oak Ridge National Laboratory, USA
Sanjay Kumar Madria	Missouri University of Science and Technology, USA
Senzhang Wang	Central South University, China
Shaoxu Song	Tsinghua University, China
Sheng Wang	New York University, USA
Shengli Wu	Jiangsu University, China
Shuyue Hu	NUS, Singapore
Taketoshi Ushiama	Kyushu University, Japan
Tao Wang	King's College London, UK
Tieyun Qian	Wuhan University, China
Ting Deng	Beihang University, China
Tingjian Ge	University of Massachusetts, Lowell, USA
Vincent Oria	NJIT, USA
Wee Siong Ng	Institute for Infocomm Research, Singapore
Wei Lu	Renmin University of China, China
Wei Song	Wuhan University, China
Wei Wang	University of New South Wales, Australia
Wen Zhang	Wuhan University, China
Xiang Lian	Kent State University, USA
Xiangmin Zhou	RMIT University, Australia
Xiaochun Yang	Northeastern University, USA
Xiaohui Tao	The University of Southern Queensland, Australia
Xiaokui Xiao	National University of Singapore, Singapore
Xiaowei Wu	University of Macau, China
Xike Xie	University of Science and Technology of China, China
Xin Cao	University of New South Wales, Australia
Xin Huang	Hong Kong Baptist University, China
Xin Wang	Tianjin University, China
Xingquan Zhu	Florida Atlantic University, USA
Xudong Mao	Xiamen University, China
Yafei Li	Zhengzhou University, China
Yajun Yang	Tianjin University, China
Yanghua Xiao	Fudan University, China
Yanghui Rao	Sun Yat-sen University, China
Yang-Sae Moon	Kangwon National University, South Korea
Yaokai Feng	Kyushu University, Japan
Yijie Wang	National University of Defense Technology, China
Yingxia Shao	BUPT, China

Yongpan Sheng	Chongqing University, China
Yongxin Tong	Beihang University, China
Yu Gu	Northeastern University, USA
Zakaria Maamar	Zayed University, United Arab of Emirates
Zhaonian Zou	Harbin Institute of Technology, China
Zhixu Li	Soochow University, China
Zouhaier Brahmia	University of Sfax, Tunisia

Contents – Part II

Emerging Data Processing Techniques

Information Extraction and Retrieval

Recommender System

Spatial and Spatio-Temporal Databases

Demo

Contents – Part I

Data Management

Topic Model and Language Model Learning

Text Analysis

Text Classification

Machine Learning 1

Machine Learning 2

Unsupervised Deep Hashing via Adaptive Clustering

Shuying Yu[1], Xian-Ling Mao[1(✉)], Wei Wei[2], and Heyan Huang[1]

[1] Beijing Institute of Technology, Beijing 100081, China
{syyu,maoxl,hhy63}@bit.edu.cn
[2] Huazhong University of Science and Technology, Wuhan 430073, China
weiw@hust.edu.cn

Abstract. Similarity-preserved hashing has become a popular technique for large-scale image retrieval because of its low storage cost and high search efficiency. Unsupervised hashing has high practical value because it learns hash functions without any annotated label. Previous unsupervised hashing methods usually obtain the semantic similarities between data points by taking use of deep features extracted from pre-trained CNN networks. The semantic structure learned from fixed embeddings are often not the optimal, leading to sub-optimal retrieval performance. To tackle the problem, in this paper, we propose a Deep Clustering based Unsupervised Hashing architecture, called DCUH. The proposed model can simultaneously learn the intrinsic semantic relationships and hash codes. Specifically, DCUH first clusters the deep features to generate the pseudo classification labels. Then, DCUH is trained by both the classification loss and the discriminative loss. Concretely, the pseudo class label is used as the supervision for classification. The learned hash code should be invariant under different data augmentations with the local semantic structure preserved. Finally, DCUH is designed to update the cluster assignments and train the deep hashing network iteratively. Extensive experiments demonstrate that the proposed model outperforms the state-of-the-art unsupervised hashing methods.

Keywords: Deep hashing · Unsupervised learning · Image retrieval

1 Introduction

With the rapid growth of visual data, how to index and retrieve them efficiently has attracted increasing attention. Exact nearest neighbor search has large time complexity when dealing with large-scale datasets. In contrast, approximate nearest neighbor (ANN) search technique can save much time, at the same time promising good search performance. Tree-based methods such as KD-tree [1] and R-tree [9] utilize the tree-structured index to speed up the search procedure. However, tree-based algorithms suffer from the curse of dimensionality in high dimensional feature space. Therefore, researchers focus more on similarity-preserved hashing algorithms in recent years. Generally, hashing maps the high

© Springer Nature Switzerland AG 2021
L. H. U et al. (Eds.): APWeb-WAIM 2021, LNCS 12859, pp. 3–17, 2021.
https://doi.org/10.1007/978-3-030-85899-5_1

dimensional features into low binary codes while preserving the relative similarities with high probabilities.

Hashing can be categorized into data-independent and data-dependent algorithms. Locality sensitive hashing (LSH) [4,7,13] is a typical data-independent method. The main idea of LSH is to increase the hashing collision probability of adjacent data points while mapping the dissimilar data points into different hashing buckets. Depart from data-independent methods, data-dependent hashing algorithms try to learn hash codes from data. Such data-dependent hashing algorithms can be further divided into supervised and unsupervised methods according to whether they use the annotated semantic labels. Existing supervised hashing methods [25,28,29,39] usually construct the semantic similarity supervision from human-annotated labels to guide the training procedure of hashing functions. With the development of deep learning, many deep learning based supervised hashing methods [2,16–18,22,35] have been proposed. Those methods have significantly improved the search performance compared to traditional models.

On the contrary, unsupervised hashing methods [8,10,24,26,33] usually train the hash model without any supervised information. The key challenge of unsupervised hashing methods is the lack of semantic labels. In real application, it is hard to obtain such expensive labels, especially for large-scale datasets. Though many previous works try to utilize the deep network to capture high-level semantic structure, we found that existing unsupervised deep hashing methods usually decouple the latent semantic relationship constructing and hash code learning into individual procedure. For example, [6,12,30,36] first analyze the semantic similarity through various ways, such as unsupervised clustering, constructing nearest neighbor graph and word embedding, and then they optimize the hash codes individually. Intuitively, the hash code learning procedure should be helpful to the semantic structure learning task because their targets are uniform. One supposed to make the similar points closer and one supposed to discriminate similar and dissimilar points. Therefore, we propose a novel unsupervised deep hashing model called DCUH in this paper. Our architecture alternates between two stages: clustering and deep hash model learning. With learning more distinctive hash codes, the network will generate more distinctive deep features. The optimized features used for clustering can help produce more accurate class labels. The more accurate pseudo class labels guide to learn more distinctive hash codes. The contributions of this paper can be summarized as follows:

- We propose a novel unsupervised hashing framework to jointly learn hash codes and perform clustering. Compared to the existing methods who fix the feature representation, our model can produce more accurate pseudo labels to guide the learning of hash codes and generate more discriminative features for clustering.
- We unveil and utilize the intrinsic semantic structure sufficiently. The hash codes of the referenced image and its transformed counterpart are supposed to be closer than arbitrary images. Meanwhile, to preserve the local aggregation structure, image pairs from the same cluster are supposed to be closer than those from different clusters.

– Extensive experiments on three public benchmark datasets prove that our
  model can achieve the best performance against the state-of-the-art baselines.

2 Related Work

2.1 Similarity-Preserving Hashing

Similarity-preserving hashing methods map data from high dimensional feature
space into Hamming space with the similarity preserved. Existing learning to
hash methods can be divided into supervised and unsupervised ways according
to whether they use the semantic labels.

Unsupervised hashing methods try to learn hash functions from unlabeled
training data. Spectral Hashing (SH) [33] is a classical traditional unsupervised
hashing algorithm, it preserves the similarity of original features by using the
Laplacian Eigenmaps. Anchor Graph Hashing (AGH) [26] and Discrete Graph
Hashing (DGH) [24] use anchor graph instead of the Laplacian matrix to improve
the computational efficiency and deal with larger scale data. K-means Hashing
(KMH) [10] combines hash codes learning with the k-means clustering algorithm.
Iterative Quantization (ITQ) [8] produces the low-dimensional features via principal component analysis (PCA) and then iteratively find a rotation matrix to
map the data to binary codes with minimum quantization error. Supervised
methods aim to learn discriminative and compact hash codes by exploring the
supervised information. Minimal Loss Hashing (MLH) [28] learns hash functions
by minimizing the triplet loss modified from the hinge loss in SVM. Latent
Factor Hashing (LFH) [39], Supervised Hashing with Kernels (KSH) [25] and
Supervised Discrete Hashing (SDH) [29] learn discrete binary hash codes by
minimizing or maximizing the Hamming distances across similar or dissimilar
pairs.

Recently, deep learning based hashing methods have shown remarkable performance in retrieval task. CNNH [35] is the first CNN based hashing algorithm,
it includes two separate stages: generating approximate hash codes by preserving
the pairwise similarities and then simultaneously learning the feature representation for images as well as the hash functions by predicting the learned hash
codes and discrete class labels. HashNet [2] is an end-to-end framework who
learns binary hash codes from imbalanced data pairs by continuation method.
However, those supervised deep hashing methods depend on human-annotated
semantic labels to train the network. Such labels are expensive to obtain, especially for large scale dataset. Unsupervised deep hashing methods adopt the
deep architectures to learn hash codes without annotations. Deep Hashing (DH)
[23] develop a multi-layer hierarchical non-linear transformations to map hash
codes. UH-BDNN [5] also build a deep network to encode binary codes and add
the decode layers to reconstruct the input samples. DeepBit [20] suppose the
hash code to be invariant with different rotations. The authors further apply
more geometry transformations including translation and scaling in paper [21].
To make the binary descriptors more distinctive, they also increase the distance
between the descriptors computed from arbitrary images. SADH [30] decomposes

the learning procedure into three stages and alternates among them. Greedy-Hash [32] adopt the greedy principle to directly optimize the discrete codes. DistillHash [37] learns a distilled data set by distilling data pairs with highly confident similarity signal. [19] propose a Bi-half Net that maximizes entropy of the binary codes to make the values of the bit are uniformly (half-half) distributed.

3   Method

3.1   Problem Definition

Given a dataset of images $\mathcal{X} = \{x_1, x_2, ..., x_N\}$, the purpose is to learn the binary hash codes $B = \{b_1, b_2, ..., b_N\} \in \{-1, +1\}^L = sgn(h_\theta(X))$. The model generates the positive samples of each original image by applying a variety of data augmentation transformations. The set of data-augmented images is denoted as $\hat{\mathcal{X}} = \{\hat{x}_1, \hat{x}_2, ..., \hat{x}_N\}$ and the corresponding hash code matrix is $\hat{B} = \{\hat{b}_1, \hat{b}_2, ..., \hat{b}_n\} \in \{-1, +1\}^L = sgn(h_\theta(\hat{X}))$, where $\hat{x}_i = T(x_i)$ and $T(\cdot)$ denotes the random data augmentation operations, such as flipping, crop and so on. As described in the introduction, the hash code should be invariant under different data augmentations, i.e. $B = \hat{B}$.

3.2   Framework

The overall framework of our proposed algorithm is shown in Fig. 1. The whole algorithm consists of two stages. At the first stage, deep features are extracted from convolutional network. Then those features are used to generate pseudo labels via unsupervised clustering algorithms. At the second stage, the pseudo labels are used to guide the softmax classifier training and update the parameters of the deep network at the same time. The output h_i of the hidden hash layer are used as the hash codes. The final output of the Softmax layer is the class prediction y'_i of each sample. The model alternates between the clustering procedure and the network training procedure. The loss functions of this model mainly consist of two parts: the classification loss and the discriminative loss. The classification loss is calculated through the labels predicted by the network and the pseudo labels. The discriminative loss contains two kinds of discrimination. The distance between hash codes of the referenced image and its transformed one should be smaller than other random images from the whole dataset. And the distance between pairs from the same category should be smaller than those pairs from different categories. Intuitively, as shown in 1, the yellow solid circle and dotted circle represent Image A and Image A' respectively, the dark blue solid circle and dotted circle represent Image B and Image B' respectively, and the baby bule solid circle and dotted circle represent Image C and Image C' respectively. Dot A and A' are closer than other points, dot B(B') is closer to C(C') than to A(A'). Following most works, AlexNet [14] is used as the backbone network in our architecture. It can be easily replaced by any other network. More details will be explained in the following subsections.

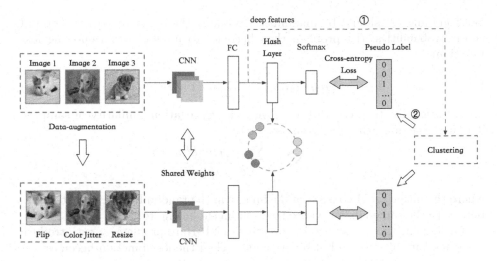

Fig. 1. The framework of our proposed model.

3.3   Discriminative Loss

Previous studies [20, 21] has demonstrated that effective hash codes being invariant under different data-augmentations. In work [21], the authors minimize the difference between hash codes which are computed from the referenced image and the augmented one. Meanwhile, the distance between hash codes computed from arbitrary images are increased. In this way, the hash codes of the instance-wise similar images will be concentrated and the hash codes of instance-wise dissimilar images will be separated. However, image retrieval tasks aim to return a ranked list of candidate images according to their similarity to the query. From this view, we suppose that the hash codes should further keep the local aggregation similarity. That is to say, the images belong to the same cluster are more similar than those in different clusters. Therefore, motivated by [34, 38], a softmax-variant loss function is used to learn discriminative hash codes. Here b_i denotes the hash code of the original image and $\hat{b}_i$ denotes the transformed one. The probability of b_i and $\hat{b}_i$ to be close is defined as:

$$P(b_i, \hat{b}_i) = \frac{exp(b_i^T \hat{b}_i / \tau)}{\Sigma_{k=1}^{M} exp(b_k^T \hat{b}_i / \tau)} \qquad (1)$$

where b_k denotes the hash code of a negative sample randomly sampled from the dataset and M is the number of selected negative samples. We choose the small batch instead of the full dataset for dynamically updating the codes. On the other hand, the probability of $\hat{b}_i$ and other instance hash code b_j $(j \neq i)$ to be separated is defined as:

$$1 - P(b_j, \hat{b}_i) = 1 - \frac{exp(b_j^T \hat{b}_i / \tau)}{\Sigma_{k=1}^{M} exp(b_k^T \hat{b}_i / \tau)} \qquad (2)$$

Both (1) and (2) should be maximize. By taking the negative log likelihood of those probabilities, the problem then becomes to minimize the following loss function:

$$L_I = -\sum_i log P(b_i, \hat{b}_i) - \sum_i \sum_{j \neq i} log(1 - P(b_j, \hat{b}_i)) \tag{3}$$

Additionally, to preserve the above local aggregation similarity of samples, The loss function can be written as:

$$L_A = -\sum_i log \frac{\sum_{m \in A} exp(b_m^T b_i / \tau)}{\sum_{k=1}^M exp(b_k^T b_i / \tau)} \tag{4}$$

where the image set A consists of the images in the randomly selected batch who belong to the same cluster where the i-th image belong to.

Optimizing the discrete codes directly is a NP-Hard problem, so we introduce the slack variables instead of binary codes. Then the loss function becomes:

$$J_1 = \alpha_1 (-\sum_i log P(u_i, \hat{u}_i) - \sum_i \sum_{j \neq i} log(1 - P(u_j, \hat{u}_i)))$$

$$+ \alpha_2 (-\sum_i log \frac{\sum_{m \in A} exp(u_m^T u_i / \tau)}{\sum_{k=1}^M exp(u_k^T u_i / \tau)}) \tag{5}$$

$$+ \alpha_3 (\|B - U\|_2^2 + \left\|B - \hat{U}\right\|_2^2)$$

where u_i is the continuous vectors and it is L2 regularized; $B = sgn(\frac{U + \hat{U}}{2}) \in \{+1, -1\}^{N \times L}$ is the hash code matrix.

Effectiveness Proof of the Loss Function. According to the definition of hamming distance: $dist_h(i, j) = \frac{L - b_i^T b_j}{2}$, where L is the length of hash code. When the value of $b_i^T b_j$ becomes larger, the hamming distance between the two hash codes becomes smaller and the hash codes are more concentrated. On the contrary, with the value of $b_i^T b_j$ becomes smaller, the hash codes become more separated. In another view, $b_i^T b_j / L$ can be regarded as the cosine similarity between hash code b_i and b_j since the L2-Norm of each code is fixed to be $\sqrt{L}$. The cosine similarity can be used to evaluate the distance between hash codes, either. Unlike the pair-wise loss and the triplet loss who face the imbalance of the positive and negative samples, our loss function naturally has discriminative capacity. On the other hand, the pair-wise similarity loss calculates the loss of every similar/dissimilar data pairs individually. Similarly, the triplet loss calculates the loss of every triple independently. Unlike those losses, for each sample, our loss function considers all positive pairs and negative pairs together.

3.4   Classification Loss

The hash code is supposed to preserve the semantic structure in the original space. Since there is no semantic labels, the model have to learn semantic relationship from the unlabeled images. Here the unsupervised clustering algorithm is used to generate the pseudo classification labels. After getting the initial deep features of original images $F^{(0)} = \{f_1^{(0)}, f_2^{(0)}, ..., f_N^{(0)}\}$, the initial cluster centroids $C^{(0)} = \{c_1^{(0)}, c_2^{(0)}, ..., c_K^{(0)}\}$ can be calculated via K-Means++. For each sample x_i, its pseudo label is $y_i = \underset{k}{argmin}\ dist(c_k^{(0)}, f_i^{(0)})$. The pseudo label of the augmented image $\hat{x}_i$ is assigned the same as x_i because they represent the same things in fact. The model tries to minimize the Cross-entropy loss of prediction label y_i', $\hat{y}'_i$ and pseudo class label y_i:

$$J_2 = l_{CrossEntropy}(Y', Y) \tag{6}$$

The predicted label matrix $Y' = \{y_1', y_2', ...y_N', \hat{y}'_1, ..., \hat{y}'_N\}$, and the pseudo label matrix $Y = \{y_1, y_2, ...y_N, y_1, ..., y_N\}$.

Combining the above Eqs. (5) and (6), the final objective function can be obtained:

$$min\ J = J_1 + \beta J_2 \tag{7}$$

To optimize the above objective function, we calculate the gradient and use the mini-batch stochastic gradient descent (SGD) method to train the network.

3.5   Cluster Reassignments

After updating the parameters of the network, the deep features of original images can be recalculated as $F^{(1)} = \{f_1^{(1)}, f_2^{(1)}, ..., f_n^{(1)}\}$ and then the centroids can be updated to $C^{(1)}$ by calculating the means of vectors in each cluster. Then each sample is reassigned to its closest cluster according to the distance between the centroids and the data points:

$$y_i^{(1)} = \underset{k}{argmin}\ dist(c_k^{(1)}, f_i^{(1)}) \tag{8}$$

After getting the new pseudo labels, the network can be trained again by calculating the gradient of Eq. (5). The whole learning procedure is summarized in Algorithm 1.

4   Experiments

We conduct experiments on several public benchmark datasets and show the results in this section. We first introduce the setup details and then analyze the experimental results.

4.1   Datasets

We select three public datasets for image retrieval task, including the CIFAR-10,[1] Flickr-25k[2] and MS-COCO.[3]

---

[1] https://www.cs.toronto.edu/~kriz/cifar.html.
[2] http://press.liacs.nl/mirflick.
[3] http://mscoco.org.

Algorithm 1. Deep Clustering based Unsupervised Hashing

Input: Training dataset $\mathcal{X} = \{x_1, x_2, ..., x_N\}$, batch-size M, hyper-parameters $\alpha_1, \alpha_2,$
      α_3, β and hash code length L.
Output: Hash codes **B**.
 1: Initialize the parameters of the network.
 2: Extract the deep features of images and perform clustering to get the initial cluster
      assignments.
 3: **for** $epoch = 0$ to max_epoch **do**
 4:    **for** $iter = 0$ to max_iter **do**
 5:       Randomly sample a mini-batch from the training dataset. Apply random data-
          augmentations on each sample.
 6:       Forward propagating both the original images and the data-augmented
          images, predicting the class labels and calculating the hash codes.
 7:       Updating the parameters of the network via backward propagation by mini-
          mizing Eq. 7.
 8:    **end for**
 9:    Recalculating the deep features and the cluster reassignments.
10: **end for**
11: **return B**.

- **CIFAR-10** is a standard dataset with 60,000 RGB images in 10 classes. Each class contains 6,000 images with size of 32×32. As usual, we randomly select 100 images from each class as the queries and 1,000 images from each class as the training set. All images except the test set are treated as the retrieval set.
- **Flickr** contains 25,000 images collected from the Flickr website. Each image is annotated with at least one of the 38 concepts provided. We randomly sample 2,000 images as the test set and the rest images are regarded as the retrieval set. From the retrieval set, we randomly select 10,000 images as the training set.
- **MS-COCO** is a dataset for image recognition, segmentation and captioning. The current release contains 82,783 training images and 40,504 validation images. Each image is labeled by some of the 80 categories. Like [2], we combine the training and validation images and obtain 12,2218 images after pruning images with no category information. We randomly choose 5,000 images as queries and the rest images are treated as the retrieval set, from which we randomly sample 10,000 images as the training set.

4.2   Baseline Methods

We compare our **DCUH** with several state-of-the-art methods, i.e., six shallow methods: AGH [26], LSH [4], BRE [15], SH [33], SpH [11] and ITQ [8]; six deep unsupervised hashing methods: UH-BDNN [5], Deepbit [20], SSDH [36], GreedyHash [32], DistillHash [37] and Bi-half [19].

For all the shallow methods, the codes implemented with MATLAB are kindly provided by the authors. For the deep method UH-BDNN, we run the

experiments with the released code. In order to have a fair comparison, we cite
the results of Deepbit, SSDH and DistillHash on CIFAR-10 and Flickr from the
literature [37]. For GreedyHash [32] and Bi-half [19], we also run the experiments
with the released code by the authors.

4.3 Evaluation

To evaluate the performance of all the hash methods, we adopt three standard evaluation criteria: Mean Average Precision (MAP), Precision-Recall curves
(PR) and Precision curves with respect to different numbers of top returned samples (P@N). The MAP is a popular criteria to evaluate the accuracy of retrieval
results. It can be calculated as follows:

$$mAP = \frac{1}{|Q|} \sum_{q \in Q} (\frac{1}{T} \sum_{r=1}^{R} (\delta(r) Precision@r)) \tag{9}$$

where T denotes the number of ground-truth relevant samples in the database
for the query and R is the length of the returned ranking list. $\delta(r)$ indicates that
whether the rth result is relevant to current query and $Precision@r$ denotes the
precision for the top r retrieved samples; Q is the query set. We adopt standard
MAP for all the datasets, R is equal to the size of the database. The Precision-
Recall curve is drawn by computing the Precision and Recall at each position in
the ranking list. And the Precision curve is drawn by computing the Precision
with respect to different numbers of top returned samples. The semantic labels
are adopted as ground truth. If two images share at least one semantic label,
they are considered to be relevant, otherwise they are irrelevant.

4.4 Implementation Details

We initialize the parameters of $conv1 - conv5$ and $fc6$, $fc7$ using the **AlexNet**
pre-trained on the ImageNet. We add a fully connected hash layer and a Softmax
classification layer. The number of nodes for the hash layer is the length of hash
codes. We set the number of clusters to K = 10, K = 5 and K = 50 for CIFAR-
10, Flickr and MS-COCO, respectively. The learning rate is fixed as 0.001 and
the momentum, batch size and weight decay are set to 0.9, 512 and 0.0005,
respectively. The hyperparameters α_1, α_2, α_3, β are set to 1, 1, 0.5 and 1.8.

For fair comparison, we adopt the deep features extracted from the $fc7$ layer
of the pretrained **AlexNet** for all the shallow methods and UH-BDNN as inputs.
The raw pixels are used as the input for our model. We resize the images into 224
× 224. Our proposed model is implemented in PyTorch.[4] The data augmentation methods include RandomResizedCrop, RandomGrayscale, ColorJitter and
RandomHorizontalFlip.

There have been several research results that unsupervised learning benefits
more from bigger models than its supervised counterpart [3]. Therefore, we also
test our model on the CIFAR-10 and Flickr datasets with **VGG16** Net [31] to
compare with other deep methods.

---

[4] https://pytorch.org/docs/stable/index.html.

4.5 Result Analysis

Results on VGG16. The MAP results of deep methods on VGG16 with different lengths of hash bits on two benchmark datasets are presented in Table 1. Our experimental settings are the same as DistillHash [37] for fair comparison. It is clear that our method outperforms the state-of-the-art deep hashing methods in most time. It can be observed that from Table 1: (1) With the growth of code length, the performance of our method increases significantly. (2) Compared with the best baseline deep method Bi-half [19], we achieve improvements 2.22% on CIFAR-10 dataset with 128 bits and 1.13% in average MAP for different bits on the Flickr dataset. (3) Compared with other deep methods, our method achieves greater improvements. Through analyzing the results, we get some conclusions: (1) Compared to other methods, GreedyHash and Bi-half have better performance. It proves that the quantization error have an obvious effect on the retrieval performance. (2) The MAP of our method nearly doubles that of SSDH on CIFAR-10 dataset. We think that the main reason is because SSDH try to construct the similarity graph by evaluating the distances between data points and deciding whether two samples are similar or dissimilar according to fixed thresholds. The performance difference between our model and SSDH proves that adaptively adjusting the learned semantic structure is important.

Table 1. Mean Average Precision (MAP) of Deep Methods with **VGG16**.

Methods	CIFAR-10				Flickr			
	16 bit	32 bit	64bit	128 bit	16 bit	32 bit	64bit	128 bit
Deepbit [20]	22.04	24.10	25.21	25.30	59.34	59.33	61.99	63.49
SSDH [36]	25.68	25.60	25.87	26.01	66.21	67.33	67.32	67.71
DistillHash [37]	28.44	28.53	28.67	28.95	69.64	70.56	70.75	69.95
GreedyHash [32]	28.50	31.67	34.53	37.28	63.26	63.13	66.50	68.35
Bi-half [19]	**41.03**	43.61	45.94	47.72	71.66	72.05	72.79	73.77
DCUH-VGG	39.57	**45.09**	**47.08**	**49.90**	**72.06**	**72.83**	**73.88**	**75.14**

Results on AlexNet. The MAP results with different lengths of hash bits on three benchmark datasets are presented in Table 2. From this table, it can be observed that: (1) It is clear that our method outperforms all baselines for all the datasets. For example, for CIFAR-10 dataset, compared to the best unsupervised non-deep hashing methods, i.e. ITQ, we achieve improvements of 8.11%, 9.11% and 6.7% for 32, 64 and 128 bit, respectively. For Flickr dataset, we achieve absolute boosts of 2.76%, 3.17% and 3.84% for 32, 64 and 128 bit, respectively. And for MS-COCO dataset, we achieve improvements of 1.56%, 2.63% and 3.36% for 32, 64 and 128 bit, respectively; (2) For most methods, with the growth of length of hash codes, the performance first increase obviously and then slowly pace down or even begin to decrease. However, AGH is the special one among

Table 2. Mean Average Precision (MAP) of Hamming Ranking for Different Number of Bits.

Methods	CIFAR-10			Flickr			MS-COCO		
	32 bit	64bit	128 bit	32 bit	64bit	128 bit	32 bit	64bit	128 bit
AGH [26]	23.32	20.57	19.66	61.47	61.24	59.53	43.63	42.01	42.54
LSH [4]	15.39	17.34	19.37	56.46	57.65	59.12	37.92	40.42	41.72
BRE [15]	22.77	25.37	25.64	59.48	61.75	63.44	42.70	43.58	47.10
SH [33]	18.23	18.16	17.97	58.21	57.92	57.51	40.02	40.43	40.20
SpH [11]	21.50	22.59	23.76	59.82	60.97	61.70	42.67	43.99	45.40
ITQ [8]	27.61	29.10	30.50	62.90	62.98	63.47	47.52	48.65	49.27
UH-BDNN [5]	26.23	27.20	29.13	62.28	62.29	62.48	47.00	48.36	48.41
DCUH	**35.72**	**38.21**	**37.57**	**65.66**	**66.15**	**67.31**	**49.08**	**51.28**	**52.63**

those methods, its performance is better when the hash code length is shorter; (3) The performances of deep methods are better in most case. By comparing the shallow methods and deep methods, we can see that deep method UH-BDNN can surpass shallow methods except ITQ; (4) Through analyzing the experimental results of the three datasets, we found that our model can achieve more improvements on single-label dataset than multi-label dataset. For example, the improvements on the CIFAR-10 dataset are much more remarkable than on the MS-COCO. Maybe it is because that discovering semantic information in single-label dataset can help more than multi-label dataset.

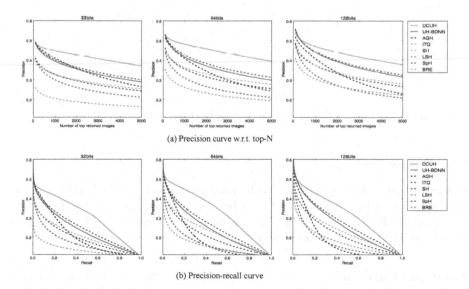

(a) Precision curve w.r.t. top-N

(b) Precision-recall curve

Fig. 2. The curves of DCUH and other methods on the CIFAR-10 dataset. (Color figure online)

Also, we draw the precision-recall and TopN-precision curves for all methods in Fig. 2 and Fig. 3. The Precision curve (P@N) presents the Precision results over top-n returned neighbors and Precision-Recall (PR) curve presents the Precision results over Recall. The full lines denote the deep methods and the dotted lines denote the shallow models. It clear that DCUH outperforms other methods by large margins in these figures. For example, Fig. 2 (a)–(b) show the Precision results over top-n returned neighbors and Precision-Recall curve with 32, 64 and 128 bit hash code length on CIFAR-10 dataset, where n ranges from 1 to 5,000. Figure 3 (a)–(d) show the Precision curve and Precision-Recall curve with 32 and 64 bit hash code length on Flickr dataset, where n ranges from 1 to 5,000. Figure 3 (e)–(h) show the Precision results over top-n returned neighbors with 32 and 64 bit hash code length on MS-COCO dataset, where n ranges from 1 to 20,000. In all the figures, the result curve of our method (blue) is always the best one.

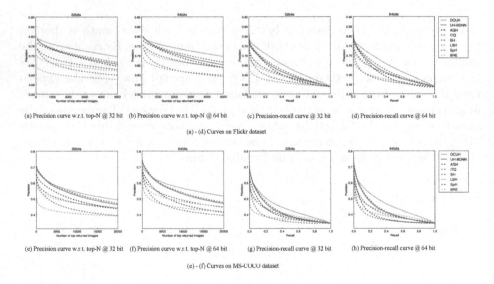

(a) Precision curve w.r.t. top-N @ 32 bit   (b) Precision curve w.r.t. top-N @ 64 bit   (c) Precision-recall curve @ 32 bit   (d) Precision-recall curve @ 64 bit

(a) - (d) Curves on Flickr dataset

(e) Precision curve w.r.t. top-N @ 32 bit   (f) Precision curve w.r.t. top-N @ 64 bit   (g) Precision-recall curve @ 32 bit   (h) Precision-recall curve @ 64 bit

(e) - (f) Curves on MS-COCO dataset

Fig. 3. The curves on the Flickr and MS-COCO datasets. (Color figure online)

4.6   Discussion

Visualization. We visualize the hash codes produced by DCUH, ITQ and UH-BDNN in Fig. 4 by t-SNE [27]. It can be clearly observed that the hash code generated by DCUH have more discriminative structures than ITQ and UH-BDNN, and hash codes of images in different categories are more separated.

Ablation Study. In this section, we analyze the influence of different part in the loss function: the hash code invariant loss, the classification loss and the local structure loss. We remove them from the objective function separately and the

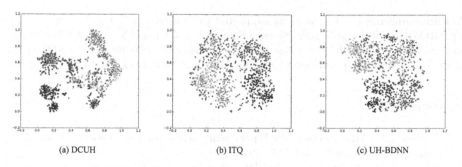

(a) DCUH   (b) ITQ   (c) UH-BDNN

Fig. 4. t-SNE of hash codes learned by DCUH, ITQ and UH-BDNN

results are shown in Table 3. DCUH-LI means that applying our model with the hash code invariant loss removed from the objective function. The performance is degraded by 2.56%, 2.98% and 1.38% with 32, 64 and 128 bits, respectively. DCUH-LA means that applying with local structure loss removed and the results is slightly lower than the complete model. DCUH-LC means that applying the model without classification loss. The performance decline sharply by 7.55%, 9.42% and 7.67% with 32, 64 and 128 bits, respectively. Through analyzing the results, we can find that the classification loss is the most important one.

Table 3. Ablation study of DCUH on the CIFAR-10 dataset.

Methods	MAP		
	32 bit	64bit	128bit
DCUH-LI	0.3316	0.3523	0.3619
DCUH-LA	0.3447	0.3660	0.3676
DCUH-LC	0.2817	0.2879	0.2990
DCUH	**0.3572**	**0.3821**	**0.3757**

5   Conclusion

This paper presented a novel unsupervised deep hashing architecture who learns the semantic structure and hash codes simultaneously. It first clusters the data points into several clusters first. And then it learns the deep hash function by keeping hash codes of data-augmented images to be invariant, minimizing the classification loss via pseudo labels and preserving the local structure. Finally, it recalculates the deep features and clusters the data points again. The proposed model alternates among the above stages with convergence guarantee. The experiment results on three popular benchmark datasets have demonstrated that the proposed algorithm outperforms the state-of-the-art baselines.

Acknowledgement. The work is supported by National Key R&D Plan (No.2018 YFB1005100), National Natural Science Foundation of China (No. 61751201, 61602197 and 61772076), Natural Science Fund of Beijing (No. Z181100008918002) and the funds of Beijing Advanced Innovation Center for Language Resources (No. TYZ19005).

References

1. Bentley, J.L.: Multidimensional binary search trees used for associative searching. Commun. ACM **18**(9), 509–517 (1975)
2. Cao, Z., Long, M., Wang, J., Yu, P.S.: HashNet: deep learning to hash by continuation. In: CVPR, pp. 5608–5617 (2017)
3. Chen, T., Kornblith, S., Norouzi, M., Hinton, G.: A simple framework for contrastive learning of visual representations. arXiv preprint arXiv:2002.05709 (2020)
4. Datar, M., Immorlica, N., Indyk, P., Mirrokni, V.S.: Locality-sensitive hashing scheme based on p-stable distributions. In: Proceedings of the Twentieth Annual Symposium on Computational Geometry, pp. 253–262 (2004)
5. Do, T.-T., Doan, A.-D., Cheung, N.-M.: Learning to hash with binary deep neural network. In: Leibe, B., Matas, J., Sebe, N., Welling, M. (eds.) ECCV 2016. LNCS, vol. 9909, pp. 219–234. Springer, Cham (2016). https://doi.org/10.1007/978-3-319-46454-1_14
6. Gattupalli, V., Zhuo, Y., Li, B.: Weakly supervised deep image hashing through tag embeddings. In: CVPR, pp. 10375–10384 (2019)
7. Gionis, A., Indyk, P., Motwani, R.: Similarity search in high dimensions via hashing. In: VLDB 1999, pp. 518–529 (1999)
8. Gong, Y., Lazebnik, S.: Iterative quantization: a procrustean approach to learning binary codes. In: CVPR, pp. 817–824 (2011)
9. Guttman, A.: R-trees: a dynamic index structure for spatial searching. In: SIGMOD 1984, pp. 47–57. ACM Press (1984)
10. He, K., Wen, F., Sun, J.: K-means hashing: an affinity-preserving quantization method for learning binary compact codes. In: CVPR, pp. 2938–2945 (2013)
11. Heo, J.P., Lee, Y., He, J., Chang, S.F., Yoon, S.E.: Spherical hashing. In: CVPR, pp. 2957–2964 (2012)
12. Hu, Q., Wu, J., Cheng, J., Wu, L., Lu, H.: Pseudo label based unsupervised deep discriminative hashing for image retrieval. In: Proceedings of the 2017 ACM on Multimedia Conference, MM, pp. 1584–1590 (2017)
13. Indyk, P., Motwani, R.: Approximate nearest neighbors: towards removing the curse of dimensionality. In: Proceedings of the Thirtieth Annual ACM Symposium on the Theory of Computing, pp. 604–613. ACM (1998)
14. Krizhevsky, A., Sutskever, I., Hinton, G.E.: ImageNet classification with deep convolutional neural networks. In: NIPS, pp. 1106–1114 (2012)
15. Kulis, B., Darrell, T.: Learning to hash with binary reconstructive embeddings. In: NIPS, pp. 1042–1050 (2009)
16. Lai, H., Pan, Y., Liu, Y., Yan, S.: Simultaneous feature learning and hash coding with deep neural networks. In: IEEE Conference on Computer Vision and Pattern Recognition, CVPR, pp. 3270–3278 (2015)
17. Li, Q., Sun, Z., He, R., Tan, T.: Deep supervised discrete hashing. In: NIPS, pp. 2482–2491 (2017)
18. Li, W., Wang, S., Kang, W.: Feature learning based deep supervised hashing with pairwise labels. In: IJCAI, pp. 1711–1717 (2016)

19. Li, Y., van Gemert, J.: Deep unsupervised image hashing by maximizing bit entropy. CoRR arxiv:abs/2012.12334 (2020)
20. Lin, K., Lu, J., Chen, C., Zhou, J.: Learning compact binary descriptors with unsupervised deep neural networks. In: CVPR, pp. 1183–1192 (2016)
21. Lin, K., Lu, J., Chen, C., Zhou, J., Sun, M.: Unsupervised deep learning of compact binary descriptors. IEEE Trans. Pattern Anal. Mach. Intell. **41**(6), 1501–1514 (2019)
22. Lin, K., Yang, H., Hsiao, J., Chen, C.: Deep learning of binary hash codes for fast image retrieval. In: CVPR, pp. 27–35 (2015)
23. Liong, V.E., Lu, J., Wang, G., Moulin, P., Zhou, J.: Deep hashing for compact binary codes learning. In: IEEE Conference on Computer Vision and Pattern Recognition, CVPR, pp. 2475–2483 (2015)
24. Liu, W., Mu, C., Kumar, S., Chang, S.: Discrete graph hashing. In: NIPS, pp. 3419–3427 (2014)
25. Liu, W., Wang, J., Ji, R., Jiang, Y., Chang, S.: Supervised hashing with kernels. In: CVPR, pp. 2074–2081 (2012)
26. Liu, W., Wang, J., Kumar, S., Chang, S.: Hashing with graphs. In: Proceedings of the 28th International Conference on Machine Learning, ICML, pp. 1–8. Omnipress (2011)
27. Van der Maaten, L., Hinton, G.: Visualizing data using t-SNE. J. Mach. Learn. Res. **9**(Nov), 2579–2605 (2008)
28. Norouzi, M., Fleet, D.J.: Minimal loss hashing for compact binary codes. In: ICML, pp. 353–360 (2011)
29. Shen, F., Shen, C., Liu, W., Shen, H.T.: Supervised discrete hashing. In: CVPR, pp. 37–45. IEEE Computer Society (2015)
30. Shen, F., Xu, Y., Liu, L., Yang, Y., Huang, Z., Shen, H.T.: Unsupervised deep hashing with similarity-adaptive and discrete optimization. IEEE Trans. Pattern Anal. Mach. Intell. **40**, 3034–3044 (2018)
31. Simonyan, K., Zisserman, A.: Very deep convolutional networks for large-scale image recognition. arXiv preprint arXiv:1409.1556 (2014)
32. Su, S., Zhang, C., Han, K., Tian, Y.: Greedy hash: towards fast optimization for accurate hash coding in CNN. In: NIPS, pp. 806–815 (2018)
33. Weiss, Y., Torralba, A., Fergus, R.: Spectral hashing. In: NIPS, pp. 1753–1760. Curran Associates, Inc. (2008)
34. Wu, Z., Xiong, Y., Yu, S.X., Lin, D.: Unsupervised feature learning via non-parametric instance discrimination. In: CVPR, pp. 3733–3742. IEEE Computer Society (2018)
35. Xia, R., Pan, Y., Lai, H., Liu, C., Yan, S.: Supervised hashing for image retrieval via image representation learning. In: Proceedings of the Twenty-Eighth AAAI Conference on Artificial Intelligence, pp. 2156–2162 (2014)
36. Yang, E., Deng, C., Liu, T., Liu, W., Tao, D.: Semantic structure-based unsupervised deep hashing. In: Proceedings of the Twenty-Seventh International Joint Conference on Artificial Intelligence, IJCAI, pp. 1064–1070 (2018)
37. Yang, E., Liu, T., Deng, C., Liu, W., Tao, D.: DistillHash: unsupervised deep hashing by distilling data pairs. In: CVPR, pp. 2946–2955 (2019)
38. Ye, M., Zhang, X., Yuen, P.C., Chang, S.: Unsupervised embedding learning via invariant and spreading instance feature. In: CVPR, pp. 6210–6219 (2019)
39. Zhang, P., Zhang, W., Li, W., Guo, M.: Supervised hashing with latent factor models. In: SIGIR, pp. 173–182 (2014)

FedMDR: Federated Model Distillation with Robust Aggregation

Yuxi Mi[1], Yutong Mu[1], Shuigeng Zhou[1(✉)], and Jihong Guan[2]

[1] Shanghai Key Lab of Intelligent Information Processing, and School of Computer Science, Fudan University, Shanghai 200438, China
{yxmi20,18210240149,sgzhou}@fudan.edu.cn
[2] Department of Computer Science and Technology, Tongji University, Shanghai 201804, China
jhguan@tongji.edu.cn

Abstract. This paper presents FedMDR, a federated model distillation framework with a novel, robust aggregation mechanism that exploits transfer learning and knowledge distillation. FedMDR adopts a weighted geometric-median-based aggregation with trimmed prediction accuracy on the server-side, which orchestrates communication-efficient training on both heterogeneous model architectures and non-i.i.d. data. The aggregation provides resilience to sharp accuracy drop of corrupted models. We also extend FedMDR to support differential privacy by adding Gaussian noise to the aggregated consensus. Results show that FedMDR achieves significant robustness gain and satisfactory accuracy, and outperforms the existing techniques.

Keywords: Federated learning · Knowledge distillation · Aggregation mechanism · Differential privacy

1 Introduction

Federated learning (FL) [15] has emerged as a leading deep learning paradigm where a multitude of clients participate collaboratively to construct a global model under the orchestration of a central server. In each communication round of FL, clients synchronize with the server and compute an update on their private data. The update is uploaded to the server and averaged to produce the updated global model. This process repeats until convergence. Clients in federated learning never explicitly share their private training datasets, thereby keep their local data autonomy and ensure a basic level of privacy. Federated learning is also optimized to reduce communication overheads among participants of a variety of scales [18,24,25].

Nevertheless, federated learning still faces various challenges [12]. Among them, the heterogeneity problem that occurs in the learning process is on the

This work was supported by Zhejiang Lab (No. 2019KB0AB05), and National Natural Science Foundation of China (No. 61972100 and No. 61772367).

L. H. U et al. (Eds.): APWeb-WAIM 2021, LNCS 12859, pp. 18–32, 2021.
https://doi.org/10.1007/978-3-030-85899-5_2

top [11,17]. This includes 1) *system heterogeneity*, where bandwidth and computational powers of participants vary considerably, 2) *statistical heterogeneity* (i.e., non-i.i.d.-ness) [3,10,13], where privately-owned data may come from distinctive distributions, and 3) *model heterogeneity* [5,21,27], i.e., the structural disparity of local models, which is the focus of this paper.

On its original purpose, federated learning asserts that all participants agree on the particular architecture of a shared global model [15]. In typical customer-oriented applications, where the clients are a massive number of low-capacity mobile devices, this assumption holds. However, it is not true in most industrial domain-specific scenarios, where participants are usually eager to design and utilize their own models [11]. Ergo, the local models are heterogeneous or even act as black boxes since their details may be concealed by participants for intellectual property and privacy concerns, which makes the standard practice of FL inapplicable.

Recently, federated model distillation (FedMD) [11] is introduced, which enables participants to learn collectively on both heterogeneous models and private data. With the help of knowledge distillation [8], FedMD establishes a "translation protocol" for deep neural networks to understand the knowledge of the others by uploading their logits instead of weight parameters. It is done without explicitly sharing data or model architectures. FedMD also addresses the data shortage problem by implementing an additional transfer learning [23] phase in the pre-training stage. Results on the FEMNIST dataset show a considerable performance gain for individual local models, compared to training without collaboration.

However, FedMD has its limitations in fault tolerance. Since the heterogeneity of models and data, during the collaboration phase, occasional yet sharp performance fluctuations can occur on one or more local models, which we call *accuracy drop*. As shown in Fig. 1(a), in each iteration of FedMD, uploaded logits are aggregated by an element-wise mean, which is sensitive to model corruption since the accuracy drop of an individual client may be propagated to the others, preventing the global model from convergence. Figure 1(b) indicates that convergence become even difficult as the number of training rounds or participants increases. Therefore, a robust aggregation mechanism is urgently required.

In this paper, we address this problem by introducing a weighted version of geometric median, which is combined with trimmed mean. During each iteration of the collaborative phase, each party does prediction on a labeled public dataset. The prediction, together with the model's accuracy, are transmitted to the server. A trimmed weight is then evaluated from the accuracy results. The server subsequently computes an updated consensus such that the sum of weighted Euclidean distances from the consensus to each model is minimized, i.e., the weighted geo-median. Extensive experiments show that our method outperforms the original FedMD, mainstream byzantine-tolerant techniques, and naïve geo-median in both accuracy and robustness.

Contributions of this paper are as follows:

1. We present FedMDR, a federated model distillation framework with robust aggregation based on weighted geometric median. It is robust to heterogeneous data and model architectures as well as participant scale.
2. We demonstrate the effectiveness of FedMDR on heterogeneous neural networks and non-i.i.d. data by extensive experiments on the FEMNIST dataset. Our framework achieves a significant robustness and accuracy gain of local models, outperforming the original FedMD and some other related approaches.
3. We further extend our FedMDR framework to privacy-preserving settings by adding Gaussian noise to the aggregated consensus. We show that the extended framework satisfies the Rényi [16] differential privacy, and validate its performance of privacy-preserving on different privacy budgets.

2   Robust Federated Model Distillation

In this section, we first give an overview of our robust federated model distillation framework, which is denoted as FedMDR in short. Then, we introduce the weighted geometric median based aggregation mechanism. Finally, we present a privacy-preserving extension of our framework.

2.1   Problem Statement

We consider the federated learning on a collection of n clients. Each client i owns a private dataset $\mathcal{D}_i$, which can be either with or without the same distribution. A relatively large labeled public dataset $\mathcal{D}_{pub}$ is accessible to all the clients. For each client, a local classification model M_i of specific architecture is trained. Neither the private data nor the parameters of all local models are allowed to share among clients.

Under this setting, a collaborative framework is adopted to improve each local model's performance by utilizing the knowledge of the other clients [11]. Our goal is to ensure such a framework maintains high robustness under various client scales, heterogeneous model architectures, and non-i.i.d. data.

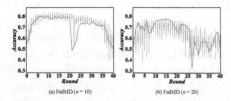

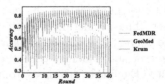

Fig. 1. Illustration of sharp accuracy drop impacting convergence. Here, the orange boxplots indicate accuracy distribution of all local models, and the green curve represents the accuracy values of a corrupted local model.

Fig. 2. Performance comparison of FedMDR with mainstream byzantine-resilient aggregations. Our method significantly outperforms Krum and GeoMed in test accuracy.

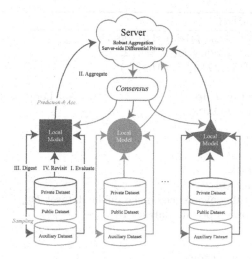

Fig. 3. The collaborative phase of FedMDR. Each client model is pre-trained locally. The straight lines represent the local data flow, and the curves represent the flow of updates between clients and the server.

2.2   The FedMDR Framework

Our FedMDR framework is illustrated in Fig. 3 and described in Algorithm 1. It consists of two phases: the *pre-training phase* and the *collaborative phase*.

The pretraining phase utilizes transfer learning to deal with the shortage of local data. It is performed on every client before the collaborative phase starts. Pretraining is completed locally: each client i trains its self-designed local model M_i first on the public dataset $\mathcal{D}_{pub}$, then on its private data $\mathcal{D}_i$.

In the collaborative phase, all clients share the knowledge of their local models via doing prediction on a fixed size subset $\mathcal{D}_{aux} \in \mathcal{D}_{pub}$ called the auxiliary dataset, which is randomly sampled by the server from the public dataset. The auxiliary dataset is introduced in practice to control the training cost. The entire public dataset can be used instead, if the data size is not too large. We show in experiments that our framework can achieve accurate prediction with a significantly smaller (public) auxiliary dataset. In general, the collaborative phase provides a federated realization of model distillation. During each iteration t of training, the following four steps are repeated until convergence:

1. **Evaluate.** Each client evaluates its local model M_i on the auxiliary dataset $\mathcal{D}_{aux}$. The prediction y_i^t on $\mathcal{D}_{aux}$ along with its accuracy a_i^t is transmitted to the central server.
2. **Aggregate.** The server calculates an updated global prediction y^{t+1} based on the local predictions $Y^t = \{y_1^t, ..., y_n^t\}$ and accuracies $A^t = \{a_1^t, ..., a_n^t\}$, by performing weighted geometric median based aggregation: $y^{t+1} = \text{AGGRE-GATE}\ (Y^t, A^t)$. The updated global prediction y^{t+1} is subsequently shared with all the clients as a public consensus.

Algorithm 1. FedMDR

Input: Public dataset $\mathcal{D}_{pub}$, private datasets $\mathcal{D}_i$
Output: Trained local models M_i, $i = 1, 2, ..., n$
1: **function** MAIN($\mathcal{D}_{pub}, \{\mathcal{D}_i\}_{i=1}^n, \{M_i\}_{i=1}^n$)
2:    PRETRAIN()
3:    **for** Each iteration t **do**   ▷ Loop continues till converges
4:       COLLABORATEONCE()
5:    **end for**
6:    **return** $\{M_i\}_{i=1}^n$
7: **end function**
8: **function** PRETRAIN
9:    **for** each client i **do**
10:       Train M_i till convergence on the public dataset $\mathcal{D}_{pub}$
11:       Train M_i on its private dataset $\mathcal{D}_i$
12:    **end for**
13: **end function**
14: **function** COLLABORATEONCE
15:    Randomly draw an auxiliary dataset $\mathcal{D}_{aux}$ from $\mathcal{D}_{pub}$
16:    **Evaluate:** Each client evaluates local model M_i on $\mathcal{D}_{aux}$, then sends prediction
       y_i^t and accuracy a_i^t to the central server
17:    **Aggregate:** Server collects $Y^t = \{y_i^t\}_{i=1}^n$ and $A^t = \{a_i^t\}_{i=1}^n$, performs
       AGGREGATE (Y^t, A^t), then redistributes updated consensus y^{t+1}
18:    **Digest:** Each client aligns M_i to y^{t+1} by training M_i on $\mathcal{D}_{aux}$ till convergence
19:    **Revisit:** Each client improves M_i on $\mathcal{D}_i$
20: **end function**

---

3. **Digest.** Each client aligns its local model M_i to the public consensus y^{t+1} by training M_i on the labeled $\mathcal{D}_{aux}$. Therefore, the knowledge of each client is shared with the other clients without explicitly exposing its private data.
4. **Revisit.** Each client improves its local model M_i on its private data $\mathcal{D}_i$ within a few epochs.

2.3   Robust Aggregation Mechanism

The procedure of our weighted geometric median based aggregation is described in Algorithm 2. It utilizes trimmed softmax as the weighting function. Basically, the aggregation returns a global prediction y^{t+1} that minimizes the sum of the weighted Euclidean distances from y^{t+1} to each individual local prediction.

The weights $W^t = \{w_1^t, ..., w_n^t\}$ are used as adjustment terms to the clients' distances, where models with lower accuracies contribute less or not at all to the aggregation. The weights are computed by mapping the local accuracies $A^t = \{a_1^t, ..., a_n^t\}$ to a distribution using trimmed softmax. Here, we use a dynamic threshold to exclude local models with sharp accuracy drop from the aggregation. Note that our method is different from byzantine-resilient methods [2], where the outliers are eliminated by distance. The threshold T is derived from the first quartile Q_1 and the third quartile Q_3 of A^t, specifically,

Algorithm 2. Weighted geometric median based aggregation

Input: Predictions $Y^t = \{y_1^t, \ldots, y_n^t\}$ and accuracies $A^t = \{a_1^t, \ldots, a_n^t\}$ of local models
Output: The updated global consensus y^{t+1}

1: **function** AGGREGATE(Y^t, A^t)
2:     $W^t \leftarrow$ TRIMMEDSOFTMAX $\left(Y^t, A^t\right)$
3:     $y^{t+1} \leftarrow \arg\min_y \sum_{i=1}^n w_i^t \left\| y_i^t - y \right\|_2$
4:     **return** y^{t+1}
5: **end function**
6: **function** TRIMMEDSOFTMAX(A^t)
7:     Calculate the threshold T from A^t
8:     **for** each client i **do**
9:         **if** $a_i^t \leq T$ **then**
10:            $w_i^t \leftarrow 0$
11:            Remove a_i^t from A_i^t
12:        **end if**
13:    **end for**
14:    **for** each a_i^t in A^t **do**
15:        $w_i^t \leftarrow \sigma_\rho \left(a_i^t\right)$
16:    **end for**
17:    **return** $W^t = \{w_1^t, \ldots, w_n^t\}$
18: **end function**

$$T = Q_1 - 1.5(Q_1 - Q_3). \tag{1}$$

The accuracies A^t are processed by a softmax function σ_ρ to derive the corresponding weights:

$$w_i^t = \sigma_\rho \left(a_i^t\right) = \frac{\exp(\rho \cdot a_i^t)}{\sum_{a_j^t \in A_{tr}^t} \exp(\rho \cdot a_j^t)}. \tag{2}$$

The hyperparameter ρ is introduced to adjust the weight distribution. Empirically, a larger ρ enables the models with higher accuracy to obtain larger weights.

Any model with a weight below the threshold will be reset to a zero weight. That is,

$$w_i^t = \begin{cases} 0, & \text{if trimmed, i.e., } w_i^t < T, \\ \sigma_\rho \left(a_i^t\right), & \text{otherwise} \end{cases}. \tag{3}$$

The distance between the supposed global prediction y and each local prediction y_i^t is defined as $\left\| y_i^t - y \right\|_2$, where $\left\| \cdot \right\|_2$ represents the Euclidean norm. The sum of weighted distances between y and Y^t by weights W^t is as follows:

$$\sum_{i=1}^n w_i^t \left\| y_i^t - y \right\|_2. \tag{4}$$

Therefore, the updated consensus y^{t+1} is evaluated by solving the following optimization problem:

$$\arg\min_y \sum_{i=1}^{n} w_i^t \left\| y_i^t - y \right\|_2 . \tag{5}$$

In our experiments, we show that our trimmed softmax aggregation outperforms the original FedMD and some other existing techniques under heterogeneous architectures of models and non-i.i.d. data.

2.4   FedMDR with Differential Privacy

In federated learning, differential privacy is the *de facto* standard approach to prevent clients' private information from inference attacks. Here, we show our FedMDR framework can realize global differential privacy with slight modification. Specifically, we add a Gaussian noise with variance β^2 to the aggregated global consensus, that is,

$$y_{DP}^{y+1} = y^{y+1} + \mathcal{N}(0, \beta^2). \tag{6}$$

We will show that FedMDR follows the definition of Rényi differential privacy [16]. Rényi differential privacy is a natural relaxation form of (ϵ, δ)-differential privacy [7]. It is well-suited for expressing guarantees of privacy-preserving algorithms and for composition of heterogeneous mechanisms. In what follows, we first introduce the Rényi divergence, which is a metric of two possibility distributions and can be regarded as the generalization of KL-divergence.

Definition 1. *(Rényi divergence)* [16]. *For two possibility distributions P and Q (with probability density functions $p(x)$ and $q(x)$, respectively) defined over $\mathcal{R}$, the Rényi divergence of order $\alpha > 1$ is*

$$D_\alpha(P\|Q) \triangleq \frac{1}{\alpha - 1} \ln \int_{\mathcal{R}} q(x) (\frac{p(x)}{q(x)})^\alpha dx \tag{7}$$

The Rényi differential privacy is defined as follows:

Definition 2. *(Rényi differential privacy)* [16]. *A randomized mechanism $f : \mathcal{X} \mapsto \mathcal{Y}$ is said to have (ϵ)-Rényi differential privacy of order α, or (α, ϵ)-RDP for short, if for any adjacent inputs $X, X' \in \mathcal{X}$, it holds that*

$$D_\alpha(f(X)\|f(X')) \le \epsilon \tag{8}$$

To show that our weighted geometric median based aggregation with differential privacy satisfies Rényi differential privacy, we denote the collection of clients as $\mathcal{C}$. Since the public dataset $\mathcal{D}_{pub}$ is available to all clients, our aggregation mechanism can be regarded as a randomized query $f : \mathcal{C} \mapsto \mathcal{D}_{pub}$, which maps the clients to the predictions of clients' local models, and the Gaussian noise $\mathcal{N}(0, \beta^2)$ can be regarded as an offset to $\mathcal{C}$. Then, we have

Theorem 1. *The weighted geometric median based aggregation with Gaussian noise $\mathcal{N}(0, \beta^2)$ satisfies $(\alpha, \frac{\alpha}{2\sigma^2})$-RDP.*

Proof. The Rényi divergence between a Gaussian distribution $\mathcal{N}(0, \beta^2)$ and its offset distribution $\mathcal{N}(\mu, \beta^2)$ is

$$
\begin{aligned}
&D_\alpha(\mathcal{N}(0, \beta^2) \| \mathcal{N}(\mu, \beta^2)) \\
&= \frac{1}{\alpha - 1} \ln \int_{-\infty}^{\infty} \frac{1}{\sigma\sqrt{2\pi}} \exp(\frac{-\alpha x^2}{2\sigma^2}) \\
&\quad \exp(\frac{-(1-\alpha)(x-\mu)^2}{2\sigma^2})dx \\
&= \frac{1}{\alpha - 1} \ln(\frac{\sigma\sqrt{2\pi}}{\sigma\sqrt{2\pi}} \exp(\frac{(\alpha^2 - \alpha)\mu^2}{2\sigma^2})) \\
&= \frac{1}{\alpha - 1} \frac{(\alpha^2 - \alpha)\mu^2}{2\sigma^2} = \frac{\alpha\mu^2}{2\sigma^2}.
\end{aligned}
\tag{9}
$$

The divergence between two adjacent clients is upbounded by

$$
D_\alpha(f(C) \| f(C')) \leq \sup_C (D_\alpha(\mathcal{N}(0, \beta^2) \| \mathcal{N}(\mu, \beta^2))) = \frac{\alpha\mu^2}{2\sigma^2}.
\tag{10}
$$

In classification tasks, the output prediction $f(C)$ is within the range $[0, 1]$. Set $\mu = 1$ and subsequently we have

$$
D_\alpha(f(C) \| f(C')) \leq \frac{\alpha}{2\sigma^2} = \epsilon.
\tag{11}
$$

It can be shown that the privacy budget ϵ_{RDP} in (α, ϵ)-RDP can be converted to the budget ϵ_{DP} in (ϵ, δ)-DP as follows [16]:

$$
\epsilon_{DP} = \epsilon_{RDP} - \frac{\ln 1/\delta}{\alpha - 1}.
\tag{12}
$$

3 Performance Evaluation

3.1 Experimental Setup

We evaluate the FedMDR framework on the MNIST and FEMNIST datasets. Specifically, MNIST is shared by all clients as the public dataset, and a small subset of FEMNIST is selected by each client as its private dataset. We consider the non-i.i.d. case, that is, each client is assigned the letters written by a certain writer in the training phase [11], while classifying the letters of all writers in the testing phase.

A collection of 10/20 clients are selected in each experiment. Each client employs a convolutional neural network (CNN) as its local model for classification, and all CNNs differ in their numbers of layers and channels, which represents the heterogeneously designed models in the real world. Starting with the transfer learning phase, each model is first pre-trained on the public dataset till convergence, which typically achieves a test accuracy of 99% on MNIST. It is then trained on its private dataset. Following that, the models go through the collaborative training phase. In each iteration of the collaborative training phase, an auxiliary dataset (i.e., a subset of the public dataset) with a default size of 5000 is randomly selected. For weighted aggregation, we set the hyper-parameter $\rho = 10$ if without extra specification. An Adam optimizer is applied with an initial learning rate $\eta = 0.001$.

In experiments, we mainly evaluate the robustness of FedMDR, and compare it with existing methods including FedMD [11], Krum [2] and GeoMed [4], in terms of the accuracies of local models. Results are presented by box plots. Particularly, we focus on the median and the variance of accuracies. Median reflects the overall performance of clients (or models), and variance reflects the stableness of the global consensus (the consensus is more stable if the predictions of local models are more consistent with each other). Methods of higher robustness are expected to have larger median and smaller variance.

3.2   Experimental Results

Performance on Auxiliary Datasets of Different Sizes. Among the challenges of federated model distillation, the lack of public data is on the top. Public datasets in industry depend heavily on cost-expensive manual extracting from papers and public databases (e.g. the ADMET database [6] for drug discovery) and labeling. We compare our FedMDR framework with the original FedMD on auxiliary datasets of different sizes $s = 4000, 5000, 6000$ and 10000 respectively, with $n = 20$ clients. The results are shown in Fig. 4. We can see that FedMD requires a considerably large auxiliary dataset to reach convergence. On the other hand, our method gets stable and consistent performance on datasets of different sizes, thus is more robust. In Fig. 4(d), both methods converge at $s = 10000$, while our method achieves slightly higher accuracy than FedMD.

Performance Comparison with Other Aggregation Methods. Here we compare our aggregation method with two other distance-based aggregation mechanisms: Krum [2] and GeoMed [4]. Krum is a byzantine-resilient aggregation. Given n participants where f are corrupted, Krum requires $n \geq 2f + 3$. At any iteration t after updates $(\gamma_1^t, ..., \gamma_n^t)$ are transmitted to the server, for each γ_i^t, the distance from it to each of the n-f-2 closest other updates are added up to output a score. The update with the smallest score is then chosen as Krum's consensus. GeoMed aggregates the local updates in three steps: (1) partitioning all received local updates into k batches where the mean of each batch is computed, (2) computing the geometric median of the k batch means, and (3) taking the geometric median as the new consensus.

The results are shown in Fig. 2 and Table 1. We can see that FedMDR performs best among the three aggregation methods. GeoMed can converge but its accuracy is much low, partly because of (1) using no weighting and (2) the batch operation that fails to work well in heterogeneous settings. Krum cannot

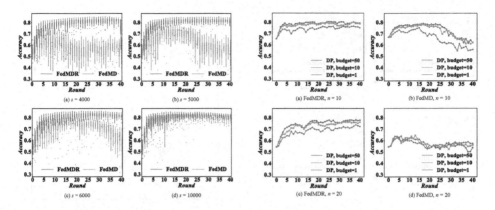

Fig. 4. FedMDR *vs.* FedMD with 20 clients and 4000, 5000, 6000 or 10000 samples respectively in the auxiliary dataset.

Fig. 5. FedMDR *vs.* FedMD for different scales of clients and different privacy budgets. Here, accuracy median values of local models are illustrated.

Table 1. Performance comparison of different aggregation methods

Method	Acc. Med.	Acc. Var.
FedMDR	**0.813**	0.0025
Krum	0.447	0.0120
GeoMed	0.760	0.0021

converge because it rashly excludes benign models from the aggregation. Further discussion will be given in Sect. 4.

Performance Comparison Under Differential Privacy Settings. Although federated learning provides basic guarantee on privacy, differential privacy can protect clients from inference attacks [1]. Here, we compare our method with FedMD under differential privacy settings of different privacy budgets. The global budget is set to $\epsilon_{RDP} = 50, 10, 1$ respectively, and then evenly distributed to each round. Both methods are trained with 10 or 20 clients for 40 rounds. Results are illustrated in Fig. 5 and Table 2. Our method performs robustly in differential privacy settings with a marginal accuracy loss, while FedMD fails to converge even under the lowest privacy budget. We note in Table 2 that the variance under a larger privacy budget can be slightly higher than a small one (e.g., $pb = 10$ and 50). This presumably occurs since the variance is influenced by both the privacy budget and the heterogeneity of models. The latter takes the dominance under a larger budget.

Ablation Study. To investigate the effectiveness of geo-median and weighting in FedMDR, we compare the three settings: FedMDR, FedMDR without geo-median and FedMDR without weighting. The results are shown in Fig. 6 and Table 3. By comparing Fig. 6(b) and (d), we can see that weighting can improve

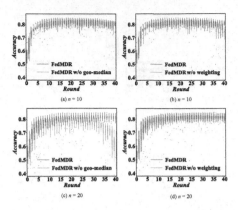

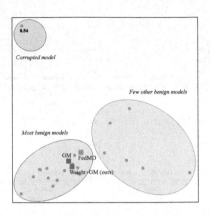

Fig. 6. Results of ablation study with 10 or 20 clients. Left: FedMDR *vs.* arithmetic mean with weighting. Right: FedMDR *vs.* geometric median without weighting.

Fig. 7. PCA results of predictions show the difference between benign and corrupted models. Gray dots represent the predictions of local models and colored squares represent consensuses of different aggregation mechanisms.

robustness when there are fewer participants, which is common in real-world business-oriented tasks. On the other hand, by comparing Fig. 6(a) and (c), we can see that geo-median takes the dominant role in aggregation as the number of participants grows. Our method is robust on different sizes of clients because of combining the merits of both techniques.

Visualization. We train FedMDR with $n = 20$ and $s = 5000$. We freeze the models after 5 communication rounds and collect the update logits of each local model. The logits represent the soft-labeled predictions on the shared auxiliary dataset. We flatten the logits by concatenating all the predictions, and perform principal component analysis (PCA) on the flattened logits of each model, then visualize the predictions with the first two principal components in Fig. 7. Here, each gray dot means the prediction of a local model. The value under the dot is the corresponding model's prediction accuracy. Dots without label have an accuracy above 0.7, indicating benign models.

The visualization is to illustrate the difference between benign and corrupted clients. Most benign clients have predictions more consistent with the consensus, so they form a cluster (the blue eclipse) in Fig. 7. Some other benign clients (in the orange eclipse) may *temporarily* have slightly different predictions from the consensus due to the heterogeneity of model architecture, making them stay a little away from the cluster. On the other hand, corrupted clients (in the red eclipse) *often* appear as isolated points. The aim of our aggregation is to exclude the corrupted models while including as many benign models as possible, as discussed in Sect. 4.

We further illustrate the consensuses of different aggregation mechanisms by squares of different colors. The orange square indicates the consensus of FedMD

Table 2. Performance comparison of FedMDR and FedMD for different scales of clients and different privacy budgets

n	pb	FedMDR		FedMD	
		Acc. Med.	Acc. Var.	Acc. Med.	Acc. Var.
10	50	0.794	0.0010	0.639	0.0053
	10	0.784	0.0004	0.626	0.0042
	1	0.761	0.0012	0.561	0.0090
20	50	0.785	0.0005	0.550	0.0046
	10	0.775	0.0019	0.573	0.0040
	1	0.742	0.0012	0.574	0.0061

Here, n: number of clients, pb: privacy budget. Fed-MDR has larger accuracy median and smaller accuracy variance than FedMD, which means that the local models of FedMD have worse performance and more difficult to reach consistent predictions.

Table 3. Results of ablation study

Method	$n = 10$		$n = 20$	
	Acc. Med.	Acc. Var.	Acc. Med.	Acc. Var.
FedMDR	0.803	0.0006	0.813	0.0025
W/o weighting	0.738	0.0012	0.811	0.0003
W/o geo-median	0.798	0.0022	0.585	0.0060

aggregated by arithmetic averaging, and the red square is the result of geometric median (GM). The consensus of our method is the blue square. We can see that our consensus is farther from the corrupted model while nearer to the center of cluster formed by most benign models than those of GM and FedMD. This shows that our aggregation mechanism is more robust.

4   Discussions

Why Combining Weighting and Geo-Median? We try to handle the scenarios with clients of different sizes. Geometric median is a mechanism to orchestrate a large number of participants, while in typical business-oriented tasks with a relatively small number of participants, weighting is more effective, where each client plays a relatively larger role in the global consensus, and the negative effect of a corrupted client may be magnified. We use weighting to alleviate or even eliminate the negative effect of corrupted models so that the benign models dominate the aggregation result. FedMDR can therefore be stable with even a very small number of clients.

About the Weighting Function. The weighting function can be of various forms. We replace the softmax in our weighting function with sigmoid, and achieve roughly similar performance. The choice of weighting function depends on how local models perform. For instance, softmax assumes that few clients have significantly higher accuracy than the others in the initial communication rounds, and thereby the weighting function should assign them larger weights. On the other hand, other weighting functions may assume that a portion of clients can perform relatively well, which should be assigned a larger weight. Although such a diversity exists, in most cases where only occasional corrupted clients occur, we do not expect a significant difference among different weighting functions.

The Limitation of Eliminating Corrupted Clients by Distance. Corrupted participants usually behave as isolated points lying far away from the consensus cluster center. Some mainstream byzantine-resilient aggregation techniques [2, 26] aim to eliminate the corrupted clients by distance. Such methods work in conventional federated learning, where the same model is employed.

However, when the architectures of models are heterogeneous, isolated models are not necessarily corrupted, because the heterogeneous nature can allow multiple "correct answers". In other words, although the corrupted models are commonly outliers, well trained models with higher accuracy (which should be kept in the aggregation) may also lie outside the cluster, as illustrated in Fig. 7. Such a situation happens especially in the early of collaborative training phase. Considering this reason, the central server should not rashly exclude all the isolated models from the aggregation, for wrong exclusion could lead to significant damage to the model's performance.

5   Related Work

Federated Frameworks Using Knowledge Distillation. Some existing works are based on the idea of knowledge distillation. For instance, compressed federated distillation (CFD) [20] is a novel communication-efficient scheme by exchanging soft-label predictions instead of model parameters. FAug [9] implements effective federated model distillation with user-generated non-i.i.d. samples by augmenting the local data via a collaboratively trained general model. These works share common grounds with ours in that all share model outputs instead of parameters. However, these works mainly aim to reduce communication overheads, none of them considers model heterogeneity.

The recently proposed FedDF [14] is an ensemble distillation scheme for model fusion, where the heterogeneous settings of models and data are discussed. In their work, the server distills the ensemble of local teacher models to one single server student model. Our method is different from FedDF in that the distillation is performed locally instead of on the server-side, without any extra global training involved. FedMD-NFDP [22] is a modified FedMD [11] with the guarantee of local differential privacy. These works, however, are still exposed to the risk of corrupted accuracy drop, which our method tries to solve.

Aggregations. In the literature there are some aggregation mechanisms, including trimmed mean, Krum, and GeoMed [2,4,26], which are all byzantine-resilient. Trimmed mean performs aggregation by coordinate-wise arithmetic averaging, while a fixed fraction of the largest and smallest elements are removed. Krum and GeoMed are both based on Euclidean distance. We have discussed them in detail in Sect. 4.

The work of [19] is related to ours, where a geo-median-based aggregation is proposed. It shows that federated learning can be made robust against byzantine adversaries by replacing the weighted arithmetic mean with an approximate geometric median. However, it is different from ours in at least three aspects: (1) it focuses on robustness against adversarial behaviors, while our work does not consider adversary. (2) It assumes a shared global model and i.i.d. data across the clients, while our method focuses on heterogeneous local model architectures and non-i.i.d. datasets. (3) It assigns the benign clients a fixed weight (equal to the number of client's samples), while in our work the weights are dynamically evaluated from accuracy results.

6   Conclusion

In this paper, we present FedMDR, a robust federated model distillation framework that allows communication-efficient training on heterogeneous model architectures and non-i.i.d. data, leveraging the idea of transfer learning and knowledge distillation. FedMDR uses a weighted geometric median-based aggregation by trimmed weights on the server-side, thus provides resilience to sharp accuracy drop of corrupted models. By extensive experiments, we show that FedMDR can achieve significant robustness gain and decent accuracy, outperforming the original federated model distillation and mainstream byzantine-resilient techniques.

References

1. Phong, L.T., Aono, Y., Hayashi, T., Wang, L., Moriai, S.: Privacy-preserving deep learning: revisited and enhanced. In: Batten, L., Kim, D.S., Zhang, X., Li, G. (eds.) ATIS 2017. CCIS, vol. 719, pp. 100–110. Springer, Singapore (2017). https://doi.org/10.1007/978-981-10-5421-1_9
2. Blanchard, P., Guerraoui, R., Stainer, J., et al.: Machine learning with adversaries: Byzantine tolerant gradient descent. In: Advances in Neural Information Processing Systems, pp. 119–129 (2017)
3. Chen, F., Dong, Z., Li, Z., He, X.: Federated meta-learning for recommendation. arXiv preprint arXiv:1802.07876 (2018)
4. Chen, Y., Su, L., Xu, J.: Distributed statistical machine learning in adversarial settings: Byzantine gradient descent. Proc. ACM Measur. Anal. Comput. Syst. **1**(2), 1–25 (2017)
5. Corinzia, L., Buhmann, J.M.: Variational federated multi-task learning. arXiv preprint arXiv:1906.06268 (2019)
6. Dong, J., et al.: ADMETlab: a platform for systematic ADMET evaluation based on a comprehensively collected ADMET database. J. Cheminformatics **10**(1), 29 (2018)

7. Dwork, C., McSherry, F., Nissim, K., Smith, A.: Calibrating noise to sensitivity in private data analysis. In: Halevi, S., Rabin, T. (eds.) TCC 2006. LNCS, vol. 3876, pp. 265–284. Springer, Heidelberg (2006). https://doi.org/10.1007/11681878_14
8. Hinton, G., Vinyals, O., Dean, J.: Distilling the knowledge in a neural network. arXiv preprint arXiv:1503.02531 (2015)
9. Jeong, E., Oh, S., Kim, H., Park, J., Bennis, M., Kim, S.L.: Communication-efficient on-device machine learning: Federated distillation and augmentation under non-IID private data. arXiv preprint arXiv:1811.11479 (2018)
10. Kang, J., Xiong, Z., Niyato, D., Yu, H., Liang, Y.C., Kim, D.I.: Incentive design for efficient federated learning in mobile networks: a contract theory approach. In: 2019 IEEE VTS Asia Pacific Wireless Communications Symposium (APWCS), pp. 1–5. IEEE (2019)
11. Li, D., Wang, J.: FedMD: heterogenous federated learning via model distillation. arXiv preprint arXiv:1910.03581 (2019)
12. Li, T., Sahu, A.K., Talwalkar, A., Smith, V.: Federated learning: challenges, methods, and future directions. IEEE Sig. Process. Mag. **37**(3), 50–60 (2020)
13. Li, T., Sahu, A.K., Zaheer, M., Sanjabi, M., Talwalkar, A., Smith, V.: Federated optimization in heterogeneous networks. arXiv preprint arXiv:1812.06127 (2018)
14. Lin, T., Kong, L., Stich, S.U., Jaggi, M.: Ensemble distillation for robust model fusion in federated learning. arXiv preprint arXiv:2006.07242 (2020)
15. McMahan, B., Moore, E., Ramage, D., Hampson, S., Arcas, B.A.: Communication-efficient learning of deep networks from decentralized data. In: Artificial Intelligence and Statistics, pp. 1273–1282. PMLR (2017)
16. Mironov, I.: Rényi differential privacy. In: 2017 IEEE 30th Computer Security Foundations Symposium (CSF), pp. 263–275. IEEE (2017)
17. Nishio, T., Yonetani, R.: Client selection for federated learning with heterogeneous resources in mobile edge. In: ICC 2019–2019 IEEE International Conference on Communications (ICC), pp. 1–7. IEEE (2019)
18. Pantelopoulos, A., Bourbakis, N.G.: A survey on wearable sensor-based systems for health monitoring and prognosis. IEEE Trans. Syst. Man Cybern. Part C (Appl. Rev.) **40**(1), 1–12 (2009)
19. Pillutla, K., Kakade, S.M., Harchaoui, Z.: Robust aggregation for federated learning. arXiv preprint arXiv:1912.13445 (2019)
20. Sattler, F., Marban, A., Rischke, R., Samek, W.: Communication-efficient federated distillation. arXiv preprint arXiv:2012.00632 (2020)
21. Smith, V., Chiang, C.K., Sanjabi, M., Talwalkar, A.S.: Federated multi-task learning. In: Advances in Neural Information Processing Systems, pp. 4424–4434 (2017)
22. Sun, L., Lyu, L.: Federated model distillation with noise-free differential privacy. arXiv preprint arXiv:2009.05537 (2020)
23. Torrey, L., Shavlik, J.: Transfer learning. In: Handbook of Research on Machine Learning Applications and Trends: Algorithms, Methods, and Techniques, pp. 242–264. IGI global (2010)
24. Yang, Q., Liu, Y., Chen, T., Tong, Y.: Federated machine learning: concept and applications. ACM Trans. Intell. Syst. Technol. (TIST) **10**(2), 1–19 (2019)
25. Yang, T., et al.: Applied federated learning: improving google keyboard query suggestions. arXiv preprint arXiv:1812.02903 (2018)
26. Yin, D., Chen, Y., Ramchandran, K., Bartlett, P.: Byzantine-robust distributed learning: towards optimal statistical rates. arXiv preprint arXiv:1803.01498 (2018)
27. Zhao, Y., Li, M., Lai, L., Suda, N., Civin, D., Chandra, V.: Federated learning with non-IID data. arXiv preprint arXiv:1806.00582 (2018)

Data Augmentation for Graph Convolutional Network on Semi-supervised Classification

Zhengzheng Tang[1,2], Ziyue Qiao[1,2], Xuehai Hong[1,3(✉)], Yang Wang[2], Fayaz Ali Dharejo[1,2], Yuanchun Zhou[2], and Yi Du[2]

[1] Computer Network Information Center, Chinese Academy of Sciences, Beijing, China
{tangzhengzheng,qiaoziyue,fayazdharejo}@cnic.cn, hxh@ict.ac.cn
[2] University of Chinese Academy of Sciences, Beijing, China
{wangyang,zyc,duyi}@cnic.cn
[3] Institute of Computing Technology, Chinese Academy of Sciences, Beijing, China

Abstract. Data augmentation aims to generate new and synthetic features from the original data, which can identify a better representation of data and improve the performance and generalizability of downstream tasks. However, data augmentation for graph-based models remains a challenging problem, as graph data is more complex than traditional data, which consists of two features with different properties: graph topology and node attributes. In this paper, we study the problem of graph data augmentation for Graph Convolutional Network (GCN) in the context of improving the node embeddings for semi-supervised node classification. Specifically, we conduct cosine similarity based cross operation on the original features to create new graph features, including new node attributes and new graph topologies, and we combine them as new pairwise inputs for specific GCNs. Then, we propose an attentional integrating model to weighted sum the hidden node embeddings encoded by these GCNs into the final node embeddings. We also conduct a disparity constraint on these hidden node embeddings when training to ensure that non-redundant information is captured from different features. Experimental results on five real-world datasets show that our method improves the classification accuracy with a clear margin (+2.5%–+84.2%) than the original GCN model.

Keywords: Data augmentation · Graph Convolutional Network · Semi-supervised classification

1 Introduction

Data augmentation can create several new feature spaces and increase the amount of training data without additional ground truth labels, which has been widely used to improve the performance and generalizability of downstream predictive

Z. Tang and Z. Qiao contributed equally to this work.

models. Many works have proposed data augmentation technologies on different types of features, such as images [7,15,28], texts [12,29], vectorized features [6,18], etc. However, how to effectively augment graph data remain a challenging problem, as graph data is more complex and has non-Euclidean structures. Graph Neural Network (GNN) is a family of graph representation learning approaches that encode node features into low-dimensional representation vectors by aggregating local neighbors' information, it has drawn increasing attention in recent years, due to the superior performance on graph data mining [10,24,25].

For graph-based semi-supervised classification, the goal is to use the given graph data to predict the labels of unlabeled nodes. The given graph data usually consists of graph topology, node attributes (also called node features in some literature, we use node attributes to avoid the confusion with graph feature), as well as the labels of a subset node. Despite the labels, graph data can be specifically described as two graph features: an adjacency matrix of graph topology $A \in \mathbb{R}^{N \times N}$ and a node attribute matrix $X \in \mathbb{R}^{N \times d}$, where N is the total number of nodes, and d is the dimension of node attribute. GNN models conduct on both of these two features simultaneously and fuse them into the final node embedding by stacking several aggregation layers. The whole model can be formulated as a multi-layer graph encoder $Z = G(A, X)$, where $Z \in \mathbb{R}^{N \times h}$ is the output node embedding matrix and h is the dimension of node embedding. In this work, we consider the most popular and representative GNN: Graph Convolutional Network(GCN), proposed by Kipf et al. [10], which is the state-of-the-art model for semi-supervised node classification. It uses an efficient layer-wise propagation rule based on a first-order approximation of spectral convolutions on graphs. The encoder function $Z = G(A, X)$ of a L-layers' GCN can be specified as:

$$Z = G(A, X) = \sigma(\hat{A}...\sigma(\hat{A}\sigma(\hat{A}XW^{(0)})W^{(1)})...W^{(L)}) \tag{1}$$

where L is the number of layers. $W^{(i)}$ is the weight matrix of the i-th layer of GCN, σ denotes an activation function. $\hat{A} = \tilde{D}^{-\frac{1}{2}}\tilde{A}\tilde{D}^{-\frac{1}{2}}$, $\tilde{A} = A + I_N$, I_N is the identity matrix and $\hat{D}$ is the diagonal degree matrix of $\tilde{A}$.

However, a fact is that as the pairwise input for the GCN model, both the original features A and X may not be positive correlated with the node labels, while GCN can not adequately learn the importance of these two features to extract the most correlated information, which dampens the performance of GCN on the classification task. Data augmentation can create new feature spaces and preserve the information in original graph data in multiple facets, some of which may contribute useful information to node classification. This leads to the question: besides the original graph features A and X, can we create new pairs of adjacency matrices and attribute matrices and adaptively choose some effective ones as new feature inputs for GCN models?

Many prior studies [6,21] in data augmentation are to capture the interactions between features by taking addition, subtraction, or cross product of two original features, which are suitable for tensorial features. The major obstacle in graph data is that the original features, graph topology, and node attributes, are two types of data, one is usually encoded by position in Euclidean space, while the other is encoded by node connectivity in non-Euclidean space. It is difficult to take combination operations on these two features to create new features. Some work [16,20,26] proposes different strategy of adding or removing edges to improve the robustness of GCN. However, these augmentation methods are limited to modifying just a part of the node featuring in the graph, which is unable to create a brand new feature space of the whole graphs for GCN.

In this paper, we first create multiple new graph topologies and node attributes from the given graph data and propose different combinations of them as inputs for specific GCN models. Then, the output node embeddings of different GCN models are assigned with different weights via an attention mechanism, to sum up to the final node embeddings. In the training, an independence measurement-based disparity constraint is integrated into the objective function to capture diverse information from different features. In this way, extensive information from the original graph is encoded into the final node embeddings to improve the semi-supervised node classification task. The main contributions of our work are summarized as follows:

1. We propose a graph data augmentation strategy to create new pairwise graph inputs for the GCN model by designing new node attributes and graph topologies from the original graph features.
2. We propose an attentional integrating model, which can learn the importance of different hidden node embeddings encoded from various pairwise graph inputs via specific GCNs, and integrate them into the final node embeddings.
3. We propose a Hilbert-Schmidt independence criterion-based disparity constraint to increase the independence between the node embeddings encoded from various pairwise graph inputs and capture more diverse information.
4. We conduct experiments to evaluate the performance of our proposed method on five datasets. Our improvement over original GCN is +2.5%–+84.2%.

2   Proposed Method

In this section, we introduce the graph data augmentation strategies for GCN, then we investigate the availability of our augmented features by intuitive cases. Finally, we introduce the whole model including the attentional integrating model and the disparity constraint.

2.1   Data Augmentation Strategy

Given the original features A and X of graph data, we aim to reconstruct the whole graph topology and node attributes. A naive and widely used way of data augmentation operation is cross operation, we first conduct cosine similarity-based cross operation on A and X to create two new features, which carry the information of global proximity of nodes with others in the views of local topology and node attributes. Specifically, for each row in A and X, we calculate the cosine similarities of it with all the other rows and concatenate these similarities as new features of its corresponding node. Finally, the new features matrices A_C and X_C of the graph can be formulated as:

$$A_{C_{ij}} = \frac{A_i \cdot A_j}{\|A_i\|\|A_j\|}, \quad X_{C_{ij}} = \frac{X_i \cdot X_j}{\|X_i\|\|X_j\|}. \tag{2}$$

where $A_C \in \mathbb{R}^{N \times N}$, $X_C \in \mathbb{R}^{N \times N}$, $A_{C_{ij}}$ and $X_{C_{ij}}$ is the element in the i-th row and j-th column of A_C and X_C respectively, A_i and X_i is the i-th row of A and X respectively. We consider A_C and X_C as new node attribute matrices, as for each node, its corresponding row in A_C preserves the information of global structural proximity with other nodes, and that in X_C preserves the information of global proximity of attribute with other nodes. To some extent, these information can be regarded as different types of node attributes.

Further, we use the obtained A_C and X_C to construct k-nearest neighbor graphs $A_T \in \{0,1\}^{N \times N}$, $X_T \in \{0,1\}^{N \times N}$, that is, we set the largest k elements in each row as 1 and set other elements as 0. A_T and X_T are considered as new adjacency matrices, where each edge in A_T represents the connecting nodes are similar in local topology and each edge in X_T represents the connecting nodes are similar in node attribute.

Finally, we combine these attribute features and adjacency features to create 9 different inputs for GNN model, as shown in the Table 1:

Table 1. Different combinations of six graph features A, X, A_C, X_C, A_T, X_T as inputs for GNN model. Adj. means the adjacency matrices, Att. means the attribute matrices. $G_i(\cdot, \cdot)$ represent the specific GNN encoder for the i-th combination of features.

Adj.	Att.		
	X	A_C	X_C
A	$G_1(A, X)$	$G_2(A, A_C)$	$G_3(A, X_C)$
A_T	$G_4(A_T, X)$	$G_5(A_T, A_C)$	$G_6(A_T, X_C)$
X_T	$G_7(X_T, X)$	$G_8(X_T, A_C)$	$G_9(X_T, X_C)$

Noted that the adjacency matrix is usually very sparse, making the cosine similarity matrix sparse, too. So before the process of data augmentation, we first use the update rule proposed in [3] through the original adjacency matrix A to build new edges between neighbors within 2-hop links, and upgrade A as a denser high-order adjacency matrix.

2.2   Feature Availability Investigation

To further investigate the availability of the attribute features A_C, X_C and the adjacency features A_T, X_T, we use a simple yet intuitive case to show the distribution and topology of these augmented features and the original graph feature A and X. Specifically, we first generate a naive graph consisting of 90 nodes, and randomly assign 3 labels to these nodes. The edge between every two nodes with the same label is created with the probability of 0.03, and that between every two nodes with different labels is created with the probability of 0.01. Each node has a feature vector of 50 dimensions. We use the Gaussian distribution to generate the node features, the Gaussian distributions for the three classes of nodes have the same covariance matrix, but three different centers far away from each other. Then, we can obtain A and X of this graph and augment new features A_C, X_C, A_T, and X_T via the operations described above. As shown in Fig. 1, the first line shows the node distribution of the attribute features X, A_C, and X_C, we use t-SNE to project them into 2-dimensional spaces. In the second line, we draw edges between nodes via the adjacency features A, A_T, and X_T to show their different graph topologies, where the node positions are set to be the same as X.

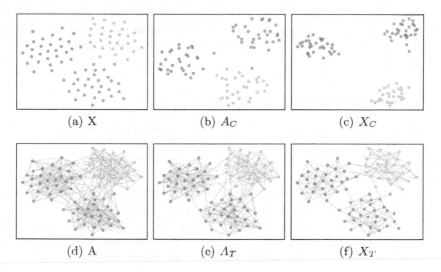

(a) X   (b) A_C (c) X_C

(d) A   (e) A_T (f) X_T

Fig. 1. Visualization of attribute features: X, A_C, and X_C, and adjacency features: A, A_T, and X_T.

Attribute Features Analysis. The attribute features are X, A_C, and X_C. First, we can observe that when X is correlated with labels, X_C can preserve the label correlation better, the nodes with the same labels are located in smaller groups and with different labels are farther away from others, we believe that is because X_C preserve the global attribute similarity of nodes with others, and the global information can better improve the node distribution for classification. We can also observe that A_C can preserve the label correlation inherited from A, but it presents a totally different node distribution with X as they contain different information. So when the graph topology is correlated with labels and the original attribute X is not, A_C may further improve the accuracy of classification if it is chosen as node attributes.

Adjacency Features Analysis. The adjacency features are A, A_T, and X_T. We can observe that comparing with A, the topology structure in the augmented feature A_T can preserve the label correlation better, the intra-class connections are denser than the inter-class connections, that may also because A_T preserve the global structural similarity of nodes with others, and the global information can better improve the graph topology for classification. Also, X_T provide another edge generation method that nodes with the higher similar attribute are more likely to connect each other. So when the node attributes are related with labels and graph topology is not, X_T may further improve the accuracy of classification if it is chosen as the adjacency matrix.

To summarize, the augmented graph features A_C, X_C, A_T, and X_T broaden the availability of the original graph features X and A, which is important because the augmentation may improve the distribution of original features for classification by introducing the global information on the one hand, on the other hand, when the distribution of some features are not correlated with the node labels, these information can provide more input choices for GNN model than the original input pair (A, X), and some of them may contribute more than (A, X) for the final task.

2.3 Attentional Integration Model

After generating the new inputs for the GNN model, the next question is how do we select useful features. In the real-world, the graph data is complex, it is hard to know which of the augmented features and original features is correlated with the final task, and time-consuming to manually choose the related ones. So we proposed an attentional integration model, which can automatically assign high weights on features with high correlation for the final task.

Specifically, given the nine combinations of GNN inputs augmented above, we use the traditional GNN encoder, Graph Convolutional Network described in Sect. 2, to encode the i-th inputs into the node embedding matrices Z_i:

$$Z_i = G_i(Adj_i, Att_i) \tag{3}$$

where $Z_i \in \mathbb{R}^{N \times h}$, h is the dimension of output node embedding, (Adj_i, Att_i) is the i-th pairwise input specified in Table 1, $G_i(\cdot, \cdot)$ represent the GNN encoder for the i-th combination of input, Noted that these nine GNN encoders do not share parameters, this help to better extract the information of different features, but without increasing the time complexity and space complexity because the parameters just increase linearly. Now we obtain the nine output of node embedding matrices: $\{Z_1, Z_2, ..., Z_9\}$ from the nine GNN encoders. Considering they may have different correlations with the node labels, we use an attention mechanism on them to learn their corresponding importance weight and weighted sum them into the final node embedding matrix:

$$Z = \alpha_1 \cdot Z_1 + \alpha_2 \cdot Z_2 + ... + \alpha_9 \cdot Z_9 \tag{4}$$

where $\{\alpha_1, \alpha_2, ..., \alpha_9\} \in \mathbb{R}^{N \times 1}$ indicate the attention weights of n nodes with embeddings $\{Z_1, Z_2, ..., Z_9\}$, respectively. To calculate α_i, We firstly transform the embeddings through a nonlinear transformation, and then use one shared attention parameter vector $\mathbf{q} \in \mathbb{R}^{h' \times 1}$ to get the attention value ω_i as follows:

$$\omega_i = q^T \cdot tanh(W_i \cdot (Z_i)^T + b_i). \tag{5}$$

where $\omega_i \in \mathbb{R}^{N \times 1}$, $W_i \in \mathbb{R}^{h' \times h}$ is the weight matrix and $b_i \in \mathbb{R}^{h' \times 1}$ is the bias vector for embedding matrix Z_i. Then we can get the the attention values $\{\omega_1, \omega_2, ..., \omega_9\}$ for embedding matrices $\{Z_1, Z_2, ..., Z_9\}$, respectively. We then normalize the attention values $\{\omega_1, \omega_2, ..., \omega_9\}$ for each node by softmax function to get the final importance weight:

$$\alpha_i^j = softmax(\omega_i^j) = \frac{exp(\omega_i^j)}{\sum_{i=1}^{9} exp(\omega_i^j)} \tag{6}$$

where α_i^j and ω_i^j represent the j-th element of α_i and ω_i, respectively. The larger α_i^j implies the corresponding node embedding in Z_i is more important for the j-th node and should contribute more to its final embedding.

2.4   Objective Function

Disparity Constraint. Firstly, we use the Hilbert-Schmidt Independence Criterion (HSIC) [17], a widely used dependency measurement [13,30], as a penalty term in the objective function to ensure the nine output node embeddings $\{Z_1, Z_2, ..., Z_9\}$ encoded from nine inputs can capture non-redundant information. HSIC is simple and reliable to compute the independency between variables and the smaller the value is, the more independent they are. The HISC of any two embeddings Z_i and Z_j is defined as:

$$HSIC(Z_i, Z_j) = (n-1)^{-2} tr(K_i H K_j H), \tag{7}$$

where $K_i, K_j \in R^{N \times N}$ are the Gram matrices with $K_i^{uv} = k_i(Z_i^u, Z_i^v)$, $K_j^{uv} = k_j(Z_j^u, Z_j^v)$, K_i^{uv} is the element in u-th row and v-th column of K_i, Z_i^u is the u-th row of Z_i, and $k_i(\cdot, \cdot)$ is the kernel function. $H = I - n^{-1}ee^T$, where e is an all-one column vector and I is an identity matrix. In our implementation, we use the inner product kernel function. Then we set the disparity constraint $\mathcal{L}_d$ by minimizing the values of HISC among nine output nodes embeddings:

$$\mathcal{L}_d = \sum_{i \neq j} HISC(Z_i, Z_j). \tag{8}$$

Optimization Objective. For semi-supervised multi-class classification, We feed the final node embeddings Z into a linear transformation and a *softmax* function. Denote classes set is C, and the probability of node i belonging to class $c \in C$ is $\hat{Y}_{ic}$, the prediction results on whole nodes $\hat{Y} = [\hat{Y}_{ic}] \in \mathbb{R}^{N \times C}$ can be calculated as:

$$\hat{Y} = softmax(W \cdot Z + b), \tag{9}$$

where $softmax(x) = \frac{exp(x)}{\sum_{c=1}^{C} exp(x_c)}$ is actually a row-wise normalizer across all classes. Then the cross-entropy loss $\mathcal{L}$ for node classification over all labeled nodes is represented as:

$$\mathcal{L}_l = - \sum_{l \in \mathcal{Y}_L} \sum_{c=1}^{C} Y_{lc} ln \hat{Y}_{lc}. \tag{10}$$

Where $\mathcal{Y}_L$ is the set of node indices that have labels, for each $l \in L$ the real one-hot encoded label is Y_l.

Finally, combining the node classification task and the disparity constraints, we have the following overall objective function:

$$\mathcal{L} = \mathcal{L}_l + \lambda \mathcal{L}_d. \tag{11}$$

where λ is parameters of the disparity constraint terms. We use a mini-batch Adam optimizer to minimize $\mathcal{L}$ and optimize the parameters in the whole model. Noted that we use HISC to calculate the pairwise independence, it would take C_9^2 times of calculation of HISC among Z_1 to Z_9 in each training step, which we think is unnecessary. We use a sampling strategy to reduce the computation that randomly selecting t pairs of the output embeddings and summing their HISC as the disparity constraints loss in each training step. Through multiple iterations, all combinations of embeddings should be sampled and all embeddings should be trained to be independent of each other.

Table 2. The statistics of the datasets

Dataset	Nodes	Edges	Classes	Attribute
Citeseer	3327	4732	6	3703
UAI2010	3067	28311	19	4973
ACM	3025	13128	3	1870
BlogCatalog	5196	171743	6	8189
Flickr	7575	239738	9	12047

3 Experiments

3.1 Experiment Setting

To adequately examine the effectiveness of our proposed data augmentation method, we evaluate the performance of our framework on five real-world benchmark datasets: Citeseer [10] is research paper citation network, UAI2010 [23] is a dataset for community detection, ACM [24] is research paper coauthor network extracted from ACM dataset, BlogCatalog [14] is a social network with bloggers relationships extracted from the BlogCatalog website, Flickr [14] is a social network with users interaction from an image and video hosting website. Basic statistics of these datasets are summarized in Table 2.

We compared our method with some GCN and node classification related baselines: GCN [10] is a classical semi-supervised graph convolutional network model, which obtains node representation through multi-layer neighbor aggregation. Chebyshev [4] learns rich feature information by superimposing multiple Chebyshev filters with GCN. GAT [22] is a graph neural network model that aggregates node features through multiple attention heads with different semantics. DEMO-Net [27] proposes a generic graph neural network model which formulates the feature aggregation into a multi-task learning problem according to nodes' degree values. MixHop [1] utilizes multiple powers of the adjacency matrix to learn the general mixing of neighborhood information, including averaging and delta operators in the feature space. We also compare our method with some related graph data augmentation based methods for semi-supervised node classification. GAug [31] is to leverage information inherent in the graph to predict which non-existent edges should likely exist, and which existent edges should likely be removed in the original graph to produce modified graphs to improve the model performance. MCGL [5] assigns pseudo-labels to some nodes in each convolutional layer, and improves the performance of the model by expanding the training set.

The weights of parameters are initialized like the original GCN [10] and input vectors are row-normalized accordingly [8]. For our model, we train nine 2-layer GCNs with the same hidden layer dimension(h_1) and the same output dimension (h_2) simultaneously, where h_1 of the UAI2010, BlogCatalog, and Flickr is 256 and the out dimension h_2 is 128. The h_1 and h_2 of ACM and Citeseer are 512 and 256 respectively. We use $5e-4$ learning rate with Adam optimizer, the dropout rate is 0.5, weight decay is $1e-4$. In addition, the hyper-parameter k for constructing k-nearest neighbor graphs is 4, t for sampling embeddings pairs is 8. For the baselines, we set the dimension of node embeddings in five datasets same as the setting of out method, and the other hyper-parameter setting are based on default values or the values specified in their own papers. We choose the number of labeled nodes per class as 20/40/60 respectively for training, and 500 nodes are used for validation and 1000 nodes for testing. All methods are repeatedly run 5 times, the average results are reported to make sure the results can reflect the performances of methods.

3.2 Semi-Supervised Classification

The semi-supervised node classification results are reported in Table 3. We report the Accuracy (ACC) and macro F1-score (F1) of the classification results. From the results, we can observe that (1) our proposed method achieves the best performance on all datasets with all label rates, showing the superiority of our method in improving the semi-supervised node classification. (2) Our method consistently outperform the original GCN on all five datasets, the improvement of ACC over Citeseer, UAI2010, ACM, BlogCatalog, Flickr is {3.0%–6.1%, 41.3%–44.9%,

Table 3. Results of semi-supervised node classification(%). (Bold: best. L/C is the number of labeled nodes per class. The results of some baselines are taken from [25].)

Datasets		Citeseer		UAI2010		ACM		BlogCatalog		Flickr	
L/C	Method	ACC	F1	ACC	F1	ACC	F1	ACC	F1	ACC	F1
20	GCN	70.30	67.50	49.88	32.86	87.80	87.82	69.84	68.73	41.42	39.95
	Chebyshev	69.80	65.92	50.02	33.65	75.24	74.86	38.08	33.39	23.26	21.27
	GAT	72.50	68.14	56.92	39.61	87.36	87.44	64.08	63.38	38.52	37.00
	DEMO-Net	69.50	67.84	23.45	16.82	84.48	84.16	54.19	52.79	34.89	33.53
	MixHop	71.40	66.96	61.56	49.19	81.08	81.40	65.46	64.89	39.56	40.13
	GAug	73.30	70.12	52.96	49.82	90.82	89.44	77.60	75.43	68.20	67.55
	MCGL	66.88	63.26	42.56	24.78	90.95	91.01	54.22	50.15	15.67	15.54
	Ours	**74.60**	**70.20**	**72.20**	**60.87**	**91.90**	**91.81**	**84.10**	**84.60**	**76.30**	**76.27**
40	GCN	73.10	69.70	51.80	33.80	89.06	89.00	71.28	70.71	45.48	43.27
	Chebyshev	71.64	68.31	58.18	38.80	81.64	81.26	56.28	53.86	35.10	33.53
	GAT	73.04	69.58	63.74	45.08	88.60	88.55	67.40	66.39	38.44	39.94
	DEMO-Net	70.44	66.97	30.29	26.36	85.70	84.83	63.47	63.09	46.57	45.23
	MixHop	71.48	67.40	65.05	53.86	82.34	81.13	71.66	70.84	55.19	56.25
	GAug	74.60	71.32	55.26	53.36	91.24	91.01	79.46	77.79	73.24	72.28
	MCGL	69.48	65.98	41.93	25.72	91.10	91.13	54.74	51.24	17.82	17.06
	Ours	**75.50**	**71.58**	**75.10**	**69.70**	**92.10**	**91.94**	**89.20**	**89.06**	**80.10**	**79.36**
60	GCN	74.48	71.24	54.40	34.12	90.54	90.49	72.66	71.80	47.96	46.58
	Chebyshev	73.26	70.31	59.82	40.60	85.43	85.26	70.06	68.37	41.70	40.17
	GAT	74.76	71.60	68.44	48.97	90.40	90.39	69.95	69.08	38.96	37.35
	DEMO-Net	71.86	68.22	34.11	29.05	86.55	84.05	76.81	76.73	57.30	56.49
	MixHop	72.16	69.31	67.66	56.31	83.09	82.24	77.44	76.38	64.96	65.73
	GAug	75.48	72.22	55.92	54.08	92.06	91.81	81.81	79.84	75.68	74.24
	MCGL	74.02	70.69	44.30	22.46	92.03	92.04	55.24	49.41	22.36	21.28
	Ours	**76.70**	**72.88**	**76.90**	**69.79**	**92.80**	**92.75**	**89.70**	**89.53**	**82.29**	**82.85**

2.5%–4.6%, 20.4%–25.1%, 71.5%–84.2%}, respectively. Indicating that the augmented graph features contain more useful information than original graph features and help to node classification. (3) We noticed that two graph augmentation methods GAug and MCGL perform well on some datasets, but also fail in some datasets, while our method consistently performs well on all datasets, showing that our whole framework is robust on different types of graphs.

We further report the visualization of learned node embeddings of the Citeseer, UAI2010, and ACM datasets in Fig. 2. We use t-SNE to project the final node embeddings of our method and original GCN into 2-dimensional spaces and color nodes differently according to their labels. We can observe that the boundaries between different classes in our method are sharper than the original GCN, and nodes in the same class are more concentrated, especially in the Citeseer dataset, which proves our method can learn better node representations to improves the node classification performance of original GCN.

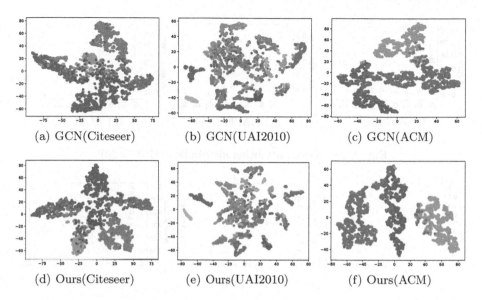

Fig. 2. Visualization of the learned final node embeddings on ACM, UAI2010, and Citeseer datasets. (L/C = 20)

3.3 Attentional Integration Model Analysis

We design nine combinations of features as inputs of GCN models and learn nine specific node embeddings for each node, then each embedding is associated with the corresponding attention values by our proposed attentional integrating model. Thus, we conduct attention distribution analysis on the ACM, UAI2010, and Citeseer datasets in Fig. 3, we report the Box-plots of the learned attention value distributions of all nodes respectively for nine GCN models $\{G_1, ..., G_9\}$. We can observe that the average of attention values for nine input combinations are evidently different, some of the combinations may have larger attention values than others, For example in ACM, the attention values of G_1, G_5, and G_9 are larger than others, which implies that the corresponding augmented inputs of (A, X), (A_T, A_C), and (X_T, X_C) contain more valuable information than other inputs for the classification task. Also, we can observe that between different datasets, the same combination input may be quite different in attention values, which proves that our proposed attentional integrating model is able to adaptively find and assign larger attention value for the important information on different datasets.

In Fig. 4, we further analyze the changing trends of attention values for different input combinations in the increasing of training epochs. We report the results of ACM, UAI2010, and Citeseer datasets as examples, we can observe that the average attention values of different combinations gradually increase or decrease when training, and finally converge to a relatively stable value. This phenomenon proves that the proposed attentional integrating model has a great fitting capability to learn attention values on different datasets.

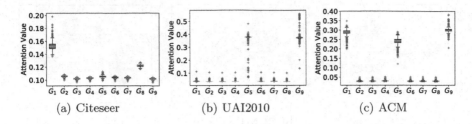

Fig. 3. Analysis of attention distribution. (L/C = 20)

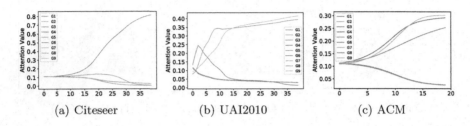

Fig. 4. The attention changing trends w.r.t epochs. (L/C = 20)

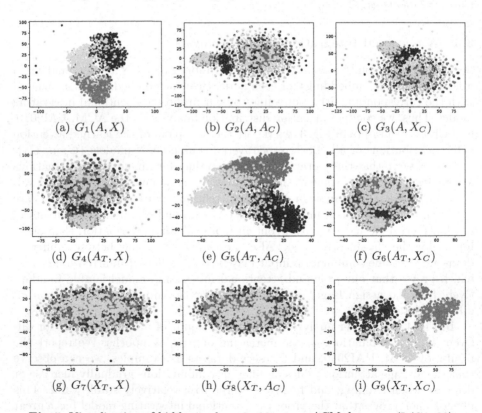

(a) $G_1(A, X)$ (b) $G_2(A, A_C)$ (c) $G_3(A, X_C)$

(d) $G_4(A_T, X)$ (e) $G_5(A_T, A_C)$ (f) $G_6(A_T, X_C)$

(g) $G_7(X_T, X)$ (h) $G_8(X_T, A_C)$ (i) $G_9(X_T, X_C)$

Fig. 5. Visualization of hidden node embeddings on ACM datasets. (L/C = 20)

We also demonstrate the distribution of the output node embeddings of nine combination inputs when the model has converged. Figure 5 shows the embedding distributions of the ACM dataset projected by t-SNE. It can be observed that the node embeddings Z_1, Z_5, and Z_9 encoded from $G_1(A, X)$, $G_5(A_T, A_C)$, and $G_9(X_T, X_C)$ is obviously well classified into three classes, so the learned attention of them in Fig. 3 is larger than others. It proves that our designed graph features can also capture useful information for node classification and the attentional integration model can adaptively integrate different information from multiple input features to improve the final classification results. Also, the distributions of nine node embeddings are significantly different from each other, showing the effectiveness of our designed disparity constraint in keeping the dependency of different embeddings.

3.4 Parameter Sensitivity

The parameter k introduced in Sect. 2.1 is used to adjust the sparsity of our augmented features A_T and X_T. In Fig. 6, we evaluate how the k impacts the performance of our method on ACM, UAI2010, and Citeseer datasets with the number of training nodes as 20/40/60, respectively. We report the ACC of our method with various numbers of k ranging from 2 to 9 and other parameters remaining the same. From the figures, we observe that when k was small, the accuracy performance of our model is relatively limited, demonstrating that a smaller size of k led to the augmented adjacency features sparser and information loss. When k is increased to 4 or 5, our model can gain the highest accuracy results. However, when k is too large, the performance decreases slightly, which may probably because denser augmented adjacency features may introduce more noisy edges. In summary, properly setting the size of k can help to generate robust features to improve the performance of our method.

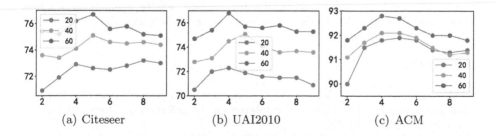

(a) Citeseer   (b) UAI2010   (c) ACM

Fig. 6. Analysis of parameter k.

4 Related Works

Graph data augmentation has drawn increasing attention in graph learning recently, it can create new graph data to improve the generalization of graph models, especially the GNN models. Existing graph augmentations mainly focus on augmenting graph structures by modifying local graph structure [2,9,16]. [32] introduce data augmentation on graphs and present two heuristic algorithms: random mapping and motif-similarity mapping, to generate more weakly labeled data for small-scale benchmark datasets via heuristic modification of graph structures. [11] propose a simple but effective solution, FLAG, which iteratively augments node features with gradient-based adversarial perturbations during training, and boosts performance at test time. [25] construct a feature graph and propose an adaptive multi-channel graph convolutional networks to improve the node embeddings. [31] shows that neural edge predictors can effectively encode class-homophilic structure to promote intra-class edges and demote inter-class edges in given graph structures, and their leverages these insights to improve performance in GNN-based node classification via edge prediction. [26] present the Node-Parallel Augmentation scheme, that creates a 'parallel universe' for each node to conduct data augmentation. [19] proposed GINN that uses supervised and unsupervised data to construct a similarity map between points in the dataset, and rebuild them to expand the dataset.

5   Conclusion

In this paper, we study to improve the performance of GCN on semi-supervised classification via graph data augmentation. We create new attribute and adjacency features base on original graph features and pairwise combine them as inputs for specific GCNs, then use attention mechanism and disparity constraint to integrate diverse information from the GCNs' outputs to the final node embeddings. From the experiments, our proposed method can better extract the rich information of graphs and improve the qualities of node representations.

Acknowledgments. This work is supported in part by the Natural Science Foundation of China under Grant No. 92046017, the Natural Science Foundation of China under Grant No. 61836013, Beijing Natural Science Foundation (4212030).

References

1. Abu-El-Haija, S., et al.: Mixhop: higher-order graph convolutional architectures via sparsified neighborhood mixing. In: International Conference on Machine Learning, pp. 21–29. PMLR (2019)
2. Chen, J., Ma, T., Xiao, C.: FASTGCN: fast learning with graph convolutional networks via importance sampling. In: International Conference on Learning Representations (2018)
3. Cheng, Y., Sun, M., Liu, Z., Tu, C.: Fast network embedding enhancement via high order proximity approximation. In: International Joint Conference on Artificial Intelligence (2017)
4. Defferrard, M., Bresson, X., Vandergheynst, P.: Convolutional neural networks on graphs with fast localized spectral filtering. In: NIPS (2016)

5. Dong, H., Ding, Z., He, X., Feng, F., Bi, S.: Data augmentation view on graph convolutional network and the proposal of monte carlo graph learning (2020)
6. Fawaz, H.I., Forestier, G., Weber, J., Idoumghar, L., Muller, P.A.: Data augmentation using synthetic data for time series classification with deep residual networks. arXiv preprint arXiv:1808.02455 (2018)
7. Frid-Adar, M., Klang, E., Amitai, M., Goldberger, J., Greenspan, H.: Synthetic data augmentation using GAN for improved liver lesion classification. In: 2018 IEEE 15th International Symposium on Biomedical Imaging. pp. 289–293 (2018)
8. Glorot, X., Bengio, Y.: Understanding the difficulty of training deep feedforward neural networks. In: Proceedings of the Thirteenth International Conference on Artificial Intelligence and Statistics, pp. 249–256 (2010)
9. Hamilton, W.L., Ying, R., Leskovec, J.: Inductive representation learning on large graphs. In: Proceedings of the 31st International Conference on Neural Information Processing Systems, pp. 1025–1035 (2017)
10. Kipf, T.N., Welling, M.: Semi-supervised classification with graph convolutional networks. arXiv preprint arXiv:1609.02907 (2016)
11. Kong, K., et al.: Flag: adversarial data augmentation for graph neural networks. arXiv preprint arXiv:2010.09891 (2020)
12. Liu, M., Xie, Z., Huang, Y., Jin, L., Zhou, W.: Distilling GRU with data augmentation for unconstrained handwritten text recognition. In: 2018 16th International Conference on Frontiers in Handwriting Recognition (ICFHR), pp. 56–61 (2018)
13. Ma, W.D.K., Lewis, J., Kleijn, W.B.: The HSIC bottleneck: Deep learning without back-propagation. In: Proceedings of the AAAI Conference on Artificial Intelligence, vol. 34, pp. 5085–5092 (2020)
14. Meng, Z., Liang, S., Bao, H., Zhang, X.: Co-embedding attributed networks. In: Proceedings of the Twelfth ACM International Conference on Web Search and Data Mining, pp. 393–401 (2019)
15. Moreno-Barea, F.J., Strazzera, F., Jerez, J.M., Urda, D., Franco, L.: Forward noise adjustment scheme for data augmentation. In: 2018 IEEE Symposium Series on Computational Intelligence (SSCI), pp. 728–734. IEEE (2018)
16. Rong, Y., Huang, W., Xu, T., Huang, J.: Dropedge: towards deep graph convolutional networks on node classification. In: International Conference on Learning Representations (2019)
17. Song, L., Smola, A., Gretton, A., Borgwardt, K.M., Bedo, J.: Supervised feature selection via dependence estimation. In: Proceedings of the 24th International Conference on Machine Learning, pp. 823–830 (2007)
18. Song, L., Minku, L.L., Yao, X.: A novel automated approach for software effort estimation based on data augmentation. In: Proceedings of the 2018 26th ACM Joint Meeting on European Software Engineering Conference and Symposium on the Foundations of Software Engineering, pp. 468–479 (2018)
19. Spinelli, I., Scardapane, S., Scarpiniti, M., Uncini, A.: Efficient data augmentation using graph imputation neural networks. In: Progresses in Artificial Intelligence and Neural Systems, p. 57
20. Srivastava, N., Hinton, G., Krizhevsky, A., Sutskever, I., Salakhutdinov, R.: Dropout: a simple way to prevent neural networks from overfitting. J. Mach. Learn. Res. 15(56), 1929–1958 (2014)
21. Summers, C., Dinneen, M.J.: Improved mixed-example data augmentation. In: 2019 IEEE Winter Conference on Applications of Computer Vision (WACV), pp. 1262–1270 (2019)
22. Veličković, P., Cucurull, G., Casanova, A., Romero, A., Lio, P., Bengio, Y.: Graph attention networks. In: ICLR (2018)

23. Wang, W., Liu, X., Jiao, P., Chen, X., Jin, D.: A unified weakly supervised framework for community detection and semantic matching. In: Phung, D., Tseng, V.S., Webb, G.I., Ho, B., Ganji, M., Rashidi, L. (eds.) PAKDD 2018. LNCS (LNAI), vol. 10939, pp. 218–230. Springer, Cham (2018). https://doi.org/10.1007/978-3-319-93040-4_18
24. Wang, X., et al.: Heterogeneous graph attention network. In: The World Wide Web Conference, pp. 2022–2032 (2019)
25. Wang, X., Zhu, M., Bo, D., Cui, P., Shi, C., Pei, J.: AM-GCN: Adaptive multi-channel graph convolutional networks. In: KDD 2020: The 26th ACM SIGKDD Conference on Knowledge Discovery and Data Mining (2020)
26. Wang, Y., Wang, W., Liang, Y., Cai, Y., Liu, J., Hooi, B.: Nodeaug: semi-supervised node classification with data augmentation. In: International Conference on Knowledge Discovery & Data Mining, pp. 207–217 (2020)
27. Wu, J., He, J., Xu, J.: Net: degree-specific graph neural networks for node and graph classification. In: Proceedings of the 25th ACM SIGKDD International Conference on Knowledge Discovery & Data Mining, pp. 406–415 (2019)
28. Xu, Y., Zhang, Y., Wang, H., Liu, X.: Underwater image classification using deep convolutional neural networks and data augmentation. In: 2017 IEEE International Conference on Signal Processing, Communications and Computing, pp. 1–5 (2017)
29. Yu, S., Yang, J., Liu, D., Li, R., Zhang, Y., Zhao, S.: Hierarchical data augmentation and the application in text classification. IEEE Access 7 (2019)
30. Zhang, C., Liu, Y., Liu, Y., Hu, Q., Liu, X., Zhu, P.: Fish-mml: fisher-hsic multi-view metric learning. In: Proceedings of the 27th International Joint Conference on Artificial Intelligence, pp. 3054–3060 (2018)
31. Zhao, T., Liu, Y., Neves, L., Woodford, O., Jiang, M., Shah, N.: Data augmentation for graph neural networks. arXiv preprint arXiv:2006.06830 (2020)
32. Zhou, J., Shen, J., Xuan, Q.: Data augmentation for graph classification. In: Proceedings of the 29th ACM International Conference on Information & Knowledge Management, pp. 2341–2344 (2020)

Generating Long and Coherent Text with Multi-Level Generative Adversarial Networks

Tianyi Tang[1,3], Junyi Li[2], Wayne Xin Zhao[2,3,4(✉)], and Ji-Rong Wen[1,2,3]

[1] School of Information, Renmin University of China, Beijing, China
[2] Gaoling School of Artificial Intelligence, Renmin University of China,
Beijing, China
{lijunyi,jrwen}@ruc.edu.cn
[3] Beijing Key Laboratory of Big Data Management and Analysis Methods,
Beijing, China
[4] Beijing Academy of Artificial Intelligence, Beijing 100084, China

Abstract. In this paper, we study the task of generating long and coherent text. In the literature, Generative Adversarial Nets (GAN) based methods have been one of the mainstream approaches to generic text generation. We aim to improve two aspects of GAN-based methods in generic text generation, namely long sequence optimization and semantic coherence enhancement. For this purpose, we propose a novel Multi-Level Generative Adversarial Networks (MLGAN) for long and coherent text generation. Our approach explicitly models the text generation process at three different levels, namely paragraph-, sentence- and word-level generation. At the top two levels, we generate continuous paragraph vectors and sentence vectors as *semantic sketches* to plan the entire content. While, at the bottom level we generate discrete word tokens for realizing the sentences. Furthermore, we utilize a Conditional GAN architecture to enhance the inter-sentence coherence by injecting paragraph vectors for sentence vector generation. Extensive experiments results have demonstrated the effectiveness of the proposed model.

Keywords: Generative Adversarial Network · Text generation

1 Introduction

The task of generic text generation is aimed to generate realistic text without inputting any condition or constraint. A main challenge for generic text generation is that it places too much burden on the generative model to capture complex semantic and structural features underlying the data distribution [5]. Recurrent Neural Network (RNN) based methods maximize the log-likelihood of each ground-truth word given prior observed words. It has shown that they are likely to suffer from *exposure bias* [6]. Hence, error accumulates as the sentence grows in length, resulting in limited capacities in generating long text.

© Springer Nature Switzerland AG 2021
L. H. U et al. (Eds.): APWeb-WAIM 2021, LNCS 12859, pp. 49–63, 2021.
https://doi.org/10.1007/978-3-030-85899-5_4

In recent years, Generative Adversarial Nets (GAN) [2,7,21,40] have been applied to improve the quality of the generated text. GAN matches the distribution of real data by introducing an adversarial game between a generator and a discriminator. However, there are still two major issues with GAN based methods on text generation. First, it is difficult to optimize GAN over long sequences with sparse, delayed rewards [7]. In prior studies [40], the discriminator can only provide the signal whether a sequence is real or not. Such a kind of feedback signal is not effective to sufficiently improve the generator, especially in a discrete generation process. Second, it is not easy to enforce the semantic coherence of long text in existing GAN-based approaches. Since these approaches usually decode the token in a sequential manner, the overall semantics of the generated text are likely to be divergent for generated text.

Considering these two issues, we design a multi-level generation process for improving GAN-based generic text generation methods. Our solution is inspired by the writing way of real users. For example, a writer usually first conceives the main idea (level 1), then designs the content flow or structure (level 2), and finally considers the grammar and word usage (level 3). Indeed, it has been widely recognized that there are multiple levels in the writing process [14,32], where level 1 and 2 are usually referred to as *content planing* and level 3 is referred to as *sentence realization*. In order to generate high-quality text, we believe an ideal text generation method should be able to mimic the real writing process and fulfill the goal at each level. Based on such an idea, we consider a three-level text generation process, where a paragraph vector (*i.e.,* embedding) is first generated to summarize the overall semantics of the content, then sentence vectors (*i.e.,* embeddings) are further generated based on the paragraph vector, and finally sentences are realized by word generation. Via such a process, we would like to enhance the capacity of GAN-based approaches on long text generation.

To this end, in this paper, we propose a novel Multi-Level Generative Adversarial Networks (MLGAN) for long and coherent text generation. As shown in Fig. 1, our approach explicitly models the text generation process at three different levels, namely paragraph-, sentence- and word-level generation. At the top two levels, we generate continuous paragraph and sentence vectors as *semantic sketches* to plan overall semantics of the entire content (*i.e.,* content planning). While, at the bottom level we generate discrete word tokens for realizing the sentences (*i.e.,* sentence realization). In this way, we decompose long text generation into multi-level smaller tasks, which are easier to learn. In order to enforce the coherence, the inter-sentence coherence has been enhanced by Conditional GAN [30] which can incorporate high-level paragraph vectors in the generation of sentence vectors. Each discriminator is designed to provide two kinds of signals, *i.e.,* whether the outputs are realistic or not and the outputs go well with the conditions or not. Finally, for sentence realization, we adopt the Gumbel-Softmax trick [10] for training the word generator on discrete data. It has been shown that Gumbel-Softmax can deal with the *non-differentiable issue* with the discrete data and overcome the unstable training in reinforcement learning [29].

To our best knowledge, it is the first GAN-based model that follows a multi-level text generation process for generating long and coherent text. We effectively address the two issues of existing GAN-based text generation models through long sequence optimization and semantic coherence enhancement. Extensive experiments on Chinese poetry and movie review datasets demonstrate that our proposed model is more capable of producing high-quality text compared with several competitive baselines.

2   Preliminaries

We consider the task of generating long text in the form of paragraphs consisting of multiple sentences, denoted by $p = \{s_i : \langle w_{i,1}, \cdots, w_{i,t}, \cdots, w_{i,n_i} \rangle\}_{i=1}^m$, where $w_{i,t}$ (from vocabulary $\mathcal{V}$) denotes the t-th word of the i-th sentence s_i, n_i is the length of the i-th sentence and m is the number of sentences in a paragraph p. For convenience, we adopt bold-fonts notations $\boldsymbol{w}_{i,t}$, $\boldsymbol{s}_i$ and $\boldsymbol{p}$ to denote the low-dimensional representations of word $w_{i,t}$, sentence s_i and paragraph p, called word vectors, sentence vectors and paragraph vectors, respectively. Such vectors can be learned or inferred using various text representation learning methods [3, 26].

Different from prior GAN-based studies on long text generation [7], our text generation process is planned at three different levels: a paragraph vector is first generated to summarize the overall semantics of the content, then sentence vectors are further generated conditioned on the paragraph vector, and finally sentences are realized by word generation. Such a generation process naturally follows the way how regular writing is performed by real users. To model this process, we design a multi-level generative adversarial network, where different generators and discriminators are incorporated for producing paragraph vectors (continuous), sentence vectors (continuous) and words (discrete). Formally, we let $G_{\theta_P}^P / D_{\phi_P}^P$, $G_{\theta_S}^S / D_{\phi_S}^S$ and $G_{\theta_W}^W / D_{\phi_W}^W$ denote the generator/discriminator components at the paragraph, sentence and word levels, respectively, which are with different parameters θ_* and ϕ_*.

In text generation, content planning is an essential stage that refers to how to select, arrange and structure the content [8, 28]. However, such a stage has seldom been considered by previous GAN-based approaches of a single generation process. As a comparison, our approach explicitly generates paragraph vectors and sentence vectors to plan the content flow. Different from previous work [19] that adopts topic words or keyphrases as semantic sketches, our sketches are continuous embeddings (*i.e.*, paragraph and sentence vectors), which are more flexible and can be automatically learned.

3   Methodology

In this section, we present the proposed Multi-Level Generative Adversarial Networks (MLGAN) for long and coherent text generation. Figure 1 presents an overview illustration of the proposed model. Next, we will first discuss how to produce paragraph vectors and sentence vectors (called *semantic sketch*) to instruct the generation of the entire content flow, and then describe the sentence realization conditioned on semantic sketch.

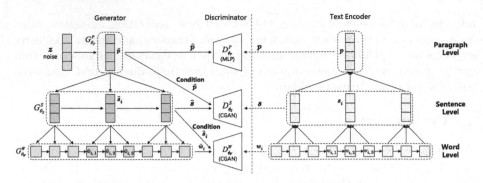

Fig. 1. Overview of the proposed Multi-Level Generative Adversarial Network.

3.1   Semantic Sketch Generation

In this part, we study how to generate the paragraph vectors and sentence vectors. The generated paragraph vector, encoding the core semantics for the entire content, will be used to enforce the inter-sentence coherence, and the generated sentence vectors are used to instruct the word generation.

Paragraph Vector Generation. Following a similar way for image generation [41], we adopt the adversarial learning for generating paragraph vectors, where a generator generates fake samples and a discriminator tries to discriminate between real and fake samples. In order to obtain real samples (paragraph vectors), we need to encode real texts. Here, we adopt the state-of-the-art bi-directional language model, BERT [3], to extract the paragraph-level features of texts. For a real (training) paragraph p, we feed p into BERT encoder and obtain the paragraph vector $\boldsymbol{p} \in \mathbb{R}^{d_P}$. Note that the implementation of the paragraph encoder is flexible and indeed independent of our approach, and we can adopt XLNet [39] or other hierarchical text encoders [35] for learning embeddings of longer text.

The paragraph generator $G_{\theta_P}^P$ is built upon a Multi-Layer Perceptron (MLP) based network. We first sample a noise input $\boldsymbol{z} \in \mathbb{R}^{d_z}$ from a normal distribution $\mathcal{N}(0,1)$. Then, we pretrain $G_{\theta_P}^P$ to produce fake paragraph vectors for fitting the real distribution by utilizing Euclidean distance as follows:

$$\min_{\theta_P} \mathbb{E}_{\boldsymbol{z} \sim \mathcal{N}(0,1)} \min_{\boldsymbol{p}_j \sim p_{para}, 1 \leq j \leq b} \|G_{\theta_P}^P(\boldsymbol{z}) - \boldsymbol{p}_j\|_2, \tag{1}$$

where p_{para} denotes the real distribution of paragraph vectors, and the latter min function means finding the nearest $\boldsymbol{p}_j$ to $G_{\theta_P}^P(\boldsymbol{z})$ among b samples. In order to improve efficiency, we employ an efficient nearest neighbor search in high-dimensional space algorithm [9]. Finally, we utilize the discriminator $D_{\phi_P}^P$ to distinguish fake paragraph vectors from the realistic ones. In the adversarial training, the generator and discriminator play a minimax game as follows:

$$\min_{\theta_P} \max_{\phi_P} \mathbb{E}_{\boldsymbol{p} \sim p_{para}} \left[\log(D_{\phi_P}^P(\boldsymbol{p}))\right] + \mathbb{E}_{\boldsymbol{z} \sim \mathcal{N}(0,1)} \left[\log(1 - D_{\phi_P}^P(G_{\theta_P}^P(\boldsymbol{z})))\right]. \tag{2}$$

Sentence Vector Generation. Similar to paragraph-level generation, we can set a sentence generator $G_{\theta_S}^S$ and sentence discriminator $D_{\phi_S}^S$, and generate the sentence vectors in a sequential manner. Here, we adopt the same method as paragraph vectors to extract the ideal sentence vectors of texts. To be specific, we apply an LSTM-based RNN to implement the sentence generator. Considering the paragraph vector contains the overall information of a text, we take p as input in sentence generator at each time step, which further enhances the inter-sentence coherence. Let $h_i^S \in \mathbb{R}^{d_S}$ denote a d_S-dimensional hidden vector for the i-th sentence, which is computed via:

$$h_i^S = \mathrm{LSTM}(h_{i-1}^S, p). \tag{3}$$

Then we use an affine transformation to generate the i-th sentence vector $\hat{s}_i \in \mathbb{R}^{d_S} : \hat{s}_i = W_l^S h_i^S + b_l^S$, where W_l^S and b_l^S are the learnable parameter matrix or vector. We compute the Euclidean distance between the real and generated sentence vectors as the pretrained loss function of $G_{\theta_S}^S$:

$$\mathcal{L}_{pre}(G_{\theta_S}^S) = \sum_{i=1}^{m} \| s_i - \hat{s}_i \|_2, \tag{4}$$

where m is the number of sentences in a paragraph.

Enforcing Inter-Sentence Coherence. Given the sentence generator described above, we can follow Eq. 2 for adversarial training. However, such a way is likely to generate incoherent text, since coherence is explicitly modeled. Therefore, we propose to utilize the conditional adversarial training for sentence vector generation conditioned on paragraph vectors. In this way, the discriminator $D_{\phi_S}^S$ would not only determine whether the sequence of sentence vectors (denoted by $\hat{s}$) is realistic or not, but also distinguish whether $\hat{s}$ is matched with the paragraph vector p or not. Specially, we adopt the Conditional Generative Adversarial Nets (CGAN) [27,30] in our approach. We decompose $D_{\phi_S}^S$ into two parts: unconditional loss representing whether $\hat{s}$ is real and conditional loss representing whether $\hat{s}$ and p are matched. To implement the discriminator, we utilize Convolutional Neural Networks (CNN) [12] to extract sentence features of $\hat{s}$, denoted by c^S. To obtain the unconditional loss, we apply an affine transformation followed by a sigmoid function via:

$$D_{\phi_S}^S(\hat{s}) = \sigma(w_u^S \odot c^S + b_u^S), \tag{5}$$

where $\sigma(x) = \frac{1}{1+e^{-x}}$ and "$\odot$" denotes the element-wise product. To determine whether p and $\hat{s}$ are matched, the conditional loss is computed as follows:

$$D_{\phi_S}^S(\hat{s}, p) = \sigma(w_c^S \odot [(W_p^S c^S) \odot p] + b_c^S). \tag{6}$$

where "⊙" denotes the element-wise product. Hence, the objective function of the discriminator consists of two parts:

$$\mathcal{L}(D_{\phi_S}^S) = - \underset{s \sim p_{sent|para}}{\mathbb{E}} \left[\log(D_{\phi_S}^S(s))\right] - \underset{\hat{s} \sim G^S}{\mathbb{E}} \left[\log(1 - D_{\phi_S}^S(\hat{s}))\right]$$
$$- \underset{s \sim p_{sent|para}}{\mathbb{E}} \left[\log(D_{\phi_S}^S(s,p))\right] - \underset{\hat{s} \sim G^S}{\mathbb{E}} \left[\log(1 - D_{\phi_S}^S(\hat{s},p))\right], \quad (7)$$

where $p_{sent|para}$ denotes the distribution of real sentence vectors given a particular paragraph vector and G^S denotes the generated distribution of sentence vectors. Finally, the generator $G_{\theta_S}^S$ is trained to generate both realistic and eligible sentence vectors that match p. Accordingly, the loss function of $G_{\theta_S}^S$ is computed as follows:

$$\mathcal{L}(G_{\theta_S}^S) = - \underset{\hat{s} \sim G^S}{\mathbb{E}} \left[\log(D_{\phi_S}^S(\hat{s}))\right] - \underset{\hat{s} \sim G^S}{\mathbb{E}} \left[\log(D_{\phi_S}^S(\hat{s},p))\right]. \quad (8)$$

3.2   Sentence Realization

Given the generated sentence vectors, we now study how to realize the sentences by word generation. In specific, we only discuss the case of a single sentence, i.e., how to generate the words $\langle w_{i,1}, \cdots, w_{i,t}, \cdots, w_{i,n_i} \rangle$ in the i-th sentence s_i based on sentence vector s_i.

Word Generation. Different from the above process, word generation is a discrete process. Following [40], we adopt the classic LSTM-based RNN as the word generator. For sentence s_i, let $h_{i,t}^W$ denote a d_W-dimensional hidden vector for the t-th word token, which is computed via: $h_{i,t}^W = \text{LSTM}(h_{i,t-1}^W, x_{i,t})$, where $x_{i,t} = s_i \oplus w_{i,t-1}$, and $w_{i,t-1}$ denotes the embedding of the previous word $w_{i,t-1}$, s_i denotes the current sentence vector, and "⊕" denotes the vector concatenation. In this way, the semantics encoded in sentence vector s_i can be utilized at each time step, enforcing the intra-sentence coherence. We apply an affine transformation followed by a softmax function to derive the generative probability of the t-th word $w_{i,t}$:

$$o_{i,t} = W^W h_{i,t}^W + b^W, \quad (9)$$
$$\hat{y}_{i,t} = \text{softmax}(o_{i,t}), \quad (10)$$

where $o_{i,t}$ is the output logits and $\hat{y}_{i,t}$ is the probability distribution of $|\mathcal{V}|$-dimension. Therefore, we aim to boost the log likelihood of the generation probability in the pretraining process:

$$\mathcal{L}_{pre}(G_{\theta_W}^W) = \sum_{i=1}^{m} \sum_{t=1}^{n_i} \mathcal{H}(y_{i,t}, \hat{y}_{i,t}), \quad (11)$$

where $y_{i,t}$ is the one-hot vector representation of word $w_{i,t}$ and $\mathcal{H}$ denotes the cross entropy loss function.

Word-Level Adversarial Training. When generating sentence words, the discrete outputs from the generator make it difficult to pass the gradients from the discriminator to the generator, so-called *non-differentiable issue*. To deal with this issue, we apply the Gumbel-Softmax, a continuous distribution on the simplex that can approximate categorical samples [10]. We first sample a vector $g_{i,t}$ from the *i.i.d.* standard Gumbel distribution. Then, the sampling in Eq. 10 can be reparametrized by relaxing the discreteness of softmax function as follows:

$$\hat{y}_{i,t} = \text{softmax}\Big(\frac{o_{i,t} + g_{i,t}}{\tau}\Big), \tag{12}$$

where $\hat{y}_{i,t} \in \mathbb{R}^{|\mathcal{V}|}$ denotes the reparametrized probability and $\tau > 0$ is a tunable parameter to make a balance between the generation quality and diversity [29]. With the Gumbel-Softmax relaxation, we are able to back-propagate from the discriminator $D_{\phi_W}^W$ to the generator $G_{\theta_W}^W$. According to the distribution $\hat{y}_{i,t}$, we can derive the corresponding embedding for the t-th token by a weighted average of word embeddings:

$$\hat{w}_{i,t} = E \cdot \hat{y}_{i,t}, \tag{13}$$

where $E \in \mathbb{R}^{d_W \times |\mathcal{V}|}$ is the word embedding lookup matrix.

Similar to sentence vector generation, we adopt CGAN to improve our word-level discriminator conditioned on the given sentence vector s_i. In the discriminator, we first obtain the word embedding for each word $w_{i,t}$ (Eq. 13) in the sentence s_i, and then combine them as a sequence of word embeddings, denoted by $\{\hat{w}_{i,t}\}$. We compute the unconditional loss to determine whether the sequence of word embeddings is realistic or not, as well as, the conditional loss to distinguish whether $\{\hat{w}_{i,t}\}$ and s_i are matched or not. Similar to Eq. 5 and 6, we apply a CNN-based feature extractor to extract features c_i^W from the i-th sentence $\{\hat{w}_{i,t}\}$ and then make the judgement based on c_i^W to implement the word discriminator:

$$D_{\phi_W}^W(\{\hat{w}_{i,t}\}) = \sigma(w_u^W \odot c_i^W + b_u^W), \tag{14}$$
$$D_{\phi_W}^W(\{\hat{w}_{i,t}\}, s_i) = \sigma(w_c^W \odot \big[(W_p^W c_i^W) \odot s_i\big] + b_c^W).$$

The loss functions for optimizing discriminator and generator are in a similar way as in Eq. 7 and 8.

3.3 Discussion and Learning

We decompose the generic text generation process into three different levels. Instead of only relying on the words, we utilize paragraph and sentence vectors learned from text encoders (*e.g.*, BERT) as additional supervision signals for generating high-level semantics. In order to associate the three levels, we utilize the Conditional GAN to incorporate higher-level semantics into lower-level generation. Another benefit is that we can focus on the content generation in a single sentence. Since only word-level optimization is discrete in our approach, it becomes more controllable and easier to learn in a shorter sequence.

Table 1. Statistics of our datasets. ASPP denotes the average numbers of sentences per paragraph, AWPS denotes the average numbers of words per sentence and AWPP denotes the average numbers of words per paragraph.

Datasets	#Paragraph	#ASPP	#AWPS	#AWPP	#Vocabulary
CHINESE POETRY	67,498	8	8	64	7,982
MOIVE REVIEW	70,808	5	17.4	87.4	18,391

During training, based on Eq. 1, 4 and 11, we first pretrain generative models at each level independently. We directly use the real paragraph vectors, sentence vectors and word vectors in pretraining process. Afterwards, we employ adversarial training between $G_{\theta_*}^*$ and $D_{\phi_*}^*$ of each level independently.

At last, for inference, we apply our model in a pipeline way: we first infer the paragraph-level vector, then predict the sentence-level vectors conditioned on the paragraph vector and finally generate each word using sentence vectors. During word-level generation process, we introduce two special symbols "START" and "END" to denote the start and end of a sentence, respectively. Once we generate the symbol "END", the word generation process will be stopped.

4   Experiments

In the following section, we first set up the experiments, and then report the results and analysis.

4.1   Experimental Setup

Datasets. To test our model's ability and quality to generate long text, the two common datasets Image COCO and EMNLP2017 WMT News [23] have limitation on sentence length (no more than 51). Instead, we use two datasets containing longer sentences, including CHINESE POETRY[1] and MOVIE REVIEW, to evaluate our model. For CHINESE POETRY, we select all the seven-character octaves as our dataset, *i.e.,* each paragraph contains eight sentences and each sentence contains eight words (plus a punctuation), and keep all the words as vocabulary. For MOVIE REVIEW, we first randomly crawl millions of reviews from IMDb[2], then select the paragraph with five sentences as our dataset, and finally remove the infrequent words occurring fewer than six times. The detailed statistics of the two datasets (after preprocessing) are summarized in Table 1.

Implementation Details. For CHINESE POETRY dataset, we employ the BERT-Small Chinese model [3] to extract 384-dimensional paragraph vectors and

---

[1] https://github.com/chinese-poetry/chinese-poetry.
[2] https://www.imdb.com.
[3] https://github.com/brightmart/albert_zh.

Table 2. Performance comparisons of different methods for text generation under two domains. "*" denotes the improvement is statistically significant compared with the best baseline (t-test with p-value < 0.05).

Datasets	Models	Generation				Coherence	
		Length	BLEU-2	BLEU-3	BLEU-4	Sen-Sim	WLCS-l
CHINESE POETRY	MLE	64.0	0.743	0.196	0.016	0.666	0.146
	SeqGAN	64.0	0.768	0.200	0.015	0.687	0.145
	RankGAN	64.0	0.713	0.160	0.010	0.706	0.127
	MaliGAN	64.0	0.654	0.145	0.007	0.676	0.134
	LeakGAN	64.0	0.772	0.201	0.016	0.695	0.147
	MLGAN	64.0	**0.819***	**0.270***	**0.029***	**0.718***	**0.154**
MOVIE REVIEW	MLE	88.0	0.924	0.619	0.299	0.904	0.097
	SeqGAN	70.5	0.946	0.654	0.305	0.898	0.103
	RankGAN	74.5	0.959	0.719	0.377	0.901	0.102
	MaliGAN	61.9	0.899	0.538	0.228	0.891	0.098
	LeakGAN	81.3	0.952	0.725	0.439	0.918	0.103
	GPT-2	79.3	0.790	0.587	0.325	0.891	0.104
	MLGAN	**96.5***	**0.968***	**0.791***	**0.515***	**0.949***	**0.106**

sentence vectors. For MOVIE REVIEW dataset, we employ the BERT-Medium English model [3] to extract 512-dimensional paragraph vectors and sentence vectors. In the paragraph level, we utilize 5-layer MLP with 384/512-dimensional hidden layer and ReLU activation function for the two datasets, respectively. In the sentence and word levels, the dimension of CNN features and the size of word embeddings are set to 1400 and 64, respectively. Finally, we adopt the Adam optimizer with the default hyper-parameters to train our model.

Baseline Models. We compare our model against a number of baseline models:

- MLE applies an RNN-based model to minimize the cross-entropy between the true and generated word distributions.
- SeqGAN [40] regards the text generation as a sequential decision making process, and applies policy gradient with Monte Carlo search to train the generator based on the guidance of a binary discriminator.
- RankGAN [21] adopts the similar reward as in SeqGAN, while changes the discriminator into a ranking model, *i.e.,* taking a softmax output over the expected cosine distances from the generated sequences to the real data.
- MaliGAN [2] uses importance sampling combined with the discriminator output to stabilize the training process and reduce the potential variance.
- LeakGAN [7] involves a high-level module and a low-level module in generator, and is guided with the leaked feature extracted by the discriminator, which aims to address the sparse reward signal in long text generation.

- GPT-2 [33] is a pretrained language model trained on large-scale corpus using Transformer decoder [37]. Since GPT-2 is originally trained on English corpus, we adopt the base version of GPT-2 and only fine-tune it on MOVIE REVIEW dataset.

We utilize text generation toolkit TextBox [16] to implement baselines.

Evaluation Metrics. To evaluate the performance of long text generation, we compute the average length of generated texts, and a common automatic *generation metrics*, BLEU-2/3/4 [31], which measures the ratios of the co-occurrences of n-grams between real and generated texts. In order to evaluate the coherence of generated texts, we adopt two automatic *coherence metrics* including Sen-Sim and WLCS-l. Sen-Sim [13] calculates the average cosine similarity between any two sentence embeddings (from BERT) among each paragraph as: Sem-Sim$(\hat{p}) = \frac{1}{M} \sum_{i,j} \cos\text{-sim}(s_i, s_j)$, where M is the number of sentence pairs $\langle s_i, s_j \rangle$ in $\hat{p}$, and WLCS-l [22] measures the extent of sequence overlapping between the real and generated texts based on Weighted Longest Common Sequence (WLCS) as: WLCS-l$(p, \hat{p}) = \frac{(1+\beta^2) R_{wlcsl} P_{wlcsl}}{R_{wlcsl} + \beta^2 P_{wlcsl}}$, $R_{wlcsl} = f^{-1}(\frac{WLCS(p,\hat{p})}{f(n)})$, $P_{wlcsl} = f^{-1}(\frac{WLCS(p,\hat{p})}{f^2(n)})$, where n is the text length, $\beta = 1.0$, and f is a weighting function of consecutive matches.

4.2   Results and Analysis

In this part, we conduct experiments to verify the effectiveness of the proposed model for long text generation.

Main Results. Table 2 presents the performance of different models for the two groups of metrics First, there exists some performance gap between the two datasets for BLEU metrics. Compared with review texts, Chinese poems, created by ancient poets, are specialized and more difficult to be fitted by these methods. Second, GPT-2 does not achieve satisfactory performance on metrics such as BLEU-2 and Sen-Sim. The reason might be that, GPT-2 is trained on large-scale corpus and has "memory" of training data, thus, it cannot fit the given dataset very well. Third, the performance of RankGAN or MaliGAN is unstable on the two datasets. We speculate that their learning processes are more unstable, which is not well-trained with our datasets. Moreover, LeakGAN outperforms the other baselines for both kinds of metrics. A major reason is that LeakGAN is specially designed for generating long texts, while the rest methods may not be effective in capturing long-range semantic dependency in text generation. Finally, our model performs better than all the baselines by a large margin. The major difference between our model and baselines lies in that we design a multi-level generation process for both long and coherent text generation. Though designed for long text generation, LeakGAN lacks the overall consideration of semantic coherence. While, other baselines do not explicitly model the two aspects for text generation.

Table 3. Ablation analysis on CHINESE POETRY dataset.

Models	BLEU-2	BLEU-4	Sen-Sim
LeakGAN	0.772	0.016	0.695
MLGAN	0.819	0.029	0.718
w/o Paragraph Vector	0.792	0.018	0.695
w/o Sentence Vector	0.812	0.026	0.713
w/o BERT, w Bi-LSTM	0.788	0.018	0.692

Table 4. Human evaluation on MOVIE REVIEW dataset.

Models	MLE	LeakGAN	MLGAN	Gold
Coherence	2.81 ± 1.07	3.25 ± 1.04	$\mathbf{3.48 \pm 0.94}$	3.98 ± 0.93
Fluency	3.22 ± 0.84	3.52 ± 0.85	$\mathbf{3.80 \pm 0.77}$	3.94 ± 0.83

Ablation Analysis. The major novelty of our model lies in the multi-level generation process, where we utilize paragraph vectors and sentence vectors as *semantic sketches*. To examine the contribution of these semantic sketches, we compare our model with two variants by removing either of the two kinds of vectors. Moreover, we have utilized BERT as the text encoder to generate the ground-truth vectors to train our model. We replace BERT with a Bi-LSTM encoder for examining whether our approach is effective with various text encoders. In Table 3, we can see that both kinds of vectors are important to improve the final performance, and paragraph vectors seem more important in our task. In our model, paragraph vectors encode the main idea of texts and essential for enhancing the inter-sentence coherence. Furthermore, based on the Bi-LSTM encoder, our model still outperforms the best baseline model, Leak-GAN, both on generation and coherence metrics, which proves the effectiveness of our proposed hierarchical architecture.

Human Evaluation. We continue to conduct human evaluation on MOVIE REVIEW dataset by using Amazon Mechanical Turk, in order to further evaluate the quality of generated texts. Following [42], we randomly choose 200 samples generated from different models, and then invite three experienced movies fans to score the texts with respect to two aspects of fluency and coherence. Fluency means how likely the text is produced by human, which can reflect some text properties such as logic and readability. Coherence evaluates how content is coherent considering both intra- and inter-sentence correlation of a paragraph [18]. The scoring mechanism adopts a 5-point Likert scale [20], ranging from 5-point ("very satisfying") to 1-point ("very terrible"). Finally, we calculate the average score among the three judges (with Cohen's Kappa of 0.78). As shown in Table 4, MLGAN produces more coherent and fluent text than other

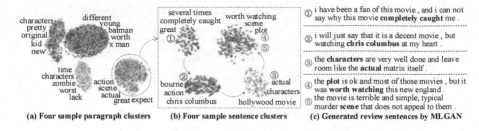

Fig. 2. Visualization of paragraph vectors, sentence vectors, and generated movie review sentences by MLGAN. The numbers denote the relative sentence positions in a paragraph. Keywords from sentence clusters in sentences are in bold font.

methods. The major reason is that we utilize semantic sketches and CGAN mechanism to effectively plan the text content, which indeed improves the fluency and coherence.

Case Study. Here, we further present a qualitative example to illustrate how the three-level generation process works in our approach. We first randomly generate 5,000 review texts for MOVIE REVIEW dataset, and keep the intermediate paragraph and sentence vectors. These paragraph vectors are projected into two-dimensional vectors for visualization with t-SNE [24]. We further cluster these paragraph vectors, and select four sample clusters for visualization. To understand the semantics of each cluster, we apply the RAKE [34] and Textrank [25] algorithms to extract high-quality keyphrases or keywords, respectively, from the generated paragraph text. As shown in Fig. 2(a), distant paragraph clusters reflect different semantics (*e.g., actual, zombie*), while close clusters share similar keywords (*e.g., kid, young*). To further understand the sentence vectors generated by our approach, we perform the similar visualization procedure. For each paragraph from the fourth cluster (in red color), we select its five sentence vectors for visualization in Fig. 2(b). Specially, we utilize different colors to denote different sentence positions (*i.e.*, $1 \sim 5$) in a paragraph. It can be observed these sentence vectors naturally form four coherent clusters according to their relative positions in a paragraph, indicating a good content planning. Specially, the semantics of sentence clusters can be considered as multi-topic fine-grained decomposition for the semantics of the paragraph clusters. Our model effectively enforces the inter-sentence coherence, since sentence clusters are relevant to each other, which together explain the semantics of paragraph vectors. Finally, we present several generated sentences from the selected paragraph cluster in Fig. 2(c). As we can see, they are fluent and informative by covering the same keyphrases or keywords of sentence clusters. These examples show that our approach is effective to capture the main semantics and content flow.

5   Related Work

Text Generation. Generic text generation is critical to many natural language processing applications, such as machine translation [38] and dialogue system [15]. Recently, due to the powerful Transformer architecture [37], pre-trained language models such as GPT-2/GPT-3 [1,33], and CTRL [11] have demonstrated the feasibility of generating high-quality text [17]. Besides, there have also been considerable efforts that generate long text with a multi-stage approach, such as review generation [19], story generation [4], and text generation [36]. However, these methods are mainly trained by MLE, which is likely to suffer from the *exposure bias* problem [6]. As a comparison, we focus on improving GAN-based generic text generation with a multi-level generation process, and study how to develop the hierarchical architecture under the GAN framework.

GAN-Based Text Generation. Many variants of GANs, including Seq-GAN [40], RankGAN [21], MaliGAN [2], and LeakGAN [7], have been proposed for text generation since adversarial learning has its advantage in optimizing over sequence data (*e.g.,* alleviating the exposure bias). Typically, they address the *non-differentiable issue* by reinforcement learning (RL) or making continuous approximation. Most RL-based GAN methods formulate text generation as a MDP, where the generator is trained with policy gradient and the discriminator provides reward signals. Considering the sparse and weak reward signal, several GAN methods reformulate the problem in continuous space and adopt the Gumbel-Softmax trick [10]. However, these methods mainly consider word-level generation, and there are seldom studies that characterize a hierarchy of paragraph-sentence-word as in our approach.

6   Conclusion

In this paper, we proposed a multi-level text generation model MLGAN for generating long and coherent text. Our approach followed a three-level generation process, where we generate paragraph vectors and sentence vectors as semantic sketches to instruct the word generation. We enforced the inter-sentence coherence by utilizing a conditional GAN architecture. Experiment results on two datasets have shown the effectiveness of our approach on long text generation. Currently, we consider a three-level generation process. As future work, it is natural to extend our approach to model a more complex hierarchy, *i.e.,* multi-paragraph generation. Besides, we will also consider combining other semantic features (*e.g.,* keywords) for content planning in order to obtain a better performance.

Acknowledgement. This work was partially supported by the National Natural Science Foundation of China under Grant No. 61872369 and 61832017, Beijing Academy of Artificial Intelligence (BAAI) under Grant No. BAAI2020ZJ0301, Beijing Outstanding Young Scientist Program under Grant No. BJJWZYJH012019100020098.

References

1. Brown, T.B., et al.: Language models are few-shot learners. In: NeurIPS (2020)
2. Che, T., et al.: Maximum-likelihood augmented discrete generative adversarial networks. arXiv preprint arXiv:1702.07983 (2017)
3. Devlin, J., Chang, M., Lee, K., Toutanova, K.: BERT: pre-training of deep bidirectional transformers for language understanding. In: NAACL-HLT (2019)
4. Dong, L., Lapata, M.: Coarse-to-fine decoding for neural semantic parsing. In: ACL (2018)
5. Garbacea, C., Mei, Q.: Neural language generation: formulation, methods, and evaluation. arXiv preprint arXiv:2007.15780 (2020)
6. Graves, A.: Generating sequences with recurrent neural networks. arXiv preprint arXiv:1308.0850 (2013)
7. Guo, J., Lu, S., Cai, H., Zhang, W., Yu, Y., Wang, J.: Long text generation via adversarial training with leaked information. In: AAAI (2018)
8. Hua, X., Wang, L.: Sentence-level content planning and style specification for neural text generation. In: EMNLP (2019)
9. Hyvönen, V., et al.: Fast nearest neighbor search through sparse random projections and voting. In: BigData (2016)
10. Jang, E., Gu, S., Poole, B.: Categorical reparameterization with gumbel-softmax. In: ICLR (2017)
11. Keskar, N.S., McCann, B., Varshney, L.R., Xiong, C., Socher, R.: Ctrl: a conditional transformer language model for controllable generation. arXiv preprint arXiv:1909.05858 (2019)
12. Kim, Y.: Convolutional neural networks for sentence classification. In: EMNLP (2014)
13. Lapata, M., Barzilay, R.: Automatic evaluation of text coherence: models and representations. In: IJCAI (2005)
14. Law, J., Charlton, J., Dockrell, J., Gascoigne, M., McKean, C., Theakston, A.: Early language development: needs, provision and intervention for pre-school children from socio-economically disadvantaged backgrounds. London Education Endowment Foundation (2017)
15. Li, J., Monroe, W., Shi, T., Jean, S., Ritter, A., Jurafsky, D.: Adversarial learning for neural dialogue generation. In: EMNLP (2017)
16. Li, J., et al.: Textbox: a unified, modularized, and extensible framework for text generation. In: ACL (2021)
17. Li, J., Tang, T., Zhao, W.X., Wen, J.: Pretrained language models for text generation: a survey. In: IJCAI (2021)
18. Li, J., Zhao, W.X., Wei, Z., Yuan, N.J., Wen, J.R.: Knowledge-based review generation by coherence enhanced text planning. In: SIGIR (2021)
19. Li, J., Zhao, W.X., Wen, J., Song, Y.: Generating long and informative reviews with aspect-aware coarse-to-fine decoding. In: ACL (2019)
20. Likert, R.: A technique for the measurement of attitudes. Arch. Psychol. (1932)
21. Lin, K., Li, D., He, X., Zhang, Z., Sun, M.T.: Adversarial ranking for language generation. In: NeurIPS (2017)
22. Liu, S., Zeng, S., Li, S.: Evaluating text coherence at sentence and paragraph levels. In: LREC (2020)
23. Lu, S., Zhu, Y., Zhang, W., Wang, J., Yu, Y.: Neural text generation: past, present and beyond. arXiv preprint arXiv:1803.07133 (2018)
24. Van der Maaten, L., Hinton, G.: Visualizing data using t-SNE. JMLR (2008)

25. Mihalcea, R., Tarau, P.: Textrank: bringing order into text. In: EMNLP (2004)
26. Mikolov, T., Sutskever, I., Chen, K., Corrado, G.S., Dean, J.: Distributed representations of words and phrases and their compositionality. In: NeurIPS (2013)
27. Miyato, T., Koyama, M.: cGANs with projection discriminator. In: ICLR (2018)
28. Moryossef, A., Goldberg, Y., Dagan, I.: Step-by-step: separating planning from realization in neural data-to-text generation. In: NAACL (2019)
29. Nie, W., Narodytska, N., Patel, A.: Relgan: relational generative adversarial networks for text generation. In: ICLR (2018)
30. Odena, A., Olah, C., Shlens, J.: Conditional image synthesis with auxiliary classifier GANs. In: ICML (2017)
31. Papineni, K., Roukos, S., Ward, T., Zhu, W.J.: Bleu: a method for automatic evaluation of machine translation. In: ACL (2002)
32. Pullum, G.K.: The land of the free and the elements of style. English Today (2010)
33. Radford, A., Wu, J., Child, R., Luan, D., Amodei, D., Sutskever, I.: Language models are unsupervised multitask learners (2019)
34. Rose, S., Engel, D., Cramer, N., Cowley, W.: Automatic keyword extraction from individual documents. Text Mining: Appl. Theory (2010)
35. Serban, I.V., Sordoni, A., Bengio, Y., Courville, A.C., Pineau, J.: Building end-to-end dialogue systems using generative hierarchical neural network models. In: AAAI (2016)
36. Shen, D., et al.: Towards generating long and coherent text with multi-level latent variable models. In: ACL (2019)
37. Vaswani, A., et al.: Attention is all you need. In: NeurIPS (2017)
38. Yang, Z., Chen, W., Wang, F., Xu, B.: Improving neural machine translation with conditional sequence generative adversarial nets. In: NAACL-HLT (2018)
39. Yang, Z., Dai, Z., Yang, Y., Carbonell, J., Salakhutdinov, R.R., Le, Q.V.: Xlnet: generalized autoregressive pretraining for language understanding. In: NeurIPS (2019)
40. Yu, L., Zhang, W., Wang, J., Yu, Y.: Seqgan: sequence generative adversarial nets with policy gradient. In: AAAI (2017)
41. Zhang, H., Xu, T., Li, H.: Stackgan: text to photo-realistic image synthesis with stacked generative adversarial networks. In: ICCV (2017)
42. Zhang, S., Dinan, E., Urbanek, J., Szlam, A., Kiela, D., Weston, J.: Personalizing dialogue agents: I have a dog, do you have pets too? In: ACL (2018)

A Reasonable Data Pricing Mechanism for Personal Data Transactions with Privacy Concern

Zheng Zhang, Wei Song$^{(\boxtimes)}$, and Yuan Shen

School of Computer Science, Wuhan University, Wuhan, China
{zhangzheng,songwei,shenyuan}@whu.edu.cn

Abstract. In the past few years, more and more data marketplaces for personal data transactions sprung up. However, it is still very challenging to estimate the value of privacy contained in the personal data. Especially when the buyer already has some related datasets, he is able to obtain more privacy by combining and analyzing the bought data and the data he already has. The main research motivation of this work is to reasonably price the data with privacy concern. We propose a reasonable data pricing mechanism which prices the personal privacy data from three aspects and is different from the existing work, we propose a new concept named 'privacy cost' to quantitatively measure the privacy information increment after a data transaction rather than directly measuring the privacy information contained in a single dataset. In addition, we use the information entropy as an important index to measure the information content of data. And we conduct a set of experiments on our personal data pricing method, and the results show that our pricing method performs better than the alternatives.

Keywords: Data pricing · Differential privacy · Data marketplace

1 Introduction

Data commodities and related analysis services are increasingly offered by the online data marketplaces in recent years, which collect personal data with privacy from data owners, process and sell them to data consumers. The privacy contained in data reflects not only the unique value but also the key information of individual like his name, age, gender, even his credit card number, therefore, the access to it should be highly restricted. As for the privacy protection, differential privacy is a standard for data releasing [10]. But we must admit that the introduced noise will perturb the personal data and lead to the inaccuracy.

What is more important, data buyer may have bought some datasets before, which may be related to the dataset he wants to buy this time and are called background datasets. Obviously, the consumer with background datasets could do some operations to obtain more privacy than another data buyer who spends

© Springer Nature Switzerland AG 2021
L. H. U et al. (Eds.): APWeb-WAIM 2021, LNCS 12859, pp. 64–71, 2021.
https://doi.org/10.1007/978-3-030-85899-5_5

the same amount of money but does not have any background dataset. It is unfair and we call this as "privacy increment issue". At present, there is not existing a pricing mechanism that can address this issue.

Based on the problems above, we propose a novel personal data pricing mechanism based on differential privacy, which takes the privacy concern into account. For the first time, we regard the background dataset as an important factor affecting the privacy cost and introduce a new personal data pricing concept named privacy cost to quantitatively measure the privacy increment caused by the union of new and old datasets.

2 Related Work

The general pricing method is subscription, however, this methods can't meet the diverse needs of users. Therefore, Koutris et al. proposed a query-based data pricing framework [4] which allows data buyers to issue different queries for the view. However, the query-based data pricing model does not give guidance on how to price the basic view. Niyato et al. combined the Stackelberg model and the classification algorithm [8]. By using the utility function, the service provider can determine the amount of data to be bought from the data provider, thereby maximizing their own profits. In addition, information entropy, as an important indicator to measure the amount of information contained in the data, has also been introduced into the data pricing model [9]. Li et al. proposed to use information entropy as a new data pricing indicator [6].

As to methods with privacy pricing, Jung et al. [3] introduced a negotiation mechanism, in which data providers and purchasers negotiate on noise scale and unit data price. Nget et al. [7] proposed the concept of data mart based on differential privacy data publishing mechanism. Li et al. [5] proposed a framework for assigning prices to noisy query answers, as a function of their accuracy, and for dividing the price amongst data owners who deserve compensation for their loss of privacy.

However, the above pricing mechanisms are not perfect, especially for the privacy increment issue brought by data union, none of the above mechanisms consider it.

3 Personal Data Pricing Mechanism

3.1 System Model

In this section we describe the basic architecture of proposed pricing mechanism, illustrated in Fig. 1.

The data publisher u_i sends a personal dataset D_i to the trusted data marketplace $\mathbf{M}$. Then $\mathbf{M}$ inserts different scales of noises into raw personal datasets to do differential privacy with different privacy budgets. Finally, the data buyer b_j issues a request $\mathbf{Q}_j(f_j, \epsilon_j)$ which includes an analysis function f_j and a data accuracy ϵ_j he can accept.

Definition 1 (data accuracy). *A privacy mechanism M gives ϵ-differential privacy, where $\epsilon \in (0,1)$ means privacy budget. Less privacy budget means more noises and implies the personal datasets will be less accurate. Therefore, the privacy budget has the same change tend with data accuracy and is positively correlated to it. So, in some extensis, data accuracy could be represented by privacy budget.*

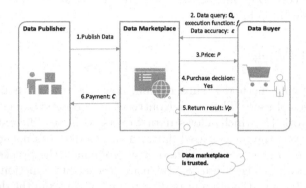

Fig. 1. Trading framework for personal data

One thing needs to be noted is that based on differential privacy [2], the risk of privacy leakage is related to the analysis function. Therefore, our pricing scheme considers not only data accuracy ϵ but also the analysis function f.

After receiving a data request $\mathbf{Q}_j(f_j, \epsilon_j)$, $\mathbf{M}$ will first find the personal dataset V_P with right privacy budget version buyer is interested in. Then the dataset price P is calculated which will be described in details in the next subsection.

3.2   Personal Privacy Data Pricing Function

In this subsection, we will explain our pricing mechanism by detailing every of three prices and the corresponding computing methods for them.

$$P = P_d + P_p + profit. \tag{1}$$

Data Value. P_d is the use value. According to [6], information entropy $H(V)$ is a more reasonable factor to measure information content and data value P_d is positively correlated with $H(V)$.

Also, we must attention one important thing. As we do differential privacy with different data accuracies ϵ, the data marketplace will insert different scales of noises V_s to dataset V, so the data has become not accuracy as it was at first [1]. There must be a accuracy loss δ after inserting noises. We use normalization of root mean square error(RMSE) to describe the accuracy loss δ and give the definition as follows:

Definition 2 (accuracy loss). *For a dataset $D^{m \times n}$, the data in it is x_{ij}, and the D' is obtained by inserting some noises D_s to the D as Eq. (9), the data in D' is x'_{ij}, and the function f is a normalized function, the accuracy loss δ we define as Eq. (7):*

$$D' = D + D_s, \tag{2}$$

$$RMSE = \sqrt{\frac{\sum_{i=0}^{m} \sum_{j=0}^{n} (x'_{ij} - x_{ij})^2}{m \times n}}, \delta = f(RMSE). \tag{3}$$

According to Eq. (7), $\delta \in [0,1]$. In our paper, inserted noise obeys Laplace distribution, namely $D_s \sim Lap(\Delta(f)/\epsilon)$.

We use $H(V)$ to represent the use value of V, and the data value P_d can be obtained by $H(V)$ subtracts the accuracy loss which is brought by inserted noises. And the function $P_d = D(H(V), \delta)$, we design as follows:

$$P_d = 100 \cdot (1 - \delta) \cdot log_2(H(V) + 1). \tag{4}$$

Privacy Cost. P_p indicates the privacy content of personal dataset. We have to pay attention to another thing that different data buyers, who bought the same personal dataset, may obtain different amounts of privacy. Because different data buyers may own different background datasets. When they merge the new dataset they bought and the background dataset, they may get different privacy increments.

Because of the background dataset, different data buyers will obtain different amount of privacy increments, that means the risks of data owners' privacy disclosure are different. Therefore, data buyer who gets more privacy increments $\Delta\theta$, should pay more privacy cost P_p, and we give initial definition of privacy content as follows:

Definition 3. *For any random function f and a dataset D with n tuples $\{t_i | i = 1, ..., n\}$, the privacy contents of t_i and D are defined as:*

$$\theta(t_i) = sup_{S,D} |log \frac{Pr(f(D) \in S}{Pr(f(t_i)) \in S}|, \tag{5}$$

$$\theta(D) = \sum_{i=1}^{n} \theta(t_i), \tag{6}$$

where S is all possible outputs of f.

However it is difficult to compute the privacy content by Definition 3, because the possibility is hard to evaluate. Chao et al. compared the output of a function with and without one data item x_i and imposed a upper bound for privacy loss [5]. The privacy loss they proposed has the same meaning with our privacy content θ, therefore, we transform the formula and introduce it into our paper. We define the function to measure θ as follow:

Definition 4 (privacy content). *For any random function f and a dataset* $\boldsymbol{D}$, *we assume the function f will execute on one attribute X, the privacy content of* $\boldsymbol{D}$ *is defined as:*

$$\theta(\boldsymbol{D}) \leq \frac{\gamma}{\Delta(f)/\epsilon}|D|, \tag{7}$$

where $\gamma = sup_{x \in X}|X|$.

Now let us compute privacy increment $\Delta\theta_j$. Let's suppose that data buyer b_j owns background dataset B_j and wants to buy dataset V_p, and then after this transaction, he will own three datasets: B_j, V_p and U_j which is obtained by doing some operations on B_j and V_p (in our paper, we restrict the operation as union which is a commonly used operation), and also owns three privacy content: $\theta(B_j)$, $\theta(V_p)$ and $\theta(U_j)$. However, b_j have paid for $\theta(B_j)$ when he bought dataset B_j. So the privacy increment $\Delta\theta_j$ he obtains in this transaction is as follows:

$$\Delta\theta_j = \theta(U_j) + \theta(V_p). \tag{8}$$

There is no doubt that P_p is positively related with $\Delta\theta_j$, and the more privacy increment $\Delta\theta_j$ buyer gets, the more he should pay. In our paper, we design the function $P_p = P(\Delta\theta_j)$ as follows:

$$P_p = \frac{\sqrt{50 + 50\Delta\theta_j}}{100}. \tag{9}$$

Profit. The data marketplace should get some remuneration as the middleman between the data publisher and data buyer. In our paper, *profit* represents the income of data marketplace, we just define *profit* as follows:

$$profit = (P_d + P_p) * l, \tag{10}$$

where $l \in (0, 1)$ is a coefficient and is decided by the data marketplace itself. In our paper, we set l as 0.25.

4   Experiments

4.1   Experimental Data and Setup

We use two personal datasets from UCI[1] contain 14 attributes as the data commodities listed on data marketplace. One is the dataset D_1 with 7840 records and the second one is the dataset D_2 with 14720 records, which are both about annual income in the USA.

There are two data buyers. b_1 wants to know the average age of the people in D_1 and b_2 wants to learn the age dispersion in D_2. We assume b_1 has no background datasets and b_2 has a background dataset B with 10000 records. For simplicity, B has the same attributes with D_2 and that means b_2 can easily merge D_2 with B. And we name the transaction on D_1 as experiment 1 and the other one is experiment 2. We compare our pricing mechanism with the baseline method and other alternatives.

---

[1] https://archive.ics.uci.edu/ml/datasets.php.

Baseline Pricing Mechanism. Just as the analysis in Definition 1, data accuracy ϵ is positively related with personal dataset price P. For simplicity, we consider the relationship between ϵ and P in the baseline pricing mechanism as direct ratio, and the function of it is defined as follows:

$$P = m * \epsilon, \tag{11}$$

where m is a coefficient and in our paper we set m as 1000.

Comparison Pricing Mechanism. We use two pricing mechanisms in our comparison experiments, one is information entropy-based data pricing mechanism [6] and the other is balanced pricing mechanisms [5].

4.2 Experimental Results

Simulation Experiment. We first simulate personal dataset transactions (Fig. 2) when data buyers choose different data accuracy ϵ. Figure 2a shows that data value P_d increases as ϵ increases. And the data value P_d increases dramatically when ϵ is 0~0.4 but then increases slightly when ϵ is 0.4~1.0. This pattern is reasonable in practice. We consider that with inserting noises into original personal dataset, the scale of noise may reach a certain threshold, then the availability of dataset will be greatly reduced, and even the dataset is no longer available.

Figure 2b shows the correlation between privacy cost P_p and ϵ. There is no doubt privacy cost P_p increases as the ϵ increases, for that higher ϵ means less privacy protection and data buyer will obtain more privacy. Remarkably, we can see that two curves in Fig. 2b are not exactly the same. When ϵ approaches 0, P_p of two transactions are particularly close, with a difference of less than \$10. When ϵ is close to 1.0, there is a large gap between P_p of the two transactions. We consider that when ϵ is low, even if the data buyer has background datasets, it is still difficult to obtain a large privacy by the background dataset. But when personal dataset is accurate, the data buyer with background datasets can easily to obtain more privacy, so they should pay more.

The last Fig. 2c shows that P increases as ϵ increases. According to Eq. (1), P is the sum of data value P_d, privacy cost P_p and transaction profit. Because $profit$ is constant, so P change trend is the function synthesis of P_d and P_p.

Comparison Experiment. We next compare the result of our personal data pricing mechanism with these of baseline pricing mechanism and other pricing mechanisms described before (Fig. 3 and Fig. 4). We can see no matter how ϵ changes, the P of information entropy-based pricing mechanism remains unchanged. Obviously, from the perspective of data accuracy, it is not reasonablepaper5 for that if two data buyers bought the same personal data with different data accuracies, and they spent the same amount of money. Also, it is not reasonable that P is just linearly related to ϵ just as what baseline pricing

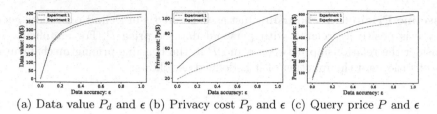

(a) Data value P_d and ϵ (b) Privacy cost P_p and ϵ (c) Query price P and ϵ

Fig. 2. Our pricing mechanism simulation

mechanism shows. When ϵ gets closer and closer to zero, the use value of personal dataset has plummeted, like what our personal data pricing mechanism and balanced pricing mechanism show. That means personal dataset has no meaning for data buyers, when data accuracy is too small, so in our pricing mechanism, it is not recommended data buyers choose too smaller ϵ.

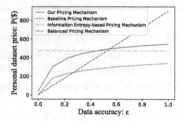
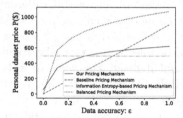

Fig. 3. Query price vs. ϵ on Experiment 1   **Fig. 4.** Query price vs. ϵ on Experiment 2

At last, we do simulations about the above mechanisms described before based on Experiment 2 to show how P changes when data buyers have the same $\mathbf{Q}(f, \epsilon)$ but different scales of background datasets.(Fig. 5). We can see that no matter how the scale of background dataset changes, the P of baseline pricing mechanism and other pricing mechanisms remain unchanged. However, from the perspective of privacy increment, this is not reasonable.

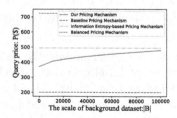

Fig. 5. Trading framework for personal data

5 Conclusion

In this paper, a reasonable data pricing mechanism for the personal data transactions from many aspects is proposed. In the pricing mechanism, we allow data buyers to choose data accuracy, which will meet their different demands. Moreover, to solve the problem of privacy increment brought by background datasets, for the first time, we propose a new concept, privacy cost, and provide the measurement method for it, which is based on differential privacy. Additionally, we consider the influence of inserted noises on the data value, which pricing data value from the perspective of information entropy and accuracy loss. Our data pricing mechanism satisfies the three requirements proposed in Section I and the rationality of it was validated by the simulation and comparison experiments.

Acknowledgement. This work is partially supported by National Key Research and Development Project of China No. 2020YFC1522602, National Natural Science Foundation of China Nos. 62072349, U1811263, and Technological Innovation Major Program of Hubei Province No. 2019AAA072.

References

1. Aperjis, C., Huberman, B.A.: A market for unbiased private data: paying individuals according to their privacy attitudes. First Monday **17**(5) (2012)
2. Dwork, C.: Differential privacy: a survey of results. In: Agrawal, M., Du, D., Duan, Z., Li, A. (eds.) TAMC 2008. LNCS, vol. 4978, pp. 1–19. Springer, Heidelberg (2008). https://doi.org/10.1007/978-3-540-79228-4_1
3. Jung, K., Lee, J., Park, K., Park, S.: PRIVATA: differentially private data market framework using negotiation-based pricing mechanism. In: Proceedings of CIKM, pp. 2897–2900 (2019)
4. Koutris, P., Upadhyaya, P., Balazinska, M., Howe, B., Suciu, D.: Query-based data pricing. J. ACM (JACM) **62**(5), 1–44 (2015)
5. Li, C., Li, D.Y., Miklau, G., Suciu, D.: A theory of pricing private data. Commun. ACM **60**(12), 79–86 (2017)
6. Li, X., Yao, J., Liu, X., Guan, H.: A first look at information entropy-based data pricing. In: Proceedings of ICDCS, pp. 2053–2060 (2017)
7. Nget, R., Cao, Y., Yoshikawa, M.: How to balance privacy and money through pricing mechanism in personal data market. In: Proceedings of the SIGIR Workshop on eCommerce (eCOM@SIGIR) (2017)
8. Niyato, D., Alsheikh, M.A., Wang, P., Kim, D.I., Han, Z.: Market model and optimal pricing scheme of big data and Internet of Things (IoT). In: IEEE International Conference on Communications (ICC), pp. 1–6. IEEE (2016)
9. Shannon, C.E.: A mathematical theory of communication. ACM SIGMOBILE Mob. Comput. Commun. Rev. **5**(1), 3–55 (2001)
10. Wang, Q., Zhang, Y., Lu, X., Wang, Z., Qin, Z., Ren, K.: Real-time and spatio-temporal crowd-sourced social network data publishing with differential privacy. IEEE Trans. Dependable Secur. Comput. **15**(4), 591–606 (2016)

Knowledge Graph

A Probabilistic Inference Based Approach for Querying Associative Entities in Knowledge Graph

JianYu Li, Kun Yue[(✉)], Jie Li, and Liang Duan

School of Information Science and Engineering, Yunnan University, Kunming, China
{jylee,jiel}@mail.ynu.edu.cn, {kyue,duanl}@ynu.edu.cn

Abstract. Querying associative entities is to provide top ranked entities in knowledge graph (KG). Many entities are not linked explicitly in KG but actually associated when incorporating outside user-generated data, which could enrich entity associations for the query processing of KG. In this paper, we leverage user-entity interactions (called user-entity data) to improve the accuracy of querying associative entities in KG. Upon the association rules obtained from user-entity data, we construct the association entity Bayesian network (AEBN), which facilitates the representation and inference of the dependencies among entities. Consequently, we formulate the problem of querying associative entities as the probabilistic inferences over AEBN. To rank the associative entities, we propose the approximate method to evaluate the association degree between entities. Extensive experiments on various datasets verify the effectiveness and efficiency of our method. Experimental results show that our proposed method outperforms some state-of-the-art competitors.

Keywords: Knowledge graph · Association entity · Association rule · Bayesian network · Probabilistic inference

1 Introduction

Recently, with a great thrive and wide applications of knowledge graph (KG), such as search engine [21] and recommender system [18], querying associative entities (AEs) over a KG has gained much attention in both academic and industrial areas [3]. Specifically, it is desirable to find a top ranked list of AEs in KG w.r.t. the query entity (QE). For example, *Avatar, Deadpool, Titanic* could be found as the AEs w.r.t. the QE *Terminator* on the KG in Fig. 1.

In view of the flexible structure and rich semantics of KG, most of the existing methods query AEs by formulating structured queries like SPARQL[1] and using keyword search [21]. However, in the scenario of KG applications, it is difficult to use these structure-based methods to query the diversified AEs accurately and holistically, since the relatively static domain knowledge in KG may not satisfy the intent of user queries. For example, a user may search the *action* movies

---

[1] https://www.w3.org/TR/rdf-sparql-query/.

© Springer Nature Switzerland AG 2021
L. H. U et al. (Eds.): APWeb-WAIM 2021, LNCS 12859, pp. 75–89, 2021.
https://doi.org/10.1007/978-3-030-85899-5_6

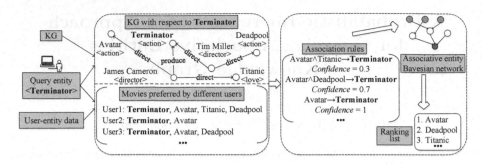

Fig. 1. Overview of our method.

directed by *James Cameron* w.r.t. *Terminator*, which are actually the answers from realistic records of social ratings, but could not be found in KG.

Undoubtedly, latent knowledge is implied or reflected in the rich user-entity interaction data, called user-entity data. For example, latent preferences could be found from the user-item interactions, and latent links between users could be found from user behavior interactions on the co-occurrence of entities [6]. This means that AEs are also implied in user-entity data outside KG, and this provides a beneficial supplement to the aforementioned structure-based methods to query AEs in KG. Simultaneously, the quantitative association degree between entities could be obtained from the user-entity data. For convenience of expression, both the explicit associations in KG and the implicit associations in user-entity data are called dependence. In this paper, we aim to obtain better ranked AEs in KG w.r.t. the given query by modeling the dependence among entities from the user-entity data.

It is worth noting that the dependence among entities is always not crisp but uncertain [10]. For example, *Avatar* is more likely to associate with *Terminator* than *Titanic*, since *Avatar* has a higher probability to co-occur with *Terminator* in the user-entity data shown in Fig. 1. Without loss of generality, the uncertainty, which could be obtained from user-entity data, reflects the association degree between entities, by which the ranking of AEs could be fulfilled. To this end, we will address the following problems:

(1) How to represent the qualitative and quantitative dependence among relevant entities w.r.t. the QE by incorporating KG and user-entity data?
(2) How to evaluate the association degree between entities effectively for AE ranking?

It is known that Bayesian network (BN), including a directed acyclic graph (DAG) and conditional probability tables (CPTs) to quantify the dependence among random variables, is widely used to represent and infer uncertain knowledge [9,22]. By adopting BN as the framework, we propose the concept of association entity Bayesian network (AEBN) to represent the dependence among entities and infer the implicit AEs effectively. In an AEBN, the entities w.r.t.

the QE are regarded as nodes, and the dependence among entities are described as edges. Importantly, we discuss the construction of AEBN from KG and user-entity data.

First, to construct the DAG w.r.t. the given QE, we propose a weighting function to score each entity in KG and obtain the candidates. Furthermore, we employ the classic frequent pattern mining algorithm [4] to find the frequent candidate entities, from which the association rules w.r.t. the QE could be generated. To achieve the dependence from the sparse user-entity data w.r.t. the QE and avoid the invalidity of classic BN learning algorithms, we employ the branch and bound algorithm to obtain the optimal set of association rules with the maximal confidence summation. Then, we express the optimal rules as Horn clauses [13], which are then transformed equivalently to the DAG of the AEBN. Following, based on the logical constraints specified by the Horn clause of each node in AEBN, we normalize the frequencies of frequent entities from user-entity data and give the method to calculate the conditional probability parameters to constitute the CPTs.

To rank AEs w.r.t. the given QE, we formulate the problem of KG query processing as the problem of probabilistic inferences over AEBN, so the association degrees between QE and AEs could be evaluated. To obtain the top ranked AEs, we propose the approximate algorithm for probabilistic inferences over AEBN based on rejection sampling [15].

Generally, the contributions of this paper are as follows:

- We provide an effective method to discover the qualitative and quantitative dependence among entities in KG by leveraging the association rules and corresponding Horn clauses in user-entity data.
- We cast the problem of querying AEs into the problem of probabilistic inferences over AEBN, and propose an efficient approximate inference algorithm over AEBN to obtain the top ranked AEs.
- We conduct extensive experiments on real-life and synthetic datasets. The results show that our framework significantly improves the accuracy of querying AEs of KG.

2 Related Work

Query Processing of KG. Query processing of KG could be regarded as the matching problem based on the highest-ranking score [17] among k subgraphs matched in KG. Jayaram et al. [7] proposed GQBE to query KG by example entities and obtained top-k tuples approximated to the maximum query graph. Jin et al. [8] proposed GStar to improve the efficiency of top-k star queries in large KGs with billions of nodes. However, these subgraph matching based methods could not describe the implicit associations among entities, which are critical to explore the diversified search intent. Many researchers embedded KG into a continuous vector space [14] to discover implicit associations among entities. But those embedding-based methods do not consider explicit logical semantics and usually have low performance in querying top-1 AEs.

Discovery of AEs. In most of the existing methods, AEs are discovered by measuring the relatedness between entities in KG. For example, Ponza et al. [12] created a small weighted subgraph that is dynamically grown around two query entities, and then used further selection or combination of known relatedness metrics to compute the weights in the subgraph. Cao et al. [1] used the heterogeneous information network to represent KG to capture the hidden semantic relations between seed entities and proposed a novel method for entity expansion based on the concatenated meta path. To discover AEs from outside data, some researchers connect implicit entities to KG based on their text-description [16] and online encyclopedias[20]. These methods show the effectiveness of discovering AEs by introducing entity associations from external data, but the quantitative associations between indirect AEs could not be achieved effectively.

Uncertainty Evaluation Among Entities. Uncertainty among entities can be evaluated by the confidences of association rules from the rich facts in KG [2]. Zhang et al. [23] used association rules to produce large amounts of evidence, based on which a factor graph could be constructed and the uncertainty between entities could be inferred. To infer new facts efficiently and accurately, Wei et al. [19] employed an embedding-based model to generate candidate sets of instances, and evaluated the uncertainty among entities of candidate sets by running a data-driven inference algorithm on the Markov logic network. To evaluate uncertainty among entities from textual Web contents, Li et al. [11] proposed EABN to represent and infer latent entity associations as well as the probabilities of associations. These methods show the effectiveness of evaluating the uncertainty among entities in KG and data, but do not consider the impact of user behaviors on the uncertainty of entity associations.

3   AEBN Construction

We first give the definitions of KG, user-entity data and AEBN as the basis of later discussions.

Definition 1. A KG is a directed graph denoted as $G = (E, R, \Lambda)$, where E is a set of entities represented as nodes and R is a set of relations between entities represented as edges. $\Lambda(e)$ represents the attributes of an entity e ($e \in E$).

Definition 2. User-entity data are characterized as a set of pairs $\Omega = \{< u, d > | u \in U, d \subseteq E\}$, where U denotes the set of users, d denotes the set of the entities of E, and the pair $< u, d >$ indicates that there is an interaction between user u and entity set d.

Definition 3. An AEBN is a pair $B = (\mathcal{G}, \theta)$, where

- $\mathcal{G} = (V, \mathcal{E})$ is a DAG, where V is the set of nodes and $\mathcal{E}$ is the set of edges. A node (i.e., variable) in V represents an entity or a conjunction of entities of $\mathcal{G}$, and $\mathcal{E}$ represents the set of dependence among the variables in V.
- θ is the set of probability parameters of the variables in V. For ease of expression, we use 1 and 0 to denote the occurrence of e in Ω or not, from which we assume that the variables in V are binary.

3.1 Generating Rules for AEBN Construction

For the given KG $G = (E, R, \Lambda)$ and the QE e_q, we first extract candidate entities that may be associated with e_q in Ω. Considering the sense of AEs, the association between a pair of entities should satisfy the following properties:

(1) A shorter hop between two entities in G leads to a larger association degree.
(2) An entity with frequent attributes is likely to be more associative with QE than that with sparse attributes in G. For example, a user who queries *James Cameron* is more likely to search *Terminator* and *Avatar* instead of *Titanic*, since most of his works are action movies.

Following, we give the weighting function that satisfies the above two properties to score an entity e in G, as follows:

$$W(e) = \frac{\log\left(Fr\left(e\right) / Fr\left(G\right)\right)}{\sqrt{len\left(e\right)}} \tag{1}$$

where $len(e)$ represents the length of the shortest path between e and e_q, $Fr(e)$ represents the frequency of $\Lambda(e)$ in G, and $Fr(G)$ represents the size of Λ in G.

By scoring the entities in G respectively, we could obtain candidate entities with the m highest scores. By employing the Apriori algorithm [4], the frequent candidates satisfying the minimum support could be obtained and denoted as L, from which the confidence of an association rule $E_u \rightarrow E_v$ could be achieved:

$$conf\left(E_u \rightarrow E_v\right) = \frac{support(E_u \cup E_v)}{support(E_u)} \tag{2}$$

where E_u and E_v represent two different itemsets of entities of G respectively, $support(E_u \cup E_v)$ is the number of d in Ω containing the entities in E_u or E_v, and $support(E_u)$ is the number of d in Ω containing the entities in E_u.

According to the basic idea of association rule mining [15], we obtain the association rules from L. By generating all nonempty subsets of each frequent itemset l in L. Furthermore, for each nonempty subset l_s of l, we generate the rule $l_s \rightarrow (l - l_s)$ if $\frac{support(l)}{support(l_s)} \geq min\_conf$, where min_conf is the threshold of the minimum confidence.

Based on the association rules generated w.r.t. e_q, we assume that each association rule between the n frequent candidate entities and e_q is described as Eq. 3, called query entity rule (QER):

$$e_1 \wedge e_2 \wedge \ldots \wedge e_n \rightarrow e_q \tag{3}$$

where $e_i \in L$ $(1 \leq i \leq n)$.

Actually, the confidence in Eq. 2 reflects the association between E_u and E_v, which motivates us to construct the AEBN based on the association rules with the confidence as maximal as possible. It is necessary to select a set of optimal QERs, since the intersection may exist among different subsets of QERs. Let Q denote the set of all QERs, Q_i represents the i-th QER in Q, and S_i

represents the set of candidate entities of Q_i. Now we consider selecting a subset of association rules by taking the total confidence as the objective function:

$$\max \sum_{i=1}^{|Q|} c_i x_i \tag{4}$$

where c_i represents the confidence of Q_i, $x_i \in \{0,1\}$ represents whether Q_i is selected.

Then, we employ the idea of the branch and bound algorithm to solve this optimal problem to obtain a subset of Q.

Solution Tree. The solution tree is a binary tree, where the i-th layer of the binary tree corresponds to the selection of Q_i, and the left and right child means whether Q_i is selected or not. The properties of a node in the solution tree are shown in Table 1.

Table 1. Properties of a node in the solution tree.

Property	Description
level	The layer of a node
child	The left or right child
tmpc	The summation of confidence
tmps	The set of selected entities

Bound. We regard the confidence as the weight of a QER, and rank all the QERs in Q by the average weight of Q_i (i.e., $c_i/|S_i|$). Suppose that a node is in the i-th level of the subset tree ($i = 0, 1, \ldots, |Q| - 1$), and the upper bound corresponding to this node is the sum of *tmpc* and the maximum weights of the selectable candidate entities:

$$tmpc + |L - tmps| \times (c_{i+1}/|S_{i+1}|) \tag{5}$$

Max Heap. In the max heap, the root has the top priority to be selected.

The above ideas are given in Algorithm 1. The execution time of steps 3–15 is $O(2^{|Q|})$. The execution time of InsertToHeap is $O(log|Q|)$. In the worst case, the complexity of Algorithm 1 is $O(log|Q| \times 2^{|Q|})$, which is far from being achieved in our experiments since a certain amount of QER cannot be generated in the sparse user-entity data.

3.2   Structure Construction

To construct the structure of AEBN that represents the dependence among entities, we consider expressing all the QERs of Q_{best} as Horn clauses, which could be transformed into the graphical structure equivalently by the logical implication. To this end, each QER $e_1 \wedge e_2 \wedge \ldots \wedge e_n \to e_q$ is expressed as a Horn

Algorithm 1. Generating the optimal QERs

Input: Q, the set of QERs; L, the set of frequent entities
Output: Q_{best}, the set of optimal QERs
1: Initialize h and a subset tree, sort QERs of Q // h is the max heap
2: $i \leftarrow 0$; $best \leftarrow 0$; $tmpc \leftarrow 0$; $tmps \leftarrow \{\}$; $Q_{best} \leftarrow \{\}$ // $best$ is the value of the objective function
3: **while** $i < |Q|$ **do**
4:     **if** $S_i \cap tmps = \emptyset$ and $tmpc + c_i > best$ **then**
5:         $best \leftarrow tmpc + c_i$; $tmps \leftarrow tmps \cup S_i$; $i \leftarrow i + 1$
6:         InsertToHeap$(h, i, tmpc + c_i, tmps, 1)$ //Generate the left child
7:     **else**
8:         $up \leftarrow tmpc + |L/tmps| \times (c_{i+1}/|S_{i+1}|)$// Calculate the upper bound up of the i-th node
9:         **if** $up > best$ **then**
10:            $i \leftarrow i + 1$; InsertToHeap$(h, i, up, tmps, 0)$ //Generate the right child
11:         **end if**
12:     **end if**
13:     $node \leftarrow DeleteMax(h)$
14:     $i \leftarrow node.level$; $tmps \leftarrow node.tmps$; $tmpc \leftarrow node.tmpc$
15: **end while**
16: **for** each $Q_i \in Q$ **do**
17:     **if** $node.child = 1$ **then**
18:         $Q_{best} \leftarrow Q_{best} \cup Q_i$; $node \leftarrow node.parent$
19:     **end if**
20: **end for**
21: **return** Q_{best}

clause $H = \overline{e_1} \vee \overline{e_2} \vee \ldots \overline{e_n} \vee e_q$. Meanwhile, H implies $e_1 \wedge e_2 \wedge \ldots \wedge e_n \rightarrow e_q$ and $e_1 \wedge e_2 \wedge \ldots \wedge e_n \rightarrow e_i (1 \leq i \leq n)$, by which H could be transformed as $\overline{e_1} \vee \overline{e_2} \vee \ldots \overline{e_n} \vee e_1 \wedge e_2 \wedge \ldots \wedge e_n \vee e_q$ equivalently, and we denote $e_1 \wedge e_2 \wedge \ldots \wedge e_n$ as *Core*. Next, we are to construct the DAG for H, as the structure specified in Definition 3 to represent the dependence between e_q and candidates in H.

In an AEBN $B = (V, \mathcal{E}, \theta)$, each node in V represents an entity or a conjunction of entities of H, and the node V_q represents e_q. Furthermore, from two different variables e_i and e_j, if $e_i \rightarrow e_j$ is implied in H, there would be a directed edge from V_i to V_j in B. Thus, H could be transformed into the logically-equivalent DAG, shown as G_1 and G_2 in Fig. 2. The above ideas are given in Algorithm 2.

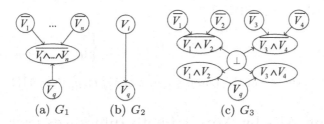

(a) G_1 (b) G_2 (c) G_3

Fig. 2. An illustrative example of DAGs constructed by QERs

Each DAG in Σ describes the dependence among entities of the corresponding QER. It is necessary to combine the DAGs in Σ to obtain the ultimate DAG of AEBN, by which the dependence between e_q and all the candidates in Q_{best}

Algorithm 2. Constructing DAG for each QER

Input: Q_{best}, the set of optimal QERs
Output: Σ, the set of DAGs
1: Transform each QER in Q_{best} as $\overline{e_1} \vee \overline{e_2} \vee \ldots \vee \overline{e_n} \vee \overline{e_1 \wedge e_2 \wedge \ldots \wedge e_n} \vee e_q$ equivalently; $\Sigma \leftarrow \{\}$
2: **for** each $\overline{e_1} \vee \overline{e_2} \vee \ldots \vee \overline{e_n} \vee \overline{e_1 \wedge e_2 \wedge \ldots \wedge e_n} \vee e_q$ in Q_{best} **do**
3:     Construct a DAG $\mathcal{G}_q$ as G_1 of Fig. 2; $\Sigma \leftarrow \Sigma \cup \mathcal{G}_q$
4: **end for**
5: **for** each $\overline{e_l} \vee e_q$ in Q_{best} **do**
6:     Construct a DAG $\mathcal{G}_q$ as G_2 of Fig. 2; $\Sigma \leftarrow \Sigma \cup \mathcal{G}_q$
7: **end for**
8: **return** Σ

---

could be described. To this end, we first replace $\overline{V_q} \to Core_i$ and $\overline{V_q} \to Core_j$ by $V_q \to \overline{Core_i}$ and $V_q \to \overline{Core_j}$ respectively. Simultaneously, we introduce identically-false node $\perp$ and make $\perp$ point to $Core_i$, $\overline{Core_i}$, $Core_j$, and $\overline{Core_j}$.

For example, suppose there exist $e_1 \wedge e_2 \to e_q$ and $e_3 \wedge e_4 \to e_q$ in Q_{best}, the DAGs obtained by Algorithm 2 for the two QERs can be combined into the structure shown as G_3 in Fig. 2.

3.3   Parameter Learning

In this section, we calculate the CPT of each node, including the node without parents and that with parents, to obtain the AEBN. Suppose V_i is a node in B and $P_a(V_i)$ is the set of the parent nodes of V_i. Conditional probability parameters in the CPT quantify the dependence between V_i and $P_a(V_i)$. We use the conditional probabilities, denoted as $P(V_i|P_a(V_i))$, to evaluate the CPT of V_i quantitatively. Moreover, all the variables are binary, (i.e. the value of V_i is v_i or $\overline{v_i}$), which represents whether V_i occurs or not respectively.

If V_i is a node without parents in B, it is straightforward to obtain the prior probabilities by normalizing the frequencies of frequent entities from user-entity data, (i.e., $v_i = N(V_i)/|\Omega|$), where $N(V_i)$ denotes the number of the entity corresponding to V_i in Ω.

If V_i is a node with parents, $P(V_i|P_a(V_i))$ is simply evaluated by the logical OR constraints represented by Boolean expressions. We give the following function to evaluate the CPT of V_i:

$$P\left(V_i = v_i | Pa\left(V_i\right) = (y_1, \ldots, y_z)\right) = f_{V_i Pa(V_i)} = \begin{cases} 1, & v_i = y_1 \vee \ldots \vee y_z \\ 0, & otherwise \end{cases} \quad (6)$$

where $Pa(V_i)$ is the set of the parents nodes of V_i, $v_i, y_j \in \{0,1\}(1 \leq i, j \leq z)$.

4   Ranking AEs by Approximate Inferences over AEBN

In an AEBN, the variable corresponding to an AE is denoted as V_a. To rank AEs w.r.t. V_q, we obtain $P(\overline{V_a} = 0 | V_q = 1)$ to evaluate V_a depending on V_q quantitatively according to G_3 in Fig. 2.

Rejection sampling [15] is an effective method to produce samples of binary variables, by which the samples w.r.t. $V_q = 1$ could be obtained the pairs of

Algorithm 3. Ranking AEs by the approximate inference over AEBN

Input: $B = (V, \mathcal{E}, \theta)$, the AEBN, where V is the set of variables of all the nodes; $V_q(V_q \in V)$, the variable in V corresponding to the QE; η, the number of samples to be generated

Output: L_p, a set of top ranked pairs $< A_k, P(\overline{A_k} = 0|V_q = 1) >$

1: Generate a value in $\{0, 1\}$ for $V_i(i = 1, 2, \ldots, |V|)$; $L_p \leftarrow \{\}$; $N(A_k) \leftarrow 0$ // $N(A_k)$ is the counter of A_k and $A(A \subseteq V)$ is the set of variables in V corresponding to AEs
2: **for** $j \leftarrow 1$ to η **do**
3:      Repeat //Generate samples
4:      **for** $i \leftarrow 1$ to $|V|$ **do**
5:          Generate a random number $\rho \in [0, 1]$
6:          **if** $\rho \leq P(V_i|Pa(V_i))$ **then**
7:              $V_i = 0$
8:          **else**
9:              $V_i = 1$
10:         **end if**
11:     **end for**
12:     Until $V_q = 1$
13:     **for** $k \leftarrow 1$ to $|A|$ **do**
14:         **if** $\overline{A_k} = 0$ **then**
15:             $N(A_k) \leftarrow N(A_k) + 1$
16:         **end if**
17:     **end for**
18: **end for**
19: **for** $k \leftarrow 1$ to $|A|$ **do**
20:     $P(\overline{A_k} = 0|V_q = 1) \leftarrow N(A_k)/\eta$
21:     $L_p \leftarrow L_p \cup \{(A_k, P(\overline{A_k} = 0|V_q = 1))\}$
22: **end for**
23: Sort L_p by $P(\overline{A_k} = 0|V_q = 1)$
24: **return** L_p

top-k AEs with association degrees by sorting $P(\overline{V_a} = 0|V_q = 1)$ in descending order. The process of approximate inferences is shown in Algorithm 3.

The time complexity of steps $4 \sim 11$ and steps $2 \sim 18$ is $O(|V|)$ and $O(\eta)$ respectively. Suppose the complexity of generating samples $V_i = 1$ in steps $3 \sim 12$ is $O(|T|)$. Then, the complexity of Algorithm 3 is $O(T \times |V| \times \eta)$. The estimation of rejection sampling will be converged as more samples are collected [15], which theoretically ensures the effectiveness of Algorithm 3.

5   Experiments

5.1   Experiment Setup

Datasets. Our experiments are conducted on two datasets: (1) users movie rating data from MovieLens [5], and (2) a user-item behavior dataset from Taobao called UserBehavior[2]. Table 2 summarizes the statistics of the two datasets. For each dataset, we adopt 70% as training data and 30% as test data. We extract part of the training data to construct KG. Specifically, in MovieLens, we create the relationship "like" between the user and movie if the ratings are greater than 4.0 (in the range between 0 and 5.0). In UserBehavior, the behavior types (click, buy, cart, favor) are served as the relationships between users and items.

---

[2] https://tianchi.aliyun.com/dataset/dataDetail?dataId=649&userId=1.

Table 2. Statistics of datasets.

Dataset	Users	Items	Categories	Records
MovieLens	162,541	62,423	1,093,360	25,000,095
UserBehavior	978,994	4,162,024	9,439	100,150,807

Evaluation Metrics

- **Precision, recall, and F1-score** are adopted to test the effectiveness of discovering AEs by probabilistic inferences over AEBN. Specifically, upon the ground truth provided by two datasets, $P@k$ denotes the proportion of the correctly discovered AEs over all top-k discovered AEs. $R@k$ denotes the proportion of the correctly discovered AEs over all correct matches [24]. $F1@k$ is the harmonic mean of $P@k$ and $R@k$:

$$F1@k = \frac{2 \times P@k \times R@k}{P@k + R@k} \qquad (7)$$

- **MAP (Mean average precision)** is adopted to measure the precision of top-k results after each relevant result is retrieved, defined as:

$$MAP = \frac{1}{|Q_s|} \sum_{1}^{|Q_s|} \frac{\sum_{i=1}^{k} P@i \times rel_i}{\mathcal{R}} \qquad (8)$$

where rel_i equals to 1 if the result at rank i is in $\mathcal{R}$ and 0 otherwise, Q_s is the set of queries, and $\mathcal{R}$ is the number of the AEs in the test data.

Comparison Methods

- **GBQE** [7] discovers a weighted hidden maximum query graph based on input query tuples, and then finds and ranks the top approximate matching answer graphs and answer tuples.
- **TSF** [12] is a two-stage framework for Wikipedia by first generating a weight subgraph w.r.t. two query entities and then computing the relatedness on the subgraph.
- **Association rule** [4] discovers AEs by mining frequent patterns from user-entity data, and the confidence evaluates the association degree.
- **Jaccard similarity** is used to find AEs from KG and user-entity data, denoted as Jaccard-KG and Jaccard-D, respectively. The association degree between entities could be obtained by calculating Jaccard similarity coefficient.

Implementation

We implement all the algorithms in Java on a machine with a 3.7 GHz Intel Core i9-10900X CPU and 128 GB of RAM.

The parameters *minimum support, size of candidate, min_conf* to 800, 100, and 0.7 on MovieLens and 5, 180, and 0.7 on UserBehavior. Each experiment is repeated for 5 times, and the average is reported.

5.2 Effectiveness Tests

To test the effectiveness of our method, we compare the precision and MAP of the top-k queries with the comparison methods. The results are shown in Table 3 and Fig. 3, respectively. We observe that:

Table 3. $P@k$ on two datasets.

Dataset	k	GQBE	TSF	Association rule	Jaccard-KG	Jaccard-D	AEBN
MovieLens	2	0.428	0.192	0.381	0.194	0.054	**0.553**
	6	0.235	0.201	0.353	0.177	0.079	**0.501**
	10	0.232	0.308	0.137	0.309	0.062	**0.442**
UserBehavior	2	0.001	0.013	0.066	0.003	0.044	**0.084**
	6	0.002	0.007	0.049	0.002	0.032	**0.073**
	10	0.001	0.005	0.039	0.003	0.030	**0.056**

(1) AEBN performs the best among all methods on both datasets. Specifically, in the top 2, 6, and 10 queries, precision could be improved via AEBN by 12.4%, 14.7%, and by 13.4% on MovieLens, and by 1.9%, 2.3%, and 1.7% on UserBehavior, respectively, compared with the second-highest method. Moreover, an average improvement in MAP could be achieved via AEBN by 7.5% and 3.5% on MovieLens and UserBehavior respectively.

(2) The precision and MAP of the comparison methods (GQBE, TSF, and Jaccard-KG) on UserBehavior are lower than those on MovieLens, since the strong randomness of the user behaviors leads to weak entity associations in the constructed KG. On the contrary, AEBN could be used to query the AEs more accurately in UserBehavior than the traditional structure-based methods by incorporating user-entity data.

(3) Compared with other comparison methods (association rule and Jaccard-D), AEBN achieves better results in terms of the precision and MAP, since the AEBN ranks AEs by probabilistic inferences based on the prior probability of entities within the user-entity data, and AEs cannot be ranked with the same confidence or Jaccard similarity coefficient.

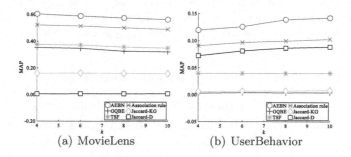

(a) MovieLens   (b) UserBehavior

Fig. 3. MAP on two datasets.

Table 4. $R@k$ on two datasets.

Dataset	k	GQBE	TSF	Association rule	Jaccard-KG	Jaccard-D	AEBN
MovieLens	2	**0.238**	0.111	0.174	0.223	0.130	0.203
	6	0.331	0.276	0.370	**0.440**	0.299	0.406
	10	0.466	0.426	0.459	0.500	0.474	**0.500**
UserBehavior	2	0.133	0.166	**0.246**	0.175	0.215	0.139
	6	0.396	0.218	**0.424**	0.248	0.353	0.345
	10	**0.500**	0.250	0.487	0.498	0.492	0.413

To further test the effectiveness of our method, we set k to 2, 6, and 10 respectively to test the recall and F1-score. Table 4 shows the effectiveness of AEBN for recalling AEs. Generally, the recall increases with the increase of k. We can see from Table 5 that AEBN performs best compared with other competitors in most cases. Specifically, AEBN improves the F1-score by 8.7% and 9.9% on MovieLens, and by 3.2% and 2.7% on UserBehavior, when k is 6 and 10 respectively.

Table 5. $F1@k$ on two datasets.

Dataset	k	GQBE	TSF	Association rule	Jaccard-KG	Jaccard-D	AEBN
MovieLens	2	**0.306**	0.141	0.239	0.207	0.077	0.297
	6	0.275	0.232	0.362	0.252	0.131	**0.449**
	10	0.324	0.300	0.369	0.215	0.110	**0.469**
UserBehavior	2	0.002	0.024	**0.103**	0.003	0.073	0.092
	6	0.003	0.013	0.088	0.002	0.057	**0.120**
	10	0.002	0.009	0.072	0.028	0.056	**0.099**

To test the effectiveness of query processing with different sized candidate entities, we test the precision by varying the size of candidate entities. As shown in Fig. 4(a) and Fig. 4(b), the precision increases with the increase of candidate entities. Specifically, precision increases by 10% when the size increases from 300 to 500 on MovieLens. On the contrary, Fig. 4(c) and Fig. 4(d) show that the recall decreases when the candidate entities increases. The recall decreases by 7% when the size increases from 300 to 500 on MovieLens. The impact of the size of candidate entities on precision and recall is fluctuating, since the UserBehavoir dataset consists of sparse user-entity behavior interactions with the randomness of real-world.

Table 6. $P@k$ of AEBN with various QERs.

Datasets	Optimal QERs	$P@2$	$P@6$	$P@10$
MovieLens	Yes (Algorithm 1)	**0.623**	**0.503**	**0.442**
	No (Random)	0.413	0.356	0.238
UserBehavior	Yes (Algorithm 1)	**0.084**	**0.049**	**0.037**
	No (Random)	0.009	0.031	0.035

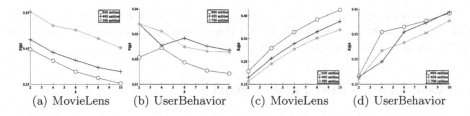

Fig. 4. $P@k$ and $R@k$ with various sizes of candidate entities on two datasets.

To test the effectiveness of the optimal QERs obtained by Algorithm 1 to improve the probabilistic inferences over AEBN, we compare the precision with the AEBN constructed by randomly selected QERs. The results are shown in Table 6. Actually, the precision of selecting the optimal QERs increases by 21%, 14.7%, and 20.4% over the set of random QERs on MovieLens when k is set to 2, 6, and 10 respectively. Moreover, the precision of selecting the optimal QERs increases by 7.5%, 1.8% and 0.2% over the set of random selected QERs on UserBehavoir when k is 2, 6, and 10 respectively. The results indicate the effectiveness of Algorithm 1 to obtain the optimal QERs for AEBN construction.

5.3 Efficiency Tests

Next, we test the efficiency of AEBN construction with different sized KGs and various parameters. Specifically, we construct KGs with the interaction records of 500, 700, and 900 users on MovieLens, and 3000, 7000, and 10000 users on UserBehavior respectively. Upon different sized KGs, we test the impact of the size of candidates and minimum support on the execution time of AEBN construction, shown in Fig. 5(a)–Fig. 5(d) respectively. We can see that the execution time increases with the increase of the candidate entities but decreases with the increase of the minimum support. The reason is that both a large sized set of candidates and a small minimum support are helpful to find more AEs from data. Moreover, under the same constraints of the minimum support and the size of candidates, there would be taking more time to construct an AEBN based on a larger KG. Precisely, the execution time of AEBN construction from the KG built by 500 users would take 3.2 times longer on average than from the KG built

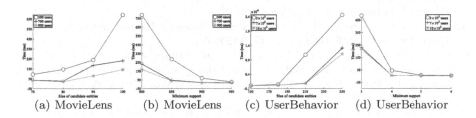

Fig. 5. Execution time of AEBN construction.

by 900 users on MovieLens. The execution time of AEBN construction from the KG built by 3000 users would take 1.9 times longer on average than from the KG built by 10000 users on UserBehavior.

6   Conclusions and Future Work

In this paper, we introduce AEBN to represent and infer the dependence between the QE and AEs with uncertainties. By expressing association rules as Horn clauses, the AEBN could be constructed from the sparse user-entity data w.r.t. the QE. By incorporating KG and user-entity data, AEBN facilitates discovering AEs with higher precision than traditional structure-based methods and provides better top ranked AEs.

Currently, only one QE is concerned in the query processing of AEBN, which should be further extended since multiple query entities are given to determine the most desirable AEs. Moreover, we consider incorporating large-scaled user-entity data based on the embedding-based methods.

Acknowledgements. This paper was supported by the National Natural Science Foundation of China (U1802271, 62002311), Major Project of Science and Technology of Yunnan Province (202002AD080002), Science Foundation for Distinguished Young Scholars of Yunnan Province (2019FJ011), China Postdoctoral Science Foundation (2020M673310), and Program of Donglu Scholars of Yunnan University.

References

1. Cao, X., Shi, C., Zheng, Y., Ding, J., Li, X., Wu, B.: A heterogeneous information network method for entity set expansion in knowledge graph. In: Phung, D., Tseng, V.S., Webb, G.I., Ho, B., Ganji, M., Rashidi, L. (eds.) PAKDD 2018. LNCS (LNAI), vol. 10938, pp. 288–299. Springer, Cham (2018). https://doi.org/10.1007/978-3-319-93037-4_23
2. Galárraga, L.A., Teflioudi, C., Hose, K., Suchanek, F.: Amie: association rule mining under incomplete evidence in ontological knowledge bases. In: Proceedings of the 22nd International World Wide Web Conference, pp. 413–422 (2013)
3. Gu, Y., Zhou, T., Cheng, G., Li, Z., Pan, J.Z., Qu, Y.: Relevance search over schema-rich knowledge graphs. In: Proceedings of the 12th ACM International Conference on Web Search and Data Mining, pp. 114–122 (2019)
4. Han, J., Kamber, M., Pei, J.: Data Mining: Concepts and Techniques, 3rd edn. Morgan Kaufmann, San Francisco (2011)
5. Harper, F.M., Konstan, J.A.: The movielens datasets: History and context. ACM Trans. Interact. Intell. Syst. **5**(4), 1–19 (2015)
6. He, G., Li, J., Zhao, W.X., Liu, P., Wen, J.R.: Mining implicit entity preference from user-item interaction data for knowledge graph completion via adversarial learning. In: Proceedings of the 29nd International World Wide Web Conference, pp. 740–751 (2020)
7. Jayaram, N., Khan, A., Li, C., Yan, X., Elmasri, R.: Querying knowledge graphs by example entity tuples. IEEE Trans. Knowl. Data Eng. **27**(10), 2797–2811 (2015)

8. Jin, J., Luo, J., Samamon, K., Dong, F., Gao, L.: GStar: an efficient framework for answering top-k star queries on billion-node knowledge graphs. World Wide Web: Internet Web Inf. Syst. **22**(4), 1611–1638 (2019). https://doi.org/10.1007/s11280-018-0611-0

9. Koller, D., Friedman, N.: Probabilistic Graphical Models - Principles and Techniques. MIT Press, Cambridge (2009)

10. Li, G., Chen, Q., Zheng, B., Zhao, X.: Reverse top-k query on uncertain preference. In: Cai, Y., Ishikawa, Y., Xu, J. (eds.) APWeb-WAIM 2018. LNCS, vol. 10988, pp. 350–358. Springer, Cham (2018). https://doi.org/10.1007/978-3-319-96893-3_26

11. Li, L., Yue, K., Zhang, B., Sun, Z.: A probabilistic approach for inferring latent entity associations in textual web contents. In: Li, G., Yang, J., Gama, J., Natwichai, J., Tong, Y. (eds.) DASFAA 2019. LNCS, vol. 11448, pp. 3–18. Springer, Cham (2019). https://doi.org/10.1007/978-3-030-18590-9_1

12. Ponza, M., Ferragina, P., Chakrabarti, S.: On computing entity relatedness in wikipedia, with applications. Knowl.-Based Syst. **188**, 105051 (2020)

13. Poole, D.: Probabilistic horn abduction and Bayesian networks. Artif. Intell. **64**(1), 81–129 (1993)

14. Ren, H., Hu, W., Leskovec, J.: Query2box: reasoning over knowledge graphs in vector space using box embeddings. In: Proceedings of the 8th International Conference on Learning Representations (2020)

15. Russell, S., Norvig, P.: Artificial Intelligence: A Modern Approach, 3rd edn. Prentice Hall Press, Hoboken (2009)

16. Shi, B., Weninger, T.: Open-world knowledge graph completion. In: Proceedings of the 32nd AAAI Conference on Artificial Intelligence, pp. 1957–1964 (2018)

17. Sun, S., Luo, Q.: Scaling up subgraph query processing with efficient subgraph matching. In: Proceedings of the 35th International Conference on Data Engineering, pp. 220–231 (2019)

18. Wang, H., Zhao, M., Xie, X., Li, W., Guo, M.: Knowledge graph convolutional networks for recommender systems. In: Proceedings of the 28th World Wide Web Conference, pp. 3307–3313 (2019)

19. Wei, Z., Zhao, J., Liu, K., Qi, Z., Sun, Z., Tian, G.: Large-scale knowledge base completion: inferring via grounding network sampling over selected instances. In: Proceedings of the 24th ACM International on Conference on Information and Knowledge Management, pp. 1331–1340 (2015)

20. Wu, T., et al.: Knowledge graph construction from multiple online encyclopedias. World Wide Web **23**(5), 2671–2698 (2019). https://doi.org/10.1007/s11280-019-00719-4

21. Yang, Y., Agrawal, D., Jagadish, H., Tung, A.K., Wu, S.: An efficient parallel keyword search engine on knowledge graphs. In: Proceedings of the 35th International Conference on Data Engineering, pp. 338–349 (2019)

22. Zhang, A., Wang, J., Li, J., Gao, H.: Aggregate query processing on incomplete data. In: Cai, Y., Ishikawa, Y., Xu, J. (eds.) APWeb-WAIM 2018. LNCS, vol. 10987, pp. 286–294. Springer, Cham (2018). https://doi.org/10.1007/978-3-319-96890-2_24

23. Zhang, R., Mao, Y., Zhao, W.: Knowledge graphs completion via probabilistic reasoning. Inf. Sci. **521**, 144–159 (2020)

24. Zheng, W., Zou, L., Peng, W., Yan, X., Song, S., Zhao, D.: Semantic SPARQL similarity search over RDF knowledge graphs. Proc. VLDB Endow. **9**(11), 840–851 (2016)

BOUNCE: An Efficient Selective Enumeration Approach for Nested Named Entity Recognition

Liujun Wang and Yanyan Shen[✉]

Shanghai Jiao Tong University, Shanghai, China
{liujunwang,shenyy}@sjtu.edu.cn

Abstract. The scenario that one entity contains other entities is known as nested entities. Nested named entity recognition is a fundamental and challenging task in various NLP applications. The state-of-the-art nested NER approach first enumerates all the text spans in a sentence and then performs classification. We realize that a large proportion of entities contain only one token which cannot be nested, and most text spans in a sentence are not entities and the full enumeration is thus costly and unnecessary. In this paper, we propose an efficient selective enumeration approach named BOUNCE. We decompose the nested NER task into two subtasks for identifying unit-length entities and the others respectively. We develop a delicate model for each subtask and perform joint training for both of them. To improve the efficiency, we employ a head detection module to locate the start points of entities, which acts as a filtering step before enumeration. We provide a detailed analysis on the time complexity of the existing nested NER techniques and conduct extensive experiments on two datasets. The results demonstrate that BOUNCE outperforms various nested NER techniques and achieves higher efficiency than the state-of-the-art method with comparable accuracy performance.

Keywords: Named entity recognition · Sequence labeling · Multi-task learning · Classification

1 Introduction

Named Entity Recognition (NER) is an essential and fundamental task in Natural Language Processing which aims to identify *entities or entity mentions* – text spans with proper semantic types such as *Person* or *Location*. This task is often treated as a sequence labeling problem where each token is tagged with a specific label and the labels indicate the recognized entities [12,19,27].

However, it has been found [16] that sequence labeling approaches fall short in dealing with *nested entity mentions* in texts, where one entity mention may include other entity mentions. As shown in Fig. 1, the *Protein* entity mention "interleukin-2" is nested in a *DNA* entity mention "Mouse interleukin-2 receptor alpha gene". While posing great challenges to the NER task, nested

© Springer Nature Switzerland AG 2021
L. H. U et al. (Eds.): APWeb-WAIM 2021, LNCS 12859, pp. 90–105, 2021.
https://doi.org/10.1007/978-3-030-85899-5_7

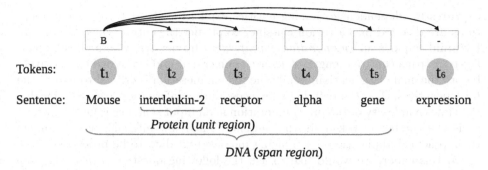

Fig. 1. An example of two nested entity mentions of *Protein* and *DNA*. "B" and "-" indicate the heads of the span regions and the others, respectively.

entities are very common in practice, especially in the biomedical domain. In the well-known ACE2005 [8] and GENIA text corpora [17], more than 20% of the sentences involve nested entity mentions. Therefore, it is crucial to develop effective approaches to the nested NER problem that can further facilitate many downstream applications such as relation extraction [13,39], reading comprehension [7,32] and translation [10,33].

There have been many attempts to recognize nested named entities, including layered sequence labeling methods [2,14], region-based classification methods [28,38] and neural methods with proprietary structures [22,24]. The layered sequence labeling methods [2,14] stacked multiple flat NER layers where innermost entity mentions are recognized in the first layer and outer entity mentions are identified in the following layers. One disadvantage of such methods is that the final performance suffers from error propagation through layers, which means the performance of a layer could be compromised if its previous layer extracts wrong entities. Later on, the region-based NER method [28] and its enhancement [38] proposed to decompose the recognition of nested entities into two steps. They first employ a single-layer sequence labeling model to detect the boundaries of entity mentions, producing candidate entities in texts. They then apply a region classification model to predict the entity type of each candidate. However, the sentence labeling model is insufficient to handle conflicting labels. For instance, the "interleukin-2" should be tagged with "B" and "I" at the same time, due to the existence of two nested entities. Some works exploited the dependencies among nested entities and developed proprietary structures such as mention hypergraph [22] or bipartite flat-graph [24], but can only achieve marginal performance improvement.

Recently, Pyramid [15] has been reported to achieve the state-of-the-art performance for nested NER. It organizes text spans of different lengths into a pyramid shape with a stack of L layers. The l-th layer predicts whether a text span of length l in the input sentence is an entity mention. The consecutive layers are inter-connected following the containment relationship of text spans, which captures the dependencies among entities explicitly. The detected entity mentions are then fed into a region classifier to predict the entity types. In general, Pyramid employs an *enumeration-classification* framework, where all the possible text spans (up to a length of L) are enumerated and examined exhaustively before the final classification. While the full enumeration is critical to reduce the false negatives, this results in high time cost during inference stages. Specifically, the time complexity of the full enumeration in an input sentence is $O(N^2)$, where N is the number of tokens in the sentence. Their low inference speed hinders their practical application when facing massive text data to be processed.

In this paper, we would like to ask the following question: *can we develop an efficient enumeration-classification approach that reaches comparable performance as Pyramid with lower time complexity?* Our work is motivated by two important observations. **First**, in practice, a number of entity mentions contain only one token, e.g., over 30% of entities have a unit length on GENIA, ACE2005 datasets. Since unit-length entities cannot be nested, conventional sequence labeling methods [1] are proficient in recognizing them with a linear time complexity of $O(N)$. This inspires us to break down the nested NER problem into two subtasks, to handle unit-length entities and the others separately. **Second**, not all the tokens in a sentence are the start points of certain entities. Instead of enumerating all the possible text spans, it would be useful to first classify whether a token is the head of at least one entity. This step plays a *filtering* role to locate possible entities in a sentence. After that, the enumeration could be performed over each of head tokens rather than all the tokens as Pyramid. Figure 1 illustrates the enumeration given the only head token "Mouse" in the sentence. Supposing the number of tokens that are heads of certain entities is S, the additional filtering step can reduce the enumeration complexity from $O(N^2)$ to $O(SN)$, and in practice S is much smaller than N.

Following our observations, this paper introduces an efficient approach named BOUNCE for nested NER. The key idea of BOUNCE is to selectively enumerate text spans rather than examine all the possible text spans exhaustively. To do this, we divide entity mentions into two types according to their lengths. We refer to entity mentions with a single token and multiple tokens as *unit regions* and *span regions*, respectively. For instance, in Fig. 1, the entity mention "interleukin-2" is a unit region and "Mouse interleukin-2 receptor alpha gene" is regarded as a span region. In a nutshell, BOUNCE solves two subtasks to recognize unit regions and span regions respectively. The two subtasks are trained jointly via multi-task learning, which enables the information sharing among entities. BOUNCE identifies unit regions by a sequence labeling model that is widely used for extracting flat (non-nested) entities. As for span regions, it first detects the head of span regions via sequence labeling and then enumerates the potential text spans (with more than one token) starting from the detected heads. As illustrated in Fig. 1, after the first token "Mouse" is detected as the only head, we enumerate $N - 1$ text spans starting from it as the candidate entity mentions to be classified afterwards (N is the sentence length). All the other text spans are ignored without examination, leading to high efficiency.

BOUNCE can be trained in an end-to-end manner via error backpropagation. To summarize, this paper makes the following major contributions.

- We propose an efficient selective enumeration approach named BOUNCE for nested NER. It separates entity mentions into unit regions and span regions, and adopts multi-task learning to detect both types of regions effectively. For span regions, BOUNCE quickly filters text spans by locating the heads of entities, which avoids the expensive full enumeration.
- We also provide a detailed analysis on the time complexity of various existing techniques for nested NER.
- We conduct extensive experiments on two real datasets. The results demonstrate that BOUNCE outperforms various existing nested NER approaches, and it achieves comparable performance as the best-performing method Pyramid with much higher efficiency[1].

2   Related Work

Deep neural networks have shown remarkable performance in plenty of applications [5,10,32,37]. Recent efforts have been devoted to developing neural network models to deal with flat named entity recognition [19,23]. However, these approaches fall short in handling nested entities where one token may refer to different entity types. Nested entities are very common in practice [21,36]. There are generally three different categories of approaches to nested NER. The first category is stacked sequence labeling methods [2,14]. Ju et al. [14] developed multiple decoding layers to label nested entities. Each layer identifies entities based on the labeling performed in the previous layers. However, the performance suffers from error propagation through layers. Joseph et al. [9] dynamically merged text spans at different encoding layers to learn higher level representation and identified the entity types of the corresponding text spans. The second category is region-based classification approaches [4,28,34]. The key idea is to identify possible entity mentions in a sentence and classify them into entity types. Zheng et al. [38] detected all potential entities based on the BIEO tag scheme and applied single-layer model to determine the entity types of those potential entities. Lin et al. [20] tackled this problem by detecting anchor words first and then determining boundaries of entities around anchor words. The third category of works used proprietary structures such as hypergraph [22] to deal with nested entities. Muis et al. [25] constructed a hypergraph structure based on multigraph representation to address the spurious structures problems.

Pyramid [15], stacking multiple LSTM and convolution layers, is a recent stacked sequence labeling method. While Pyramid has been reported to achieve the state-of-the-art performance, the time complexity of enumerating all the text spans for nested NER is high. In this paper, we propose to separate entities into unit regions and span regions. And we selectively enumerate text spans based on the detected head tokens that are the start points of at least one entities, leading to high efficiency.

---

[1] Our code is available at https://github.com/LiujunWang/BOUNCE.

Table 1. The summary of notations.

Notation	Description
N	The length of sentence
C	The set of entity types
h_i	The hidden state of i-th token in a sentence
$[h_i; h_j]$	The concatenated representation of h_i and h_j
σ	ReLU activation function
$*$	1D convolutional operator

3 BOUNCE Approach to Nested NER

In this section, we present our BOUNCE approach to nested NER. We divide entity mentions into two types, *unit region* and *span region*, according to their lengths. The unit region entities contain only one token and the span region entities involve more than one tokens. It is important to notice that unit region entities cannot be nested. At a high level, BOUNCE aims to *selectively enumerate text spans and classify their entity labels* to reduce the inference time costs. Figure 2 depicts the BOUNCE architecture, which consists of three major modules: (i) *unit region classification* is responsible for identifying unit region entities and associating them with correct entity types; (ii) *span region head detection* tries to locate the head of possible entities; and (iii) *span region classification* enumerates span region entities according to the detected heads and classify them into types. There are two novel attempts in BOUNCE. First, we decompose the challenging nested NER task into two subtasks for handling unit region entities and span region entities, respectively. This allows us to tailor more appropriate models to each subtask. Second, we enumerate possible entity mentions following the detected region span heads, which is beneficial to reduce false alarms and enhance the efficiency. It is worth mentioning that BOUNCE is fully differentiable and can be optimized via error backpropagation. In what follows, we present the details of our BOUNCE approach. Table 1 summarizes all the notations used throughout the paper.

3.1 Token Representation

We consider a N-length sentence $\{t_1, t_2, \cdots, t_N\}$ as the raw input. Initially, each token $t_i (1 \leq i \leq N)$ is encoded using the one-hot vector. We transform it into the *context-aware latent vector*. First, we compute the word-level embedding x_i^w of t_i as: $x_i^w = E^w(t_i)$, where E^w is the word embedding lookup matrix. We initialize E^w with pre-trained language models as in [15].

Second, we consider the character-level embedding x_i^c of t_i following [19], which are useful to capture the orthographic and morphological features of the tokens and represent out-of-vocabulary words. Let c_j^i be the j-th character in token t_i. We compute the initial embedding of c_j^i as $E^c(c_j^i)$, where E^c is the

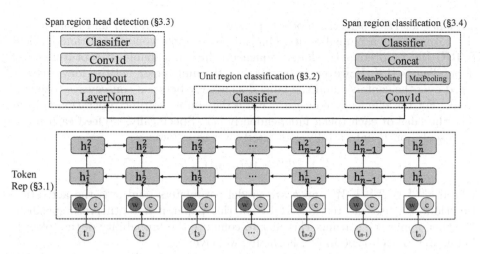

Fig. 2. Model architecture of our BOUNCE model. h represents the hidden states of inputs. The superscript and subscript of h denotes the layers of bi-LSTM, position of tokens respectively.

character embedding lookup table and we initialize it randomly. We then supply the character sequence of t_i into a bidirectional LSTM [11]. The character-level embedding x_i^c of t_i is computed by concatenating the last hidden states of the bi-LSTM as follows:

$$x_i^c = [\overrightarrow{h_{|t_i|}}; \overleftarrow{h_{|t_i|}}] \tag{1}$$

Finally, we employ a stack of L bi-LSTM layers to transform the two-level embedding $x_i = (x_i^w, x_i^c)$ of t_i into its context-aware latent vector. The first-layer transformation is formulated as follows:

$$\overrightarrow{h_i^1} = \overrightarrow{LSTM}\left(x_i, \overrightarrow{h_{i-1}^1}; \overrightarrow{\theta^1}\right)$$
$$\overleftarrow{h_i^1} = \overleftarrow{LSTM}\left(x_i, \overleftarrow{h_{i+1}^1}; \overleftarrow{\theta^1}\right) \tag{2}$$
$$h_i^1 = [\overrightarrow{h_i^1}; \overleftarrow{h_i^1}]$$

where $i \in [1, N]$ and θ terms denote the parameters to be learned. The l-th layer simply replaces x_i in Eq. (2) with the corresponding hidden state h_i^{l-1} in the lower layer. The output of the L-th layer is $\{h_1^L, h_2^L, \cdots, h_N^L\}$, where h_i^L is the context-aware token representation of t_i. Henceforth, we use h_i to denote h_i^L for ease of description.

3.2   Unit Region Classification

The unit region classification module aims at identifying unit region entities. The input to this module is the context-aware token representations $H = \{h_1, \cdots, h_N\}$. Let C denote the set of entity types. We try to predict the label sequence for H, where the labels belong to $C^* = C \cup \{none\}$ and *none* means the token is not a named entity. One way is to apply conditional random field (CRF) [18] to predict the label sequence, which is capable of capturing label dependencies [19]. However, in our setting, the unit region entities may be scattered over the sentence and the label dependency between consecutive tokens is weak. For the efficiency concern, we use the simple softmax operation to predict the label of each token independently [35]. Specifically, we feed each token representation h_i into a fully-connected layer as follows:

$$z_i^{unit} = W(\sigma(h_i)) + b \tag{3}$$

where $z_i^{unit} \in \mathbb{R}^{|C^*|}$, W and b are model parameters, and σ is the activation function. We use the rectifier ReLU in this paper if not otherwise specified. We then apply the softmax classifier to compute the probability of the token t_i belonging to each type in C^*. Formally, we have:

$$y_{ij}^{unit} = P(c_j \in C^* \mid h_i) = \frac{\exp(z_{ij}^{unit})}{\sum_{k=1}^{|C^*|} \exp(z_{ik}^{unit})} \tag{4}$$

where y_{ij}^{unit} is the probability of the token t_i belonging to type c_j.

We compute the cross-entropy loss to optimize this module, and the loss for H is formulated as:

$$\mathcal{L}_{unit}(H) = -\sum_{i=1}^{N} \sum_{j=1}^{|C^*|} \tilde{y}_{ij}^{unit} \log y_{ij}^{unit} \tag{5}$$

where $\tilde{y}_i^{unit}$ is the truth unit region label vector of the token t_i.

3.3   Span Region Head Detection

We propose to enumerate span region entities (with more than one tokens) in a selective manner. The span region head detection module is to identify the head (i.e., the first token) of at least one span region entities. The input to this module is the token representations $H = \{h_1, \cdots, h_N\}$. We adopt a sequence labeling model to assign each token with a binary label indicating whether it is a head or not. We first perform layer normalization followed by a dropout layer over each token representation h_i in H:

$$\tilde{h}_i = Dropout\left(LN(h_i)\right) \tag{6}$$

To capture the label dependency between adjacent tokens, we further apply 1D convolution with a window size of two over $\tilde{H}$:

$$z_i^{head} = W^c * [\tilde{h}_{i-1}; \tilde{h}_i] + b^c \tag{7}$$

where $*$ denotes the convolutional operator. W^c and b^c are respectively the kernel matrix and bias to be learned.

We then feed z_i^{head} into a fully-connected layer followed by a softmax layer, which is formulated as follows:

$$y_i^{head} = softmax(W(\sigma(z_i^{head})) + b) \tag{8}$$

where $y_i^{head} \in [0,1]^2$ and $W \in \mathbb{R}^{|h_i| \times 2}$ and b are model parameters.

Similar to Eq. (5), we adopt the cross-entropy loss to optimize the span region head detection module, which is defined as:

$$\mathcal{L}_{head}(H) = -\sum_{i=1}^{N}\sum_{j=1}^{2} \tilde{y}_{ij}^{head} \log y_{ij}^{head} \tag{9}$$

where $\tilde{y}_i^{head}$ is the ground-truth binary label vector of the token t_i being the head of any span region entities.

3.4 Span Region Classification

Based on results predicted by the span region head detection module, we construct candidate span regions as illustrated in Fig. 1. Specifically, for each detected head token, we enumerate all the text spans starting from it till the last token in the sentence, which are regarded as *candidate span region entities*. The span region classification module takes each candidate as input and produces its entity type in C^*. Note that we leverage the ground-truth labels of tokens being the head of any span regions during training, while the actual predicted head labels are used for testing. It is also worth mentioning that our method does not require to construct a pyramid-like structure to propagate information among candidate entity mentions, which is time-consuming. Instead, we avoid unnecessary enumeration and classification of span region candidates, and capture the dependencies among entities through shared token representation module and the overall joint training paradigm.

To deal with the problem that candidate span region entities have different lengths, a commonly adopted strategy to obtain the representation of span regions is simply averaging the representations for the involved tokens like in [38]. However, applying average pooling directly would dismiss the local features of entities. Hence, in our design, we first employ the convolution neural network with different kernel sizes to extract local features of candidate span regions. We consider a candidate region span entity with the token representations $H_c = (h_{c1}, \cdots, h_{ck})$, where $c1$ is the index of the head token and ck is the index of the end token, satisfying $ck - c1 = k - 1$ (a continuous text span).

To simply the description, we define the convolutional operator with a window size of two as an illustration, which is the following:

$$z_{ci}^{span} = W^{cs} * [h_{c(i-1)}; h_{ci}] + b^{cs} \tag{10}$$

where $*$ is the convolutional operator. W^{cs} and b^{bs} are model parameters. Then we utilize both max-pooling and mean-pooling to normalize the candidate representations into the same dimension and further concatenate the pooling results, which are defined in the following equations:

$$H_c^{max} = \mathcal{F}^{max}([z_{c1}^{span} : z_{ck}^{span}]) \tag{11}$$

$$H_c^{mean} = \mathcal{F}^{mean}([z_{c1}^{span} : z_{ck}^{span}]) \tag{12}$$

$$\bar{H}_c = H_c^{max} \oplus H_c^{mean} \tag{13}$$

where $[z_{c1}^{span} : z_{ck}^{span}]$ denotes the output of the convolutional operator. $\mathcal{F}^{max}$ and $\mathcal{F}^{mean}$ are the two pooling operations. $\oplus$ means the concatenation.

Now that we obtain the representation of the candidate region span entities $\bar{H}_c$, we supply it to the softmax classifier to produce its type in C^*. Formally, we have:

$$y_c^{span} = softmax(W(\sigma(\bar{H}_c)) + b) \tag{14}$$

where y_c^{span} is a $|C^*|$-dimensional vector. The loss function of the span region classification module is defined as follows:

$$\mathcal{L}_{span} = -\sum_c \sum_{j=1}^{|C^*|} \tilde{y}_{cj}^{span} \log y_{cj}^{span} \tag{15}$$

where $\tilde{y}_{cj}^{span}$ denotes the ground-truth label vector of the candidate.

Overall, the loss function to optimize the parameters of all the modules consists of three parts in Eq. (5), Eq. (9) and Eq. (15), which is defined as follows:

$$\mathcal{L} = \alpha_1 \mathcal{L}_{unit} + \alpha_2 \mathcal{L}_{head} + \alpha_3 \mathcal{L}_{span} \tag{16}$$

where α terms are used to reweigh the losses of the respective modules.

3.5   Time Complexity Analysis

In this section, we discuss the time complexity of the main computational blocks in processing one sentence, including bi-LSTM layer, convolution layer, pooling layer and fully connected layer. We ignore other layers like embedding layer since the main computational blocks are the dominate factors in the time complexity.

Given token representations of a sentence with length N, the time complexity of the computational blocks to obtain the sequence representation is $O(N)$. Therefore, the time complexity of bi-LSTM layer, pooling layer and convolution layer are $O(N)$. For N candidate entities, the time complexity of the fully connected layer predicting tokens' labels is also $O(N)$.

Similarly, the time complexity of the Pyramid-Basic model [15] is $O(LN)$ since it stacks L layered bi-LSTMs and L convolution layers, which will produce LN candidate entities with L being the number of the stacked layers. They set L to 16 in their experiments, and hence the time complexity of Pyramid-Basic is approximately $O(MN)$, where M is the maximum length of entity mentions. Assuming the number of head tokens is S, our BOUNCE model produces SN candidate span region entities. Besides, we only need to process N-length sequence once to obtain all the pooling results of candidate span region entities which share the same head token during pooling step. Therefore, the time complexity of our BOUNCE approach is $O(SN)$. We also discuss the time complexity of various existing NER methods. The analysis results are summarized in Table 4.

Table 2. The statistics of the datasets used in the experiments. A sentence is considered as nested if it contains nested entities.

	ACE2005			GENIA		
	Train	Dev	Test	Train	Dev	Test
#sentences	7285	968	1058	15022	1669	1855
#nested sentences	2797	352	339	3222	328	448
	(38%)	(36%)	(32%)	(21%)	(20%)	(24%)
#entities	24708	3218	3029	47006	4461	5596
#unit region entities	13625	1793	1671	21863	1507	2132
	(55%)	(56%)	(55%)	(47%)	(34%)	(38%)
#span region entities	11083	1425	1358	25143	2954	3464
	(45%)	(44%)	(45%)	(53%)	(66%)	(62%)
Maximum entity length	51	31	31	20	20	15

4 Experiments

4.1 Datasets and Experimental Settings

Datasets. We evaluate our model on two nested NER datasets[2]: ACE2005, GENIA. Table 2 provides the statistical details of the datasets.

- **ACE2005** involves 7 fine-grained entity types. We used the same splits of documents (8:1:1 for train/dev/test sets) as in the previous work [15].
- **GENIA** is from GENIAcorpus3.02p[3]. Following the previous studies [15,22], we split it into 8.1:0.9:1 for train/dev/test sets. It contains 5 entity types. The DNA, RNA and protein subtypes are collapsed into *DNA*, *RNA* and *Protein* respectively, while cell line and cell type are kept.

Comparison Methods and Metrics. We compare our proposed BOUNCE approach with 15 different NER methods as listed in Table 4. We use precision (P), recall (R) and $F1$-score (F1) as the performance metrics. An entity mention is recognized correctly if its start index, end index and entity type are all predicted correctly. We also measure the *inference speed* by the number of processed tokens per second for efficiency comparison.

Model Settings. Table 3 summarizes the hyperparameters and their values used in our experiments. We adopted the stochastic gradient descent (SGD) as our optimizer for model training. For GENIA dataset, we initialized the word embeddings with pre-trained 200-dimensional vectors [6] like the previous works [15,38]. For ACE2005 datasets, we used the publicly pre-trained 100-dimensional GloVe word embeddings [26]. All the dropout rates in our experiments were set to 0.5. We set all the α terms in Eq. (16) to be one by default.

---

[2] The NNE and ACE2004 datasets are inaccessible due to lack of license.
[3] http://www.geniaproject.org/genia-corpus/pos-annotation.

Table 3. Hyperparameters used in our experiments. When two values are given, they are used for ACE2005, GENIA datasets, respectively.

Hyperparameter	Value
Token embedding size	100, 200
Char embedding size	30, 50
Dropout rate	0.5
bi-LSTM hidden size	200
Stacked bi-LSTM layers	2
Batch size	4
Learning rate	0.015, 0.004
Momentum	0.9
Gradient clipping	5.0

We updated the learning rate by time decay, where the decay_rate was set to 0.05. We also performed early stopping to prevent overfitting. Pyramid-Full, containing an inverse pyramid, is an enhancement of Pyramid-Basic. All the performance results of the comparison methods are directly obtained from the original papers.

Experimental Environment. We conducted the experiments on a 64-bit Linux machine with a Intel(R) Xeon(R) CPU E5-2620 v4 @ 2.10 GHz processor and a NVIDIA TITAN Xp with 12 GB of available RAM. We ran all the experiments 10 times and reported the averaged results.

4.2   Comparison Results

Performance Evaluation. Table 4 shows the performance comparison results of different methods on two datasets. Missing results on some datasets represent that corresponding model has no evaluation on that datasets. We have the following key observations. First, our BOUNCE approach consistently outperforms all the existing NER methods except Pyramid on the two datasets, which proves the effectiveness of our selective enumeration method in handling nested entities. Though Seq2seq is trained using train+dev sets on GENIA, it is still inferior to our method. Second, BOUNCE achieves comparable performance to the two Pyramid methods on GENIA, and the performance is slightly below Pyramid on ACE2005. This is because Pyramid constructs a pyramid structure to explicitly capture the dependencies among entities and enumerates all the text spans to avoid false negatives. However, the time complexity of Pyramid is higher than BOUNCE, and hence our BOUNCE approach is more desirable when the efficiency is a major concern. Third, all the approaches report the highest F1-score on GENIA. The possible reasons are that GENIA contains more training data, and its maximum entity length is much smaller than those in ACE2005. Besides, we present the performance of our span region head detection module on two

Table 4. Performance comparison results on ACE2005, GENIA. M is the maximum length of entity mentions and N refers to the sentence length. For time complexity, Q and S denote the average numbers of entity mentions and span region entities per sentence, respectively. K denotes the average number of anchor words [20] per sentence ($S < Q < K < M < N$ and $Q \ll N$). The time complexity of Cascaded-CRF is not listed as it varies over datasets.

	ACE2005			GENIA			Time complexity
	P	R	F1	P	R	F1	
Hypergraph [22]	66.3	59.2	62.5	74.2	66.7	70.3	$O(N)$
Multi-hypergraph [25]	69.1	58.1	63.1	75.4	66.8	70.8	$O(N)$
Multi-CRF [19]	69.7	61.3	65.2	73.1	64.9	68.8	$O(N)$
FOFE [34]	76.9	62.0	68.7	74.0	65.5	69.5	$O(N^2)$
Transition [31]	74.5	71.5	73.0	78.0	70.2	73.9	$O(N)$
Cascaded-CRF [14]	74.2	70.3	72.2	78.5	71.3	74.7	–
LH [16]	70.6	70.4	70.5	79.8	68.2	73.6	$O(N)$
SH [30]	76.8	72.3	74.5	77.0	70.3	75.1	$O(N^2)$
Exhaustive [28]	–	–	–	73.3	68.3	70.7	$O(N^2)$
Merge & Lable [9]	75.1	74.1	74.6	–	–	–	$O(N)$
Anchor-region [20]	76.2	73.6	74.9	75.8	73.9	74.8	$O(N + KN)$
Boundary-aware [38]	–	–	–	75.9	73.6	74.7	$O(N + Q^2)$
Seq2seq [29]	–	–	75.4	–	–	76.4	$O(N)$
BiFlaG [24]	75.0	75.2	75.1	77.4	74.6	76.0	$O(N + M^2)$
Pyramid-basic [15]	79.27	79.37	79.32	77.91	77.20	77.55	$O(MN)$
Pyramid-full [15]	80.01	78.85	79.42	78.60	77.02	77.78	$O(2MN)$
BOUNCE	80.46	75.20	77.74	77.80	76.10	76.94	$O(SN)$

Table 5. Results of the span region head detection module on ACE2005 and GENIA.

Head detection	ACE2005			GENIA		
	P	R	F1	P	R	F1
B	90.7	84.6	87.5	82.3	85.4	83.8

datasets in Table 5. The head detection accuracy on GENIA is slightly lower than that on ACE2005. This is reasonable since GENIA contains more span regions in the test set. However, the final performance of BOUNCE on GENIA shows that the slightly inferior performance of the head detection is acceptable.

Efficiency Evaluation. We evaluate the inference speed of our BOUNCE approach and the best-performing methods Pyramid-Basic and Pyramid-Full using different batch sizes on ACE2005 and GENIA datasets. We keep the same dimensions in token representation and hidden state of bi-LSTM for all the methods. The inference efficiency of Pyramid was measured in the same experimental environment as BOUNCE. The results are provided in Fig. 3.

We can observe that BOUNCE achieves the highest inference speed on both datasets. On average, the inference speed of BOUNCE is about 3.3× and 5× than those of Pyramid-Basic and Pyramid-Full respectively for all the batch sizes on GENIA. The efficiency improvements are more significant on ACE2005, which contains smaller number of span region entities. As the batch size becomes larger, the efficiency improvement of BOUNCE tends to decrease slightly. This is reasonable as the bi-LSTM used for token representation occupy more time cost in the total inference time. Besides, Pyramid-Full runs slower than Pyramid-Basic on all the cases because it contains an inverse pyramid, which means that the time complexity of Pyramid-Full is about twice as much as Pyramid-Basic.

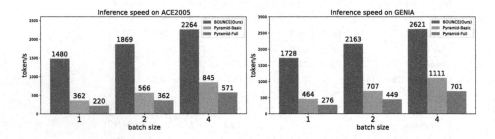

Fig. 3. Efficiency comparison results on ACE2005 and GENIA datasets.

Table 6. Ablation study results on GENIA dataset.

	P	R	F1	ΔF1
BOUNCE	77.80	76.10	76.94	
w/o separation	77.09	75.30	76.19	(-0.75)
w/o character	77.45	74.19	75.78	(-1.16)
w/o max-pooling	78.01	74.73	76.33	(-0.61)
w/o mean-pooling	77.80	75.42	76.60	(-0.34)
w/o layerNorm	77.00	76.09	76.54	(-0.40)

4.3 Ablation Study

We conduct ablation study on GENIA dataset to verify the benefits of separating entity mentions into two types according to their lengths and confirm the effectiveness of different components in BOUNCE including character-level bi-LSTM in Eq. (1), max-pooling layer in Eq. (11), mean-pooling layer in Eq. (12) and layer normalization in Eq. (6). We present the results in Table 6. And all these components have positive effects on the final performance of our model. The separation can improve the F1-score to a certain extent and it can also avoid invalid enumeration. Character-level features provide significant contributions because it captures orthographic and morphological information of tokens.

Max-pooling layer achieves larger improvement gain than mean-pooling layer in term of F1-score, which demonstrates that max-pooling reserves more discriminative features than mean-pooling in our model. Layer normalization also improves the F1-score and it can speed up the training process [3].

5 Conclusion

In this paper, we propose an efficient selective enumeration approach named BOUNCE for nested NER. BOUNCE divides named entities of different lengths into two types, unit region and span region. It devises delicate models to identify each type of entities effectively and performs joint training for better information sharing. BOUNCE follows the filtering-enumeration-classification framework for identifying span region entities, thus avoiding unnecessary text span examination. We further analyze the time complexity of various existing NER techniques and prove the efficiency of BOUNCE. Our experiments on two real datasets demonstrate that our BOUNCE approach can achieve comparable performance to the best-performing Pyramid method, with much higher inference speed.

Acknowledgements. This work is supported by the National Key Research and Development Program of China (No. 2018YFC0831604), NSFC (No. 61602297), and the Tencent Wechat Rhino-Bird Focused Research Program.

References

1. Akbik, A., Blythe, D., Vollgraf, R.: Contextual string embeddings for sequence labeling. In: COLING (2018)
2. Alex, B., Haddow, B., Grover, C.: Recognising nested named entities in biomedical text. In: BioNLP (2007)
3. Ba, J.L., Kiros, J.R., Hinton, G.E.: Layer normalization. arXiv preprint arXiv:1607.06450 (2016)
4. Byrne, K.: Nested named entity recognition in historical archive text. In: ICSC (2007)
5. Chen, R., Shen, Y., Zhang, D.: GNEM: a generic one-to-set neural entity matching framework. In: WWW (2021)
6. Chiu, B., Crichton, G., Korhonen, A., Pyysalo, S.: How to train good word embeddings for biomedical NLP. In: BioNLP (2016)
7. Clark, C., Gardner, M.: Simple and effective multi-paragraph reading comprehension. In: ACL (2018)
8. Doddington, G.R., Mitchell, A., Przybocki, M., Ramshaw, L., Strassel, S., Weischedel, R.: The automatic content extraction (ACE) program-tasks, data, and evaluation. In: LREC (2004)
9. Fisher, J., Vlachos, A.: Merge and label: a novel neural network architecture for nested NER. In: ACL (2019)
10. He, D., et al.: Dual learning for machine translation. In: NIPS (2016)
11. Hochreiter, S., Schmidhuber, J.: Long short-term memory. Neural Comput. **9**, 1735–1780 (1997)

12. Huang, Z., Xu, W., Yu, K.: Bidirectional LSTM-CRF models for sequence tagging. arXiv preprint arXiv:1508.01991 (2015)
13. Ji, H., Grishman, R.: Refining event extraction through cross-document inference. In: ACL (2008)
14. Ju, M., Miwa, M., Ananiadou, S.: A neural layered model for nested named entity recognition. In: NAACL (2018)
15. Jue, W., Shou, L., Chen, K., Chen, G.: Pyramid: a layered model for nested named entity recognition. In: ACL (2020)
16. Katiyar, A., Cardie, C.: Nested named entity recognition revisited. In: EMNLP (2018)
17. Kim, J.D., Ohta, T., Tateisi, Y., Tsujii, J.: Genia corpus–a semantically annotated corpus for bio-textmining. In: ISMB (2003)
18. Lafferty, J.D., McCallum, A., Pereira, F.C.N.: Conditional random fields: probabilistic models for segmenting and labeling sequence data. In: ICML (2001)
19. Lample, G., Ballesteros, M., Subramanian, S., Kawakami, K., Dyer, C.: Neural architectures for named entity recognition. In: NAACL (2016)
20. Lin, H., Lu, Y., Han, X., Sun, L.: Sequence-to-nuggets: nested entity mention detection via anchor-region networks. In: ACL (2019)
21. Liu, L., et al.: Heterogeneous supervision for relation extraction: a representation learning approach. In: EMNLP (2017)
22. Lu, W., Roth, D.: Joint mention extraction and classification with mention hypergraphs. In: EMNLP (2015)
23. Luo, Y., Xiao, F., Zhao, H.: Hierarchical contextualized representation for named entity recognition. In: AAAI (2020)
24. Luo, Y., Zhao, H.: Bipartite flat-graph network for nested named entity recognition. In: ACL (2020)
25. Muis, A.O., Lu, W.: Labeling gaps between words: Recognizing overlapping mentions with mention separators. In: EMNLP (2017)
26. Pennington, J., Socher, R., Manning, C.D.: Glove: Global vectors for word representation. In: EMNLP (2014)
27. Peters, M., Ammar, W., Bhagavatula, C., Power, R.: Semi-supervised sequence tagging with bidirectional language models. In: ACL (2017)
28. Sohrab, M.G., Miwa, M.: Deep exhaustive model for nested named entity recognition. In: EMNLP (2018)
29. Straková, J., Straka, M., Hajic, J.: Neural architectures for nested NER through linearization. In: ACL (2019)
30. Wang, B., Lu, W.: Neural segmental hypergraphs for overlapping mention recognition. In: EMNLP (2018)
31. Wang, B., Lu, W., Wang, Y., Jin, H.: A neural transition-based model for nested mention recognition. In: EMNLP (2018)
32. Wang, Z., Mi, H., Hamza, W., Florian, R.: Multi-perspective context matching for machine comprehension. arXiv preprint arXiv:1612.04211 (2016)
33. Wu, Y., et al.: Google's neural machine translation system: bridging the gap between human and machine translation. arXiv preprint arXiv:1609.08144 (2016)
34. Xu, M., Jiang, H., Watcharawittayakul, S.: A local detection approach for named entity recognition and mention detection. In: ACL (2017)
35. Yang, J., Liang, S., Zhang, Y.: Design challenges and misconceptions in neural sequence labeling. In: COLING (2018)
36. Zhang, Y., Qi, P., Manning, C.D.: Graph convolution over pruned dependency trees improves relation extraction. In: EMNLP (2018)

37. Zhao, Y., Shen, Y., Zhu, Y., Yao, J.: Forecasting wavelet transformed time series with attentive neural networks. In: ICDM (2018)
38. Zheng, C., Cai, Y., Xu, J., Leung, H.F., Xu, G.: A boundary-aware neural model for nested named entity recognition. In: EMNLP-IJCNLP (2019)
39. Zhou, G., Su, J., Zhang, J., Zhang, M.: Exploring various knowledge in relation extraction. In: ACL (2005)

PAIRPQ: An Efficient Path Index
for Regular Path Queries
on Knowledge Graphs

Baozhu Liu, Xin Wang$^{(\boxtimes)}$, Pengkai Liu, Sizhuo Li, and Xiaofei Wang

College of Intelligence and Computing, Tianjin University, Tianjin, China
{liubaozhu,wangx,liupengkai,lszskye,xiaofeiwang}@tju.edu.cn

Abstract. With the growing popularity and application of knowledge-based artificial intelligence, the scale of knowledge graph data is dramatically increasing. A Regular Path Query (RPQ) allows for retrieving vertex pairs with the paths between them satisfying regular expressions. As an essential type of queries for RDF graphs, RPQs have been attracting increasing research efforts. Since the complexity of RPQs is in polynomial time with respect to the scale of the knowledge graphs, currently, there has been no efficient method to process RPQs on large-scale knowledge graphs. In this paper, we propose a novel indexing solution by leveraging *frequent path mining*. Unlike the existing RPQ processing methods, our approach makes full use of frequent paths as the basic indexing facility. The frequent paths extracted from data graphs will be indexed to accelerate RPQs. Meanwhile, since no RPQ benchmark available, we create a micro-benchmark on synthetic and real-world data sets. The experimental results show that PAIRPQ improves the query efficiency by orders of magnitude than the state-of-the-art RDF storage engines.

Keywords: Knowledge graphs · Path index · Regular path queries

1 Introduction

With the proliferation of Knowledge Graphs (KG), the applications of KGs have a rapid growth in recent years. In the Semantic Web community, the *Resource Description Framework* (RDF) [1] becomes a de facto standard format for KGs and has been extensively applied. As an essential type of queries for RDF graphs, Regular Path Queries (RPQs) have been attracting increasing research efforts. RPQs explore RDF graphs in a navigational manner, which is an indispensable building block in most graph query languages. SPARQL 1.1 [2] is the standard query language on the RDF graphs, providing the *property path* [3] feature which is actually an implementation of RPQ semantics. In particular, answering an RPQ $Q = (x, r, y)$ over an RDF graph G is to find a set of pairs of resources (v_0, v_n) such that there exists a path ρ in G from v_0 to v_n, where the label of ρ, denoted by $\lambda(\rho)$, satisfies the regular expression r in Q.

© Springer Nature Switzerland AG 2021
L. H. U et al. (Eds.): APWeb-WAIM 2021, LNCS 12859, pp. 106–120, 2021.
https://doi.org/10.1007/978-3-030-85899-5_8

Although theoretical aspects of RPQs have been well studied, few practical techniques exist, such as efficient RPQ evaluation and optimization. Several methods with prune and filter techniques are proposed to tackle RPQs, such as the approach in [4]. However, the existing methods focus on the query optimization approaches rather than consider the statistics of data, leading to differences in the query performance over different KGs. In contrast with other path index methods, the path indexes built by PAIRPQ are on the top of frequent paths existing in the KGs, which will alleviate the query performance differences over data sets since the indexed items are adaptive to the data.

For capturing the statistical features of the data, we adopt the path index technique, which has been successfully applied in the area of XML and semistructured data management. For constructing this index, we consider frequent paths that exhibit in the KG, as shown in Fig. 1. It is noteworthy that PAIRPQ only captures the frequent paths and leaves the rare paths not indexed, which will save the storage space. To deal with various kinds of queries, two tables, PST and PTS, are constructed to record the paths, source vertices, and target vertices, while the first two columns of PST and PTS are indexed using B-tree. For the paths in the input query statements, we divide them into several indexed paths to make full use of the query efficiency advantages of PAIRPQ. The join order between the several parts of the divided paths is determined by the histogram of the data. The detailed method for path division is presented in Sect. 4.3. The processed query statements are executed over PAIRPQ to obtain the subgraphs that conform to the specified paths, and the final results are output in the form of a relation table.

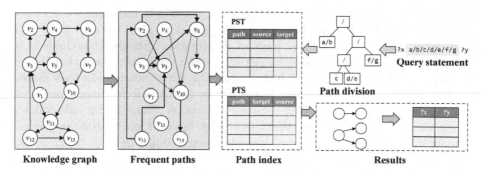

Fig. 1. The overflow of PAIRPQ

Our contributions in this paper can be summarized as follows:

(1) In order to accelerate RPQs, path indexes on frequent paths are built, i.e., PAIRPQ, which takes advantage of statistics of the underlying KGs. With the path indexes, all RPQs will be divided into several indexed parts, reducing intermediate calculations and improving query efficiency.
(2) The *Brzozowski's derivatives* [5] is utilized to divide paths into parts, while the join order between the several parts is determined by the histogram of the data, leading to high efficiency.

(3) Since there are no explicit benchmarks targeted for RPQs over RDF graph yet, we provide a micro-benchmark over synthetic and real-world data sets to measure the performance of the query processing method proposed.
(4) Extensive experiments are carried out to verify the effectiveness and efficiency of the proposed methods. The experimental results show that PAIRPQ and the query processing algorithm over PAIRPQ outperform the state-of-the-art methods.

The rest of this paper is organized as follows. Section 2 reviews related works. In Sect. 3, we introduce preliminary definitions. In Sect. 4, we describe the PAIRPQ index method for RPQs on RDF graphs and query processing techniques over PAIRPQ in detail. Section 5 shows the experimental results, and we conclude in Sect. 6.

2 Related Work

In this section, we discuss the related works, including path index methods and RDF storage engines.

2.1 Path Index

Recent years have witnessed great advances in path index techniques, which can be classified into the following categories: (1) DataGuide (2) T-index (3) k-bisimilarity index.

DataGuide. A DataGuide [6,7] for an data graph d is an summary graph s such that every label path of d has exactly one data path instance in s, and every label path of s is a label path of d. Moreover, Strong DataGuide is a class of DataGuide that is more restrictively, where each label path that shares the same extent in the DataGuide is exactly the set of label paths that shares the same target set in the source. Nevertheless, DataGuide requires a powerset construction over the underlying database. Moreover, DataGuides only follows the structural information from the data graphs, however, paths that are queried frequently should be attached more weights when building indexes, which is one of our key contributions in PAIRPQ.

T-Index. T-index [8] (*template index*) is proposed to answer queries for specified path template. The most simple template index, 1-index, is a rooted and labeled summary graph s where nodes are equivalence classes of the nodes in the original data graph d, assuring that for each edge in d there exists an edge in s. In 2-index, each node represents the equivalence class for a 2-length path. T-index, generalizing both 1-index and 2-index, only builds indexes on those having high percentage accessed queries rather than indexing all the paths. T-index leverages query logs to filter out the paths that should be indexed, however, query logs are not available in several data sets, which hinders the wider application of T-index. In contrast with T-index, all the requirements can be extracted from the data graphs in PAIRPQ, which assures the availability of PAIRPQ.

k-Bisimilarity Index. DataGuide and T-index, which are designed to answer RPQs accurately, leads to increased size and complexity with little added value. To deal with the shortcomings of DataGuide and T-index, A(k)-index [9], D(k)-index [10], and M(k)-index [11] are proposed based on k-bisimilarity. In A(k)-index, vertices are grouped based on the incoming paths of length up to k. For paths no longer than k, A(k)-index could get exact answers. While for paths longer than k, the A(k)-index becomes approximate. D(k)-index is an adaptive structural summary utilizing the query load, which can dynamically adjust its structure optimally to achieve reduced index size and improved performance. M(k)-index allows different k values for different index vertices having the same label, which makes M(k)-index not over-refined for irrelevant indexes or data vertices. Compared with the aforementioned methods, we not only consider the statistical features of data graphs but also reduce the dependence on query log, ensuring the applicability of PAIRPQ.

2.2   RDF Storage Engine

With the widespread application of knowledge graphs, various RDF storage engines have emerged. Virtuoso [12] is a commercial open source RDF storage engine based on a SQL engine, facilitating multi-model data management, and supporting the property path feature in SPARQL 1.1. However, due to the defects of structural features, the query efficiency over Virtuoso is unsatisfactory. In addition, gStore [13] is a prototype system that uses VS*-tree to speed up query processing and supports SPARQL 1.1. Nevertheless, not all syntax in SPARQL 1.1 can be parsed in gStore, particularly, the property path is beyond the ability of gStore system. Moreover, KGDB [14] is another prototype system that accommodates RDF graphs and property graphs and supports basic queries of SPARQL and Cypher, in which property path is allowed. However, no query optimization methods for RPQs are available in KGDB, which limits the query efficiency of RPQs. Virtuoso and KGDB, which facilitate the property path, are included in the experiments to verify the effectiveness and efficiency of PAIRPQ.

3   Preliminaries

In this section, we introduce the definitions of relevant background knowledge. Table 1 gives the main notations used throughout this paper.

Definition 1 (RDF Graph). *Consider three disjoint infinite sets U, B, and L representing Uniform Resource Identifiers (URI), blank nodes, and literals, respectively. RDF graph is a finite set of RDF triples $(s,p,o) \in (U \cup B) \times U \times (U \cup B \cup L)$, in which s is the subject, p is the predicate, and o is the object. A triple (s,p,o) is a statement of a fact, which means there is a connection p between s and o or the value of property p for s is o.*

Given an RDF graph $G = (V, E, \Sigma)$, where V, E, and Σ denote the set of vertices, edges, and edge labels in G, respectively. Formally, $V = \{s \mid (s,p,o) \in$

Table 1. List of notations.

Notation	Description
$t = (s, p, o)$	A triple t in knowledge graph G
$a^{-1}R$	The derivative of regular expression R
$minSup$	Minimum support threshold for frequent path mining
$\lambda(\rho)$	The labels of path ρ
S_ρ	The source vertices of path ρ
T_ρ	The target vertices of path ρ

$T\} \cup \{o \mid (s, p, o) \in T\}$, $E = \{(s, o) \mid (s, p, o) \in T\}$ and $\Sigma = \{p \mid (s, p, o) \in T\}$. In addition, we define an infinite set Var of variables that is disjoint from U and L. An example RDF graph G is shown in Fig. 2(a), which consists of 21 triples (i.e., edges). For instance, (v_1, a, v_4) is an RDF triple as well as an edge with label a in G, $V = \{v_i \mid 1 \le i \le 14\}$, and $\Sigma_G = \{\mathsf{a}, \mathsf{b}, \mathsf{c}\}$.

Definition 2 (Regular Path Queries). *Let $Q = (x, R, y)$ be a regular path query over an RDF graph $G = (V, E, \Sigma)$, where $x, y \in Var$ are variables, and R is a regular expression over the alphabet Σ. Regular expression R is recursively defined as $R ::= \varepsilon \mid p \mid R/R \mid R|R \mid R^*$, where $p \in \Sigma$ and $/$, $|$, and $*$ are concatenation, alternation, and the Kleene's closure, respectively. The shorthands R^+ for R/R^* and $R?$ for $\varepsilon|R$ are also allowed. $L(R)$ denotes the language expressed by R and $\lambda(\rho)$ is the label of path ρ. The answer set of Q under the standard semantics, denoted by $[\![Q]\!]_G$, is defined as $\{(x, y) \mid \exists$ a path ρ in T from x to y s.t. $\lambda(\rho) \in L(R)\}$. The set of source vertices of path ρ is defined as $S_\rho = \{x \mid \exists$ a path ρ in T from x to y s.t. $\lambda(\rho) \in L(R)\}$, while the set of target vertices is $T_\rho = \{y \mid \exists$ a path ρ in T from x to y s.t. $\lambda(\rho) \in L(R)\}$*

Definition 3 (Frequent Path Mining). *Given an RDF graph $G = (V, E, \Sigma)$ and a minimum support threshold $minSup$, the problem of frequent path mining over G is to find a set of paths $P = \{\rho_1, \rho_2, \ldots, \rho_n\}$. P can be divided into m multiple equivalence classes $C_1, C_2, \ldots, C_m$, within which each path has a similar structure, assuring that the size of each equivalence class should larger than $minSup$, i.e., $|C_1|, |C_2|, \ldots, |C_m| > minSup$.*

Definition 4 (Regular Expression Derivatives). *For any given regular expression R and any string u, the derivative $u^{-1}R$ can be computed recursively as follows:*

$$(ua)^{-1}R = a^{-1}(u^{-1}R) \quad \text{for a symbol } a \text{ and a string } u$$

$$\varepsilon^{-1}R = R$$

Using the previous two rules, the derivative with respect to an arbitrary string is explained by the derivative with respect to a single-symbol string a. The latter can be computed as follows:

$$a^{-1}\varepsilon = \phi$$

$$a^{-1}\phi = \varepsilon$$

$$a^{-1}b = \begin{cases} \varepsilon & \text{if } a = b \\ \phi & \text{otherwise} \end{cases}$$

$$a^{-1}(R)^* = (a^{-1}R)R^*$$

$$a^{-1}(R/S) = \begin{cases} (a^{-1}R)S + a^{-1}S & \text{if } R \text{ can be } \varepsilon \\ (a^{-1}R)S & \text{otherwise} \end{cases}$$

$$a^{-1}(R|S) = (a^{-1}R)|(a^{-1}S)$$

4   Path Index for Regular Path Queries

In this section, we propose a path index for RPQs on KGs, which employs the frequent paths in graphs. First, we describe the frequent path mining method on KGs, then the path index building approach will be presented. Finally, we explain the query processing algorithm adapted to the path index.

4.1   Frequent Path Mining

Although there exists several Frequent Path Mining (FPM) algorithms, most of them are applied to the scenario where multiple data graphs are involved. Among single graph-based FPM algorithms [15], few of them can be directly adopted to KG. In order to support the path index building process and the benchmark queries, a greedy FPM algorithm is introduced in this paper.

Generally speaking, the SPARQL queries with a low number of triples (from 0 to 2) have a significant noticeable share within the total amount of queries per data set [16]. Therefore, in order to minimize the execution time and complexity of Algorithm 1, we only consider the paths ρ that $|\lambda(\rho)| \leq 3$, i.e., up to 3 labels involved in the path.

Algorithm 1 presents the greedy FPM method adopted in PAIRPQ. Intuitively speaking, JOIN two edges with larger number of occurrences will get more results than the few number of occurrences ones. Thus, we assume that the frequent paths only exist in the JOIN results of two edges that appear more than $minSup$ times. Given a KG G, Algorithm 1 traverses the triples, extracts edges between entities, and records the number of the appearance of each edge label (line 1–4). The edge labels will be processed in descending order of the number of occurrences (line 5–11). A JOIN operation will be executed on each pair of edges (line 7). If the number of occurrences of the candidate paths $P_{candidate}$ obtained after the JOIN operation is greater than $minSup$, $P_{candidate}$ would be included in the result (line 9–11). The calculation will be executed repeatedly until the number of occurrences of any edge label participating in the JOIN operation is less than or equal to $minSup$. Algorithm 1 shows the method for mining 2-length frequent paths. For frequent paths longer than 2, we can use an iterative method to continuously increase the length of frequent paths.

Algorithm 1: Frequent Path Mining on KG

Input: Knowledge graph $G = \{t \mid t = (s, p, o)\}$ and a minimum support threshold $minSup$

Output: Frequent paths P

1 **for** *each* $t = (s, p, o)$ **do**
2   **if** p *is not* $rdf\text{:}type$ *and* $o \notin L$ **then**
       // p represents for the action between two entities
3   count$[p]$++;
       // count the appearance of the edge labels

4 sort(count);
   // sort the edge labels in descending order of the number of occurrences
5 $p_1, p_2 \leftarrow$ getProNext(count);
   // retrieve two edge labels with highest number of occurrences (p_1, p_2 can be same)
6 **while** count$[p_1] > minSup$ *and* count$[p_2] > minSup$ **do**
    // the number of occurrences of the two edge labels involved in the calculation is greater than the threshold
7     $P_{candidate} \leftarrow \{(s_1, p_1 p_2, o_2) \mid \forall t_1 = (s_1, p_1, o_1), t_2 = (s_2, p_2, o_2) \in G \land o_1 = s_2\}$;
8     $n \leftarrow |P_{candidate}|$;
    // join the two edge and record the appearance of the joined path
9   **if** $n > minSup$ **then**
10        $P \cup P_{candidate}$;
11     $p_1, p_2 \leftarrow$ getProNext(count);
12 **return** P;

Complexity Analysis. The time complexity of the greedy FPM algorithm on KG is bounded by $O\left((1 + \log(|E|))|E| + m^2\right)$, where $|E|$ is the number of edges in KG, m is the number of edge labels that occur more than $minSup$ times.

Proof. (Sketch) The time complexity of greedy FPM algorithm on KG consists of three parts: (1) The algorithm firstly traverses the graph by edges, which complexity is $O(|E|)$; (2) The edges are sorted by descending order of the number of occurrence, with complexity of $O(|E|\log(|E|))$; (3) The edges that occur more than $minSup$ times will be joined, with complexity of $O(m^2)$. Hence, the overall time complexity of the proposed algorithm is $O\left((1 + \log(|E|))|E| + m^2\right)$. □

Example 1. As shown in Fig. 2, given $minSup = 6$ and a graph G, Algorithm 1 will traverse G to obtain the statistics in Fig. 2(b). In a greedy way, the edges will be joined and determined by $minSup$. The frequent paths shown in Fig. 2(c) will be available after the FPM procedure completed. As illustrated in Fig. 2(c), there are two kinds of frequent paths in Fig. 2(a), i.e., paths with label a/b and b/a.

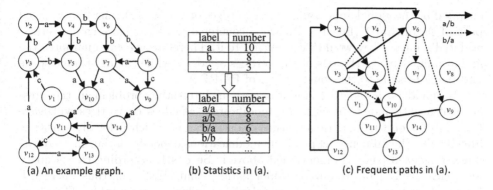

(a) An example graph.   (b) Statistics in (a).   (c) Frequent paths in (a).

Fig. 2. Greedy FPM on KG

4.2 Index Scheme

To cope with the frequent paths extracted from data, we propose a path index method, i.e., PAIRPQ. We assume that the queries and the data show a consistent distribution, thus, with most frequent paths indexed, PAIRPQ will accelerate most RPQs.

Example 2. As shown in Fig. 3, the frequent paths are recorded twice in two relation tables (i.e., PST and PTS), so that the path indexes can adapt to queries with fixed subjects or objects. The first two columns of PST or PTS relation tables are indexed using B-tree, thus, the contents of the same entries will be placed together, increasing query efficiency. The first column of PST and PTS records the labels $\lambda(\rho)$ of the paths ρ, which is extracted from data graphs as frequent paths, while the second column is about S_ρ (or T_ρ), and the third column indicates T_ρ (or S_ρ).

path	source	target
a/b	v_2	v_5
a/b	v_2	v_6
a/b	v_3	v_5
a/b	v_3	v_6
a/b	v_{10}	v_{13}
a/b	v_{12}	v_2
a/b	v_{12}	v_5

path	source	target
b/a	v_3	v_4
b/a	v_3	v_{10}
b/a	v_4	v_{10}
b/a	v_6	v_7
b/a	v_6	v_9
b/a	v_6	v_{10}

path	target	source
a/b	v_5	v_2
a/b	v_6	v_2
a/b	v_5	v_3
a/b	v_6	v_3
a/b	v_{13}	v_{10}
a/b	v_2	v_{12}
a/b	v_5	v_{12}

path	target	source
b/a	v_4	v_3
b/a	v_{10}	v_3
b/a	v_{10}	v_4
b/a	v_7	v_6
b/a	v_9	v_6
b/a	v_{10}	v_6

(a) Path Source Target tables (PST)   (b) Path Target Source tables (PTS)

Fig. 3. PAIRPQ index

B-tree is usually used for equivalent and range queries on sortable data, so it is suitable for indexing ID columns that are often stored in the digital form. In order to utilize the convenience of B-tree and compress the storage space PAIRPQ requires, the URIs of the vertices and edges in PST and PTS are encoded by the global appearance order of edges or vertices. During the traversal part of Algorithm 1 (line 1–4), if we encounter a newly added edge or vertex, a globally unique key would be attached to it. Therefore, we can guarantee the global uniqueness of the IDs of the vertices or edges, while saving storage space and being feasible to the construction of PAIRPQ.

It should be noted that updates pose an interesting problem in the presence of a path index. In fact, the modification of edges or vertices will leave little impact on the statistical feature of data graphs, which is locally sensitive. Specifically, the influence scope of the modifications depends on the length of the longest indexed path. As mentioned above in Sect. 4.1, according to the query analytical study [16], we only consider paths ρ that $|\lambda(\rho)| \leq 3$, thus, there will be few statistics that need to be recalculated, which is acceptable. Therefore, the modifications of the data will not affect the performance of PAIRPQ.

4.3 Query Processing

With PAIRPQ, it is obvious that the most paths in data graphs should be indexed and the paths can be divided into parts with lengths ranging from 1 to 3. According to the analytical study mentioned above, the indexed items should be able to solve the vast majority of queries. However, in order to improve the applicability of PAIRPQ, we still need to consider the processing method for longer-length queries.

The query processing method for dividing the paths into independent parts for processing is often applied in distributed query processing scenarios. Inspired by this, we exploit *Brzozowski's derivative* [5] to query over PAIRPQ. As shown in Sect. 3, the derivative of a regular expression with respect to a character computes a new regular expression that matches the same results as the original one, assuming the character as the prefix of the original regular expression.

In order to reduce the complexity of query processing and increase the query efficiency, we only consider the first few steps in *Kleene's closure*. For other types of operators in regular expressions, we use derivatives denoted in Definition 4 to compute the final results in a prefix-matching way. The division and assemble method can be found in [17], which leverages histogram of the data to obtain the optimal path division results and join order.

Algorithm 2 presents the path division method utilized in this paper. For a regular expression containing alternation operators, a prefix-matching procedure is first applied to extracted the prefix by the *Brzozowski's derivative* to reduce the intermediate calculation and speed up the query processing (line 2–3). To obtain the final result, path division algorithm described in [17] will be recursively called and executed for each sub-part (line 6–7).

Complexity Analysis. The time complexity of the Algorithm 2 is bounded by $O\left(l^2\right)$, where l is the max length of the sub-parts of R separated by alternation operators.

Proof. (Sketch) The time complexity of Algorithm 2 consists of three parts: (1) If there exists alternation operators '|', the regular expression is divided into parts by complexity of $O(1)$. (2) The algorithm finds the longest common sub-string of each part that seperated by alternation operators, which complexity is $O\left(l^2\right)$. (3) For each part, the path division problem can be regarded as a knapsack problem, with complexity of $O(l^2)$. Hence, the overall time complexity of the proposed algorithm is $O\left(l^2\right)$. □

Algorithm 2: Path division algorithm `divide(R)`

Input: regular expression R
Output: modified regular expression R'
1   **if** $R = R_1|R_2|\dots|R_\alpha$ **then**
     // R contains alternation operators '|' and can be divided into α
     parts that connect with '|'
2   **if** *the prefix of* $R_1, R_2, \dots, R_\alpha$ *can be the same string* S **then**
3       $R' \leftarrow S/\left(\texttt{divide}\left(\left(S^{-1}R_1\right)|\left(S^{-1}R_2\right)|\dots|\left(S^{-1}R_\alpha\right)\right)\right)$
4   **else**
5       $R' \leftarrow \texttt{divide}(R_1)|\texttt{divide}(R_2)|\dots|\texttt{divide}(R_\alpha);$
6
7   **else**
     // R does not contains alternation operators '|'
8     $R' \leftarrow R_1/R_2/\dots/R_\beta;$
     // $R_1/R_2/\dots/R_\beta$ are the optimal division results of R according
     to the histogram of the data
9   **return** $R';$

Example 3. As shown in Fig. 4, the original regular expressions in the query statements will go through three phases and be divided into indexed paths: (1) The common prefix will be extracted to reduce intermediate computation; (2) Path division algorithm will be recursively applied to sub-parts separated by alternation operators; (3) By assembling the path division results of each sub-part, the final path division result will be obtained.

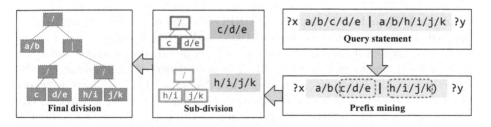

Fig. 4. Path division procedure

5   Experiments

In this section, we implement our method and verify the effectiveness and efficiency of PAIRPQ, and compare with the baselines on several data sets.

5.1   Experimental Settings

The proposed path index method was implemented on the top of KGDB [14], which is deployed on a single-node server. The server has an 8-core Intel(R) Xeon(R) Platinum 8255C@ 2.5 GHz CPU, with 32 GB of memory, running 64-bit CentOS 7.6 operating system.

Data Sets. Our experiments were conducted on both benchmark and real-world data sets. LUBM [18] consists of customizable and repeatable synthetic data, and allows users to define the size of the data set. Five LUBM data sets of different sizes (i.e., LUBM10, LUBM20, LUBM30, LUBM40 and LUBM50) are adopted in the experiments. DBpedia [19] is a real-world data set extracted from Wikipedia. In our experiment, a subset of the DBpedia data set is used. The statistics of the data sets is presented in Table 2.

Table 2. Data sets.

Data set	#Triples	#Vertices	#Edges
LUBM10	1,316,700	207,429	630,757
LUBM20	2,782,126	437,558	1,332,030
LUBM30	4,109,002	645,957	1,967,309
LUBM40	5,495,742	864,225	2,630,657
LUBM50	6,890,640	1,082,821	3,298,814
DBpedia	23,445,441	2,257,499	6,876,041

Baselines. We compare the efficiency and effectiveness of PAIRPQ against two KG databases. Virtuoso [12] is a hybrid database management system that supports a variety of data models. KGDB [14] is a KG database, which implements a unified storage scheme for KGs that can accommodate both RDF graphs and property graphs.

Benchmark Queries. To evaluate PAIRPQ and the query processing method proposed, 16 benchmark queries[1] on LUBM and DBpedia are created, respectively. As shown in Table. 3, the queries are proposed in accordance with the result of FPM mentioned in Sect. 4.1. The precedence of all operators in the regular expression is based on the rules in SPARQL 1.1 [2], without brackets changing the precedence, i.e., the regular expression containing brackets needs to be rewritten to obtain support. According to the nature of RPQ, the benchmark queries proposed are mainly chain queries, while star and complex queries are also included.

---

[1] https://github.com/tjuliubaozhu/PAIRPQ

Table 3. Benchmark queries.

Query	Type	Feature	Diagram[i]
$Q1$	chain	2-length index	
$Q2$	star	type-limited, 2-length index	
$Q3$	chain	3-length index	
$Q4$	chain	2-length index, not-indexed item	
$Q5$	chain	2-length index, not-indexed item, literal variable	
$Q6$	chain	without index, closure operator	
$Q7$	complex	3-length index, alternation operator	
$Q8$	chain	2-length index, not-indexed item, closure operator	

[i] The solid circles represent the edge labels, the dotted circles represent the entity variables (dotted circle with t means the entity is type-limited), the dotted squares represent the literal variables, the rings represent the closures, and the lines with options represent the alternation operators.

5.2 Experimental Results

Exp 1. Index Construction. As shown in Fig. 5, with the amount of data increasing, the storage space and FPM time required for index construction also increase with a linear trend. The construction of PAIRPQ is closely related to the results of FPM. In the selected data sets of LUBM, the final size of all indexes are basically the same as the space occupied by the original data. Although PAIRPQ is not dominant in the storage space, the overhead paid on the index is worthwhile to compare to the gain in the efficiency of queries.

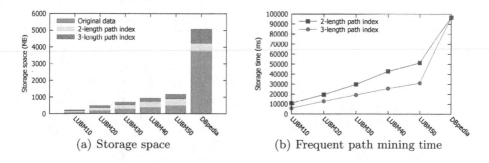

(a) Storage space   (b) Frequent path mining time

Fig. 5. The experimental results of storage space and time

As shown in Fig. 5(b), on LUBM data sets, with the scale of the data sets increasing, the increasing trend of the construction time and space of the 3-length path index is gradually lower than that of the 2-length path index, which proves that it makes sense for us to focus on shorter paths. For the real-world data set, DBpedia, the time required to construct a 2-length or 3-length path index is basically the same.

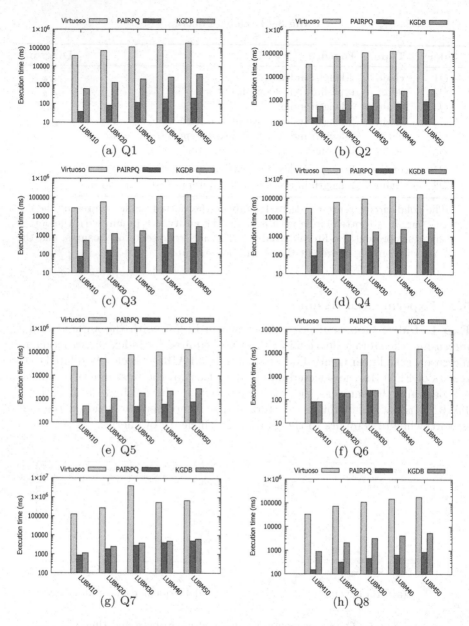

Fig. 6. The results of query execution time on LUBM (logarithmic scale)

Exp 2. Query Efficiency. As shown in Fig. 6 and Fig. 7, for all the benchmark queries we create, PAIRPQ can increase the query efficiency by three orders of magnitude than Virtuoso on LUBM. Moreover, for most queries, PAIRPQ can inprove the query efficiency by one order of magnitude on average than KGDB on LUBM, in which no path indexes are constructed. PAIRPQ can deal with Q6

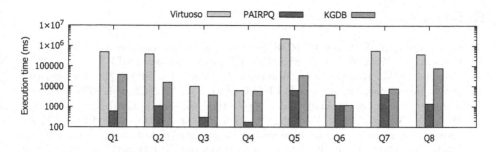

Fig. 7. The results of query execution time on DBpedia (logarithmic scale)

in the same execution time as KGDB, since $Q6$ does not involve path indexes. For DBpedia, the query efficiency of PAIRPQ is at least double that of KGDB and more than three times that of Virtuoso.

In Virtuoso, all data is stored in the form of triple tables, i.e., a three-column table is built to accommodate all KG data. To accelerate query processing, five index structures are built in Virtuoso, including PSOG, POSG, SP, OP, and GS indexes. (S, P, O, and G stands for subject, property, object, and graph, respectively.) Obviously, when a query involving multiple edges is executed in Virtuoso, more time-consuming JOIN operations are required, since the relation table with more rows is involved. Unlike Virtuoso, all KG data is classified and stored according to the types of vertices or edges in KGDB, while the B-tree indexes being constructed on the IDs of the vertices or edges. By this type-based storage scheme, the query efficiency of KGDB is significantly improved, which is also adopted in PAIRPQ and further improved by constructing the path indexes.

6 Conclusion

In this paper, we propose PAIRPQ, a path index method for RPQs on knowledge graphs. With frequent paths extracted using a greedy FPM algorithm, path indexes are built, which takes advantage of the statistics of underlying KGs. Furthermore, the Brzozowski's derivatives are utilized to divide paths, and the join order between the several parts is determined by the histogram of the data. Micro-benchmarks over LUBM and DBpedia are proposed to verify the efficiency and effectiveness of PAIRPQ and the query processing method. The experimental results show that PAIRPQ and the query processing algorithm over PAIRPQ outperform the state-of-the-art methods by orders of magnitude.

Acknowledgements. This work is supported by the National Key Research and Development Program of China (2019YFE0198600) and National Natural Science Foundation of China (61972275).

References

1. Consortium, W.W.W., et al.: RDF 1.1 concepts and abstract syntax (2014)
2. Consortium, W.W.W., et al.: SPARQL 1.1 query language (2013)
3. Kostylev, E.V., Reutter, J.L., Romero, M., Vrgoč, D.: SPARQL with property paths. In: Arenas, M., et al. (eds.) ISWC 2015, Part I. LNCS, vol. 9366, pp. 3–18. Springer, Cham (2015). https://doi.org/10.1007/978-3-319-25007-6_1
4. Wang, X., Wang, S., Xin, Y., Yang, Y., Li, J., Wang, X.: Distributed Pregel-based provenance-aware regular path query processing on RDF knowledge graphs. World Wide Web **23**(3), 1465–1496 (2019). https://doi.org/10.1007/s11280-019-00739-0
5. Brzozowski, J.A.: Derivatives of regular expressions. J. ACM (JACM) **11**(4), 481–494 (1964)
6. Goldman, R., Widom, J.: Dataguides: enabling query formulation and optimization in semistructured databases. Tech. rep., Stanford (1997)
7. Goldman, R.: Approximate dataguides. In: Workshop on Query Processing for Semistructured Data and Non-standard Data Formats (1999). http://www-db.stanford.edu/pub/papers/adg.ps
8. Milo, T., Suciu, D.: Index structures for path expressions. In: Beeri, C., Buneman, P. (eds.) ICDT 1999. LNCS, vol. 1540, pp. 277–295. Springer, Heidelberg (1999). https://doi.org/10.1007/3-540-49257-7_18
9. Kaushik, R., Shenoy, P., Bohannon, P., Gudes, E.: Exploiting local similarity for indexing paths in graph-structured data. In: Proceedings 18th International Conference on Data Engineering, pp. 129–140. IEEE (2002)
10. Chen, Q., Lim, A., Ong, K.W.: D(k)-index: an adaptive structural summary for graph-structured data. In: Proceedings of the 2003 ACM SIGMOD International Conference on Management of Data, pp. 134–144 (2003)
11. He, H., Yang, J.: Multiresolution indexing of xml for frequent queries. In: Proceedings of 20th International Conference on Data Engineering, pp. 683–694. IEEE (2004)
12. Erling, O., Mikhailov, I.: RDF support in the virtuoso DBMS. In: Pellegrini, T., Auer, S., Tochtermann, K., Schaffert, S. (eds.) Networked Knowledge - Networked Media. Studies in Computational Intelligence, vol. 221. Springer, Heidelberg (2009). https://doi.org/10.1007/978-3-642-02184-8_2
13. Das, S., Agrawal, D., El Abbadi, A.: G-store: a scalable data store for transactional multi key access in the cloud. In: Proceedings of the 1st ACM Symposium on Cloud Computing, pp. 163–174 (2010)
14. Liu, B., Wang, X., Liu, P., Li, S., Zhang, X., Yang, Y.: KGDB: knowledge graph database system with unified model and query languages. Ruan Jian Xue Bao/J. Softw. **32**(3), 781–804 (2021). (in Chinese)
15. Zhu, F., Qu, Q., Lo, D., Yan, X., Han, J., Yu, P.S.: Mining top-k large structural patterns in a massive network. Proc. VLDB Endow. **4**(11), 807–818 (2011)
16. Bonifati, A., Martens, W., Timm, T.: An analytical study of large SPARQL query logs. VLDB J. **29**(2), 655–679 (2020)
17. Fletcher, G.H., Peters, J., Poulovassilis, A.: Efficient regular path query evaluation using path indexes. In: 19th International Conference on Extending Database Technology (EDBT 2016), pp. 636–639. OpenProceedings.org (2016)
18. Guo, Y., Pan, Z., Heflin, J.: LUBM: a benchmark for owl knowledge base systems. J. Web Semant. **3**(2–3), 158–182 (2005)
19. Lehmann, J., et al.: DBpedia-a large-scale, multilingual knowledge base extracted from Wikipedia. Semant. Web **6**(2), 167–195 (2015)

A Hybrid Semantic Matching Model for Neural Collective Entity Linking

Baoxin Lei[1], Wen Li[1], Leung-Pun Wong[2], Lap-Kei Lee[2], Fu Lee Wang[2], and Tianyong Hao[1(✉)]

[1] School of Computer Science, South China Normal University, Guangzhou, China
{2019022603,wli66,haoty}@m.scnu.edu.cn
[2] School of Science and Technology, The Open University of Hong Kong, Hong Kong, China
{s1243151,lklee,pwang}@ouhk.edu.hk

Abstract. The task of entity linking aims to correctly link mentions in a text fragment to a reference knowledge base. Most existing methods apply single neural network model to learn semantic representations on all granularities in contextual information, which neglecting the trait of different granularities. Also, these solely representation-based methods measure the semantic matching based on the abstract vector representation that frequently miss concrete matching information. To better capture contextual information, this paper proposes a new neural network model called Hybrid Semantic Matching (HSM) for the entity linking task. The model captures two different aspects of semantic information via representation and interaction-based neural semantic matching models. Furthermore, to consider the global consistency of entities, a recurrent random walk is applied to propagate entity linking evidences among related decisions. Evaluation was conducted on three publicly available standard datasets. Results show that our proposed HSM model is more effective compared with a list of baseline models.

Keywords: Entity linking · Hybrid Semantic Matching · Joint Model

1 Introduction

Entity Linking (EL) is the task of assigning entity mentions in a text to corresponding entries in a knowledge base (KB). For example, the word "Florida" can refer to the Florida city, university of Florida or Florida Gators football. With specific context in a phrase "The Supreme Court in Florida today refused the application", the mention "Florida" should be linked to Florida city. In general, entity linking is typically performed in two steps: obtaining candidate entities for each mention and identifying true entities to reference knowledge bases.

A key challenge for successful entity linking is the need to capture semantic and background information at various levels of granularity. Recently, the studies of EL have evolved from the conventional statistical models to the neural network-based models in virtue of the excellent capacity of encoding semantic representation. Gupta et al. [1] leveraged a LSTM model as local context encoder to learn a unified dense representation for each entity. Xue et al. [2] and Agarwal et al. [3] utilized a CNN and Bert

© Springer Nature Switzerland AG 2021
L. H. U et al. (Eds.): APWeb-WAIM 2021, LNCS 12859, pp. 121–134, 2021.
https://doi.org/10.1007/978-3-030-85899-5_9

model respectively to learn semantic representation among various granularities to measure similarity. Except from considering local contextual information only, some other researches propose to measure the relevance among all entities in a document. Le et al. [4] treated relations among mentions as latent variables to model the relevance between different EL decisions, and Cao et al. [5] utilized a graph convolutional network to measure the topical coherence throughout the entire document. Through the combination of local features and global evidences, the disambiguation information can be better obtained. However, these methods tend to utilize solely model as the encoder that are incapable to take advantage of trait of different granularities to capture the representation of local information. Meanwhile these representation-based methods neglect some concrete matching information, which can help to measure the compatibility between mentions and entities as the complement.

In this paper, an end-to-end neural collective model called HSM is proposed, which take both representation semantic matching and word-level abstract concrete matching information into account to measure relevance. The representation-based method in HSM hybrids the convolution neural network and Bert to consider the trait of each granularity among mention surfaces, local contexts, mention text in datasets and Wikipedia page of entities. Then a bilateral multi-head attention method is introduced to obtain the concrete matching information between two pieces of texts. After that, two matching models work jointly to measure conditional probability of a mention referring to a specific entity. To consider global consistency of entities, a recurrent random walk layer is applied to propagate the EL decisions among related entities. In that case, both local semantic correspondence between mentions and entities and global interdependence between different EL decisions can be fully exploited.

The main contribution of this paper lies on the following aspects: 1) A new model HSM is proposed by utilizing the characteristics of different models to capture the semantic representation of local information in various granularities. 2) A bilateral multi-head attention-based method is incorporated into the HSM model to capture word-level concrete information between mentions and entities. 3) Extensive experiments show that the HSM model outperforms baseline methods on three publicly available datasets.

2   Related Work

Entity linking (EL) can be typically regarded as a task of linking a mention to its correct entity in a reference knowledge base (KB). Most researches contain two main lines of approach to resolve the EL problems, namely local approach, and global approach. The local component focuses on modeling the semantic relatedness between mentions and candidate entities. Early studies tackled this task based on lexical matching between the mention's surrounding words and entity description text [6, 7]. However, these methods could only capture the surface matches, with incapable to obtain deep semantic relationship. Recently, with the development of neural network, semantic matching powered by DNN showed promising improvement on entity linking task. The common approaches were to learn latent representations of local context and entity, respectively. Then, the semantic matching between a mention and an entity was conducted by utilizing similarity measures [8, 9]. Radhakrishnan et al. [10] proposed ELDEN model to improve the entity embedding by using information available on the web to enhance the structure of an original knowledge base.

Apart from the methods that training the embeddings of mention and entity to evaluate similarity, some researches resorted to neural network as encoder to learn semantic representation to measure the relevance. For example, Sun et al. [11] and Francis-Landau et al. [12] leveraged the rich parameterization of convolutional networks to exploit various kinds of text information. Gupta et al. [1] utilized a LSTM model as encoder to form local context and document-level representation of mentions. These neural models had been proposed as a way to support better generalization over sparse features, nevertheless it still lacked of capturing complex text features. Recently, modern pre-trained language models such as ELMO, BERT, ALBERT, etc., were used widely for NLP tasks by providing rich text representations through replacing static word embeddings with deep contextualized word embeddings. The current trend in research was to investigate all aspects of these language models or their applications to various domains. In entity linking task, Sevgili et al. [13] summarized widely-used entity embedding techniques and novel applications of EL for enhancing word representation models like Bert. Yamada et al. [14] and Washio et al. [15] used Bert model to produce contextualized embeddings for words and entities in input text and trained models as a masked entity prediction task. Broscheit et al. [16] and Zhao et al. [17] proposed an extreme simplification of the entity linking setup to cast it as a per token classification over the entire entity vocabulary, and treated the EL task as an end-to-end model. These methods improved the capacity of models to learn semantic representation of mention and entity. Although these methods had achieved considerable performance on EL task, they mainly focused to utilize NN model to learn semantic representation of various text granularities like context or document, with little attention on measuring concrete word-level match information. Guo et al. [18] discussed the differences of semantic matching and relevance matching. Further, Nie et al. [19] introduced the relevance matching in EL and proposed representation-based and interaction-based neural matching model, these two different aspects of semantic information could work jointly for entity disambiguation.

These works treated each entity as a separate unit with little attention paid on the interdependence between these different EL decisions. To tackle this problem, some approaches based on global entity consistency had been proposed. Yang et al. [20] utilized structured gradient tree boosting algorithm to produce globally optimized entity assignments for mentions in a document. Belief propagation (BP) and its variant loopy belief propagation (LBP) had been used by [21] and [5] respectively. By virtue of using random walks, Guo et al. [22] leveraged indirect connections between nodes in the disambiguation graph to measure similarity. Guo et al. [23] utilized random walk with restart on a graph to propagate information along the edges and Xue et al. [2] further employed recurrent random walk to model the semantic interdependence between different EL decisions by introducing external knowledge. Note that modeling entity-entity coherence is very challenging, as the long-range dependencies between entities correspond to exponentially large search space.

To address the method that solely relied on semantic matching, this work exploits a hybrid neural network model to enhance the semantic representation learning from contextual information. Differ from these exiting methods, our model considers the traits of different text and applies different models for different granularities. Then, an interaction-based method is applied to build local interactions (e.g., word-level similarity) between two pieces of text. These two matching methods work jointly to reinforce the capacity of model to capture disambiguation information.

3   The HSM Model

This paper proposes a new model named Hybrid Semantic Matching (HSM) for the entity linking task. The model can be divided into two components: one is to model semantic and concrete matching information between mentions and entities, and the other to capture relationships between global entities using an external knowledge base, as shown in Fig. 1. More specifically, the semantic representation of mentions and entities is firstly learned on multiple granularities through hybrid CNN and Bert models, which is designed to capture abstract -level semantic matching information. Then, apart from merely measuring similarity based on semantic representation, an interaction-focused method is introduced to capture the concrete matching information. These two methods are combining with other statistical features to measure conditional probability of a mention referring to a specific entity. Then, in the global model, a probability graph model based on random walk is applied to model the global dependence between entities,

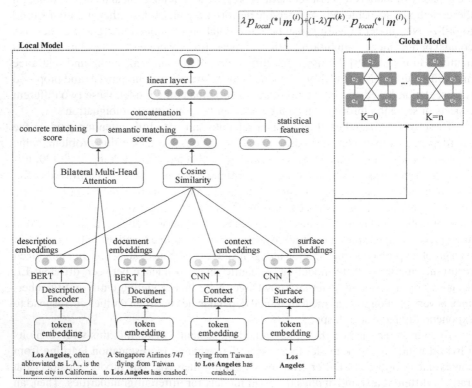

Fig. 1. The architecture of the HSM model containing a local component and a global component for entity linking.

which can propagate the evidences among related decisions with the help of external knowledge base to adjust the score obtained by the local model.

3.1 Local Mention-to-Entity Model

To better describe our model, some annotation information to be used in model is first defined. We use d to denote the original text where the mention is, $m(d) = \{m_1, m_2, \ldots, m_N\}$ to represent the set of all mentions contained in a document. In addition, for each mention m_i, its candidates set is defined as $T(m_i) = \{e_1, e_2, \ldots, e_N\}$, where each entity e_j has a corresponding Wikipedia page p_j. The semantic information of mention m_i is represented at three granularity levels: s_i, c_i, d_i, where s_i represents the surface string of m_i, c_i is the context within a predefined window of m_i, and d_i is the entire document contains m_i. For the entity, the entity description text b_j in the Wikipedia page is used to represent it. Each word is mapped to its embedding via the pre-trained embedding GloVe[1]. Using EL model, the exception is to map correctly for each mention to its corresponding entity in the reference knowledge base.

Hybrid CNN and Bert

For each granularity, we consider to conceive different methods based on its text characteristic to better capture the semantic representation. For s_i and c_i, a convolution neural network is applied to convert the sequence of words in the surface and context into a distributed representation. Given a sequence of words $w_1, w_2, .., w_n$, each word w_i is represented as an embedding vector v_i fixed to h-dimension. Then, the sequence of words is transformed to a matrix representation M, where $M = (v_1, v_2, \ldots, v_n) \in R^{h*N}$. Here N is the word number of each granularity text. The convolution operation is performed on M with a filter bank $M_l \in R^{u \times h}$, where window size is l and u is the number of filters. Then the result of each filter is concatenated and applies the rectified linear unit (ReLU) function to obtain the feature matrix $H \in R^{(u*(n-l+1))}$:

$$\overrightarrow{h_j} = \max\{0, M_{j(j+l)}\} \tag{1}$$

$$H = [\overrightarrow{h_1}, \overrightarrow{h_2}, \ldots, \overrightarrow{h_{n-l+1}}] \tag{2}$$

In the equations, the $v_{(j:j+l)}$ is a concatenation of the given word vectors and the max is element-wise. Each convolution granularity (s_i, c_i) has a distinct set of filter parameters. From above process, the word-level n-gram features from the text are captured. Then the average pooling function is utilized to transform feature matrix H into a fixed length vector to represent the semantic embedding of s_i and c_i.

For d_i and e_j, these granularities equipped with more rich and complex text features need to be captured. Thus, a pre-trained language model Bert is introduced to better learn the text distributed representation. Firstly, the model represents the sequence as a sequence of input embeddings contains standard components: wordpiece vectors, position and segment embeddings, one for each token, and generates a contextualized output embedding for each token by using a stack of Transformer layers. Please note that, the

---

[1] https://nlp.stanford.edu/projects/glove/.

output of model is the average value of each token output embedding t_i to represent the semantic embedding of d_i and e_j rather than merely using the output embedding of [CLS] token. Then, a fixed length vector for d_i and e_j are obtained, which the dimension is equaled with s_i and c_i in convenience for subsequent cosine similarity calculation. N denotes the number of tokens.

$$Avg_{output} = \frac{1}{N} \sum_{i=1}^{N} t_i \qquad (3)$$

After obtaining the embedding above, the cosine similarity function is used to calculate the local similarity among the above granularities.

$$sim(m_i, p_j) = [\cos(\overline{s}_{cnn_i}, \overline{b}_{bert_j}), cos(\overline{c}_{cnn_i}, \overline{b}_{bert_j}), cos(\overline{d}_{bert_i}, \overline{b}_{bert_j})] \qquad (4)$$

In the equation, the $\overline{s}_{cnn_i}$, $\overline{c}_{cnn_i}$, $\overline{d}_{bert_i}$, and $\overline{b}_{bert_j}$ denote the distributed representation of s_i, c_i, d_i, b_j respectively and the model that it used. Through aforementioned methods, the HSM model can capture the rich contextual information to represent the semantic representation of different granularities.

The Bilateral Multi-head Attention
Even though the above models can capture distinguishable information from both mentions and entities side, some concrete matching information are lost (e.g., exact match), since the matching between two texts is generated through their abstract semantic representations. The interaction-focused method tries to build local interactions (e.g., word-level similarity) between two pieces of text, and then uses neural networks to learn the final matching score based on the local interactions. To enhance the representation-based method, a bilateral multi-head attention method is introduced to measure the relevance between d_i and e_j. Before that some pre-processes are done to make the raw text included as a bag of words in the document that are non-stop words. Then, given a sequence of words $[w_1^d, \ldots, w_n^d] \in D$ and $[w_1^e, \ldots, w_m^e] \in E$, where D, E represents the document of mention and Wikipedia page of entity respectively. For each word w_i^d, the method of dot product attention model is leveraged to calculate the inner product of the embedding vector of w_j^e to express the similarity between two words. The output matrix $M_{att} \in \mathbb{R}^{n \times m}$ is the concatenation of similarity vector of each w_i^d, which represents the word-level similarity between two granularities. Then, the max similarity score for each w_j^e as follows:

$$u(w_j^e) = \max_{i \in n} x_i^{d^T} x_j^e \qquad (5)$$

x represents the embedding of each word. The max operation is from the intuition that the weight is high if the word in Wikipedia page is strongly related to at least one word in document of mention. Also, to reduce the noisy of non-informative words, the Top K words with the highest scores $u\left(w_j^e\right)$ are left to form the relevance information and then transform it to attention weights as follows:

$$\overline{e} = \{w \in E | u(w) \in topK(u)\} \qquad (6)$$

$$\begin{cases} a(w_j^e) = \dfrac{\exp[u(w_j^e)]}{\sum_{k\in\bar{e}}\exp[u(w_k^e)]}, \textit{if } w_j^e \in \bar{e} \\ \quad\quad 0, \textit{ otherwise} \end{cases} \tag{7}$$

Finally, an attention weighted of entity side text-level embedding is obtained as:

$$x_e = \sum_{j\in\bar{e}} a(w_j^e) * x_j^e \tag{8}$$

The bilateral means that both the entity side and document side are considered. The same process above is utilized to produce a document side text-level embedding x_d, except the matrix M_{att} which is calculated by $x_j^{e^T} \cdot x_i^d$. Then the two vectors are concatenated and feed into a two linear layer with the rectified linear unit (ReLU) activate function in the middle. Finally, the output unit is feed into a sigmoid function to get the interaction-based bilateral attention score $att\_score(d, e)$.

After the above steps, through the combination of representation-based and interaction-based methods, the abundant relevance information of local mention-to-entity compatibility can be obtained. The next step is to propagate this information by leveraging the global consistency of all entities in a document.

3.2 Global Model

Considering the global consistency of the candidate entities, a recurrent random-walk layer is utilized to propagate EL evidence to capture the global dependencies between different EL decisions. To transfer the evidence of different EL decisions, a $N * N$ transition matrix T is defined, where N represents all candidate entity sets under a document and T_{ij} is calculated by hyperlinks of each entity to represent the evidence propagation ratio from e_i to e_j.

To be specific, for two candidate entity e_i and e_j, the traditional Wikipedia Link-based Measure (WLM) formula is used to calculate the semantic relevance score between entities:

$$Sim_{hyperlink}(e_i, e_j) = 1 - \frac{\log(\max(|I|, |J|)) - \log(|I \cap J|)}{\log(|W|) - \log(\min(|I|, |J|))} \tag{9}$$

I and J are the sets of all entities that links to p_i and p_j in Wikipedia respectively, and W is the size of entire Wikipedia. Then normalize these relevance scores by entity to generate T:

$$T_{ij} = \frac{sim(e_i, e_j)}{\sum_{j'\in N_{e_i}} sim(e_i, e_{j'})} \tag{10}$$

N_{e_i} is the set of neighbor entities of entity e_i. Note that, in order to reduce the error of introducing unrelated entities, the top 4 candidate entities with the highest scores generated by local model are only considered to propagate the evidence. By leveraging the transition matrix T, the random walk layer is used to propagate the information between different EL decisions. The formula is as follows:

$$p^{(k+1)}(*|m^{(i)}) = \lambda p_{local}(*|m^{(i)}) + (1 - \lambda)T^{(k)} \cdot p_{local}(*|m^{(i)}) \tag{11}$$

In the equation, the $p_{local}(*|m^{(i)})$ is the predicted entity distribution of m_i at the k iteration. Both the weighted parameter λ and the transition matrix T are updated with the training process to obtain the optimal value of the hyperparameter. By using the random walk layer as global model, the dependency relationship between global entities can be captured, so as to update the score obtained under the local model.

4   Experiments and Results

4.1   Datasets

To evaluate the performance of the proposed HSM model, various datasets are utilized. The training dataset is AIDA-CoNLL, which is a widely adopted corpus consisting of 946 documents for training (as AIDA-train). Three popular publically available datasets including AQUAINT, MSNBC, and ACE2004 are used for testing. AQUAINT, MSNBC, and ACE2004 are three datasets utilizing Wikification, which is the process of transforming plain content into understandable, linked, interactive content suitable for a wiki. The statistical characteristics of the datasets are presented in Table 1.

Table 1. The statistics of a training dataset AIDA-train and three test datasets.

Datasets	#mentions	#documents	#mentions per doc	#words per doc
AIDA-train	18448	946	19.5	217
ACE2004	257	36	7.1	430
AQUAINT	727	50	14.5	243
MSNBC	656	20	32.8	632

Wikipedia Dump[2] on December 2019 is used as the reference knowledge base. The first 200 words in each Wikipedia page of an entity are utilized as entity description. The English word tokenizer in NLTK by default is used to tokenize each Wikipedia page. The mentions in the above datasets that have no matched entities in the Wikipedia Dump are excluded.

4.2   Settings

Our proposed HSM model is compared with the following baseline models:

- Hofmann et al. [8] introduced a Local Model with Neural Attention and implemented LBP network as a global model.
- Le et al. [4] treated relations as latent variables in a neural entity-linking model and optimized an entity-linking system in an end-to-end manner.

---

[2] https://dumps.wikimedia.org/.

- Yang et al. [20] presented a gradient-tree-boosting-based structured learning model for jointly disambiguating named entities in a document.
- Yang et al. [24] proposed a simple yet effective model called Dynamic Context Augmentation (DCA) for collective entity linking, requiring only one passthrough mentions in a document.
- Feng et al. [25] proposed a method named FGS2EE to inject fine-grained semantic information into entity embeddings to reduce the distinctiveness and to facilitate the learning of contextual commonality.
- Yamada et al. [15] treated the entity linking task as predicting randomly masked entities in entity-annotated texts obtained from Wikipedia with a Bert model.

In order to match the dimensionality of CNN to bert output, we used 768 filters with the window size as 4 for the convolution operation and the non-linear transformation function ReLU when employed CNN to learn the distributed representations of inputs. Meanwhile, to learn the entity representation by Bert through utilizing the entity descriptions in Wikipedia pages, first 512 words are used to fit to the BERT model. The CNN model is used to learn distributed representation at two granularities: mention surfaces and local contexts. For each granularity, the CNN kernel size is set to 2 and 4, respectively. The $bert\text{-}base\text{-}uncased$ version is chosen as our Bert model ($L = 12, H = 768, A = 12$, and total parameters $= 110M$). Particularly, we keep top 10 candidates for each mention based on their prior probabilities, while keep top 3 candidates for each mention m_i according to $p_{local}(*|m^{(i)})$ during propagating the evidence. The learning rate α is set to $1e-5$ and Adam as optimizer.

The pretrained Glove word embedding is used to map each word into a distributed representation. The entity embedding is captured from [8] and Wikipedia2Vec[3] which are publicly released. The dimensionality of the word and entity embedding is set to 300. Note that the embedding is updated during training.

The assessment of entity linking methods is usually performed in terms of evaluation measures, such as precision, recall and F1-measure. Given the ground truth T and output of entity linking systems O, the standard precision, recall and Micro F1 are calculated as follows:

$$Precision = \frac{|T \cap O|}{|O|} \tag{12}$$

$$Recall = \frac{|T \cap O|}{|T|} \tag{13}$$

$$Micro\ F_1 = \frac{2 \times Precision \times Recall}{Precision + Recall} \tag{14}$$

4.3 Results

For optimizing the parameter K as the number of random-walk layers, it is set from 0 to 4 with an incremental interval of 1 each time. The Micro F1 scores of the HSM model on the three test datasets are reported in Fig. 2. Note that no random-walk is available

---

[3] https://github.com/wikipedia2vec/wikipedia2vec.

when K is set to 0. The model achieves the best performance when $K = 2$. This result indicates that graph-based evidence propagation makes contribution to the improvement of our HSM model.

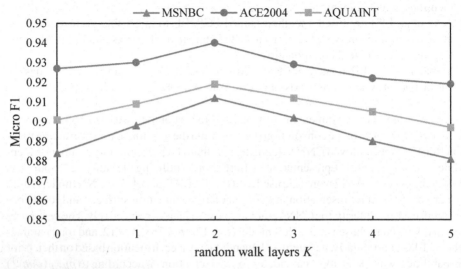

Fig. 2. Performance of the HSM model using different numbers of random-walk layers as K on the three test datasets.

To evaluate the effectiveness of utilizing the global model and the local model, a comparison experiment by using the local model and the global model separately is conducted. As shown in Table 2, the global model outperforms the local model by 0.4%, 1.8% and 2.8%, respectively on the three test datasets. Also, to investigate the effectiveness of the global model more specifically, wrong output mentions in the local model but correct in the global model after propagating decisions are analyzed. For example, the mention *Italy* in a test text is originally linked to entity *Italy* (city) from the output of the local model. However, the mention accompanies with the mention *FIFA* and *World Cup* in the same text context. By considering the global consistency of all entities, the link to the wrong entity *Italy* (city) is corrected to *Italy nation football team*.

Table 2. Performance of the local and global model in terms of F1 score on the three test datasets.

	ACE2004	AQUAINT	MSNBC
Local model	0.936	0.901	0.884
Global model	0.940	0.919	0.912

To explore the effective of our hybrid strategy in combining CNN and Bert using different granularities of local information, solely CNN model and Bert model are used to encode the semantic representation of four granularities. The compression result is report in Table 3. The hybrid strategy obtains performance gains and achieves the best result on all three datasets. The performance of using the hybrid strategy outperforms the best results of the solely models by 1.3%, 1.6 and 1.9% respectively on the three test datasets. The text of mention surfaces and contexts is relative short. The Bert model with complex parameters tends to be overfitting in learning semantic representation on these two granularities. Meanwhile, for long text of documents and Wikipedia pages, the convolution network captures contextual dependence within fixed window size, thus it is incapacity to learn semantic dependence of long-distance words. Through the combination of the two models, the HSM model can take advantages of the trait of each granularity and strength the semantic representations.

Table 3. Performance comparison of using the CNN model, the Bert model, and the hybrid strategy.

	ACE2004	AQUAINT	MSNBC
CNN only	0.923	0.885	0.865
Bert only	0.920	0.880	0.860
Hybrid strategy	0.936	0.901	0.884

To analyze the difference between the two semantic matching methods empirically, an experiment by comparing using the representation-based method and the hybrid method (representation + interaction-based method) is conducted. The result, as reported in Table 4, shows that the hybrid representation method obtains various improvement and achieves the best performance on all the three test datasets by 0.9%, 1.3% and 1.0%, respectively. To be specific, the interaction-based method captured the concrete match information (e.g., word-level similarity) between text content of mention and entity. For example, considering a mention named *Bremen*, which is a city of German, in a document of AIDA-train dataset. This document contains the words like airfreight, flown and airports which are similarity with the word airport, airfield, flights that appeared in Wikipedia page of entity *Bremen Airport*. By capturing the word-level similarity feature to measure relevance, the entity *Bremen Airport* is expected to output as the correct candidate entity of mention *Bremen*. The result also demonstrates the benefits when combining the two semantic matching methods.

Table 4. Performance comparison of using representation-based method and the combination method.

	ACE2004	AQUAINT	MSNBC
Representation-based method	0.927	0.888	0.874
Representation + interaction-based method	0.936	0.901	0.884

The performance of our HSM model is compared with all the baseline methods on the test dataset. As shown in Table 5, Yamada (2020) obtains a Micro-F1 score of 0.907 on the Ace2004, and a Micro-F1 score of 0.915 on the AQUAINT. Our HSM model achieves an improvement of 3.3% and 0.40% on the two datasets, respectively. On the dataset MSNBC, the DCA model of Yang (2019) achieves the best performance as 0.948. To investigate the reason, we analyze the model in the experiments. The model mainly focuses on designing the global model to capture the relatedness between entities. For example, the multi-relational model [4] utilizes the relations between mentions in a document to decide if linking decisions are compatible. In comparison, our HSM model mainly focuses on capturing local features by utilizing the hybrid strategy and two semantic matching methods. Table 1 presents that the number of mentions per documents of MSNBC dataset is the largest, which indicates that the consistency of global entities can provide rich disambiguation evidence. While the number of mentions in per documents of former two datasets are smaller, thus the local feature plays a more important role to disambiguate and our HSM model achieves the improvement.

Table 5. Performance comparison on the three test datasets using the Micro F1 score.

	Ace2004	AQUAINT	MSNBC
LBP Hofmann et al. (2017)	0.888	0.889	0.938
Multi-relational model Le et al. (2018)	0.903	0.888	0.941
SGTB Yang et al., (2018)	0.892	0.905	0.924
DCA Yang et al. (2019)	0.901	0.887	**0.948**
FGS2EE Feng et al. (2020)	0.903	0.889	0.944
Contextual model Yamada et al. (2020)	0.907	0.915	0.941
HSM model	**0.940**	**0.919**	0.912

5   Conclusion

This paper proposed a novel end-to-end neural network HSM for collective entity linking. In contrast to existing methods, HSM model devised different models for different text granularities to learn rich semantic information. To reinforce the methods based on solely semantic matching, an interaction-based method was introduced to capture local concrete match information between two pieces of text. The two different aspects of semantic information work jointly for disambiguation. Finally, both local semantic match information and global interdependence were incorporated. Experiment results demonstrated the effectiveness of the proposed HSM model for entity linking.

Acknowledgements. This work was supported by National Natural Science Foundation of China (No.61772146) and Natural Science Foundation of Guangdong Province (2021A1515011339).

References

1. Gupta, N., Singh, S., Roth, D.: Entity linking via joint encoding of types, descriptions, and context. In: Proceedings of Conference on Empirical Methods in Natural Language Processing, pp. 2681–2690 (2017)
2. Xue, M., et al.: Neural collective entity linking based on recurrent random walk network learning. In: Proceedings of IJCAI, pp. 5327–5333 (2019)
3. Agarwal, O., Bikel, D.M.: Entity linking via dual and cross-attention encoders. arXiv preprint arXiv:2004.03555 (2020)
4. Le, P., Titov, I.: Improving entity linking by modeling latent relations between mentions. In: Proceedings of Annual Meeting of the Association for Computational Linguistics, pp. 1695–1604 (2018)
5. Cao, Y., Hou, L., Li, J., Liu, Z.: Neural collective entity linking. In: Proceedings of International Conference on Computational Linguistics, pp. 675–686 (2018)
6. Bunescu, R., Pasca, M.: Using encyclopedic knowledge for named entity disambiguation. In: Proceedings of Conference of the European Chapter of the Association for Computational Linguistics (EACL), pp. 9–16 (2006)
7. Mihalcea, R., Csomai, A.: Wikify! Linking documents to encyclopedic knowledge. In: Proceedings of ACM conference on Conference on information and knowledge management, pp. 233–242 (2007)
8. Ganea, O.E., Hofmann, T.: Deep joint entity disambiguation with local neural attention. In: Proceedings of Conference on Empirical Methods in Natural Language Processing, pp. 2619–2629 (2017)
9. Yamada, I., Shindo, H., Takeda, H., Takefuji, Y.: Joint learning of the embedding of words and entities for named entity disambiguation. In: Proceedings of SIGNLL Conference on Computational Natural Language Learning, pp. 250–259 (2016)
10. Radhakrishnan, P., Talukdar, P., Varma, V.: Elden: improved entity linking using densified knowledge graphs. In: Proceedings of Conference of the North American Chapter of the Association for Computational Linguistics: Human Language Technologies, vol. 1 (Long Papers), pp. 1844–1853 (2018)
11. Sun, Y., Lin, L., Tang, D., Yang, N., Ji, Z., Wang, X.: Modeling mention, context and entity with neural networks for entity disambiguation. In: Proceedings of IJCAI, pp. 1333–1339 (2015)
12. Francis-Landau, M., Durrett, G., Klein, D.: Capturing semantic similarity for entity linking with convolutional neural networks. In: Proceedings of Conference of the North American Chapter of the Association for Computational Linguistics: Human Language Technologies, pp. 1256–1261 (2016)
13. Sevgili, O., Shelmanov, A., Arkhipov, M., Panchenko, A., Biemann, C.: Neural entity linking: a survey of models based on deep learning. arXiv preprint arXiv:2006.00575 (2020)
14. Yamada, I., Asai, A., Shindo, H., Takeda, H., Matsumoto, Y.: LUKE: deep contextualized entity representations with entity-aware self-attention. In: Proceedings of Conference on Empirical Methods in Natural Language Processing (EMNLP), pp. 6442–6454 (2020)
15. Yamada, I., Washio, K., Shindo, H., Matsumoto, Y.: Global entity disambiguation with pre-trained contextualized embeddings of words and entities. arXiv preprint arXiv:1909.00426 (2019)
16. Broscheit, S.: Investigating entity knowledge in BERT with simple neural end-to-end entity linking. In: Proceedings of Conference on Computational Natural Language Learning (CoNLL), pp. 677–685 (2019)

17. Zhao, Chen, H., Li, X., Gregoric, A.Z., Wadhwa, S.: Contextualized end-to-end neural entity linking. In: Proceedings of Conference of the Asia-Pacific Chapter of the Association for Computational Linguistics and International Joint Conference on Natural Language Processing, pp. 637–642 (2020)
18. Guo, J., Fan, Y., Ai, Q., Croft, W.B.: A deep relevance matching model for ad-hoc retrieval. In: Proceedings of ACM international on conference on information and knowledge management, pp. 55–64 (2016)
19. Nie, F., Zhou, S., Liu, J., Wang, J., Lin, C.Y., Pan, R.: Aggregated semantic matching for short text entity linking. In: Proceedings of Conference on Computational Natural Language Learning, pp. 476–485 (2018)
20. Yang, Y., Irsoy, O., Rahman, K.S.: Collective entity disambiguation with structured gradient tree boosting. In: Proceedings of Conference of the North American Chapter of the Association for Computational Linguistics: Human Language Technologies, vol. 1 (Long Papers), pp. 777–786 (2018)
21. Ganea, O.E., Ganea, M., Lucchi, A., Eickhoff, C., Hofmann, T.: Probabilistic bag-of-hyperlinks model for entity linking. In: Proceedings of International Conference on World Wide Web, pp. 927–938 (2016)
22. Guo, Z., Barbosa, D.: Robust named entity disambiguation with random walks. Semantic Web. 9(4), 459–479 (2018)
23. Guo, Z., Barbosa, D.: Robust entity linking via random walks. In: Proceedings of ACM International Conference on Conference on Information and Knowledge Management, pp. 499–508 (2014)
24. Yang X., et al.: Learning dynamic context augmentation for global entity linking. In: Proceedings of Conference on Empirical Methods in Natural Language Processing and the 9th International Joint Conference on Natural Language Processing (EMNLP-IJCNLP), pp. 271–281 (2019)
25. Hou, F., Wang, R., He, J., Zhou, Y.: Improving entity linking through semantic reinforced entity embeddings. In: Proceedings of Annual Meeting of the Association for Computational Linguistics, pp. 6843–6848 (2020)

Multi-space Knowledge Enhanced Question Answering over Knowledge Graph

Ye Ji[1], Bohan Li[1,3,4(✉)], Yi Liu[1], Yuxin Zhang[1], and Ken Cai[2]

[1] Nanjing University of Aeronautics and Astronautics, Nanjing, China
bhli@nuaa.edu.cn
[2] Zhongkai University of Agriculture and Engineering, Guangzhou, China
[3] Key Laboratory of Safety-Critical Software, Jiangsu, China
[4] Ministry of Industry and Information Technology, Collaborative Innovation Center
of Novel Software Technology and Industrialization, Jiangsu, China

Abstract. Knowledge graph question answering (KG-QA) accesses the substantial knowledge to return a comprehensive answer in a more user-friendly solution. Recently, the embedding-based methods to KG-QA have always been hot issues. Traditional embedding-based methods can not make full use of knowledge since they incorporating the knowledge by using a single semantic translation model to embed entities and relations. Semantic translation models based on non-Euclidean spaces can capture more kinds of latent information because they can focus on the characteristics of different aspects of knowledge. In this paper, we propose the multi-space knowledge enhanced question answering model and mine the latent information of knowledge in different embedding spaces to improve the KG-QA. In addition, Transformer is used to replace the traditional Bi-LSTM to obtain the vector representation of question, and specially designed attention mechanism is used to calculate the score of candidate answers dynamically. The experiment conducted on the WebQuestions dataset shows that compared with other state-of-art QA systems, our method can effectively improve the accuracy.

Keywords: Question answering · Knowledge graph · Embedding model

1 Introduction

Knowledge graph question answering (KGQA) [10] involves answering questions posed in natural language using existing knowledge graphs, given natural language questions, the goal of KGQA is to automatically find answers from the KG. The approach to tackle the KGQA task can be classified into two main groups: semantic parsing based (SP-based) approaches and information retrieval based (IR-based) approaches. IR-based approaches can scale better to large and complex KGs since they do not need hand-made rules [7]. However, the use of knowledge graph embedding methods in IR-based approaches is inadequate. Existing approaches mainly

© Springer Nature Switzerland AG 2021
L. H. U et al. (Eds.): APWeb-WAIM 2021, LNCS 12859, pp. 135–140, 2021.
https://doi.org/10.1007/978-3-030-85899-5_10

choose to use knowledge graph embedding methods based on semantic translation in euclidean space, of which the TransE model [3] is the most representative
method, whereas embedding methods in other spaces is neglected.

We assume that different embedding spaces are helpful for better representing knowledge graphs. Specifically, models in complex vector space are more
suitable for knowledge reasoning and models in hyperbolic space can better capture structural information of knowledge graphs. Compared to existing KGQA
methods that use the traditional TransE [3] model to encode knowledge graph
into euclidean space, we introduce a novel attention network that comprehensively utilize information of knowledge graph in different embedding spaces. To
this end, we choose models in three different embedding spaces to represent the
knowledge graph in answer end. Built on top of that, we design a attention network to dynamically adjust the weights of embedding vectors in different embedding spaces. Besides, we apply a stacked transformer network [9] to obtain the
representation of the input question. The candidate answers are represented in
four different aspects and the input question is used to help calculate the weights
of different answer aspects.

In summary, we highlight our contributions as follows: 1) we prove that the
embedding spaces of knowledge graph have certain influence on the KGQA task,
which is caused by differences of spatial features; 2) we propose a novel attention network for the task of KGQA, which is intended to simultaneously utilize
information of knowledge graph in multiple embedding spaces; 3) the experimental results on the WebQuestions dataset demonstrate the effectiveness of
our approach.

2   Our Approach

The overview of our model is shown as the Fig. 1. The top part is the stacked
Transformer neural networks for question representation learning. The bottom
part is the KG embedding matrix and attention networks. We use deep neural
network based on Transformer to learn the representations of questions and the
representation of input question q is denoted as q. The whole knowledge graph
is embedded into three different vector spaces, traditional euclidean space E,
complex vector space V and hyperbolic space H. For every candidate answer a
in C_q, four different aspects are applied to represent it and they are denoted as
a_e, a_r, a_t and a_c. Then we get twelve vector representations in three embedding
spaces and four answer aspects to help represent the candidate answer, vector
embeddings in euclidean space are denoted as E_e, E_r, E_t, E_c, vector embeddings
in complex vector space [8] are denoted as V_e, V_r, V_t, V_c, vector embeddings in
hyperbolic space [6] are denoted as H_e, H_r, H_t, H_c. Two attention networks
are employed to learn the representation of the candidate answer, one attention
network is called answer aspect attention and is used to aggregate the information in different answer aspects, the other attention network is called multi-space
attention and is used to aggregate the information in different embedding spaces.
Finally, we can compute the score for the question-answer pair (q, a).

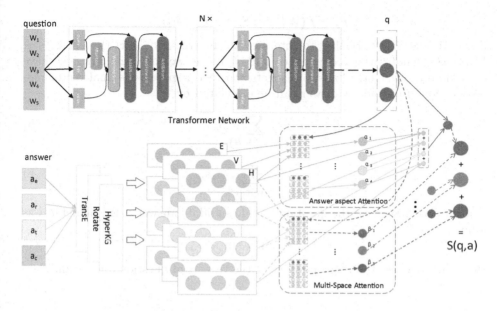

Fig. 1. The whole architecture of our model.

2.1 Answer Aspect Attention Network

In terms of answer aspects, since the extent of attention should be measured by the relatedness between representation of input question q and answer aspect embeddings $E_i, V_i, H_i, i \in \{e, r, t, c\}$. We calculate the weights using the following formulas:

$$\alpha_i = \frac{\exp(\eta_i)}{\sum_{j \in \{e,r,t,c\}} \exp(\eta_j)} \tag{1}$$

$$\eta_i = f\left(W_1^T [q; E_i; V_i; H_i] + b_1\right) \tag{2}$$

Here, $[u; v]$ denotes the concat of vector u and vector v, $W_1^T \in \mathbb{R}^{4d \times d}$ denotes an intermediate matrix and b_1 is the offset. The intermediate matrix and offset are randomly initialized and updated in the training process. The vector q is the representation of input question and is output by the Transformer network. $f(\cdot)$ is an activation function which is non-linear and $j \in \{e, r, t, c\}$ is the answer aspect. α_i denotes the weight of answer aspect, which indicates the importance of the aspect towards question.

2.2 Multi-space Attention Network

In terms of vector spaces, we calculate the weights with all the information of answer while the information of question is abandoned since question has no direct connection with the vector space. The formulas we propose is as follows:

$$\beta_s = \frac{\exp(\theta_s)}{\sum_{s \in \{E,V,H\}} \exp(\theta_s)} \tag{3}$$

$$\theta_s = f\left(W_2^T\left[S_e; S_r; S_t; S_c\right] + b_2\right) \tag{4}$$

Here, $W_2^T \in \mathbb{R}^{4d \times d}$ is also an intermediate matrix and b_2 is the offset. $s \in \{E, V, H\}$ denotes the vector space and β_s is the weight of it. Since we have calculated the weights of answer aspects and vector spaces, the final vector representation of candidate answer can be calculated by:

$$\mathrm{a} = \sum_{s \in \{E, V, H\}} \beta_s \gamma_s \tag{5}$$

$$\gamma_s = \sum_{i \in \{e, r, t, c\}} \alpha_i s_i \tag{6}$$

The similarity score of the question q and candidate answer a can be defined as follows:

$$S(q, a) = \mathrm{h(q, a)} \tag{7}$$

Here, $\mathrm{h}(\cdot)$ denotes the inner product of the vectors of question q and candidate answer a.

2.3   Model Training

For every input question q, we divide the candidate answer set C_q into correct answer set R_q and wrong answer set W_q. For every correct answer $a \in R_q$, we randomly select k wrong answers $a' \in W_q$ and use them as negative examples. Then we can using the training data to conduct pairwise training. To be more specific, the training loss is a hinge loss as follows:

$$L\left(q, a, a'\right) = \left[m - S(q, a) + s\left(q, a'\right)\right]_+ \tag{8}$$

Here, $\mathrm{s}(\cdot)$ is the scoring function, m is the margin parameter used to regularize the gap between positive and negative examples and $[z]_+$ means $\max(0, z)$. The objective function is:

$$\min \sum_q \frac{1}{|R_q|} \sum_{a \in R_q} \sum_{a' \in W_q} L\left(q, a, a'\right) \tag{9}$$

Moreover, stochastic gradient descent (SGD) based on minibatch is applied as optimizer in the training process.

3   Experiments

The WebQuestions dataset and FB2M knowledge graph are used to conduct experiments to evaluate our model. As for baseline, we focus on the information retrieval based approaches proposed in recent years. In the training process, we perform the knowledge graph embedding models and question answering model in turn. All the knowledge graph embedding models utilize pair-wise training strategy, we use the provided code in their papers to perform the training process and the embedding dimension is set to 250. For the question answering training part, we also set the embedding size $d = 250$. The minibatch size and learning rate are set to 50 and 0.01, respectively. Negative sample number k is set to 1000 and the margin parameter m is set to 0.7. Besides, hyperbolic tangent function is used as the activation function $f(\cdot)$.

3.1 Performance Comparison

Table 1. Results on the WebQuestions dataset.

Methods	Macro F1
Bordes et al., 2014	39.2 ± 1.8
Dong et al., 2015	40.8 ± 1.2
Bordes et al., 2015	42.2 ± 0.7
Hao et al., 2017	42.9 ± 0.9
Our approach	$\mathbf{44.1} \pm 0.6$

To evaluate the effectiveness of our approach, we compare F1 of our model with state-of-art IR-based methods. Bordes et al., 2014 [1] apply subgraph embeddings for answer representation, while the learning process of both question and answer is a simplified bag of word model. Dong et al. [4] improve the ability of question representation by using multi-column convolutional neural network and the answer representation contains the information of answer path, answer type and answer context. Bordes et al., 2015 [2] introduce a much larger dataset called SimpleQuestions and use the Memory Network to construct their model. Note that they also conduct experiments on WebQuestions and achieve higher F1 score. Hao et al. 2017 [5] use answer aspects to help represent question and apply Bi-LSTM to get the embedding vector of question. Besides, they employ TransE to combine the global KG information. We utilize three embedding spaces to enhance knowledge in answer end, Transformer network in question end and attention network to calculate final score.

As is shown in Table 1, our method achieve higher F1 score than baseline methods on WebQuestions. Our model takes the advantage of attention network proposed by Hao et al. [5], while we improve the way of combing the global KG information. Hao et al. focus on using the answer aspect information to help represent question and they apply TransE to encode the KG in order to combine global knowledge. Based on the previous work done by Zhang et al. [11], we realize that the euclidean space of TransE is not the best way to embed knowledge graph and the spatial information in different embedding spaces differs, so we employ three embedding spaces to enhance the information of answer in KG and design a novel attention network to dynamically aggregate information in these embedding spaces. Besides, we replace the Bi-LSTM with Transformer network. The results show that our proposed approach can achieve the best performance compared with other state-of-art methods.

4   Conclusion

In this work, we propose a novel model that comprehensively utilizes information in knowledge graph for the task of KGQA. Firstly, we consider the impacts of different embedding spaces on KG representation, and design a multi-space attention network to aggregate information in three embedding spaces. Then, we represent candidate answer through different answer aspects and apply question vector to help represent candidate answer. Finally, we improve the neural network in question end according to the latest sequential model. The experiments on the WebQuestions dataset show that the proposed approach achieves better performance compared with other state-of-art methods.

References

1. Bordes, A., Chopra, S., Weston, J.: Question answering with subgraph embeddings. arXiv preprint arXiv:1406.3676 (2014)
2. Bordes, A., Usunier, N., Chopra, S., Weston, J.: Large-scale simple question answering with memory networks. arXiv preprint arXiv:1506.02075 (2015)
3. Bordes, A., Usunier, N., Garcia-Duran, A., Weston, J., Yakhnenko, O.: Translating embeddings for modeling multi-relational data. In: Neural Information Processing Systems (NIPS), pp. 1–9 (2013)
4. Dong, L., Wei, F., Zhou, M., Xu, K.: Question answering over freebase with multi-column convolutional neural networks. In: Proceedings of the 53rd Annual Meeting of the Association for Computational Linguistics and the 7th International Joint Conference on Natural Language Processing (Volume 1: Long Papers) (2015)
5. Hao, Y., Zhang, Y., Liu, K., He, S., Zhao, J.: An end-to-end model for question answering over knowledge base with cross-attention combining global knowledge. In: Proceedings of the 55th Annual Meeting of the Association for Computational Linguistics (Volume 1: Long Papers) (2017)
6. Kolyvakis, P., Kalousis, A., Kiritsis, D.: HyperKG: hyperbolic knowledge graph embeddings for knowledge base completion. arXiv preprint arXiv:1908.04895 (2019)
7. Meng, W., Jingting, W., Yinlin, J., Guilin, Q.: Hybrid human-machine active search over knowledge graph. J. Comput. Res. Dev. **57**(12), 2501 (2020)
8. Sun, Z., Deng, Z.H., Nie, J.Y., Tang, J.: Rotate: knowledge graph embedding by relational rotation in complex space. arXiv preprint arXiv:1902.10197 (2019)
9. Vaswani, A., et al.: Attention is all you need. arXiv (2017)
10. Wang, R., Wang, M., Liu, J., Chen, W., Cochez, M., Decker, S.: Leveraging knowledge graph embeddings for natural language question answering. In: Li, G., Yang, J., Gama, J., Natwichai, J., Tong, Y. (eds.) DASFAA 2019. LNCS, vol. 11446, pp. 659–675. Springer, Cham (2019). https://doi.org/10.1007/978-3-030-18576-3_39
11. Zhang, Y., et al.: Fine-grained evaluation of knowledge graph embedding model in multiple types of downstream tasks. Big Data Res. **25**, 100218 (2021)

Emerging Data Processing Techniques

A Distribution-Aware Training Scheme for Learned Indexes

Youyun Wang, Chuzhe Tang, and Xujia Yao$^{(\boxtimes)}$

Shanghai Jiao Tong University, Shanghai, China
{wyy.stephen,t.chuzhe,yaoxj}@sjtu.edu.cn

Abstract. The recent proposal of the learned index leads us to a new direction to optimize indexes. With the help of learned models, it has demonstrated promising performance improvement compared with traditional indexes. However, the skewed query distribution and ever-changing data distribution common in real-world workloads pose additional challenges to the learned index. The missing consideration of these 'distributions' can notably obscure the learned index's high performance. To solve this issue, we propose a Distribution-Aware Training scheme for the learned index (called DATum). DATum can produce a tuned model for a specific query and data distribution. Central to DATum are two designs. First, it stretches the training data according to access frequencies to incorporate the skewed query patterns. Second, it combines a model cache and a classic grid search to efficiently find the best model architecture for the ever-changing datasets. Our experimental results show that, DATum can improve the learned index's performance by 51.1% and reduce its model rebuilding time to less than 1%.

Keywords: Learned index · Skewed query · Data distribution shifting · Model training

1 Introduction

The recent study of the learned index [11] presents us with a novel way of building indexes with the help of machine learning models. Range indexes can be seen as mappings from keys to positions. The basic idea is to leverage machine learning models such as neural networks to overfit the mappings. Hence, to perform a query, it first predicts a position with the learned model; then it employs a local search surrounding the predicted position to find the target record. The learned index shows excellent performance. It achieves up to 3× performance than B-Tree while saving more than 90% memory footprint [11].

Although the learned index and successive works [4,8,9,16] have shown promising performance compared with traditional indexes, we argue that existing model training schemes yield poorly learned models, thus unsatisfactory performance under real-world workloads. The model training scheme plays a critical role in learned indexes as the trained model directly determines their performance. Under real-world workloads, the query distribution tends to be skewed

© Springer Nature Switzerland AG 2021
L. H. U et al. (Eds.): APWeb-WAIM 2021, LNCS 12859, pp. 143–157, 2021.
https://doi.org/10.1007/978-3-030-85899-5_11

(some keys are more frequently accessed than others), and data distribution is constantly evolving due to inserts and removes [3,7,12,22]. However, existing training schemes lack the consideration of these distributions. First, under skewed query distribution, the performance can drop greatly if hot models (i.e., sub-models containing hot keys) are poorly learned. Typical learned indexes (e.g., RMI [4,11,16]) need to construct a hierarchy of sub-models, with each sub-model responsible for a small range of the total dataset. The model errors differ across different leaf-stage sub-models. The performance can drop substantially if the leaf-stage sub-models with a large error are frequently accessed, which is also confirmed in [16]. Second, the best model architecture varies for different data distributions. A number of hyperparameters can be used to tune the model architecture, such as the number of sub-models, the type of each sub-model (from simple linear regression to complex neural networks). The complex model can provide better accuracy for complex data distribution, but is also penalized by high computation costs. Hence, using a fixed model architecture gives unsatisfactory performance after the change of data distribution.

To tackle this issue, we propose DATum, a Distribution-Aware Training scheme for learned indexes. At its core, DATum achieves distribution awareness in two ways. First, to incorporate the skewed query distribution of real-world workloads, DATum adopts a novel method named *data stretching*. It improves the accuracy of hot models by augmenting the distances between keys according to their access frequencies. Second, to accommodate the ever-changing data distribution, DATum employs a model cache and the classic grid search to efficiently find the best model architecture for each dataset. The model cache buffers pre-tuned models, thus avoiding costly grid search when a similar data distribution is encountered again. The preliminary results show the effectiveness of DATum. With the model trained by DATum with data stretching, the learned index can achieve up to 51.1% performance improvement under skewed query patterns. By reusing previously trained models, DATum can reduce the model rebuilding time of the learned index to less than 1%.

In summary, this paper makes the following contributions:

- An in-depth analysis to manifest that, the learned index's performance is sub-optimal without considering query and data distribution while training.
- A distribution-aware training system for learned indexes, which unleashes the performance through data stretching and model cache.
- A set of experimental results that demonstrates the effectiveness of DATum.

The following of this paper is organized as follows: Sect. 2 introduces the basic background of the learned index; Sect. 3 quantitatively shows the issue of the existing training scheme. Section 4 presents our system with the data stretching (Sect. 4.1) and the model cache (Sect. 4.2); Sect. 5 presents some evaluation results; Sect. 6 summarizes related works, and Sect. 7 concludes this paper.

2   The Learned Index

In this section, we give some basics of the learned index [11].

Kraska et al. [11] observe that traditional range indexes such as B-Tree can be regarded as models: they map keys to positions in sorted order. However, B-Tree constructs this mapping using a hierarchy of nodes and does not exploit the characteristics of the data. Base on this, they propose to replace the hierarchical nodes with machine learning models such as neural networks, thus leading to the novel index structure called the learned index[1]. Specifically, assuming an array of records sorted by keys, the learned index leverages machine learning models to approximate the cumulative distribution function (CDF) of the data. With the estimated CDF F, the position p of a key K can be predicted as $p = \lfloor F(K) * N \rfloor$, where N is the total number of keys.

To put this idea into practice, several key techniques have been proposed.

First, the learned index uses a local search around the predicted location to accommodate the prediction errors of models. Since models may not perfectly learn the CDF, it could predict a wrong position. The learned index corrects this wrong prediction by a local search. During training, it maintains the maximum error max_err and the minimum error min_err. Then for any key whose predicted position is pos, the target record is guaranteed to reside within the range $[pos + min\_err, pos + max\_err]$ if it exists. Hence, for each lookup, a simple binary search within the bounded error range is used to locate the records. The error bound, which equals $log_2(max\_err + min\_err)$, determines the effectiveness of the learned model.

Second, the learned index introduces a new model structure called *Recursive Model Indexes (RMI)* to improve the prediction accuracy and thus the performance. Using a single model over the entire CDF can result in a large error bound, degrading lookup efficiency. To overcome this, the RMI constructs multiple levels (termed *stage*) of models (termed *sub-model* in the following), and assigns different parts of the CDF into different leaf-stage sub-models. Each leaf-stage sub-model only needs to approximate a small range of the entire CDF, which means a better prediction accuracy. The sub-models in the leaf stage also maintain the minimum and the maximum error of the corresponding CDF range. In an RMI, each internal sub-model takes a given key as input and picks the sub-model in the next stage, while each leaf-stage sub-model gives the predicted CDF value. The specific RMI architecture is determined by the number of stages, the number of models and the choice of each sub-model[2]. It can be tuned for each data distribution during model training. For example, sub-model in the upper stages can use complex models to learn a wide range of complex CDF, while the bottom ones can use simple linear regression models.

The learned index shows excellent performance compared with traditional indexes [11]. It achieves up to 3× performance than B-Tree with orders of

---

[1] We focus on the range index in this paper.

[2] The choice of each sub-model can vary, ranging from the simplest model such as a linear regression model, to a more complex model such as a multi-layer neural network.

magnitude smaller index size. Many successive works have been proposed to further boost its performance under a wide range of scenarios [4,5,8–10,13,14,16,20]. For all these systems, the model training process is critical as 1) many of them [4,9,16] require frequent model retraining after data modifications to fully employ the indexing capabilities of learned models, and 2) the trained model directly determines their performance. However, no work has been done to improve the performance of the learned index through a better training scheme. We show that existing training schemes do not fully exploit the performance benefits, and a distribution-aware training scheme can obtain better performance.

3   The Problem

In this section, we present the problem of existing training schemes under real-world workloads in detail through some experiments.

We use a two-staged RMI to illustrate the challenges, which is also the default configuration in [11]. The second stage of the RMI contains 200 K linear regression models. We vary the type of sub-model in its first stage and use the following three model architectures in experiments: LIN (linear regression model) and NN8/NN16 (one-hidden-layer neural network of width 8/16). Four datasets are used in our experiments; each of them is generated by randomly sampling from several normal distributions with different parameters ($\sigma \in [0,10], \mu \in [0,1]$). The numbers are scaled to 1 B (i.e., 10^9) as done in [11]. Each dataset has 200M integer keys. Figure 1 shows their CDFs.

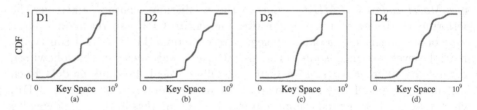

Fig. 1. The CDFs of datasets D1, D2, D3 and D4. The x-axis indicates the key space, and the y-axis is the normalized CDF for each dataset.

The training process plays an important role in the learned index's high performance, especially under real-world workloads. The real-world workloads consist of skewed queries and ever-changing data distribution. However, existing training schemes are not distribution-aware. **Without considering the query and data distributions during training, the learned index can yield sub-optimal performance.**

3.1   Query Distribution

The performance is unpredictable under skewed query distribution, as it is dominated by these hot models' error bound. In a typical RMI, there can be thousands

Table 1. Latency (in nanoseconds) of different model architectures under different skewed query workloads. The dataset is D1 (Fig. 1a) The skewed workloads (Skewed 1, Skewed 2 and Skewed 3) have 95% queries reading 5% hot keys, but in different ranges. The Uniform workload access all keys with equal probability.

Model arch	Workload			
	Skewed 1	Skewed 2	Skewed 3	Uniform
LIN	1120	252	331	406
NN16	321	310	282	375

of sub-models in the leaf stage, and the error bounds of these sub-models differ. The *hot model* is defined as the leaf-stage sub-model that holds the hot (frequently accessed) keys. If the hot models have a large error bound, the learned index needs to binary search within a larger range. More memory references are required with the increasing search range, thus degrading the performance. On the other hand, the learned index can achieve excellent performance if the hot models have a small error bound, even though all the other 'cold' models are poorly learned.

To better illustrate the problem, we evaluate the performance of the learned index with two different model architectures (LIN and NN16) under skewed query patterns. In skewed workloads, 95% of queries only access 5% of keys in different ranges. The hot range is 0th to 5th, 20th to 25th, and 60th to 65th percentile of the sorted keys array for Skewed 1, Skewed 2 and Skewed 3. Table 1 presents the query latency under workloads, and Fig. 2 shows the error bounds of the two model architecture among the key space. The performance variance across different workloads is large even with the same model architecture. LIN performs 37.9% better under Skewed 2 than under Uniform. But under Skewed 1, the query latency of LIN is 75.8% higher than under Uniform, which is even 82.8% higher than B-Tree (396 ns). The differences in error bounds cause this performance fluctuation. As shown in Fig. 2, the error bound of the key range from 0 B to 0.23 B (which covers the hot range of Skewed 1) is much larger than the average error bound (24 vs. 6.58). Comparing the two different models, NN16 has better performance than LIN under Uniform workload (375 ns vs. 406 ns). But under skewed workloads, NN16 can perform worse than LIN (310 ns vs. 252 ns under Skewed 2). The reason is that, NN16 has a smaller average error bound than LIN (5.32 vs. 6.58). However, for the key range from 0.35 B to 0.46 B (which covers the hot range of Skewed 2), LIN's error bound is smaller than NN16's (4.56 vs. 4.86, which is zoomed out in the figure).

Existing works [4,9,16] all assume a uniform access pattern while building machine learning models. Therefore, they can suffer from performance issues under skewed query distribution. PGM-Index [8] is the only learned index so far that considers query distribution while training. However, it couples with the design of the Piecewise Geometric Model, thus can not serve as a general training scheme for various model architectures.

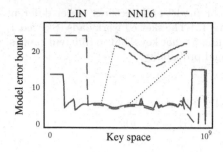

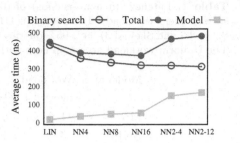

Fig. 2. Errors of two model configurations (LIN and NN16). The x-axis is the key space, and the y-axis is the error bound $(log_2(max\_err + min\_err))$ of the sub-model having the key.

Fig. 3. The search time ('Total') under different model architectures. It consists of binary search time ('Binary') and model computation time ('Model'). NN2-4/NN2-12 means using two-hidden-layer neural network of width 4/12 as the root-stage model.

3.2   Data Distribution

Without considering data distribution during training, learned indexes may use a sub-optimal model architecture, thus obtaining a sub-optimal performance. Frequent write requests cause the shifting of data distribution, but the best model architecture varies for different data distributions. On the one hand, even with a small hyperparameter space (e.g., the number of sub-models, type of sub-models), we can easily obtain hundreds even thousands of different model architectures. On the other hand, complex models are not always a good choice. The complexity of data distributions varies. Complex models (e.g., neural networks) can approximate complex CDFs more precisely, thus expecting a smaller average error bound. However, the performance of learned indexes is not only directly correlated with the accuracy of the model (i.e., binary search cost), but also with the complexity of the model (i.e., inference cost). Complex models introduce higher computation costs, which can cancel out its advantages in binary search time. Figure 3 shows query latency breakdown (which consists of binary search time and model computation time) with different model architectures under dataset D1. With the increase of complexity of the first-stage model (from LIN to NN2-12), the binary search time decreases. But the model inference costs also increases dramatically. This tradeoff makes it hard to choose the best model architecture for different data distributions.

Table 2 shows the best model architecture and the corresponding query latency under different datasets. The best architecture differs across different datasets and even different workloads. For example, for dataset D3, though NN16 spends less time in binary search than LIN (317 ns vs. 336 ns), LIN still has lower query latency than NN16 (350 ns vs. 367 ns). NN16 is penalized by the high inference cost (50 ns vs. 14 ns).

Table 2. The best model architecture and its corresponding average search time (in nanoseconds) under different datasets and workloads.

Dataset	Workload							
	Skewed 1		Skewed 2		Skewed 3		Uniform	
	Arch	Time(ns)	Arch	Time(ns)	Arch	Time(ns)	Arch	Time(ns)
D1	NN16	321	LIN	252	NN16	282	NN16	375
D2	NN8	319	NN8	316	NN8	301	LIN	344
D3	LIN	293	LIN	281	LIN	278	LIN	350
D4	NN8	314	LIN	289	LIN	288	NN8	376

Hence, under real-world workloads where data distribution is constantly evolving, using a fixed model architecture can result in sub-optimal performance. The best architecture should be detected during model retraining. Intuitively, we can apply some basic search techniques such as grid search to find the best model architecture upon the change of data distribution. However, it can easily take 10–100× the model training time [1], which significantly impacts the responsiveness of learned indexes.

4   DATum

To unleash the performance of the learned index, we propose a distribution-aware training system for learned indexes called DATum.

Figure 4 shows the architecture of DATum. It consists of three main components: *Dataset Augmentor*, *Model Tuner* and *Model Trainer*. DATum adopts two key mechanisms to achieve distribution-awareness while training models. First, DATum "stretches" the dataset according to query patterns and trains models with a stretched dataset to improve the performance of hot models (*Dataset Augmentor* and *Model Trainer*, Sect. 4.1). Second, DATum reuses the pre-found best model architecture for the same data distribution to avoid the costly grid search once the data distribution changes (*Model Tuner*, Sect. 4.2).

The overall workflow of DATum is as follows. The *Dataset Augmentor* first stretches the dataset according to the query pattern and generates the new training dataset. Then *Model Tuner* finds the best model architecture for the stretched dataset through *Model Cache* (previously been found) or *Auto-tuner* (not found in the cache). The *Model Tuner* returns the tunned model to *Model Trainer*. Finally, *Model Trainer* retrains the leaf-stage sub-models of the tunned model with the original dataset to repair the position information.

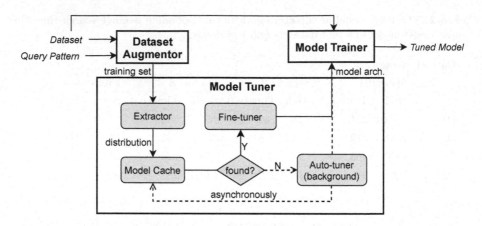

Fig. 4. Architecture of DATum.

4.1   Data Stretching

Our key observation is that, improving the performance under skewed workloads requires reducing hot models' error bounds instead of improving the prediction accuracy of individual keys. This insight comes from an intuition solution, which increases the contribution of hot keys during training. To incorporate query patterns, the intuitive solution duplicates hot keys in the training set according to their access frequency. For example, for a dataset with three keys {a, b, c} in a sorted order, if the access frequencies of the keys are 0.25 : 0.5 : 0.25, then we can simply create two copies of b to generate the training set. The final training set becomes {(a, 0), (b, 1), (b, 1), (c, 2)}, in the format of (key, position) pairs. Then, the hot key b can contribute two times than the other keys during training, which is much more likely to improve its prediction accuracy. We evaluate this solution under the three skewed workloads (Table 2), but find that the performance rarely improves compared to previous best model architectures. The underlying reason is that the intuitive solution hardly improves hot models' error bounds, which actually determines the search time.

Base on the observation, DATum adopts a novel approach called data stretching to incorporate the query distribution. The goal of data stretching is to reduce the number of keys handled by hot models in the leaf stage, as leaf-stage sub-models tend to have smaller error bound with fewer keys. To achieve this, DATum increases the distance between these hot keys and their neighbors (i.e., keys before and after them). It simply shifts the position labels according to the access frequencies. For the above training set {(a, 0), (b, 1), (c, 2)} with access ratio of 0.25 : 0.5 : 0.25 (i.e., 1:2:1), DATum will augment it to {(a, 0.5), (b, 2), (c, 3.5)}. Figure 5 shows the effect of data stretching on dataset D1 under workload Skewed 3. The hot range is stretched according to the query pattern, as shown in the right CDF. More formally, we define the query pattern as $Q = \{(k_i, f_i)\}_{i=1,...,n}$ where $0 < f_i < 1$ is the access ratio, and

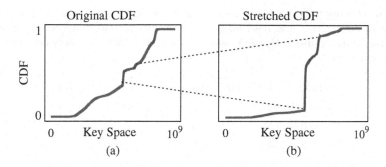

Fig. 5. The left figure shows the CDF of the original dataset D1. The corresponding CDF of D1 after stretching is shown in the right figure.

cdf as the stretched CDF. Then DATum will augment the dataset to satisfy the following formula:

$$\frac{cdf(k_{i+1}) - cdf(k_i)}{cdf(k_i) - cdf(k_{i-1})} = \frac{f_{i+1} + f_i}{f_i + f_{i-1}}, \ \forall i > 1 \tag{1}$$

Then in the augmented CDF, the distances between any adjacent keys are determined by their access ratios.

The *Dataset Augmentor* takes query patterns and dataset as input. It applies the above data stretching to the dataset and generates the augmented training set. Then it sends the training set to *Model Tuner* to get a tuned model (Sect. 4.2). Since the position labels in the stretched training set differ from the real dataset, DATum needs to repair these position information at the final step. It retrains the leaf-stage sub-model of the returned model with the original dataset in *Model Trainer*, and finally outputs the ready-to-use model.

4.2   Model Cache

DATum leverages a model cache and the classic grid search to efficiently find the best model architecture upon data distribution shifting (*Model Tuner* in Fig. 4). The model cache maintains mappings from data distribution to the already-found best model architectures and parameters. DATum uses grid search to find the best model architecture for a new data distribution given a hyperparameter search space, then adds the search result to the model cache. When a similar data distribution is encountered again, DATum just directly returns the entry in the model cache, thus avoiding the costly grid search.

The *Model Tuner* contains three modules that work synergistically: *Extractor, Model Cache, Fine-tuner* and *Auto-tuner*.

The *Extractor* extracts the distribution information of the dataset by uniformly sampling K keys from the augmented training set. Empirically, choosing a higher sample rate can bring higher fidelity as to the real distribution, but also means higher storage and computation overhead.

Table 3. The query latency (in nanoseconds) of the learned index using different methods to incorporate the read access pattern. Origin does not consider the query distribution while training. Baseline refers to the method which simply creates multiple copies of hot keys.

Workload	Origin (ns)	Baseline (ns)	Stretching (ns)
Skewed 1	321	288	157
Skewed 2	252	260	222
Skewed 3	282	270	237

The *Model Cache* maintains pre-trained models for already-seen data distributions. Each entry in the cache consists of a sampled dataset and the corresponding tuned model. When getting a new dataset from *Extractor*, it tries to find an entry in the cache with the most similar data distribution based on two-sample tests such as Kolmogorov–Smirnov test. If the similarity is larger than a user-given threshold, the cache simply returns the found model to *Fine-tuner*. Otherwise, DATum will start a grid search in the background, which is conducted by *Auto-tuner*.

The *Fine-tuner* gets the pre-trained model from *Model Cache*. It incrementally trains the model with the augmented training set.

The *Auto-tuner* is used to perform the grid search. It starts a grid search in the background to find the best model architecture for a given data distribution and stores the result into the cache asynchronously. Based on the observation shown in Fig. 3, *Auto-tuner* tries to find the best tradeoff between model complexity and accuracy. Specifically, given a hyperparameter search space, *Auto-tuner* increases the complexity of the model (such as increasing the number of stages/models, using a neural network with more layers) until the increase in the model inference cost overwhelms the reduction in binary search cost. Though not the focus of this paper, this process can also be optimized by techniques such as parallel execution and early abort [6].

5   Experiments

In this section, we present preliminary evaluation results of DATum to show its effectiveness. The default setup is the same as that in Sect. 3. All the experiments are run on a server with two 20-core Intel Xeon E5-2650 v3 CPUs, each with 25 MB LLC.

5.1   Data Stretching

Table 3 shows the query latency of the learned index under dataset D1 (Fig. 1a) after incorporating the read access pattern. Baseline refers to the intuitive method mentioned in Sect. 4.1, which simply increases the frequency of hot keys in the training set. Origin is the original method without considering the read

Table 4. The execution time of *Model Tuner* under different configurations. The ratio column represents the ratio between the execution time of *Model Tuner* and the time of using the grid search.

Sample size	# of entries in *Model Cache*					
	1K		5K		10K	
	Time(s)	Ratio(%)	Time(s)	Ratio(%)	Time(s)	Ratio(%)
1K	0.01	0.01	0.02	0.01	0.05	0.03
10K	0.05	0.03	0.25	0.13	0.51	0.27
50K	0.23	0.12	1.24	0.65	2.54	1.32
100K	0.51	0.26	2.55	1.30	4.88	2.49
200K	0.95	0.48	4.78	2.41	9.48	4.77

access pattern. Note that we only present the optimization result based on the best model architecture under Origin (NN16 for Skewed 1 & 3, LIN for Skewed 2). From the table, we can see that data stretching can improve the query latency of the learned index by 51.1%, 11.9%, 15.9% for the three workloads, respectively. For the workload Skewed 1, the average error bound of the hot models after data stretching is 7.76, which is 24.9% smaller than that of Origin (10.34). As a comparison, Baseline barely improves the performance and even increases the query latency for Skewed 2. For the workload Skewed 1, the average error bound of Baseline is 10.08, similar to that of Origin. This is because Baseline tries to improve the prediction accuracy of hot keys, but fails to reduce the error bound. The error bound of one model is only determined by the keys with the worst accuracy (the minimum and the maximum error elaborated in Sect. 2), which decides the search time.

5.2   Model Cache

Next, we conduct experiments on the model cache. In this experiment, we first populate the cache by employing grid search to find the best model for different datasets. The datasets are generated by randomly replacing half of the existing elements in one normal distribution with different normal distributions. The parameter of normal distributions are the same as those in Sect. 3, and the average size is 1M. Then we use existing datasets as input to ask *Model Tuner* for the best model. To narrow down the search space for the grid search, we use a two-stage RMI and set only two kinds of hyperparameters: the number of sub-models in the second stage (10K to 500K, with a step of 10K) and the type of each sub-model (including the root-stage model).

Table 4 shows the execution time of *Model Tuner* under different configurations, namely sample size and the number of entries in *Model Cache*. Overall, DATum can find the tuned model architecture quickly. DATum can reduce the model rebuilding time to less than 1% of the classic grid search in most cases. With the increasing sample size and the number of entries, the execution time

Table 5. The execution time of *Model Trainer* with different configurations.

Data size	# of models in the leaf stage			
	10K	50K	100K	200K
10M	0.06 s	0.07 s	0.08 s	0.09 s
50M	0.33 s	0.30 s	0.31 s	0.34 s
100M	0.68 s	0.63 s	0.60 s	0.61 s
200M	1.36 s	1.21 s	1.25 s	1.22 s

tends to increase. When the sample size is 200K, and the number of entries is 10K, it accounts for up to 4.77% of the grid search. This is because DATum has to find the entry in *Model Cache* with the most similar data distribution to the input dataset, which currently requires iterating over all the entries. As to memory consumption, it consumes more space with the increase of sample size and entry size. When the sample size is 10K, and the number of entries is 5K, DATum requires around 0.49 GB space. The storage cost increases to 15.1 GB for 200K sample size and 10K entries. A larger sample size introduces longer execution time and larger storage consumption, but brings higher accuracy. Small sample size may break the distribution, which leads to DATum finding a suboptimal model in the cache (i.e., a model with a different data distribution). For example, when the sample size increases from 10K to 100K, the average percent of finding the wrong entry is reduced from 10% to 4%.

Table 5 present the execution time of *Model Trainer* under different data sizes and different numbers of leaf-stage sub-models in the RMI. The *Model Trainer* only needs to retrain the leaf-stage sub-models with the original datasets, which takes less time than retraining the whole RMI model. For example, it only takes 4 μs to train a linear model with 1000 keys. As a result, we can conclude that the total execution time of DATum is still far shorter than that of the grid search within a given space.

6   Related Works

Learned Indexes. The proposal of the learned index [11] has stimulated a surge of researches on indexes. Some works [5,8] have tried to improve performance under skewed query distributions. PGM-Index [8] proposes a Piecewise Geometric Model (PGM), which orchestrates an optimal number of linear models in a recursive structure. It can train a PGM based on the query distributions. Compared with it, DATum is a general model training framework that can apply to all types of model architectures. Tsunami [5] is a learned multi-dimensional index specially optimized for data correlation and query skew, while our work focuses on one-dimensional indexes. There are also some works [4,8,16] that consider the dataset shifting at runtime. XIndex [16] provides an efficient and non-blocking compaction (including data sorting and model retraining) scheme for the learned index to handle writes under concurrent scenarios. ALEX [4] constructs an adaptive RMI for indexing, where data are stored in leaf nodes with a gapped array layout for insertions. XIndex and ALEX both adopt some structure adjustment strategies such as node split to accommodate workload characteristics at runtime. As a comparison, our work is orthogonal to theirs as 1) we provide a new way of training model with better accuracy, which can be applied to existing systems to further boost their performance; and 2) we do not pose any additional restrictions to the data structure layout.

Besides, works have been done for the learned index on other different aspects. FITing-Tree [9] uses piecewise linear functions to approximate an index with bounded error. It allows a DBA to tune the index to balance performance and space overhead. Shift-Table [10] provides an enhancement layer for learned indexes to improve the precision of a learned model which contains the drift values to correct predictions. LIPP [20] leverages a tree structure to make the prediction of the model precise, thus eliminating the 'last mile' search. LISA [13] makes use of the learned index to accelerate spatial query processing. Flood [14] builds multi-dimensional indexes with the help of machine learning models. SIndex [18] is a learned index specially optimized for string keys. BOURBON [2] applies the learned index into an LSM-based key-value store based on a series of in-depth measurements and analyses. XStore [19] uses the learned index as the client-side cache for RDMA-based key-value stores and leverages a hybrid structure to handle writes. All of them focus on different scopes compared with ours, and our approaches can be used to achieve more performance benefits.

Workload-Aware Data Structures. Skewed access pattern exhibits itself in common real-world workloads. A hybrid index structure [22] has been proposed to deal with skewed patterns, which uses a flexible structure to index hot records and a compact and read-only structure to hold the cold data. H-Store [3] uses "anti-caching" to detect hot and cold tuples and moves cold data to disk to save memory space. VoltDB [15] employs a similar approach but uses virtual memory paging to swap data to disk. Siberia [12] uses sampling to detect hot/cold data and uses SQL Server's buffer pool to swap the data to/from disk as needed.

Data Augmentation. Data Augmentation is a commonly used yet powerful technique to avoid overfitting and increase the generalization performance of machine learning models. Hundreds of methods have been explored, such as geometric and photometric transformations [17], example interpolation [21], random erasing [23]. Different from them, our data stretching does not improve generalizability, but improves the prediction accuracy of frequently accessed sub-models.

7   Conclusion

This paper presents a new way to improve the learned index's performance under real-world workloads through a distribution-aware training scheme. The Distribution-Aware Training system, called DATum, takes both the query distribution and data distribution into consideration while training model. Experimental results have shown the effectiveness of DATum's designs.

References

1. Bergstra, J., Bardenet, R., Bengio, Y., Kégl, B.: Algorithms for hyper-parameter optimization. In: Proceedings of the 24th International Conference on Neural Information Processing Systems, NIPS 2011, pp. 2546–2554. Curran Associates Inc., Red Hook (2011)
2. Dai, Y., et al.: From wisckey to bourbon: a learned index for log-structured merge trees. In: 14th USENIX Symposium on Operating Systems Design and Implementation (OSDI 2020), pp. 155–171. USENIX Association, November 2020
3. DeBrabant, J., Pavlo, A., Tu, S., Stonebraker, M., Zdonik, S.: Anti-caching: a new approach to database management system architecture. Proc. VLDB Endow. **6**(14), 1942–1953 (2013). https://doi.org/10.14778/2556549.2556575
4. Ding, J., et al.: Alex: an updatable adaptive learned index. In: Proceedings of the 2020 ACM SIGMOD International Conference on Management of Data, SIGMOD 2020, pp. 969–984. Association for Computing Machinery, New York (2020). https://doi.org/10.1145/3318464.3389711
5. Ding, J., Nathan, V., Alizadeh, M., Kraska, T.: Tsunami: a learned multidimensional index for correlated data and skewed workloads. Proc. VLDB Endow. **14**(2), 74–86 (2020). https://doi.org/10.14778/3425879.3425880
6. Duan, S., Thummala, V., Babu, S.: Tuning database configuration parameters with ituned. Proc. VLDB Endow. **2**(1), 1246–1257 (2009). https://doi.org/10.14778/1687627.1687767
7. Eldawy, A., Levandoski, J., Larson, P.R.: Trekking through Siberia: managing cold data in a memory-optimized database. Proc. VLDB Endow. **7**(11), 931–942 (2014). https://doi.org/10.14778/2732967.2732968
8. Ferragina, P., Vinciguerra, G.: The PGM-index: a fully-dynamic compressed learned index with provable worst-case bounds. Proc. VLDB Endow. **13**(8), 1162–1175 (2020). https://doi.org/10.14778/3389133.3389135
9. Galakatos, A., Markovitch, M., Binnig, C., Fonseca, R., Kraska, T.: Fiting-tree: a data-aware index structure. In: Proceedings of the 2019 International Conference on Management of Data, SIGMOD 2019, pp. 1189–1206. Association for Computing Machinery, New York (2019). https://doi.org/10.1145/3299869.3319860
10. Hadian, A., Heinis, T.: Shift-table: a low-latency learned index for range queries using model correction. arXiv preprint arXiv:2101.10457 (2021)
11. Kraska, T., Beutel, A., Chi, E.H., Dean, J., Polyzotis, N.: The case for learned index structures. In: Proceedings of the 2018 International Conference on Management of Data, SIGMOD 2018, pp. 489–504. Association for Computing Machinery, New York (2018). https://doi.org/10.1145/3183713.3196909
12. Levandoski, J.J., Larson, P.Å., Stoica, R.: Identifying hot and cold data in mainmemory databases. In: 2013 IEEE 29th International Conference on Data Engineering (ICDE), pp. 26–37. IEEE (2013)
13. Li, P., Lu, H., Zheng, Q., Yang, L., Pan, G.: Lisa: a learned index structure for spatial data. In: Proceedings of the 2020 ACM SIGMOD International Conference on Management of Data, SIGMOD 2020, pp. 2119–2133. Association for Computing Machinery, New York (2020). https://doi.org/10.1145/3318464.3389703
14. Nathan, V., Ding, J., Alizadeh, M., Kraska, T.: Learning multi-dimensional indexes. In: Proceedings of the 2020 ACM SIGMOD International Conference on Management of Data, SIGMOD 2020, pp. 985–1000. Association for Computing Machinery, New York (2020). https://doi.org/10.1145/3318464.3380579

15. Stoica, R., Ailamaki, A.: Enabling efficient os paging for main-memory OLTP databases. In: Proceedings of the Ninth International Workshop on Data Management on New Hardware. DaMoN 2013. Association for Computing Machinery, New York (2013). https://doi.org/10.1145/2485278.2485285
16. Tang, C., et al.: Xindex: a scalable learned index for multicore data storage. In: Proceedings of the 25th ACM SIGPLAN Symposium on Principles and Practice of Parallel Programming, PPoPP 2020, pp. 308–320. Association for Computing Machinery, New York (2020). https://doi.org/10.1145/3332466.3374547
17. Taylor, L., Nitschke, G.: Improving deep learning with generic data augmentation. In: 2018 IEEE Symposium Series on Computational Intelligence (SSCI), pp. 1542–1547 (2018). https://doi.org/10.1109/SSCI.2018.8628742
18. Wang, Y., Tang, C., Wang, Z., Chen, H.: Sindex: a scalable learned index for string keys. In: Proceedings of the 11th ACM SIGOPS Asia-Pacific Workshop on Systems, APSys 2020, pp. 17–24. Association for Computing Machinery, New York (2020). https://doi.org/10.1145/3409963.3410496
19. Wei, X., Chen, R., Chen, H.: Fast RDMA-based ordered key-value store using remote learned cache. In: 14th USENIX Symposium on Operating Systems Design and Implementation (OSDI 2020), pp. 117–135. USENIX Association, November 2020
20. Wu, J., Zhang, Y., Chen, S., Wang, J., Chen, Y., Xing, C.: Updatable learned index with precise positions. arXiv preprint arXiv:2104.05520 (2021)
21. Zhang, H., Cisse, M., Dauphin, Y.N., Lopez-Paz, D.: mixup: beyond empirical risk minimization. arXiv preprint arXiv:1710.09412 (2017)
22. Zhang, H., Andersen, D.G., Pavlo, A., Kaminsky, M., Ma, L., Shen, R.: Reducing the storage overhead of main-memory OLTP databases with hybrid indexes. In: Proceedings of the 2016 International Conference on Management of Data, SIGMOD 2016, pp. 1567–1581. Association for Computing Machinery, New York (2016). https://doi.org/10.1145/2882903.2915222
23. Zhong, Z., Zheng, L., Kang, G., Li, S., Yang, Y.: Random erasing data augmentation. In: Proceedings of the AAAI Conference on Artificial Intelligence, vol. 34, no. 07, pp. 13001–13008 (2020). https://doi.org/10.1609/aaai.v34i07.7000

AIR Cache: A Variable-Size Block Cache Based on Fine-Grained Management Method

Yuxiong Li[1], Yujuan Tan[1,3(✉)], Congcong Xu[1], Duo Liu[1], Xianzhang Chen[1],
Chengliang Wang[1], Mingliang Zhou[2], and Leong Hou U[2]

[1] College of Computer Science, Chongqing University, Chongqing, China
{liuduo,wangcl}@cqu.edu.cn
[2] State Key Lab of Internet of Things for Smart City,
University of Macau, Macau, China
mingliangzhou@cqu.edu.cn, ryanlhu@um.edu.mo
[3] Wuhan National Laboratory for Optoelectronics, Wuhan, China

Abstract. Recently, adopting large cache blocks has received widespread attention in server-side storage caching. Besides reducing the management overheads of cache blocks, it can significantly boost the I/O throughput. However, although using large blocks has advantages in management overhead and I/O performance, existing fixed-size block management schemes in storage cache cannot effectively handle them under the complicated real-world workloads. We find that existing fixed-size block management methods will suffer from the fragmentation within the cache block and fail to identify hot/cold cache blocks correctly when adopting large blocks for caching.

Therefore, aiming to solve this problem, we propose AIR cache, which is a variable-size block cache based on fine-grained management method. AIR cache contains three major parts, Multi-Granularity Writer (MGW), Multi-Granularity Eviction (MGE) and Fine-Grained Recorder (FGR) where FGR is dedicated to record the data popularity using fine-grained data sections, MGW writes data at different granularity, and MGE is responsible for evicting the data at dynamic granularity. Our experiments with real-world traces demonstrate that AIR cache can increase the read cache hit ratio by up to 6.97X and the cache space utilization rate by up to 3.63X over the traditional fixed-size block management methods.

Keywords: Storage cache · Fine-grained management · Variable size block

1 Introduction

Storage cache is a component that resides in a relatively fast but expensive device and is used to store recently used data [1,3,4,13,15,16,21]. In this way, future requests can quickly access commonly used data without having to access them from slower devices. Nowadays, storage cache is a must-have component of

© Springer Nature Switzerland AG 2021
L. H. U et al. (Eds.): APWeb-WAIM 2021, LNCS 12859, pp. 158–177, 2021.
https://doi.org/10.1007/978-3-030-85899-5_12

various storage systems [19, 20, 22]. For example, in datacenters, SSDs are used as storage cache of HDD; in distributed systems, a portion of local memory/storage is used as storage cache for remote data access. Cache block is the basic data processing unit of storage cache, and existing cache management methods set its size as 4KB for a long time [2, 5, 6, 11, 12, 17, 18, 23].

Recently, adopting large blocks for caching has attracted widespread attention for three important reasons. First, with the advancement in storage technology, storage devices are moving towards high capacity and low cost. When the size of the device to be used for caching is large, increasing the block size can significantly reduce the total number of blocks and the associated overhead of managing these blocks. Second, with the explosive growth of data and the popularity of big data applications, more and more users are pursuing high I/O throughput. Increasing the size of cache block can achieve higher data read/write bandwidth and increase I/O throughput. Third, some storage devices no longer support processing relatively small data units. For example, with the development of semiconductor technology and the improvement in flash memory manufacturing technology, the page size of some NAND Flash SSDs has steadily increased from the original 2 KB or 4 KB to 8KB and 16 KB [8, 10].

Although using large blocks has benefits in management overhead and I/O performance, existing cache management methods in storage cache cannot effectively use large cache blocks. The main limitation is that it manages data with a fixed-size block granularity. When the cache block becomes larger, it is difficult to effectively utilize the cache space for the two problems.

The first problem is the internal fragmentation of the cache block. Existing cache management methods in storage cache process cache data in block granularity and operating any part of the cache block requires operations on the entire cache block. Therefore, when data is written to the cache, the data needs to be touched as a whole block. If the size of written data is smaller than cache block size, some parts of the cache block are not used, thus causing the internal fragmentation problem. Obviously, this internal fragmentation will result in low cache utilization. In addition, the larger the cache block, the worse the internal fragmentation, and the lower the cache space utilization rate. Our preliminary studies show that most large blocks have internal fragmentation. In particular, the cache space utilization rate using the traditional ARC algorithm is only 56.2% when the cache block size is 16 KB (see Sect. 2).

The second problem is that hot/cold cache blocks cannot be identified correctly. Existing cache management methods record data popularity in block granularity. It means that no matter how much data is accessed, they will increase the popularity of the entire cache block. This makes it difficult to capture accurate data access patterns. Our preliminary studies show that the cache block partial hits (only a part of the block is accessed) account for an average of 52.43% of the total hits (see Sect. 2). As a result, when the cache is full, it is difficult to find the correct cold block to delete. Sometimes the blocks to be deleted from the cache may be hotter than the blocks to be retained. In this case, the block replacement algorithm is inefficient and reduces cache performance.

Based on these observations, we propose a variable-size block cache based on fine-grained management method, called AIR cache. It consists of three components, Fine-Grained Recorder (FGR), Multi-Granularity Writer (MGW) and Multi-Granularity Eviction (MGE). FGR focuses on recording data access popularity based on fine-grained data sections in each block, which can help better capture data access patterns and correctly record access popularity. MGW is responsible for writing multi-granularity data according to the size of the I/O requests of the upper-layer applications. When the cache is full, MGE focuses on evicting multi-granularity cold data. It selects the cold data to delete based on the access popularity recorded by the FGR. Combing FGR, MGW, and MGE, AIR cache can effectively manage variable-size cache blocks to make full use of cache space and improve cache performance.

To evaluate our AIR cache approach, we have implemented an AIR cache prototype and integrated two modified cache replacement algorithms based on the traditional replacement algorithms LRU and ARC, called AIR-LRU and AIR-ARC, respectively. Our experiments through the FIU [9] trace show that AIR-LRU and AIR-ARC outperform LRU and ARC [14], by up to 6.97X in read cache hit ratio, with an average of 3.21X, and up to 3.63X in cache space utilization rate, with an average of 1.77X.

2   Related Work

Caching has been widely used as a performance accelerator. Over the years, many cache replacement algorithms have been proposed to capture the characteristics of different workloads. LRU algorithm is the most widely used algorithm at present. In the existing system, basically LRU algorithm or LRU-like algorithm is adopted. However, LRU has some limitations, such as not considering the frequency. Variants of LRU such as 2Q [7], MQ [23], LIRS [18]and ARC [14] are proposed to improve LRU. 2Q has two queues, one is the FIFO queue and the other is the LRU queue. On the first reference to a page, the 2Q algorithm places it in the FIFO queue. If a page in the FIFO queue is referenced, the page is moved to the LRU queue. Otherwise, it will be removed from the FIFO queue. MQ uses a skewed frequency distribution in the second-level buffer cache to enhance high-frequency blocks to improve cache hit ratios. LIRS retains data with a small reuse distance and replace data with a large reuse distance, because data with a small reuse distance is more likely to be accessed in the future. ARC is anti-scanning. It consists of two partitions. On a hit, it upgrades the block from one partition to another and resizes the partition to fit the workload. Although these cache replacement algorithms can potentially significantly improve cache performance, there are still gaps in effectively managing large cache blocks because they process all cached data with a fixed size block granularity without exception. Our work, the AIR cache, can bridge this gap by managing and storing cached data in cache blocks of multiple sizes.

3   Motivation

Existing cache management methods based on a fixed-size cache block design
and managing cache data with a fixed-size block granularity cannot effectively
utilize large cache blocks. Specifically, writing a small amount of data to a large
cache block causes fragmentation within the cache block, while fixed-size cache
data processing units will have difficulty capturing accurate data access patterns,
which will lose the ability to identify hot/cold blocks. Next, we will describe these
two issues in detail.

3.1   Internal Fragmentation

Problem Description. In storage cache, the purpose of using large cache
blocks is to improve I/O throughput by accessing large amounts of data at once.
However, if the requested data is smaller than the cache block, the entire block
still needs to be touched. Specifically, when a request is missing, it needs to read
the data from the underlying storage system into the cache. At this time, if the
data written to the cache is smaller than one block, it needs to be written to the
entire block. As a result, except for the data part, other parts of the cache block
are not used, which may cause severe fragmentation inside the cache block. We
call a cache block with unused portions named fragmented block.

A fragmented block occupies the space of the entire cache block, but contains
less useful data. Obviously, storing these fragmented blocks wastes cache space.
In addition, the larger the cache block, the larger the fragmentation of the block.
Using large blocks for caching can cause very low cache utilization. At the same
time, as the intensity of modern workloads increases, the demand for cache
capacity is bound to grow rapidly. The cache space is so precious that we need
to explore it effectively. However, reviewing existing cache management methods,
they process cached data with a fixed-sized block granularity, regardless of how
much valid data exists in each block. Therefore, it is not efficient to use fixed-size
block management methods to manage large cache blocks.

Statistical Evidence. To evaluate the internal fragmentation of cache block,
we implement a storage cache in DRAM using the traditional replacement algorithms LRU and ARC with fixed-size cache blocks. In our preliminary studies,
we evaluated the cache space utilization and cache hit ratios using WebVM from
the FIU trace. The characteristics of the workload are described in Table 2 in
Sect. 4. The cache size is set to 20%, 30%, 40% of the working set size and the
size of the cache block is set from 8 KB to 64 KB.

Figure 1 shows the cache space utilization rate. As shown in Fig. 1, no matter
what the cache block size is, it cannot use the LRU or ARC algorithm to completely occupy the cache space. For example, when the cache size is 30% of the
working set size and the block size is 8KB, the cache space utilization rate using
LRU algorithm is only 83.95% and using ARC algorithm is only 78.30%. When
the block size is increased to 16 KB, 32 KB and 64 KB, the cache space utilization rate using the LRU algorithm is reduced to 66.57%, 49.48%, 34.43%, and

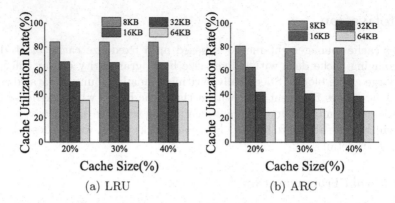

Fig. 1. Cache space utilization rate of LRU and ARC as a function of the block size and cache size.

the cache space utilization rate using the ARC algorithm is reduced to 57.18%, 40.36%, and 27.55%. These results show that when the block size increases from 8 KB to 64 KB, there are much more fragmented blocks in the cache. It proves that the larger the cache block, the more severe the fragmentation, and the lower the cache space utilization rate.

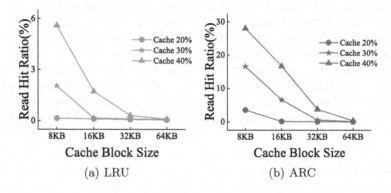

Fig. 2. Read hit ratios of LRU and ARC as a function of the block size and cache size.

To evaluate the impact of cache space utilization on cache performance, we further evaluate the read hit ratios using the same experimental settings as the cache space utilization rate. Figure 2 shows the experimental results, the read hit ratio decreases as the block size increases. For example, when the block size is 8 KB and the cache size is 40% of the working set size, the read hit ratio using the ARC algorithm is 28.04%. But when the block size increases to 16 KB, the read hit ratio using the ARC algorithm is only 16.56%, and when the block size is increased above 16 KB, the ratio continues to decrease. This is because as the block size increases, block fragmentation becomes worse. It results in less useful data being stored in the cache and fewer requests can be served by the cache.

3.2 False Positives in Identifying Hot Cache Blocks

Problem Description. Existing cache management methods use access frequency and access recency to identify hot/cold cache blocks, like LRU and ARC algorithms. The main limitation of these methods is that they track access frequency and access recency at a fixed-size block granularity. That is, for each cache block, if any data content is accessed recently, the whole block is labeled as recently accessed. They do not care about how much data is accessed in the cache block and what data is accessed. In fact, each time a different amount of the access data and different actual access data content have different effects on the access popularity of the entire cache block. It is incorrect to calculate the popularity of local data access in each block as the popularity of the entire block access. This can lead to many false positives on identifying hot cache blocks, especially if the cache block is large.

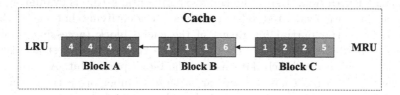

Fig. 3. An example of incorrectly identifying hot/cold blocks.

Figure 3 uses an extreme example to illustrate this situation. In the figure, there are three blocks, A, B, and C, in the cache, and each block contains four data parts. The number marked in each part represents the corresponding reference count. For blocks B and C, since their first part is frequently accessed (reference count are 6 and 5, respectively), even if most of their data parts are cold, they are still identified as hot blocks and promoted to the MRU position. In addition, when using the LRU algorithm to select a block as the victim block, although block A is a real hot block, it will be evicted from the cache first, which will reduce the cache hit ratio.

These misidentified hot blocks will affect the cache performance for two reasons. First, these misidentified hot blocks can pollute the cache space. This is because these blocks may contain data that will never be accessed. Therefore, storing this cold data wastes cache space. Second, these misidentified hot blocks can affect the cache hit ratio. This is because when the cache is full, these blocks will not be evicted to make room, but deleting other blocks that are indeed hotter than these misidentified hot blocks, thereby hurting the cache hit ratio.

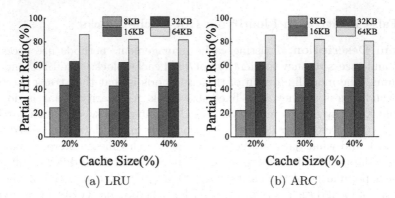

Fig. 4. Partial hit ratios of cache block.

Statistical Evidence. Using the same experimental setup as evaluating block fragmentation, we evaluated false positives on identifying hot cache blocks. Figure 4 shows the partial hit ratios of the cache block (accessing only part of the data in the cache block). Here, we define that each request accesses less than 50% of the cache block data as a cache block partial hit. As can be seen from the Fig. 4, in most cases, there are a large number of partial cache block hits in LRU and ARC. For example, when the cache size is set to 20% of the working set size and the cache block is 16 KB, the partial hits of the cache block using the LRU algorithm account for 43.34% of the total hits, and the partial hits of the cache block using ARC algorithm account for 41.37% of the total hits. When the block size is increased to 32 KB, the partial hit ratio is increased to 63.29% and 62.58% respectively. These results indicate that in existing fixed-size block management methods, there are many partial cache block hits, and treating these partial cache block hits as the entire cache block hit will generate many false positives when identifying hot cache blocks.

These observations motivate us to propose a variable-size block cache based on fine-grained management method to support variable-sized data caching instead of using one fixed-size cache blocks as existing block management method. In fact, with the diversification of storage devices and data applications, the size of read/write request units has become more and more diverse. Using cache blocks of variable sizes can better capture data access patterns and increase cache hit ratios. Therefore, it is necessary for storage cache to provide cache blocks of variable sizes to support variable-size data caching. In the next section, we will describe our proposed cache management method AIR-cache in detail.

4   AIR Cache Design

Existing cache management methods manage the data at a fixed-size block granularity, leading to internal fragmentation problems and inability to correctly identify the hot/cold cache blocks. To address these two problems, we propose a variable-size block cache based on fine-grained method, called AIR cache. In this section, we will describe in detail the three components of the AIR cache: Fine-Grained Recorder, Multi-Granularity Writer, and Multi-Granularity Eviction.

4.1   Fine-Grained Recorder

To manage variable sized blocks to store variable size data, the AIR cache uses Fine-Grained Recorder (FGR) to record the data access status and popularity of small data portions within each block. Specifically, FGR divides each block into multiple small portions and uses an array to record the access count of each portion. The access count for each portion represents the data popularity of each portion, which can help identify and delete the cold data with finer granularity. The size of each small data portion can be preset or set dynamically based on feedback of the data access characteristics.

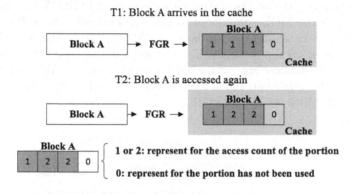

Fig. 5. Function of FGR.

Figure 5 shows an example to illustrate the function of FGR. FGR divides the block A into four portions and records the access count of each portion. There are two cases in FGR. In the first case, when the block first reaches the cache, only one bit is needed per portion to identify whether to store data. As shown in Fig. 5, when Block A arrives, the first three portions have valid data, and their corresponding access count is set to 1, and the last portion is not used, so the corresponding access count is set to 0. In the second case, when the block is accessed again, FGR records the access count. Here the FGR only increases the access frequency number of the re-accessed data, and does not increase the entire block as in the traditional cache management method. As shown in Fig. 5, only the second and the third portion of the Block A are accessed again, so only the access count of these two portions are increased from 1 to 2. Note that block A here is a fragmented block because the fourth data portion is not used. Next, we will show how AIR cache uses Multi-Granularity Writer to resolve this fragmentation problem.

4.2 Multi-Granularity Writer

Multi-Granularity Writer (MGW) is responsible for finding the appropriate cache space to store variable-size data written. To reduce the internal fragmentation of the cache block, the size of the cache space allocated to write data must be close to the size of the data itself. Therefore, MGW uses the following two steps to find and allocate cache space.

In the first step, MGW uses the access status recorded by the FGR to check whether there are some cached blocks, whose unused portion size is close to the incoming data size. If such a cache block exists, the MGW will directly write data to the unused portions of the found cache block, and then update the access record. This can help reduce internal fragmentation of cache blocks. However, if such cache block does not exist, the MGW will switch to the second step to find other cache block.

In the second step, MGW needs to allocate a new cache block and create a new record to store the access status with the help of FGR. When the cache is full, it waits for the MGE component to delete some cold data to free space. In addition, if the written data is too large, MGW will use multiple cache blocks to store the data; on the contrary, if the written data is too small, MGW will still allocate the smallest size cache block provided by the AIR cache to store it. Generally, the minimum block size is usually equal to the size of the data portion of each block set by the FGR.

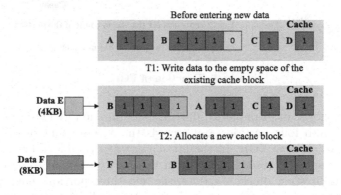

Fig. 6. A working example of MGW.

Figure 6 provides an example to illustrate how MGW works. For simplicity, the cache here can only store 32 KB of data; each portion of the cache block is set to 4 KB. Before new data enters the cache, it has stored four blocks, namely Block A (8 KB size), Block B (16 KB size), Block C (4 KB size), and Block D (4 KB size). At time T1, Data E (4 KB size) needs to enter in the cache, and MGW performs the first step to find a cache block whose unused portion size is close to the size of data E. Since the remaining unused space of the Block B is 4 KB, the MGW writes the data E into the unused portion of Block B and updates the corresponding access status. At time T2, data F (8 KB size) is written to the cache. At this time, the MGW cannot find a cache block with an appropriate unused space close to the size of the data F, so the MGW needs to perform the second step to allocate a new cache block of 8KB to store the data F. Before allocating new blocks, the AIR cache needs to use the MGE component to evict cold blocks Block C and Block D to make room for data F.

4.3   Multi-Granularity Eviction

Multi-Granularity Eviction (MGE) is responsible for finding and deleting cold data to free space when the cache is full. It uses the access status recorded by the FGR component and combines the access frequency and recency of small data portions within each block to help identify the cold/hot data. Specifically, MGE is composed of two parts, namely Cold Data Identification (CDI) and Cold Data Removal Multi-Grained Removal (MGR), which will be described below. As a side note, because MGE uses the same method to identify all hot and cold data of all cache blocks of various sizes, when describing MGE, we did not specify the block size and the number of data segments in each block.

Cold Data Identification. Cold Data Identification (CDI) is responsible for identifying cold data. CDI is dedicated to identifying the cold data of the cache block located at the LRU (last recently used) location, because in the traditional algorithm, the block at the LRU location is considered the coldest block. Using the block access count recorded by the FGR component, CDI takes three steps to process each block that reaches the LRU location. Algorithm 1 shows how it works, while Table 1 defines the symbols used in the algorithm.

Table 1. Symbols definition.

Symbol	Definition
C	Cache
Bi	A block in cache
BL	The block in the LRU position in cache
Pi	A data portion in the cache block
APi	The access count of Pi
Ave	The average access count of all Pi in cache
λ	The threshold to measure cold data portions
FPtr	The starting address used to store new data
FP(Bi)	Find the size of multiple consecutive and invalid portions in Bi

As a first step, CDI will reduce the number of accesses to all portions of the block. The reduced value is equal to the average access count for all portions of the cache. This is because when a block reaches the LRU position, the entire block is likely to be deleted in the traditional algorithm. Therefore, when the block reaches the LRU position, CDI first reduces the access count of all portions of the block by the same value to reduce its popularity.

In the second step, CDI checks the access count of each portion and identify cold data portions in the block. For each portion, if the access count is less than the preset cold threshold, CDI will directly identify the portion as a cold data portion and set the access count to zero; otherwise, if the access count is not less than the preset cold threshold, CDI will not change its access count.

In the third step, CDI moves the block based on the cold data recognition results. There are two cases. First, if all data portions are identified as cold data portions, or if the access count of all data portions are zero, the block are identified as cold block and CDI will move the block to the candidate free list. Otherwise, for the second case, if the access count of some data portions is larger than the preset cold threshold, the entire block will be moved to the MRU position and have a chance to remain in the cache.

Algorithm 1: The pseudocode of CDI

Input: A list of cache block in C.
Initialization: Set $B_i = B_L$;
foreach P_i *in* B_i **do**
  $A_{Pi} = A_{Pi}$ - Ave;
  if $A_{Pi} \leq \lambda$ **then**
    $A_{Pi} = 0$;
    P_i will be marked as a cold data portion;

if *Each A_{Pi} in B_i is 0* **then**
  B_i will be marked as a cold block;
  Remove B_i to the candidate free list;
else
  Move B_i to the MRU position;

Multi-Grained Removal. Multi-Grained Removal (MGR) is responsible for removing cold data with multiple granularity through CDI. MGR works when new data is written to the cache but there is no free space in the cache. MGR focuses on removing cold data located at the LRU position. For each block at the LRU position, if the CDI identifies a portion of the block as a cold portion, MGR will invalidate the data portion. When the size of the invalid portion in the block or the cumulative size of multiple consecutive portions is not less than the size of the newly written data, or when all portions of the entire block are invalidated and the cumulative size of multiple cold blocks in the candidate free list is not less than the size of the newly written data, MGR will remove these related cold portions or cold blocks to make room for the new data. Otherwise, the MGR will continue to check the block at the LRU position until enough space is found to store new data written to the cache. Algorithm 2 shows how it works.

Algorithm 2: The pseudocode of MGR

Input: The size of cache space for writing new data.
Output: FPtr
Initialization: Set $B_i = B_L$, FPtr=NULL;
while *FPtr is NULL* **do**
    foreach P_i *in* B_i **do**
        if A_{P_i} *is cold* **then**
            P_i will be marked as a invalid data portion;

    FPtr=FP(Bi);
    if *FPtr is not NULL* **then**
        return FPtr;

    else
        Find next B_i in the LRU position;

---

5 Experimental Evaluation

5.1 Experimental Setup

Prototype Built. We have built an AIR cache prototype in Linux, based on block device virtualization. To evaluate the performance of the AIR cache, we implemented it based on stack algorithm LRU and non-stack algorithm ARC, called AIR-LRU and AIR-ARC, respectively. When using the AIR-LRU and AIR-ARC algorithms, the MGE component of the AIR cache determines the LRU and MRU locations based on the traditional LRU and ARC algorithms. In addition to the AIR cache, we also built another conventional cache prototype that manages and operates cache data with a fixed-size cache block granularity and integrates traditional LRU and ARC algorithms as baseline methods.

Experimental Workload. We have replayed the public FIU [9] traces to evaluate the performance of the AIR cache. These traces were collected from a VM hosting the departmental websites for webmail and online course management (WebVM), a file server used by a research group (Homes), and a departmental mail server (Mail). Table 2 shows the statistical characteristics of these traces. In our experiments, we set the cache size to 20% to 80% of the working set size. In addition, since the I/O request size in the FIU trace is only 4 KB, we merge I/O requests with consecutive source addresses to generate larger I/O requests for larger cache blocks.

Table 2. Statistical characteristics of the datasets.

Name	Total I/Os(GB)	Working Set(GB)	Write-to-read ratio	Unique Data(GB)
WebVM	54.5	2.1	3.6	23.4
Homes	67.3	5.9	31.5	44.4
Mail	1741	57.1	8.1	171.3

Performance Metrics. We compared the AIR cache with the baseline method on two performance metrics: hit ratio and cache space utilization rate.

Cache hit ratio is a key indicator of cache performance for cache management methods. A cache with a higher cache hit ratio means faster access to more data to reduce data access latency. In addition, since the size of each I/O request is variable in our experiments, the hit ratio here is defined as the amount of hit data divided by the amount of requested data, not the number of hits in the cache divided by the total I/O requests. We compared the read hit ratio, write hit ratio, and the total hit ratio of both the AIR cache and baseline methods.

Cache space utilization rate is defined as the amount of data stored in the cache divided by the total size of the cache. Generally, if all cache blocks are fully used, the cache space utilization rate is 1. Cache space utilization rate is less than 1 when some fragmented blocks exist. Therefore, the cache space utilization rate is an indicator of the severity of fragmentation within the cache block.

5.2   Performance Results

In this section, we will compare the performance results of AIR cache using AIR-LRU and AIR-ARC algorithms and the baseline methods using traditional LRU and ARC algorithms in terms of cache hit ratio and cache space utilization rate. For the AIR cache, we show the experimental results when the maximum size of used cache blocks is 8 KB, 16 KB, and 32 KB respectively. For the baseline method, because it uses a fixed-size block granularity to manage cached data instead of using multiple-sized cache blocks, we show the experimental results when the block sizes are 8 KB, 16 KB, and 32 KB respectively. Therefore, a performance comparison between the AIR cache and the baseline method is performed only when the maximum block size of the AIR cache is equal to the block size used by the conventional cache. In addition, in the AIR cache, the FGR component divides each block into 4 KB sized data parts (because the minimal size of the I/O request size 4 KB in FIU trace), and the preset threshold is set to the average number of accesses to all data parts in the cache.

Read Hit Ratios. Figure 7 compares the read hit ratios of AIR-ARC and ARC, AIR-LRU and LRU with WebVM, Mail and Homes traces, when the block size is from 8 KB to 32 KB and the cache size is set to 20% to 80% of the working set size. It can be seen from the results that for all cache settings and all three datasets, the read hit ratios of AIR-ARC and AIR-LRU are higher than ARC and LRU, respectively. Especially for WebVM, AIR-ARC and AIR-LRU have much higher read hit ratios than ARC and LRU, respectively. For example, when the blocks size is 8 KB (here the 8KB block size is the maximum cache block size used by AIR cache and the fixed block size used by the baseline method) and the cache size is 30%, the read hit ratios of AIR-ARC and AIR-LRU are 2.46X and 1.54X higher than the read hit ratios of ARC and LRU respectively. The high read hit ratios of AIR-ARC and AIR-LRU can be contributed to the AIR cache, which can correctly identify and delete cold data, and retain the correct

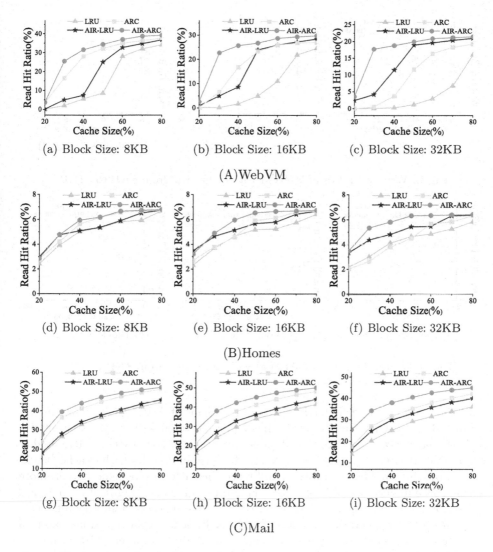

Fig. 7. Read hit ratios of WebVM, Homes and Mail with block sizes from 8 KB to 32 KB.

hot data in the cache to improve the hit ratio. In addition, by analyzing the experimental results, the AIR cache has two other characteristics in improving the read hit ratios.

First, as the cache size increases, the improvement in the AIR cache's read hit ratios becomes more pronounced compared to the baseline method. Taking the results of the WebVM dataset as an example, when the cache size is set to 20% of the working set size and the block size is 16KB, compared with LRU and ARC, the read hit ratios of AIR-LRU and AIR-ARC have increased by 1.22X and 1.65X respectively. When the cache size has increased to 30% of the working set

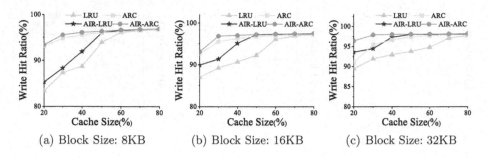

Fig. 8. Write hit ratios of WebVM with block sizes from 8 KB to 32 KB.

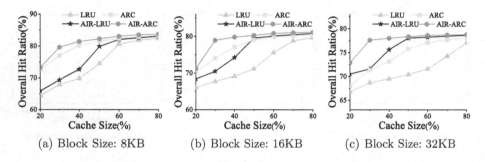

Fig. 9. Overall hit ratios of WebVM with block sizes from 8 KB to 32 KB.

and the block size is still 16 KB, the read hit ratios of AIR-ARC is 3.34X higher than ARC, and when the cache size has increased to 50% of the working set size and the block size is still 16 KB, the read hit ratios of AIR-LRU is 5.04X higher than that of LRU. This is because, for the baseline method, the cache blocks have worse internal fragmentation, and when the cache size becomes larger, more cache space in the cache block is left blank due to internal fragmentation issues. Therefore, as the cache size increases, the baseline method cannot significantly improve the read hit ratio. However, for the AIR cache, it has much less internal fragmentation. Therefore, when the cache size becomes larger, AIR cache can better explore the increased cache space and store cache data more efficiently, thereby significantly improving the read hit ratios and cache performance.

Second, when the cache size is fixed, as the block size increases (the largest block size used by the AIR cache and the fixed block size used by the baseline method), the advantage of the AIR cache in terms of read hit ratio becomes more apparent. Taking WebVM as an example, when the cache size is set to 60% of the working set size and the block size is 16 KB, compared with LRU and ARC, the read hit ratios of AIR-ARC and AIR-LRU have increased by 2.43X and 1.12X respectively. When the block size increases to 32 KB and the cache size is still 60% of the working set size, compared with LRU and ARC, the read hit ratios of AIR-ARC and AIR-LRU have increased by 6.97X and 1.27X respectively. This significant improvement is because AIR cache makes full use of the cache space by identifying and deleting the right cold data and reducing internal fragmentation. Unlike the AIR cache, the baseline method manages the cache data with a fixed-sized block granularity, and a mismatch between the size of the I/O request and the size of the cache block can cause serious internal fragmentation issues and failure to identify the cold data. In addition, the larger the cache block, the larger the size mismatch between the cache block and the data request, so it is more difficult for the baseline method to explore the cache space and effectively manage the cache data. Therefore, compared with the baseline method, as the block size increases, AIR cache can better improve the read hit ratios.

Write Hit Ratios and Overall Hit Ratios. Figure 8 and Fig. 9 show the write hit ratios and overall hit ratios of the WebVM dataset using the AIR-ARC, AIR-LRU, ARC and LRU algorithms. Due to the high similarity, the results of Mail and Homes traces are not shown here. As can be seen from the Fig. 8, these results show three characteristics. First, the write hit ratios of the AIR-ARC and AIR-LRU algorithms are only slightly higher than that of the ARC and LRU algorithms. Second, the write hit ratios produced by all replacing algorithms are high. Third, when the cache size is increased to 30% or 40%, the write hit ratios will reach 90%, and it will not increase as the cache size continues to increase. These results come from two reasons. First, most write requests from WebVM access large amounts of data. When the baseline method is used, almost all sized blocks have no internal fragmentation, and since the size of each write request is large and not smaller than the size of the cache block, the hot/cold data identification can be correct. Therefore, compared to the baseline methods, the AIR cache has a limited effect on improving the write hit ratio. Second, most write requests from WebVM have a strong access locality. Therefore, when the cache size is 30% or 40%, all cache replacement algorithms can produce a high write hit ratio.

In Fig. 9, compared to LRU and ARC, the overall hit ratios of AIR-ARC and AIR-LRU increase in the same trend as the increase of read hit ratios. The only difference is that the improvement in overall hit ratio is not significant compared to the increase in read hit ratio, which can be attributed to two important reasons. First, in our experimental dataset, write requests are very dense, and all cache replacement algorithms can handle them well, so the AIR cache's improvement in write hit ratio is very limited. Second, the proportion of write requests is much higher than the proportion of read requests(see Table 2), so the contribution of the read hit ratio to the overall hit ratio is much smaller than the write hit ratio. Therefore, the AIR cache does not improve the overall hit ratio as significantly as the read hit ratio.

Cache Space Utilization Rate. Figure 10 shows the cache space utilization rate of AIR-ARC and ARC, AIR-LRU and LRU with WebVM, Homes and Mail traces. Cache space utilization rate measures the internal fragmentation of blocks stored in the cache. It can be seen from the results that the cache space

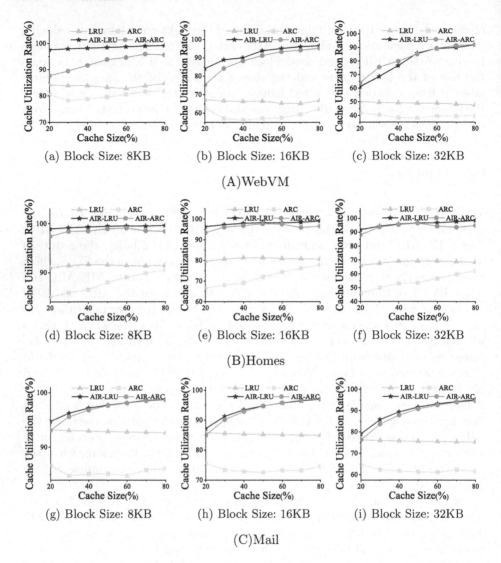

Fig. 10. Cache space utilization rate of WebVM, Homes and Mail with block sizes from 8 KB to 32 KB.

utilization rate of AIR-ARC and AIR-LRU is higher than that of LRU and ARC in all cases. On average, AIR-LRU and AIR-ARC outperform LRU and ARC by 1.18X and 1.15X for 8 KB blocks, 1.39X and 1.51X for 16 KB blocks, 1.65X and 2.09X for 32KB blocks, respectively. These results clearly show that AIR cache generates much less fragmentation than the baseline methods because the data is written to AIR cache at different granularity. In addition, the results of cache utilization have two other characteristics. First, regardless of the AIR cache or baseline method, the performance of ARC related algorithms is usually worse than that of LRU related algorithms. As can be seen from the Fig. 10, the cache space utilization rate of AIR-ARC and ARC is lower than that of AIR-LRU and LRU respectively. This is because in ARC, there are two lists, T1 and T2, and the T2 list is used to capture data with high temporal locality have retained many fragmented blocks, so the cache space utilization rate is lower. In addition, we compared the cache space utilization rate of the blocks stored in the T1 list and the T2 list in Fig. 11. As shown in Fig. 11, regardless of the block size and cache size, the cache space utilization rate of the blocks in the T2 list is always lower than the blocks in the T1 list.

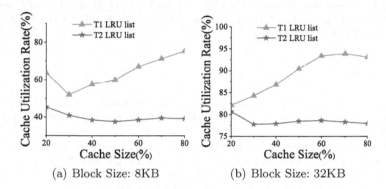

(a) Block Size: 8KB   (b) Block Size: 32KB

Fig. 11. Cache space utilization rate of the blocks in T1 list and the blocks in T2 list for WebVM.

Second, although the cache space utilization rate of AIR-ARC and ARC is lower than that of AIR-LRU and LRU respectively, the hit ratios of AIR-ARC and ARC are higher than that of AIR-LRU and LRU respectively. This is because, for these traces, there are a large amount of I/O scan requests, especially scan read requests. Therefore, non-stacked ARC related algorithms that excel at processing scan I/O request can produce higher hit ratios than LRU related algorithms.

6 Conclusion

Existing server-side storage caching methods process all cached data by a fixed-size block granularity. As a result, operating any part of the cache block is treated as touching the entire cache block. This behavior results in a large amount of cache blocks with internal fragmentation and incorrectly identifies hot/cold cache blocks, especially when the cache block becomes large. Therefore, in this work, we proposed AIR cache, which is a variable-size block cache based on fine-grained management method. It consists of three components, Fine-Grained Recorder (FGR), Multi-Granularity Writer (MGW) and Multi-Granularity Eviction (MGE). FGR is dedicated to recording data popularity using fine-grained data parts. MGW is responsible for writing multi-granularity data to eliminate internal fragmentation in large blocks. MGE is used to accurately identify and evict cold cache data. Our extensive experimental results show that the AIR cache is very effective in improving the cache hit ratio and cache space utilization rate. Compared to the existing fixed-size block management methods driven by real-world datasets, the AIR cache can increase the read cache hit ratio by up to 6.97X and the cache space utilization rate by up to 3.63X.

Acknowledgements. This work was supported by grants from Natural Science Foundation of China No. 62072059, Open Project Program of Wuhan National Laboratory for Optoelectronics No. 2019WNLOKF009, Natural Science Foundation of Chongqing No. cstc2020jcyj-msxmX0897, the Fundamental Research Funds for the Central Universities No. 2020CDJLHZZ-050.

References

1. Byan, S., et al.: Mercury: host-side flash caching for the data center. In: 2012 IEEE 28th Symposium on Mass Storage Systems and Technologies (MSST), pp. 1–12. IEEE (2012)
2. Cao, P., Irani, S.: Cost-aware www proxy caching algorithms. In: Usenix Symposium on Internet Technologies and Systems, vol. 12, pp. 193–206 (1997)
3. Holland, D.A., Angelino, E., Wald, G., Seltzer, M.I.: Flash caching on the storage client. In: Proceedings of the 2013 USENIX Conference on Annual Technical Conference (2013)
4. Huang, S., Wei, Q., Dan, F., Chen, J., Cheng, C.: Improving flash-based disk cache with lazy adaptive replacement. ACM Trans. Storage **12**(2), 1–24 (2016)
5. Jaleel, A., Theobald, K.B., Steely Jr., S.C., Emer, J.: High performance cache replacement using re-reference interval prediction (RRIP). In: ACM SIGARCH Computer Architecture News, vol. 38, pp. 60–71. ACM (2010)
6. Jiang, S., Zhang, X.: LIRS: an efficient low inter-reference recency set replacement policy to improve buffer cache performance. ACM SIGMETRICS Perform. Eval. Rev. **30**(1), 31–42 (2002)
7. Johnson, T., Shasha, D., et al.: 2Q: a low overhead high performance buffer management replacement algorithm. In: Proceedings of the 20th International Conference on Very Large Data Bases, pp. 439–450 (1994)
8. Kang, D., et al.: 256 Gb 3 b/cell V-NAND flash memory with 48 stacked WL layers. IEEE J. Solid-State Circuits **52**(1), 210–217 (2016)
9. Koller, R., Rangaswami, R.: I/o deduplication: utilizing content similarity to improve i/o performance. In: 8th USENIX Conference on File and Storage Technologies, San Jose, CA, USA, 23–26 February 2010 (2010)
10. Lee, S., et al.: 7.5 A 128Gb 2b/cell NAND flash memory in 14nm technology with tPROG= 640μs and 800MB/s I/O rate. In: 2016 IEEE International Solid-State Circuits Conference (ISSCC), pp. 138–139. IEEE (2016)
11. Li, C.: DLIRS: improving low inter-reference recency set cache replacement policy with dynamics. In: Proceedings of the 11th ACM International Systems and Storage Conference, pp. 59–64. ACM (2018)
12. Li, W., Jean-Baptise, G., Riveros, J., Narasimhan, G., Zhang, T., Zhao, M.: CacheDedup: in-line deduplication for flash caching. In: 14th {USENIX} Conference on File and Storage Technologies ({FAST} 2016), pp. 301–314 (2016)

13. Luo, T., Ma, S., Lee, R., Zhang, X., Liu, D., Zhou, L.: S-CAVE: effective SSD caching to improve virtual machine storage performance. In: Proceedings of the 22nd International Conference on Parallel Architectures and Compilation Techniques, pp. 103–112. IEEE (2013)
14. Megiddo, N., Modha, D.S.: ARC: a self-tuning, low overhead replacement cache. In: FAST, vol. 3, pp. 115–130 (2003)
15. Meng, F., Zhou, L., Ma, X., Uttamchandani, S., Liu, D.: vCacheShare: automated server flash cache space management in a virtualization environment. In: 2014 {USENIX} Annual Technical Conference ({USENIX}{ATC} 2014), pp. 133–144 (2014)
16. Saxena, M., Swift, M.M., Zhang, Y.: Flashtier: a lightweight, consistent and durable storage cache. In: Proceedings of the 7th ACM European Conference on Computer Systems, pp. 267–280. ACM (2012)
17. Smaragdakis, Y., Kaplan, S., Wilson, P.: EELRU: simple and effective adaptive page replacement. In: SIGMETRICS, vol. 99, pp. 1–4. CiteSeer (1999)
18. Song, J., Zhang, X.: LIRS: an efficient low inter-reference recency set replacement policy to improve buffer cache performance. ACM SIGMETRICS Perform. Eval. Rev. **30**(1), 31–42 (2002)
19. Wang, T., Wang, Y., Wang, X., Cao, Y.: A detailed review of D2D cache in helper selection. World Wide Web **23**(4), 2407–2428 (2020). https://doi.org/10.1007/s11280-019-00756-z
20. Yan, T., Chen, W., Zhao, P., Li, Z., Liu, A., Zhao, L.: Handling conditional queries and data storage on hyperledger fabric efficiently. World Wide Web **24**(1), 441–461 (2021). https://doi.org/10.1007/s11280-020-00844-5
21. Yang, Q., Ren, J.: I-cash: intelligently coupled array of SSD and HDD. In: 2011 IEEE 17th International Symposium on High Performance Computer Architecture, pp. 278–289. IEEE (2011)
22. Ye, F., Li, Q., Chen, E.: Benefit based cache data placement and update for mobile peer to peer networks. World Wide Web **14**(3), 243–259 (2011). https://doi.org/10.1007/s11280-010-0103-3
23. Zhou, Y., Philbin, J., Li, K.: The multi-queue replacement algorithm for second level buffer caches. In: USENIX Annual Technical Conference, General Track, pp. 91–104 (2001)

Learning an Index Advisor with Deep Reinforcement Learning

Sichao Lai[1], Xiaoying Wu[1], Senyang Wang[1], Yuwei Peng[1], and Zhiyong Peng[1,2(✉)]

[1] School of Computer Science, Wuhan University, Wuhan, China
{sichaolai,xiaoying.wu,whuwsy,ywpeng,peng}@whu.edu.cn
[2] Big Data Institute of Wuhan University, Wuhan University, Wuhan, China

Abstract. Indexes are crucial for the efficient processing of database workloads and an appropriately selected set of indexes can drastically improve query processing performance. However, the selection of beneficial indexes is a non-trivial problem and still challenging. Recent work in deep reinforcement learning (DRL) may bring a new perspective on this problem. In this paper, we studied the index selection problem in the context of reinforcement learning and proposed an end-to-end DRL-based index selection framework. The framework poses the index selection problem as a series of 1-step single index recommendation tasks and can learn from data. Unlike most existing DRL-based index selection solutions that focus on selecting single-column indexes, our framework can recommend both single-column and multi-column indexes for the database. A set of comparative experiments with existing solutions was conducted to demonstrate the effectiveness of our proposed method.

Keywords: Index selection · Deep reinforcement learning · Performance tuning

1 Introduction

Database indexes are additional data structures that can provide fast access to the desired data and are one of the most important aspects of database physical design. Although indexes may be beneficial, they also consume storage space, and need to be maintained, i.e., having more indexes is not always a better choice. Thus, it is important to choose an appropriate index configuration (i.e. a set of indexes) for the database to ensure an overall performance improvement. And the term Index Selection Problem (ISP, also be referred to as index tuning or index recommendation) is defined to address this problem and still one of the most important problems in the field of database physical design and database performance tuning.

ISP is challenging for many reasons: Firstly, ISP can be considered an optimization problem and has already been proven to be NP-Hard and even hard to approximate [1]. In ISP, the number of possible index configurations grows exponentially along with the size of the database schema (for example, the number of database tables and columns), and it's also expensive and impractical to choose an optimal index configuration by evaluating all configuration candidates. Secondly, there are possible interactions between

© Springer Nature Switzerland AG 2021
L. H. U et al. (Eds.): APWeb-WAIM 2021, LNCS 12859, pp. 178–185, 2021.
https://doi.org/10.1007/978-3-030-85899-5_13

indexes, both positively and negatively [2]. For example, several indexes can be used together via index intersection to answer a single query, while a single query can also be answered using different individual indexes. Thirdly, most ISP solutions are dependent on the optimizer's cost estimation, but the optimizer of modern DBMS is complex, and inaccurate cost estimation (may come from the errors of cardinality estimation and cost model [3]) may cause performance regressions [4], i.e. the real performance of the DBMS may degrade despite an expected improvement by the optimizer.

The importance and challenges of the ISP have interested researchers for continuous exploration, yet existing methods all have their limitations. Most traditional automated ISP solutions (e.g. AutoAdmin [5], DB2Advis [6], Relaxation [7]) use heuristics to reduce configuration search space and guide the searching process of the optimal index configuration. However, these methods often miss good configurations, since they rely on manually-designed heuristics which are fixed and unable to learn from past experiences. Recent work in deep reinforcement learning may bring a new perspective on this problem since data-driven DRL solutions can learn a flexible strategy tailored to data and workloads. Many researchers [8–10] have proposed their DRL-based solutions for index recommendation, but most of them only considered single-column indexes. However, multi-column indexes like covering indexes can make index-only accesses possible and greatly reduce the time to fetch desirable data without table lookups. Hence it is important to support the selection of multi-column indexes when designing and training an agent for index selection. Although Hai Lan et al. [10] addressed the recommendation of multi-column indexes, that paper lacks details of agent modeling and training, which makes it hard to follow up.

In this paper, we study the ISP in the context of reinforcement learning and develop an end-to-end DRL-based framework to recommend indexes. The main contributions of this paper can be summarized as follows:

(1) We formulate the ISP as a Markov Decision Process and proposed an end-to-end DRL solution, where both single-column indexes and multi-column indexes are considered.
(2) We design workload-dependent state representations for indexes and a reward formulation that considers the possible interactions among indexes.
(3) We conducted comparative experiments with several index selection solutions to demonstrate the effectiveness of our proposed solution.

2 Problem Formalization

The traditional index selection problem is about finding a set of indexes for a given workload that has the maximum benefit for the workload while considering certain constraints, like the storage constraint or the tuning time constraint. Before we give a formal definition of the index selection problem, we introduce terminologies used in this paper. A database D contains a set of relations (tables) $\{T_1, T_2, \ldots, T_d\}$, each of which contains a set of attributes (columns) $\{c_1, c_2, \ldots, c_m\}$, and a workload W is a set of SQL statements $\{q_1, q_2, \ldots, q_n\}$. A set of indexes $\{i_1, i_2, \ldots, i_k\}$ is termed as an index configuration I for the database, which may contain different single-column or multi-column indexes from different tables. A set of certain constraints of ISP are denoted as

$\{b_1, b_2, \ldots, b_j\}$ and the benefit of a configuration over a query (workload) $G_I(W)$ is defined as the reduced execution time of a query (workload) under that configuration. We now give a formal definition of the index selection problem as follows:

Definition 1. *(Index Selection Problem, ISP). Given a database $D = \{T_1, T_2, \ldots, T_d\}$ and a workload $W = \{q_1, q_2, \ldots, q_n\}$. The aim is to find an index configuration $I^* = \{i_1, i_2, \ldots, i_k\}$ such that $I^* = \arg\max_I G_I(W)$ while satisfying all constraints $B = \{b_1, b_2, \ldots, b_j\}$.*

3   Learning Index Selection

3.1   ISP as a DRL Problem

We formulated the ISP as an episodic reinforcement learning task, i.e. broke the agent-environment interaction naturally into subsequences (called episodes) [11]. In each round of interaction between the agent (index tuner) and the environment (DBMS), the agent will take one action (recommend one index) according to current state and policy, and the environment (DBMS) will assign a reward to the agent as an evaluation of that action. When reaching the terminal state of an episode (e.g., getting an index configuration), an episode ends, then the environment is reset (drop all recommended indexes, and reset the state) and a new episode begins. This training process continues until the stop criterion is met, e.g., the policy (a mapping from states to probabilities of selecting each possible action [10], which tells the agent to select an index) stabilizes, and the expected return converges. Once the training is done, the recommending of index configurations for a new workload can be computed leveraging the policy. This process is end-to-end and can be "in-sync" with the optimizer (since an index is only beneficial when the optimizer uses it to answer queries), which can improve the efficiency and maintainability of the solution.

3.2   Index Agent for Indexes

In our design, the action space of the index selection agent is consistent with the search space of all possible beneficial indexes in the database. Since the state observed by the agent determines the action of the agent, we include two parts of information in our state representation: 1) the current index configuration of the database. The current index configuration indicates the indexes that already existed in the database, since it is meaningless for an agent to recommend existed indexes, and the action to recommend an existed index should be discouraged. 2) the selectivity of indexes. The selectivity, or the filter factor of an index, is a good indicator of possible future benefits since an index with a high filter factor can filter out a large portion of undesirable records in advance and reduce the fetching time of the desired data.

A single-column index can be identified by the only index key, which is chosen among all columns in the database schema. In this situation, an index can be intuitively represented as a one-hot vector, where the 1-valued slot indicates the indexed column (the index). Then an index configuration (denoted as I_{conf}) can be represented as a 0–1 vector by adding all representations of the indexes included in the configuration.

However, a multi-column index contains plural index keys, and the order of the index keys also matters, i.e., each permutation of the index keys represents a distinct index. Therefore, we developed a strategy to build a one-to-one correspondence between possible indexes and the combinatorial numbers (i.e. a combinatorial number system, and there are already many algorithms that can do this [12]). The size of index vectors will be the size of the number system and the rest can be handled similarly as for the case of the single-column indexing scheme. Hence, both single-column indexes and multi-column indexes can be encoded and considered by the index agent.

We design a selectivity matrix is designed to include the information of both the workload and the index keys:

$$Sel_{n*m} = \begin{bmatrix} sel(q_0, c_0) & \cdots & sel(q_0, c_{m-1}) \\ \vdots & \ddots & \vdots \\ sel(q_{n-1}, c_0) & \cdots & sel(q_{n-1}, c_{m-1}) \end{bmatrix} \tag{1}$$

$$Sel_i = \begin{bmatrix} sel(q_i, c_0), & \ldots, sel(q_i, c_{m-1}) \end{bmatrix}_{1*m}, 0 \le i \le n-1 \tag{2}$$

$$sel(q_i, c_j) = \begin{cases} \frac{count(c_j, q_i)}{count(c_j)}, & \textit{if there're predicates on } c_j \textit{ in } q_i, \\ 1, \textit{otherwise.} \end{cases} \tag{3}$$

Where n is the number of queries in the workload, and m is the number of columns in the database, the $count(c_j, q_i)$ is the number of records returned if there are predicates on the column c_j in the query q_i, and the $count(c_j)$ is the total number of records in the table with column c_j, so $sel(q_i, c_j)$ implies the filtering effect of the index key c_j for the query q_i, and Sel_i, Sel_{n*m} describes the selectivity of index keys for query q_i and the whole workload respectively (the selectivity of a multi-column index is implicitly represented in the selectivity of corresponding index keys). Now, the state S can be represented as a concatenation of these two parts: $S = Sel_{n*m} \oplus I_{conf}$.

When the index agent selects an index according to the current state and current policy, the corresponding position of the new index in I_{conf} will be set to 1. Then the agent will be assigned a reward for this index and finish a round of interaction. To handle the huge space of state and action, we use a neural network to represent the policy of the agent, where the input to the neural network is the representation of the state and the output is the representation of the recommended index.

3.3 Reward Design

The use of a reward signal to formalize the idea of a goal is one of the most distinctive features of reinforcement learning, and the success of a reinforcement learning application strongly depends on how well the reward signal accesses progress in reaching the goal [11]. The goal of the ISP is to select a set of indexes to decrease the execution time of the workload to the maximum, so we use the reduction of cost after the deployment of recommended indexes as the reward signal:

$$\mathcal{R}(I_{conf}) = \max\left(\frac{cost(\emptyset)}{cost(I_{conf})} - 1, 0\right) \tag{4}$$

Where $cost(\emptyset)$ means the cost of workload execution when there are no indexes in the database, the $cost(I_{conf})$ means the cost of the workload after the recommended indexes have all been deployed. The maximum function guarantees that the reward is always non-negative in case of some run-time fluctuations.

In our design, the intermediate reward is always 0 and the reward is only computed and assigned when an episode ends. This design is based on the following thinking: there are possible interactions among indexes, and if a positive reward is assigned per episode step, the reward of one step will be correlated with the future steps. Hence, it needs careful reward shaping to avoid biasing the learning, which is rather tricky [13].

3.4 Reinforcement Learning Training

After all elements of reinforcement learning have been modeled, a reinforcement learning algorithm is needed to train the agent, then the agent will learn to recommend indexes. Due to the combinatorial explosion of candidate indexes, the state space is huge. Therefore, traditional tabular reinforcement learning methods become inefficient to maintain a large value table (or action-value table) and fill them accurately [11]. Thus, we use DRL to address this problem, i.e., a neural network is used as an approximation function to deal with the large search space problem. Specifically, we adopted Proximal Policy Optimization (PPO) [14] to train the index selection agent, which is a policy-based off-the-shelf state-of-the-art DRL technique. The main advantage of PPO are (1) it can converge fast and (2) it has reliable performance.

4 Experiments

4.1 Experimental Setup

Implementation. We have implemented our proposed index advisor in Python on an Ubuntu machine with an Intel Xeon 6240 CPU@2.6 GHZ and 768 GB RAM. PostgreSQL is our DBMS of choice and we used the HypoPG[1] extension of PostgreSQL to provide a similar what-if index mechanism [15] of AutoAdmin (i.e. we use cost estimation of the optimizer to compute rewards in the training process, and avoid the overhead of actual query execution and index creation). For reinforcement learning, we design the RL environments on the top of the OpenAI Gym[2] package, use TensorFlow, Ray (RLlib) package[3] to train agents.

---

[1] https://github.com/HypoPG/hypopg.

[2] https://gym.openai.com/.

[3] https://github.com/ray-project/ray.

Experimental Data and Workload Generation. The data of DBMS were generated with a scale factor of 1 following the standard procedure of the TPC-H benchmark. The workload queries were randomly generated following a pattern of SELECT tbl_x.col_y FROM ... WHERE .... In the WHERE clause, predicates can be an equality selection (e.g., l_discount = 0.01) or a range selection (e.g., l_quantity > 46) or a join (l_partkey = p_partkey). The target column (col_y) and the target table (tbl_x) were randomly selected from the tables in the FROM clause. The training and testing workloads are generated both with 20 queries.

Comparative Algorithms. We used the evaluation platform of traditional ISP algorithms developed by Jan Kossmann et al. [16], which includes the implementation of AutoAdmin [5], DB2Advis [6], Relaxation [7] (a top-down index recommendation approaches). We measured the performance improvement of workload runtime (i.e. improvement rate) after the deployment of recommended indexes as used in AutoAdmin [5], since the improvement rate, as a metric, alleviates the influence of hardware on the execution of queries to a degree.

4.2 Reinforcement Learning Training Details

We designed the policy as a multiple-layered neural network. In this neural network, there are 3 hidden layers, each hidden layer is composed of 8 neurons with the RELU activation function, and the activation function of the output layer is SOFTMAX. To evaluate our RL modeling approach, we measured the convergence of RL training using the logged statistics. We set the maximum number of indexes in a configuration to 3 in the following experiments. The agent was trained with RLlib in 500 iterations, which took around 2.8 h.

Figure 1 shows the changes in the episode reward during the training process, where the middle line is the mean value of episode rewards bounded by the maximum and minimum value of episode rewards. We can see that, as the number of time steps increases, the performance of the algorithm improves. The maximum value of the rewards reaches the peak quickly, and the fluctuating minimum value of the reward indicates the continuous exploration behavior of the agent. At around the 300th iteration, the mean value of the episode reward begins to stabilize and converge.

4.3 Performance Comparative Evaluation

In this section, we describe comparative evaluation experiments between selected traditional ISP solutions and our proposed solution (denoted as PPO-MC). For those solutions that take storage consumption as a constraint parameter, we pick their best configuration with comparative storage consumption for comparison.

We tested our solution considering the recommendation of multi-column indexes. As we can see from Fig. 2 and Fig. 3, PPO-MC performs best both in the improvement rate and the algorithm runtime performance. In Fig. 4, although the storage consumption of our solution is not the smallest, however, we argue that we trade reasonable storage consumption for better performance.

184   S. Lai et al.

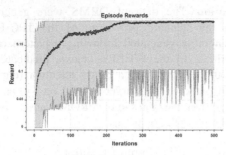

Fig. 1. Episode reward

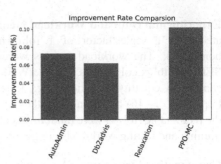

Fig. 2. Improvement rate

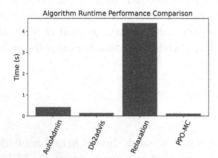

Fig. 3. Algorithm runtime

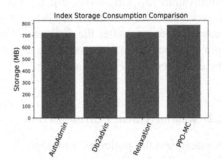

Fig. 4. Storage consumption

5 Conclusions

Index selection is one important aspect of physical database design. In this paper, we proposed an index advisor based on deep reinforcement learning, which is capable of learning to recommend beneficial indexes under various situations. The design of our index advisor proposal takes into account the challenges of ISP. Our solution can recommend both single-column and multi-column and shows very promising results.

To further explore the possibilities of employing DRL to the ISP, the investigation of a more sophisticated design of agent modeling and reward shaping is worthwhile. The exploration of more advanced DRL techniques is also our current and future work.

Acknowledgments. This work is supported by the National Natural Science Foundation of China (No. U1811263) and CCF-Huawei Database System Innovation Research Plan (CCF-HuaweiDBIR003A).

References

1. Chaudhuri, S., Datar, M., Narasayya, V.: Index selection for databases: a hardness study and a principled heuristic solution. IEEE Trans. Knowl. Data Eng. **16**, 1313–1323 (2004). https://doi.org/10.1109/TKDE.2004.75

2. Schnaitter, K., Polyzotis, N., Getoor, L.: Index interactions in physical design tuning: modeling, analysis, and applications. Proc. VLDB Endow. **2**, 1234–124512 (2009)
3. Lan, H., Bao, Z., Peng, Y.: A survey on advancing the DBMS query optimizer: cardinality estimation, cost model, and plan enumeration. Data Sci. Eng. **6**(1), 86–101 (2021). https://doi.org/10.1007/s41019-020-00149-7
4. Ding, B., Das, S., Marcus, R., Wu, W., Chaudhuri, S., Narasayya, V.R.: AI meets AI: leveraging query executions to improve index recommendations. In: Proceedings of the 2019 International Conference on Management of Data - SIGMOD 2019, pp. 1241–1258. ACM Press, Amsterdam (2019). https://doi.org/10.1145/3299869.3324957
5. Chaudhuri, S., Narasayya, V.R.: An efficient cost-driven index selection tool for Microsoft SQL server. In: Proceedings of 23rd International Conference on Very Large Data Bases, VLDB 1997, August 25–29, 1997, Athens, Greece, pp. 146–155 (1997)
6. Valentin, G., Zuliani, M., Zilio, D.C., Lohman, G., Skelley, A.: DB2 advisor: an optimizer smart enough to recommend its own indexes. In: Proceedings of 16th International Conference on Data Engineering (Cat. No. 00CB37073), pp. 101–110. IEEE Computer Society, San Diego, CA, USA (2000). https://doi.org/10.1109/ICDE.2000.839397
7. Bruno, N., Chaudhuri, S.: Automatic physical database tuning: a relaxation-based approach. In: Proceedings of the ACM SIGMOD International Conference on Management of Data, Baltimore, Maryland, USA, June 14–16, 2005, pp. 227–238 (2005). https://doi.org/10.1145/1066157.1066184
8. Sharma, A., Schuhknecht, F.M., Dittrich, J.: The case for automatic database administration using deep reinforcement learning. arXiv:1801.05643 [cs] (2018)
9. Paludo Licks, G., Colleoni Couto, J., de Fátima Miehe, P., de Paris, R., Dubugras Ruiz, D., Meneguzzi, F.: SmartIX: a database indexing agent based on reinforcement learning. Appl. Intell. **50**(8), 2575–2588 (2020). https://doi.org/10.1007/s10489-020-01674-8
10. Lan, H., Bao, Z., Peng, Y.: An index advisor using deep reinforcement learning. In: Proceedings of the 29th ACM International Conference on Information & Knowledge Management, pp. 2105–2108. Association for Computing Machinery, New York (2020). https://doi.org/10.1145/3340531.3412106
11. Sutton, R.S., Barto, A.G.: Reinforcement Learning: An Introduction, 2nd edn. MIT Press, Cambridge (2018)
12. Knuth, D.E.: Generating all combinations and partitions, vol. 4, fascicle 3 of the art of computer programming (2005)
13. Irpan, A.: Deep reinforcement learning doesn't work yet (2018). https://www.alexirpan.com/2018/02/14/rl-hard.html
14. Schulman, J., Wolski, F., Dhariwal, P., Radford, A., Klimov, O.: Proximal policy optimization algorithms. arXiv:1707.06347 [cs] (2017)
15. Chaudhuri, S., Narasayya, V.: AutoAdmin "What-if" index analysis utility. In: Proceedings of the 1998 ACM SIGMOD International Conference on Management of Data, pp. 367–378. ACM, New York (1998). https://doi.org/10.1145/276304.276337
16. Kossmann, J., Halfpap, S., Jankrift, M., Schlosser, R.: Magic mirror in my hand, which is the best in the land? An experimental evaluation of index selection algorithms, vol. 14 (2020)

SardineDB: A Distributed Database on the Edge of the Network

Min Dong[1,2(✉)], Haozhao Zhong[1], Boyu Sun[1], Sheng Bi[1,2], and Yi Cai[2,3]

[1] School of Computer Science and Engineering, South China University
of Technology, Guangzhou 510006, Guangdong, China
{hollymin,picy}@scut.edu.cn
[2] Key Laboratory of Big Data and Intelligent Robot, Ministry of Education,
Guangzhou 510006, Guangdong, China
ycai@scut.edu.cn
[3] School of Software Engineering, South China University of Technology,
Guangzhou 510006, Guangdong, China

Abstract. In the past few years, the number of sensors is rapidly increasing on the edge of the network. IoT(Internet of things) devices play not only data producers but also data consumers. It is valuable to deploy a distributed database on the edge of the network. However, flash memory is the mainstream storage medium on the edge, which is different from cloud environment. Flash memory can wear out through repeated writes while large amount of data are written on the edge per day. Thus, in this paper, SardineDB is presented, which is a decentralized distributed database optimized for edge. The engine of SardineDB is SardineCore, which is a flash-optimized key-value separation storage based on LevelDB. SardineCore has low GC (garbage collection) burden, which can be used to low the write amplification and improve the write performance on the edge. From evaluation results, the write performance and random read performance of SardineDB have great advantages compared with existing distributed databases on the edge. As a result, SardineDB is very suitable for edge because it has high write performance, low GC burden and low write amplification.

Keywords: IOT · Edge computing · LevelDB · Distributed database · Sensor · Flash memory

1 Introduction

Nowadays, IoT devices play a role of not only data producer, but also data consumer. Some ways for data processing on the edge are presented such as fog computing [5] and edge computing [10]. They both move data processing tasks to the edge of the network, in which data are stored and processed on the edge. In order to store and manage data on the edge, a new way for storage has emerged: edge storage [9]. Edge storage is a new type of distributed storage for big data on the edge of the network [6]. Compared to the cloud storage, edge storage

© Springer Nature Switzerland AG 2021
L. H. U et al. (Eds.): APWeb-WAIM 2021, LNCS 12859, pp. 186–193, 2021.
https://doi.org/10.1007/978-3-030-85899-5_14

reduces data transmission distance during the process of production, processing and consumption. The network traffic produced on the edge will be reduced drastically by edge storage which means network transmission delay and network fluctuation will be reduced. Hence, the performance of applications on the edge will be improved by edge storage. Edge storage is different from cloud storage in terms of storage mediums, hardware performance and application scenarios. These differences bring new challenges to existing data storage technologies.

There are already some databases designed for edge storage. The most popular open-source product for edge storage is RedisEdge. RedisEdge is a purpose-built, multi-model database for the demanding conditions at the edge. Based on Redis, RedisEdge provides many modules including streams, time series and AI. In industry, Microsoft provides Azure SQL Database Edge [11], which is a relational database system(RDBMS) optimized for IoT devices on the edge. Almost all current databases can be split into three types according to their data management choices on the edge: Redis-based database, B-tree-based database and LSM-tree-based (Log-structured merge tree-based) [8] database.

However, Redis is closer to an in-memory database (IMDB), as the number of items grows, the memory allocation of Redis is big while the size of the device's memory is always small on the edge. Moreover, persistence of Redis relies on Redis-RDB, which is not steady as there is a delay before data persistence. B-tree and LSM-tree are designed for external storage and commonly used in classic hard-disk drivers (HDD). But the storage medium is usually flash memory [3] on the edge. B-tree and LSM-tree lead to big write amplification which can wear out the flash memory quickly. Therefore, in this paper we design SardineDB, a new distributed database for data on the edge of the network. SardineDB is optimized for the storage medium of edge storage and it also has high performance when processing data on the edge. Moreover, SardineDB is generic and easily extensible, which can be deployed in most applications on the edge.

As a database on the edge of network, SardineDB has these main features:

- **Flash optimized**: SardineDB is designed for flash memory such as NAND. Thus, SardineDB has a low write amplification to decrease the life deterioration of the flash memory. Moreover, SardineDB is optimized to take full advantage of the flash memory.
- **Data synchronization**: SardineDB is a decentralized distributed database, data synchronization can happen between any two nodes in the cluster of SardineDB so that all ways for data processing can work well upon SardineDB.
- **IoT optimized**: For data on the edge, simple key-value database is not enough. Most data on the edge is IoT data which belongs to time series data. Therefore, SardineDB can work as a time series database to manage IoT data better. Moreover, in order to adapt to existing applications on the edge, SardineDB is universality and flexible, providing many different ways to manage data.
- **High performance**: Performance is most important for a database. As the frequency of writes is much higher than the frequency of reads on the edge of the network, SardineDB is designed as a high write performance database

and its read performance also meets the requirement of applications on the edge.

The rest of this paper is organized as follows. Section 2 explains architecture of SardineDB. Then, the performance evaluation of SardineDB is shown in Sect. 3. At last, we conclude the work in Sect. 4.

2   Architecture of SardineDB

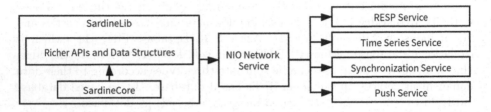

Fig. 1. The architecture of SardineDB

2.1   Architecture of SardineDB

The architecture of a node of SardineDB is shown in Fig. 1. It can be seen that a node of SardineDB is composed of these parts:

- **SardineCore**: SardineCore is the engine of SardineDB. It is developed based on LevelDB. Compared to LevelDB, SardineCore reduces write amplification by key-value separation so that it is more suitable to use in flash memory.
- **SardineLib**: Based on SardineCore, SardineLib is a programming library which has richer APIs and various data structures such as hash map, sorted set and queue.
- **NIO Network Service**: NIO Network Service is an independent TCP network service based on NIO. It provides network interfaces by calling APIs in SardineLib. All upper layer services are implemented based on NIO Network Service.
- **RESP Service**: Based on NIO Network Service, we implement RESP [2] protocol which is the protocol for redis client. Therefore, SardineDB can be visited easily by redis clients and some convenient redis tools can be used in SardineDB directly.
- **Time Series Service**: Time Series Service provides time series APIs so that users can manage data in SardineDB by time series.
- **Synchronization Service**: Synchronization Service is used for synchronous replication between nodes of SardineDB. Master-slave synchronization and multi-master synchronization are supported by this service.
- **Push Service**: Push Service is an active pushing service developed based on NIO Network Service. It is necessary for a database on the edge of the network because there are many messages which should be pushed to the cloud actively in the scenario of IoT applications.

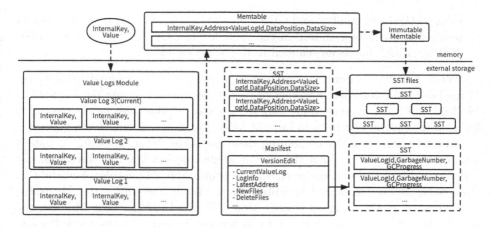

Fig. 2. The architecture of SardineCore

2.2 Architecture of SardineCore

To improve the lifetime of flash memory, SardineCore adopts a key-value separation architecture. The design of SardineCore is shown in Fig. 2. SardineCore is composed of these modules: Memtable, Immutable Memtable, Sorted String Table(SST) files, Manifest files and the Current file, which is similar to LevelDB. However, Log file of LevelDB is replaced by Value Logs Module in SardineCore. The obviously differences between SardineCore and LevelDB are shown as follow:

- **Log file is replaced by Value Logs Module**: Value Logs Module is a module composed of many value logs. Values of SardineCore are saved in value logs with their keys. Every value log file is ordered by its unique ValueLogId in Value Logs Module. In addition, similar to the log file, when the log function is used, the value log file in the Value Logs module is also a write-ahead log (WAL). All data written to SardineCore will be written to the value log file in the form of key-value pairs before being written to Memtable.
- **Data in Memtable, Immutable Memtable and SST files are key-address pairs**: After an item is written to Value Logs Module, the address of the item in Value Logs Module will be sent to Memtable with its key. Key-address pairs will be sorted in Memtable. Once the size of the Memtable reaches the threshold, the Memtable will be transferred to the Immutable Memtable. Then, the Immutable Memtable will be transferred to a SST files which is saved in external storage.
- **Content of Manifest file is different between SardineCore and LevelDB**: Compared to LevelDB, the VersionEdit of SardineCore saves three additional parameters: The first parameter is CurrentValueLog, which is used to identify current value log file. The second parameter is LatestAddress, which shows the address of latest item in external storage. The last parameter is LogInfo, which is a table and is used to control Garbage Collection(GC). For each item of LogInfo, the key is ValueLogId, the value is composed of two

integer: GarbageNumber and GCProgress. GarbageNumber is the number of items which can be removed in the value log file. GCProgress is the number of items which has been scanned in the value log file.

When writing an item, key-value pair is written to the current value log in Value Logs Module. Then, SardineCore gets three messages from the Value Logs Module: the id of current value log, the position of the item in current value log and the size of the item in current value log. Next, SardineCore generates an address of the item by combining these messages. Next, key-address pair is written to Memtable. When the size of Memtable reaches the threshold, the full Memtable will be transferred to the Immutable Memtable. Any data in Immutable Memtable cannot be edited again. Finally, the Immutable Memtable will be saved in the external storage as a SST file. In Value Logs Module, the maximum size of a value log is fixed which is configured by users. Once the size of current value log reaches the maximum size, it will be replaced by a new value log. The old value log will not be deleted until the GC condition is met. There are many advantages of SardineCore's GC on the edge of the network:

- GC is triggered by the number of removed items. SardineCore does not scan the whole database, which lows the impact of GC, the probability of performance fluctuation is reduced. The performance overhead of GC can be ignored in SardineCore.
- The progress of GC is maintained by VersionEdit and Manifest files, which will not effect LSM-tree. The unnecessary write amplification is avoided.
- In most realistic scenarios on the edge, data which should be removed is often centralized in a part of records, GC of SardineCore is very effective in this scenario as only one or several value logs are impacted by GC.

3 Experiments

3.1 Experimental Setup

All experiments happen in NanoPC-T4 [1]. NanoPC-T4 is a type of RK3399 mainboard. To emulate scenes of most devices on the edge, memory for testing is limited to 1 GB and all data are saved in external 32 GB TF card, which is a commonly storage medium on the edge. All program run in docker [7] container to ensure the consistency of environment in tests.

To show the performance of this platform clearly, we test read/write performance of this platform by 30000 data blocks whose size is 8 KB. The speed of write is about 13.7 MB/S and the speed of read is about 60.2 MB/s. These data can be a contrast for performance of databases.

3.2 Performance of SardineCore

SardineCore is a standalone static library so we evaluate the performance of SardineCore compared with LevelDB. The benchmark tool provided by LevelDB is used in this test. Random read/write and sequential read/write are tested. The result is shown in Table 1.

Table 1. Performance of SardineCore and LevelDB

Kernel	Evaluation type			
	Random write (MB/s)	Sequential write (MB/s)	Random read (MB/s)	Sequential read (MB/s)
LevelDB	2.1	7.5	7.8	**247.2**
SardineCore	**7.8**	**12.8**	**9.1**	47.6

From the result, it can be known that SardineCore has advantages in random write, sequential write and sequential read compared to LevelDB. This result meets our expectations. Benefited by the reducing of write amplification, the random write performance of SardineCore is much higher than LevelDB. Moreover, the sequential write performance of SardineCore is very high and it is close to the write performance of hardware platform. For random reads, the performance of SardineCore has a little advantage compared with LevelDB because each level of LSM-tree can accommodate more items of SardineCore, the depth of SardineCore is smaller than LevelDB. In addition, items of SardineCore is smaller compared with LevelDB, thus Memtable of SardineCore can save more items, which lows the read amplification of external storage. The sequential read performance of SardineCore is lower than LevelDB because of its sequential read amplification. It is acceptable as the frequency of writes is higher than reads on the edge.

3.3 Performance of SardineDB

To evaluate the performance of SardineDB, we compare its performance with MySQL and Redis using YCSB (Yahoo! Cloud Serving Benchmark) [4] at the IoT device. YCSB is an open source standard benchmark tool for almost all mainstream RDBMS and NoSQL. In this test, SardineDB works in RESP mode. Considering the realistic scene of data on the edge, Sizes of test cases are 0.5 KB, 1 KB, 4 KB, 16 KB and 64 KB. Table 2 summarizes performance evaluation result of SardineDB.

From the results of evaluation, the write performance of SardineDB and Redis is totally higher than MySQL on the edge. Moreover, SardineDB has a little advantage compared with Redis because of its low write amplification.

For random reads, as the memory is small, SardineDB still has best performance because more items of SardineDB can be held in the memory. The random read speed of SardineDB is about two times of MySQL.

Table 2. Performance evaluation result of SardineDB

Evaluation type	Database	Test cases				
		0.5 KB	1 KB	4 KB	16 KB	64 KB
Random write (KB/s)	MySQL	8.09	15.72	51.68	113.12	252.16
	Redis	74.11	158.96	594.6	1481.92	4271.36
	SardineDB	**107.76**	**216.21**	**833.6**	**2333.76**	**5142.4**
Random read (KB/s)	MySQL	89.78	165.32	497.16	1908.8	4049.28
	Redis	156.895	295.56	855.16	2600.32	6409.6
	SardineDB	**244.725**	**499.92**	**1696**	**3870.4**	**7244.16**
Sequential read (KB/s)	MySQL	**3745**	**7870**	**14280**	**25760**	**46080**
	Redis	455	670	1680	7520	23680
	SardineDB	505	990	2360	8000	15360

For sequential read performance, RDBMS has a natural advantage because traditional RDBMS is optimized for sequential read performance. Thus, compared with SardineDB and Redis, MySQL has a very high sequential read performance. However, as write performance of RDBMS is less than satisfactory on the edge, it is also meaningful to pay attention to Redis and SardineDB although their sequential read performance is not as high as MySQL. Both SardineDB and Redis are NoSQL databases, the sequential read performance of SardineCore and Redis are very close. When test cases are smaller, the sequential read performance of SardineDB is better. Considering most data are small on the edge, SardineDB is more suitable for data on the edge. As the sequential read performance of Redis is acceptable on the edge. It can be inferred that the sequential read performance of SardineDB is also enough for applications on the edge.

4   Conclusion

Nowadays, data are rapidly increasing on the edge of the network. A database optimized for the edge is very valuable. In this paper, SardineDB is designed as a decentralized distributed database for data on the edge and its engine SardineCore is a low GC burden key-value separation storage optimized for flash memory based on LevelDB. Compared with LevelDB, SardineCore lows the write amplification and improves the write performance so that SardineDB is more suitable for devices and scenes on the edge. Moreover, SardineDB has higher write performance compared with many currently popular databases on the edge and various different interfaces are supported by SardineDB so that data can be managed more conveniently on the edge. Because the deployment of SardineDB's production environment is more difficult than traditional cloud services, we hope to develop a unified publishing platform for edge networks in the future, so that we can manage, maintain, and update edge applications like SardineDB in a unified manner.

Acknowledgements. This research work is supported by Guangdong province science and technology plan projects (2020A0505100015), National Natural Science Foundation of China (61703168).

References

1. NanoPC-T4-FriendlyARM wiki. http://wiki.friendlyarm.com/wiki/index.php/NanoPC-T4. Accessed 7 Mar 2020
2. Redis protocol specification. https://redis.io/topics/protocol. Accessed 6 May 2019
3. Bez, R., Camerlenghi, E., Modelli, A., Visconti, A.: Introduction to flash memory. Proc. IEEE **91**(4), 489–502 (2003)
4. Cooper, B.F., Silberstein, A., Tam, E., Ramakrishnan, R., Sears, R.: Benchmarking cloud serving systems with YCSB. In: Proceedings of the 1st ACM Symposium on Cloud Computing, pp. 143–154 (2010)
5. Jalali, F.: Energy consumption of cloud computing and fog computing applications. Ph.D. thesis (2015)
6. Liu, D., Yang, J., Tan, Y.: A survey on the storage issues in edge computing. ZTE Technol. J. **25**(3), 15–22 (2019)
7. Merkel, D.: Docker: lightweight Linux containers for consistent development and deployment. Linux J. **2014**(239), 2 (2014)
8. O'Neil, P., Cheng, E., Gawlick, D., O'Neil, E.: The log-structured merge-tree (LSM-tree). Acta Informatica **33**(4), 351–385 (1996)
9. Panetta, K.: Top trends in the Gartner hype cycle for emerging technologies, Gartner, Stamford, US (2017)
10. Shi, W., Cao, J., Zhang, Q., Li, Y., Xu, L.: Edge computing: vision and challenges. IEEE Internet Things J. **3**(5), 637–646 (2016)
11. Stackowiak, R.: IoT edge devices and microsoft. In: Azure Internet of Things Revealed, pp. 55–72. Apress, Berkeley (2019). https://doi.org/10.1007/978-1-4842-5470-7_3

DLSM: Distance Label Based Subgraph Matching on GPU

Shijie Jiang🆔, Yang Wang🆔, Guang Lu🆔, and Chuanwen Li$^{(\boxtimes)}$🆔

School of Computer Science and Engineering, Northeastern University,
Shenyang, China
lichuanwen@mail.neu.edu.cn

Abstract. Graphs have been prevalently used to represent complex data, such as social networks, citation networks and biological protein interaction networks. The subgraph matching problem has wide applications in the graph data computing area. Recently, many parallel matching algorithms have been proposed to speed up subgraph matching queries, among which the filter-join framework is attracting increasingly attentions in recent years. Existing filtering strategies are able to compress candidate vertex sets to a certain size. However, quite a few invalid vertices are still left, leading to unnecessary computation in later joining phases. We observed that the shortest distance between vertices can act as an important condition to further refine the candidate set. In this paper, we propose a method of shortest distance estimation based on the observation and design a new method based on distance coding. By this means we improve the efficiency of subgraph matching. The experimental results suggests that our method is more efficient and scalable than the state-of-the-art method.

Keywords: Subgraph matching · GPU · Parallel computing · Shortest diatance

1 Introduction

Graph is a powerful data structure that can depict relationships concisely and powerfully. Graph database has been widely used as an important tool for modeling and querying complex graph data in many applications, e.g., social network, semantic web and biological network. Finding all matching or embedding problems of query graph in large data graph has been widely used in various practical applications, such as semantic query, program analysis and compound search. To speed up this process, a number of algorithms have been proposed [1,3,5], most of which greatly improve the efficiency of subgraph matching.

We observe that there is a problem in the existing "filter-join" framework: when selecting candidate sets for query graph vertices in the filtering phase, the positional relationship between vertices is not considered. Consider the query graph Q and data graph G in Fig. 1. Whether we choose v_2 or v_7 as the mapping vertex of u_1, v_{13} cannot be a vertex in the matching result. This is because

© Springer Nature Switzerland AG 2021
L. H. U et al. (Eds.): APWeb-WAIM 2021, LNCS 12859, pp. 194–200, 2021.
https://doi.org/10.1007/978-3-030-85899-5_15

the length of the shortest path from v_{13} to v_2 and v_7 is 4 (the edge weights are all considered as 1), while the upper limit of the shortest path from u_1 to other vertices of Q is 1. However, the existing filtering methods can not filter out vertices like v_{13}. Based on the above observation, we propose an efficient GPU subgraph matching algorithm DLSM based on edge-oriented join strategy. We use a "filter-join" framework that is more suitable for GPU.

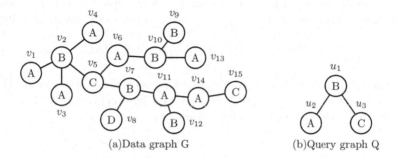

(a)Data graph G   (b)Query graph Q

Fig. 1. An example of Data graph G and Query graph Q

2 Distance Label Based Subgraph Matching (DLSM)

2.1 Problem Definition

In this paper we study undirected graphs, where each vertex is labeled and each edge is unlabeled. We use $G = \{V, E, L, L_v\}$ to denote graph G, where V is the set of all vertices in the graph, E is the set of edges, L is the set of vertex labels, and L_v is the label function that maps each vertex in V set to the label in L.

Definition 1 (Subgraph Isomorphism). *Given a query graph $Q = \{V, E, L, L_v\}$ and a data graph $G = \{V', E', L', L_v'\}$, and $|Q| \leq |G|$. Subgraph isomorphism means finding an injective function H: $V(Q) \rightarrow V(G)$, which maps each vertex of Q to a unique vertex of G, thus satisfying the following conditions: 1) $\forall(u, v) \in E, (H(u), H(v)) \in E'$; 2) item $Lv(u) = Lv'(H(u)), Lv(v) = Lv'(H(v))$.*

Given a query graph $Q = \{V, E, L, L_v\}$ and a data graph $G = \{V', E', L', L_v'\}$, and $|Q| \leq |G|$. The task of **subgraph matching** is to find all subgraphs isomorphic to Q in G. For example, Fig. 1 (a) and Fig. 1 (b) are given data graph G and query graph Q respectively, then all results on matching with $\{u_1, u_2, u_3\}$ are: $\{v_2, v_1, v_5\}, \{v_2, v_3, v_5\}, \{v_2, v_4, v_5\}$ and $\{v_7, v_{11}, v_5\}$.

Definition 2 (Shortest Distance). *Given the vertices v_a and v_b in a connected graph M, we define the shortest distance between v_a and v_b as $SD(M, V_a, V_b)$.*

2.2 Distance Label Based Filtering

Since a graph is a metric space, the shortest distance between any three vertices on a graph satisfies the triangular inequality. In other words, for any three dissimilar vertices v_x, v_y, v_z in the data graph G, the following conditions are satisfied:

$$|SD(G, v_x, v_z) - SD(G, v_y, v_z)| \leq SD(G, v_x, v_y) \tag{1}$$

We can easily extend the above inequality to multiple vertices. For example, if we extend v_z to n vertices $v_{z_1}, v_{z_2}...v_{z_n}$, we can get the following results:

$$\max_{1 \leq i \leq n} |SD(G, v_x, v_{z_i}) - SD(G, v_y, v_{z_i})| \leq SD(G, v_x, v_y) \tag{2}$$

Theorem 1. *If data graph G has subgraphs isomorphic to query graph Q, then for any two vertices u_x, u_y in Q, their corresponding vertices $v_x = H(u_x)$, $v_y = H(u_y)$ in G satisfy the following conditions:*

$$SD(G, v_x, v_y) \leq \varphi(u_x) \wedge SD(G, v_x, v_y) \leq \varphi(u_y) \tag{3}$$

Where $\varphi(u)$ is the height of the breadth first spanning tree of vertex u (excluding the root node).

Proof. The above two inequalities are equivalent. We only need to prove one and then use symmetry to deduce the other. Here we give the proof of the first inequality: we know that $\varphi(u_x)$ is the breadth first spanning tree height of the query graph vertex u_x (excluding the root node). In other words, $\varphi(u_x)$ can be regarded as the maximum of the shortest path from u_x to all other vertices of the query graph Q, that is, $SD(G, u_x, u_y) \leq \varphi(u_x)$. Since $SD(G, v_x, v_y) \leq SD(G, u_x, u_y)$, it can be inferred that the above Theorem 1 holds.

Theorem 2. *If data graph G has subgraphs isomorphic to query graph Q, then for any vertex u_x, u_y, u_z in Q and their corresponding vertices v_x, v_y, v_z in G, there must be:*

$$|SD(G, v_x, v_z) - SD(G, v_y, v_z)| \leq \varphi(u_x) \tag{4}$$

Proof. Theorem 2 can be derived from inequality (1) and Theorem 1, as well as the transitivity of inequality.

Similarly, we can extend it to multiple vertices just like Theorem 1. For example, if we extend v_z to n vertices $v_{z_1}, v_{z_2}...v_{z_n}$, we can get the following results:

$$\max_{1 \leq i \leq n} |SD(G, v_x, v_{z_1}) - SD(G, v_y, v_{z_1})| \leq \varphi(u_x) \tag{5}$$

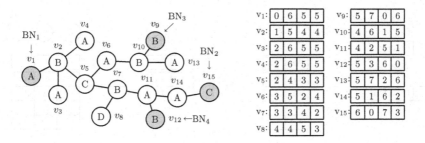

Fig. 2. Distance code of Data graph G

Constructing Distance Coding. From inequality (5), we can know that the distance relationship between the vertices in the data graph and the height of the breadth first traversal spanning tree of the vertices in the query graph is unequal. The following is the construction method of distance coding in preprocessing.

(1) In the data graph G, any vertex v_1 with the smallest degree is found as the first fixed vertex;
(2) In the process of traversal, the distance from each vertex to v_1 is filled in the first column of the coding table. At the end of traversal, any vertex v_2 which is farthest from v_1 is selected as the second fixed vertex;
(3) In the same analogy, the next step n starts with v_n for breadth first traversal. In the traversal process, the distance from each vertex to v_n is filled in the nth column of the coding table. At the end of traversal, the vertex v_{n+1} with the largest sum of distances from any vertex to the first n vertices is selected as the $(n + 1)$th fixed vertex and iterated in turn.

Figure 2 shows the coding situation when n = 4. We find that the good filtering effect can be achieved when n = 4.

3   DLSM Overview

The framework of DLSM includes the filtering phase and joining phase. Our solution follows the GPU friendly "filter-join" strategy. In the filtering phase, we construct the candidate vertex set of $V(Q)$; in the joining phase, we transform the candidate vertex set of the query graph into the candidate edge set, which will be connected according to the constraint of subgraph isomorphism (Fig. 3).

The overhead of parallel joining is closely related to the effect of candidate set filtering in the previous phase. We establish candidate vertex set C (u) for each query vertex u in query graph Q. In this work, we propose a distance based approach to achieve efficient filtering and pruning. We design a four bit distance code for each vertex in G, which is used to estimate the distance between any two vertices in the query graph. The specific coding and usage will be given in the fifth chapter. The candidate set of all query vertices can be found through the filtering phase. In Fig. 1, the candidate sets are $C(u_1) = \{v_2, v_7\}$, $C(u_2) =$

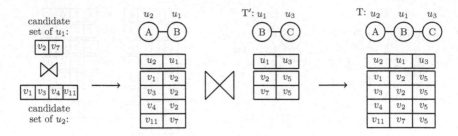

Fig. 3. An example of check edge and edge-oriented join

$\{v_1, v_3, v_4, v_{11}\}$, and $C(u_3) = \{v_5\}$. Because of the edge-oriented join strategy, after the candidate vertex set is determined, the edges should be checked according to the constraint conditions and converted to the candidate edge set C (E) of each query edge E. We find the candidate set for each edge of the query graph. The candidate set of edges (u_1, u_2) is $\{(v_2, v_1), (v_2, v_3), (v_2, v_4), (v_7, v_{11})\}$, and the candidate set of edges (u_1, u_3) is $\{(v_2, v_5), (v_7, v_5)\}$. Finally, all the final matching solutions $\{v_1, v_2, v_5\}, \{v_3, v_2, v_5\}, \{v_4, v_2, v_5\}$ and $\{v_{11}, v_7, v_5\}$ are obtained by joining the candidate sets of query graph edges.

4   Experimental Results

In this section, we will evaluate our method (DLSM) by comparing it with the state-of-the-art subgraph matching algorithms. We compare our method with the advanced algorithm GpSM [3] in the "filter-join" framework.

4.1   Experimental Setup

We perform the experiments on a computer with Intel Core i5-8250u CPU (1.66GHz × 8), NVIDIA geforce MX150 GPU (6 GB), 8 GB RAM, Ubuntu 16.04 and CUDA 10.2 toolkit. The code is written by G++ 8.1.0, and all the algorithms are implemented by C++.

Synthetic Data Sets. We use the RMAT model [2] to generate a synthetic dataset, and the graph generated by this model follows a power-law distribution. To match the computing power of the device, we set $|V(Q)|$ from 4 to 32 and $|V(G)|$ from 1,000 to 10,000. The total number of label sets is set to 300, and then a label is randomly selected from the label set and assigned to each vertex. Our experiment changes $|V(Q)|$ and $|V(G)|$ to test the performance of DLSM when other variables are constant.

Real World Data Sets. A total of four real-world datasets were selected, include Yeast, Human, HPRD and WordNet. They are all graphs with vertex labels. Among them, the smallest is Yeast, which has 3,112 vertices and 12,519 edges, and the total number of label is 71. The largest is WordNet, which has 76,853 vertices and 120,399 edges, with a total number of 5 labels.

4.2   Results on Synthetic and Real World Datasets

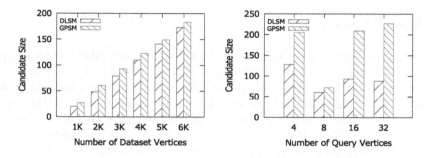

Fig. 4. Experiment result on synthetic dataset (candidate set size)

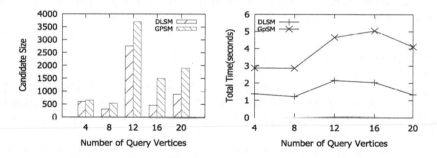

Fig. 5. Experiment result on Human dataset

In the experiment of changing $|V(G)|$ on the synthetic dataset, Fig. 4 shows that the performance of DLSM is significantly better than that of GpSM. Let's recall the distance coding in chapter two, the global location information filtering combination is more powerful than GpSM. Therefore, the filtration time of DLSM is better than that of GpSM. In the real-world data experiment, Fig. 5 shows the experimental results on the human dataset. The selected evaluation indexes are the total number of vertices and the total time (filter + join) of the candidate set. DLSM is still better than GpSM in the total number of candidate vertices, which is consistent with the results of the composite dataset.

5 Related Work

The subgraph matching problem has been widely studied in recent year. [4] designs a distributed algorithm based on recursive backtracking framework. Lai et al. GpSM [3] works on GPU, and stands out among many algorithms through breadth first search and edge-oriented join. GSI [5] proposes the improvement in this idea, which changes the edge-oriented join into the vertex-oriented join, so as to solve the problem of memory pre allocation.

6 Conclusion

This paper proposes a filtering method based on distance label coding to optimize the sub graph matching problem based on the "filter-join" framework. We call this method DLSM. The method can achieve fast subgraph matching query by virtue of the high efficiency parallelism of graphics processor. DLSM considers global and local location information in the filtering phase, and achieves a stronger filtering effect. The experimental results on a large number of synthetic and real data sets show that the method is effective. In the future, we will further solve some limitations of DLSM, such as how to deal with the non connected graph data and try to adopt vertex-orient join strategy in the joining phase.

Acknowledgements. This work is supported by the National Nature Science Foundation of China (61872071, 61872070).

References

1. Carletti, V., Foggia, P., Ritrovato, P., Vento, M., Vigilante, V.: A parallel algorithm for subgraph isomorphism. In: Conte, D., Ramel, J.-Y., Foggia, P. (eds.) GbRPR 2019. LNCS, vol. 11510, pp. 141–151. Springer, Cham (2019). https://doi.org/10.1007/978-3-030-20081-7_14
2. Chakrabarti, D., Zhan, Y., Faloutsos, C.: R-mat: a recursive model for graph mining. In: Proceedings of the 2004 SIAM International Conference on Data Mining, pp. 442–446. SIAM (2004)
3. Tran, H.-N., Kim, J., He, B.: Fast Subgraph Matching on Large Graphs using Graphics Processors. In: Renz, M., Shahabi, C., Zhou, X., Cheema, M.A. (eds.) DASFAA 2015. LNCS, vol. 9049, pp. 299–315. Springer, Cham (2015). https://doi.org/10.1007/978-3-319-18120-2_18
4. Wang, Z., Gu, R., Hu, W., Yuan, C., Huang, Y.: BENU: distributed subgraph enumeration with backtracking-based framework. In: 2019 IEEE 35th International Conference on Data Engineering (ICDE), pp. 136–147. IEEE (2019)
5. Zeng, L., Zou, L., Özsu, M.T., Hu, L., Zhang, F.: GSI: GPU-friendly subgraph isomorphism. In: 2020 IEEE 36th International Conference on Data Engineering (ICDE), pp. 1249–1260. IEEE (2020)

Information Extraction and Retrieval

Distributed Top-k Pattern Mining

Xin Wang[1]([✉]), Mingyue Xiang[2], Huayi Zhan[3], Zhuo Lan[1], Yuang He[1],
Yanxiao He[1], and Yuji Sha[1]

[1] Southwest Petroleum University, Chengdu, China
`xinwang@swpu.edu.cn`,
{202022000326,202022000311,202022000283,202025000059}@`stu.swpu.edu.cn`
[2] Southwest Jiaotong University, Chengdu, China
`mingyuexiang@my.swjtu.edu.cn`
[3] Sichuan ChangHong Electric Co. Ltd., Mianyang, China
`huayi.zhan@changhong.com`

Abstract. Frequent pattern mining (FPM) on a single large graph has
been receiving increasing attention since it is crucial to applications in a
variety of domains including *e.g.*, social network analysis. The FPM problem is defined as finding all the subgraphs (*a.k.a.* patterns) that appear frequently in a large graph according to a user-defined frequency threshold. In
recent years, a host of techniques have been developed, while most of them
suffers from high computational cost and inconvenient result inspection.
To tackle the issues, in this paper, we propose an approach to mining top-k
patterns from a single graph G under the distributed scenario. We formalize the distributed top-k pattern mining problem by incorporating viable
support and *interestingness* metrics. We then develop a parallel algorithm,
that preserves *early termination* property, to efficiently discover top-k patterns. Using real-life and synthetic graphs, we experimentally verify that
our algorithm is rather effective and outperforms traditional counterparts
in both efficiency and scalability.

1 Introduction

Frequent pattern mining, which is to find subgraphs whose appearances exceed a
user defined threshold, has been at the core of data mining research for a period.
Existing work considers the problem under two different settings: transactional-
based and single-graph-based. In recent years, more attention has been paid to the
latter setting, as it plays a crucial role in a variety of applications such as bioinfor-
matics, cheminformatics, web analysis, social network analysis, etc. Most of prior
methods follow the combinatorial pattern enumeration paradigm. In real world
applications such as social network analysis, the complete enumeration of patterns
is practically infeasible, as the mining results are explosive in size [18,31].

Indeed, it is often unnecessary to enumerate all the patterns. Consider a
frequent pattern Q, all its subgraphs must be frequent as well. If Q is returned,
why do we need to identify its sub-patterns? Moreover, users are often only
interested in a few typical patterns, instead of the overwhelmed pattern set [32].

Another challenge for the FPM problem lies in that large graphs are often
distributive stored, which hinders the application of centralized solutions and

© Springer Nature Switzerland AG 2021
L. H. U et al. (Eds.): APWeb-WAIM 2021, LNCS 12859, pp. 203–220, 2021.
https://doi.org/10.1007/978-3-030-85899-5_16

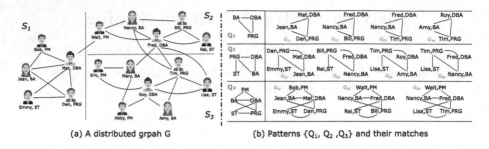

(a) A distributed grpah G   (b) Patterns {Q₁, Q₂ ,Q₃} and their matches

Fig. 1. A distributed social graph G & a set of patterns along with their matches

calls for distributed techniques. Indeed, under the distributed scenario, costly mining computation may benefit from parallel computation.

These highlight the need for *distributed top-k pattern mining*: given a distributed graph G, a support threshold θ and an integer k, it is to find k patterns, that not only satisfy support constraint but also are most interesting to the users. Furthermore, if an algorithm for the problem preserves the *early termination property, i.e.,* it discovers top-k patterns without identifying the entire pattern set, then we do not have to pay the price of costly pattern mining.

Example 1. A fraction of a social graph G is shown in Fig. 1 (a), where each node denotes a person with name and job title (*e.g.,* project manager (PM), database administrator (DBA), programmer (PRG), business analyst (BA) and software tester (ST)); and each edge indicates friendship, *e.g.,* (Bob, Mat) indicates that Bob and Mat are friends. As is shown, G is distributively stored at sites S_1, S_2 and S_3, respectively. To identify frequent patterns, centralized approaches no longer work, *e.g.,* one match G_{33} of the pattern Q_3 (shown in Fig. 1 (b)), that crosses S_2 and S_3 can not be identified, thus the support of Q_3 may not be correctly computed. Moreover, together with Q_3, Q_1 and Q_2 (as sub-patterns of Q_3) are considered as redundant patterns, and unworthy to pay extra cost for identification and inspection.   □

This example calls for techniques for *distributed top-k pattern mining*. To tackle the issue, several questions have to be answered. (1) How to efficiently perform frequent pattern mining in a distributed scenario? (2) How to develop effective method such that mining computation can terminate as soon as k "best" patterns have been identified? (3) What metric can be easily used to measure goodness of a pattern?

Contributions. The paper investigates the *distributed top-k pattern mining problem* and provides an effective approach for it.

(1) We introduce viable *support* and *interestingness* metrics to measure patterns. Based on the metrics, we formalize the *distributed top-k pattern mining* (TopKPM) problem (Sect. 2).

(2) We investigate the TopKPM problem and develop a parallel algorithm, that is based on *partial evaluation* for it (Sect. 3). The algorithm has desirable

performances: its computational cost is influenced by a factor n (number of pattern extensions), that is often small in practice and it preserves *early termination property*.

(3) Using real-life and synthetic graphs, we experimentally verify the performance of our algorithms (Sect. 4). We find the following. (a) Our mining algorithm scales well with the increase of processors (n): they are on average 1.94, 2.14 and 2.22 times faster than a counterpart on three real-world social networks, when n increases from 4 to 20. (b) Our algorithm works reasonably well on large graphs. For example, on a graph with 4 million nodes and 53.5 million edges, our algorithm spends less than 219 s to discover frequent patterns using 20 processors.

Related Work. The problem of FPM on single large graphs has been well studied and a host of techniques have been proposed. We next review them as follows.

Centralized Techniques. Typical centralized FPM approaches can be classified into two categorizes, *i.e.*, [5,12,21] for static graphs and [4,24] for evolving graphs. (I) On static graphs, a novel approach GRAMI is first introduced by [12]. GRAMI applies a minimum-image-based support metric, that preserves anti-monotonic property and models FPM problem as a constraint satisfaction problem. To address the issue on weighted graphs, [5,21] proposed approaches to mining weighted frequent subgraphs, on edge-weighted single large graphs. (II) Over evolving graphs, [24] proposed an algorithm StreamFSM to continuously discover frequent patterns. StreamFSM applies a strategy to cope with areas with updates and supports batch updates only. [4] introduced another dynamic algorithm IncGM+, which separates the input graph into frequent and infrequent updated subgraphs and prunes the update area by adjusting the boundary subgraphs named "fringe". This approach keeps small memory overhead.

Distributed Techniques. In recent years, distributed FPM techniques over single large graphs are intensively studied. Typical methods are listed as follows. [26] proposed a parallel subgraph listing framework PSgL, which deals with subgraph listing in a divide-and-conquer fashion, thereby avoiding the costly join operation. Another distributed platform Arabesque [28] employs a high-level filter-process model to facilitate mining computation. DISTGRAPH [27] uses a set of optimizations and efficient collective communication operations to minimize total amount of messages shipped among different sites. [16] presents a distributed framework with expressive graph API to effectively reduce memory overhead and improve system performance. [3] proposed a scalable system ScaleMine. The system leverages the approximate and exact phases to achieve better load balance and more efficient evaluation for candidate patterns. Gemini [33] is another distributed and synchronous graph processing framework. It uses a low-overhead edge-cut partitioning strategy to distribute graph data, and applies a co-scheduling mechanism to alleviate the computing bottleneck. Extended from [16], G-Miner [8] provides an expressive API as well as a novel task-pipeline that removes the synchronization barrier and hides the overheads of network and disk I/O and achieves high performance. Similar to ours, [22] introduced an approach to mining the top-k uncertain frequent patterns from uncertain databases. This approach combines the mining and ranking phases as a whole and proposes effective threshold raising strategies to enhance the mining time and reduce the memory usage. [6] studied approximate k-vertex frequent pattern mining on a dynamic graph with high probability in a given time. PrefixFPM framework [30] fully utilizes the CPU cores in a multicore machine and adopts the prefix projection approach pioneered by PrefixSpan to achieve high performance. There also exist a host of techniques [7,11,20] developed on MapReduce. [7] introduced FSM-H, a novel iterative MapReduce-based frequent subgraph mining algorithm. Along the similar line, [11] introduces MR-SimLab, a scalable approach for representative subgraph selection based on MapReduce. In particular, MR-SimLab takes advantage of the similarity between node labels to support approximate isomorphism checking. [20] describes Pegasus, a graph mining system on top of MapReduce with the key component GIM-V.

Our work differs with [22,27] in the following: we leverage both partial evaluation and asynchronous message passing to identify matches of candidate pattern in distributive environment, instead of level-wise evaluation; moreover frequent patterns are our intermediate results.

2   Graphs, Patterns and Pattern Mining

In this section, we first review graphs, patterns, graph pattern matching; we then formalize the pattern mining problem.

2.1   Graph Pattern Matching

Graph. A *data graph* (or simply *graph*) is defined as $G = (V, E, L)$, where (1) V is a set of nodes; (2) $E \subseteq V \times V$ is a set of *undirected* edges ; and (3) each node v in V carries a tuple $L(v) = (A_1 = a_1, \cdots, A_n = a_n)$, where $A_i = a_i (i \in [1, n])$ represents that the node v has a value a_i for the attribute A_i, and is denoted as $v.A_i = a_i$, e.g., v.name = "Bill", v.job_title = "PM".

A graph $G' = (V', E', L')$ is a *subgraph* of $G = (V, E, L)$, denoted by $G' \subseteq G$, if $V' \subseteq V$, $E' \subseteq E$, and moreover, for each $v \in V'$, $L'(v) = L(v)$.

Distributed Graph. In practice a big graph G is often fragmented into a collection of subgraphs and stored in different sites [19,25]. A *fragmentation* $\mathcal{F}$ of a graph $G = (V, E, L)$ is $(F_1, \ldots, F_n)$, where each *fragment* F_i is specified by $(V_i \cup F_i.O, E_i, L_i)$ such that (a) $(V_1, \ldots, V_n)$ is a partition of V, (b) $F_i.O$ is the set of nodes v' such that there exists an edge $e = (v, v')$ or $e = (v', v)$ in E, $v \in V_i$ and node v' is in *another fragment*; we refer to v' as a *virtual node*, e as a *crossing edge* and cE_i as the set of crossing edges; and (c) $(V_i \cup F_i.O, E_i, L_i)$ is a subgraph of G induced by $V_i \cup F_i.O$.

For the fragmentation, we denote $V_f = \bigcup_{i \in [1,n]} F_i.O$ as the set of all virtual nodes in $\mathcal{F}$, E_f as the set of all crossing edges in $\mathcal{F}$, and $|\mathcal{F}|$ as the number of fragments in $\mathcal{F}$.

Pattern. A *pattern* Q is defined as a graph (V_p, E_p, f_v), where V_p and E_p are the set of nodes and edges, respectively; for each u in V_p, it is associated with a predicate $f_v(u)$ defined as a conjunction of atomic formulas of the form of '$A = a$' such that A denotes an attribute of the node u and a is a value of A. Intuitively, $f_v(u)$ specifies search conditions imposed by u.

A pattern $Q' = (V_p', E_p', f_v')$ is *subsumed by* another pattern $Q = (V_p, E_p, f_v)$, denoted by $Q' \sqsubseteq Q$, if (V_p', E_p') is a subgraph of (V_p, E_p), and function f_v' is a restriction of f_v. Then, Q' is referred to as a sub-pattern of Q if $Q' \sqsubseteq Q$.

Graph Pattern Matching. Consider graph G and pattern Q, a node v in G satisfies the search conditions of a pattern node u in Q, denoted as $v \sim u$, if for each atomic formula '$A = a$' in $f_v(u)$, there exists an attribute A in $L(v)$ such that $v.A = a$.

We adopt subgraph isomorphism [10] as the matching semantic. A *match* of pattern Q in graph G is a *bijective function* ρ from the nodes of Q to the nodes of a subgraph G, such that (1) for each node $u \in V_p$, $\rho(u) \sim u$, and (2) (u, u') is an edge in Q if and only if $(\rho(u), \rho(u'))$ is an edge in G. When an isomorphism ρ from pattern Q to a subgraph G_s of G exists, we say G *matches* Q, and denote G_s as a *match* of Q in G. Abusing notations, we say v in G_s as a *match* of u in Q, when $\rho(u) = v$.

We denote by $M(Q, G)$ the set of matches G_s of Q in G. Then, for each node u in E_p, we derive a set $\{v | v \in \rho(Q), \rho(Q) \in M(Q, G), v = \rho(u)\}$ from match set $M(Q, G)$, and denote it by $\mathsf{img}(u)$. Intuitively, $\mathsf{img}(u)$ contains a set of *distinct* nodes v in G as matches of u in Q.

Example 2. Recall graph G in Fig. 1 (a). It is distributed into three sites *i.e.*, S_1, S_2 and S_3. Taking S_1 as example, it maintains not only local nodes and edges, but also a *crossing edge* (Mat, Walt) that connects a *virtual node* Walt. Given patterns Q_1, Q_2 and Q_s in Fig. 1 (b), one may verify that Q_1, Q_2 are *subsumed by* Q_3, and moreover, $M(Q_1, G) = \{G_{11}, G_{12}, G_{13}, G_{14}\}$, $M(Q_2, G) = \{G_{21}, G_{22}, G_{23}, G_{24}\}$ and $M(Q_3, G) = \{G_{31}, G_{32}, G_{33}\}$.

DFS Tree. Given a pattern Q, its DFS tree T_Q can be built via a depth-first search in Q from a node u. Then, edges that are in T_Q are referred to as *forward edges* and the remaining edges in Q are denoted as *backward edges*.

Thus, the *forward extension* on a pattern Q essentially introduces a new edge from one node in Q; while the *backward extension* includes a new edge from two existing nodes. For example, a pattern Q_c with edge set $\{(\mathsf{BA}, \mathsf{DBA}), (\mathsf{DBA}, \mathsf{PRG})\}$ can be generated via *forward extension* from a pattern with edge $(\mathsf{BA}, \mathsf{DBA})$; with Q_c, another pattern Q_1 (shown in Fig. 1(b)) is generated via *backward extension*.

We will use the following notations. (1) The *size* $|G|$ of G (resp. $|Q|$ of Q) is $|V| + |E|$ (resp. $|V_p| + |E_p|$), the total number of nodes and edges in G (resp. Q). (2) A graph G (resp. pattern Q) is a *complete* graph (resp. pattern), if there exists an edge for each pair of nodes in it. (3) In a directed tree T, the height of a node v is the length of the longest downward path to a leaf node from v. Then the height h of T is the largest height among all tree nodes.

2.2 Frequent Pattern Mining

We start from the *support* metric, followed by the frequent pattern mining problem.

Support. The support of a pattern Q in a single graph G, denoted by $\mathsf{sup}(Q,G)$, indicates the appearance frequency of Q in G. Analogous to the association rules for itemsets, the support metric for patterns should be *anti-monotonic*, *i.e.*, for patterns Q and Q', if $Q' \sqsubseteq Q$, then $\mathsf{sup}(Q',G) \geq \mathsf{sup}(Q,G)$ for any G, to facilitate search space pruning.

Several pattern-based *anti-monotonic* support metrics exist, *e.g.*, minimum image (mni) [12], harmful overlap [14] and maximum independent sets [17]. In this work, mni is used, since it can be more efficiently calculated.

$$\mathsf{sup}(Q,G) = \mathsf{min}\{|\mathsf{img}(u)| \mid u \in V_p\}, \tag{1}$$

where $\mathsf{img}(u)$ is the image of pattern node u in G. It can be easily verified that this support measure is *anti-monotonic*.

Example 3. Recall graph G, pattern Q_1 and its matches in Fig. 1. It can be easily verified that for Q_1, $\mathsf{img}(\mathtt{DBA}) = \{\mathtt{Mat},\mathtt{Fred},\mathtt{Roy}\}$, $\mathsf{img}(\mathtt{BA}) = \{\mathtt{Jean},\mathtt{Nancy},\mathtt{Amy}\}$, $\mathsf{img}(\mathtt{PRG}) = \{\mathtt{Dan},\mathtt{Bill},\mathtt{Tim}\}$, which leads to $\mathsf{sup}(Q_1,G) = 3$ rather than 4.

Problem. The frequent pattern mining (FPM) problem can be stated as follows. Given a graph G and support threshold θ, it is to discover a set $\mathbb{S}$ of frequent patterns Q in G such that $\mathsf{sup}(Q,G) \geq \theta$ for any Q in $\mathbb{S}$.

In practice, FPM problem faces three big challenges: (1) the underlying graphs G are typically very large, moreover the FPM problem is intractable, it is hence very costly to identify all the frequent patterns on such large graphs; (2) big graphs are often distributively stored, thus centralized approaches for the FPM problem no longer work; and (3) it is not easy to set a viable support threshold θ, as a large (resp. small) θ will lead to too few (resp. many) patterns [31]. In light of these, we study the *distributed top-k pattern mining* (TopKPM) problem.

2.3 Problem Formalization

We introduce the *interestingness* metric, along with the formalization of the problem.

Interestingness. As observed by [31], on a large graph, there may exist excessive frequent patterns, which brings trouble to the investigation and application, in the meanwhile, people are more interested in those patterns which are top ranked. This calls for a metric to measure the *interestingness* of a pattern. Indeed, a host of *interestingness* metrics have been introduced. For example, a formalization of *subjective interestingness* was first introduced by [29], followed by several similar counterparts, all of which were based on information theory and are very costly for evaluation. In contrast to *subjective interestingness*, [9,18] proposed an objective metric which is a combination of "closeness" and "maximality", and essentially closely related to the pattern size. Motivated by this, we propose the following metric to measure how interesting a pattern Q is.

$$\text{itrs}(Q) = |Q| \tag{2}$$

Intuitively, the *interestingness* of a pattern Q is defined as its size, indicting that patterns with large size are more favored. This is reasonable since information brought by smaller patterns is less than that of larger ones.

Problem. The *distributed top-k pattern mining* (TopKPM) problem is stated as follows.

- Input: A distributed graph G, support threshold θ and integer k.
- Output: A set $\mathbb{S}_k$ of patterns Q in G such that $|\mathbb{S}_k| \leq k$, $\text{sup}(Q, G) \geq \theta$ for any Q in $\mathbb{S}_k$ and $\arg\max_{\mathbb{S}_k \subseteq \mathbb{S}} \sum_{Q \in \mathbb{S}_k} \text{itrs}(Q)$.

The TopKPM problem is to find at most k (specified by users) patterns that not only satisfy support constraint but also are most interesting.

3   Distributed Top-k Pattern Mining

In this section, we first show hardness of the TopKPM problem. Nonetheless, we next present a parallel algorithm, with *early termination* property to discover top-k patterns.

Proposition 1: *The decision problem of* TopKPM *is NP-hard.*   □

To see Proposition 1, observe that the subgraph isomorphism (ISO) problem is embedded in TopKPM problem, thus TopKPM problem must be at least as hard as ISO problem. Since ISO is an NP-complete problem [10], thus TopKPM problem must be NP-hard.

Intuitively, one may develop such an algorithm to identify top-k patterns. The algorithm, denoted as Naive, applies a "find-all-select" strategy: it discovers a complete set $\mathbb{S}$ of frequent patterns, ranks them according to their interestingness values and picks k best ones. Though straightforward, this algorithm has to mine all the frequent patterns and hence is costly for big graphs. While one can rectify this by incorporating *early termination* property.

Theorem 2. *Given a graph G, a parameter θ as support threshold and an integer k, there exists a parallel algorithm for the* TopKPM *problem, that finds a set $\mathbb{S}_k$ of patterns such that (a) $\text{sup}(Q, G) \geq \theta$ for each Q in $\mathbb{S}_k$ and $\Sigma_{Q \in \mathbb{S}_k} \text{itrs}(Q)$ is maximized, (b) the support computation is in $O(|V|^n \cdot n^{n+1})$ time (n refers to the expansion times), and (c) can terminate as soon as k patterns are discovered.*

Proof. We show Theorem 2 by presenting an algorithm as a constructive proof.

Algorithm DisMiner /* executed at the *coordinator* */

Input: Fragmented graph $\mathcal{F} = \{F_1, \cdots, F_n\}$ of G, support threshold θ and k.
Output: A set of no more than k patterns.
1. initialize $\mathsf{S}^{[1]}:=\emptyset$; $T_1 := \emptyset$; $T_2 := \emptyset$; $\mathbb{S}_k := \emptyset$; flag := false; $\mathcal{T}$ as an empty tree;
2. collect partial results S_e^i from each *worker* S_i; $\mathsf{S}^{[1]} := \bigcup_{i \in [1,n]} S_e^i$;
3. remove Q from $\mathsf{S}^{[1]}$ if $\sup(Q, G) < \theta$; update $\mathcal{T}$;
4. **while** (flag $\neq$ True) **do**
5. $L := \mathsf{TreeGen}(\mathsf{S}^{[1]}, \mathcal{T})$;
6. $\mathcal{P} := \mathcal{P} \bigcup \mathsf{LMiner}(L, \theta, \mathcal{T})$; /*executed at each worker in parallel*/
7.   **for each** pattern Q_c in L **do**
8.   **for each** map $\mathcal{H}$ in $\mathcal{P}$ **do**
9.   retrieve $\langle I_b, \mathsf{frq} \rangle$ from $\mathcal{H}(Q_c)$; $T_1 := T_1 \cup I_b$; $T_2 := T_2 \cup \mathsf{frq}$;
10. $\mathsf{ParEva}\ (T_1, Q_c)$; $\mathsf{SuppEva}\ (T_2, Q_c)$;
11.   update T_1, T_2; update $\mathcal{T}$ with Q_c (support $\geq \theta$);
12. **if** $\mathcal{T}$ is not updated **then** flag := true;
13. $\mathbb{S}_k := \mathsf{TopkSch}(\mathcal{T}, \mathsf{S}^{[1]}, \theta, k)$;
14. **return** $\mathbb{S}_k$.

Procedure TopkSch
Input: A tree $\mathcal{T}$, a set $\mathsf{S}^{[1]}$, support threshold θ, k.
Output: A set of patterns.
1. initialize Terminate:=false; $\mathbb{S}_k := \emptyset$; h as the height of $\mathcal{T}$;
2. **while** (Terminate $\neq$ True) **do**
3.   **for each** v at level h **do**
4. $L_p:=\mathsf{NonTreeGen}(Q_{[v]}, \mathsf{S}^{[1]}, \mathcal{T})$;
5.   **for each** Q_c in L_p **do**
6.   **if** Q_c was not generated before **then**
7.   verify support of Q_c in parallel;
8.   **if** Q_c is a qualified pattern **then** $\mathbb{S}_k := \mathbb{S}_k \bigcup \{Q_c\}$;
9.   **if** termination condition is satisfied **then**
10.   Terminate:=true; update $\mathbb{S}_k$; **break** ;
11. update h;
12. **return** $\mathbb{S}_k$;

Fig. 2. Algorithm DisMiner

The algorithm is denoted as DisMiner and shown in Fig. 2. It implements parallel computation by employing one processor as *coordinator* (S_c) and a set of processors as *workers* (S_i). In contrast to the traditional BSP-based models, DisMiner (a) combines parallel mining with *partial evaluation* [13] to ease mining processing; and (b) incrementally identifies top-k patterns in a step-by-step manner. We next illustrate the details of the algorithm.

Algorithm. DisMiner takes a fragmented graph $\mathcal{F}$, support threshold θ and k as input and outputs a set $\mathbb{S}_k$ of patterns with $|\mathbb{S}_k| \leq k$, $\sup(Q, G) \geq \theta$ for each Q in $\mathbb{S}_k$ and maximized $\sum_{Q \in \mathbb{S}_k} \mathsf{itrs}(Q)$.

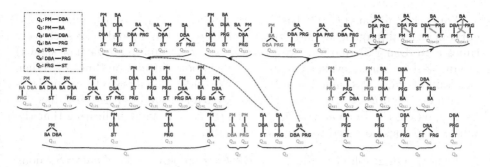

Fig. 3. A tree $\mathcal{T}$ showing the hierarchical structure of candidate patterns

Messages. In the distributed scenario, messages are broadcast between the *coordinator* and *workers*. In particular, each *worker* S_i sends *local frequency* of each candidate pattern to S_c. The *local frequency* of a pattern Q at S_i is defined as follows.

$$\mathsf{frq}(Q, F_i) = \{(u, |\mathsf{img}(u)|) \mid u \in V_p\} \tag{3}$$

Initialization. DisMiner first initializes a set of parameters: set $\mathsf{S}^{[1]}$ for maintaining single-edge (*a.k.a.* "seed") patterns, sets T_1 and T_2 for recording intermediate results, set $\mathbb{S}$ for keeping track of top-*k* patterns, a Boolean variable flag to control **while** loop and an empty tree $\mathcal{T}$ (line 1). It then invokes each *worker* to perform local evaluation to identify the support of "seed" patterns, in parallel and collects all the local frequencies (line 2). After *global supports* are calculated, DisMiner removes those "seed" patterns whose supports are below θ and expands the tree $\mathcal{T}$ with nodes, who correspond to "seed" patterns in $\mathsf{S}^{[1]}$ (line 3).

Tree Pattern Mining. Based on $\mathsf{S}^{[1]}$, DisMiner repeatedly produces "tree" patterns and verifies their supports, following a *level-wise* strategy (lines 4–12). During the iteration, LMiner is employed by each *worker* for local mining (line 6). We now present details.

In each round iteration, DisMiner firstly generates a set L of "tree" patterns as candidates with procedure TreeGen (not shown). Specifically, TreeGen produces candidate patterns by expanding frequent "tree" patterns that locate at the top level of $\mathcal{T}$ with "seed" patterns in $\mathsf{S}^{[1]}$, following *forward expansion* (line 5). The *coordinator* S_c then broadcasts L to all *workers* and invokes LMiner at each *worker* for local mining (details of LMiner will be given shortly). After local mining, the response from each *worker* consists of the following two types of information for each candidate pattern Q_c (line 6).

- frequency $\mathsf{frq}(Q_c, F_i)$ of Q_c at S_i.
- virtual match $\tilde{G}[Q_c]$ of Q_c, which is a set of node pairs with special elements (u, x). Here, (u, x) indicates that there does not exist a local match of u at F_i, but may exist an unknown match x at other site (details of virtual match will be illustrated shortly).

For each candidate Q_c in L, DisMiner retrieves a pair $\langle I_b, \mathsf{fre} \rangle$ from map $\mathcal{H}$, and gathers its local frequencies and "virtual matches" in sets T_1 and T_2, respectively (lines 8–9). Using T_1 and T_2, two procedures ParEva and SuppEva (not shown) are invoked for partial evaluation and global support calculation (line 10). When the support of Q_c is obtained, DisMiner sets T_1 and T_2 as empty sets and updates $\mathcal{T}$ with Q_c if $\mathsf{sup}(Q_c, G) \geq \theta$ (line 11). After current round finished, if $\mathcal{T}$ has not been updated, the Boolean flag flag is then changed to false, indicating that the **while** loop does not need to continue (line 12).

Example 4. On graph G of Fig. 1 (a), DisMiner employs a *coordinator* S_c along with *workers* S_1, S_2, S_3 to identify candidate patterns. At S_c, it first assembles partial results from each worker and initializes the set $\mathsf{S}^{[1]}$ with patterns Q_1–Q_7 (shown in Fig. 3), as their supports all equal to 3. Then, DisMiner applies TreeGen to generate candidate patterns following *forward extension*, in a *level-by-level* manner. For example, using pattern Q_1, S_c generates candidate patterns by enlarging Q_1 with other frequent single-edge patterns and produces L = $\{Q_{11}, Q_{12}, Q_{13}, Q_{14}\}$. Four levels of "nontrivial" candidate patterns (patterns without duplicate node labels) are shown in Fig. 3, where patterns marked with blue are considered infrequent (with support less than 3).

Top-k Mining. Using frequent "tree" patterns, DisMiner employs procedure TopkSch (shown in Fig. 4) to mine top-k patterns. More specifically, TopkSch first initializes a Boolean variable Terminate, an empty set $\mathbb{S}_k$ and an integer h as the height of $\mathcal{T}$ (line 1). It then simulates the procedure for discovering "tree" patterns to repeatedly identify qualified non-tree patterns (lines 2–11). In each round, TopkSch selects a node v, which corresponds to a "tree" pattern $Q_{[v]}$, at level h of $\mathcal{T}$, and generates a set L_p of candidate patterns with procedure NonTreeGen (line 4). Note that NonTreeGen works in the similar way as TreeGen, but only enlarges pattern $Q_{[v]}$ with "seed" patterns via *backward expansion*. For each candidate pattern Q_c in L_p, TopkSch verifies whether Q_c has been generated before and computes its support along the same line as before (line 7). To facility existence verification of a pattern, we apply a heuristic strategy for fast pruning. For each pattern Q, that is generated before, we record its statistic information, *e.g.,* label distribution, degree distribution, diameter and use it for comparison. If Q_c is a qualified pattern, TopkSch then enriches $\mathbb{S}_k$ with it (line 8). TopkSch next verifies whether the termination condition, specified by Proposition 3, is satisfied.

Proposition 3: *Given parameters θ, k and a tree $\mathcal{T}$, whose nodes correspond to the set $\mathbb{S}^t$ of frequent "tree" patterns, a k-element set $\mathbb{S}_k$ is the top-k pattern set, if (1) $\mathsf{sup}(Q, G) \geq \theta$ for each Q in $\mathbb{S}_k$, and (2) $\min\{\mathsf{itrs}(Q) | Q \in \mathbb{S}_k\} \geq \max\{\mathsf{itrs}(\widehat{Q_t}) | Q_t \in \mathbb{S}^t \setminus \mathbb{S}_k\}$).* □

Here $\widehat{Q_t}$ indicates a *complete* pattern that is expanded from a tree pattern Q_t in $\mathbb{S}^t \setminus \mathbb{S}_k$. Intuitively, Proposition 3 states that when the minimum interestingness value of a pattern in $\mathbb{S}_k$ is already no less than the maximum interestingness of

---

Procedure LMiner /* executed at each working site S_i in parallel */
Input: Fragment F_i, a set L of candidate patterns, support threshold θ, tree $\mathcal{T}$.
Output: A map $\mathcal{H}$.
1. initialize an empty map $\mathcal{H}$;
2. **for each** candidate pattern Q_c in L **do**
3.   identify a parent Q'_c of Q_c in $\mathcal{T}$; $I_b := \emptyset$;
4.   **for each** match G_s of Q'_c **do**
5.   **if** G_s can be locally extended as a match of Q_c **then**
6. $M(Q_c, F_i) := M(Q_c, F_i) \cup \{G'_s\}$;
7.   **elseif** G_s can not be locally determined as a match of Q_c **then**
8. $I_b := I_b \cup \tilde{G}[Q_c]$;
9.   compute $\mathsf{frq}(Q_c, F_i)$; $\mathcal{H}(Q_c) := \langle I_b, \mathsf{frq} \rangle$;
10. **return** $\mathcal{H}$;

Fig. 4. Procedure LMiner

any pattern possibly generated from existing tree patterns, then $\sum_{Q \in \mathbb{S}_k} \mathsf{itrs}(Q)$ is already maximized and no further exploration is needed.

If the termination condition is satisfied, TopkSch sets Terminate as true, eliminates redundant patterns in $\mathbb{S}_k$ if $|\mathbb{S}_k| > k$, breaks the **while** loop (line 10) and returns $\mathbb{S}_k$ as final result (line 12). Otherwise, after all the nodes on level h are processed, TopkSch decreases h by 1 for next round iteration (line 11).

Example 5. To identify the top-1 pattern, TopkSch first generates new candidate patterns, *e.g.*, Q_{33411}, Q_{33412}, Q_{33413} by expanding Q_{3341}, at the top level ($h = 3$) of $\mathcal{T}$ via *backward extension*. Assume that these candidates have not been generated before, TopkSch then evaluates their supports following the descending order of itrs and obtains $\mathbb{S}_k = \{Q_{33413}\}$. The above process can terminate until candidates generated from "tree" patterns at level 2 are all processed, as the remaining candidates can not have higher itrs values.

Local Mining. When a set L of candidate patterns are generated, the *coordinator* sends L to all *workers* and invokes procedure LMiner at each *worker* for local mining. At a working site S_i, LMiner takes F_i, L, θ and $\mathcal{T}$ as input, and works as follows. It first initializes an empty map $\mathcal{H}$, which is used for maintaining local supports of candidate patterns (line 1). It then computes the local support for each candidate pattern Q_c (lines 2–9). Specifically, LMiner identifies one parent node Q'_c of Q_c in $\mathcal{T}$, whose matches will be used for support evaluation and initializes an empty set I_b, which is used for recording "virtual matches" (line 3). For each match G_s of Q'_c, LMiner checks whether G_s can be extended as a match G'_s of Q_c and includes G'_s in match set $M(Q_c, F_i)$ if G'_s exists (lines 5–6). Otherwise, LMiner includes the "virtual match" $\tilde{G}[Q_c]$ in I_b (lines 7–8). When all the matches of Q'_c are processed, LMiner computes local support frq of Q_c and initializes $\mathcal{H}(Q_c)$ with a pair $\langle I_b, \mathsf{frq} \rangle$ (line 9). The map $\mathcal{H}$ is returned as final result after all the candidate patterns are evaluated (line 10).

Partial Evaluation. For a candidate pattern Q_c and its sub-pattern Q'_c, when a match G_s of Q'_c can not be *locally* determined as a match of Q_c, G_s is referred to as a *partial match* of Q_c and has to be verified from global perspective. To do this, we introduce a method based on partial evaluation [13] as follows.

At each *worker* S_i, it first constructs a "virtual match" $\tilde{G}[Q_c]$ of Q_c and then sends $\tilde{G}[Q_c]$ along with pattern Q_c to the *coordinator*. Here, $\tilde{G}[Q_c]$ (or simply $\tilde{G}$ when it is clear from context) is defined as below:

$$\tilde{G}[Q_c] = \{(u,v)|u \in V'_c, v \in V_s\} \bigcup \{(\tilde{u},x)|\tilde{u} \in V_c \backslash V'_c\}, \tag{4}$$

where V_c, V'_c and V_s are the node sets of Q_c, Q'_c and G_s, respectively, and x is a variable indicting a possible match of node $\tilde{u}$ of Q_c.

At the *coordinator*, S_c first collects all the "virtual matches" of each candidate pattern and then checks whether all the variables in $\tilde{G}$ can be instantiated with concrete nodes in G. This is warranted by the fact that if *partial matches* from different workers can be merged as a whole, all the variables in $\tilde{G}$ must be able to instantiated by nodes from neighbor sites (add proof if necessary).

Example 6. Recall Example 4. Upon receiving a candidate pattern Q_{123}, LMiner at S_2 first identifies its "parent" Q_{12} on tree $\mathcal{T}$ along with its local matches G_{s1} : (Walt, Mat, *), G_{s2} : (Walt, Fred, Rei), G_{s3} : (Walt, Fred, Lisa). Here, "*" in G_{s1} indicates that it is a *virtual* match of ST at S_2. Then, LMiner repeatedly enlarges $G_{s1} - G_{s3}$ with $Q_1 - Q_7$. After loop, a new match (Walt, Fred, Rei, Bill) of Q_{123}, which is enlarged locally from G_{s2}, is generated, while global extension on G_{s1} and G_{s3} are still needed. Thus, S_2 generates two "virtual matches", *i.e.*, {(PM, Walt), (DBA, Mat), (ST, *), (PRG, x)}, {(PM, Walt), (DBA, Fred), (ST, Lisa), (PRG, x)} from G_{s1}, G_{s3}, and sends them along with *local frequency* to S_c.

Correctness. The correctness of DisMiner is warranted by the following observations. (1) DisMiner will never miss any qualified pattern. (2) The support computation with *partial evaluation* is correct. (3) The strategy used by top-k pattern selection will never choose a pattern whose interestingness is less than any top-k pattern.

Complexity. For a pattern Q_c with vertex set V_{p_c}, there may exist at most $|V|^{|V_{p_c}|}$ matches in a graph G. Thus, it takes $O(|V|^{|V_{p_c}|+1})$ time to identify matches of a candidate pattern Q'_c ($Q_c \sqsubseteq Q'_c$). If Q_c is a "tree" pattern, there may generate at most $|V_{p_c}||\mathcal{L}|$ candidate patterns after *forward extension*; otherwise, at most $O(|V_{p_c}|^2)$ candidate patterns will be generated through *backward extension*. In the meanwhile, it still needs $O(|V|^{|V_{p_c}|+1} \cdot (|V_{p_c}|+1)^{|V_{p_c}|+1})$ time to verify whether Q_c has been generated before, since at most $|V|^{|V_{p_c}|+1}$ candidate patterns may be generated before and each round isomorphism checking needs $O((|V_{p_c}|+1)^{|V_{p_c}|+1})$ time. By induction, it takes DisMiner $\sum_{i\in[1,n]}(|V_{p_c}|+i-1)|V|\cdot|V|^{|V_{p_c}|+i}(1+(|V_{p_c}|+i)^{|V_{p_c}|+i})$ times to verify all the subsequent patterns for a candidate Q_c, where n refers to the extension times and is bounded by

$|V|$, $|\mathcal{L}|$ and $|V_{p_c}|$ are bounded by $|V|$. As the iteration starts from single-edge patterns Q_c and at most $|V|^2$ different Q_c exists, hence DisMiner is bounded by $O(|V|^n \cdot n^{n+1})$ time.

The analysis above completes the proof of Theorem 2.   □

4 Experimental Study

Using real-life and synthetic data, we conducted comprehensive experimental studies to evaluate: efficiency, data shipment and scalability of algorithm DisMiner.

Experimental Setting. We used three real-life graphs: (a) *Amazon* [1], a product co-purchasing network with 0.55 million nodes and 1.79 million edges. The total size of *Amazon* is 0.95GB. (b) *Pokec* [2], a social network with 1.63 million nodes, and 30.6 million edges. Its size is 2.2 GB. (c) *Google+* [15], a social graph whose size is 2.6 GB, has 4 million entities and 53.5 million links.

We designed a generator to produce synthetic graphs $G=(V, E, L)$, controlled by the numbers of nodes $|V|$ and edges $|E|$, where L is taken from an alphabet of $1K$ labels.

Algorithms. We implemented the following, all in Java. Algorithm DisMiner, compared with (a) GRAMI$_{ND}$, which is a naive distributed algorithm, that ships all fragments to the *coordinator*, and applies centralized technique GRAMI [12] to find all frequent patterns and then select top-k ones; and (b) GRAMI$_D$, another distributed FPM algorithm that works as follows. At S_c, GRAMI$_D$ first requests each *worker* to compute support of single-edge patterns, in parallel. After assembling the results from *workers*, S_c identifies infrequent single-edge patterns and notifies all the *workers* to perform local update, *i.e.*, eliminate local edges corresponding to infrequent patterns and ship updated fragments to the *coordinator*. The *coordinator* then merges updated fragments together and invokes GRAMI to find frequent patterns in a centralized way and choose k best patterns.

Graph Fragmentation and Distribution. We used the algorithm of [23] to partition a graph G into n fragments, and distributed them to n sites ($n \in [1, 20]$). Each site is powered by 8 cores Intel(R) Xeon(R) 2.00 GHz CPU with 128 GB of memory and 1 TB hard disk, using Debian Linux 3.2.04 system. Each experiment was run 5 times and the average is reported.

Experimental Results. We next report our findings. Note that we used the *logarithmic scale* for the y-axis in the figures for RT (response time).

Varying n. Fixing $k = 50$ and $\theta = 0.3K$, $3K$ and $0.8K$ for *Amazon*, *Pokec* and *Google+*, respectively, we varied n from 4 to 20 in 4 increments and evaluated efficiency and data shipment of DisMiner vs. GRAMI$_D$ and GRAMI$_{ND}$.

Figures 5(a)–(c) report the RT of all the algorithms on *Amazon*, *Pokec* and *Google+*, respectively, which tells us the following. (1) The more sites (processors) that are available, the less time DisMiner takes. This is because DisMiner gains benefits from parallel computation. For example, DisMiner is, on average,

1.94, 2.14 and 2.22 times faster than $\mathsf{GRAMI_D}$ when n increases from 4 to 20 on *Google+*, *Pokec* and *Amazon*, respectively. Moreover, DisMiner requires only 219 s to identify frequent patterns over *Google+*, when it is distributed over 20 sites. (2) $\mathsf{GRAMI_{ND}}$ and $\mathsf{GRAMI_D}$ are indifferent to n since they ship local fragments from each *worker* to the *coordinator* and apply a centralized algorithm to identify the matches. However, $\mathsf{GRAMI_D}$ is, on average, 2.94 times faster than $\mathsf{GRAMI_{ND}}$, as it effectively reduces local fragment at each *worker*.

Figures 5(d)–(f) show the results *w.r.t.*DS (data shipment) of the algorithms over *Amazon*, *Pokec* and *Google+*, respectively. We find that DisMiner ships, on average, 17.2% (resp. 13%, 14.2%) data of $\mathsf{GRAMI_D}$, on *Amazon* (resp. *Pockec* and *Google+*). The DS of $\mathsf{GRAMI_{ND}}$ trivially equals to the size of entire graph, hence is not reported.

Varying θ. Fixing $n = 4$ and $k = 50$, we varied the support threshold θ from $0.1K$ to $0.5K$ in $0.1K$ increments, $2K$ to $4K$ in $0.5K$ increments and $0.6K$ to $1.0K$ in $0.1K$ increments on *Amazon*, *Pokec* and *Google+*, respectively.

Figures 5(g)–(i) show results on RT and reveal the following. (1) All the algorithms take longer with a small θ, because more candidate patterns and their matches have to be verified. (2) DisMiner outperforms $\mathsf{GRAMI_D}$ and $\mathsf{GRAMI_{ND}}$ in all cases and is less sensitive to the increase of θ because DisMiner maximizes parallelism for support computation, while $\mathsf{GRAMI_D}$ (resp. $\mathsf{GRAMI_{ND}}$) simply assembles a part of (resp. entire) fragment from each *worker* and verifies support with the costly centralized method.

The results given in Figs. 5(j)–(l) show the results of DS over *Amazon*, *Pokec* and *Google+*, respectively. We find that (1) DisMiner and $\mathsf{GRAMI_D}$ ship less data when θ increases, since larger θ means stronger constraint and less verification cost; and (2) DisMiner incurs 14.8% DS of $\mathsf{GRAMI_D}$, on average, the reason for this lies in that DisMiner only ships necessary information for global verification, rather than assembling a large part of fragment from each *worker*.

Varying k. Fixing $n = 4$ and $\theta = 0.3K$, $3K$ and $0.8K$ for *Amazon*, *Pokec* and *Google+*, respectively, we varied k from 10 to 50 in 10 increments, and compared DisMiner with $\mathsf{GRAMI_D}$ and $\mathsf{GRAMI_{ND}}$, *w.r.t.* RT and DS.

Results shown in Figs. 5(m)–(o) tell us following. (1) DisMiner runs much more efficiently than $\mathsf{GRAMI_D}$ and $\mathsf{GRAMI_{ND}}$, owing to its *early termination* property. For example, at *google+*, DisMiner only takes on average 49.4% time of $\mathsf{GRAMI_D}$. (2) DisMiner is sensitive to the increase of k, since it has to verify more candidate patterns before termination condition can be satisfied. (3) $\mathsf{GRAMI_D}$ and $\mathsf{GRAMI_{ND}}$ are insensitive to the change of k, as both of them apply the naive "find-all-select" strategy.

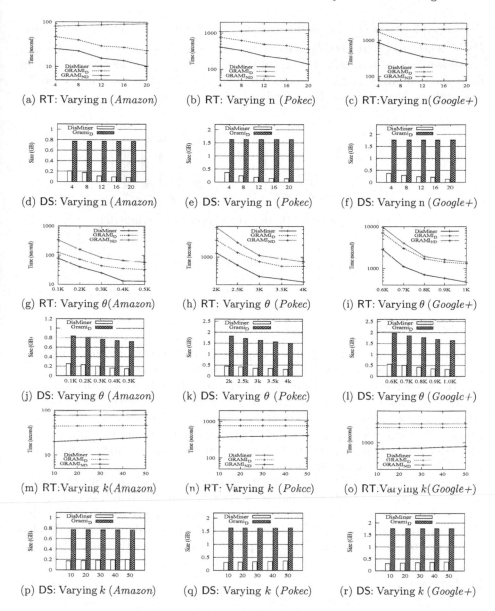

Fig. 5. Performance of DisMiner on real-life graphs

Figures 5(p)–(r) report results on DS of all the algorithms. We find the following. (1) Unlike the trend on RT, DisMiner is not very sensitive to the increase of k w.r.t. DS, as it needs slightly more information to verify supports of candidates which are introduced by the increase of k. (2) GRAMI$_D$ and GRAMI$_{ND}$ are not influenced by the varying of k w.r.t. DS, since the data shipment remains unchanged for both of them.

Varying $|G|$ (Synthetic). Fixing $n = 4$, $k = 50$ and $\theta = 1K$, we varied $|G|$ from $(10M, 20M)$ to $(50M, 100M)$ with $10M$ and $20M$ increments on $|V|$ and $|E|$. As shown in Figs. 6(a) and (b), (1) all the algorithms take longer time and ship more data on larger graphs, as expected; and (2) DisMiner is less sensitive to $|G|$ than others, *w.r.t.* RT and DS, showing better scalability.

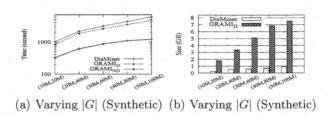

(a) Varying $|G|$ (Synthetic) (b) Varying $|G|$ (Synthetic)

Fig. 6. Scalability of DisMiner

5   Conclusion

We have proposed a distributed technique to identify top-k patterns from large graphs. To do this, we have introduced a metric to measure "interestingness" of a pattern; we have also developed an algorithm with *early termination* property to efficiently discover top-k patterns. In particular, the algorithm combines the strategy of "look-ahead & backtracking" and "partial evaluation" to discover frequent pattern. Our experimental study has verified the efficiency, effectiveness and scalability of the algorithm. We hence contend that our approach yields a promising tool for big graph analysis.

The study of TopKPM is still in its infancy. One topic for future work is to diversify patterns such that patterns identified are not only interesting but also as diverse as possible. Another topic concerns early pruning for generation and supports verification of candidate patterns. The third topic is to develop techniques to efficiently maintain top-k patterns from frequently updated graphs.

References

1. Amazon. http://snap.stanford.edu/data/amazon-meta.html
2. Pokec social network. http://snap.stanford.edu/data/soc-pokec.html
3. Abdelhamid, E., Abdelaziz, I., Kalnis, P., Khayyat, Z., Jamour, F.T.: ScaleMine: scalable parallel frequent subgraph mining in a single large graph. In: West, J., Pancake, C.M. (eds.) Proceedings of the International Conference for High Performance Computing, Networking, Storage and Analysis, SC, pp. 716–727. IEEE Computer Society (2016)

4. Abdelhamid, E., Canim, M., Sadoghi, M., Bhattacharjee, B., Chang, Y., Kalnis, P.: Incremental frequent subgraph mining on large evolving graphs. IEEE Trans. Knowl. Data Eng. **29**(12), 2710–2723 (2017)
5. Ashraf, N., et al.: WeFreS: weighted frequent subgraph mining in a single large graph. In: Perner, P. (ed.) Advances in Data Mining - Applications and Theoretical Aspects, 19th Industrial Conference, ICDM, pp. 201–215. IBAI publishing (2019)
6. Aslay, Ç., Nasir, M.A.U., Morales, G.D.F., Gionis, A.: Mining frequent patterns in evolving graphs. In: Cuzzocrea, A., et al. (eds.) Proceedings of the 27th ACM International Conference on Information and Knowledge Management, CIKM, pp. 923–932. ACM (2018)
7. Bhuiyan, M., Hasan, M.A.: An iterative MapReduce based frequent subgraph mining algorithm. IEEE Trans. Knowl. Data Eng. **27**(3), 608–620 (2015)
8. Chen, H., Liu, M., Zhao, Y., Yan, X., Yan, D., Cheng, J.: G-miner: an efficient task-oriented graph mining system. In: Oliveira, R., Felber, P., Hu, Y.C. (eds.) Proceedings of the Thirteenth EuroSys Conference, EuroSys, pp. 32:1–32:12. ACM (2018)
9. Chi, Y., Xia, Y., Yang, Y., Muntz, R.R.: Mining closed and maximal frequent subtrees from databases of labeled rooted trees. IEEE Trans. Knowl. Data Eng. **17**(2), 190–202 (2005)
10. Cordella, L.P., Foggia, P., Sansone, C., Vento, M.: A (sub)graph isomorphism algorithm for matching large graphs. TPAMI **26**(10), 1367–1372 (2004)
11. Dhifli, W., Aridhi, S., Nguifo, E.M.: MR-Simlab: scalable subgraph selection with label similarity for big data. Inf. Syst. **69**, 155–163 (2017)
12. Elseidy, M., Abdelhamid, E., Skiadopoulos, S., Kalnis, P.: GRAMI: frequent subgraph and pattern mining in a single large graph. PVLDB **7**(7), 517–528 (2014)
13. Fan, W., Wang, X., Wu, Y.: Performance guarantees for distributed reachability queries. PVLDB **5**(11), 1304–1315 (2012)
14. Fiedler, M., Borgelt, C.: Subgraph support in a single large graph. In: Workshops Proceedings of the 7th IEEE International Conference on Data Mining, pp. 399–404. IEEE Computer Society (2007)
15. Gong, N.Z., et al.: Evolution of social-attribute networks: measurements, modeling, and implications using google+. In: IMC (2012)
16. Gonzalez, J.E., Xin, R.S., Dave, A., Crankshaw, D., Franklin, M.J., Stoica, I.: Graphx: graph processing in a distributed dataflow framework. In: 11th USENIX Symposium on Operating Systems Design and Implementation (2014)
17. Gudes, E., Shimony, S.E., Vanetik, N.: Discovering frequent graph patterns using disjoint paths. IEEE Trans. Knowl. Data Eng. **18**(11), 1441–1456 (2006)
18. Huan, J., Wang, W., Prins, J., Yang, J.: Spin: mining maximal frequent subgraphs from graph databases. In: SIGKDD (2004)
19. Husain, M.F., Doshi, P., Khan, L., Thuraisingham, B.M.: Storage and retrieval of large RDF graph using Hadoop and MapReduce. In: CloudCom, pp. 680–686 (2009)
20. Kang, U., Faloutsos, C.: Big graph mining: algorithms and discoveries. SIGKDD Explor. **14**(2), 29–36 (2012)
21. Le, N., Vo, B., Nguyen, L.B.Q., Fujita, H., Le, B.: Mining weighted subgraphs in a single large graph. Inf. Sci. **514**, 149–165 (2020)
22. Le, T., Vo, B., Huynh, V., Nguyen, N.T., Baik, S.W.: Mining top-k frequent patterns from uncertain databases. Appl. Intell. **50**(5), 1487–1497 (2020)
23. Rahimian, F., Payberah, A.H., Girdzijauskas, S., Jelasity, M., Haridi, S.: Ja-be-ja: a distributed algorithm for balanced graph partitioning. In: SASO (2013)

24. Ray, A., Holder, L., Choudhury, S.: Frequent subgraph discovery in large attributed streaming graphs. In: Proceedings of the 3rd International Workshop on Big Data, Streams and Heterogeneous Source Mining: Algorithms, Systems, Programming Models and Applications, volume 36 of JMLR Workshop and Conference Proceedings, pp. 166–181 (2014)
25. Rowe, M.: Interlinking distributed social graphs. In: Proceedings of Linked Data on the Web Workshop, WWW (2009)
26. Shao, Y., Cui, B., Chen, L., Ma, L., Yao, J., Xu, N.: Parallel subgraph listing in a large-scale graph. SIGMOD (2014)
27. Talukder, N., Zaki, M.J.: A distributed approach for graph mining in massive networks. Data Min. Knowl. Discov. **30**(5), 1024–1052 (2016)
28. Teixeira, C.H.C., Fonseca, A.J., Serafini, M., Siganos, G., Zaki, M.J., Aboulnaga, A.: Arabesque: a system for distributed graph mining. In: Miller, E.L., Hand, S. (eds.) Proceedings of the 25th Symposium on Operating Systems Principles, pp. 425–440. ACM (2015)
29. van Leeuwen, M., Bie, T.D., Spyropoulou, E., Mesnage, C.: Subjective interestingness of subgraph patterns. Mach. Learn. **105**(1), 41–75 (2016)
30. Yan, D., Qu, W., Guo, G., Wang, X.: Prefixfpm: a parallel framework for general-purpose frequent pattern mining. In: 36th IEEE International Conference on Data Engineering, ICDE, pp. 1938–1941. IEEE (2020)
31. Yan, X., Han, J.: Closegraph: mining closed frequent graph patterns. In: Proceedings of the Ninth ACM SIGKDD International Conference on Knowledge Discovery and Data Mining, pages 286–295. ACM (2003)
32. Zhu, F., Qu, Q., Lo, D., Yan, X., Han, J., Yu, P.: Mining top-k large structural patterns in a massive network. VLDB **4**(11), 807–818 (2011)
33. Zhu, X., Chen, W., Zheng, W., Ma, X.: Gemini: a computation-centric distributed graph processing system. In: Keeton, K., Roscoe, T. (eds.) 12th USENIX Symposium on Operating Systems Design and Implementation, OSDI 2016, pp. 301–316. USENIX Association (2016)

SQKT: A Student Attention-Based and Question-Aware Model for Knowledge Tracing

Qize Xie[1], Liping Wang[1($\boxtimes$)], Peidong Song[1], and Xuemin Lin[1,2]

[1] Shanghai Key Laboratory of Trustworthy Computing, East China Normal University, Shanghai, China
{51194501074,51205902112}@stu.ecnu.edu.cn, lipingwang@sei.ecnu.edu.cn, lxue@cse.unsw.edu.au
[2] The University of New South Wales, Sydney, Australia

Abstract. The goal of Knowledge Tracing (KT) is to trace student's knowledge states in relation to different knowledge concepts and make prediction of student's performance on new exercises. With the growing number of online learning platforms, personalized learning is more and more urgently required. As a result, KT has been widely explored for recent decades. Traditional machine learning based methods and Deep Neural Network based methods have been constantly introduced for improving prediction accuracy of KT models and have achieved some positive results. However, there are still some challenges for KT research, such as information representation of high-dimentional question data, consideration of personalized learning ability, and so on. In this paper we propose a novel Student attention-based and Question-aware model for KT (SQKT), which can address the challenges by estimating student attention on different type of questions through history exercise trajectory. Firstly, we devise a weighted graph and propose a weighted deep-walk method to get the question embedding which is combined with the correlated skills as question representation. Secondly, we propose a novel student attention mechanism, which is dedicated for the updating of student's knowledge state. Finally, comprehensive experiments are conducted on 4 real world datasets, the results demonstrate that our SQKT model outperforms the state-of-the-art KT models on all datasets.

Keywords: Knowledge Tracing · Deep learning · Graph embedding · Attention-based model

1 Introduction

Knowledge Tracing (KT) [5] aims to estimate student's mastery of knowledge and predict student's future performance, which is a combination of artificial intelligence (AI) and education. As KT is one of the basic techniques for student behavior analysis, it can be widely used for knowledge recommendation, personalized learning path generation and learning evaluation, etc. Recently, with the

© Springer Nature Switzerland AG 2021
L. H. U et al. (Eds.): APWeb-WAIM 2021, LNCS 12859, pp. 221–236, 2021.
https://doi.org/10.1007/978-3-030-85899-5_17

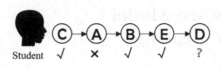

Question	Skill
A	Probability, Function
B	Function, Inequality
C	Function, Inequality
D	Function, Monotonicity
E	Function, Inequality, Monotonicity

Fig. 1. A simple example of knowledge tracing process. Left shows a the exercising records of a student, where he has done question A, B, C and E, the right box shows the corresponding skills of each question, knowledge tracing is used to predict his performance on the new coming question D.

popularity of various online learning platforms, personalized learning is more and more urgently required. As a result, KT has attracted wide attention from related researchers for recent decades.

Generally, the data for KT mostly comes from student's behaviors on the online learning platforms, which contain the questions, responses, timestamps, etc. The questions are usually tagged to skills which is introduced to better represent the knowledge concepts, as is shown in Fig. 1. The algorithm of KT would utilize student's history behaviors and the info or structures about skills for study to predict student's future performance. During early-stage, the traditional machine learning methods is devised for KT. Representative work is Bayesian Knowledge Tracing (BKT) [5] which models knowledge states as a set of binaries, each representing the student's mastery of a single knowledge concept. In recent years, the Deep Neural Network (DNN) [21]-based methods is widely explored. Long short-term memory (LSTM) [8], as its sensitivity for time sequence, has been successfully introduced to update knowledge state at each timestamp. Moreover, skills and their relationships can be modeled as graph and Graph Neural Network (GNN) [24] based-methods is devised to aggregate the student's knowledge state of related skills.

Although the combination with LSTM and GNN has make KT more effective and accurate, challenges for KT research still remain: 1) Due to the high dimension and sparsity of questions data, most of existing methods only use related skills to represent a question. To a certain extent, skills can roughly replace questions for its closer relevance to Knowledge Concepts (KC), and the skills-based methods have achieved a fine empirical performance. However, the abandon of characteristics of questions may cause much information loss and performance degrade. For instance, in Fig. 1, question B and C have the same skills, but they are 2 totally different questions. Therefore, the feature extraction and utilization of questions is very important. 2) The existing KT models lack the ability to trace the latent variation of student's knowledge state. Either a set of binaries or a memory matrix can not fully represent the knowledge states of a student. We noticed that student havs attention when doing exercises, keep practicing on same-type questions can make student more concentrated on the type of questions. 3) The existing GNN based methods have a high dependence on dataset, thus lack of scalability.

In this paper, we devise a novel knowledge tracing model to address the above challenges. Specifically, our model provides a graph-based embedding method for feature extraction and question representation, which can consider comprehensive info of student behaviors on various questions. Additionally, we propose a novel attention mechanism to estimate the student's learning ability on different knowledge concepts and this attention mechanism is dedicated for the updating of student's knowledge state. Our main contributions are summarized as follows:

1) To comprehensively represent the questions, we devise a weighted graph, propose a weighted deepwalk method to get the question embedding and combine it with the correlated skills as question representation. Our question representation can catch the latent relevance while solve the high dimension problem.
2) To enhance the ability of tracing the latent variation of student's knowledge state, we propose a student attention mechanism to add an attention weight when updating the knowledge state. Our student attention mechanism can cooperate with the traditional attention methods well.
3) Extensive and comprehensive experiments are conducted on 4 real world datasets, the experimental results demonstrate the effectiveness of proposed SQKT model. And the comparison to the state-of-the-art KT methods shows that our model achieves higher prediction accuracy.

2   Related Work

In this section, we introduce the progress of the development of Knowledge Tracing methods.

Traditional Knowledge Tracing Methods. Traditional machine learning methods always use logistic regression to classify the questions and skills by regarding each question or skill as a binary variable thus can signify whether the student has mastered the skill or not. Bayesian Knowledge Tracing (BKT) [5] is probably the most popular model in traditional knowledge tracing methods, which update the knowledge state for each student through a Hidden Markov Model (HMM). Based on the BKT model, Pardos et al. [18] introduced the item difficulty to the knowledge tracing model, and Baker et al. [2] utilized contextual estimation of slip and guess probabilities to improve the accuracy. Student individualization is also modeled as an implementation in IBKT [28] and MIBKT [17,28]. Factor Analysis models aim to learn common relations between different features such as (user, skills) pair, and use these common factors as predictors in logistic regression. E.g. Item Response Theory (IRT) [7] model simply use the difference between the mastery degree of student and the difficulty of skill. Multi-dimensional Item Response Theory (MIRT) [6] model has extended the IRT model to multidimensional abilities. Additive factor model (AFM) [3] has taken the student's number of attempts into account, on the basis of AFM, Pavlik et al. propose Performance Factors Analysis (PFA) [19] model which utilizes different bias for the number of the successful and failed attempts.

The methods of logistic regression have strong interpretability and expansibility and the traditional KT models based on BKT [5] have performed reasonably well. However, the explosion of educational data in recent times naturally benefited the deep neural network (DNN) models.

Deep Neural Network. Deep Knowledge Tracing (DKT) [21] first applies deep neural network in knowledge tracing, which utilizes a Recurrent Neural Network (RNN) [27] for KT that can extract the variation of the knowledge state from student's past learning history. Dynamic Student Classification Memory Networks (DSCMN) [12] model, as an extension of DKT, takes the side information of question difficulty into consideration. Dynamic Key-Value Memory Networks (DKVMN) [29] model proposes a Memory-Augmented Neural Network (MANN) [23] instead of traditional RNN. On the basis of DKVMN, Sequential Key-Value Memory Networks (SKVMN) [1] model uses a Hop-LSTM layer that can jump ahead in a sequence of related history records when training. Self-Attentive Knowledge Tracing (SAKT) [15] model utilizes the relevance of past interactions as attention for high-performance in sparse data. Relation-aware self-attention for Knowledge Tracing (RKT) [16] model takes the time interval between two interactions into account to improve the accuracy. Exercise-aware Knowledge Tracing (EKT) [9,25] framework proposes a EERNNA model which uses a bi-directional LSTM to learn the hidden word state of questions in order to distinguish different questions.

With the development of Graph Neural Network (GNN) [24], some GNN-based methods are proposed. Graph-based Knowledge Tracing (GKT) [14] method structures a graph to represent skills and uses GNN to aggregate the student's knowledge state of related skills. On the basis of EKT, Hierarchical exercise Graph for Knowledge Tracing (HGKT) [26] model utilizes a hierarchical graph to tackle with the question representation problem. Both of the two models use the text of the questions while no public dataset contains these text. Therefore, these two models can only test their effectiveness on specific datasets, which means the methods are not universally adaptable.

The SQKT model proposed in this paper differs from all models above, which uses a Weighted Graph Neural Network to represent the high-dimension question data and adds a global attention mechanism to focus on both student attention and question attention. To the best of knowledge, our SQKT model is the first work to propose the idea about weighted graph embedding and student attention mechanism.

3   Problem Formulation

In an Interactive Educational System (IES) with $|S|$ students and $|Q|$ questions, each question contains one or more knowledge skills, every interaction of student will be recorded, our goal is to trace student's knowledge state based on his history records.

Here we denote the history records of one student as $R_s = \{(q_1, a_1, t_1), (q_2, a_2, t_2), ..., (q_N, a_N, t_N)\}, s \in S$, where $q_n \in Q$ represents the n-th question in the history record of student s , $a_n \in (0, 1)$ represents the correctness, if the student answers correctly, a_n equals to 1, else a_n equals to 0, and t_n represents the timestamp when student answers the question. To trace student's mastery of each knowledge unit, knowledge skills are used to represent knowledge units. The knowledge skills that are included by the questions was counted by the online educational platform. Each question q_n can contain one or more corresponding knowledge skills $s_1, s_2, ...s_k$, while a knowledge skill can be included by many questions. Generally, the amount of knowledge skills is far less than the amount of questions.

Based on the above description, the problem about KT can be formally defined as follows: given the history record of a student $R_s = \{(q_1, a_1, t_1), (q_2, a_2, t_2), ..., (q_{n-1}, a_{n-1}, t_{n-1})\}$ and the knowledge skills related to each question $S_q = s_1, s_2, ..., s_k$, our goal is to trace student's mastery of knowledge and predict whether the student can answer the coming question q_n correctly.

4   The SQKT Method

In this section, we introduce the specific improvements of our SQKT model. The overall framework is shown in Fig. 2. We first construct a weighted graph by the relationship of questions, then use weighted-deepwalk to learn question representations. After get the question representations, we use Recurrent Neural Network (RNN) [27] with both student attention and question attention to update the knowledge state of the student and to predict his performance on the coming question. Here we just explain the main idea of the model, the detail about question representation and student attention mechanism is described in Sect. 4.1 and Sect. 4.2.

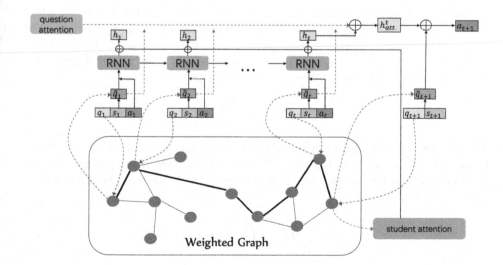

Fig. 2. An illustration of SQKT, which use a weighted graph and a Recurrent Neural Network (RNN) with question and student attention mechanism to get prediction.

4.1   Question Representation

From the perspective of pedagogy, whether a student can answer a question correctly depends on both the question and the student's ability. For question representation, we not only use the related skills, but also focus on the latent relationship that can not be represented by skills. To catch the unique features of each question, we construct a weighted graph $G = (V, E)$ that shows the latent relevance between questions. In the weighted graph, each node represents a question, when question q_i and q_j follows $|t_i - t_j| < T$, we add 1 on the weight w_{ij} of edge e_{ij} between node v_i and node v_j. Figure 3 shows the overview of question representation process.

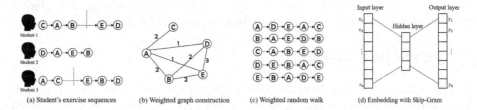

Fig. 3. The overview of question representation process: (a) Students' exercise records, the dashed line means the time span of two exercise exceeded the threshold; these records are used to construct the weighted graph; (b) The weighted graph, where the number on the edges represents the weights; (c) The sequences generated from the weighted graph, the larger the weight, the more likely the edge will be chosen; (d) Use Skip-Gram algorithm to get question embedding

In the weighted graph, nodes represent questions and the weight of edges represent the correlation degree between the nodes at both ends. Improved on the basis of DeepWalk [20], we use a weighted deepwalk method to get the structural characterization of our weighted graph. We take each node as a starting point for random walk with the transition probability defined as:

$$p(v_i|v_j) = \frac{w_{ij}}{\sum_{k \in N_i} w_{ik}} \tag{1}$$

After generating the question sequences by random walk, we utilize the Skip-Gram [10,11] algorithm to learn the embeddings, which maximizes the co-occurence probability of two questions in an obtained sequence. The optimization goal is as follow:

$$\underset{\Phi}{minimize} - log \prod_{j=i-s, j \neq i}^{i+s} \Pr(v_j \mid \Phi(v_i)) \tag{2}$$

where s is the window size of the context questions in the sequences.

The embeddings of nodes in the weighted graph can reflect the latent relevance between questions, for each interaction at timestamp t, we concatenate the node embedding $\widetilde{\mathbf{q}}_t$ with the one-hot encoding of related skills $\mathbf{s}_t$ and project to d-dimension through a non-linear transformation as complete question representation:

$$\mathbf{q}_t = \text{ReLU}\left(\mathbf{W}\left([\widetilde{\mathbf{q}}_t, \mathbf{s}_t]\right) + \mathbf{b}\right) \tag{3}$$

4.2 Student Attention Mechanism

Learning is a very complicated process. During the process of education, educators always divide the questions into lectures and teach systematically. Generalized by experience, keeping practice on questions of same lecture can be more effective than picking up questions randomly. Therefore, we assume that the learner's absorption of knowledge is based on his attention which generated from his history exercise record in a period of time. The devise of the student attention mechanism can guarantee that learners whose attention is on the same question type can absorb more knowledge than those who are not.

We first choose a hyper parameter T as the time threshold, at each timestamp t_{n+1}, the history question record $q_k \in R_s$ would be regarded as an influence to students's attention if $|t_{n+1} - t_k| < T$. The influence of history record on student's current attention is related to the time gap, the shorter time gap is, the more influence it will have. We use the following formulation to measure the extent of k-th history record's influence on student's current attention:

$$E_k = \text{RelU}(\mathbf{W}\frac{1}{t_{n+1} - t_k} + \mathbf{b}) \tag{4}$$

where E_k presents the influence extent of k-th history record on student attention. Then we add the influence of all eligible history record with the coefficient of its influence extent to get students's current attention:

$$Att_s^t = \sum_{t_i > t - T} E_i * q_i \tag{5}$$

where t is the current timestamp and q_i can be calculated by Eq. (3).

Finally we use the cosine similarity between student's current attention Att_s^t and current question q_t as attention weight to measure his absorption of the question when updating knowledge state:

$$W_{att}^t = cos(Att_s^t, q_t) \tag{6}$$

As is shown in Fig. 4, orange nodes present questions from lecture A, green nodes present questions from lecture B, red nodes present student's attention. The blue thick line depicts student's exercise sequence while the red dotted line depicts student's attention sequence calculated by the equations above. When student transits from lecture A to lecture B when doing question 3, the attention weight W_{att}^3 declines correspondingly.

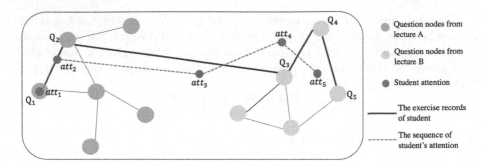

Fig. 4. Student attention sequence generated from his exercise records.

4.3   Modeling Process of SQKT

In this section, we will systematically elaborate SQKT modeling process. SQKT use weighted graph to better represent the questions, trace and update student knowledge state by RNN with both student attention and question attention mechanism.

Question-Answer Embedding. In SQKT model, we maintain a weighted graph which represent the latent relationship of questions, and use a weighted deepwalk method with Skip-Gram [11] algorithm to get the question embedding. When student has done a new question at timestamp t, the triplet (q_t, s_t, a_t) would be generated, we get the question embedding Q_t with dimension d_v from q_t and s_t through the weighted graph, extent the embedding vector to dimension $2d_v$ through a_t:

$$\widetilde{Q}_t = \begin{cases} [Q_t \oplus \mathbf{0}] & \text{if} \quad a_t = 1 \\ [\mathbf{0} \oplus Q_t] & \text{if} \quad a_t = 0 \end{cases} \tag{7}$$

where $\mathbf{0} = (0, 0, ..., 0)$ is a vector of all zeros with dimension d_v and $\oplus$ means concatenate, the embedding vector $\widetilde{Q}_t$ is the question-answer embedding which represent the complete triplet (q_t, s_t, a_t).

Knowledge State Evolution. After we get the question-answer embedding $\widetilde{Q}_t$, we use LSTM [8] to trace the knowledge state of student:

$$\mathbf{i}_t = \sigma \left(\mathbf{W}_i \left[\widetilde{Q}_t \mathbf{h}_{t-1}, \mathbf{c}_{t-1} \right] + \mathbf{b}_i \right) \tag{8}$$

$$\mathbf{f}_t = \sigma \left(\mathbf{W}_f \left[\widetilde{Q}_t, \mathbf{h}_{t-1}, \mathbf{c}_{t-1} \right] + \mathbf{b}_f \right) \tag{9}$$

$$\mathbf{o}_t = \sigma \left(\mathbf{W}_o \left[\widetilde{Q}_t, \mathbf{h}_{t-1}, \mathbf{c}_{t-1} \right] + \mathbf{b}_o \right) \tag{10}$$

$$\mathbf{c}_t = \mathbf{f}_t \mathbf{c}_{t-1} + \mathbf{i}_t \tanh \left(\mathbf{W}_c \left[\widetilde{Q}_t, \mathbf{h}_{t-1} \right] + \mathbf{b}_c \right) \tag{11}$$

$$\mathbf{h}_t = \mathbf{o}_t \tanh (\mathbf{c}_t) \tag{12}$$

where i_t, o_t, f_t, c_t, h_t represents input gate, output gate, forget gate, cell state, hidden state respectively.

We introduce the concept of student attention, which can measure student's absorption of knowledge state. Using student attention when updating knowledge state, the Eq. (12) can be updated to:

$$\mathbf{h}_t = W_{att}^t \mathbf{o}_t \tanh(\mathbf{c}_t) \tag{13}$$

where W_{att}^t is the attention weight calculated by Eq. (6)

Prediction Output. Through markov property, we use student's current knowledge state h_t to predict whether he can answer question q_{t+1} correct or not, the prediction probability can be calculated as follow:

$$y_{T+1} = \text{ReLU}\left(\mathbf{W_1} \cdot [h_T \oplus x_{T+1}] + \mathbf{b_1}\right) \tag{14}$$

where W_1, b_1 are parameters and $\oplus$ is concatenation operation.

Note that questions have attentions too and students may get similar score on similar questions. We consider the knowledge state h_t as a weighted sum aggregation of history questions based on its similarity with current question:

$$h_{att}^T = \sum_{i=1}^{T} \alpha_i h_i \tag{15}$$

where $\alpha_i = cos(x_{T+1}, x_i)$. After obtaining the attention mechanism, Eq. (14) can replace the h_t with h_{att}^t:

$$y_{T+1} = \text{ReLU}\left(\mathbf{W_1} \cdot [h_{att}^T \oplus x_{T+1}] + \mathbf{b_1}\right) \tag{16}$$

We use the Sigmoid function $\sigma(x) = \frac{1}{1+\exp(-x)}$ to normalize the result as prediction probability:

$$\tilde{y}_{T+1} = \sigma\left(\mathbf{W_2} \cdot y_{T+1} + \mathbf{b_2}\right) \tag{17}$$

The student's answer to this question will be predicted to be correct if $\tilde{y}_{T+1} > 0.5$, else will be predicted to be wrong.

4.4 Optimization

We use gradient decent to optimize the parameters in our model. The overall loss can be formulated as:

$$\mathcal{L} = -\sum_{t=1}^{T} \left(a_t \log \tilde{y}_t + (1 - a_t) \log(1 - \tilde{y}_t)\right) \tag{18}$$

where a_t is the actual binary score, while $\tilde{y}_t$ is our predicted score.

5 Experiments

In this section, we conduct several experiments to evaluate the performance of our model on the following aspects: 1) The accuracy of prediction comparison between SQKT and the other baseline models. 2) The representation ability of proposed question embedding method based on weighted graph. 3) The effectiveness of our student attention mechanism.

5.1 Datasets

To evaluate the prediction accuracy, we test the proposed SQKT model and other baseline methods on 4 real world datasets. The datasets were carefully selected that comprehensively covers mathematics, programming and many other fields.

Mynereus[1] is a dataset collected from Mynereus programming Platform, with a total of 86772 records from 202 students on 184 questions. There are 48 skills about these questions.

ASSISTments2009[2] is a dataset collected from the ASSISTments online tutoring platform during the school year 2009–2010. Due to the duplicated record problem, we removed the duplicated records and the rest dataset has 4151 students with 110 questions on 123 type of skills.

ASSISTments2015[3] is collected from the same tutoring platform with ASSISTments2009 during year 2015–2016. In ASSISTments2015 dataset, each question only related to one skill. After dataprocess for duplicated records, there are 161,723 records from 4,210 students reserved in the dataset.

Ednet[4] is a dataset collected over 2 years by Santa, which is a multi-platform AI tutoring service. The dataset includes total 131,441,538 interactions from 784,309 students and 13,169 questions on 293 type of skills. Since the Ednet dataset is too large, we randomly choose 5,000 students with 1,079,483 records.

The dataset statistics are shown in Table 1.

Table 1. Dataset statistics

Dataset	#Questions	#Students	#Skills	#Records
Mynereus	184	202	48	86,772
ASSISTments2009	13016	4,151	110	325,637
ASSISTments2015	9073	4,210	100	161,723
Ednet	11187	5000	187	1,079,483

5.2 Baselines

The following KT models are chosen as baselines to measure the performance of the proposed SQKT model:

– **BKT** [5] models knowledge state as a set of binaries and use a Hidden Markov Model to update knowledge state.

---

[1] Mynereus: http://code.mynereus.com.

[2] ASSISTments2009: https://sites.google.com/site/assistmentsdata/home/assistment-2009-2010-data/skill-builder-data-2009-2010.

[3] ASSISTments2015: https://sites.google.com/site/assistmentsdata/home/2015-assistments-skill-builder-data.

[4] Ednet: https://github.com/riiid/ednet.

- **KTM** [22] is the most comprehensive factor analysis model of KT, which has taken much side information into consideration.
- **DKT** [21] is the first deep learning KT method, which utilize a Recurrent Neural Network to extract the variation of the knowledge state.
- **DKVMN** [13] as an expansion of DKT, proposed a Mempry-Augmented Neural Network (MANN) [23] to represent the knowledge state of a student.
- **SKVMN** [1] as an expansion of DKVMN, use Hop-LSTM network in its sequence modeling.
- **GKT** [14] is a Graph Neural Network (GNN) based KT model, which casting the knowledge structure as a graph.

5.3   Metrics

We use AUC (the area under the Receiver Operating Characteristic (ROC) curve) to evaluate the KT models' prediction accuracy. The AUC score varies from 0 to 1, the higher the number is, the better the model performs. When the AUC score equals 0.5, the predictive model's accuracy is as same as random guess.

5.4   Model Evaluation

During experiments, each dataset was split into two parts: 70% for training and validation and 30% for testing. We used 5-fold cross validation to separate each training and validation subset, we divide the subset into 5 equal-sized parts, use 4 parts for training and 1 part for validation in turn.

Here the hyperparameters are chosen by grid search, we chose 0.01 as the learning rate, 0.1 as the epsilon value for Adam optimizer, 0.5 as the lambda for L2 loss, 5000 as the time threshhold, 5 as the window size of deep walk, and 100 as question embedding dimension.

Table 2. The AUC score of all KT models on all Datasets

Model	Mynereus	ASSISTments09	ASSISTments15	Ednet
BKT	0.7132	0.6271	0.6304	0.7401
KTM	0.7854	0.7169	0.6830	0.7829
DKT	0.8082	0.7961	0.7131	0.8519
DKVMN	0.8187	0.8157	0.7268	0.8721
GKT	0.8023	0.7940	0.7172	0.8790
SKVMN	0.8174	0.8348	0.7469	0.8760
SQKT	**0.8312**	**0.8416**	**0.7527**	**0.8841**

The overall performances of all KT models are shown in Table 2 and Fig. 5. From the result, we can sum up the following conclusions.

First of all, deep learning models generally outperform the traditional knowledge tracing models with an average improvement of 9.36% on AUC score, due

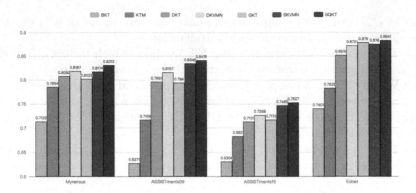

Fig. 5. The AUC score results of 7 KT models over 4 datasets

to the deep neural network's ability to learn complex student learning patterns. Second, the existing graph-based KT model such as GKT [14] and other DL models have advantages and disadvantages of each, GKT has a better score on Ednet dataset, while DKVMN and SKVMN performs better on ASSISTments datasets, which shows that the existing graph based methods are not perfect. Third, DL models with memory structure (such as DKVMN [29] and SKVMN [1]) performs better than no memory structure models (such as DKT), which shows the effectiveness of memory structure in storing student knowledge units. Last but not least, the proposed SQKT model outperforms all other existing models on all 4 datasets, the usage of question information and student attention have enhanced the prediction accuracy with an average of 0.8% in comparison to the state of art SKVMN model.

5.5   Ablation Studies

We also designed several ablation studies to further investigate the effect of our question representation and student attention module.

First, we compare our question representation module with 3 other methods, separately using random generalized embedding matrix, GCN (Graph convolutional network) and GAT (Graph attention network) to get the question embeddings. We denote these models as SQKT-Rand, SQKT-GCN and SQKT-GAT. The comparative experiment on 3 models is shown in Table 3.

Table 3. The AUC score of 3 comparative models and SQKT on all datasets

Dataset	SQKT-Rand	SQKT-GCN	SQKT-GAT	SQKT
Mynereus	0.8210	0.8307	0.8311	**0.8312**
ASSISTments09	0.8371	0.8386	0.8392	**0.8416**
ASSISTments15	0.7480	0.7516	0.7511	**0.7527**
Ednet	0.8769	0.8820	0.8824	**0.8841**

Next, we remove the student attention module, treat student's attention weight on all questions as the same, and denote this model as QKT. The comparative experiment result on QKT and SQKT model is shown in Table 4.

Table 4. The AUC score of QKT and SQKT on all datasets

Dataset	QKT	SQKT
Mynereus	0.8301	**0.8312**
ASSISTments09	0.8357	**0.8416**
ASSISTments15	0.7461	**0.7527**
Ednet	0.8760	**0.8841**

From the results, we can find that our question representation method achieved the best auc score among all 4 methods, while the attention module has proved to be effective through ablation experiment. It is worth mentioning that the student attention mechanism achieves a better improvement on larger dataset with longer time span. The comparative and ablation experiments have demonstrate the effectiveness of the modules we have proposed.

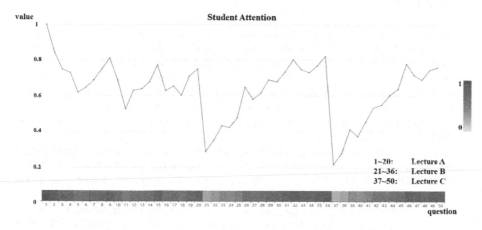

Fig. 6. The visualization of student attention through a student's exercise record

Figure 6 visualizes the variation of a student's attention during his learning process from Ednet [4] dataset. We intercepted the first 50 questions of the students' exercise record, and shows the attention on each question on the picture. The darker the red is, the more attention the student get, which means he can learn more on the question. The 50 questions are from 3 different lectures and the student finish these 3 lectures in turn. From the Fig. 6, we can see that the student attention have a clear reduction when he switch to a new lecture (around question 21 and 37). This phenomenon is very close to the actual human learning process, that keeping practice systematically on same-type questions can be more effective than practising randomly.

6 Conclusion

In this paper, we introduced a novel Student attention-based and Question-aware model for Knowledge Tracing (SQKT). In SQKT model, we first proposed a question representation method, which use Weighted Deep Walk method with Skip-Gram algorithm based on a weighted graph constructed from questions relationship. Then we introduced a student attention mechanism to measure attention weight when updating student knowledge state. Finally we use RNN with question attention to predict student's performance on the new coming question. Abundant experiments and ablation studies were conducted on SQKT model, the experiment result shows that SQKT model outperformed the state-of-the-art models over all datasets, and the ablation study proves the reasonableness and effectiveness of the proposed methods. For future work, more side information could be taken into consideration, and the structure of RNN network can be further optimized.

Acknowledgments. This work was supported by NSFC 61401155.

References

1. Abdelrahman, G., Wang, Q.: Knowledge tracing with sequential key-value memory networks. In: Proceedings of the 42nd International ACM SIGIR Conference on Research and Development in Information Retrieval, pp. 175–184 (2019)
2. Baker, R.S.J., Corbett, A.T., Aleven, V.: More accurate student modeling through contextual estimation of slip and guess probabilities in Bayesian knowledge tracing. In: Woolf, B.P., Aïmeur, E., Nkambou, R., Lajoie, S. (eds.) ITS 2008. LNCS, vol. 5091, pp. 406–415. Springer, Heidelberg (2008). https://doi.org/10.1007/978-3-540-69132-7_44
3. Cen, H., Koedinger, K., Junker, B.: Learning factors analysis – a general method for cognitive model evaluation and improvement. In: Ikeda, M., Ashley, K.D., Chan, T.-W. (eds.) ITS 2006. LNCS, vol. 4053, pp. 164–175. Springer, Heidelberg (2006). https://doi.org/10.1007/11774303_17
4. Choi, Y., et al.: EdNet: a large-scale hierarchical dataset in education. In: Bittencourt, I.I., Cukurova, M., Muldner, K., Luckin, R., Millán, E. (eds.) AIED 2020. LNCS (LNAI), vol. 12164, pp. 69–73. Springer, Cham (2020). https://doi.org/10.1007/978-3-030-52240-7_13
5. Corbett, A.T., Anderson, J.R.: Knowledge tracing: modeling the acquisition of procedural knowledge. User Model. User-Adap. Inter. **4**(4), 253–278 (1994)
6. Desmarais, M.C., d Baker, R.S.: A review of recent advances in learner and skill modeling in intelligent learning environments. User Modeling User-Adapted Interact. **22**(1), 9–38 (2012)
7. Embretson, S.E., Reise, S.P.: Item Response Theory. Psychology Press, London (2013)
8. Hochreiter, S., Schmidhuber, J.: Long short-term memory. Neural Comput. **9**(8), 1735–1780 (1997)
9. Liu, Q., et al.: EKT: exercise-aware knowledge tracing for student performance prediction. IEEE Trans. Knowl. Data Eng. **33**(1), 100–115 (2019)

10. Mikolov, T., Chen, K., Corrado, G., Dean, J.: Efficient estimation of word representations in vector space. arXiv preprint arXiv:1301.3781 (2013)
11. Mikolov, T., Sutskever, I., Chen, K., Corrado, G., Dean, J.: Distributed representations of words and phrases and their compositionality. arXiv preprint arXiv:1310.4546 (2013)
12. Minn, S., Desmarais, M.C., Zhu, F., Xiao, J., Wang, J.: Dynamic student classification on memory networks for knowledge tracing. In: Yang, Q., Zhou, Z.-H., Gong, Z., Zhang, M.-L., Huang, S.-J. (eds.) PAKDD 2019. LNCS (LNAI), vol. 11440, pp. 163–174. Springer, Cham (2019). https://doi.org/10.1007/978-3-030-16145-3_13
13. Minn, S., Yu, Y., Desmarais, M.C., Zhu, F., Vie, J.J.: Deep knowledge tracing and dynamic student classification for knowledge tracing. In: 2018 IEEE International conference on data mining (ICDM), pp. 1182–1187. IEEE (2018)
14. Nakagawa, H., Iwasawa, Y., Matsuo, Y.: Graph-based knowledge tracing: modeling student proficiency using graph neural network. In: 2019 IEEE/WIC/ACM International Conference on Web Intelligence (WI), pp. 156–163. IEEE (2019)
15. Pandey, S., Karypis, G.: A self-attentive model for knowledge tracing. arXiv preprint arXiv:1907.06837 (2019)
16. Pandey, S., Srivastava, J.: RKT: relation-aware self-attention for knowledge tracing. In: Proceedings of the 29th ACM International Conference on Information & Knowledge Management, pp. 1205–1214 (2020)
17. Pardos, Z.A., Heffernan, N.T.: Modeling individualization in a Bayesian networks implementation of knowledge tracing. In: De Bra, P., Kobsa, A., Chin, D. (eds.) UMAP 2010. LNCS, vol. 6075, pp. 255–266. Springer, Heidelberg (2010). https://doi.org/10.1007/978-3-642-13470-8_24
18. Pardos, Z.A., Heffernan, N.T.: KT-IDEM: introducing item difficulty to the knowledge tracing model. In: Konstan, J.A., Conejo, R., Marzo, J.L., Oliver, N. (eds.) UMAP 2011. LNCS, vol. 6787, pp. 243–254. Springer, Heidelberg (2011). https://doi.org/10.1007/978-3-642-22362-4_21
19. Pavlik Jr, P.I., Cen, H., Koedinger, K.R.: Performance factors analysis-a new alternative to knowledge tracing. Online Submission (2009)
20. Perozzi, B., Al-Rfou, R., Skiena, S.: Deepwalk: online learning of social representations. In: Proceedings of the 20th ACM SIGKDD International Conference on Knowledge Discovery and Data Mining, pp. 701–710 (2014)
21. Piech, C., et al.: Deep knowledge tracing. arXiv preprint arXiv:1506.05908 (2015)
22. Rendle, S.: Factorization machines. In: 2010 IEEE International Conference on Data Mining, pp. 995–1000. IEEE (2010)
23. Santoro, A., Bartunov, S., Botvinick, M., Wierstra, D., Lillicrap, T.: Meta-learning with memory-augmented neural networks. In: International Conference on Machine Learning, pp. 1842–1850. PMLR (2016)
24. Scarselli, F., Gori, M., Tsoi, A.C., Hagenbuchner, M., Monfardini, G.: The graph neural network model. IEEE Trans. Neural Netw. 20(1), 61–80 (2008)
25. Su, Y., et al.: Exercise-enhanced sequential modeling for student performance prediction. In: Proceedings of the AAAI Conference on Artificial Intelligence, vol. 32 (2018)
26. Tong, H., Zhou, Y., Wang, Z.: HGKT: introducing problem schema with hierarchical exercise graph for knowledge tracing. arXiv preprint arXiv:2006.16915 (2020)
27. Williams, R.J., Zipser, D.: A learning algorithm for continually running fully recurrent neural networks. Neural Comput. 1(2), 270–280 (1989)

28. Yudelson, M.V., Koedinger, K.R., Gordon, G.J.: Individualized Bayesian knowl-edge tracing models. In: Lane, H.C., Yacef, K., Mostow, J., Pavlik, P. (eds.) AIED 2013. LNCS (LNAI), vol. 7926, pp. 171–180. Springer, Heidelberg (2013). https://doi.org/10.1007/978-3-642-39112-5_18
29. Zhang, J., Shi, X., King, I., Yeung, D.Y.: Dynamic key-value memory networks for knowledge tracing. In: Proceedings of the 26th International Conference on World Wide Web, pp. 765–774 (2017)

Comparison Question Generation Based on Potential Compared Attributes Extraction

Jiayuan Xie[1,2], Wenhao Fang[1,2], Yi Cai[1,2(✉)], and Zehang Lin[3]

[1] Key Laboratory of Big Data and Intelligent Robot (South China University of Technology), Ministry of Education, Guangzhou, China
ycai@scut.edu.cn
[2] South China University of Technology, Guangzhou, China
[3] The Hong Kong Polytechnic University, Kowloon, Hong Kong

Abstract. Question generation (QG) aims to automatically generate questions from a given passage, which is widely used in education. Existing studies on the QG task mainly focus on the answer-aware QG, which only asks an independent object related to the expected answer. However, to prompt students to develop comparative thinking skills, multiple objects need to be simultaneously focused on the QG task, which can be used to attract students to explore the differences and similarities between them. Towards this end, we consider a new task named comparison question generation (CQG). In this paper, we propose a framework that includes an attribute extractor and an attribute-attention seq2seq module. Specially, the attribute extractor is based on Stanford CoreNLP Toolkit to recognize the attributes related to the multiple objects that can be used for comparison. Then, the attribute-attention seq2seq module utilizes an attention mechanism to generate questions with the assistance of the attributes. Extensive experiments conducted on the HotpotQA dataset manifest the effectiveness of our framework, which outperforms the neural-based model and generates reliable comparison questions.

Keywords: Question generation · Potential compared attributes extraction

1 Introduction

Question generation (QG) is a dual task of question answering [2,11,19,22], which aims to generate natural and relevant questions from natural language text [7,20]. It can generate various types of questions to help for the knowledge testing in education [7,8]. Specially, there is a kind of question named comparison question that is commonly featured in standardized tests, e.g., the English exams for middle and high school, which is required to compare the differences and similarities between multiple objects. According to the existing studies in the area of education, these questions can be used as good materials for students to begin developing the comparative thinking skill [6], which is an important high-order thinking skill that can

L. H. U et al. (Eds.): APWeb-WAIM 2021, LNCS 12859, pp. 237–252, 2021.
https://doi.org/10.1007/978-3-030-85899-5_18

Passage: **Arthur's Magazine** (<u>1844–1846</u>) was an <u>American</u> literary periodical published in Philadelphia in the 19th century. **First for Women** is a woman's magazine published by Bauer Media Group in the <u>USA</u>. The magazine was started in <u>1989</u>. Radio City is India's first private FM radio station and was started on 3 July 2001...

Question: Which magazine was started first, **Arthur's Magazine** or **First for Women?**
Answer: Arthur's Magazine

Fig. 1. An example of comparison questions generation in HotpotQA dataset [25]. We highlight the compared objects in **bold** and <u>underline</u> fragments related to the compared attributes.

help students achieve their highest potential [18]. Therefore, it is necessary for us to investigate a new task named comparison question generation (CQG).

Existing studies on QG for knowledge testing are mainly focusing on the answer-aware QG, which generates a question according to the given passage that targets an expected answer [4,9,26,27]. Take the passage shown in Fig. 1 as an example, annotators may generate a question (i.e., "when was First for Women established?") and an expected answer (i.e., "1989") based on the passage, which guides students to explore the attribute (i.e., "the date of establishment") of the object (i.e., "First for Women") that related to the answer. We can find that these studies only ask about certain attributes of an independent object related to the expected answer. However, not only the multiple objects in a given passage but also the attributes that can be used to explore the differences and similarities between them should be taken into account when raising a comparison question, which is quite different from the existing studies.

Comparing with conventional methods of the QG task, CQG has three unique characteristics. Firstly, the CQG task needs to focus on multiple objects for comparison at the same time while conventional methods only asking questions about a single object. Secondly, the CQG task requires extracting some suitable potential compared attributes from all attributes related to each object to explore the differences and similarities between them. However, conventional methods mainly focus on the relationship between an object and its attribute rather than the relationship between multiple objects. As shown in Fig. 1, an appropriate attribute (i.e., DATE) related to the specific fragments (i.e., "1844–1846" and "1989") will be extracted from multiple attributes contained in the passage, which can be used to explore the differences between the establishment date of the different magazine. Thirdly, the CQG task demands to ensure that the objects used for comparison and one of the potential compared attributes can be included in the generated question while conventional methods on the QG task lack relevant and effective mechanisms.

To tackle the characteristics mentioned above, we propose a novel framework consisting of two modules, an attribute extractor and an attribute-attention seq2seq module, which can simultaneously consider multiple objects. To extract the potential compared attributes between the multiple objects, the attribute extractor first utilizes the Stanford CoreNLP Toolkit [14] to recognize the types of entities in target sentences, which describes the relevant attributes of an object in the passage. Specifically, we use the types of entities related to the compared objects as the attributes of them, because each entity type is a description of the object in certain aspects, such as LOCATION, DATE, and COUNTRY. As shown in Fig. 1, we can recognize the types of entities COUNTRY and DATE corresponding to the two entities "USA" and "1989" respectively in the target sentence (the second sentence in the passage) as the attributes of the object "First of Women". In addition, to ensure that the generated question is about comparing multiple objects on a certain potential compared attribute, the attribute-attention seq2seq module utilizes an attention mechanism to focus on the specific fragments of the input, e.g., the fragments related to potential compared attributes and compared objects, to generate comparison questions.

To summarize, our contributions are as follows:

- We introduce a new task of comparison question generation (CQG), which is crucial for students to develop comparative thinking skills in education and can potentially provide datasets for future relevant research.
- We propose a novel framework for the CQG task by formulating the QG task with an auxiliary task of compared attributes extraction, which can be used to explore the differences and similarities between multiple objects.
- We conduct analytical experiments on the HotpotQA dataset to verify the effectiveness of the proposed method. The experimental results prove the effectiveness of our framework: the potential compared attributes extracted from the attribute extractor are given more attention by the attribute-attention seq2seq module, which can significantly improve the quality of the generated questions.

2   Related Work

Recently, question generation (QG) has mainly tackled with end-to-end deep learning neural network, especially the encoder-decoder architecture [4,9,20,26,27]. Du et al. [4] firstly use a sequence-to-sequence model with an attention mechanism for the task of QG and achieve better performance than most rule-based question generation methods [8]. However, these models only use the passage information for question generation, which makes it difficult to control the generation of the question for the specific fragments of the input.

After, a lot of studies add the answer information as assistance to generate appropriate questions [9,21,27]. In detail, Zhou et al. [27] utilize some features related to the answer (i.e., named entity recognition (NER) and part-of-speech (POS) tagging [23]) for their model, which makes the generated questions related to the target answer. Kim et al. [9] propose an answer-separate model that separates the target answer from the passage to make better use of the answer information. These methods generate questions based on a single passage-answer pair and focus on how to better utilize passages to generate questions related to the answer.

In addition to utilizing the information of answer, Zhao et al. [26] propose that more sentences or paragraphs should be used for question generation, which combined more abundant contextual information. Cho et al. [3] propose choosing different tokens as the focuses in the passage and generating questions according to different focus-answer pairs, which can make the generated questions more specific and increase the diversity of questions. These methods provide more information for question generation, but they still ask questions about an object.

In conclusion, the questions generated by the above methods all tested an independent object in the passage. To the best of our knowledge, none of the previous studies has focused on the issue that generates a comparison question, which needs a model to generate questions based on multiple fragments and their relationships.

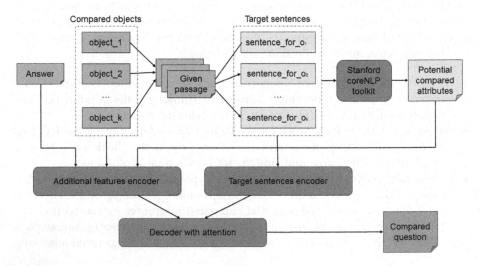

Fig. 2. Overview of our framework. The top half part is the attribute extractor, and the bottom half part is the attribute-attention seq2seq module. The original input is shown in green; the modules are shown in blue; the intermediate files to be generated are shown in yellow; the generated question are shown in red. (Color figure online)

3 Framework

Given a passage $X^p = (x_1^p, ..., x_n^p)$, an expected answer $A = (x_1^a, ..., x_m^a)$ and k compared objects $O = \{o_1, ..., o_k\}$, where $o_i = (x_1^{o_i}, ..., x_w^{o_i}) \subset X^p$, CQG aims to generate a question Y that compares a certain attribute of these compared objects O and can be answered with the expected answer A. The overall framework is shown in Fig. 2.

The framework can be divided into two parts from top to bottom: an attribute extractor and an attribute-attention seq2seq module. The workflow starts from the attributes extractor. Firstly, the attribute extractor extracts one or more target sentences related to each compared object from the given passages. Then, the attribute extractor extracts the potential compared attributes among compared objects from the target sentences and conveys them to the attribute-attention seq2seq module as assistance for question generation. Secondly, the attribute-attention seq2seq module generates questions based on the target sentences. Considering that some specific fragments in the target sentences are crucial for generating comparison questions, e.g., the fragments related to potential compared attributes, the module employs an attention mechanism to focus on the additional features, i.e., potential compared attributes, compared objects and expected answers. In the following parts, we will introduce the two modules in detail.

3.1   Attribute Extractor

To generate questions that can attract students to explore the differences and similarities between multiple objects, the model should extract attributes that can reflect the differences and similarities between objects in the passage before constructing the question. The attribute extractor uses Stanford CoreNLP Toolkit [14] to recognize the entity types of entities other than the object itself from the target sentences, where these target sentences are the sentences in the passage corresponding to each compared object. Then we define these entity types as the attributes of the object. As shown in Fig. 1, we identify related entities (e.g., "USA" and "1989") in the target sentence corresponding to the compared object (i.e., "First of Women"), and then utilize the types of these entities (i.e., COUNTRY and DATE) as the attributes of the object. Then, we use the shared entity types in each target sentence as the potential compared attributes. Specially, when the shared entity type is empty, we utilize all the entity types that have appeared in each corresponding sentence to represent the potential compared attributes.

3.2   Attribute-Attention Seq2seq Module

After extracting the potential compared attributes from the attribute extractor, the attribute-attention seq2seq module (AAs2s) utilizes the potential compared attributes, compared objects, and answers as additional features to generate questions. AAs2s is based on a basic encoder-decoder framework, which consists of three components: additional features encoder, target sentences encoder, and decoder with attention. The overall framework is shown in Fig. 3. In the following section, we will introduce AAs2s in detail.

Additional Features Encoder. We take a special token $\langle s \rangle$ to concatenate the additional features, i.e., expected answer A, the compared objects O and the potential compared attributes C as input $X^a = [A, \langle s \rangle, O, \langle s \rangle, C]$. The encoder uses an one-layer bi-directional LSTM (bi-LSTM),

$$\overrightarrow{h_i^a} = \overrightarrow{\text{LSTM}}(X_i^a, \overrightarrow{h_{i-1}^a}) \tag{1}$$

$$\overleftarrow{h_i^a} = \overleftarrow{\text{LSTM}}(X_i^a, \overleftarrow{h_{i+1}^a}) \tag{2}$$

$$h_i^a = \left[\overrightarrow{h_i^a}; \overleftarrow{h_i^a}\right] \tag{3}$$

where $\overrightarrow{h_i^a}$ is the hidden state at time step i for the forward LSTM, $\overleftarrow{h_i^a}$ for the backward.

Target Sentences Encoder. Similarly, the same special token $\langle s \rangle$ is used to concatenate the target sentences as input $X^s = [s_1, \langle s \rangle, ..., s_k] \subset X^p$, where s_i is the target sentence corresponding to o_i. The encoder uses another individual one-layer bi-LSTM, and the hidden state of the encoder in the last time step h_{final}^s is used to represent the whole input X^s,

$$\overrightarrow{h_j^s} = \overrightarrow{\text{LSTM}}(X_j^s, \overrightarrow{h_{j-1}^s}) \tag{4}$$

$$\overleftarrow{h_j^s} = \overleftarrow{\text{LSTM}}(X_j^s, \overleftarrow{h_{j+1}^s}) \tag{5}$$

$$s_0 = h_{final}^s = \left[\overrightarrow{h_m^s}; \overleftarrow{h_m^s} \right] \tag{6}$$

where $\overrightarrow{h_j^s}$ is the hidden state at time step j for the forward LSTM, $\overleftarrow{h_j^s}$ for the backward. The $\overrightarrow{h_m^s}$ and $\overleftarrow{h_m^s}$ are the hidden state at last time step.

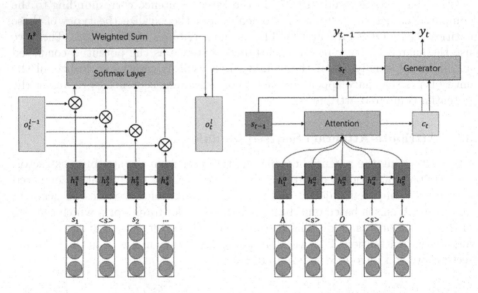

Fig. 3. Overview of attribute-attention seq2seq module. The bottom left part is the target sentences encoder, the bottom right part is the additional features encoder, and the top half part is the decoder.

Decoder with Attention. After encoding the additional features and the target sentences by encoders, the decoder uses a one-layer uni-directional LSTM with attention modules to generate the questions employing the above encoded features.

$$s_t = \text{LSTM}(y_{t-1}, s_{t-1}, c_t, o_t^l) \tag{7}$$

where y_{t-1} is the output token of previous time step, s_{t-1} is the hidden state of previous time step, c_t is the context vector, o_t^l is the keyword vector that are passed through the decoder to compute the decoder hidden state at current time step s_t. By the way, we initialize the decoder hidden state s_0 with the final hidden state of target sentences encoder h_{final}^s.

The context vector c_t is a representation of the content related to the additional feature. We obtain c_t by calculating s_{t-1} and h_i^a,

$$e_{ti} = v^T \tanh(W_a s_{t-1} + U_a h_i^a) \tag{8}$$

$$\alpha_{ti} = \frac{\exp(e_{ti})}{\sum_{k=1}^{n} \exp(e_{tk})} \tag{9}$$

$$c_t = \sum_{i=1}^{n} \alpha_{ti} h_i^a \tag{10}$$

where W_a and U_a are trainable matrices, v^T is a trainable vector. e_{ti} is computed as the matching score between s_{t-1} and h_i^a, α_{ti} is computed with normalization and we take the weighted average of h_i^a as context vector c_t.

The keyword vector o_t^l captures key information related to X^a in the target sentences X^s. We obtain o_t^l by attention mechanism termed keyword-net [9] as follows,

$$o_t^0 = c_t \tag{11}$$

$$p_{tj}^l = \text{Softmax}((o_t^{l-1})^T h_j^s) \tag{12}$$

$$o_t^l = \sum_j p_{tj}^l h_j^s \tag{13}$$

We initialize keyword vector in the first layer o_t^0 with context vector of current time step c_t. Afterward, a normalization matching score between o_t^{l-1} and h_j^s is computed and we take the weighted average of h_i^s as keyword vector o_t^l in current layer l.

In order to make up for the shortcoming of the sequence-to-sequence model which tends to memorize sequence patterns without reflecting the meaning of words, Ma et al. [13] proposed a retrieval style word generation layer. Based on the current decoder structure, we then replace the existing output layer in the decoder with this word generator layer.

The generator layer utilizes the decoder hidden state s_t and the context vector c_t to calculate the query q_t. Then, by querying q_t to each of the word embedding e_k, we can calculate the correlation score between q_t and e_k. Finally, the normalized value of the scoring function can be used to represent the generation probability of each word,

$$q_t = \tanh(W_q[s_t; c_t]) \tag{14}$$

$$\text{score}(q_t, e_k) = q_t^T W_s e_k \tag{15}$$

$$p(y_t) = \text{Softmax}(\text{score}(q_t, e_k)) \tag{16}$$

where W_q and W_s are the trainable matrices.

4   Experiment

In this section, we discuss (i) the dataset we used in our experiment, (ii) implementation details, (iii) several evaluation metrics mainly used to assess the quality of generated questions, and (iv) the models for comparison.

4.1   Dataset

Our experiments are conducted on the HotpotQA dataset [25], which is constructed for the task of reading comprehension originally. Each sample includes a passage, a question, two compared objects, and an expected answer. The question can be answered according to the target sentences in the passage, which correspond to the two compared objects. The expected answer to the question includes "yes", "no", or one of the compared objects. According to the different methods of constructing passages, the HotpotQA dataset includes two settings: distractor and full-wiki.

(1) **Distractor setting (D-s)**: The passage includes two target sentences corresponding to the two compared objects and eight sentences retrieved from Wikipedia using TF-IDF [15].

(2) **Full-wiki setting (F-s)**: All sentences in the passage are retrieved from Wikipedia and a compared object may correspond to multiple target sentences, which will introduce noise.

The dataset contains 10,740 samples for training, 1,487 for testing under distractor setting, and 1,487 for development under full-wiki setting. We randomly split the training set into 90% (9,666 samples) for training and 10% (1,074 samples) for validation.

4.2   Experimental Details

We implement our model in Tensorflow and train the model with a single GTX 2080 Ti. The hyperparameters of our proposed model are described as follows.

In AAs2s, the number of hidden units in two encoders and the decoder is 350. For both encoder and decoder, we only keep 30k most frequent words that appeared in the training corpus and replace the rest with <UNK> token. Besides, 300-dimensional GloVe embeddings [17] pre-trained on 6 billion-token corpus are used for initialization and frozen during training. Weight normalization is applied to the attention module and the dropout layer with $P_{drop}=0.4$ is also applied for both LSTMs and the attention module. The layer size of the keyword-net is set to 4.

During training, we optimize the cross-entropy loss function with the gradient descent algorithm using Adam optimizer [10], with an initial learning rate of 0.001. The mini-batch size is set to 128 and the model is trained up to 10 epochs.

4.3   Evaluation

In order to evaluate the quality of the generated questions, we use automatic metrics and human evaluation criteria.

Automatic Metrics. We conduct an automatic evaluation using five metrics: BLEU(1-4) [16] and ROUGE-L [12], which are standard evaluation metrics for generating tasks, e.g., machine translation and text summarization. BLEU-n measures the quality of the candidate by counting the matching n-grams between the candidate and the reference text. ROUGE-L assesses the candidate based on the longest common sub-sequence shared by both the candidate and the reference text. Specially, we use an evaluation package released by [1] to compute them.

Human Evaluation Criteria. In addition to the automatic evaluation, we also recruit human annotators to judge the quality of responses generated by different models based on 100 samples [24]. We invite five volunteers with rich educational experience to evaluate. The samples generated by different models are pooled and randomly shuffled for each volunteer. Volunteers refer to the questions and judge the quality of the responses according to the following criteria [5]:

+**2**: The question is meaningful and matches the compared objects described in the passage.

+**1**: The question more or less is consistent with the differences and similarities between the two compared objects described in the passage, or has little mistakes (e.g., with little grammatical errors or UNK).

+**0**: The question neither makes sense nor matches the passage or compared objects.

4.4   Comparative Models for Generation Task

To demonstrate the effectiveness of our framework, we make a comparison for several generation models.

- **S2S** [4] uses the complete passage as input for the encoder-decoder model with an attention mechanism to generate questions.
- **NQG** [27] selects all target sentences as input, and uses the attributes extracted by attributes extractor as additional features for question generation based on S2S.
- **S2S-A-AT-MP-GSA** [26] utilizes complete passage as input, and includes copy mechanism, maxout pointer mechanism and gated self-attention to generate questions based on S2S.
- **Answer-Separated Seq2Seq (ASs2s)** [9] selects all target sentences as input, and utilizes the attention mechanism to pay more attention to the answer information separated from the input for question generation based on S2S.
- **Attribute Extractor+Attribute-Attention Seq2Seq Module (AE+AAs2s)** is our proposed generation framework, which utilizes the attributes, objects, and answers as additional features to generate a comparison question.

To prove the effectiveness of each part of the additional features, we also did some ablation experiments based on Attribute-Attention Seq2Seq Module (AAs2s) as follows:

- **AAs2s** contains no additional feature, filled with "PAD".
- **AAs2s-o** only contains the additional feature of two compared objects.
- **AAs2s-a** only contains the additional feature of the target answer.
- **AAs2s-c** only contains the additional feature of the potential compared attributes.

5   Results and Analysis

To effectively evaluate the results of multiple models, we utilize automatic metrics and human evaluation to evaluate the results separately.

Table 1 gives the result of automatic metrics. We have several findings:

1) Performances of all models in D-s are better than F-s in terms of all the five metrics. This is because each object in D-s is different from F-s that only corresponds to one related sentence, which will not introduce other disturbing sentences to bring the noise.
2) Performance of NQG is better than that of S2S in terms of all the five metrics, which proves that the additional features we extracted can help the model generate better comparison questions.
3) Performance of AE+AAs2s is better than that of NQG in terms of all five metrics. We consider that AE+AAs2s utilizes the attention mechanism better than the method of directly tagging the position of the fragments in the input paragraphs.
4) Compared with ASs2s and S2S-A-AT-MP-GSA, our proposed model AE+AAs2s produces the best results of all five evaluation metrics. This confirms the effectiveness of our proposed framework for comparison question generation.

Table 1. Main automatic metrics results of baselines and our model on HotpotQA dataset. **Bold**: the best performance in the column.

Model	BLEU-1		BLEU-2		BLEU-3		BLEU-4		ROUGE-L	
	F-s	D-s	F-s	D-s	F-s	D-s	F-s	D-s	F-s	D-s
S2S	19.5	22.3	11.2	12.3	6.2	8.1	3.4	4.5	19.8	20.9
NQG	31.2	33.8	19.8	21.7	12.6	15.7	8.9	10.3	30.8	32.6
S2S-A-AT-MP-GSA	36.6	36.7	23.1	23.3	15.5	15.8	10.8	10.9	31.8	32.6
ASs2s	34.5	35.8	21.9	23.0	14.4	15.0	9.6	9.7	31.9	32.3
AAs2s	25.7	33.5	15.3	19.1	9.8	14.3	6.5	10.5	22.2	28.7
AAs2s-o	33.1	34.2	21.1	22.8	13.8	16.2	9.4	11.8	31.6	33.3
AAs2s-a	34.6	36.8	22.2	23.3	14.7	15.6	9.9	10.5	32.3	32.8
AAs2s-c	29.4	32.8	18.9	21.8	12.9	15.2	8.9	10.9	28.7	29.9
AE+AAs2s	**47.8**	**48.1**	**31.6**	**32.2**	**19.9**	**21.8**	**14.5**	**16.2**	**47.8**	**49.2**

Table 2. The human evaluation results of baselines and our model in each category in 100 samples. **Bold**: the maximum value in the column.

Model	+2		+1		+0		AVG	
	F-s	D-s	F-s	D-s	F-s	D-s	F-s	D-s
NQG	66	86	167	153	267	261	0.60	0.65
S2S-A-AT-MP-GSA	71	78	159	162	270	260	0.60	0.63
ASs2s	59	73	142	151	**299**	**276**	0.52	0.59
AAs2s	56	81	172	162	272	257	0.57	0.65
AE+AAs2s	**106**	**117**	**198**	**201**	196	182	**0.82**	**0.87**

Table 2 shows the human evaluation result. We have the following findings:

1) The performance of AE+AAs2s is better than that of ASs2s in terms of the human evaluation metrics. This indicates that ASs2s is making full use of the information of the answer, but neglects to ensure that the compared objects corresponding to the answer appear in the generated question, which leads to poor results of human evaluation.
2) The performance of S2S-A-AT-MP-GSA is similar to that of NQG in terms of the human evaluation metrics, which shows that using all the sentences in the passage for question generation brings more noise while introducing more information contained in the sentences.
3) The gap between NQG and AE+AAs2s will be smaller than the automatic metrics. This shows that the question with attributes that are selected to be different from ground truth for comparison among potential compared attributes is also worth asking in human evaluation.
4) The average scores of automatically generated questions are all lower than the value of "+1", i.e., the generated questions only have certain fragments that are consistent with the two objects described in the passage. This indicates that there is still a large room for the question generation system to improve.

5.1 Additional Features

To demonstrate the effectiveness of the additional features (i.e., answer, compared objects, and potential compared attributes), we performed compared experiments on each of them.

Table 3. The percentage result of the accuracy (%) of different question-types in AAs2s and AAs2s-a. **Bold:** the best performance in the column.

Model	what		which		are/is	
	D-s	F-s	D-s	F-s	D-s	F-s
AAs2s	5.3	11.5	53.7	58.2	23.2	13.9
AAs2s-a	**46.5**	**46.5**	**73.7**	**88.4**	**61.8**	**74.7**

Table 4. The percentage result of the probability (%) that the two compared objects appear in a generated question in AAs2s and AAs2s-o. **Bold:** the best performance in the column.

Model	o_1		o_2		$o_1 \& o_2$	
	F-s	D-s	F-s	D-s	F-s	D-s
AAs2s	69.8	71.9	70.2	73.2	66.1	68.9
AAs2s-o	**93.7**	**95.0**	**92.4**	**93.7**	**86.5**	**89.7**

Answer. As shown in Table 3, the accuracy of the question type (e.g., "what/which/ who/are/is") of the questions generated by AAs2s-a is higher than that of AAs2s. This shows that the target answer as additional features can help our model to generate the same type of questions as the ground truth. Besides, as shown in Fig. 5a, the weight of the words "dirty pretty things" in input sentences will increase.

Compared Objects. As shown in Table 4, the question generated by AAs2s-o contains compared objects (i.e., o_1 and o_2) with a higher probability than model AAs2s under the two settings. This indicates that the keyword-net can help AAs2s-o to focus on the compared objects in the target sentences for question generation. As shown in Fig. 5b, when we use an object (e.g., "pretty things") as additional features, the weight of the words in the passage corresponding to these two compared objects will be larger.

Compared Attributes. As shown in a case in Fig. 4, when we only utilize the same attributes (i.e., COUNTRY) as the additional information for the ground truth, AE+AAs2s can use the information to generate a question like ground-truth. When the potential compared attribute COUNTRY as the additional features, as shown in Fig. 5c, the weight of words "English" related to the compared attribute in the sentences will increase.

5.2   Case Study

As shown in Fig. 4, we show the output question of our model AE+AAs2s and other comparative models (i.e., NQG, S2S-A-AT-MP-GSA, and ASs2s) on an example from the HotpotQA dataset. Firstly, the results generated by S2S-A-AT-MP-GSA include "BBC", which indicates that additional noise is introduced when we take the complete passage as input. Secondly, ASs2s cannot ask two compared objects in the question, which shows that the method of separating the answers of the model will prevent the compared object corresponding to the answer appearing in the question. Thirdly, our model AE+AAs2s can generate a question similar to the ground truth, which proves the effectiveness of our model.

Passage: **Fireflight** is an American Christian rock band formed in Eustis, Florida in 1999...In 2014 he announced the creation of his new band, The Tackals. **Dirty Pretty Things** were an English band fronted by Carl Barât...In 2006, it was used as the theme tune to the BBC series "sorted".

Ground Truth: Which band is from England, Fireflight or Dirty Pretty Things?
Answer: Dirty pretty things.

NQG: Was Fireflight or Christian rock started first?
AAs2s-o: Who was announced first, Fireflight or Pretty Things?
S2S-A-AT-MP-GSA: Who was in BBC Fireflight or Fireflight?
ASs2s: Which band was formed first, Fireflight or Fireflight?

Potential Compared Attributes: LOCATION; DATE; NATIONALITY
AE+AAs2s: Which band is in England, Fireflight or Dirty Pretty Things?

Fig. 4. Case study of sample output questions generated by human (i.e., ground truth questions), baselines and our models. We highlight the compared objects in **blod**.

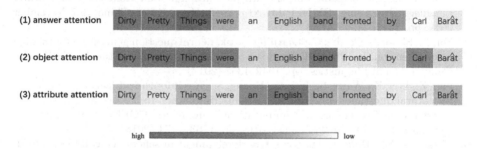

Fig. 5. (a), (b) and (c) represent the score of the keyword-net after adding the target answer, compared objects, and compared attributes from a text span in the passage of the case in Fig. 4, respectively

6 Conclusions

In this paper, we conduct a preliminary study on the comparison question generation and discuss the challenges encountered when generating. The challenges encountered are divided into two aspects: the first is how to extract potential compared attributes that can be used to explore the differences and similarities between multiple objects and the second is how to utilize the potential compared attributes as additional information to generate a reliable comparison question. To address these challenges, we propose a novel framework that can not only effectively extract potential compared attributes through an attribute extractor, but also effectively utilize these attributes as the additional feature to the CQG task through an attribute-attention seq2seq module. Experiments demonstrate the effectiveness of our method on HotpotQA, which can greatly outperform benchmarks on QG tasks.

Acknowledgement. This work was supported by National Natural Science Foundation of China (No. 620761 00), National Key Research and Development Program of China (Standard knowledge graph for epidemic prevention and production recovering intelligent service platform and its applications), the Fundamental Research Funds for the Central Universities, SCUT (No. D2201300, D2210010), the Science and Technology Programs of Guangzhou(201902010046), the Science and Technology Planning Project of Guangdong Province (No. 2020B0101100002).

References

1. Chen, X., et al.: Microsoft COCO captions: data collection and evaluation server. CoRR abs/1504.00325 (2015)
2. Chiang, M., Peng, W., Yu, P.S.: Exploring latent browsing graph for question answering recommendation. World Wide Web **15**(5–6), 603–630 (2012)
3. Cho, J., Seo, M.J., Hajishirzi, H.: Mixture content selection for diverse sequence generation. In: Proceedings of the 2019 Conference on Empirical Methods in Natural Language Processing and the 9th International Joint Conference on Natural Language Processing, EMNLP-IJCNLP 2019, Hong Kong, China, 3–7 November 2019, pp. 3119–3129 (2019)
4. Du, X., Shao, J., Cardie, C.: Learning to ask: neural question generation for reading comprehension. In: Proceedings of the 55th Annual Meeting of the Association for Computational Linguistics, pp. 1342–1352 (2017)
5. Fan, Z., Wei, Z., Wang, S., Liu, Y., Huang, X.: A reinforcement learning framework for natural question generation using bi-discriminators. In: Proceedings of the 27th International Conference on Computational Linguistics, COLING 2018, Santa Fe, New Mexico, USA, 20–26 August 2018, pp. 1763–1774 (2018)
6. Fischer, K.W., Bullock, D.: Cognitive development in school-age children: conclusions and new directions. In: Development During Middle Childhood: The Years from Six to Twelve, pp. 70–146 (1984)
7. Gao, Y., Li, P., King, I., Lyu, M.R.: Interconnected question generation with coreference alignment and conversation flow modeling. In: Proceedings of the 57th Annual Meeting of the Association for Computational Linguistics, pp. 4853–4862 (2019)
8. Heilman, M., Smith, N.A.: Good question! statistical ranking for question generation. In: Human Language Technologies: The 2010 Annual Conference of the North American Chapter of the Association for Computational Linguistics (NAACL), pp. 609–617 (2010)
9. Kim, Y., Lee, H., Shin, J., Jung, K.: Improving neural question generation using answer separation. In: The Thirty-Third AAAI Conference on Artificial Intelligence (AAAI 2019), pp. 6602–6609 (2019)
10. Kingma, D.P., Ba, J.: Adam: a method for stochastic optimization. In: 3rd International Conference on Learning Representations, ICLR 2015, San Diego, CA, USA, 7–9 May 2015, Conference Track Proceedings (2015)
11. Li, L., Zhang, M., Chao, Z., Xiang, J.: Using context information to enhance simple question answering. World Wide Web **24**(1), 249–277 (2021)

12. Lin, C.Y.: Rouge: a package for automatic evaluation of summaries. In: Proceedings of the ACL-04 Workshop. Association for Computational Linguistics, Barcelona, Spain, pp. 74–81 (2004)
13. Ma, S., Sun, X., Li, W., Li, S., Li, W., Ren, X.: Query and output: generating words by querying distributed word representations for paraphrase generation. In: Proceedings of the 2018 Conference of the North American Chapter of the Association for Computational Linguistics: Human Language Technologies, Volume 1 (Long Papers), vol. 1, pp. 196–206 (2018)
14. Manning, C., Surdeanu, M., Bauer, J., Finkel, J., Bethard, S., McClosky, D.: The Stanford CoreNLP natural language processing toolkit. In: Proceedings of 52nd Annual Meeting of the Association for Computational Linguistics: System Demonstrations, pp. 55–60 (2014)
15. Martineau, J., Finin, T.: Delta TFIDF: an improved feature space for sentiment analysis. In: Proceedings of the Third International Conference on Weblogs and Social Media, ICWSM 2009, San Jose, California, USA, 17–20 May 2009 (2009)
16. Papineni, K., Roukos, S., Ward, T., Zhu, W.: Bleu: a method for automatic evaluation of machine translation. In: Proceedings of the 40th Annual Meeting of the Association for Computational Linguistics, Philadelphia, PA, USA, 6–12 July 2002, pp. 311–318 (2002)
17. Pennington, J., Socher, R., Manning, C.: Glove: global vectors for word representation. In: Proceedings of the 2014 Conference on Empirical Methods in Natural Language Processing (EMNLP), pp. 1532–1543 (2014)
18. Seif, A.A.A.: Evaluating the higher order thinking skills in reading exercises of English for palestine grade 8 (2012)
19. Tang, D., Duan, N., Qin, T., Yan, Z., Zhou, M.: Question answering and question generation as dual tasks. arXiv preprint arXiv:1706.02027 (2017)
20. Wang, S., Wei, Z., Fan, Z., Liu, Y., Huang, X.: A multi-agent communication framework for question-worthy phrase extraction and question generation. In: The Thirty-Third AAAI Conference on Artificial Intelligence, AAAI 2019, The Thirty-First Innovative Applications of Artificial Intelligence Conference, IAAI 2019, The Ninth AAAI Symposium on Educational Advances in Artificial Intelligence, EAAI 2019, Honolulu, Hawaii, USA, 27 January–1 February 2019, pp. 7168–7175 (2019)
21. Wang, Z., Hamza, W., Florian, R.: Bilateral multi-perspective matching for natural language sentences. In: Proceedings of the Twenty-Sixth International Joint Conference on Artificial Intelligence, IJCAI 2017, Melbourne, Australia, 19–25 August 2017, pp. 4144–4150 (2017)
22. Wenyin, L., Hao, T., Chen, W., Feng, M.: A web-based platform for user-interactive question-answering. World Wide Web 12(2), 107–124 (2009)
23. Wu, X., Cai, Y., Li, Q., Xu, J., Leung, H.: Combining weighted category-aware contextual information in convolutional neural networks for text classification. World Wide Web 23(5), 2815–2834 (2020)
24. Xing, C., et al.: Topic aware neural response generation. In: Proceedings of the Thirty-First AAAI Conference on Artificial Intelligence, San Francisco, California, USA, 4–9 February 2017, pp. 3351–3357 (2017)
25. Yang, Z., et al.: Hotpotqa: a dataset for diverse, explainable multi-hop question answering. In: Proceedings of the 2018 Conference on Empirical Methods in Natural Language Processing, Brussels, Belgium, 31 October–4 November 2018, pp. 2369–2380 (2018)

26. Zhao, Y., Ni, X., Ding, Y., Ke, Q.: Paragraph-level neural question generation with maxout pointer and gated self-attention networks. In: Proceedings of the 2018 Conference on Empirical Methods in Natural Language Processing (EMNLP), pp. 3901–3910 (2018)
27. Zhou, Q., Yang, N., Wei, F., Tan, C., Bao, H., Zhou, M.: Neural question generation from text: a preliminary study. In: Natural Language Processing and Chinese Computing - 6th CCF International Conference, NLPCC, pp. 662–671 (2017)

Multimodal Encoders for Food-Oriented Cross-Modal Retrieval

Ying Chen[1], Dong Zhou[1]($\boxtimes$) (iD), Lin Li[2], and Jun-mei Han[3]

[1] School of Computer Science and Engineering, Hunan University of Science and Technology, Xiangtan 411201, Hunan, China
dongzhou@hnust.edu.cn, dongzhou1979@hotmail.com
[2] School of Computer Science and Technology, Wuhan University of Technology, Wuhan 430070, Hubei, China
[3] National Key Laboratory for Complex Systems Simulation, Department of Systems General Design, Institute of Systems Engineering, Beijing 100101, China

Abstract. The task of retrieving across different modalities plays a critical role in food-oriented applications. Modality alignment remains a challenging component in the whole process, in which a common embedding feature space between two modalities can be learned for effective comparison and retrieval. Recent studies mainly utilize adversarial loss or reconstruction loss to align different modalities. However, insufficient features may be extracted from different modalities, resulting in low quality of alignments. Unlike these methods, this paper proposes a method combining multimodal encoders with adversarial learning to learn improved and efficient cross-modal embeddings for retrieval purposes. The core of our proposed approach is the directional pairwise cross-modal attention that latently adapts representations from one modality to another. Although the model is not particularly complex, experimental results on the benchmark Recipe1M dataset show that our proposed method is superior to current state-of-the-art methods.

Keywords: Food oriented computing · Cross-modal retrieval · Multimodal encoders · Modality alignment

1 Introduction

Food plays a vital role in human's daily life and is closely connected with our health. With the increasing amount of multimodal data on the World Wide Web, people face billions of food images, videos, and recipes [1]. Therefore, an appropriate method is highly desired to retrieve accurate contents across different modalities. Cross-modal retrieval aims to retrieve relevant items that are of different modalities [2, 3]. In this task, the heterogeneity gap between different modalities leads to inconsistent feature distributions. To solve this particular problem, modality alignment is necessary to make the feature distributions of different modalities consistent [2–5]. The existing research methods for modality alignment can be roughly divided into two categories. One type of methods [6–8] uses adversarial loss [9] to map food images and recipes to eliminate

© Springer Nature Switzerland AG 2021
L. H. U et al. (Eds.): APWeb-WAIM 2021, LNCS 12859, pp. 253–266, 2021.
https://doi.org/10.1007/978-3-030-85899-5_19

the gaps between them. In this way, modalities can be corrected aligned to achieve direct matching between different modalities. Another type of methods [7, 8, 10] mainly uses reconstruction loss [11] to complement modality alignment. This group of methods firstly assumes a fixed distribution and then regenerates the modal features according to their respective distributions.

Despite the promising performance of the methods mentioned above, there are still some shortcomings. 1) It is well-known that the adversarial learning methods are not stable [9]. This makes the whole model difficult to train; 2) The reconstruction method needs to regenerate the features based on predefined distributions [11], which is somewhat idealized. It can be found that modality alignment can be defined as two processes: feature extraction and modality matching. While previous methods mainly focus on the latter. However, if insufficient information is extracted, modality alignment will be challenging.

Unlike previous methods that primarily focus on the modality matching process, we emphasize the importance of feature extraction in this paper. We propose a method that utilizes multimodal encoders to extract sufficient information from different modalities. Then we adopt adversarial learning to achieve the modality alignment. The core of our proposed method is directional pairwise cross-modal attention. Specifically, we use the cross-modal attention mechanism to latently adapt streams from one modality to another. Then multiple multimodal encoders are stacked to reinforce the consistency between different modalities repeatedly. The self-attention mechanism [12] is also used to capture the internal features in one modality. The modal features are repeatedly strengthened through modal interaction in the whole process, and then the information is further consolidated and supplemented. Ultimately, sufficient feature information can be extracted before the subsequent adversarial learning process. This makes the whole model relatively stable. We conduct experiments on the benchmark Recipe1M [13], and results demonstrate that the proposed method outperforms the state-of-the-art methods using adversarial and reconstruction learning.

Our contributions in this paper can be summarized as follows:

(1) We propose to use multimodal encoders to capture the inter- and intra-modality features. With adversarial learning, our method aims to enhance the very heart component, i.e. modality alignment in cross-modal retrieval.
(2) We propose to use stacked multiple encoders to improve the effect of feature extraction. Ablation experiments show that multiple encoders are pretty effective and necessary.
(3) Experiments on a benchmark dataset show that our proposed method is significantly superior to the state-of-the-art cross-modal retrieval methods with less sufficient feature information extracted.

2   Related Work

Cross-modal retrieval aims to retrieve results in one modality by using queries from another modality, such as using text to retrieve related images [1–3]. Due to the heterogeneous gap among different media types, the distributions of different modalities are usually inconsistent. This makes it difficult to measure the similarity of different modalities directly. Therefore, in cross-modal retrieval tasks [14, 15], the modality alignment method is crucial to make the distributions of features from different modalities consistent. Adversarial learning commonly uses Generative Adversarial Networks (GAN) [9] to map the features from different modalities to eliminate the gap between them [15]. The adversarial Cross-Modal Retrieval (ACMR) method [6] first proposes to use adversarial learning to learn an effective common subspace for cross-modal retrieval. The adversarial Cross-Modal Embedding (ACME) [8] method further improves the aligning process by introducing cross-modal translation consistency. Recipe Retrieval with Generative Adversarial Network (R2GAN) method [7] is also a GAN-based method. It consists of one generator and two discriminators. In this way, features may be aligned to finish direct matching between different modalities.

Reconstruction methods encourage the embedding of one modality to cover the corresponding information of another modality, enhance modality alignment during this process. For example, in ACME, new images or texts are regenerated according to existing features and then used to enhance modality alignment. Modality-Consistent Embedding Network (MCEN) method [10] proposes to use the latent variable model to reconstruct the latent representations with learned embeddings.

Although these approaches perform well, there are still some problems. It is well-known that adversarial learning-based methods are not stable [9]. It makes the whole model difficult to train. The reconstruction method needs to regenerate features based on fixed distributions [10]. This makes the whole process complicated. It is also somewhat idealized.

The attention mechanism is firstly proposed to use in machine translation for translation and alignment [12]. From a macro perspective, the attention mechanism is borrowed from the study of human visual perception [12]. In fact, humans selectively focus on parts of a message, not all of it. In particular, the self-attention mechanism is quite effective in various cross-modal tasks [16–18].

The co-attention mechanism has also been widely used in cross-modal tasks [19, 20]. For example, Zhang et al. [19] utilize the co-attention network to perform the hashtag recommendation for multimodal microblogs. Cross-modal attention is initially designed to study the problem of image-text matching [21]. Lee et al. [22] present a stacked cross-attention mechanism to discover the whole latent alignments to infer the image-text similarity. The MCEN method [10] uses cross-modal attention to capture the semantic alignment relationships between images and recipes. Though effective, there is a lack of studies on using multiple cross-modal attention and self-attention for cross-modal retrieval.

The original Transformer [12] model is an encoder-decoder [23] structure for sequence-to-sequence tasks, such as translation from one language to another. Inspired by the powerful presentation capabilities of Transformer, it has now been extended to the field of computer vision [24, 25] and multimodal tasks [26, 27]. However, unlike the original Transformer structure, the multimodal encoders do not adopt an encoder-decoder structure. Instead, it is based on the encoding of Transformer sequences and consists of multiple stacked cross-modal attention blocks that are directional and appear in pairs [12].

In recent years, multimodal encoders have been applied to some specific multimodal tasks. For example, Tsai et al. [26] propose to apply multimodal encoders to the analysis of human multimodal languages. They adapt elements across modalities via the attention mechanism to achieve multimodal interaction on unaligned language sequences. There are also studies on using multimodal encoders for image captioning [27]. Deep-stacked attention blocks are used to perform complex multimodal reasoning to ensure the accuracy of captions.

Transformers are pretty compelling. However, most of the previous work directly replaces all complicated modules with Transformers. They have not been used as feature extractors and in modality alignment before.

3   Model Framework

This section introduces the proposed cross-modal retrieval framework, which combines multimodal encoders and adversarial learning to implement modality alignment.

3.1   Overview of the Overall Framework

Problem Formulation. Given a set of image-recipe pairs (v_i, r_i) for $i = 1, 2, 3, \ldots, N$, where a food image $v_i \in V$ and a recipe $r_i \in R$ (V and R correspond to the image and recipe domains, respectively). The cross-modal retrieval task is to use the data from one modality (such as v_i) as a query to find the data in another modality (such as r_i) that related to it. Due to the heterogeneous gap between different modalities, the feature distributions of v_i and r_i are usually inconsistent. Our goal is to make the feature distributions of $V \to E^v$ and $R \to E^r$ consistent after modality alignment, where $E^v \in \mathbb{R}^d$ and $E^r \in \mathbb{R}^d$ denote the distributions of d-dimensional image embedding and recipe embedding, respectively. For simplicity purpose, in this paper, we use v to represent a food image v_i, and r to represent a recipe r_i.

Overall Framework. The proposed framework is shown in Fig. 1. Our framework has four components: initial embedding generation, multimodal encoders, modality alignment, and cross-modal learning. In the first component, images and texts are processed to obtain their initial semantic vectors using traditional deep neural network models. Then these vectors are input into the multimodal encoders to acquire sufficient inter- and intra-modal feature information. These features are then passed through the modality

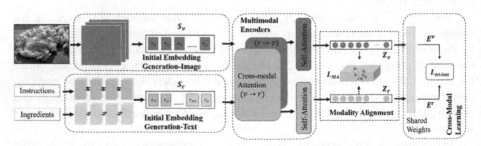

Fig. 1. Our proposed framework

alignment component to make features from different modalities consistent and comparable. Finally, we use the cross-modal learning component to implement the retrieval and sort the retrieval results.

3.2 Initial Embedding Generation

We now describe the four components in detail. We use the convolutional neural network (CNN) ResNet-50 [28] to extract the initial features of food image v. We denote the extracted vector by S_v. Unlike previous methods, we use the output of the last residual block of ResNet-50 to facilitate the inputs into multimodal encoders. We denote the output sequence as $S_v = (v_{i1}, v_{i2}, v_{i3}, \ldots, v_{in})$, where $v_{i1}, v_{i2}, v_{i3}, \ldots, v_{in}$ represent the elements in a n-dimensional visual vector.

The recipes typically consist of raw materials (in the form of words) and operation instructions (in the form of sentences). We process them separately. The operation instructions are extracted with LSTM [29], and the raw materials are transformed into embedded vectors with bi-directional LSTM. The original feature embedding of the recipes is the concatenation of vectors of operation instructions and raw materials, denoted as $S = (S_{ins}, S_{ing})$, where $S_{ins} = (S_{ins}^1, S_{ins}^2, \ldots, S_{ins}^m)$, $S_{ing} = (S_{ing}^1, S_{ing}^2, \ldots, S_{ing}^t)$. The final recipe embedding is then obtained through a full connection layer, denoted as $S_r = (r_{i1}, r_{i2}, r_{i3}, \ldots, r_{in})$, where $r_{i1}, r_{i2}, r_{i3}, \ldots, r_{in}$ denote the elements in a n-dimensional recipe vector.

3.3 Multimodal Encoders

We now describe the core of our method. The overall structure of the multimodal encoders is shown in Fig. 2. This component is composed of multi-layer cross-modal attention modules together with a self-attention layer. It is worth mentioning that all the attention mechanisms involved in this component are multi-head attention mechanisms. They can capture more accurate latent relationships and contextual semantics from different angles than the single-head attention mechanism [12]. The cross-modal attention modules repeatedly reinforce the sequence features in the target modality with the influence of the source modality through the stacked network. The multi-layer structure makes sure that the fine-grained features of both modalities can be extracted. After interactions between different modalities, the self-attention layer further models the intra-modal information inside each modality. The features can be further enriched to supplement the semantic information by correctly capture long-range dependencies.

As mentioned before, S_v and S_r obtained from the first component are taken as inputs into the multimodal encoders. After passing through the cross-modal attention modules, we can obtain a set of new feature vectors $Z_{v'}$ and $Z_{r'}$. By further enhanced through the self-attention layer with more intra-modal information considered, we finally get the feature vectors Z_v and Z_r with sufficient semantic information. This process can be viewed as the first alignment stage before we pass them through the modality alignment component.

A cross-modal attention layer allows one modality to receive the information provided by the fine-grained relationships between itself and another modality. For example,

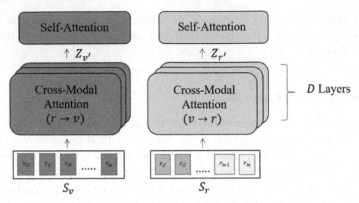

Fig. 2. Cross-modal encoder component

"whole kernel corn" in a recipe (r) should correspond to the part of "corn kernels" in a food image (v). According to these fine-grained relationships, more attention can be paid to the corresponding parts from the source and the target modality. In this way, the influence of the input order can be eliminated with much less computational load. The cross-modal attention in the component is directional and pairwise. This means that the recipe features can help to reinforce the food image features and vice versa. Besides, stacked cross-modal attention modules ensure the feature information can be enhanced through repeat interaction between modalities.

More formally, we define the Querys as $Q_v = S_v W_{Q_v}$, Keys as $K_r = S_r W_{K_r}$, and Values as $V_r = S_r W_{V_r}$, where $W_{Q_v} \in R^{d_v \times d_k}$, $W_{K_r} \in R^{d_r \times d_k}$, and $W_{V_r} \in R^{d_r \times d_k}$ are weights. The process of image features reinforce recipe features can be formulated as follows:

$$Y_r = ME_{v \to r}(S_v, S_r) = softmax\left(\frac{Q_v K_r^T}{\sqrt{d_k}}\right)V_r = softmax\left(\frac{S_v W_{Q_v} W_{K_r}^T S_r^T}{\sqrt{d_k}}\right)S_r W_{V_r} \quad (1)$$

Here $ME_{v \to r}$ is single-head cross-modal attention from image to recipe, the Querys are from the image, and the Keys and Values are from the recipe.

Similarly, the process of recipe features reinforce image features can be formulated as follows:

$$Y_v = ME_{r \to v}(S_r, S_v) = softmax\left(\frac{Q_r K_v^T}{\sqrt{d_k}}\right)V_v = softmax\left(\frac{S_r W_{Q_r} W_{K_v}^T S_v^T}{\sqrt{d_k}}\right)S_v W_{V_v} \quad (2)$$

Here $ME_{r \to v}$ is also single-head cross-modal attention from recipe to image.

As shown in Eqs. (1) and (2), Querys come from the source modality, while Keys and Values come from the target modality. When the multimodal encoders are stacked with D layers, the calculation of the feed-forward network from layer 1 to D is as follows (take image to recipe as an example):

$$Z_{v \to r}^{[0]} = S_r = S_r^{[0]}$$

$$\hat{Z}_{v \to r}^{[i]} = ME_{v \to r}^{[i],mul}\left(LN\left(Z_{v \to r}^{[i-1]}\right), LN\left(S_v^{[0]}\right)\right) + LN\left(Z_{v \to r}^{[i-1]}\right)$$

$$Z_{v \to r}^{[i]} = f_{\theta_{v \to r}^{[i]}}\left(LN\left(\hat{Z}_{v \to r}^{[i]}\right)\right) + LN\left(\hat{Z}_{v \to r}^{[i]}\right) \tag{3}$$

where f_θ is a feed-forward sublayer parametrized by θ, and $ME_{v \to r}^{[i],mul}$ means a multi-head version of $ME_{v \to r}$ at layer i $(1 \leq i \leq D)$. LN denotes the layer normalization.

Multimodal encoders contain a self-attention module in this last layer. This is used to consolidate and supplements the features $Z_{r'} = Z_{v \to r}^{[D]}$, $Z_{v'} = Z_{r \to v}^{[D]}$ to the final vectors Z_v and Z_r. Note that the inputs to the self-attention layer come from cross-modality results in only one direction (i.e., $Z_{r'}$ or $Z_{v'}$). It is defined as:

$$Z_v = softmax\left(\frac{Q_{v'}K_{v'}^T}{\sqrt{d_k}}\right)V_{v'}$$
$$= softmax\left(\frac{Z_{v'}W_{Q_{v'}}W_{K_{v'}}^T Z_{v'}^T}{\sqrt{d_k}}\right)Z_{v'}W_{V_{v'}} \tag{4}$$

$$Z_r = softmax\left(\frac{Q_{r'}K_{r'}^T}{\sqrt{d_k}}\right)V_{r'}$$
$$= softmax\left(\frac{Z_{r'}W_{Q_{r'}}W_{K_{r'}}^T Z_{r'}^T}{\sqrt{d_k}}\right)Z_{r'}W_{V_{r'}} \tag{5}$$

where Querys $Q_{v'}$ come from the image feature $Z_{v'}$, calculated as $Q_{v'} = Z_{v'}W_{Q_{v'}}$. Keys and Values are also from the image feature $Z_{v'}$, calculated as $K_{v'} = Z_{v'}W_{K_{v'}}$, $V_{v'} = Z_{v'}W_{V_{v'}}$. $W_{Q_{v'}}$, $W_{K_{v'}}$ and $W_{V_{v'}}$ are weights. The notaions for $Z_{r'}$ have the same meaning.

3.4 Modality Alignment

After we obtain the enhanced feature vectors from the multimodal encoders, adversarial learning can be used to enforce the distribution consistency of the two modalities. Specifically, the food image features and recipe features finally obtained are input into the GAN for modality alignment. In this paper, WGAN-GP [9] is used to train the GAN. For food images and recipes with similar semantics, adversarial learning tries to achieve a feature representation such that a discriminator D_Z cannot distinguish whether the feature representation was obtained from the image or the recipe. Finally, features from different modalities can be correctly aligned.

We define the loss function for the modality alignment component as follows:

$$\mathcal{L}_{MA} = E_{v \sim p_{image}}[log D_Z(Z_v(v))] + E_{r \sim p_{recipe}}[1 - log D_Z(Z_r(r))] \tag{6}$$

and solved by a min-max optimization:

$$\min_{Z_v, Z_r} \max_{D_z} \mathcal{L}_{MA}$$

Unlike previous works [7, 8, 30], the modal features inputted into this GAN network[31] have been aligned by multimodal encoders. Compared with the unaligned features, the aligned version can make adversarial learning more stable and accurate. The reason for unstable comes from the fact that the distributions of true and false data are distinct at the beginning of the training process. The discriminator can distinguish them very quickly, leading to the result that the generator will optimize slowly or even stop updating. In this paper, the pre-aligned features ensure that the distributions of two modalities are not far away. They even have a certain amount of overlaps, so the discriminator will be difficult to distinguish between these features, making the whole process in a relatively stable state.

3.5 Cross-Modal Learning

After modality alignment, the final features E^v and E^r are obtained through a full connection layer with shared weights. We use the triplet loss with hard sample mining [8] to minimize the distances between the embeddings of different modalities with similar or identical semantic and maximize the distances between the embeddings of different modalities with dissimilar semantic. A triplet comprises one feature embedding as an anchor point in one modality, a positive and a negative feature embedding from another modality. As shown in Eq. (7), E_a^v represents an anchor point from the food image features, while E_p^r and E_n^r represent a positive sample and a negative sample from the recipe features correlated with the anchor point or uncorrelated with the anchor point, respectively. The positive instance corresponds to the one we want to be similar to the anchor point, and the negative instance should be dissimilar to the anchor point. In our case, we also have another type of triplets by using the recipe feature as the anchor point. The loss $\mathcal{L}_{tri-loss}$ is defined as:

$$
\mathcal{L}_{tri-loss} = \min_{E^v, E^r} \left(\sum_V \left[d\left(E_a^v, E_p^r\right) - d\left(E_a^v, E_n^r\right) + \alpha \right] \right.
$$
$$
\left. + \sum_R \left[d\left(E_a^r, E_p^v\right) - d\left(E_a^r, E_n^v\right) + \alpha \right] \right)
\tag{7}
$$

Here $d(.)$ is the Euclidean distance, subscripts a, p, and n refer to anchor, positive and negative samples, respectively, and α is the margin of error. To improve learning convergence, we use the triplet loss with hard sample mining to give preference to the most distant positive instances and the closest negative instances during the training procedure.

3.6 Training and Inference

The total training objective of our framework is formulated as:

$$
\mathcal{L} = \lambda \mathcal{L}_{MA} + \mathcal{L}_{tri-loss}
\tag{8}
$$

where λ is the trade-off parameter. Cross-modal learning component $\mathcal{L}_{tri-loss}(E^v, E^r)$ receives two high-level feature vectors E^v for images and E^r for recipes, and computes the retrieval loss. Modality alignment component $\mathcal{L}_{MA}(Z_v, Z_r)$ aims to achieve modality-invariance using an adversarial loss to align the two distributions. The feature representations E^v and E^r are used for retrieval tasks.

4 Experiments

4.1 Dataset and Evaluation Metrics

We evaluate the effectiveness of our proposed method on the benchmark Recipe1M dataset. The dataset is made up of about a million food images and recipe pairs. It is one of the largest collections of public available recipe data along with food images. In this paper, we use the separation of the original data splits [13], using 238,999 pairs of image-recipe pairs for training, 51,119 pairs of image-recipe pairs for validation and 51,303 pairs for testing.

We evaluate our proposed method and all baseline methods using widely adopted metrics as in prior works [7, 8, 10]. We compute median rank (MedR) and recall rate at top K (R@K) on sample subsets in the test partition to evaluate the retrieval performance. MedR measures the median retrieval rank position of true positives over all test samples, and the ranking position starts from 1. R@K refers to the percentage of queries for which matching instances are ranked among the top K results. We report results on 1,000 (1K) randomly selected pairs of samples and 10,000 (10K) pairs of samples in the test sets. The L2 distances between the embedding vectors of one modality and the embedding vectors of another modality are calculated. The ranking results are sorted in descending order. Moreover, it should be noted that we do not incorporate the additional semantic labels used by prior work [7, 8, 10], such as food-classes and labels of commonly used ingredients.

Table 1. Main results.

Test set size	Baselines	Image to recipe				Recipe to image			
		MedR	R@1	R@5	R@10	MedR	R@1	R@5	R@10
1K	CCA	15.7	14.0	32.0	43.0	24.8	9.0	24.0	35.0
	R2GAN	2.0	39.1	71.0	81.7	2.0	40.6	72.6	83.3
	ACME	2.0	44.3	72.9	81.7	2.0	45.4	73.4	82.0
	MCEN	2.0	48.2	75.8	83.6	1.9	48.4	76.1	83.7
	Ours	**1.0**	**56.8**	**80.6**	**88.4**	**1.0**	**57.5**	**80.6**	**89.3**
10K	R2GAN	13.9	13.5	33.5	44.9	12.6	14.2	35.0	46.8
	ACME	10.0	18.1	39.9	50.8	9.2	20.1	41.5	51.9
	MCEN	7.2	20.3	43.3	54.4	6.6	21.4	44.3	55.2
	Ours	**4.0**	**24.2**	**59.9**	**79.7**	**4.0**	**26.1**	**60.6**	**79.1**

4.2 Baselines

We compare against several state-of-the-art baselines:

CCA [32]: In this method, cross-modal retrieval is calculated by Canonical Correlation Analysis. It aims at maximizing the correlation between similar pairs.

R2GAN [7]: R2GAN is a GAN-based method for cross-modal retrieval. It consists of a generator and two discriminators to learn cross-modal embeddings. At the same time consider semantic dependencies.

ACME [8]: This method is a state-of-the-art method for cross-modal food retrieval tasks. It improves the modality alignment and translation consistency by using multiple GAN components.

MCEN [10]: This method uses a latent variable model to achieve interaction between different modalities and enhance modality alignment by the reconstruction method.

4.3 Implementation

For the image initial embedding generation, ResNet-50 is used to embed the food images. It consists of $7 \times 7 = 49$ columns of 2048 dimensional convolutional outputs. We add a full connection layer to obtain an embedding with 1024 dimensions. For the recipes, LSTM and bi-directional LSTM are used to encode the operation instructions and raw materials of the recipe respectively. After concatenating, an embedding with 1024 dimensions was also obtained for recipes. We use three layers and four attention heads for our multimodal encoders as it gives better results. We present the ablation studies in Sect. 4.5 to analyze the effects of different layers. The margin of error α in the triplet loss function of the cross-modal learning component is set to 0.3. In Eq. (8), the trade-off parameter λ in the model loss function is set to 0.005.

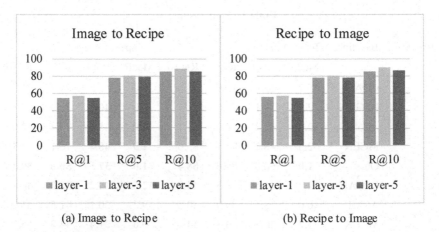

(a) Image to Recipe   (b) Recipe to Image

Fig. 3. Ablation study: multimodal encoders with different layers.

4.4 Main Results

We present the results of our proposed method against various representative baseline methods in Table 1. We show the results for image to recipe retrieval and recipe to image retrieval separately. As can be seen from the table, the performance of the method presented in this paper outperforms all baselines on all evaluation metrics with different test sizes. On the 1K test dataset, we obtain the MedR value of 1.0, which demonstrates the best performance. The performance of our method by using the $R@K$ metric is also better than all other methods. The value of $R@1$ is nearly 8% higher than the best-performed baseline MCEN. The results in the top 10 of the retrieval results ($R@10$) are nearly 5% higher. This indicates that our method can retrieve more number of matched results in the top 10 results for both image to recipe and recipe to image retrieval tasks. These results show that using multimodal encoders for enhanced modality alignment is quite adequate for the cross-modal retrieval task. Sufficient semantic feature information can be extracted by using this component to further help modality alignment on top of adversarial learning.

We now turn to the results on the 10K setting. It is obvious that the performance of all methods decreases significantly since the retrieval task becomes much more challenging. It may be caused by the difficulty of finding matched results in a large number of similar samples. However, we notice that the performance decrease of our method is much less than that of other methods. The value of MedR reaches 4.0, and the values of $R@1$ to $R@10$ are gradually increasing, more quickly when comparing with other baseline methods. Although $R@1$ was only 4% (Image to Recipe) to 5% (Recipe to Image) better than the best-performed baseline MCEN, the results of $R@5$ and $R@10$ are 16% and 24% better than MCEN, respectively. It shows that in a larger dataset, our method focuses more on the characteristics of different modalities from multiple angles. It can use particular regions on images to locate the most similar samples.

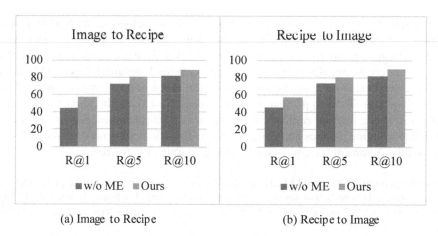

(a) Image to Recipe   (b) Recipe to Image

Fig. 4. Ablation study: results with and without multimodal encoders.

4.5 Ablation Studies

The core part of our framework is the multimodal encoders. To evaluate the influence of different sizes of cross-modal encoder layers, we conduct ablation studies on several variants of architectures. As shown in Fig. 2, the cross-modal encoders are composed of D layers. When the number of layers is 1, it means that initial embeddings are only passed through cross-modal attention and a self-attention layer. The number of 3 or 5 layers indicates these cross-modal encoders are actually stacked. Figure 3 presents the results of 1, 3 and 5 layers with different R@K metrics, where Fig. 3(a) shows Image to Recipe retrieval, Fig. 3(b) shows Recipe to Image retrieval. In either direction, it can be seen from the results that the method with 3 layers outperforms methods with all other number of layers.

Intuitively, the larger number of layers means that the model is deeper to capture more complex semantic relationships between different modalities. Henceforth, the extracted information should be more sufficient than a shallow model. However, on the other side, a deeper model means that there is a greater danger of overfitting. This is confirmed in our experiments that the method with 5 layers works worse than the method with 3 layers. This may be due to the repeated extraction.

To demonstrate the importance of using multimodal encoders to extract information before adversarial learning, we compare the performance of our full method with a method that the multimodal encoders removed (denote as w/o ME).

The experimental results are shown in Fig. 4. We can see that our method is always better than w/o ME in all R@K results. Removing multimodal encoders will lead to insufficient feature information extraction. It is obvious that the multimodal encoders in our method play a vital role in modality alignment.

5 Conclusion

In this paper, we propose a novel cross-modal retrieval method in the health domain. We use multimodal encoders to capture the inter- and intra-modality features. With adversarial learning, our method aims to enhance the very heart component, i.e., modality alignment in cross-modal retrieval. Experiments on the benchmark Recipe1M dataset with different evaluation metrics demonstrate the efficiency and effectiveness of our proposed method. We also present ablation studies to examine the impact of different numbers of layers and our multimodal encoders as a complete component. We aim to thoroughly examine the pros and cons of using both multimodal encoders and decoders for modality alignment for cross-modal retrieval purposes in the future.

Acknowledgements. We would like to thank anonymous reviewers for their helpful comments and suggestions. This work was supported by the National Natural Science Foundation of China under Project No. 61876062 and General Key Laboratory for Complex System Simulation under Project No. XM2020XT1004.

References

1. Carvalho, M., Cadène, R., Picard, D., Soulier, L., Thome, N., Cord, M.: Cross-modal retrieval in the cooking context: learning semantic text-image embeddings. In: Proceedings of the 41st International ACM SIGIR Conference on Research and Development in Information Retrieval, pp. 35–44 (2018)
2. Peng, Y., Huang, X., Zhao, Y.: An overview of cross-media retrieval: concepts, methodologies, benchmarks, and challenges. IEEE Trans. Circuits Syst. Video Technol. **28**(9), 2372–2385 (2017)
3. Wang, Y., Lin, X., Wu, L., Zhang, W.: Effective multi-query expansions: collaborative deep networks for robust landmark retrieval. IEEE Trans. Image Process. **26**(3), 1393–1404 (2017)
4. Wang, Y., Lin, X., Wu, L., Zhang, W., Zhang, Q.: LBMCH: learning bridging mapping for cross-modal hashing. In: Proceedings of the 38th international ACM SIGIR conference on research and development in information retrieval, pp. 999–1002 (2015)
5. Wu, L., Wang, Y., Shao, L.: Cycle-consistent deep generative hashing for cross-modal retrieval. IEEE Trans. Image Process. **28**(4), 1602–1612 (2018)
6. Wang, B., Yang, Y., Xu, X., Hanjalic, A., Shen, H.T.: Adversarial cross-modal retrieval. In: Proceedings of the 25th ACM international conference on Multimedia, pp. 154–162 (2017)
7. Zhu, B., Ngo, C.H., Chen, J.J., Hao, Y.: R2GAN: cross-modal recipe retrieval with generative adversarial network. In: Proceedings of the IEEE Conference on Computer Vision and Pattern Recognition, pp. 11477–11486 (2019)
8. Wang, H., Sahoo, D., Liu, C.H., Lim, E.P., Hoi, S.C.H.: Learning cross-modal embeddings with adversarial networks for cooking recipes and food images. In: Proceedings of the IEEE Conference on Computer Vision and Pattern Recognition, pp. 11572–11581 (2019)
9. Gulrajani, I., Ahmed, F., Arjovsky, M., Dumoulin, V., Courville, A.: Improved training of wasserstein gans. arXiv:1704.00028 (2017)
10. Fu, H., Wu, R., Liu, C., Sun, J.: MCEN: bridging cross-modal gap between cooking recipes and dish images with latent variable model. In: Proceedings of the IEEE/CVF Conference on Computer Vision and Pattern Recognition, pp. 14570–14580 (2020)
11. Ghifary, M., Kleijn, W.B., Zhang, M., Balduzzi, D., Li, W.: Deep reconstruction-classification networks for unsupervised domain adaptation. In: Leibe, B., Matas, J., Sebe, N., Welling, M. (eds.) ECCV 2016. LNCS, vol. 9908, pp. 597–613. Springer, Cham (2016). https://doi.org/10.1007/978-3-319-46493-0_36
12. Vaswani, A., et al.: Attention is all you need. arXiv:1706.03762 (2017)
13. Salvador, A., et al.: Learning cross-modal embeddings for cooking recipes and food images. In: Proceedings of the IEEE Conference on Computer Vision and Pattern Recognition, pp. 3020–3028 (2017)
14. Zou, F., Bai, X., Luan, C., Li, K., Wang, Y., Ling, H.: Semi-supervised cross-modal learning for cross modal retrieval and image annotation. World Wide Web **22**(2), 825–841 (2018)
15. Xu, X., He, L., Lu, H., Gao, L., Ji, Y.: Deep adversarial metric learning for cross-modal retrieval. World Wide Web **22**(2), 657–672 (2018)
16. Yu, Z., Wang, W., Li, G.: Multi-step self-attention network for cross-modal retrieval Based on a limited text space. In: Proceedings of the IEEE International Conference on Acoustics, Speech and Signal Processing, pp. 2082–2086 (2019)
17. Ye, L., Rochan, M., Liu, Z., Wang, Y.: Cross-modal self-attention network for referring image segmentation. In: Proceedings of the IEEE/CVF Conference on Computer Vision and Pattern Recognition, pp.10502–10511 (2019)
18. Gao, X., Mu, T., Goulermas, J., Wang, M.: Attention driven multimodal similarity learning. Inf. Sci. **432**, 530–542 (2018)

19. Zhang, Q., Wang, J., Huang, H., Huang, X., Gong, Y.: Hashtag recommendation for multimodal microblog using co-attention network. In: Proceedings of the International Joint Conference on Artificial Intelligence, pp. 3420–3426 (2017)
20. Zhang, Q., Fu, J., Liu, X., Huang, X.: Adaptive co-attention network for named entity recognition in tweets. In: Proceedings of the AAAI Conference on Artificial Intelligence (2018)
21. Ma, R., Zhang, Q., Wang, J., Cui, L., Huang, X.: Mention recommendation for multimodal microblog with cross-attention memory network. In: Proceedings of the 41st International ACM SIGIR Conference on Research & Development in Information Retrieval, pp. 195–204 (2018)
22. Lee, K., Chen, X., Hua, G., Hu, H., He, X.: Stacked cross attention for image-text matching. In: Proceedings of the European Conference on Computer Vision, pp. 201–216 (2018)
23. Sutskever, I., Vinyals, O., Le, Q.V.: Sequence to sequence learning with neural networks. arXiv:1409.3215 (2014)
24. Lu, J., Batra, D., Parikh, D., Lee, S.: ViLBERT: pretraining task-agnostic visiolinguistic representations for vision-and-language tasks. arXiv:1908.02265 (2019)
25. Sun, C., Myers, A., Vondrick, C., Murphy, K., Schmid, C.: VideoBERT: a joint model for video and language representation learning. In: Proceedings of the IEEE/CVF International Conference on Computer Vision, pp. 7464–7473 (2019)
26. Tsai, Y.H.H., et al.: Multimodal transformer for unaligned multimodal language sequences. In: Proceedings of the 57th Conference of the Association for Computational Linguistics, pp. 6558–6569 (2019)
27. Yu, J., Li, J., Yu, Z., Huang, Q.M.: Multimodal transformer with multi-view visual representation for image captioning. IEEE Trans. Circuits Syst. Video Technol. 30(12), 4467–4480 (2019)
28. He, K., Zhang, X., Ren, S., Sun, J.: Deep residual learning for image recognition. In: Proceedings of the 2016 IEEE conference on computer vision and pattern recognition, pp. 770–778 (2016)
29. Hochreiter, S., Schmidhuber, J.: Long short-term memory. Neural Comput. 9(8), 1735–1780 (1997)
30. Zan, Z., Li, L., Liu, J., Zhou, D.: Sentence-based and noise-robust cross-modal retrieval on cooking recipes and Food Images. In: Proceedings of the 2020 International Conference on Multimedia Retrieval, pp.117–125 (2020)
31. Rezende, D.J., Mohamed, S., Wierstra, D.: Stochastic backpropagation and approximate inference in deep generative models. In: Proceedings of the 31th International Conference on Machine Learning, pp.1278–1286 (2014)
32. Hotelling, H.: Relations between two sets of variates. In: Breakthroughs in Statistics, pp. 162–190. Springer, New York (1992). https://doi.org/10.1007/978-1-4612-4380-9_14

Data Cleaning for Indoor Crowdsourced RSSI Sequences

Jing Sun$^{(\boxtimes)}$, Bin Wang, Xiaoxu Song, and Xiaochun Yang

School of Computer Science and Engineering,
Northeastern University, Liaoning 110819, China
sunjing@stumail.neu.edu.cn, {binwang,yangxc}@mail.neu.edu.cn

Abstract. Received Signal Strength Indication (RSSI) has been increasingly deployed in indoor localization and navigation. Comparing with traditional fingerprint-based methods, crowdsourced method can collect RSSIs without expert surveyors and designated fingerprint collection points low-costly and efficiently. However, the crowdsourced RSSIs may contain some false and incomplete data. In this paper, we focus on two quality types of indoor crowdsourced RSSI sequences: missing values and false values. For the received signal strength values, we propose a RSSI sequences alignment and matching method to complete the missing values. For the location labels, we construct an indoor logical graph to capture the indoor topology and spatial consistent. To repair the missing and false location labels, we design a AP distribution based mapping method to map crowdsourced RSSIs to floor plan.

Keywords: Data cleaning · RSSI · Indoor localization · Crowdsourcing

1 Introduction

Crowdsourcing is a low-cost and efficient way to collect the RSSIs of indoor space from crowd participants without expert surveyors [5,6]. The RSSIs collected by crowdsourced users are consist of received signal strength values and location labels. However, the crowdsourced RSSIs may contain some false and missing values, which hinder the process of further localization and navigation. Hence it is of fundamental importance to clean the indoor crowdsourced RSSI sequences. We use the following example to introduce the problem of indoor crowdsourced RSSI sequences cleaning.

Example 1. Figure 1 shows a set of crowdsourced RSSI sequences S. Given m APs, a RSSI is an m-dimensional vector of signal strength values received from m APs with a partition-level location label. Assuming that topological floor plan is known and shown in Fig. 2. The crowdsourced RSSI sequences data may have some missing and false values: the RSSIs from f_{113} to f_{115} of u_1 and f_{210} of u_2 have missing received signal strength values. The RSSI f_{14} of u_1 and f_{23} to f_{27} of u_2 have missing location labels in single RSSI and continuous multiple RSSIs. The RSSI f_{16} has false location label. The goal is to complete the missing values and repair the false values. The ground truth is shown in Fig. 1.

© Springer Nature Switzerland AG 2021
L. H. U et al. (Eds.): APWeb-WAIM 2021, LNCS 12859, pp. 267–275, 2021.
https://doi.org/10.1007/978-3-030-85899-5_20

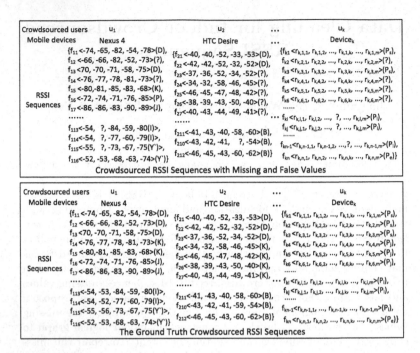

Fig. 1. Example of crowdsourced RSSI sequences with missing and false values.

To alleviate these above problems, we propose a cleaning method for the missing and false values of indoor crowdsourced RSSI sequences. The main idea is cleaning the location labels with the RSSI values and the logical floor plan, and cleaning the RSSI values with location labels and the logical floor plan. To complete the missing received signal strength values, we propose a RSSI sequence alignment method to match the overlap segments of different RSSI sequences, and estimate the missing values with the aligned RSSIs. To solve the device diversity, we propose a novel RSSI distance metric. To detect the false location labels, we construct a logical graph of floor plan to capture indoor topology and spatial constraint. To repair the missing and false location labels, we propose a mapping method which can map RSSIs to partitions of floor plan. We consider the property of AP distribution and the order relationship of RSSI sequence.

Related Work. There are several work about indoor data cleaning [9]. Asif [2] studied data cleaning for indoor RFID tracking data which focused on two relevant tasks: temporal redundancy elimination and spatial ambiguity reduction. Asif [1] also presented a learning-based approach to clean raw indoor RFID data. They proposed the Indoor RFID Multivariate Hidden Markov Model to capture the uncertainties of indoor RFID data. However, these RFID data cleaning methods cannot clean the missing and false RSSI data and location labels. At present, there is no work about RSSI data cleaning and crowdsourced RSSI sequence cleaning. The most similar work is that Ge Yan [3] proposed a least square localization method for wireless sensor networks using RSSI with the aid of the condition number of coordinate matrix to avoid the appearance of outliers. However, this work can only avoid the outliers in RSSIs, and cannot repair the false values and missing values.

2   Preliminaries and Problem Statement

In this section, we formalize the data cleaning for crowdsourced RSSI sequences.

Definition 1. Crowdsourced RSSI Sequence with Location Label: *A crowdsourced RSSI sequence* $s_i = \{<f_{i1}, p_{i1}>, <f_{i2}, p_{i2}>, ..., <f_{in}, p_{in}>\}$ *is a sequence of n crowdsourced RSSIs with location labels. Each RSSI f_{ij} in s_i is a vector of received signal strength values received from m APs at location p_i denoted as $< f_i > =<(r_{i1}, r_{i2}, ..., r_{im})>$, and f_{ij} has a time stamp t_{ij} and a partition-level location label p_{ij}.*

Definition 2. Data Cleaning for Crowdsourced RSSI sequences: *Given a set of crowdsourced RSSI sequences $S = \{s_1, s_2, ..., s_n\}$ where $s_i = \{<f_{i1}, p_{i1}>, <f_{i2}, p_{i2}>, ..., <f_{ik}, p_{ik}>\}$ and $< f_i, p_i> = <(r_{i1}, r_{i2},..., r_{im}), p_i>$. Some received signal strength values r_{ij} $(1 \leq j \leq m)$ of single RSSI f_i and some $\{r_{1j}, r_{2j},..., r_{sj}\}$ $(1 \leq s \leq k)$ of continuous multiple RSSIs are missing, some location labels p_{qj} of single RSSI f_q and some $\{p_{1j}, p_{2j},..., p_{tj}\}$ $(1 \leq q,t \leq k)$ of continuous multiple RSSIs are missing or false. We want to complete the missing r_{ij}, and repair missing and false p_{qj}.*

3   Cleaning the Received Signal Strength Values

In this section, we introduce how to clean the missing received signal strength values in single RSSI and continuous multiple RSSIs. When the missing received signal strength value is in single RSSI, we estimate the missing values with average of the relative entries of two adjacent RSSIs.

3.1   Alignment and Matching of RSSIs in Different RSSI Sequences

To complete the missing received signal strength values in continuous multiple RSSIs, we propose a RSSI sequence alignment and matching method and utilize the RSSIs from aligned and matched RSSIs to estimate the missing values.

To solve the problem of device diversity, based on [4,7], we consider not only absolute RSSI values, but also the signal strength differences from different APs. We construct the signature vectors to measure signal difference between different APs, where $\widehat{r_{ist}} = r_{is} - r_{it}$ and $\widehat{r_{jst}} = r_{js} - r_{jt}$ $(1 \leq s \leq m - 1, 2 \leq t \leq m)$. We propose the RSSI distance metric as following and set $\alpha = \beta = 1/2$.

$$dis(f_i, f_j) = \alpha \sqrt{\sum_{k=1}^{m} (r_{ik} - r_{jk})} + \beta \sqrt{\sum_{s=1}^{m-1} (\widehat{r_{ist}} - \widehat{r_{jst}})}$$

Given two RSSI sequences, $s_1 = \{f_{11}, f_{12}, f_{13}, ..., f_{1p}\}$ and $s_2 = \{f_{21}, f_{22}, f_{23}, ..., f_{2q}\}$. We want to find the overlap RSSIs of s_1 and s_2. Given two RSSI sequences s_1 and s_2, to match two different RSSI sequences, For $f_{1,i}$ in s_1 and $f_{2,j}$ in s_2, we compute the following *bound* to restrict the aligned RSSIs.

$$bound = \frac{1}{4}(dis(f_{1,i}, f_{1,i-1}) + dis(f_{1,i}, f_{1,i+1}) + dis(f_{2,j}, f_{2,j-1}) + dis(f_{2,j}, f_{2,j+1}))$$

We compare $dis(f_{1,i}, f_{2,j})$ with *bound*. If $dis(f_{1,i}, f_{2,j}) \leq bound$, we can match and align $f_{1,i}$ with $f_{2,j}$.

3.2   Cleaning Missing Values in Continuous Multiple RSSIs

Given a RSSI sequence s_i, there are missing values from $f_{i,p+1}$ to $f_{i,q-1}$ in s_i. We align and match $f_{i,p-1}$ and $f_{i,q+1}$ of s_i with RSSI sequences in S, and get k crowdsourced RSSI sequences $S' = \{s_1, s_2,..., s_k\}$ whose segments are aligned and matched with s_i. For each missing r_{ij}, we use the average of these k matched RSSIs to estimate the missing values as $r_{ij} = (\sum_{l=1}^{k} r_{lj})/k$.

4   Cleaning the Location Labels

In this section, we introduce how to clean the missing and false location labels.

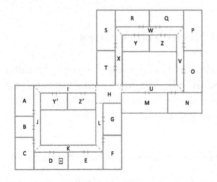
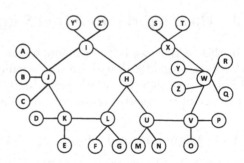

Fig. 2. Example of indoor floor plan.   **Fig. 3.** The logical graph of the floor plan.

4.1   Logical Graph G_l: Topology and Constraints of Indoor Space

Given the topological floor plan, we divide the indoor space into partitions with rooms and walls. Each partition p_i is a small piece of independent space, p_i is represented as a node. There is an edge e_k between two adjacent partitions p_i and p_j. Then we can construct the logical graph G_l as shown in Fig. 3.

Lemma 1. *Given a RSSI sequence s and logical graph G_l, for each two adjacent location labels p_i and p_j of s, if p_i and p_j are the same partition or there is an edge e_k between p_i and p_j in G_l, then s is spatial consistent for location labels.*

With Lemma 1, given a RSSI sequence s and logical graph G_l, for each two adjacent p_i and p_j in s, if they are not in the same partition and there is no edge between them in G_l, then p_i and p_j are marked as candidate false location labels. Those location labels which are marked twice are false location labels.

4.2 Repair of False and Missing Location Label for Single RSSI

For a false or missing location label, if its previous and next RSSIs are in the same partition, we repair it with its previous RSSI. If they are in different partitions, we utilize the following distance metric to compute their difference.

$$d(f_i, f_j) = \sqrt{\sum_{k=1}^{m}(r_{ik} - r_{jk})^2/(t_j - t_i)} \tag{1}$$

Given a RSSI f_j and its previous RSSI and next RSSI are f_i and f_k, the location labels of f_i and f_k are p_i and p_k. If $d(f_i, f_j) < d(f_j, f_k)$, the location label of f_j is repaired as p_i, otherwise, the location label of f_j is repaired as p_k.

4.3 Repair of False and Missing Location Labels for Continuous Multiple RSSIs

To repair the false and missing location labels for continuous multiple RSSIs, we transform the problem to map RSSIs without location labels to floor plan.

Definition 3. Floor Plan Mapping with Crowdsourced RSSI Sequence: *Given a RSSI sequence $s_i = \{f_{i1}(p_s), f_{i2}, ..., f_{ik}(p_e)\}$, the first and last RSSI have position labels p_s and p_e. The topological floor plan is consist of indoor partitions $P = \{p_1, p_2, ..., p_j\}$ which are connected together. We want to map each RSSI f_i in s_i to the partitions in P, and add partition label for each RSSI.*

Since the APs are deployed in different partitions, we can construct the *AP distribution* of RSSI sequence and connection path. Given a RSSI sequence s with n RSSIs, base on the triangulation theory, we construct *AP distribution of RSSI sequence* $s_{ap} = \{AP_i, ..., AP_k, ..., AP_l\}$ which is the sequence of APs which are the top-3 strongest signal strength APs for each f_i in s. Given two vertexes p_i and p_j in G_l, the *connection path* $cp = < p_i, p_k, ..., p_l, p_j >$ from p_i to p_j is a sequence of consecutive vertexes that can connect p_i and p_j on G_l. We can also construct *AP distribution for connection path* $cp_{ap} = \{AP_j, ..., AP_p, ..., AP_l\}$ which is the sequence top-3 strongest signal strength APs for each p_i in cp.

Lemma 2. *Given RSSI sequence s and connection path cp, their AP distributions are s_{ap} and cp_{ap}, if s_{ap} can match with cp_{ap}, then s can match with cp.*

Based on the observation that the similarity two adjacent RSSIs in two different partitions is smaller than that in the same partition, we can divided RSSI sequence into segments and map the RSSIs in s_i to the partitions. Given a RSSI sequence s_i, with Eq. 1, we can compute the *difference sequence* of each two adjacent RSSIs in s_i as $d_{seq} = (d_{12}, d_{23}, ..., d_{n-1,n})$, where $d_{ij} = d(f_i, f_j)$.

Lemma 3. *Given a RSSI sequence $s = \{f_1, f_2, ..., f_i, f_j, ..., f_n\}$ and its difference sequence $d_{Seq} = \{d_{12}, d_{23}, ..., d_{n-1,n}\}$, if $d_{i,j} > d_{i-1,j-1}$ and $d_{i,j} > d_{i+1,j+1}$, the s_i can be divided by f_i and f_j as $s = \{< f_1, f_2, ..., f_i >, < f_j, ..., f_n >\}$.*

With Lemma 3, if knowing the number of segments num_s of s, we can divide s into num_s segments by the top-$(num_s - 1)$ RSSI distances d_{ij}. We match the AP distributions of RSSI sequence and connection path, and divide s into segments and match each segment with the partition p_i in the floor plan. Algorithm 1 describes the procedure of mapping RSSIs to the indoor partitions.

Algorithm 1: Floor plan mapping for RSSI sequences

Input: A RSSI sequence s and topological floor plan graph G_l

Output: The mapping pairs $< f_i, p_i >$ between f_i in s and p_i in G_l

1 $Hdis \leftarrow \infty$, $num_s \leftarrow 0$, $num_p \leftarrow 0$;
2 Find the non-redundant RSSI sequence s' for s;
3 **for** *each RSSI f_i in s'* **do**
4 $\quad\lfloor$ Find the $\{AP_i, AP_j, AP_k\}$ which have the top-3 strongest signal strength;

5 Construct the AP distribution s_{ap} of s';
6 Find the non-redundant connection paths $CP = \{cp_1, cp_2, ..., cp_k\}$ from p_s to p_e;
7 **for** *each non-redundant connection path cp_i* **do**
8 $\quad$ Construct the AP distribution cp_{ap_i} of cp_i;
9 $\quad$ **if** $hamDis(cp_{ap_i}, s_{ap}) <= Hdis$ **then**
10 $\quad\quad$ $Hdis = hamDis(cp_{ap_i}, s_{ap})$;
11 $\quad\quad$ Count the num_p of cp_i;
12 $\quad\quad$ $num_s = num_p$;

13 **for** *each RSSI f_i in s'* **do**
14 $\quad\lfloor$ Compute $d(f_i, f_{i+1})$;

15 Construct the difference sequence d_{seq};
16 Find the top-(num_s-1) entries d_{ij} in d_{seq};
17 Divide s' into num_s segments with d_{ij};
18 Map the f_i in each segment to the relative partitions p_i;
19 **return** the mapping pairs $< f_i, p_i >$;

---

5 Experimentation and Evaluation

In the experiments, we use the following two real indoor RSSI data sets: **UJIIndoorLoc Data Set** [8]: We extract 500 RSSIs as crowdsourced RSSIs and construct 50 crowdsourced RSSI sequences with 5 different devices. We select 9 APs and use the RSSIs with coordinates as the ground truth. **Wi-Fi Received Signal Strength measurements:** The indoor RSSIs are collected in our building. We select 5 APs and use four different mobile devices and collect 50 location-tagged RSSIs sequences with total 500 location-tagged RSSIs as the ground truth. For each data set, we randomly delete received signal strength values in single RSSI and continuous multiple RSSIs of 50 RSSIs, and randomly delete and modify location labels in single RSSI and continuous multiple RSSIs of 100 RSSIs. All the algorithms were implemented using C++. The experiments were run on a PC with an Intel 2.93 GHz Quad Core CPU i7 and 4 GB memory with a 500 GB disk. **RClean** is our proposed method, where **RClean-5** and **RClean-9** are with 5 APs and 9 APs. **LSOP** is the method proposed by [3]. **L2 Dist** method locates user's position with L2 distance without data cleaning.

5.1 Accuracy of Location Labels Cleaning

We evaluate the accuracy of the location labels cleaning by evaluating the accuracy of mapping RSSIs to floor plan. We compute the mapping average accuracy:

$$Mapping\ accuracy = \frac{number\ of\ RSSIs\ repaired\ with\ right\ location\ labels}{number\ of\ RSSIs\ with\ false\ and\ missing\ location\ labels}$$

Figure 4(a) and Fig. 5(a) show the mapping accuracy when varying the number of RSSIs. **Label cleaning** is the our propose location labels cleaning method. **Nearby cleaning** is the method which directly uses the adjacent location labels to repair the missing location labels. The accuracy of repairing RSSIs to right location labels is larger than 95% with different number of RSSIs.

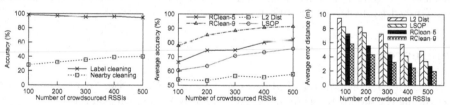

(a) Accuracy of Cleaning (b) Accuracy of Localization(c) Average Error Distance

Fig. 4. The result on UJIIndoorLoc data set.

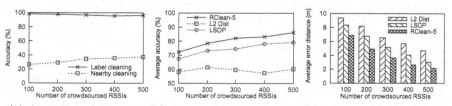

(a) Accuracy of Cleaning (b) Accuracy of Localization(c) Average Error Distance

Fig. 5. The result on Wi-Fi Received Signal Strength measurements data set.

5.2 Accuracy of Localization

To evaluate the accuracy of cleaning the missing received signal strength values, we evaluate the average accuracy of indoor localization [7]. We compute the *Average accuracy* with 100 randomly generated localization queries. Figure 4(b) and Fig. 5(b) show the average accuracy when varying the number of RSSIs. With the increase of RSSI number, the localization accuracy of out proposed method is range from 80% to 90%.

5.3 Average Error Distance

We compute the distance between the localization position with the ground truth position. Figure 4(c) and Fig. 5(c) show the average error distance when varying the number of RSSIs. We can find that the average error distance is less than 4 m when the number of RSSIs is large than 300.

6 Conclusion

In this paper, we propose a cleaning method for the missing and false values of crowdsourced RSSI sequences. To complete the missing received signal strength values, we propose a RSSI sequences alignment and matching method. To repair the missing and false location labels, we construct an indoor logical graph and propose a floor plan mapping method.

Acknowledgement. The work is partially supported by the National Natural Science Foundation of China (62072088), Fundamental Research Funds for the Central Universities (No. N171602003), Ten Thousand Talent Program (ZX20200035), and Liaoning Distinguished Professor (XLYC1902057).

References

1. Baba, A.I., Jaeger, M., Lu, H., Pedersen, T.B., Ku, W.-S., Xie, X.: Learning-based cleansing for indoor RFID data. In: ACM SIGMOD, pp. 925–936 (2016)
2. Baba, A.I., Lu, H., Xie, X., Pedersen, T.B.: Spatiotemporal data cleansing for indoor RFID tracking data. In: MDM, vol. 1, pp. 187–196. IEEE (2013)
3. Ge, Y., Zheng, Z., Yan, B., Yang, J., Yang, Y., Meng, H.: An RSSI-based localization method with outlier suppress for wireless sensor networks. In: IEEE International Conference on Computer and Communications, pp. 2235–2239 (2016)
4. Laoudias, C., Piche, R., Panayiotou, C.G.: Device self-calibration in location systems using signal strength histograms. J. LBS **7**(3), 165–181 (2013)
5. Li, X., Zhao, Y., Zhou, X., Zheng, K.: Consensus-based group task assignment with social impact in spatial crowdsourcing. Data Sci. Eng. **5**(4), 375–390 (2020). https://doi.org/10.1007/s41019-020-00142-0
6. Sun, J., Wang, B., Yang, X.: Practical approximate indoor nearest neighbour locating with crowdsourced RSSIs. World Wide Web **24**(3), 747–779 (2021). https://doi.org/10.1007/s11280-021-00868-5

7. Sun, J., Yang, X., Wang, B.: Crowdsourced indoor localization for diverse devices with RSSI sequences. In: Ni, W., Wang, X., Song, W., Li, Y. (eds.) WISA 2019. LNCS, vol. 11817, pp. 614–625. Springer, Cham (2019). https://doi.org/10.1007/978-3-030-30952-7_62

8. Torres-Sospedra, J., et al.: UJIIndoorLoc: a new multi-building and multi-floor database for WLAN fingerprint-based indoor localization problems. In: IPIN, pp. 261–270. IEEE (2014)

9. Wu, Y., Lin, X., Yang, Y., He, L.: Cleaning uncertain graphs via noisy crowdsourcing. World Wide Web **22**(4), 1523–1553 (2018). https://doi.org/10.1007/s11280-018-0624-8

Recommender System

A Behavior-Aware Graph Convolution Network Model for Video Recommendation

Wei Zhuo[1], Kunchi Liu[2,3], Taofeng Xue[2,3], Beihong Jin[2,3(✉)], Beibei Li[2,3], Xinzhou Dong[2,3], He Chen[1], Wenhai Pan[1], Xuejian Zhang[1], and Shuo Zhou[1]

[1] MX Media Co., Ltd., Singapore, Singapore
[2] State Key Laboratory of Computer Science, Institute of Software, Chinese Academy of Sciences, Beijing, China
Beihong@iscas.ac.cn
[3] University of Chinese Academy of Sciences, Beijing, China

Abstract. Interactions between users and videos are the major data source of performing video recommendation. Despite lots of existing recommendation methods, user behaviors on videos, which imply the complex relations between users and videos, are still far from being fully explored. In the paper, we present a model named Sagittarius. Sagittarius adopts a graph convolutional neural network to capture the influence between users and videos. In particular, Sagittarius differentiates between different user behaviors by weighting and fuses the semantics of user behaviors into the embeddings of users and videos. Moreover, Sagittarius combines multiple optimization objectives to learn user and video embeddings and then achieves the video recommendation by the learned user and video embeddings. The experimental results on multiple datasets show that Sagittarius outperforms several state-of-the-art models in terms of recall, unique recall and NDCG.

Keywords: Recommender system · Graph convolution network · Video recommendation

1 Introduction

In recent years, online streaming platforms develop rapidly. On the mainstream online streaming platforms (e.g., YouTube and MX Player), the number of daily active users can easily reach hundreds of millions, where users are constantly changing their needs of cultural entertainment and tastes. In order to improve user experience and increase user stickiness to platforms, video recommendation becomes an indispensable part of the online streaming platforms.

This work was supported by the National Natural Science Foundation of China under Grant No. 62072450 and the 2019 joint project with MX Media.

Video recommendation, in common with other item recommendation tasks, has to face a large amount of sparse user-video interactions which contain multiple user behaviors such as clicking, sharing and downloading videos. Further, we note that the behaviors in the video recommendation more or less indicate user preferences, although their roles differ from ones in the e-commerce scenarios where some behaviors such as place-an-order clearly reveal the user preferences.

In general, the interactions between users and videos are the most important data source for top-k video recommendation, since they imply user preferences on videos and prevailing trends of videos. To maintain the characteristics of original user-video interactions to the greatest extent, we plan to model interactions as a bipartite user-video graph and learn embeddings of users and videos from the graph first, and then achieve the video recommendations. Logically, the videos interacted with a user can be used to enrich the user's embedding, because these interactions might reflect the user preference on the videos. On the other hand, a group of users who have interacted with a video can also be regarded as the side information of the video to measure the collaborative similarity between videos, therefore they can also be used to enrich the embedding of the video. For digging out the influence between users and videos from a large-scale sparse bipartite user-video graph, we turn to a convolutional neural network on the graph to learn embeddings of users and videos. As a result, we propose a model named Sagittarius. The contributions of our work are summarized as follows.

- We highlight that the different user behaviors imply the different degrees of user preferences on videos. To fully understand user preferences on videos, we quantify the behaviors as weights on the edges while building the bipartite graph, and then design a graph convolution network (GCN) to propagate the embeddings of users and videos across the edges of the bipartite user-video graph, so as to mine the influence between users and videos.
- We highlight that top-k video recommendation can be optimized from different ranking metrics. Further, we adopt a combination of multiple optimization objectives (including one major and two minor objectives) to guide the embedding learning. In particular, we propose to add weights of user behaviors to optimization objectives.
- We conduct extensive offline experiments and online A/B tests. The offline experimental results on five datasets show that Sagittarius outperforms several state-of-the-art models in terms of recall, unique recall and NDCG. Moreover, we conduct online A/B test in MX Player. Sagittarius behaves better than two existing models in MX Player, which proves the effectiveness of Sagittarius in a real-world production environment.

The rest of the paper is organized as follows. Section 2 introduces the related work. Section 3 describes our Sagittarius model. Section 4 gives the experimental results and analyses. Finally, the paper is concluded in Sect. 5.

2 Related Work

Our work is related to the research under two non-orthogonal topics: GNN (Graph Neural Network)-based collaborative filtering, video recommendation.

GNN-based collaborative filtering combines representation learning on graphs [7] and collaborative filtering. The basic procedure is to model user-item interactions as one or multiple graphs, design a graph neural network (e.g., a GCN) to learn the node embeddings, and then apply the learned embeddings of items and users to achieve recommendation tasks.

Obviously, item graphs can be constructed from user-item interactions where nodes denote the items that users interact with and directed edges indicate the relations between two item nodes. For example, Equuleus [22] constructs a homomorphic video graph and then develops a node attributed encoder network to generate video embeddings. SR-GNN [18] builds the directed item graphs for interaction sequences and then develops a GNN to capture complex item transition and an attention mechanism to fuse user's long-term and short-term interests. GC-SAN [19], an improved version of SR-GNN, borrows the self-attention structure from Transformer and combines a multi-layer self-attention network with original SR-GNN.

Besides item graphs subordinated to homomorphic graphs, heteromorphic graphs can be built. Taking the work on bipartite graphs as an example, Berg et al. present a graph auto-encoder GCMC [2], where the encoder contains a graph convolution layer that constructs user and item embeddings through message passing on the bipartite user-item graph and the bilinear decoder predicts the labeled links in the graph. Wang et al. propose NGCF [16] which models the high-order connectivity on the bipartite user-item graph. By stacking multiple embedding propagation layers, NGCF can generate the embeddings of users and items on the user-item graph, which encodes the collaborative signal between user and item. Wei et al. propose MMGCN [17] for micro-videos, which constructs a bipartite user-item graph for each modality, yields modal-specific embeddings of users and videos by the message passing of graph neural networks, enriching the representation of each node with the topological structure and features of its neighbors, and then obtains final node embeddings by a combination layer. Moreover, MBGCN [9] builds a unified heterogeneous graph where an edge indicates the behavior between a user and an item or the relation between items. In particular, the complex behavior-aware message propagations are designed for the GCN in MBGCN.

Recently, for exploring the intrinsic relations of interaction data and/or fusing various side information, some work develops different types of graphs, such as semi-homogenous graphs in Gemini [20], the directed multigraph and the shortcut graph in LESSR [4], the item graph, category graph, and shop graph in M2GRL [15], and attribute graphs in Murzim [5].

In addition, He et al. propose LightGCN [8], a simplified version of NGCF, which deletes feature transformation and nonlinear activation in NGCF so as to decrease the unnecessary complexity of the network architecture. The authors claim that LightGCN can achieve better recommendation performance than NGCF. Similarly, Chen et al. propose LR-GCCF [3] which is a linear residual graph convolutional neural network based on graph collaborative filtering. By removing nonlinear transformations in the network, it reduces multiple parameter matrices of different layers of the network into a single matrix, thereby effectively reducing the amount of learnable parameters.

As for video recommendation, recent progress mainly depends on deep learning. For example, Gao et al. [6] adopt recurrent neural networks and consider video semantic embedding, user interest modeling and user relevance mining in a unified framework. Li et al. [11] present a model which is composed of a novel temporal graph-based LSTM and multi-level interest layers to model diverse and dynamic user interest and multi-level user interest. Moreover, Li et al. [10] employ GCNs to recommend long-tail hashtags for micro-videos.

Video recommendation is also a hot spot in the industry. For example, Baluja et al. [1] propose a random walk-based model for video click-through rate prediction in YouTube, Xu et al. [21] adopt GATs (Graph Attention Networks) and the knowledge graph to generate video recommendations for the store-shelf and autoplay scenarios in Hulu, and Xue et al. [23] develop a spatio-temporal collaborative filtering approach for offline on-demand cinemas of iQIYI.

Comparing to existing work, our Sagittarius model falls in the scope of GNN-based collaborate filtering, and designs a new graph convolution network to distinguish user behaviors and employs multiple optimization objectives. Further, differing from the recommendation models which exploits multi-behavior data, our model adopts a lightweight way to fuse user behavior semantics.

3   Sagittarius Model

3.1   Problem Formulation

In the top-k video recommendation scenario, we model user-video interactions as a bipartite user-video graph, denoted by $\mathcal{G} = (\mathcal{U} \cup \mathcal{V}, \mathcal{E}, \mathcal{R})$, where $\mathcal{U}$ is the set of users, $\mathcal{V}$ is the set of videos, and $\mathcal{U} \cup \mathcal{V}$ constitutes the set of nodes. Edge (u, v, r) in $\mathcal{E}$ represents that the type of the interaction between user $u \in \mathcal{U}$ and video $v \in \mathcal{V}$ is $r \in \mathcal{R}$, where $\mathcal{R}$ is a set of all interactive behavior types, including clicking, giving a like, sharing, downloading and etc. In addition, we define a priori function $\phi(r) : \mathcal{R} \rightarrow \mathbb{R}$, which maps an interactive behavior to a score. The function is used to measure the degree of user preference by the user behavior, and higher scores indicate greater user interest. Particularly, the score of non-interaction is set to 0. While building the bipartite graph, we take the value of $\phi(r)$ as the weight W_{uv} of edge (u, v, r). Our goal is to learn the embeddings of the users and videos and apply the embeddings to recommending top-k videos for users.

3.2   Model Architecture

Sagittarius consists of the embedding layer, the convolution layers, the combination layer, and the prediction layer. Figure 1 shows the architecture of our Sagittarius model.

Embedding Layer. The embedding layer provides the initial embeddings of users and videos. Formally, we denote the user embedding matrix by $\mathbf{E}_u \in \mathbb{R}^{|\mathcal{U}| \times \bar{d}}$ and the video embedding matrix by $\mathbf{E}_v \in \mathbb{R}^{|\mathcal{V}| \times \bar{d}}$, where $\bar{d}$ denotes the initial embedding size. $\mathbf{E}_u$ and $\mathbf{E}_v$ are initialized randomly. In this way, given the user u and its ID one-hot vector $\mathbf{x}_u \in \mathbb{R}^{|\mathcal{U}|}$, its embedding $\mathbf{e}_u \in \mathbb{R}^{\bar{d}}$ is set to $\mathbf{e}_u = \mathbf{E}_u^T \mathbf{x}_u$. Similarly, for the ID one-hot vector $\mathbf{x}_v \in \mathbb{R}^{|\mathcal{V}|}$ of video v, its embedding is expressed as $\mathbf{e}_v = \mathbf{E}_v^T \mathbf{x}_v$.

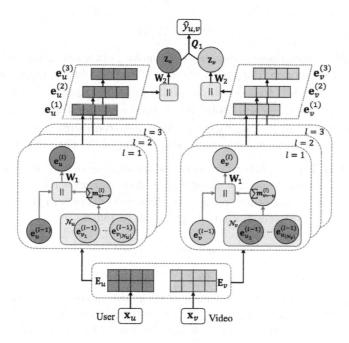

Fig. 1. The architecture of Sagittarius

Convolution Layers. Each convolution layer is responsible for performing the convolution operation on each node and its neighbors of the bipartite graph so that the embeddings will be passed and transformed across edges of the graph. In particular, for a certain user-video interaction pair (u, v), in the l-th graph convolution layer, we propagate embedding information from the neighbor node v to the target node u by Eq. (1).

$$\mathbf{m}_{u \leftarrow v}^{(l)} = c_{uv} \mathbf{e}_v^{(l-1)} \tag{1}$$

In Eq. (1), $\mathbf{m}_{u \leftarrow v}^{(l)}$ denotes the message passed from node v to u, and $\mathbf{e}_v^{(l-1)}$ is the embedding of node v output by the $(l-1)$-th convolution layer. In particular, $\mathbf{e}_v^{(0)} = \mathbf{e}_v$, $\mathbf{e}_v$ is the initial embedding of the video v output by the embedding layer. c_{uv} is the scaling factor, which is defined in Eq. (2) where $\mathcal{N}_u$ and $\mathcal{N}_v$ are the sets of neighbors of node u and node v, respectively.

$$c_{uv} = \sqrt{\frac{\phi(r)}{|\mathcal{N}_u||\mathcal{N}_v|} \frac{\mathbf{e}_u^{(l-1)T}\mathbf{e}_v^{(l-1)}}{||\mathbf{e}_u^{(l-1)}||_2||\mathbf{e}_v^{(l-1)}||_2}} \tag{2}$$

Further, we combine the aggregated neighbor information with the information of the node u by Eqs. (3)–(4).

$$\mathbf{h}_u^{(l)} = \mathbf{e}_u^{(l-1)} || \sum_{v \in \mathcal{N}_u} \mathbf{m}_{u \leftarrow v}^{(l)} \tag{3}$$

$$\mathbf{e}_u^{(l)} = \text{ReLU}(\mathbf{W}_1 \mathbf{h}_u^{(l)}) \tag{4}$$

In the above equations, $||$ denotes the concatenation operation, $\mathbf{e}_u^{(l-1)}$ is the embedding of the node u output by the $(l-1)$-th convolution layer, and matrix $\mathbf{W}_1 \in \mathbb{R}^{\bar{d} \times 2\bar{d}}$ maps $\mathbf{h}_u^{(l)}$ to the $\bar{d}$-dimensional embedding space, which is a learnable parameter. By these equations, $\mathbf{e}_u^{(l-1)}$ is concatenated with the aggregated information $\sum_{v \in \mathcal{N}_u} \mathbf{m}_{u \leftarrow v}^{(l)}$, and then the concatenated result is sent to a nonlinear transformation, obtaining the user embedding of the current layer.

Combination Layer. After the iterative operations of multiple convolution layers, we can obtain the output of each layer of the L convolution layers, namely $\{\mathbf{e}_u^{(1)}, \mathbf{e}_u^{(2)}, \dots, \mathbf{e}_u^{(L)}\}$. In order to improve the expressiveness of the embeddings, we perform a layer-wise combination operation as follows.

$$\mathbf{h}_u = \mathbf{e}_u^{(1)} || \mathbf{e}_u^{(2)} || \cdots || \mathbf{e}_u^{(L)} \tag{5}$$

$$\mathbf{z}_u = \mathbf{W}_2 \mathbf{h}_u \tag{6}$$

Specifically, we apply the concatenation operation shown in Eq. (5) to concatenate the embeddings output by different layers, and perform the linear transformation shown in Eq. (6) to combine the low-order embeddings extracted from the low-level convolution layers and the high-order embeddings extracted from the high-level convolution layers. The achieved effect is that the embeddings output by different layers can predict the score cooperatively. In Eq. (6), $\mathbf{W}_2 \in \mathbb{R}^{d \times L\bar{d}}$ maps $\mathbf{h}_u$ to a d-dimensional embedding space, where d is the dimension of the embeddings. Thus, the finally learned $\mathbf{z}_u$ combines the information of the user node u itself and the collaboration information from the multi-order neighborhood nodes. In the same way, we can obtain the embedding $\mathbf{z}_v$ of the video v.

Prediction Layer. We adopt the following bilinear decoder to calculate the affinity score of each user-video pair, sort videos by the score, and then filter the videos that the user has interacted with to get top-k recommendations.

$$\hat{y}_{u,v} = g_1(\mathbf{z}_u, \mathbf{z}_v) = \mathbf{z}_u^T \mathbf{Q}_1 \mathbf{z}_v \tag{7}$$

In Eq. (7), $\mathbf{Q}_1$ is a parameter that needs to be learned, $\mathbf{z}_u$ and $\mathbf{z}_v$ are the embeddings of the node u and the node v obtained from Eq. (6).

3.3   Learning Objectives

Generally speaking, the recommended videos should be the top-k videos ranked by a certain metric or score. We choose the probability of the next click on each video as the metric, where the probability can be estimated based on the set of videos that user has interacted with or based on the sequence of videos that the user has interacted with. While employing a score, we can say that given a specific user, the score of the video that the user has interacted with should be greater than the score of the video that has not been interacted with. Therefore, we construct three objective functions, i.e., video partial order preserving function, video click-through rate prediction function and next click video prediction function.

Video Partial Order Preserving Function. In practical, we measure the partial order between videos instead of total order of videos, not only because the total order is often unavailable or costs high, but also because the partial order relationship between videos is enough to determine the relative ranking of recommended videos and alleviate the problem of positional deviation.

We adopt the BPR [13] loss function to optimize the partial order relationship between videos. Thus, for each user-video interaction (u, v, r), i.e., one positive sample, we randomly select 10 negative samples to construct a set $\mathcal{O}$ containing 10 quadruple (u, v, r, w), where user u performs no behavior on video w.

In addition, we regard the preference score difference between the positive sample and the negative sample, i.e. $W_{uv} - W_{uw} = \phi(r) - 0 = \phi(r)$ as the weight of this quadruple, where $\phi(r)$ is the function defined in Sect. 3.1.

Finally, we define the BPR loss function $\mathcal{L}_1$ for optimizing the ordering of videos as follows:

$$\mathcal{L}_1 = -\frac{1}{|\mathcal{O}|} \sum_{(u,v,r,w) \in \mathcal{O}} \phi(r) \ln \sigma \left(g_1\left(\mathbf{z}_u, \mathbf{z}_v\right) - g_1\left(\mathbf{z}_u, \mathbf{z}_w\right) \right) \tag{8}$$

In Eq. (8), $g_1\left(\mathbf{z}_u, \mathbf{z}_v\right) = \mathbf{z}_u^T \mathbf{Q}_1 \mathbf{z}_v$, and σ is the sigmoid activation function. This function is our major learning objective.

Video Click-Through Rate Prediction Function. In the video recommendation scenario, most of the user-video interactions are very sparse and mainly focus on click behaviors. Considering that clicking can reflect the user's degree of interest in the video to a large extent, we recognize the necessity for optimizing the prediction of the click-through rate of users on the video. We adopt the binary cross entropy loss function to predict the video click-through rate.

Specifically, we reuse the negative samples sampled for Eq. (8). For each quadruple $(u, v, r, w) \in \mathcal{O}$, we define the cross entropy loss function as follows.

$$\mathcal{L}_2 = -\frac{1}{|\mathcal{O}|} \left(\sum_{(u,v,r,w) \in \mathcal{O}} \phi(r) \cdot \log \sigma \left(g_2\left(\mathbf{z}_u, \mathbf{z}_v\right) \right) + \log \left(1 - \sigma \left(g_2\left(\mathbf{z}_u, \mathbf{z}_w\right) \right) \right) \right) \tag{9}$$

In Eq. (9), $g_2(\mathbf{z}_u, \mathbf{z}_v) = \mathbf{z}_u^T \mathbf{Q}_2 \mathbf{z}_v$ where $\mathbf{Q}_2$ is a learnable parameter, and $\phi(r)$ is used as the weight of the positive sample, and the weight of the negative sample is set to 1.

Next Click Video Prediction Function. User-video interactions can be viewed as a sequence which implies the change of user preferences on videos over time. Therefore, we can set the prediction of the next click video by the interaction sequences as an optimization objective.

Given that a user has the interaction sequence $(v_1, v_2, \ldots, v_T) \in \mathcal{S}$, where $\mathcal{S}$ is the set of interaction sequences, for predicting the next click video, we apply the standard single layer GRU, taking $\mathbf{z}_{v_1}, \mathbf{z}_{v_2}, \ldots, \mathbf{z}_{v_{T-1}}$ as input, and then regard the hidden state representation output by the GRU at the last time step as the embedding $\mathbf{q}_{v_T}$ of the video sequence. Next, we send $\mathbf{q}_{v_T}$ to a fully connected layer and then apply softmax to predict the distribution of the next click video v_T. The corresponding equations are as follows.

$$\mathbf{q}_{v_T} = \mathrm{GRU}(\mathbf{z}_{v_1}, \mathbf{z}_{v_2}, \ldots, \mathbf{z}_{v_{T-1}}) \tag{10}$$

$$p(v_T | v_1, v_2, \ldots, v_{T-1}) = softmax(\mathbf{W}_s \mathbf{q}_{v_T}) \tag{11}$$

In Eq. (11), $\mathbf{W}_s^{|\mathcal{V}| \times d}$ maps the sequence representation $\mathbf{q}_{v_T}$ to the $|\mathcal{V}|$ dimension space of the video set. Furthermore, we take the negative log likelihood of v_T as the function to be optimized, i.e., the sequence loss, as shown below.

$$\mathcal{L}_3 = -\frac{1}{|\mathcal{S}|} \left(\sum_{(v_1, v_2, \ldots, v_T) \in \mathcal{S}} \log p(v_T | v_1, v_2, \ldots, v_{T-1}) \right) \tag{12}$$

Loss Function. The loss function of the Sagittarius model is the weighted summation of the three optimization functions, as shown below.

$$\mathcal{L} = \lambda_1 \mathcal{L}_1 + \lambda_2 \mathcal{L}_2 + \lambda_3 \mathcal{L}_3 \tag{13}$$

In Eq. (13), λ_1, λ_2 and λ_3 denote the coefficients, which specify the importance of different functions, respectively.

3.4 Recommendation Acceleration

When facing large-scale users, it will take a lot of time to generate recommendation results if only using a single machine. In order to speed up the generation of recommendation results, we perform the generation on Spark engine. The detailed implementation is as Algorithm 1.

4   Evaluation

In this section, we evaluate the top-k video recommendation performance of Sagittarius by conducting offline experiments and online A/B tests. We list corresponding results and discussions, answering the following four research questions (RQs):

Algorithm 1. Generating top-k video recommendations

1: According to the obtained embeddings $\mathbf{z}_u, \mathbf{z}_v$, construct the list $\mathbf{Y}$ in the form of $\left[(u_1, \mathbf{z}_{u_1}), \ldots, \left(u_{|\mathcal{U}|}, \mathbf{z}_{u_{|\mathcal{U}|}} \right) \right]$, and form final video embedding matrix $\mathbf{Z} \in \mathbb{R}^{|\mathcal{V}| \times d}$.

2: For each user $u \in \mathcal{U}$, obtain the historical interacted video collection $\mathcal{S}_u$, and then organize them into the form of $\left[(u_1, \mathcal{S}_{u_1}), \ldots, \left(u_{|\mathcal{U}|}, \mathcal{S}_{u_{|\mathcal{U}|}} \right) \right]$.

3: Perform a concatenation operation of $\mathbf{Y}$ in Step (1) with the result of Step (2), and the result is like $[(u, \mathbf{z}_u, \mathcal{S}_u), \ldots]$.

4: Broadcast parameters $\mathbf{Z}$ and $\mathbf{Q}_1$ in $g_1(\mathbf{z}_u, \mathbf{z}_v) = \mathbf{z}_u^T \mathbf{Q}_1 \mathbf{z}_v$ to each executor.

5: For each user $u \in \mathcal{U}$, this is, each $[(u, \mathbf{z}_u, \mathcal{S}_u), \ldots]$ in the result of Step (3), perform the following Map operation:

  5.1 According to $\mathbf{z}_u, \mathbf{Z}$ and $\mathbf{Q}_1$, calculate the affinity score $g_1(\mathbf{z}_u, \mathbf{z}_v)$ of u for each video $v \in \mathcal{V}$.

  5.2 Traverse the set of videos which are sorted in descending order of the affinity score. For each video v, if $v \in \mathcal{S}_u$ then it is filtered, else it is added to the top-k recommendation result. When the number of recommended videos reaches k, the loop ends.

6: Perform the Reduce operation and output the recommendation result of each user to the storage file (e.g., S3 in MX Player).

RQ1: How well does Sagittarius perform for the top-k video recommendation, compared to the state-of-the-art GNN models?

RQ2: What is the impact of the design choices of Sagittarius on the performance of the top-k video recommendation?

RQ3: What is the impact of the hyper-parameters of Sagittarius on the recommendation performance?

RQ4: How does Sagittarius perform in the live production environment, e.g., when serving MX Player, one of India's largest streaming platforms?

4.1 Experimental Setup

Datasets. We adopt four publicly available datasets, i.e., MovieLens-100K and MovieLens-10M from MovieLens [12], and Amazon-Beauty and Amazon-Digital Music from Amazon Product Review[14]. For the latter two datasets, we filter out items which are reviewed less than five times and users who give less than five reviews. For these four datasets, we split them into train, validation and test sets by a ratio of nearly 7:1:2.

Besides, we construct a dataset MXPlayer-4D-5M from the MX Player log, which contains four-day data from Oct. 31st, 2020 to Nov. 3rd, 2020. We take the data in the first three days as a train set from which we take 10% as a validation set, and then take the data of the last day as a test set.

Table 1 lists the statistics of these five datasets. Roughly, we can classify datasets by density into dense and sparse datasets, where MovieLens-100K and MovieLens-10M belong to the former and Amazon-Beauty, Amazon-Digital Music and MXPlayer-4D-5M datasets belong to the latter. In addition, as shown

Table 1. Statistics of datasets

Dataset	#User	#Item	#Ratings	Density	Rating levels
MovieLens-100K	943	1682	100,000	0.0630	$1, 2, \ldots, 5$
MovieLens-10M	69,878	10,677	10,000,054	0.0134	$0.5, 1, 1.5, 2 \ldots, 5$
Amazon-Beauty	12,008	3,570	92,512	0.0022	$1, 2, \ldots, 5$
Amazon-Digital Music	4,325	1,662	38,722	0.0054	$1, 2, \ldots, 5$
MXPlayer-4D-5M	5,534,825	13,463	29,471,665	0.0004	$0.5, 1, 1.5, 2 \ldots, 5$

in the last column of Table 1, we set different $\phi(r)$ for different datasets. Taking MXPlayer-4D-5M as an example, we set $\phi(r)$ to 0.5, 1.0, 1.5, 2.0, 2.5, 3.0, 3.5, 4.0, 4.5 and 5 for user's single click, multiple clicks, watching whose duration is between 10 s and 1 min, watching whose duration is between 1 min and 5 min, favorite, watching whose duration is between 5 min and 30 min, watching whose duration is greater than 30 min, sharing, like, and download, respectively.

Metrics. We adopt Recall@K, URecall@K (Unique Recall@K) and NDCG@K (Normalized Discounted Cumulative Gain@K) as evaluation metrics. As for URecall@K, we say that for a user, if there is at least one positive sample among the top-k recommended items, then the URecall@K is 1, otherwise it is 0. The Unique Recall@K of the recommendation system is the average of Unique Recall@K values of each user. That is, Unique Recall@K is equivalence to Hit@K.

4.2 Competitors

For each dataset, we search the optimal parameters for each model using the train set and validation set, and then conduct the comparative experiments on the test set using the models under optimal parameters.

We choose the following state-of-the-art models which are built on bipartite user-item interaction graphs as the competitors:

1. **GCMC** [2]: a graph auto-encoder which predicts labeled links in the bipartite user-item graph. To apply GCMC to our scenario, we treat different user behaviors in our scenario as different labeled links in GCMC.
2. **NGCF** [16]: a GCN based method which refines embeddings of users and items by embedding propagation.
3. **LightGCN** [8]: a simplified version of NGCF which omits the feature transformation and nonlinear activation.
4. **MMGCN** [17]: a GCN based method which generates separate node embeddings for each modality and then combines them into the final ones. To apply MMGCN to our scenario, we treat each category of user behaviors in our scenario as a modality individually.

To be fair, for Sagittarius and all the above methods, we adopt 2-layer convolutional neural networks, set the dimensions of user and video embedding to 64, and set the number of negative samplings in BPR loss function to 10. We adopt Adam optimizer, setting the learning rate to 0.01.

4.3 Performance Comparison

We conduct performance comparison experiments, comparing Sagittarius with four competitors. Table 2 lists the recommendation performance of Sagittarius and all the competitors.

Table 2. Recommendation Performance. The best performance in each row is in bold, and the second best performance in each row is underlined.

Datasets	Metrics	GCMC	NGCF	LightGCN	MMGCN	Sagittarius	Improvement
MovieLens-100K	**Recall@10**	0.0356	0.0361	<u>0.0367</u>	0.0343	**0.0382**	4.09%
	URecall@10	0.4542	0.4657	<u>0.4683</u>	0.4497	**0.4751**	1.45%
	NDCG@10	0.3207	0.3219	<u>0.3285</u>	0.3108	**0.3392**	3.26%
MovieLens-10M	**Recall@10**	0.0068	<u>0.0074</u>	0.0073	0.0072	**0.0076**	2.70%
	URecall@10	0.4651	<u>0.5081</u>	0.5058	0.4981	**0.5142**	1.20%
	NDCG@10	0.2502	<u>0.2863</u>	0.2761	0.2714	**0.2963**	3.49%
Amazon-Beauty	**Recall@10**	0.0362	0.0340	0.0357	<u>0.0372</u>	**0.0445**	19.62%
	URecall@10	0.0661	0.0652	0.0658	<u>0.0681</u>	**0.0768**	12.78%
	NDCG@10	0.0573	0.0562	0.0571	<u>0.0587</u>	**0.0604**	2.90%
Amazon-Digital Music	**Recall@10**	0.0257	0.0251	0.0254	<u>0.0265</u>	**0.0311**	17.36%
	URecall@10	<u>0.0723</u>	0.0701	0.0716	0.0713	**0.0815**	12.72%
	NDCG@10	0.0995	0.0887	0.0913	<u>0.1004</u>	**0.1016**	1.20%
MXPlayer-4D-5M	**Recall@10**	0.1653	0.1539	0.1367	<u>0.1710</u>	**0.1794**	4.91%
	URecall@10	0.2975	0.2913	0.2748	<u>0.3014</u>	**0.3147**	4.41%
	NDCG@10	0.2139	0.2094	0.1985	<u>0.2172</u>	**0.2261**	4.10%

From Table 2, we can make the following observations and inferences:

1. On dense datasets, Sagittarius, LightGCN and NGCF outperform GCMC and MMGCN. However, on sparse datasets, Sagittarius and MMGCN behave better than GCMC, LightGCN and NGCF, which shows that, in the scenarios with sparse datasets, differentiating between different interactive behaviors and model them separately are effective.
2. LightGCN does not perform as well as NGCF on datasets except MovieLens-100K, Amazon-Beauty and Amazon-Digital Music. These results are different from the ones in [8], which illustrate that deleting the feature transformation and nonlinear activation will not always obtain the stable improvement in performance and the actual effect of LightGCN might depend on the datasets or scenarios.
3. Whether it is for dense datasets or sparse datasets, Sagittarius outperforms other comparison models in all metrics. The reasons can be summarized as follows. Firstly, Sagittarius quantifies interactions of users on items and applies the quantitative values to the messages needed to be propagated in the GCN. Secondly, Sagittarius quantifies interaction behaviors in weights to guide the objective function to pay more attention to samples with the high interaction value. Thirdly, Sagittarius adopts a combination of multiple optimization

objectives to tradeoff the relationship between different objectives, thereby fully mining the information in the interactions and improving the concentration level of the model.

4.4 Ablation Analyses

We conduct the ablation study to observe the effectiveness of different components in Sagittarius including three optimization objectives (denoted as CTR, Sequence, BPR, respectively), behavior weighting (denoted as Behavior). Table 3 shows the detailed results of the ablation study.

Table 3. Ablation study of Sagittarius. The best performance in each row is the number in bold, and the worst performance in each row is underlined.

Datasets	Metrics	Sagittarius	- CTR	- Sequence	- BPR	- Behavior
MovieLens-100K	**Recall@10**	**0.0382**	0.0376	0.0374	0.0362	0.0377
	URecall@10	**0.4751**	0.4687	0.4652	0.4575	0.4691
	NDCG@10	**0.3392**	0.3314	0.3279	0.3217	0.3354
MovieLens-10M	**Recall@10**	**0.0076**	0.0074	0.0072	0.0069	0.0074
	URecall@10	**0.5142**	0.5068	0.4976	0.4753	0.5117
	NDCG@10	**0.2963**	0.2907	0.2883	0.2648	0.2935
Amazon-Beauty	**Recall@10**	**0.0445**	0.0423	0.0378	0.0365	0.0382
	URecall@10	**0.0768**	0.0751	0.0739	0.0724	0.0735
	NDCG@10	**0.0604**	0.0591	0.0579	0.0571	0.0587
Amazon-Digital Music	**Recall@10**	**0.0311**	0.0295	0.0274	0.0254	0.0287
	URecall@10	**0.0815**	0.0783	0.0746	0.0703	0.0765
	NDCG@10	**0.1016**	0.0967	0.0912	0.0897	0.0924
MXPlayer-4D-5M	**Recall@10**	**0.1794**	0.1643	0.1624	0.1452	0.1712
	URecall@10	**0.3147**	0.2916	0.2937	0.2758	0.3024
	NDCG@10	**0.2261**	0.2105	0.2088	0.1936	0.2193

From Table 3, we find that removing the BPR optimization objective leads to the largest drop in performance metrics and no matter which optimization objective is removed, the performance decreases on all datasets, which shows that combining multiple optimization objectives actually can help improve performance.

On the other hand, on the sparse datasets, the performance of Sagittarius-behavior which removes the weighting of interaction behavior is not as good as the one of intact Sagittarius, which is our expectation. On the dense dataset, the performance of the Sagittarius-behavior has not much difference from the intact model. This shows that on sparse datasets, the behavior-aware strategy, i.e., differentiating from interaction behaviors and converting interaction behaviors into weights to guide learning objectives to pay more attention to high-affinity user-item pairs, can indeed improve recommendation performance.

4.5   Impact of Hyper-parameters

In this section, we analyze the impact of hyper-parameters. Due to the limit of space, we only select three important hyper-parameters, that is, λ_1, λ_2, and λ_3, and conduct experiments to observe the performance under different values of λ_1, λ_2, and λ_3.

For the convenience of experiments, we change one of three parameters from 0.7 to 1.3 with the increment of 0.1 while setting the rest parameters to 1. Figures 2(a)–(c) show the results on MovieLens-100K and Figs. 2(d)–(f) show the results on Amazon-Beauty, where all the blue lines with solid circles show the performance under different λ_1 but $\lambda_2 = 1$ and $\lambda_3 = 1$, all the orange lines with solid squares show the performance under different λ_2 but $\lambda_1 = 1$ and $\lambda_3 = 1$, and all the grey lines with solid pentagons show the performance under different λ_3 but $\lambda_1 = 1$ and $\lambda_2 = 1$.

From Fig. 2, we find no matter which parameter is adjusted, the change trends of different performance metrics are the same, that is, with the change of any hyper-parameter value from small to large, the performance varies from a low value to a high one and finally moves to a low one. This observation illustrates that substantially increasing or decreasing the parameter value to emphasize or weaken some objective will slow down the performance. In addition, as shown in Fig. 2, when values of three parameters are within [0.9, 1.1], the performance is relatively good. Therefore, we assign the same value (i.e., 1) to these three parameters.

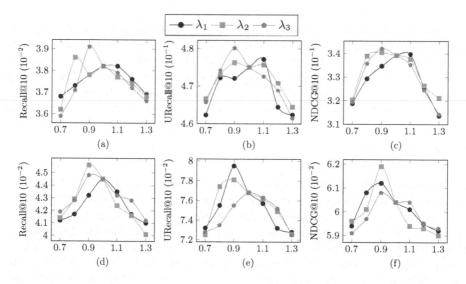

Fig. 2. The influence of λ_1, λ_2 and λ_3 on MovieLens-100K and Amazon-Beauty

4.6   Online A/B Test

We have deployed Sagittarius in the production environment of MX Player to serve top-k video recommendation scenarios. We observe the difference in performance between Sagittarius and two existing recommendation models in MX Player. One comparison model is to recommend top-k videos based on the videos clicked by users recently, and the other one is to recommend videos according to user profiles. Figure 3 shows the CTRs of three models recommending movie-type videos from Sep. 13rd, 2020 to Sep. 23rd, 2020.

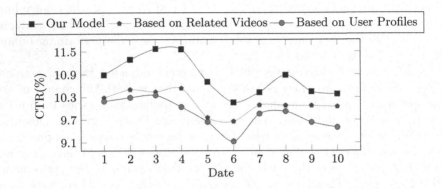

Fig. 3. Online A/B Test (Sep. 13th, 2020–Sep. 23th, 2020)

From Fig. 3, we can see that the CTRs of Sagittarius are significantly better than the existing recommendation models. During the ten-day observation, Sagittarius is always in the first place, which shows the effectiveness of Sagittarius. Currently, the recommendation results obtained by Sagittarius are used to generate user's personalized card. This personalized card is entitled "Movies Based on Your Viewing" and shown on the start screen in the MX Player App.

5   Conclusion

To improve the performance of top-k video recommendation in MX Player, we propose a model named Sagittarius in the paper. Sagittarius extracts the collaborative relations in the bipartite user-item graph to the node embeddings through the convolution layers. Meanwhile, in Sagittarius, we quantify the behaviors in the user-video interactions and apply them to guide the message propagation and the optimization of the recommendation task. More importantly, for the top-k video recommendation, we propose to choose the videos by multiple metrics and adopt a combination of three optimization objects to drive the training of the model. Results from offline experiments and online A/B tests illustrate that Sagittarius is suitable for top-k recommendation scenarios with sparse data, in addition to MX Player.

References

1. Baluja, S., et al.: Video suggestion and discovery for Youtube: taking random walks through the view graph. In: Proceedings of the 17th International Conference on World Wide Web, pp. 895–904 (2008)
2. Berg, R.V.D., Kipf, T.N., Welling, M.: Graph convolutional matrix completion. In: Proceedings of the 24th ACM SIGKDD International Conference on Knowledge Discovery, pp. 1–7 (2018)
3. Chen, L., Wu, L., Hong, R., Zhang, K., Wang, M.: Revisiting graph based collaborative filtering: a linear residual graph convolutional network approach. In: Proceedings of the AAAI Conference on Artificial Intelligence, vol. 34, pp. 27–34 (2020)
4. Chen, T., Wong, R.C.W.: Handling information loss of graph neural networks for session-based recommendation. In: Proceedings of the 26th ACM SIGKDD International Conference on Knowledge Discovery & Data Mining, pp. 1172–1180 (2020)
5. Dong, X., Jin, B., Zhuo, W., Li, B., Xue, T.: Improving sequential recommendation with attribute-augmented graph neural networks. In: Proceedings of the 25th Pacific-Asia Conference on Knowledge Discovery and Data Mining (2021)
6. Gao, J., Zhang, T., Xu, C.: A unified personalized video recommendation via dynamic recurrent neural networks. In: Proceedings of the 25th ACM International Conference on Multimedia, pp. 127–135 (2017)
7. Hamilton, W.L., Ying, R., Leskovec, J.: Representation learning on graphs: methods and applications. IEEE Data Eng. Bull. **3**, 52–74 (2017)
8. He, X., Deng, K., Wang, X., Li, Y., Zhang, Y., Wang, M.: LightGCN: simplifying and powering graph convolution network for recommendation. In: Proceedings of the 43rd International ACM SIGIR Conference on Research and Development in Information Retrieval, SIGIR 2020, pp. 639–648 (2020)
9. Jin, B., Gao, C., He, X., Jin, D., Li, Y.: Multi-behavior recommendation with graph convolutional networks. In: Proceedings of the 43rd International ACM SIGIR Conference on Research and Development in Information Retrieval, pp. 659–668 (2020)
10. Li, M., Gan, T., Liu, M., Cheng, Z., Yin, J., Nie, L.: Long-tail hashtag recommendation for micro-videos with graph convolutional network. In: Proceedings of the 28th ACM International Conference on Information and Knowledge Management, pp. 509–518 (2019)
11. Li, Y., Liu, M., Yin, J., Cui, C., Xu, X.S., Nie, L.: Routing micro-videos via a temporal graph-guided recommendation system. In: Proceedings of the 27th ACM International Conference on Multimedia, pp. 1464–1472 (2019)
12. MovieLens (2018). https://grouplens.org/datasets/movielens/
13. Rendle, S., Freudenthaler, C., Gantner, Z., Schmidt-Thieme, L.: BPR: Bayesian personalized ranking from implicit feedback. In: Proceedings of the Twenty-Fifth Conference on Uncertainty in Artificial Intelligence, pp. 452–461. AUAI Press (2009)
14. Amazon Product (2014). http://jmcauley.ucsd.edu/data/amazon/links.html
15. Wang, M., Lin, Y., Lin, G., Yang, K., Wu, X.M.: M2GRL: a multi-task multi-view graph representation learning framework for web-scale recommender systems. In: Proceedings of the 26th ACM SIGKDD International Conference on Knowledge Discovery & Data Mining, pp. 2349–2358 (2020)

16. Wang, X., He, X., Wang, M., Feng, F., Chua, T.S.: Neural graph collaborative filtering. In: Proceedings of the 42nd International ACM SIGIR Conference on Research and Development in Information Retrieval, pp. 165–174 (2019)
17. Wei, Y., Wang, X., Nie, L., He, X., Hong, R., Chua, T.S.: MMGCN: multi-modal graph convolution network for personalized recommendation of micro-video. In: Proceedings of the 27th ACM International Conference on Multimedia, pp. 1437–1445 (2019)
18. Wu, S., Tang, Y., Zhu, Y., Wang, L., Xie, X., Tan, T.: Session-based recommendation with graph neural networks. In: Proceedings of the AAAI Conference on Artificial Intelligence, vol. 33, pp. 346–353 (2019)
19. Xu, C., et al.: Graph contextualized self-attention network for session-based recommendation. In: IJCAI, vol. 19, pp. 3940–3946 (2019)
20. Xu, J., Zhu, Z., Zhao, J., Liu, X., Shan, M., Guo, J.: Gemini: a novel and universal heterogeneous graph information fusing framework for online recommendations. In: Proceedings of the 26th ACM SIGKDD International Conference on Knowledge Discovery & Data Mining, pp. 3356–3365 (2020)
21. Xu, X., Chen, L., Zu, S., Zhou, H.: Hulu video recommendation: from relevance to reasoning. In: Proceedings of the 12th ACM Conference on Recommender Systems, pp. 482–482 (2018)
22. Xue, T., et al.: Feedback-guided attributed graph embedding for relevant video recommendation. In: Proceedings of the European Conference on Machine Learning and Principles and Practice of Knowledge Discovery in Databases (2020)
23. Xue, T., Jin, B., Li, B., Wang, W., Zhang, Q., Tian, S.: A spatio-temporal recommender system for on-demand cinemas. In: Proceedings of the 28th ACM International Conference on Information and Knowledge Management, pp. 1553–1562 (2019)

GRHAM: Towards Group Recommendation Using Hierarchical Attention Mechanism

Nanzhou Lin, Juntao Zhang, Xiandi Yang[(⊠)], Wei Song, and Zhiyong Peng

School of Computer Science, Big Data Institute, Wuhan University,
Wuhan, Hubei, China
{linnzh,juntaozhang,xiandiy,songwei,peng}@whu.edu.cn

Abstract. Group recommendations extend individual user recommendations to groups, which have become one of the most prevalent topics in the recommender system and widely applied in catering, tourism, movies, and many other fields. The key to group recommendation is how to aggregate the preferences of different group members and calculate the group's preferences. However, the existing aggregation strategy is static and simple. First, they ignore that the preferences of members will change over time. Second, they fail to consider that member's influence is different when the group makes decisions on different activities. To this end, this paper proposes a new novel model for Group Recommendation using Hierarchical Attention Mechanism (GRHAM), which can dynamically adjust the weight of members in group decision-making. Our model consists of two layers of attention neural networks, the first attention layer learns the influence weights of members when the group makes the decision, and the second attention layer learns the influence weights between group members. Besides aggregating the preference of group members, we further learn group topic preferences from the historical data. We conduct experiments on two real datasets, and the experimental results show that our model outperforms other group recommendation models.

Keywords: Group recommendation · Recommender system ·
Attention mechanism · Preferences aggregation

1 Introduction

Recommender systems have played an important role in the information systems owing to their excellent ability to handle the information overload issue. Recommender systems can provide personalized information services for users and helps service providers to adjust their strategy to gain more income, both users and service providers benefit from it. At present, recommender systems have been widely used in many fields, such as social networks, e-commerce, news, and information, etc.

Existing research on recommender systems are mainly focused on recommending items to individual users, such as mobile recommender systems,

© Springer Nature Switzerland AG 2021
L. H. U et al. (Eds.): APWeb-WAIM 2021, LNCS 12859, pp. 295–309, 2021.
https://doi.org/10.1007/978-3-030-85899-5_22

context-aware recommender system, social recommender system and so on [12,16,20,25]. However, the recommended items are not intended for personal in many circumstances, but rather for group activities. For example, watching movies with family, planning a trip with other travelers, having dinner with friends. Therefore, the recommended item is extended from a user to a group, and the system that recommends to the group is called the group recommender system [11]. Personalized recommendation methods can be applied to group recommendation by treated each group as a virtual user. However, they only perform well for persistent groups with sufficient persistent group-item interaction records, and perform poorly for occasional groups with only a few or even no historical group-item interactions in group recommendation. Traditional personalized recommendation methods do not meet the demand of groups.

Different from individual recommendation systems, there are two key challenges in group recommendation. One is how to aggregate the preferences of all the members for making group recommendation. Group recommendation needs to consider the preferences of each member in the group and make the recommendation results meet the needs of all members as much as possible. Another one is how to model the complex and dynamic group decision-making process. Each member plays a different role in the group, so it will show different influences when getting the final results in group decision-making process. Such as user A may have a higher impact weight than user B when the group decides on which place in Asia to travel, but have a lower impact weight than user B when the group decides on which place in Europe to travel. Because user A often travels to Asia, user B often travels to Europe. Besides, the interaction among group members will also affect group decision-making. For example, user C has a closer relationship with user A than user B, user C has more impact weight on user A when the group makes a decision. In general, the preference aggregation method can be divided into two categories: model aggregation and recommendation aggregation. The model aggregation is first to fuse the member preference model according to a fixed strategy for generating a group preference model. The recommendation aggregation is to first calculate a prediction score for each group member and then use a predefined strategy to generate a group prediction score. Existing approaches mainly applied a predefined and fixed strategy to aggregate the preferences of group members, Such as average [3,11], least misery [1], maximum satisfaction [5], and so on. However, these aggregation strategies can not dynamically adjust the weight of members' decisions and capture the complex and dynamic decision-making process. Recently, the neural attention mechanism has been widely used in deep learning. Cao et al. [6] proposed a group recommendation model based on attention mechanism, which uses attention mechanism to dynamically adjust the weight of users in the group decision-making process which is more flexible. But it ignores the interaction between group members and not consider influence between group members.

To solve the above problems, we propose a novel model for Group Recommendation using Hierarchical Attention Mechanism(GRHAM). It uses a hierarchical attention mechanism to learn group preferences from the historical data that included user-user interaction, user-item interaction, and group-item interaction.

Our model consists of two layers of attention neural networks. The first attention layer learns the influence weights of members when the group decides so that the group members have different contributions and the group members' weight can adjust dynamically in the group decision-making, and the second attention layer learns the weights of influence between group members. Besides aggregating the preference of group members, we further learn group topic preferences from the historical data. Furthermore, GRHAM explores the interactions between groups and items with neural collaborative filtering for group recommendation. The main contributions of this work are summarized as follows:

- We propose a novel model for the group recommendation called GRHAM, which uses the hierarchical attention mechanism to implements group recommendation.
- We develop a solution to compute the influence of weights between group members by using the user-user interactions, which are aggregated with members' preferences to generate group preferences.
- We perform experiments on two datasets and demonstrate the effectiveness of our model.

2   Related Work

2.1   Group Recommendation

Group recommendation has been aroused widely concern in recent years. In general, existing group recommendations can be classified into two categories - memory-based and model-based methods.

Memory-based methods can be further divided into score aggregation [18] and preference aggregation [23]. The score aggregation first computes a score of an item for each user and then aggregates the scores of members in a group via predefined strategies to represent the group recommendation score of the item. While preference aggregation first aggregate all user preferences and then employ individuals recommendation techniques to make group recommendation. Aggregation strategies can be divided into three types basic, weighted and mixed. Basic aggregation strategies mainly include average, least misery, maximum satisfaction. The weighting strategy is to assign different weights to each group member according to the characteristics, role, influence and other factors of the group members [2,4]. A mixed strategy is using multiple basic strategies to solve the shortcomings of a single strategy [15]. But these aggregation strategies are predefined and lack flexibility, they can not dynamically adjust the weight of members' decisions and capture the complex and dynamic decision-making process.

Model-based methods explore the interaction among the group by modeling the generative process of a group. The personal impact topic (PIT) [13] model assumes that the most influential member should be representative of a group and has the largest influence on making recommendations for the group. A probabilistic model named COM [23] is proposed to model the generative process of group activities and make group recommendations. It assumes that the group decided on the topic of a group's preferences and its members' preferences.Qin et al. [17] divided a big group into different interest subgroups and proposed a dynamic group aggregation scheme that integrate the recommended media lists of all interest subgroups as the final group recommendation results.

2.2 Attention Mechanism for Recommendation

Deep learning is widely used in various fields [8,19,21], including recommendation systems. Attention mechanism is one of the most exciting recent advancements in deep learning. Attention mechanism have been extensively applied in recommender systems [6,9,10,24]. He et al. [13] propose an enhanced item similarity model by distinguishing the different importance of interacted items in contributing to a user's preference via attention network. Chen et al. [9] propose a novel CF framework named Attentive Collaborative Filtering (ACF) for multimedia recommendation, which can automatically assign weights to the two levels of feedback. The above studies are about the individual recommendation system. It shows a good idea for the combination of attention mechanism and group recommendation systems. Cao et al. [6] proposed the AGREE model, which uses an attention mechanism to optimize groups' representations and learns interactions between groups and items under a neral collaborative filtering framework. Another recent work is SIGR [22], which adopts the attention mechanism to learn each user's social influence and adapt their social influences to different groups. But these methods ignores the interaction between group members, and not consider influence between group members is dynamic.

3   GRHAM Model

In this section, we first present the notations and formulate the group recommendation problem to be solved in Sect. 3.1. Then we introduce our proposed model in Sect. 3.2. Lastly, we discuss the optimization method in Sect. 3.3.

3.1   Notations and Problem Formulation

Notations. We use bold capital letters (e.g., $\mathbf{X}$) and bold lowercase letters (e.g., $\mathbf{x}$) to denote matrices and vectors. We employ non-bold lowercase letters (e.g., x) to represent scalars. Table 1 shows the notations and corresponding descriptions used in this paper.

Problem Formulation. Suppose there are a set of users $\mathcal{U}$, a set of groups $\mathcal{G}$ and a set of items $\mathcal{V}$ in the group recommender system. The l-th group $g_l \in \mathcal{G}$ consists of a set of users. There are three kinds of observed interactions among $\mathcal{U}$, $\mathcal{V}$ and $\mathcal{G}$, that is user-item interactions, group-item interactions, and user-user interactions. We use $\mathbf{R}$ to denote the user-item interactions, $\mathbf{Y}$ to denote the

Table 1. Notations and denotations

Notation	Description	Notaion	Description
$\mathcal{U} = \{u_1, u_2, ..., u_n\}$	User set	$\mathcal{V} = \{v_1, v_2, ..., v_m\}$	Item set
$\mathcal{G} = \{g_1, g_2, ..., g_s\}$	Group set	$|g_l|$	The size of group g_l
$H_l = \{h_{l,1}, h_{l,2}, ...\}$	Group g_l members with user indexes	$K_i = \{k_{i,1}, k_{i,2}, ...\}$	User indexes with user i
$D_l = \{d_{l,1}, d_{l,2}, ...\}$	Group g_l members with item indexes	$\mathbf{R} = [r_{ij}]_{n \times m}$	User-item interactions
$\mathbf{Y} = [y_{lj}]_{s \times m}$	Group-item interactions	$\mathbf{Z} = [z_{ik}]_{n \times n}$	User-user interactions

group-item interactions, and $\mathbf{Z}$ to denote the user-user interactions (i.e., user social network). Figure 1 illustrates the group recommendation task which we address in this paper. Given a target group g_t, our task is to recommend a ranked list of items that group g_t may be interested in. The group recommendation problem can be defined as follows:

Input: Users $\mathcal{U}$, groups $\mathcal{G}$, items $\mathcal{V}$, user-item interactions $\mathbf{R}$, group-item interactions $\mathbf{Y}$ and user-user interactions $\mathbf{Z}$.

Output: A personalized ranking function that maps an item to a ranking score for a target group $f_g : \mathcal{V} \longrightarrow \mathbb{R}$

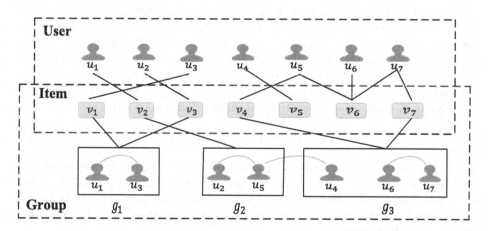

Fig. 1. Illustration of the input data of group recommendation task, which contains user-item interactions, user-user interactions and group-item interactions.

3.2   Model Framework

This subsection introduces our proposed model for group recommendation. The motivation of our model is to enable group-level recommendations by modeling three kinds of interactions.

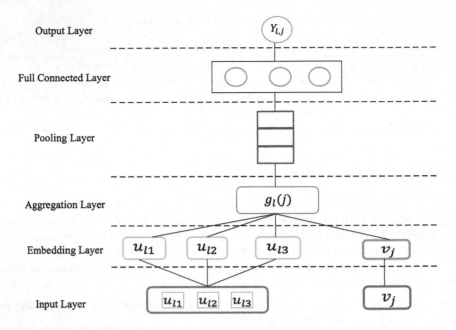

Fig. 2. The architecture of GRHAM for group recommendation

Our proposed model is based on the representation learning (RL) framework. In the RL framework, each entity is described as an embedding vector that encodes the inherent preferences of the entity(e.g., the interest of a user or a group). The embedding can be learned from historical data. Figure 2 illustrates the architecture of GRHAM. Let $\mathbf{u}_m$ and $\mathbf{v}_j$ be the embedding vector for user u_m and item v_j. Our target is to obtain an embedding vector $\mathbf{g}_l$ for each group to estimate its preference on item v_j. Formally, it can be defined as:

$$\mathbf{g}_l(j) = f_a\left(\{\mathbf{u}_m\}_{m \in H_l}, \mathbf{v}_j\right) \qquad (1)$$

where $\mathbf{g}_l$ denotes the representation learning of group g_l which represents its preference on item v_j; H_l contains the user indexes of group g_l, and f_a is the aggregation to be specified. In GRHAM, we design the group embedding $\mathbf{g}_l$ as consisting of two components - user embedding aggregation $\mathbf{q}_l$ and group topic preference embedding $\mathbf{p}_l$.

$$\mathbf{g}_l = \mathbf{q}_l + \mathbf{p}_l \qquad (2)$$

Figure 3 illustrates user embedding aggregation and group topic preference embedding, we next elaborate on the components.

User Embedding Aggregation. We perform a weighted sum on the embeddings of group g_l's member, where the coefficient $\beta(j, t)$ denotes the influence of member user u_t in deciding the group's choice on item v_j. The user embedding aggregation can be defined as:

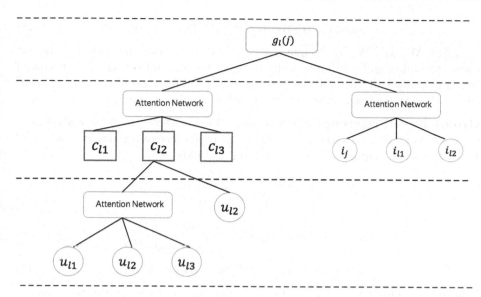

Fig. 3. Illustrates user embedding aggregation and group topic preference embedding

$$\mathbf{q}_l(j) = \sum_{t \in \mathcal{H}_l} \beta(j,t)\mathbf{u}_t \qquad (3)$$

$$u_t = \sum_{i \in K_t} \alpha(t,i)\mathbf{c}_i + \mathbf{c}_t \qquad (4)$$

Embedding $\mathbf{u}_t$ encodes the member user's preference and embedding $\mathbf{v}_j$ encodes the member target item's property, we parameterize $\beta(j,t)$ as a neural attention work with $\mathbf{u}_t$ and $\mathbf{v}_j$ as the input:

$$\beta(j,t) - \mathrm{softmax}(b(j,t)) = \frac{\exp b(j,t)}{\sum_{t' \in \mathcal{H}_l} \exp b(j,t')} \qquad (5)$$

$$b(\mathrm{j},\mathrm{t}) = h^T \,\mathrm{ReLU}\left(W_v^1 v_j + W_u^1 u_t + b\right) \qquad (6)$$

where $\mathbf{W}_v^1$ and $\mathbf{W}_u^1$ are weight matrices of the attention network that convert item embedding and user embedding to the hidden layer, and $\mathbf{b}$ is the bias vector of the hidden layer. We use ReLU as the activation of the hidden layer and project it to a score $b(j,t)$ with a weight vector $\mathbf{h}$. Lastly, we normalize $b(j,t)$ using Softmax function.

In the group decision process, the user's choice depends on self preference and other user's influences. We define the user embedding as formula 4. Where $\mathbf{c}_t$, $\mathbf{c}_i$ denote the member user u_t and u_i historical preference, the coefficient $\alpha(t,i)$ represent weight the influence of member user u_i to u_t. Similar to the first attention, the second attention score is also a two-layer network and is formularized as:

$$\alpha(t,i) = \mathrm{softmax}(a(t,i)) = \frac{\exp a(t,i)}{\sum_{t' \in K_t} \exp a(t,t')} \qquad (7)$$

$$a(t, i) = \boldsymbol{h}^T \text{ReLU} \left(\boldsymbol{W}_c^2 \boldsymbol{c}_t + \boldsymbol{W}_u^2 \boldsymbol{c}_i + \boldsymbol{b} \right) \tag{8}$$

where $\mathbf{W}_c^2$ and $\mathbf{W}_u^2$ are weight matrices of the attention network that convert user embedding and user embedding to hidden layer, and $\mathbf{b}$ is the bias vector of the hidden layer. ReLU is utilized as the activation function of the hidden layer, and is then projected to a score $\alpha(t, i)$ with a weight vector $\mathbf{h}$.

Group Topic Preference Embedding. Besides aggregating the embeddings of group members, we further take the topic preference of a group into account. We define the group preference embedding as follow $\boldsymbol{p}_l$:

$$\boldsymbol{p}_l = \sum_{t \in D_l} \gamma(j, t) \boldsymbol{v}_t \tag{9}$$

$$\gamma(j, t) = \text{softmax}(r(j, t)) = \frac{\exp r(j, t)}{\sum_{t' \in D_l} \exp a(t, t')} \tag{10}$$

$$r(j, t) = \boldsymbol{h}^T \text{ReLU} \left(\boldsymbol{W}_j^3 \boldsymbol{v}_j + \boldsymbol{W}_t^3 \boldsymbol{v}_t + \boldsymbol{b} \right) \tag{11}$$

Where the coefficient $\gamma(j, t)$ denote the correlation between item v_j and item v_t, where $\mathbf{W}_j^3$ and $\mathbf{W}_t^3$ are weight matrices of the attention network that convert item embedding and item embedding to the hidden layer, and $\mathbf{b}$ is the bias vector of the hidden layer. ReLU is utilized as the activation function of the hidden layer, and is then projected to a score $\gamma(t, i)$ with a weight vector $\mathbf{h}$.

The NCF applied to learn user-item interactions for item recommendation can model interactions better than the simple inner product of vectors, In GRHAM, the interaction learning procedure consists of two layers: a pooling layer and a prediction layer.

Pooling layer: The pooling layer models the interaction behaviors between groups and items. The pooling layer first performs element-wise product on their embeddings, and then concatenates it with the original embeddings:

$$\boldsymbol{e}_0 = \varphi_{\text{pooling}} \left(g_l(j), v_j \right) = \begin{bmatrix} \boldsymbol{g}_l(j) \odot \boldsymbol{v}_j \\ \boldsymbol{g}_l(j) \\ \boldsymbol{v}_j \end{bmatrix} \tag{12}$$

Prediction layer: The score of a group g_i for item v_j can be predicted by

$$\hat{y}_{ij} = \text{Prediction} \left(\boldsymbol{e}_0 \right) \tag{13}$$

where Prediction(*) is a fully connected layer with an activation function.

3.3 Model Optimization

Objective Function. We use the pairwise learning method for optimizing model parameters, assuming that observed interactions are ranked higher than their unobserved counterparts. We apply the regression-based pairwise loss:

$$L = \sum_{(l,j,s) \in \mathcal{O}} (y_{ljs} - \widehat{y_{ljs}})^2 = \sum_{(l,j,s) \in \mathcal{O}} (\widehat{y_{lj}} - \widehat{y_{ls}} - 1)^2 \tag{14}$$

where $y_{ljs} = y_{lj} - y_{ls}$, $\widehat{y_{ljs}} = \widehat{y_{lj}} - \widehat{y_{ls}}$, and $\mathcal{O}$ is the set of training instances. Each instance (l, j, s) in $\mathcal{O}$ means that there are interaction data between group g_l and item v_j but no interaction data between group g_l and item v_s. The value of each observed interaction to be 1, and the value of unobserved interaction to be 0, we have $y_{ljs} = y_{lj} - y_{ls} = 1$.

4   Experiments

In this section, we report experimental results of comparing GRHAM and state-of-the-art techniques on two datasets. In general, the goal of our experiments is to answer the following research questions (**RQ**):

- **RQ1: How does GRHAM perform as compared to existing advanced methods?**
- **RQ2: How do the hyper-parameters affect the performance of GRHAM?**

4.1   Datasets

We conduct experiments on two real-world datasets: Mafengwo and Douban-Event. Mafengwo[1] is a tourism website where users can record their traveled venues, create or join a group trip. Douban-Event is one of the largest online event-based social networks in China that helps people publish and participate in social events. Mafengwo is from the paper [7], it retained the groups which have at least 2 members and have traveled at least 3 venues, and collected their traveled venues. Douban-Event does not contain explicit group information, extracted the implicit group activities by assuming that if a set of users who are connected on the social network attend the same event (or visit the same restaurant). At the same time, they are members of a group and the corresponding activities are group activities. During pre-processing, we filter out groups and venues with less than 3 interactions each. The detailed statistics of these two datasets are shown in Table 2.

Table 2. Statistics of Mafengwo and Douban-Event

Statistics	Mafengwo	Douban-Event
# Users	5,275	1,698
# Items/Events	39,761	41,317
# Groups	995	851
Avg. # group size	7.19	4.84
Avg. # interactions per user	7.54	338.59
Avg. # friends per user	10.09	40.86
Avg. # interactions per group	3.61	5.85

---

[1] https://www.mafengwo.com.

4.2   Evaluation

We used the leave-one-out evaluation protocol, which has been widely used to evaluate the performance of the top-k recommendation. To evaluate the performance of the top-k recommendation, we employed the widely used metric—Hit Ratio (HR) and Normalized Discounted Cumulative Gain(NDCG), large values indicate better performance. In the leave-one-out evaluation, HR measures whether the testing item is ranked in the top-K list. The Hit ratio is defined as follows:

$$\text{Hits } @K = \frac{\#hit@K}{|\mathcal{D}_{\text{test}}|} \tag{15}$$

where $\# hit@K$ denotes the number of hits in the test set, and $|\mathcal{D}_{\text{test}}|$ is the total number of test cases in the test set. The higher Hits@K is denoted that recommend result is well. NDCG accounts for the position of the hit by assigning a higher score to hit at top positions. It is calculated as follows:

$$DCG = \sum_{i=1}^{N} \frac{2^{rel_i} - 1}{\log_2(i + 1)} \tag{16}$$

$$NDCG = \frac{DCG}{IDCG} \tag{17}$$

where $rel_i = 1$ if the ith item in the recommendation list is accepted by the group, and $rel_i = 0$ otherwise. IDCG is the maximum possible discounted cumulative gain (DCG) with the top N relevant items.

4.3   Baselines

To verify the effectiveness of our model, we compared it with the following state-of-the-art methods.

- **Consensus model(COM):** COM is a generative model that considers the group's topic influence and individual preferences influences in the final group decision.
- **Neural Collaborative Filtering(NCF):** NCF [14] is a state-of-the-art collaborative filtering model that uses a neural architecture to model the interactions between users and items.
- **NCF+avg:** NCF+avg [3] is denote "NCF combined with average". It is the simplest aggregation strategy that averages the preferences of group members as the group preferences, and it supposes that each member contributes equally to the final group decision.
- **NCF+lm:** It adopts the least misery strategy [1] in which the least satisfied member determines the final group decision, which is the well-known cask principle.
- **NCF+ms:** It applies the maximum satisfaction strategy [5] and tries to maximize the satisfaction of group members.

- **AGREE:** AGREE [6] is the first to use the attention mechanism for group recommendation. This model considers the group members have different weights for different items in the final group decision.
- **SoAGREE:** SoAGREE [7] is extended by AGREE and the social followee information is further incorporated into the user representation learning via another attention network.

Table 3. Top-k performance both recommendation tasks for groups on Mafengwo

Ovrall Performance Comparison (Mafengwo)				
Model	HR@5	NDCG@5	HR@10	NDCG@10
COM	0.4420	0.2169	0.5434	0.3727
NCF	0.4701	0.3657	0.6269	0.4141
NCF+avg	0.4774	0.3669	0.6222	0.414
NCF+lm	0.4744	0.3631	0.6302	0.4152
NCF+ms	0.47	0.3616	0.6281	0.4114
AGREE	0.4814	0.3747	0.64	0.4244
SoAGREE	0.4898	0.3807	0.6481	0.4301
GRHAM	**0.6603**	**0.5504**	**0.7025**	**0.5703**

Table 4. Top-k performance both recommendation tasks for groups on Douban-Event

Ovrall Performance Comparison (Douban-Event)				
Model	HR@5	NDCG@5	HR@10	NDCG@10
COM	0.2301	0.1598	0.4569	0.2220
NCF	0.2401	0.1657	0.4641	0.2241
NCF+avg	0.2574	0.1669	0.4703	0.2260
NCF+lm	0.2544	0.1631	0.4682	0.2252
NCF+ms	0.2598	0.1616	0.4764	0.2285
AGREE	0.2996	0.1743	0.5064	0.2345
SoAGREE	0.3290	0.2010	0.5137	0.2423
GRHAM	**0.3367**	**0.2077**	**0.5324**	**0.2543**

4.4 Overall Performance Comparison(RQ1)

On Two datasets, we compared the GRHAM model with other baseline methods, as shown in Table 2, 3. We have the following observations: (1) Our GRHAM model achieves the best on all datasets, which is better than the current advanced methods. This shows our model has clearly improved in terms of performance;

(2) In the score aggregation-based solutions, there no obvious outstand solution. An aggregation strategy might work well in some datasets but perform poorly in others. For example, the least misery aggregation strategy outperforms the other two predefined aggregations on Mafengwo dataset, while the average aggregation achieves the best performance among the three predefined aggregation strategies on Douban-Event dataset; (3) The performance of model use attention mechanism batter than models that de not use attention mechanism, this demonstrates the superiority of attention mechanism; (4) On the two dataset, the AGREE and SoAGREE models are inferior to our GRHAM model, because they ignores the interaction between group members and not consider influence between group members (Table 4).

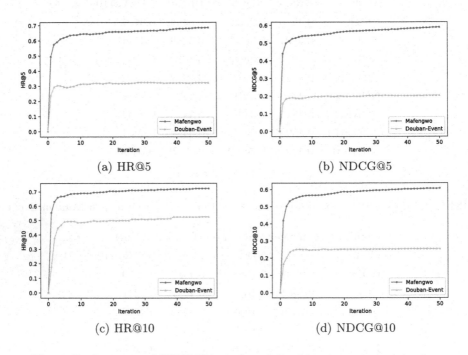

(a) HR@5   (b) NDCG@5

(c) HR@10   (d) NDCG@10

Fig. 4. Performance of GRHAM in each training iteration on two datasets.

4.5 Model Performances for Different Hyper-Parameters (RQ2)

In order to demonstrate the robustness and effectiveness of our proposed model, we investigated the convergence of GRHAM and studied the sensibility of several factors, such as the number of negative samples and Dimension of Embedding.

Convergence. We record the value of HR@5, HR@10, NDCG@5, NDCG@10 along with each iteration. Figure 4 shows the HR@5, HR@10, NDCG@5, NDCG@10 with the increasing number of iterations on the two datasets. The results show that our model GRHAM converges fast in the fast 20 interactions and reaches its optimal results around the 45th iteration. This presents the ratio-nality of our model.

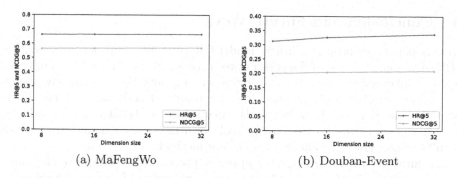

(a) MaFengWo   (b) Douban-Event

Fig. 5. Impact of Dimension of Embedding: HR@5 and NDCG@5 of GRHAM model on two datasets.

Impact of Dimension of Embedding. In order to study the effect of dimension of embedding, we test vary the dimension of embedding to investigate its influence on recommendations on different datasets. The results are shown in Fig. 5. The results show that increate dimension size in some range can help improve performance, which indicates that a larger dimension size is likely to encode more information.

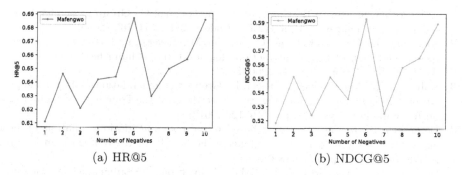

(a) HR@5   (b) NDCG@5

Fig. 6. Impact of Number of Negative: HR@5 and NDCG@5 of GRHAM model on Mafengwo.

Impact of Negative Samples: It randomly samples various numbers of missing data as negative samples to pair with each positive instance. To illustrate the impact of negative sampling of GRHAM, we run the experiments where different negative sample ratios on Mafengwo datasets. AS shown in Fig. 6. We have the following observations: 1) It is obviously seen that one negative sample for each positive instance is not optimal performance. 2) With more negative samples selected, the performance of GRHAM reaches its optimal results.

5   Conclusion and Future Work

In this paper, we proposed a new model GRHAM for group recommendation. GRHAM considers the influences between its members. Instead of simply use a user's inherent preference as its preference in group. We dynamically learned the impact weights of all members in a group for distinctly target items via the attention mechanism. To validate the effectiveness of GRHAM, we conducted a wide range of experiments on two real-world datasets, and the experimental results demonstrate the effectiveness of our method.

In future work, we will further optimize the model and improve the model recommendation performance. At the same time, we will focus on the cold start problem of general preference modeling in group recommendation and study how to solve this problem effectively to improve the accuracy and efficiency of group recommendation.

Acknowledgements. This work is partially supported by National Natural Science Foundation of China Nos. U1811263, 62072349, National Key Research and Development Project of China No. 2020YFC1522602. We also thank anonymous reviewers for their helpful reports.

References

1. Amer-Yahia, S., Roy, S.B., Chawlat, A., Das, G., Yu, C.: Group recommendation: semantics and efficiency. Proc. VLDB Endow. **2**(1), 754–765 (2009)
2. Ardissono, L., Goy, A., Petrone, G., Segnan, M., Torasso, P.: Intrigue: personalized recommendation of tourist attractions for desktop and hand held devices. Appl. Artif. Intell. **17**(8–9), 687–714 (2003)
3. Baltrunas, L., Makcinskas, T., Ricci, F.: Group recommendations with rank aggregation and collaborative filtering. In: Proceedings of the Fourth ACM Conference on Recommender Systems, pp. 119–126 (2010)
4. Berkovsky, S., Freyne, J.: Group-based recipe recommendations: analysis of data aggregation strategies. In: Proceedings of the fourth ACM Conference on Recommender Systems, pp. 111–118 (2010)
5. Boratto, L., Carta, S.: State-of-the-art in group recommendation and new approaches for automatic identification of groups. In: Soro, A., Vargiu, E., Armano, G., Paddeu, G. (eds.) Information Retrieval and Mining in Distributed Environments, pp. 1–20. Springer, Heidelberg (2010). https://doi.org/10.1007/978-3-642-16089-9_1
6. Cao, D., He, X., Miao, L., An, Y., Yang, C., Hong, R.: Attentive group recommendation. In: The 41st International ACM SIGIR Conference on Research & Development in Information Retrieval, pp. 645–654 (2018)
7. Cao, D., He, X., Miao, L., Xiao, G., Chen, H., Xu, J.: Social-enhanced attentive group recommendation. IEEE Trans. Knowl. Data Eng. (2019)
8. Chen, J., et al.: Co-purchaser recommendation for online group buying. Data Sci. Eng. **5**(3), 280–292 (2020)
9. Chen, J., Zhang, H., He, X., Nie, L., Liu, W., Chua, T.S.: Attentive collaborative filtering: multimedia recommendation with item-and component-level attention. In: Proceedings of the 40th International ACM SIGIR Conference on Research and Development in Information Retrieval, pp. 335–344 (2017)

10. Devlin, J., Chang, M.W., Lee, K., Toutanova, K.: Bert: pre-training of deep bidirectional transformers for language understanding. arXiv preprint arXiv:1810.04805 (2018)

11. Garcia, I., Pajares, S., Sebastia, L., Onaindia, E.: Preference elicitation techniques for group recommender systems. Inf. Sci. **189**, 155–175 (2012)

12. Ge, Y., Xiong, H., Tuzhilin, A., Xiao, K., Gruteser, M., Pazzani, M.: An energy-efficient mobile recommender system. In: Proceedings of the 16th ACM SIGKDD International Conference on Knowledge Discovery and Data Mining, pp. 899–908 (2010)

13. He, X., He, Z., Song, J., Liu, Z., Jiang, Y.G., Chua, T.S.: Nais: neural attentive item similarity model for recommendation. IEEE Trans. Knowl. Data Eng. **30**(12), 2354–2366 (2018)

14. He, X., Liao, L., Zhang, H., Nie, L., Hu, X., Chua, T.S.: Neural collaborative filtering. In: Proceedings of the 26th International Conference on World Wide Web, pp. 173–182 (2017)

15. Jameson, A.: More than the sum of its members: challenges for group recommender systems. In: Proceedings of the Working Conference on Advanced Visual Interfaces, pp. 48–54 (2004)

16. Papadimitriou, A., Symeonidis, P., Manolopoulos, Y.: A generalized taxonomy of explanations styles for traditional and social recommender systems. Data Min. Knowl. Disc. **24**(3), 555–583 (2012)

17. Qin, D., Zhou, X., Chen, L., Huang, G., Zhang, Y.: Dynamic connection-based social group recommendation. IEEE Trans. Knowl. Data Eng. **32**(3), 453–467 (2020)

18. Seo, Y.D., Kim, Y.G., Lee, E., Seol, K.S., Baik, D.K.: An enhanced aggregation method considering deviations for a group recommendation. Expert Syst. Appl. **93**, 299–312 (2018)

19. Tian, S., Mo, S., Wang, L., Peng, Z.: Deep reinforcement learning-based approach to tackle topic-aware influence maximization. Data Sci. Eng. **5**(1), 1–11 (2020)

20. Wang, C.S.: An AR mobile navigation system integrating indoor positioning and content recommendation services. World Wide Web **22**(3), 1241–1262 (2019)

21. Wu, S., Zhang, Y., Gao, C., Bian, K., Cui, B.: Garg: anonymous recommendation of point-of-interest in mobile networks by graph convolution network. Data Sci. Eng. **5**(4), 433–447 (2020)

22. Yin, H., Wang, Q., Zheng, K., Li, Z., Yang, J., Zhou, X.: Social influence-based group representation learning for group recommendation. In: 2019 IEEE 35th International Conference on Data Engineering (ICDE), pp. 566–577. IEEE (2019)

23. Yuan, Q., Cong, G., Lin, C.Y.: Com: a generative model for group recommendation. In: Proceedings of the 20th ACM SIGKDD International Conference on Knowledge Discovery and Data Mining, pp. 163–172 (2014)

24. Zhai, S., Chang, K.H., Zhang, R., Zhang, Z.M.: Deepintent: learning attentions for online advertising with recurrent neural networks. In: Proceedings of the 22nd ACM SIGKDD International Conference on Knowledge Discovery and Data Mining, pp. 1295–1304 (2016)

25. Zhou, X., Chen, L., Zhang, Y., Qin, D., Cao, L., Huang, G., Wang, C.: Enhancing online video recommendation using social user interactions. VLDB J. **26**(5), 637–656 (2017)

Multi-interest Network Based on Double Attention for Click-Through Rate Prediction

Xiaoling Xia, Wenjian Fang[(✉)], and Xiujin Shi[(✉)]

Donghua University, Shanghai, China
2191925@mail.dhu.edu.cn, sxj@dhu.edu.cn

Abstract. Whether in the field of personalized advertising or recommender systems, click through rate (CTR) prediction is a very important task. In recent years, Alibaba Group has done a lot of advanced research on the prediction of click through rate, and proposed a technical route includes kinds of deep learning models. For example, in the deep interest network (DIN) proposed by the Alibaba Group, the sequence of users' browsing behaviors is used to express their interest features, and this sequence is made up of items clicked by users. Usually, the item is mapped into a static vector, but the fixed length embedded vector is difficult to express the user's dynamic interest features. In order to solve this problem, Alibaba Group introduced the attention mechanism in the field of natural language processing (NLP) into deep interest network (DIN), and designed a unique activation unit to extract the important informations in the user's historical behavior sequence, and use these important informations to express user's dynamic interest features. In this paper, we propose a novel deep learning model: Multi-Interest Network Based on Double Attention for Click-Through Rate Prediction (DAMIN), which based on Deep Interest Network (DIN) and combined with multi-head attention mechanism. In the deep interest network (DIN), the attention weight between the candidate item vector and the item vector of the user's historical behavior sequence is learned by fully connected neural network. Different from deep interest network (DIN), we design a new method, which uses the reciprocal of Euclidean Distance to represent the attention weight between two item vectors. Then, the item vectors in user's historical behavior sequence are weighted by the attention weights and meanwhile the candidate item vectors are also weighted by the attention weights. In the next, we can obtain new item vectors by add the weighted item vectors of user's historical behavior sequence and weighted candidate item vectors, and those new item vectors are used to represent user's dynamic interest feature vectors. In the end, the user's dynamic interest features are send into the three multi-head attention layers, which can extract users' various interest features. We have conducted a lot of experiments on three real-world datasets of Amazon and the results show that the model proposed by this paper acquires a better performance than some classical models. Compared with DIN, the model proposed in this paper improves the average of AUC by 4%–5%, which proves that the model proposed in this paper

© Springer Nature Switzerland AG 2021
L. H. U et al. (Eds.): APWeb-WAIM 2021, LNCS 12859, pp. 310–322, 2021.
https://doi.org/10.1007/978-3-030-85899-5_23

is effective. In addition, a large number of ablation experiments have been carried out to prove that each module of the proposed model is effective.

Keywords: Recommender system · Click-through rate prediction · Attention · Euclidean distance

1   Introduction

In deep interest network and other CTR models proposed by Alibaba Group[1], the user's historical behavior sequence is composed of the items that they have clicked, and those sequences are regarded as user's interest features. In traditional deep learning models, the items are mapped into vectors with fixed length. However, user's interests are variable and diverse, so the vectors with fixed length are difficult to express the user's dynamic interests. In order to solve this problem, a very important activation unit in deep interest network is designed based on the attention mechanism in the field of natural language processing. And the activation unit can calculate the attention weight with any two item vectors, then the weight is used to weight the item vectors in user's historical behavior sequence. Since those weights are variable, the weighted user's historical behavior sequence can represent user's dynamic interest features.

It is one of the biggest disadvantages that traditional recurrent neural network (RNN) can not run in parallel, so the training speed of RNN model is very slow. In order to solve this problem, Google Group proposed new model named Transformer [2] in its paper *Attention is all you need* published in 2017. The core of transformer model is multi-head attention layer, which is composed of several parallel self-attention layers, so it can realize the parallel training of the model. In addition, each self-attention layer can extract the context information of words, so the multi-head attention layer composed of several parallel self-attention layers can extract various semantic information of words in different contexts. Similarly, in the scene related to the user browsing sequence, the user's interest features will change in different contexts. Therefore, this paper introduces the multi-head attention mechanism and hopes to learn the user's interest features in different contexts.

This paper proposes a novel model: Multi-Interest Network Based on Double Attention for Click-Through Rate Prediction (DAMIN), which based on Deep Interest Network (DIN) and combined with multi-head attention mechanism. And the main contributions of this paper are summarized as follows:

- We change the calculation method of activation unit in deep interest network, and use the reciprocal of the square of Euclidean distance as the attention weight of two item vectors in this paper, and the experimental results show that Euclidean distance can effectively calculate the similarity between two item vectors;

- We set a part for calculate the attention weight between item vectors in user's historical behavior sequence and candidate items before the multi-head attention layers, and extract the user's dynamic interest features as the input of the multi-head attention mechanism, which can highlight the effective information and suppress the useless information;
- In order to make the multi-head attention layer make full use of the information of candidate item vector, we add the item vector in user's historical behavior sequence and candidate item vector, and the result is a new vector. Then this new vector is weighted by the attention weight between item vector clicked by user and candidate item vector, and the new weighted vector is used as the input of multi-head attention layer. By summing the weighted candidate item vector with the weighted item vector clicked by user, the similarity will be greater between the two similar item vectors in user's historical behavior sequence, and the difference will be also greater between the two dissimilar item vectors in user's historical behavior sequence.

2   Related Work

In the field of recommendation systems, collaborative filtering is one of the most classic algorithms. Recommendation algorithms based on collaborative filtering can be roughly divided into three categories, and first category algorithm is user-based collaborative filtering (UCF) recommendation algorithm [3], second category algorithm is item-based collaborative filtering (ICF) recommendation algorithm [4], third category algorithm is model-based collaborative filtering recommendation algorithm [5]. Collaborative filtering has a lot of advantages, for instance, collaborative filtering can recommend new information for users and find unknown interests not found by users. But at the same time, collaborative filtering also has some weaknesses, such as data sparsity, cold start and so on.

In the field of click through rate (CTR) prediction and recommendation systems, the early algorithms include logistic regression (LR) algorithm [6], naive bayes algorithm [7] and gradient boosting decision tree (GBDT) [8] belongs to tree models, etc. In 2014, the Facebook Group combined logistic regression (LR) algorithm with GBDT algorithm [9], and achieved good performance in the actual production environment. The main idea is to use the output of GBDT as the input features of LR, which saves the time and steps of manual feature searching and feature interaction.

In 2010, factorization machines (FM) algorithm [10] proposed by Osaka University has achieved a great success and become one of the most classic algorithms in the field of click through rate (CTR) prediction and recommendation systems. Among them, the logistic regression algorithm only realizes a linear weighted interaction of all features, and does not consider the relationship between features. And factorization machines algorithm focuses on the relationship between different features and realizes the interaction of different features. So, factorization machines can improve the learning ability of model and obtains a better performance than logistic regression. However, the factorization machine algorithm also has some disadvantages, such as: (1) Due to the limitation of computing power, the factorization machine algorithm only realizes the second-order feature interaction, and does not realize the higher-order feature interaction; (2) Every feature interaction is regarded as equivalent in factorization machine algorithm, but in fact, not all feature interactions are effective. On the contrary, some interactions of different features are harmful noise for the model, and may make the performance of the model worse.

Deep learning has gradually become popular after 2015, and the combination of factorization machines algorithm and deep learning has become a mainstream research trend. The common factorization machines algorithm only realizes the second-order feature interaction, but after combining the factorization machines algorithm with deep learning, it can easily realize higher-order feature interaction, and improve the learning ability of model. And the relevant deep learning models include: Wide & Deep [11], PNN [12], DeepFM [13], xDeepFM [14], etc.

In recent years, attention mechanism has been successfully applied in natural language processing, recommendation system, computer vision and other fields, and achieved a good performance. In order to solve the problem that the factorization machine algorithm can't distinguish the importance of different feature interactions, attention mechanism is successfully applied in relevant recommendation algorithms and CTR models. By combining attention mechanism with factorization machine algorithm based on deep learning, the attention weight of the interaction of different features can be calculated. And the relevant deep learning models mainly include AFM [15], FAT-Deep-FFM [16] and so on.

For the processing of discrete features, the traditional method is using the one-hot coding to map discrete features into one-hot vectors, but one-hot coding has some very serious disadvantages, such as: (1) There are a lot of 0 values in one-hot vectors, so this encoding method wastes storage space; (2) The cosine similarity between any two one-hot vectors is 0 and so on. In order to solve this problem, Google Group opened a tool named word2vec [17] in 2013. The main function of the tool is to map words or other discrete features into vectors, and it can well calculate the similarity weights between word vectors. Among them, mapping words into vectors is an embedding process. In formally, embedding is to transform high-dimensional and sparse data into low-dimensional and dense space.

The algorithms related to factorization machine algorithm mainly focus on the interaction of features, and do not involve the scenes related to sequence. And there are a large number of user's browsing and clicking behaviors in Taobao, Tmall and other online shopping platforms. The items clicked by users constitute the user's behavior sequence, which can be used to express the user's interest features. User's behavior sequence is a kind of typical data with time sequence characteristics, because the items clicked by users have sequence. So how to mine the user's interests from the user's behavior sequence is an urgent task. In order to solve this problem, Alibaba Group proposed the deep interest network (DIN) in 2018, and other deep learning model such as DIEN [18], DSIN [19], BST [20], DMIN [21] are also proposed base on DIN.

3   Model of This Paper

This paper proposes a deep learning model: Multi-Interest Network Based on Double Attention for Click-Through Rate Prediction (DAMIN), which consists of two attention parts. And first attention part is used to extract users' dynamic interest features, second attention part is used to acquire users' multi interest features base on first attention part. The innovation of this paper is first attention part, which uses the reciprocal of Euclidean distance square between item clicked by user and candidate item as their attention weight. Finally, the experimental results show that the computing method of attention weight in this paper achieves better performance than the computing method of attention weight in deep interest network. Therefore, Euclidean distance can mine the relationship in any two item vectors very well. Besides, the attention weight in deep interest network (DIN) is learned through several full-connected neural network layers. So, it needs more memory space to store training variables, and consumes more computing and time resources. On the contrary, the calculation method of attention weight in this paper directly calculates the attention weight of any two item vectors and without some training variables to store, so this calculation method of attention weight spends less time in training process.

3.1   Embedded Layer

Usually, the embedding layer is the first layer in most deep learning models, and its main function is to map high-dimensional sparse discrete features into low dimensional dense vectors. In this paper, we use the API named Embedding in tensorflow 2.x to transform high-dimensional and sparse discrete features. For instance, we can map the item id into a dense vector, and the item id can be expressed as the vector $x_b = [x_1, x_2, ..., x_d]$, d is the dimension of the vector.

Figure 1 is the architecture of the model in this paper, it contains three parts, include embedding layer, user's dynamic interest extraction layer and multi interest extraction layer. And the attention unit is used to calculate the reciprocal of the square of Euclidean distance as the attention weight of two item vectors.

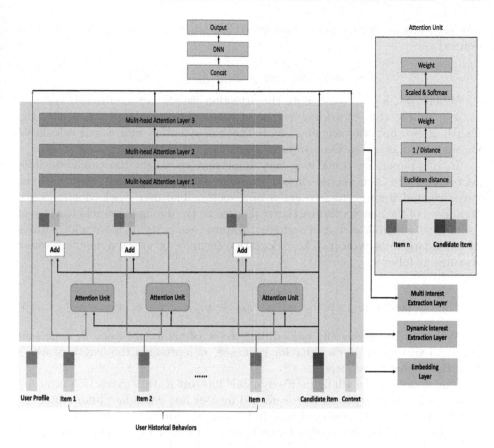

Fig. 1. The architecture of DAMIN.

3.2 Users' Dynamic Interest Features Extraction Layer

In this paper, we use the reciprocal of the Euclidean distance square between the candidate item vector and the item vector clicked by user as the attention weight w of the two item vectors. From the viewpoint of geometric, if the Euclidean distance of the two item vectors is smaller, the similarity of the two item vectors is higher. So, we use the reciprocal of its Euclidean distance square as the attention weight between item in user's behavior sequence, and the attention weight defined as:

$$w = \frac{1}{(x_1 - y_1)^2 + (x_2 - y_2)^2 + ... + (x_d - y_d)^2}, \tag{1}$$

Where, $\{x_1, x_2, ..., x_d\}$ denotes the embedding vector of item clicked by user, $\{y_1, y_2, ..., y_3\}$ denotes the vector of the candidate item, d denotes the dimension of the embedding vector.

Then, we can use the attention weight to weight the item vectors in user's behavior sequence and use the weighted item vectors to express user's dynamic interest features. In deep interest network (DIN), users' dynamic interest features defined as:

$$I = \{w_1 * x_{b1},\ w_2 * x_{b2},\ ...,\ w_n * x_{bn}\}, \qquad (2)$$

Where, w_1, w_2, ..., w_n denote the attention weight between items, x_{b1}, x_{b2}, ..., x_{bn} denote the embedding vector of items clicked by users, n denote the length of user behavior sequence. Note that the attention weight w is calculated through the method in Deep Interest Network.

In this paper, we think it is very important to weight the candidate item vector and the item vector clicked by users at the same time, then add the two weighted item vectors to get a new vector. The user's behavior sequence composed of the new vectors can better represent the dynamic interest features of users. And we think such user's interest features can carry on more informations of candidate item vectors. The calculation formula of user's dynamic interest features as follows:

$$I = \{w_1 * (x_{b1} + y),\ w_2 * (x_{b2} + y),\ ...,\ w_n * (x_{bn} + y)\}, \qquad (3)$$

Where, y represents the embedding vector of candidate item, x_b represent the item vectors in user's behavior sequence, n represents the length of user's historical behavior sequence.

The details of the whole user's dynamic interest feature extraction layer are shown in Fig. 2, every item vector clicked by user and candidate item vector are weighted by their attention weights. In the end, we add the weighted item vector clicked by user and the weighted candidate item vector to get new vectors.

3.3 Multi-interest Extraction Layer

The model named transformer proposed by Google Group in 2017 solved this problem that RNN [22], LSTM [23] and GRU [24] can not be trained in parallel, and the core part of this model is the multi-head attention mechanism. In the scene of machine translation, multi-head attention mechanism can be used to extract various semantic informations of some words in different contexts.

Similarly, in the scenario of click-through rate prediction, user's interests are also diverse in different contexts. So, we can use the multi-head attention mechanism to extract users' kinds of interest features. And multi-head attention mechanism is composed of several parallel self-attention networks, every self-attention network may learn different user's interest features. Finally, the learning results of those parallel self-attention networks are concated as the outputs of multi-head attention layer. In order to parallelize the computation, we concat item vectors $\{x_{b1}, x_{b2}, ..., x_{bn}\}$ clicked by users into a matrix. At the same time, the matrix is copied into three matrixs for the convenience of calculation and expressed by Q, K and V respectively . The outputs of single self-attention layer as follows:

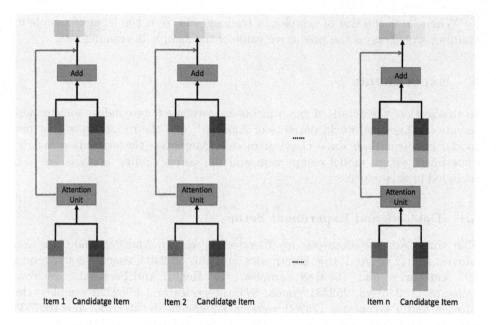

Fig. 2. The architecture of users' dynamic interest feature extraction layer.

$$head_i = Softmax(\frac{Q * K^T}{\sqrt{d_k}}) * V,\qquad(4)$$

Where, d_k is the dimension of the item embedding vector, $Q * K^T$ is the attention weights matrix , and $Q * K^T$ is used to weight the matrix V to get the result of every self-attention. Finally, the weighted matrix V of several self-attention layers are concated as the outputs of multi-head attention layer.

Moreover, the multi-head attention network of this paper includes three multi-head attention layers, and every multi-head attention layer is composed of four parallel self-attention layers, and the dimension of the item embedding vector 128. At the same time, we add residuals in two multi-head attention layer, residuals is an important part of the residuals neural network [25]. In the end, experimental results show that those settings achieves the best performance.

3.4   Loss Function

Click-through rate prediction (CTR) is a typical binary classification task. Therefore, the classical cross entropy is chosen as the loss function of the model in this paper. And cross entropy is defined as:

$$Loss = -\frac{1}{n}(\sum_{i=1}^{n} y_i log f(x_i) \ + \ (1 - y_i)log f(1 - f(x_i)))\qquad(5)$$

Where, n is the size of samples in training sets, y_i is the label of sample in training sets, $f(x_i)$ is the predictive value of the sample in training sets.

4   Experiments

In this section, the details of experiments are presented, we conduct some experiments on three real-world datasets of Amazon[1], and the results show that our model is better than some classical models. Moreover, the evaluation metric, experiment setup, model comparison and the corresponding analysis are also included in this paper.

4.1   Datasets and Experiment Setup

The three Amazon datasets are Electronics, Health_And_Personal_Care and Movies_And_TV. And the Electronics contains 192403 users, 63001 goods, 801 categories and 1689188 samples, the Health_And_Personal_Care contains 1851132 users, 252331 goods, 977 categories and 2982326 samples, the Movies_And_TV contains 123960 users, 50052 goods, 29 categories and 1697533 samples. And the following table is the statistical informations of those datasets, Users is the number of users, Goods is the number of items, Categories is the number of categories of items, and Samples is the number of datasets.

For all models, the learning rate is set between 0.1 and 1, the dimension embedding vector is set to 128, the training batch size is set to 32. In terms of memory and time, the maximum browsing length of all users is limit 500.

Table 1. Statistics of datasets used in this paper.

Datasets	Users	Goods	Categories	Samples
Electronics	192403	63001	801	1689188
Health_And_Personal_Care	1851132	252331	977	2982326
Movies_And_TV	123960	50052	29	1697533

4.2   Competitors

In order to verify the effectiveness of the model in this paper, we have carried out some comparative experiments. Therefore, some classical deep learning models in field of click-through rate prediction and recommender systems are chosen in comparative experiments, and those deep learning models include Wide&Deep, PNN, DeepFM, and DIN. And the BaseModel we choosen is to map the item in users' historical behavior sequence into a static vector directly.

---

[1] http://jmcauley.ucsd.edu/data/amazon/.

4.3 Evaluation Metrics

In the field of recommender systems and click through prediction (CTR), AUC is the most common metrics used to evaluate the model, which is defined as the area under the ROC curve and surrounded by the coordinate axis. Generally, the value range of AUC is between 0.5 and 1. If the value of AUC is closer to 1, the authenticity of the detection method is higher.

4.4 Comparative Experimental Results

From the experimental results of Table 2, we can know that the model of this paper achieves better performance than other classical deep learning models in CTR. In Table 2, DIN represents the original model proposed by Alibaba Group, DIN_EMB indicates that the embedding layer adopts the API named Embedding in tensorflow 2.x based on DIN, and DAMIN is the model proposed by us in this paper. And the experimental results show that DIN_EMB can get a better performance than DIN, and the DAMIN get the best performance.

Table 2. Comparative experimental results (AUC) on three real-world datasets.

Model	Electronics	Health_And_Personal_Care	Movies_And_TV
BaseModel	0.8651	0.8774	0.8837
Wide& Deep	0.8627	0.8701	0.8562
PNN	0.8639	0.8794	0.8794
DeepFM	0.8709	0.8743	0.9021
DIN	0.8758	0.8811	0.8976
DIN_EMB	0.9141	0.9289	0.9306
DAMIN	0.9501	0.9386	0.9564

4.5 Ablation Experimental Results

In addition, in order to verify the function and effectiveness of each module of DAMIN in this paper, we have conducted a large number of ablation experiments. For each ablation experiment, we trained it for 10 epochs and took the average value of AUC as the final experimental result in Table 3. Among them, DIN_EMB indicates that the embedding vector of DIN was embedd by the API named Embedding in tensorflow 2.x, DIN_O_EMB adopts the novel calculation method to calculate the reciprocal Euclidean distance of any two item vectors as their attention weight, DAMIN_NO_CAN means that candidate item vectors are not weighted into the item vectors of user's behavior sequence. In the end, DAMIN is the final model proposed by us in this paper.

Table 3. Ablation experimental results AUC (mean±std) on three real-world datasets.

Model	Electronics	Health_And_Personal_Care	Movies_And_TV
DIN_EMB	0.8766 ± 0.0343	0.8783 ± 0.0516	0.8971 ± 0.0196
DIN_O_EMB	0.8789 ± 0.0348	0.8837 ± 0.0515	0.8843 ± 0.0190
DAMIN_NO_CAN	0.9086 ± 0.0388	0.9045 ± 0.0456	0.9103 ± 0.0243
DAMIN	0.9234 ± 0.0408	0.9176 ± 0.0380	0.9289 ± 0.0308

Based on the experimental results in Table 3, we can obtain a conclusion that every modul of DAMIN is effective. In the first place, we can find the performance of DIN_O_EMB is slightly better than DIN_EMB on two common datasets. So, those experimental results prove it is effective to use the reciprocal of Euclidean distance as the attention weight between two item vectors. Then, the multi-head attention layer is added in DAMIN_NO_CAN, and the performance of DAMIN_NO_CAN is better than the DIN_O_EMB. And the experimental results show that multi-head attention layer makes the average of AUC of DAMIN_NO_CAN increase by 1%–3%. And the possible reason is that multi-head attention layer can effectively learn the relationship between any two items in user's historical behavior sequence and capture user's kinds of interests. In the end, DAMIN is the final model proposed by us in this paper. Compared with DAMIN_NO_CAN, the candidate item vector is also weighted in DAMIN. In order to make full use of the information of the candidate item vector, we add the weighted candidate item vector and the weighted item vector in user's behavior sequence to get a new vector, and the new vector is used as the input of the multi-head attention layer. The advantage of adding the weighted candidate item vector and the weighted item vector clicked by users is that the similarity will be greater between the two similar item vectors in user's historical behavior sequence, and the difference will be also greater between the two dissimilar item vectors in user's historical behavior sequence. And the experiment results show that the performance of DAMIN is better than DAMIN_NO_CAN, the average value of DAMIN is about improved by 1%–2%.

5   Conclusion

In this paper, we combined Deep Interest Network proposed by Alibaba Group and multi-head attention mechanism of transformer proposed by Google Group, and made some improvements based on those deep learning models. Compared with Deep Interest Network, we change the calculation method of the activation unit, and adopt the reciprocal of Euclidean distance square as the attention weight of two item vectors. In addition, we weight the item vector clicked by user and candidate item vector, then add the two weighted item vectors, and we think the results can represent users' dynamic interest feature. Meanwhile, we set the activation unit before the multi-head attention layer. And the advantage of this method is that it can highlight the effective information and suppress the invalid information. The information of users' dynamic interest feature extraction layer is more conducive to the multi-head attention layer to extract users' various interests. Finally, the experimental results show that our model achieves better performance than some classical models.

References

1. Zhou, G., et al.: Deep interest network for click-through rate prediction. In: Proceedings of the 24th ACM SIGKDD International Conference on Knowledge Discovery & Data Mining, pp. 1059–1068 (2018)
2. Vaswani, A., et al.: Attention is all you need. arXiv preprint arXiv:1706.03762 (2017)
3. Zhao, Z.-D., Shang, M.-S.: User-based collaborative-filtering recommendation algorithms on Hadoop. In: 2010 Third International Conference on Knowledge Discovery and Data Mining, pp. 478–481. IEEE (2010)
4. Sarwar, B., Karypis, G., Konstan, J., Riedl, J.: Item-based collaborative filtering recommendation algorithms. In: Proceedings of the 10th international conference on World Wide Web, pp. 285–295 (2001)
5. Mobasher, B., Burke, R., Sandvig, J.J.: Model-based collaborative filtering as a defense against profile injection attacks. In: AAAI, vol. 6, p. 1388 (2006)
6. Kleinbaum, D.G., Dietz, K., Gail, M., Klein, M., et al.: Logistic Regression. Statistics for Biology and Health, Springer, New York (2002). https://doi.org/10.1007/b97379
7. Rish, I., et al.: An empirical study of the Naive Bayes classifier. In: IJCAI 2001 Workshop on Empirical Methods in Artificial Intelligence, vol. 3, pp. 41–46 (2001)
8. Ke, G., et al.: LightGBM: a highly efficient gradient boosting decision tree. Adv. Neural. Inf. Process. Syst. **30**, 3146–3154 (2017)
9. He, X., et al.: Practical lessons from predicting clicks on ads at Facebook. In: Proceedings of the Eighth International Workshop on Data Mining for Online Advertising, pp. 1–9 (2014)
10. Rendle, S.: Factorization machines. In: 2010 IEEE International Conference on Data Mining, pp. 995–1000. IEEE (2010)
11. Cheng, H.-T., et al.: Wide & deep learning for recommender systems. In: Proceedings of the 1st Workshop on Deep Learning for Recommender Systems, pp. 7–10 (2016)
12. Qu, Y., et al.: Product-based neural networks for user response prediction. In: 2016 IEEE 16th International Conference on Data Mining (ICDM), pp. 1149–1154. IEEE (2016)
13. Guo, H., Tang, R., Ye, Y., Li, Z., He, X.: DeepFM: a factorization-machine based neural network for CTR prediction. arXiv preprint arXiv:1703.04247 (2017)
14. Lian, J., Zhou, X., Zhang, F., Chen, Z., Xie, X., Sun, G.: xDeepFM: combining explicit and implicit feature interactions for recommender systems. In: Proceedings of the 24th ACM SIGKDD International Conference on Knowledge Discovery & Data Mining, pp. 1754–1763 (2018)
15. Xiao, J., Ye, H., He, X., Zhang, H., Wu, F., Chua, T.-S.: Attentional factorization machines: learning the weight of feature interactions via attention networks. arXiv preprint arXiv:1708.04617 (2017)
16. Zhang, J., Huang, T., Zhang, Z.: Fat-deepfFM: field attentive deep field-aware factorization machine. arXiv preprint arXiv:1905.06336 (2019)

17. Mikolov, T., Chen, K., Corrado, G., Dean, J.: Efficient estimation of word representations in vector space. arXiv preprint arXiv:1301.3781 (2013)
18. Zhou, G., et al.: Deep interest evolution network for click-through rate prediction. Proc. AAAI Conf. Artif. Intell. **33**, 5941–5948 (2019)
19. Feng, Y., et al.: Deep session interest network for click-through rate prediction. arXiv preprint arXiv:1905.06482 (2019)
20. Chen, Q., Zhao, H., Li, W., Huang, P., Ou, W.: Behavior sequence transformer for e-commerce recommendation in Alibaba. In: Proceedings of the 1st International Workshop on Deep Learning Practice for High-Dimensional Sparse Data, pp. 1–4 (2019)
21. Xiao, Z., Yang, L., Jiang, W., Wei, Y., Hu, Y., Wang, H.: Deep multi-interest network for click-through rate prediction. In: Proceedings of the 29th ACM International Conference on Information & Knowledge Management, pp. 2265–2268 (2020)
22. Zaremba, W., Sutskever, I., Vinyals, O.: Recurrent neural network regularization. arXiv preprint arXiv:1409.2329 (2014)
23. Hochreiter, S., Schmidhuber, J.: Long short-term memory. Neural Comput. **9**(8), 1735–1780 (1997)
24. Cho, K., et al.: Learning phrase representations using RNN encoder-decoder for statistical machine translation. arXiv preprint arXiv:1406.1078 (2014)
25. He, K., Zhang, X., Ren, S., Sun, J.: Deep residual learning for image recognition. In: Proceedings of the IEEE Conference on Computer Vision and Pattern Recognition, pp. 770–778 (2016)

Self-residual Embedding
for Click-Through Rate Prediction

Jingqin Sun[1], Yunfei Yin[1(✉)], Faliang Huang[2(✉)], Mingliang Zhou[1],
and Leong Hou U[3]

[1] College of Computer Science, Chongqing University, Chongqing, China
{yinyunfei,mingliangzhou}@cqu.edu.cn
[2] School of Computer and Information Engineering, Nanning Normal University,
Nanning 530100, China
[3] State Key Lab of Internet of Things for Smart City, University of Macau, Taipa,
Macau 999078, China
ryanlhu@um.edu.mo

Abstract. In the Internet, categorical features are high-dimensional and sparse, and to obtain its low-dimensional and dense representation, the embedding mechanism plays an important role in the click-through rate prediction of the recommendation system. Prior works have proved that residual network is helpful to improve the performance of deep learning models, but there are few works to learn and optimize the embedded representation of raw features through residual thought in recommendation systems. Therefore, we designed a self-residual embedding structure to learn the distinction between the randomly initialized embedding vector and the ideal embedding vector by calculating the self-correlation score, and applied it to our proposed SRFM model. Extensive experiments on four real datasets show that the SRFM model can achieve satisfactory performance compared with the superior model. Also, the self-residual embedding mechanism can improve the prediction performance of some existing deep learning models to a certain extent.

Keywords: CTR prediction · Self-residual embedding · Neural network

1 Introduction

Item recommendation and advertising ranking are essential for many Internet companies (Amazon, Alibaba, and Google, etc.). Click-through rate (CTR) prediction plays a crucial role in many recommendation systems [1,5,9,13]. Logistic Regression [16] (LR), Bayesian Model [4] and Factorization Machines(FM) [18]

Supported by National Natural Science Foundation of China (61702059, 61962038), Guangxi Bagui Teams for Innovation and Research (201979), Science and Technology Development Fund Macau (SKL-IOTSC-2021-2023), University of Macau (MYRG2019-00119-FST).

L. H. U et al. (Eds.): APWeb-WAIM 2021, LNCS 12859, pp. 323–337, 2021.
https://doi.org/10.1007/978-3-030-85899-5_24

have been used to accomplish this task. Based on the FM model, the field-aware Factorization Machines [11] (FFM) model allows each feature to be mapped to multiple vectors, which are associated with each other feature. Since FM model has only a shallow structure, the expressive power of such models is limited by the cost of computing. Deep Neural Network (DNN) can extract hidden structures and inherent patterns of different levels of abstraction from training data, and can implicitly learn high-order feature interactions [6,7,9,13]. Therefore, many CTR prediction models based on neural networks have been proposed. For example, the "Wide & Deep" [1] (WD) model proposed by Google takes into account the exploration of the interaction between low-order features and high-order features by Logical Regression and Deep Neural Network respectively. The Factorization Machine Supported Neural Networks [25] (FNN) proposed by Zhang et al. takes the implicit vector in FM as the initialization value of the embedding layer. The Product-based Neural Networks [17] (PNN) proposed by Qu et al. are used to model the interaction patterns of features through "Inner Product" and "Outer Product" operations in the "Product" layer. Xiao et al. assign different importance to different feature interactions in the model of Attentional Factorial Machines [24] (AFM), and introduce the attention mechanism into the feature interaction part. Residual Network has been successfully applied in image processing, the "Deep & Cross" Network [23] (DCN) proposed by Wang et al. extends the residual Network. Meanwhile, a novel "Cross Network" is proposed to explicitly conduct feature interaction at each layer of the model. The DeepFM [9] model proposed by Guo et al. combines the functions of FM and DNN in parallel to model low-order features and high-order features respectively. The Neural Factorization Machine [6] (NFM) proposed by He et al. is similar to FNN in that they both combine the advantages of FM and DNN. Lian et al. designed a Compressed Interaction Network (CIN) in the proposed Extreme Deep Factorization Machine (xDeepFM) [13] model to explicitly learn high-order feature interactions. Cheng et al. proposed an Adaptive Factorization Network (AFN) [2], which can adaptively learn any low-order and high-order cross features from data. The Automatic Feature Interaction [20] (AutoInt) model proposed by Song et al. can automatically learn the high-order Interaction of input features. Then the input features are explicitly modeled using a multi-head self-attention neural network with residual connections.

To model the raw categorical feature, what the above models have in common is to obtain a low-dimensional dense embedding vector to represent it through an embedding mechanism. The generation of embedding vectors is to randomly generate a set of feature vectors through some strategies. This approach may not be sufficient to obtain the optimal embedding vector. Some studies [20,22,27] have shown the successful application of residual modules in deep learning. Inspired by this, we proposed a self-residual embedding method to better learn and optimize feature embedding. The main contributions of this paper are as follows:

- A method of *Self-residual Embedding* is proposed to better learn and optimize of original feature embedding vector. On this basis, combined with *Deep Neural Network*, we designed a novel *Self-residual Embedding Factorization*

Machines model. Extensive experiments on four real-world datasets demonstrate the effectiveness of the proposed method.

- For different application scenarios, some baseline models combined with the method of *Self-residual Embedding* can improve the predictive performance of these models to a certain extent.

2 Problem Definition

In the recommendation system, predicting the likelihood of a user clicking on an item (e.g. product, advertisement) is called the click-through rate estimation. The click-through rate (CTR) prediction can be defined as: let $\mathbf{x}$ represent all the features of the user u and all the features of the item v in a record, where $\mathbf{x} \in \mathbb{R}^m$, m is the total number of all the different features. The purpose of click-through rate prediction is to predict the probability $\hat{y}_{uv}$ of users u clicking items v according to the feature vectors of users and items, which can be used as the ranking basis for products, news, and advertisements displayed to users by the system.

3 Methodology

In this section, we will describe the architecture of *Self-residual Embedding Factorization Machines*(SRFM). It includes *Embedding layer, Self-residual Embedding layer, Second-order Feature Interaction layer, and Hidden layer*. The complete SRFM model is shown in Fig. 1.

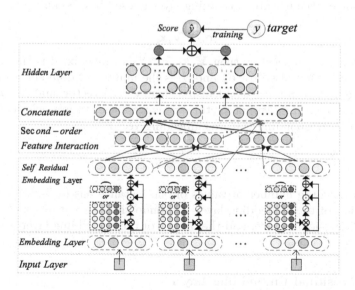

Fig. 1. The overview architecture of SRFM

3.1   Input and Embedding Layer

The raw input features include numerical features and categorical features. Therefore, the typical processing method is to convert the categorical features of users and items into a vector, which is encoded by *one-hot* or *multi-hot*. These vectors are usually high-dimensional and sparse. Finally, all the encoded features are concatenated to obtain the corresponding feature vectors $\mathbf{x} = [\mathbf{x}_1, \mathbf{x}_2, \cdots, \mathbf{x}_m]$. Where m is the total number of features, $\mathbf{x}_i$ representing the i-th feature. If the i-th feature is categorical, then $\mathbf{x}_i$ is a one-hot or multi-hot vector, and if the i-th feature is a numerical feature, then $\mathbf{x}_i$ is a scalar. Since the one-hot or multi-hot vector adopted usually has a very high dimension, in order to reduce the feature dimension, the raw feature needs to be embedded into a low-dimensional and dense space to obtain a real-value vector of the corresponding feature, as shown in the Fig. 2.

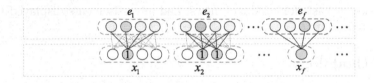

Fig. 2. The architecture of embedding

In order to map the high-dimensional sparse vector $\mathbf{x}_i$ to a low-dimensional dense vector $\mathbf{e}_i$, the feature embedding layer is used to accomplish this task, as follows:

$$\mathbf{e}_i = \mathbf{V}_i \mathbf{x}_i .\tag{1}$$

If $\mathbf{x}_i$ is a one-hot vector, then $\mathbf{V}_i \in \mathbb{R}^{d \times n_i}$ is a matrix, d is the dimension of the low-dimensional vector $\mathbf{e}_i$, and n_i is the number of different values of the i-th feature. If $\mathbf{x}_i$ is a numerical feature, then $\mathbf{V}_i$ is a vector, and the dimension of $\mathbf{V}_i$ is d. If $\mathbf{x}_i$ is a multi-hot vector, we express the feature field as the mean value of the corresponding feature embedding vector:

$$\mathbf{e}_i = \frac{1}{z} \mathbf{V}_i \mathbf{x}_i .\tag{2}$$

where z denote the number of values of one instance has for i-th feature field. The function of the embedding layer is to map the raw features $\mathbf{x}$ of the input to a low-dimensional space, and the output of the embedding layer is expressed as $\mathbf{e} = [\mathbf{e}_1, \mathbf{e}_2, \cdots, \mathbf{e}_m]$.

3.2   Self-residual Embedding Layer

In order to obtain sufficient expressive power of features and optimize the original embedding vector of features to transform input features into advanced features, we propose a *Self-residual Embedding* mechanism, as shown in the Fig. 3. We can take the feature embedded in each dimension of the vector as an implicit attribute corresponding to this feature, and learn the dimensional interaction among the feature vector attributes of the sample with auxiliary parameters. A score is calculated by the activation function, which is called the self-correlation score s of the corresponding feature. Then the s is integrated with the original embedding vector, and finally, the new embedding vector is obtained by adding the original embedding vector. Detailed calculation steps are as follows:

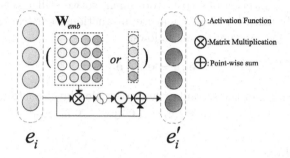

Fig. 3. The overview of self-residual embedding unit

First of all, for each feature field $\mathbf{e_j}$, we calculate the self-correlation score s_i of the feature. The formalized steps are as follows:

$$\mathbf{s}_i = \sigma(\mathbf{W}_{emb} \otimes \mathbf{e}_i) . \tag{3}$$

where $\otimes$ denotes matrix multiplication. If $\mathbf{W}_{emb} \in \mathbb{R}^{d \times d}$, this is an self-correlation score s calculated at the vector level, we call it a "vector-wise score" $\mathbf{s}_v \in \mathbb{R}^d$. If $\mathbf{W}_{emb} \in \mathbb{R}^{1 \times d}$, this is the self-correlation score calculated at the bit level, we call it the "bitwise-wise score" $s_b \in \mathbb{R}$. The σ is the non-linear activation function. The difference between the original embedding vector of the feature and the optimal representation of the feature field is calculated with the self-correlation score s.

$$\mathbf{e}'_i = \mathbf{s}_i \odot \mathbf{e}_i + \mathbf{e}_i . \tag{4}$$

where $\mathbf{e}'_i$ is the new embedding vector obtained through the transformation of the *Self-residual Embedding layer*, corresponding to the original embedding vector $\mathbf{e}_i$. $\odot$ represents the element-wise product of two vectors. So we can get the output $\mathbf{e}' = [\mathbf{e}'_1, \mathbf{e}'_2, \cdots, \mathbf{e}'_m]$ of the *Self-residual Embedding layer*.

3.3 Second-Order Feature Interaction

Then, we send the embedding vector set obtained by the *Self-residual Embedding layer* into the *Second-order Feature Interaction layer*, aiming to capture the lower-order feature interaction. In order to reduce the time complexity, the higher-order feature interaction realizes implicit exploration through DNN. According to the existing research work [14, 15, 20], there are less effective explicit low-order feature interactions and higher-order feature interactions. Liu et al. found that for Avazu datasets (Avazu published in Kaggle's click-through prediction contest), the removal of about 70% of the second-order explicit cross features not only reduces the training time of FM and DeepFM models, but leads to further performance improvements [14] too. Further research shows that less than one tenth of the effective third-order explicit cross features are effective, and the ineffective interaction features introduce noise. Explicit learning of all high-order feature interactions costs too much, so we still use the DNN structure to implicitly learn high-order feature interactions. For features $\mathbf{e}'_i$ and $\mathbf{e}'_j$, feature interaction is formalized as follows:

$$\mathbf{e}'_{i,j} = \mathbf{e}'_i \odot \mathbf{e}'_j . \tag{5}$$

The result $\mathbf{e}'_{cross}$ of the second-order interaction layer contains $m\,(m-1)\,/2$ cross feature vectors, $\mathbf{e}'_{cross} = [\mathbf{e}'_{1,2}, \cdots, \mathbf{e}'_{i,j}, \cdots, \mathbf{e}'_{m-1,m}]$.

3.4   Hidden Layer

Next, $\mathbf{e}'_{\mathbf{cross}}$ and $\mathbf{e}'$ are fed to two sets of multilayer perceptrons, respectively. The input of the multilayer perceptron is $\tilde{\mathbf{e}}^0(\mathbf{e}'_{\mathbf{cross}}$ or $\mathbf{e}')$. The hidden layers are made up of multiple fully connected layers that can be stacked to learn advanced interactions between features. The output of each layer is defined as follows:

$$\tilde{\mathbf{e}}^{(l+1)} = \sigma \left(BN \left(\mathbf{W}^l \tilde{\mathbf{e}}^l + \mathbf{b}^l \right) \right) . \tag{6}$$

where $\mathbf{W}^l$, $\tilde{\mathbf{e}}^l$ and $\mathbf{b}^l$ are input, model weight and bias of the l-th layer respectively. The $\tilde{\mathbf{e}}^{l+1}$ is the output of layer l-th and serves as the input of layer $(l+1)$-th. Finally, the outputs of the two sets of multilayer perceptrons are added together to obtain y_{mlp}. σ is the activation function. In order to avoid the problem of gradient disappearance, the Batch Normalization (BN) keeps the input of each layer of neural network the same distribution through certain Normalization methods during the training of the model [10]. Using BN to train deep neural network can achieve fast convergence and better performance [14, 19]. BN is formalized as follows:

$$\hat{x}_i = \frac{x_i - \mu_B}{\sqrt{\sigma_B + \varepsilon}} . \tag{7}$$

$$y_i = \gamma \hat{x}_i + \beta . \tag{8}$$

where x_i is the input, μ_β and σ_β are the mean and standard deviation of x_i on a mini-batch B, respectively. γ and β are two adjustment parameters corresponding to *Scale* operation and *Shift* operation respectively. ε is a numerical constant. We use the Dropout mechanism [21] in each layer of the hidden layer to alleviate the occurrence of overfitting and achieve the regularization effect to some extent.

3.5   Output Layer

Finally, the output of hidden layer y_{mlp} is mapped to a scalar between 0 and 1, which serves as the final prediction score $\hat{y}$:

$$\hat{y} = \frac{1}{1 + e^{-y_{mlp}}} .$$ (9)

3.6   Model Training

We use *Logloss* as the loss function, which is defined as follows:

$$L = -\frac{1}{N} \sum_{i=1}^{N} \left(y_i \log\left(\hat{y}_i\right) + (1 - y_i) \log\left(1 - \hat{y}_i\right) \right) .$$ (10)

where N represents the total number of samples, i represents the index of training samples, y_i represents the actual label when users click on the i-th sample, and $\hat{y}_i$ represents the estimated estimate of the probability of the i-th sample being clicked by the model. In order to alleviate the over-fitting of the model and increase the generalization ability of the model, some regularization methods are adopted. The optimization objective function of the final model is as follows:

$$\mathcal{L} = L + \lambda \|\mathbf{W}\|^2 .$$ (11)

where $\|\mathbf{W}\|^2$ represents the L_2 regularization term of the model to avoid over-fitting, and λ is the hyper-parameter of the regularization term.

4   Experiments

In this section, we conduct experiments to answer the following questions: (1) Whether our proposed SRFM method can achieve satisfactory prediction performance compared with other state-of-the-art click-through rate prediction methods. (2) The influence of hyper-parameters and different network structures on the performance of the proposed SRFM model. (3) Whether the Self-residual Embedding mechanism can enhance the click-through rate prediction performance of other baseline models.

4.1   Experimental Settings

Datasets. To evaluate the performance of the SRFM algorithm, we conducted experiments on four data sets: 1) *Avazu Dataset*[1]: It has 40,428,967 records, each of which has 23 categorical fields. This data set was released in Kaggle's click-through estimation contest. 2) *Criteo dataset*[2]: It contains 45,840,617 records, each of which has 39 categorical fields. The feature field, consisting of numerical

---

[1] https://www.kaggle.com/c/avazu-ctr-prediction/data.
[2] https://www.kaggle.com/c/criteo-display-ad-challenge/data.

features and categorical features, serves as the benchmark dataset for the Click-through Rate Prediction (CTR) algorithm and has been used in the Display Advertising Challenge hosted by Kaggle.

For *Avazu* and *Criteo* dataset, categorical feature values with less than 20 times of feature occurrence are uniformly replaced with the same categorical value "NULL". 3) *Movielens1M dataset*[3]: It contains 10,0209 anonymous ratings for 3,900 movies from 6,040 users. It is necessary to binarize users' ratings of the movie. We regard the samples with ratings less than or equal to 3 as negative samples, indicating that users do not like the movie. We regard the samples with ratings greater than 3 as positive samples, indicating that users like the movie. 4) *Book-Crossing dataset*[4]: It contains 278,858 anonymous user rating records for approximately 271,379 books. Similarly, those with a score greater than 5 are considered positive samples, and those with a score less than or equal to 5 are considered negative samples. According to the ratio of 8:1:1, we divided all data sets into training data, validation data, and test data respectively.

Baselines. We chose the following widely used click-through rate prediction models to compare with our proposed SRFM model: LR [16] is a linear approach to modeling only individual features. Some models take into account second-order feature interactions, such as FM [18], AFM [24]. Models that explore higher-order complex feature interactions, such as WD [1], AFI [20], AFN [2], DCN [23], DeepFM [9], FNN [25], xDeepFM [13], NFM [6], and DRM [26] are also included.

Metrics. In the click-through rate prediction task, AUC [3] and *Logloss* are often used to evaluate the prediction performance of the model. AUC: It refers to the area under the ROC curve, which represents the possibility that the prediction score of positive examples is higher than that of negative samples. The better the model performance, the higher the AUC value. *Logloss*: Its formal definition is shown in formula (10), and refers to the logarithmic loss. The smaller the *Logloss* value, the better the performance of the model.

Some prior works [8,14,20,26] also show that in the CTR prediction task of the recommendation system, the increase of AUC or the decrease of Logloss at **0.001-level** or **0.0001-level** will bring significant improvement.

Implementation Details. All methods are implemented in PyTorch. The dimension of the embedding vector of all the baseline models is $d = 16$. The parameter of learning rate is selected from {1e-3, 1e-4, 1e-5}, the coefficient λ of L_2 regularization is selected from {1e-3,1e-4,1e-5,1e-6}, and the batch size is selected from {2e12, 2e10, 2e7}. Set the same structural parameters for all baseline methods involving hidden layers (16, 16, 1). We use Adam [12] to optimize all deep neural network-based models. The conditions for the algorithm to

---

[3] https://grouplens.org/datasets/movielens/1m/.
[4] https://grouplens.org/datasets/book-crossing/.

stop: AUC values in the validation data converge or decrease, and perform early stopping if necessary. The optimal model obtained from the validation data was used to evaluate the test data.

4.2   Experimental Results

In this part, in order to answer Question 1, we demonstrate the performance improvement of the SRFM relative to the selected baseline model. The experiments are conducted on Avazu, Criteo, Movielens1M, and BookCrossing datasets. The results are shown in Table 1.

Table 1. Effectiveness comparison of different algorithms. *AVG* column denotes the average *AUC* increase and average *LogLoss* decrease of the *SRFM* relative to other baseline models on different datasets

Model	Avazu		Criteo		MovieLens1M		BookCrossing		AVG	
	AUC	LogLoss	AUC	LogLoss	AUC	LogLoss	AUC	LogLoss	AUC	LogLoss
LR	0.7576	0.3922	0.7942	0.4561	0.7900	0.5426	0.7752	0.5126	**0.0216**	**−0.0184**
FM (2010)	0.7810	0.3794	0.8035	0.4482	0.7987	0.5338	0.7772	0.5095	**0.0107**	**−0.0102**
WD (2016)	0.7817	0.3788	0.8050	0.4464	0.8001	0.5307	0.7816	0.5090	**0.0087**	**−0.0087**
FNN (2016)	0.7810	0.3793	0.8044	0.4504	0.8008	0.5305	0.7842	0.5038	**0.0082**	**−0.0085**
AFM (2017)	0.7769	0.3825	0.8048	0.4465	0.8014	0.5306	0.7730	0.5148	**0.0118**	**−0.0111**
DCN (2017)	0.7829	0.3787	0.8064	0.4454	0.8085	0.5219	0.7871	0.5003	**0.0046**	**−0.0041**
DeepFM (2017)	0.7860	0.3764	0.8059	0.4459	0.8104	0.5224	0.7838	0.5049	**0.0043**	**−0.0049**
NFM (2017)	0.7853	0.3766	0.8097	0.4420	0.8037	0.5277	0.7727	0.5123	**0.0080**	**−0.0072**
xDeepFM (2018)	0.7872	0.3766	0.8102	0.4420	0.8070	0.5247	0.7879	0.5019	**0.0028**	**−0.0038**
AFI (2019)	0.7858	0.3770	0.8106	0.4412	0.8087	0.5214	0.7868	0.5014	**0.0029**	**−0.0028**
AFN (2020)	0.7822	0.3801	0.8115	0.4403	0.8079	0.5221	0.7852	0.5027	**0.0041**	**−0.0038**
DRM (2020)	0.7851	0.3769	0.8096	0.4425	0.8072	0.5229	0.7868	0.5010	**0.0036**	**−0.0034**
SRFM (ours)	**0.7881**	**0.3750**	**0.8119**	**0.4399**	**0.8115**	**0.5186**	**0.7918**	**0.4964**	–	–

From the data in Table 1, we can observe that: 1) Compared with other baseline methods, the SRFM proposed in this paper has achieved satisfactory results on different datasets. Compared with other baseLine models, the average AUC increase value and average Logloss decrease value of SRFM on different datasets are both significant at 0.001-level. The slight increase of AUC in the offline experiment may also bring a great increase in the click rate when tested online [14], which brings significant benefits in the context of large user groups on the Internet. 2) By comparing the experimental results of its baseline method with LR, it can be observed that: for Avazu dataset, the suboptimal xDeepFM improved by 3.89% on AUC and 3.96% on Logloss on average. SRFM improved by 4.02% on AUC and 4.37% on LogLoss. For the Criteo dataset, the suboptimal AFN improved by an average of 2.18% on AUC and 3.46% on Logloss. SRFM improved by 2.23% on AUC and 3.56% on LogLoss. For the Movielens1M dataset, the suboptimal DeepFM improved by an average of 2.18% on AUC and 3.46% on Logloss. SRFM improved by 2.23% on AUC and 3.56% on LogLoss.

For the BookCrossing dataset, DRM improved by an average of 1.5% over LR on AUC and 2.26% on LogLoss. SRFM improved 2.15% on AUC and 3.16% on LogLoss. From the perspective of improvement relative to LR, SFRM is higher than the suboptimal model. 3) On the four datasets, the experimental results of all deep learning models are better than LR, indicating that it is meaningful to explore second-order feature interactions or even higher-order complex feature interactions.

4.3   Influence of the Network Structure

In order to further study the influence of network structure and model parameters on the performance of SRFM, we conducted several experiments.

Ablation Study. The *Self-residual Embedding layer* and the *Second-order Feature Interaction* layer are removed from the proposed *SRFM* model respectively, and the new structural models are respectively called *SRFM*1* and *SRFM*2*. We compared the performance of *SRFM*, *SRFM*1* and *SRFM*2* in the four datasets, and the results are shown in Table 2. For different datasets, we observed that the *Self-residual Embedding layer* and the *Second-order Feature Interaction* layer generally reduce the performance of the complete structure SRFM at 0.001-level. Compared with the *Self-residual Embedding layer*, the *Second-order Feature Interaction layer* can bring more obvious improvement.

Table 2. Ablation experiments about *SRFM*. $\Delta1(\Delta2)$ column denotes the *AUC* increase and *LogLoss* decrease of the *SRFM* relative to *SRFM*1(SRFM*2)* on different datasets.

Model		SRFM	SRFM*1	$\Delta1$	SRFM*2	$\Delta2$
Avazu	AUC	0.78812	0.78875	−0.00063	0.783807	0.00431
	LogLoss	0.37503	0.37518	0.00015	0.378091	−0.00306
Criteo	AUC	0.81189	0.81141	0.00049	0.807194	0.00470
	LogLoss	0.43985	0.44131	−0.00145	0.444322	−0.00447
MovieLens1M	AUC	0.81152	0.81066	0.00086	0.807119	0.00440
	LogLoss	0.51861	0.51927	−0.00066	0.522878	−0.00427
BookCrossing	AUC	0.79180	0.79048	0.00133	0.785926	0.00588
	LogLoss	0.49643	0.49760	−0.00117	0.501284	−0.00486

Self-correlation Score. We conducted experiments to study the effects of different activation functions and different self-correlation scores, $\mathbf{s}_v$ and s_b, on the performance of SRFM. The experimental results are shown in Table 3. We observed that the best results were obtained using *sigmoid* and $\mathbf{s}_v$ on the

Movielens1M and BookCrossing datasets. For Movielens1M and BookCrossing datasets, the combination of activation functions and self-correlation scores yielded mean AUC scores of about *0.81051* and *0.79021*, respectively, still higher than other baseline models. To explore the best performance, an experimental search is required to determine which σ and which s are used on the self-residual embedding layer for different datasets.

Table 3. Effects of *Self-residual Embedding* layer with different *activation functions* σ and *Self-correlation Scores* s on *SRFM* performance

σ		MovieLens1M		BookCrossing	
		s_v	s_b	s_v	s_b
sigmoid	AUC	**0.81152**	0.81003	**0.79180**	0.79098
	LogLoss	**0.51860**	0.52032	**0.49643**	0.49715
Softmax	AUC	0.81080	0.81078	0.78893	0.79098
	LogLoss	0.52038	0.51896	0.49938	0.49715
tanh	AUC	0.81124	0.80972	0.78866	0.79017
	LogLoss	0.51875	0.54474	0.50027	0.49786
relu	AUC	0.81072	0.80928	0.78993	0.79027
	LogLoss	0.52084	0.52752	0.49778	0.49788

Embedding Size. We set the embedding size of the feature embedding layer from 8 to 64 to study the impact of different feature embedding dimensions on the performance of SRFM model, as shown in Fig. 4. It can be observed that for the Movielens1M dataset, the model performance tends to be stable as the embedding dimension increases, and the model performance is generally higher when the "vector-wise score" is adopted. For the BookCrossing dataset, the results of the two self-correlation scores were similar. On both datasets, the optimal performance can be achieved when the feature dimension is set to 16. This indicates that SRFM can obtain the optimal result with a small number of parameters.

Stacking Self-residual Embedding Layer. We stack the self-residual embedding layer to study its effect on the performance of the SRFM model. As shown in Fig. 5, the model's performance did not improve significantly on the Movielens1M dataset and decreased somewhat on the BookCrossing dataset as the number of self-residual embedding layer increased. This shows that the stacking of the self-residual embedding layer is not necessarily efficient and only one layer can be used.

The Extensibility of the Self-residual Embedding Layer. A helpful approach should not only improve performance, but also have better extensibility.

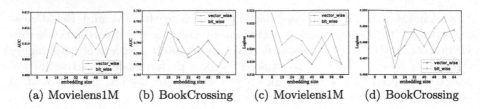

(a) Movielens1M   (b) BookCrossing   (c) Movielens1M   (d) BookCrossing

Fig. 4. The performance of *SRFM* on different *embedding sizes.* (a), (b), (c) and (d) respectively represent *AUC on Movielens1M*, *AUC on BookCrossing*, Logloss on Movielens1M and *Logloss on BookCrossing* in different embedding size

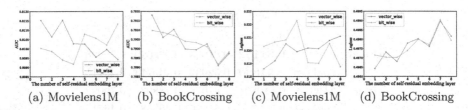

(a) Movielens1M   (b) BookCrossing   (c) Movielens1M   (d) BookCrossing

Fig. 5. Effect of stacked *Self-residual Embedding layer* on model performance. (a), (b), (c) and (d) respectively represent *AUC on Movielens1M*, *AUC on BookCrossing*, Logloss on Movielens1M and *Logloss on BookCrossing* in different number of *Self-residual Embedding layers*

In this section, we investigate whether the self-residual embedding layer can be migrated to some widely used deep learning model for click-through rate prediction, with the aim of improving its performance. We transfer the method proposed in Sect. 3.2 to other models such as Wide & Deep, AFM, DCN, and NFM. The new name for the model is called "Model*". Table 4 lists the experimental results of the original model and the new model "Model*" on different datasets.

By observation of the experimental results in Table 4, it can be seen that "model*" has different degrees of improvement in AUC and Logloss compared with the original model, and can reach an improvement of orders of magnitude from 0.0001-level to 0.001-level in different scenarios. Note that this is not always valid, and DeepFM* and xDeepFM* show some performance degradation on the Avazu and Criteo datasets. The performance of DCN* and WD* on MovieLensm is degraded. We have also carried out experiments on other models, and the results show that the self-residual embedding layer is also not stable in these models, and maybe the optimal network parameter that cannot be searched. These experiments show that under certain scenarios, the *Self-residual Embedding layer* can improve the performance of some known click-through rate prediction models and has a certain expansibility.

Table 4. *model** vs *model*. Performance improvements are indicated in **bold** text.

Model	Avazu		Criteo		Movielens1m		Bookcrossing	
	AUC	LogLoss	AUC	LogLoss	AUC	LogLoss	AUC	LogLoss
WD	0.78172	0.37879	0.80498	0.44635	0.80006	0.53073	0.78162	0.50903
WD*	**0.78214**	**0.37866**	**0.80532**	**0.44601**	0.79996	0.53067	**0.78406**	**0.50357**
AFM	0.77689	0.38246	0.80482	0.44653	0.80135	0.53062	0.77295	0.51485
AFM*	**0.77995**	**0.38087**	**0.80536**	**0.44606**	**0.80176**	0.53097	**0.77619**	**0.51216**
DeepFM	0.78597	0.37642	0.80585	0.44586	0.81042	0.52243	0.78383	0.50486
DeepFM*	0.78547	0.37698	0.80196	0.44999	0.80699	0.52320	**0.78638**	**0.50135**
DCN	0.78288	0.37871	0.80638	0.44538	0.80852	0.52190	0.78711	0.50032
DCN*	**0.78328**	**0.37808**	**0.80656**	**0.44526**	0.80745	0.52246	**0.78821**	**0.49938**
NFM	0.78533	0.37660	0.80967	0.44200	0.80368	0.52772	0.77265	0.51231
NFM*	**0.78619**	**0.37615**	**0.80994**	**0.44173**	**0.80574**	**0.52538**	0.77179	0.51254
xDeepFM	0.78716	0.37664	0.81022	0.44200	0.80695	0.52468	0.78791	0.50194
xDeepFM*	0.78595	0.37716	0.80971	0.44237	**0.81244**	**0.51899**	**0.79158**	**0.50001**

5 Conclusion

The embedding layer is an important part of most CTR models. Good input affects the upper limit of model performance. In order to better represent and model the raw features, we propose SRFM model for CTR prediction. Extensive offline experiments on large-scale standard datasets show that the proposed model has a satisfactory performance. The second-order feature interaction layer of SRFM can bring more significant improvement, but its computational complexity is nonlinear. The self-residual feature embedding mechanism can improve the performance of some models and has certain expansibility. At present, the performance of the CTR prediction task has reached a bottleneck. In the future, we will further study the method to learn and optimize feature embedding representation, aiming to better optimize the current CTR prediction model in terms of performance and efficiency.

References

1. Cheng, H.T., et al.: Wide & deep learning for recommender systems. In: Proceedings of the 1st Workshop on Deep Learning for Recommender Systems, pp. 7–10 (2016)
2. Cheng, W., Shen, Y., Huang, L.: Adaptive factorization network: learning adaptive-order feature interactions. In: Proceedings of the AAAI Conference on Artificial Intelligence vol. 34, no. (04), pp. 3609–3616 (2020)
3. Hand, D.J., Till, R.J.: A simple generalisation of the area under the roc curve for multiple class classification problems. Mach. Learn. **45**, 171–186 (2001)
4. Graepel, T., Candela, J.Q., Borchert, T., Herbrich, R.: Web-scale Bayesian click-through rate prediction for sponsored search advertising in microsoft's bing search engine. In: Proceedings of the 27th International Conference on Machine Learning (ICML-10), 21–24 June 2010, Haifa, Israel, pp. 13–20 (2010)

5. Han, Y., Gu, P., Gao, W., Xu, G., Wu, J.: Aspect-level sentiment capsule network for micro-video click-through rate prediction. World Wide Web, 1–20 (2021)
6. He, X., Chua, T.S.: Neural factorization machines for sparse predictive analytics. In: Proceedings of the 40th International ACM SIGIR Conference on Research and Development in Information Retrieval, pp. 355–364 (2017)
7. Huang, F., Li, X., Yuan, C., Zhang, S., Zhang, J., Qiao, S.: Attention-emotion-enhanced convolutional LSTM for sentiment analysis. IEEE Trans. Neural Netw. Learn. Syst., 1–14 (2021). https://doi.org/10.1109/TNNLS.2021.3056664
8. Huang, T., She, Q., Wang, Z., Zhang, J.: GateNet: gating-enhanced deep network for click-through rate prediction (2020)
9. Huifeng, G., Ruiming, T., Yunming, Y., Zhenguo, L., Xiuqiang, H.: DeepFM: a factorization-machine based neural network for CTR prediction. In: Proceedings of the 26th International Joint Conference on Artificial Intelligence, pp. 1725–1731. AAAI Press (2017)
10. Ioffe, S., Szegedy, C.: Batch normalization: accelerating deep network training by reducing internal covariate shift. In: Proceedings of the 32nd International Conference on Machine Learning, vol. 37, pp. 448–456 (2015)
11. Juan, Y., Zhuang, Y., Chin, W.S., Lin, C.J.: Field-aware factorization machines for CTR prediction. In: Proceedings of the 10th ACM Conference on Recommender Systems. ACM, September 2016
12. Kingma, D., Ba, J.: Adam: a method for stochastic optimization. Comput. Sci. (2014)
13. Lian, J., Zhou, X., Zhang, F., Chen, Z., Xie, X., Sun, G.: xDeepFM: combining explicit and implicit feature interactions for recommender systems. In: Proceedings of the 24th ACM SIGKDD International Conference on Knowledge Discovery & Data Mining, pp. 1754–1763 (2018)
14. Liu, B., et al.: AutoFIS: automatic feature interaction selection in factorization models for click-through rate prediction. In: Proceedings of the 26th ACM SIGKDD International Conference on Knowledge Discovery & Data Mining. ACM (2020)
15. Luo, Y., et al.: AutoCross: automatic feature crossing for tabular data in real-world applications. In: Proceedings of the 25th ACM SIGKDD International Conference on Knowledge Discovery & Data Mining, pp. 1936–1945 (2019)
16. Park, H.-A.: An introduction to logistic regression. J. Korean Acad. Nurs. **43**(2), 154–164 (2013)
17. Qu, Y., et al.: Product-based neural networks for user response prediction. In: 2016 IEEE 16th International Conference on Data Mining (ICDM), pp. 1149–1154 (2016)
18. Rendle, S.: Factorization machines. In: 2010 IEEE 10th International Conference on Data Mining (ICDM), pp. 995–1000 (2010)
19. Sheng, X.R., et al.: One model to serve all: star topology adaptive recommender for multi-domain CTR prediction (2021)
20. Song, W., et al.: AutoInt: automatic feature interaction learning via self-attentive neural networks. In: Proceedings of the 28th ACM International Conference on Information and Knowledge Management. ACM, November 2019
21. Srivastava, N., Hinton, G., Krizhevsky, A., Sutskever, I., Salakhutdinov, R.: Dropout: a simple way to prevent neural networks from overfitting. J. Mach. Learn. Res. **15**(1), 1929–1958 (2014)
22. Vaswani, A., et al.: Attention is all you need. CoRR abs/1706.03762 (2017)
23. Wang, R., Fu, B., Fu, G., Wang, M.: Deep & cross network for ad click predictions. In: ADKDD 2017 (2017)

24. Xiao, J., Ye, H., He, X., Zhang, H., Wu, F., Chua, T.: Attentional factorization machines: learning the weight of feature interactions via attention networks. CoRR abs/1708.04617 (2017)
25. Zhang, W., Du, T., Wang, J.: Deep learning over multi-field categorical data. In: Ferro, N., et al. (eds.) ECIR 2016. LNCS, vol. 9626, pp. 45–57. Springer, Cham (2016). https://doi.org/10.1007/978-3-319-30671-1_4
26. Zhao, Z., Fang, Z., Peng, C., Bao, Y., Yan, W.: Dimension relation modeling for click-through rate prediction. In: The 29th ACM International Conference on Information and Knowledge Management, CIKM 2020 (2020)
27. Zhou, G., Wu, K., Bian, W., Yang, Z., Zhu, X., Gai, K.: Res-embedding for deep learning based click-through rate prediction modeling. In: The 1st International Workshop (2019)

GCNNIRec: Graph Convolutional Networks with Neighbor Complex Interactions for Recommendation

Teng Mei[1], Tianhao Sun[1]($\boxtimes$), Renqin Chen[1], Mingliang Zhou[1], and Leong Hou U[2]

[1] Chongqing University, Chongqing 400044, China
{TengMei,sthing,laird,mingliangzhou}@cqu.edu.cn
[2] State Key Lab of Internet of Things for Smart City,
University of Macau, Macau 999078, China
ryanlhu@um.edu.mo

Abstract. In recent years, tremendous efforts have been made to explore features contained in user-item graphs for recommendation based on Graph Neural Networks (GNN). However, most existing recommendation methods based on GNN use weighted sum of directly-linked node's features only, assuming that neighboring nodes are independent individuals, neglecting possible correlations between neighboring nodes, which may result in failure of capturing co-occurrence signals. Therefore, in this paper, we propose a novel Graph Convolutional Network with Neighbor complex Interactions for Recommendation (GCNNIRec) focused upon capturing possible co-occurrence signals between node neighbors. Specifically, two types of modules, the Linear-Aggregator module and the Interaction-Aggregator module are both inside GCNNIRec. The former module linearly aggregates the features of neighboring nodes to obtain the representation of target node. The latter utilizes the interactions between neighbors to aggregate the co-occurrence features of nodes to capture co-occurrence features. Furthermore, empirical results on three real datasets confirm not only the state-of-the-art performance of GCNNIRec but also the performance gains achieved by introducing Interaction-Aggregator module into GNN.

Keywords: Recommender system · Graph neural networks · Neighbor interactions

1 Introduction

To cope with information overload, recommender systems are widely used in life. Collaborative filtering is one of the most commonly used techniques in many modern recommendation systems [1]. It assumes that similar people tend to own similar preferences on similar items. The interactions between users and items can naturally be regarded as a graph structure, therefore graph neural networks [2–4] can be applied in recommendation. STAR-GCN [5] utilizes GNN to aggregate the structural information. NGCF [6] uses stacked graph convolutional layers to obtain the high-order relationship information.

© Springer Nature Switzerland AG 2021
L. H. U et al. (Eds.): APWeb-WAIM 2021, LNCS 12859, pp. 338–347, 2021.
https://doi.org/10.1007/978-3-030-85899-5_25

These models show the remarkable ability of GNN in aggregating feature information in recommendation systems. Based on assumption that neighboring nodes are independent individuals, these approaches take a weighted sum of all neighbors' features to obtain the representation of the target node. In fact, there are latent interactions between some neighboring nodes. The interactions may be a strong signal of the characteristics of target node, which can indicate the user's preferences. The example below shows that the interactions between neighbors can be a strong signal—user's preferences.

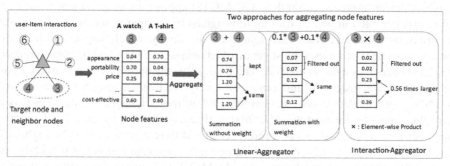

Fig. 1. A shopping example: (Left) A transaction graph. (Right) Two aggregation methods, linear aggregation and interaction aggregation.

Figure 1 illustrates a scenario in a shopping dataset. A user purchased two items as the picture depicted, which are a watch and a T-shirt. It can be seen from the figure that the user paid more attention to the feature "cost-effective" when purchasing the watch and the T-shirt. In the case of linear aggregation that takes summation without weight in Fig. 1, it can be found that the user paid attention to features such as "price", "cost-effective", "portability" and "appearance", but it fails to correctly capture user preferences. Employing the linear aggregation method that takes weighted summation, it can filter out some irrelevant features such as "appearance" and "portability", but also fail to capture the user's main preference characteristics; In the case of interaction aggregation, it can capture the co-occurrence feature—"cost-effective" between the two products and filter out two irrelevant features, "appearance" and "portability". Therefore, the potential interactions between neighbor nodes may be a strong cooperative signal, which contribute to the learning of user preference features. But most recommendations based on GNN failed to capture such signals.

To obtain user preference information, we propose an end-to-end deep model GCN-NIRec, which can capture co-occurrence signals between neighboring nodes. Specifically, the key component of GCNNIRec consists of two modules: Linear-Aggregator module and Interaction-Aggregator module. Given a user-item interaction graph, the Linear-Aggregator module takes the weighted sum of the features of the connected nodes to obtain general feature representation of target node; The Interaction-Aggregator module utilizes the interactions between neighbors to learn the co-occurrence feature information for target nodes. Moreover, a sparse regularizer [7] is applied to solve the over-parameterization and over-fitting problems.

2 Related Works

Graph neural networks have been widely used in recommendation system, and have made remarkable achievements. Lots of previous works based on GNN are to obtain node features by linearly aggregating features of neighbors, which may fail to capture some co-occurrence features between neighbors.

According to the method of information aggregation in GNN, the existing recommendation models are mainly divided into unweighted linear aggregation models and weighted linear aggregation models. GC-MC [8] applies the graph neural network to the matrix completion, which uses an unweighted linear aggregator to aggregate node feature information and treats each adjacent node equally, which may lead to the introduction of some noise caused by some disliked items. GAT [4] could be considered as a weighted linear aggregation method, which can solve the noise problem caused by non-weighted linear aggregation, and it makes the weighted linear aggregator more common in GNN recommendation system. GraphRec [9] utilizes a dynamic attention network to learn the impact of different neighbor nodes. HGMAP [10] uses a multi-head attention mechanism to distinguish users' preferences for different aspects of POI. LightGCN [11] applies a simple weighted linear aggregator to aggregate features of neighbors and learns node features efficiently and quickly. MCCF [12] uses a hierarchical attention network to learn multiple potential purchase intentions. Linear aggregation method is widely used in graph neural networks.

GraphSage [3] also proposed several nonlinear aggregation methods such as pooling aggregation and LSTM aggregation. GATNE-T [13] utilizes the mean aggregator and max-pooling aggregator to obtain edge embedding. The mean aggregation and pooling aggregation method can learn the main characteristics, but they cannot learn the possible co-occurrence preference characteristics of neighbor nodes.

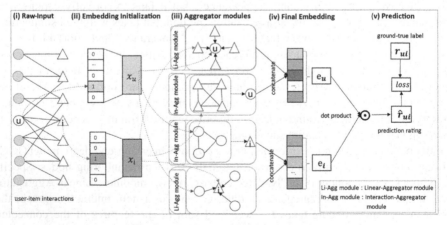

Fig. 2. The framework of GCNNIRec.

3 Our Approach

Figure 2 provides an overview of GCNNIRec. In the following, this paper will introduce each part of GCNNIRec in detail.

3.1 Raw Input and Embedding Initialization

GCNNIRec requires user-item bipartite graph G as input. The raw input of user node or item node is a one-hot vector, a high-dimensional sparse vector, which is not conducive to the calculation and representation of the model. Therefore, an embedding layer is applied to convert it into a low-dimensional dense vector to obtain user node's initial embedding x_u and item's initial embedding x_i.

After obtaining the initial embedding of each node, the target node can update its feature embedding by message passing and message aggregation. The following section will introduce two message aggregation methods respectively.

3.2 Linear-Aggregator Module

GNN has been extensively employed in recommendation systems and achieved great success. For graph attention networks (GAT) [4], users can give different attentions to different purchased items, which can reduce the noise caused by some disliked items. Therefore, we apply GAT to Linear-Aggregator module to learn feature information of target node by aggregating the features between neighboring nodes, as shown in formula (1).

$$LiAgg(h_v) = h_v = LinearAgg\left(\{h_i\}_{i \in \tilde{N}(v)}\right) = \sum_{i \in \tilde{N}(v)} a_{iv} h_i W \qquad (1)$$

Where h_v represents target node v; $\tilde{N}(v)$ is the set of expanded adjacent nodes of node v, including target node v; W is a weight matrix (a trainable parameter) to do feature transformation; a_{iv} is the attention coefficient of the target node v to neighboring node i, which can be calculated by formula (2).

$$a_{iv} = \frac{\exp\left(\text{ReLU}\left(\vec{a}^T \left[W\vec{h_v} \| W\vec{h_i}\right]\right)\right)}{\sum_{k \in N(v)} \exp\left(\text{ReLU}\left(\vec{a}^T \left[W\vec{h_v} \| W\vec{h_k}\right]\right)\right)} \qquad (2)$$

Where h_i denotes the representation of the neighbor node i; $N(v)$ represents the neighbors of node v; $\|$ is the concatenation operation; $\vec{a}$ is a weight vector; $.^T$ represents transposition; ReLU is an activation function.

Applying Linear-Aggregator module, GCNNIRec can learn general feature information from all neighboring nodes. But Linear-Aggregator module cannot learn the co-occurrence feature information (a strong signal) from purchased items. Therefore, we introduce a new information aggregation method, interaction aggregation.

3.3 Interaction-Aggregator Module

We designed a new Interaction-Aggregator module for GCNNIRec. This module utilizes the interactions between neighbors to aggregate the co-occurrence features of nodes.

As shown in Fig. 3, we first utilize a weighted random sample strategy [14] on user-item ratings to select a fixed number of neighboring nodes for efficiency of model training. Then, we will generate a complete graph based on the target node and the fixed number of neighboring nodes selected by the sampling. After that, we will use formula (3) to make all nodes on the graph interact in pairs, and finally perform a weighted summation of the interactive results to obtain the aggregated characteristics of the target node.

$$h_v = InteractionAgg\left(\{h_i\}_{i \in N(v)}\right) = \sum\nolimits_{i \in N(v)} \sum\nolimits_{j \in N(v) \& i < j} h_i W \odot h_j W \qquad (3)$$

Where $N(v)$ represents the set of directly connected neighbors of node v; i and j are node index from $N(v)$; $\odot$ denotes element-wise product.

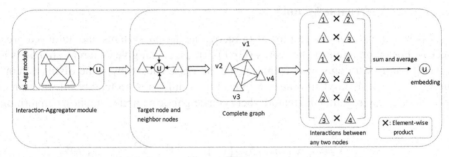

Fig. 3. The framework of Interaction-Aggregator module.

Inspired by BGNN [15], we consider interactions between target nodes and all neighboring nodes, as shown in Eq. (4).

$$h_v = InteractionAgg\left(\{h_i\}_{i \in \tilde{N}(v)}\right) = \frac{1}{n_v} \sum\nolimits_{i \in \tilde{N}(v)} \sum\nolimits_{j \in \tilde{N}(v) \& i < j} h_i W \odot h_j W \qquad (4)$$

Where $\tilde{N}(v) = N(v) \cup \{v\}$; i and j are node index from $\tilde{N}(v)$; n_v denotes the number of all interactions. Interaction-Aggregator module has a high computational time complexity, which is not conducive to model training. Inspired by [15], We can rewrite formula (4) equivalently as follows:

$$InteractionAgg\left(\{h_i\}_{i \in \tilde{N}(v)}\right) = \frac{1}{2n_v}\left(\sum\nolimits_{i \in \tilde{N}(v)} \sum\nolimits_{j \in \tilde{N}(v)} s_i \odot s_j - \sum\nolimits_{i \in \tilde{N}(v)} s_i \odot s_i\right) \qquad (5)$$

$$InAgg(h_v) = h_v = \frac{1}{2n_v}\left(\underbrace{\left(\sum\nolimits_{i \in \tilde{N}(v)} s_i\right)^2}_{o\left(|\tilde{N}(v)|\right)} - \underbrace{\sum\nolimits_{i \in \tilde{N}(v)} s_i^2}_{o\left(|\tilde{N}(v)|\right)}\right) \qquad (6)$$

Where $s_i = h_i W$ denotes the transformed feature vector of node i. We can compute the Interaction-Aggregator module in linear time and the complexity is the same as the Linear-Aggregator module.

3.4 Final Embedding

We can learn lots of node features from the Linear-Aggregator module and the Interaction-Aggregator module. Specifically, from the Linear-Aggregator module, we can obtain some general feature information; From the Interaction-Aggregator module, we can obtain some co-occurrence features and capture the user's possible preferences. Then, we obtain the final embedding of the target node by weighted sum of the two embeddings obtained by the two modules, as shown in Eq. (7).

$$e_v = (1 - \alpha) * LiAgg(h_v) + \alpha * InAgg(h_v) \tag{7}$$

Where α is a hyper-parameter, which controls the ratio of node embedding obtained from the Interaction-Aggregator module and from the Linear-Aggregator module.

3.5 Rating Prediction

Once getting the final embedding of the user u and the item i (i.e., e_u and e_i), according to Matrix Factorization (MF) model, we utilize the dot product between user final embedding and item embedding to predict the user-item interaction rating, as shown in formula (8).

$$\hat{r}_{ui} = e_u * e_i \tag{8}$$

Objective Function. Our task is the rating prediction. The objective function is as follows:

$$Loss_r = \frac{1}{2|o|} \sum_{(u,i) \in o} \left(r_{ui} - \hat{r}_{ui} \right)^2 \tag{9}$$

where O donates the set of observed interaction ratings, and r_{ui} is the ground truth rating of the user u on the item i. To alleviate overfitting and over-parametrization, the $L0$ regularization [7] is introduced in our objective function.

The final objective function is shown below.

$$\min_{\Theta} Loss = Loss_r + \lambda \|\Theta\|_0 \tag{10}$$

where Θ denotes the trainable model-parameter set and λ is a hyper-parameter, which controls the strength of $L0$ regularization to alleviate overfitting. We adopt the Adam as the optimizer to optimize and update the model.

4 Experiments

4.1 Experimental Settings

Datasets. The effectiveness of our model is evaluated on three real datasets: Yelp, Movielens-100K, Amazon. Yelp is a business recommendation dataset that contains 30838 ratings from 1286 users to 2614 items. Movielens-100K is an extensively adopted movie dataset in recommendation, which consists of 100,000 ratings from 943 users to 1682 movies. Amazon is a product recommendation dataset containing 65170 ratings from 1000 users to 1000 items. In each dataset, 80% of historical ratings are randomly selected as training set, and the remaining are the test set.

Metrics. In our rating prediction task, we adopt two widely-used evaluation metrics: Root Mean Squared Error (RMSE) and Mean Absolute Error (MAE) [12].

Baselines. We compare GCNNIRec with the following approaches:

- BiasMF [16] is an improved method based on MF model, which takes into account the biases of different users and items.
- AUTOREC [17] is an auto-encoder based method. In our experiments, we use I-AUTOREC to represent, for it has better performance than U-AUTOREC.
- GC-MC [8] is a collaborative filtering model based on graph convolutional networks, which linearly aggregates features of neighboring nodes to encode nodes.
- MCCF [12] is a novel recommendation approach based on graph attention networks, which employs hierarchical attention networks to explore user intents.

4.2 Performance Comparison

Table 1. Performance comparison of rating prediction.

	Yelp		ML-100K		Amazon	
	RMSE	MAE	RMSE	MAE	RMSE	MAE
BiasMF	0.3862	0.1494	0.9217	0.7238	0.9021	0.6752
AUTOREC	0.3814	0.1185	0.9383	0.7319	0.9163	0.7024
GC-MC	0.3837	0.1264	0.9145	0.7126	0.8915	0.6601
MCCF	0.3806	0.1029	0.9070	0.7050	0.8876	0.6428
GCNNIRec-LA	0.3750	0.1069	0.9135	0.7103	0.8895	0.6521
GCNNIRec-IA	0.3801	0.1103	0.9226	0.7215	0.8864	0.6408
GCNNIRec	**0.3636**	**0.0997**	**0.9012**	**0.7028**	**0.8823**	**0.6312**

We compare the recommended performance of all models mentioned above. GCNNIRec-LA and GCNNIRec-IA are two variants of GCNNIRec. Specifically,

GCNNIRec-LA removed the complex interactions between neighboring nodes from GCNNIRec and only retained the linear aggregator. On the contrary, GCNNIRec-IA only kept the interaction aggregator. From Table 1, we can see experimental results of all methods and compare these models in terms of RMSE and MAE. We have several observations.

- Our model GCNNIRec consistently outperforms all benchmark methods, which shows the significance of introducing interactions between neighboring nodes to recommender systems.
- It is observed that MCCF and GC-MC outperform BiasMF, which indicates the power of neural network models. Among these baselines, MCCF and GC-MC show significant performance, suggesting that the GNNs and attention mechanism are powerful in representation learning for graph data.
- GCNNIRec outperforms GCNNIRec-LA, which suggests that the model GCNNIRec with the Interaction-Aggregator module has more powerful representation capabilities and implies that the complex interactions between neighbors are effective for improving the recommendation performance. Similarly, since it ignores the Linear-Aggregator module, GCNNIRec-IA performs worse than GCNNIRec. We can see that both the Interaction-Aggregator module and the Linear-Aggregator module contribute to the improvement of the model performance.

4.3   Hyper-Parameter Analysis of GCNNIRec

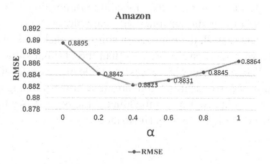

Fig. 4. Impact of the hyper-parameter α on Amazon dataset.

Impact of the Hyper-Parameter α. The hyper-parameter α controls the contributions of Interaction-Aggregator module and Linear-Aggregator module to the model. When α is greater than 0.5, the Interaction-Aggregator module contributes more to the model. When α is 1, the model only contains Interaction-Aggregator module; When α is less than 0.5, the model is more contributed by Linear-Aggregator module. When α is 0, the model only consists of Linear-Aggregator module. In Fig. 4, we can see that when α is 0.4, GCNNIRec achieves the best performance, which means that the model learns more from the Linear-Aggregator module. Since user's purchase behavior is usually affected by many intentions, the Interaction-Aggregator module can only learn the main co-occurrence preference features such as the "cost-effective" feature in Fig. 1, while the Linear-Aggregator module can learn all features such as "appearance", "price" and "cost-effective", although it cannot capture co-occurrence preference information; when α is close to 0 or 1, the model performance will gradually deteriorate, suggesting that when only learning the general features or co-occurrence features of neighboring nodes, the model cannot get the optimal performance. It demonstrates the effectiveness of Interaction-Aggregator module and Linear-Aggregator module.

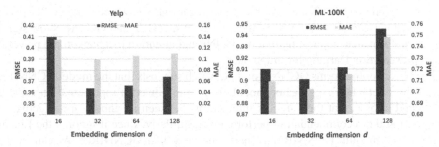

Fig. 5. Impact of embedding dimension d on Yelp and Movielens-100K datasets.

Impact of the Hyper-Parameter d (Embedding Dimensions). Since the embedding dimension d plays a key role in controlling the complexity and expressive capacity of GCNNIRec, we evaluate how it impact on recommendation performance. Generally speaking, when we gradually increase the embedding dimension d, its performance will be improved, since a smaller dimension is not capable of expressing the features of nodes, and when d is increased, the expression ability of each node will be improved to an optimal value. However, when d is greater than the optimal value, increasing d will affect performance. When d further increases, the node expression ability will be further enhanced, which may lead to overfitting and introduce corresponding noise. Figure 5 can prove this. Therefore, an appropriate embedding dimension d is employed to balance the trade-off between complexity and performance.

5   Conclusion

In this paper, we proposed a novel model GCNNIRec based on GNN for recommendation, which explores features contained in user-item bipartite graph by utilizing complex interactions between neighboring nodes. Specifically, GCNNIRec contains two designed modules, Linear-Aggregator module and Interaction-Aggregator module. The former module uses a weighted sum of the features of the connected nodes to represent the target node. The latter utilizes the interactions between neighboring nodes to aggregate the co-occurrence features, which can capture possible co-occurrence signals between neighboring nodes. And then combine the modules to extract node features. Our experimental results demonstrate that our model outperforms existing models in terms of recommendation metrics, RMSE and MAE.

Acknowledgments. This work was supported by the Science and Technology Development Fund Macau (SKL-IOTSC-2021–2023) and University of Macau (MYRG2019-00119-FST).

References

1. Pan, Y., He, F., Yu, H.: Learning social representations with deep autoencoder for recommender system. World Wide Web **23**(4), 2259–2279 (2020)
2. Kipf, T., Welling, M.: Semi-supervised classification with graph convolutional networks. In: ICLR (2017)
3. Hamilton, W., Ying, R., Leskovec, J.: Inductive representation learning on large graphs. In: NIPS (2017)
4. Veličković, P., Cucurull, G., Casanova, A., Romero, A., Lio, P., Bengio, Y.: Graph attention networks. In: ICLR (2017)
5. Zhang, J., Shi, X., Zhao, S., King, I.: STAR-GCN: stacked and reconstructed graph convolutional networks for recommender systems. In: IJCAI, pp. 4264–4270 (2019)
6. Wang, X., He, X., Wang, M., Feng, F., Chua, T.: Neural graph collaborative filtering. In: SIGIR, pp. 165–174 (2019)
7. Louizos, C., Welling, M., Kingma, D.: Learning sparse neural networks through L0 regularization. In: ICLR (2018)
8. Berg, R., Kipf, T., Welling, M.: Graph convolutional matrix completion. In: KDD (2018)
9. Fan, W., et al.: Graph neural networks for social recommendation. In: WWW, pp. 417–426 (2019)
10. Zhong, T., Zhang, S., Zhou, F.: Hybrid graph convolutional networks with multi-head attention for location recommendation. World Wide Web **23**(6), 3125–3151 (2020)
11. He, X., Deng, K., Wang, X., Li, Y.: LightGCN: simplifying and powering graph convolution network for recommendation. In: SIGIR, pp. 639–648 (2020)
12. Wang, X., Wang, R., Shi, C., Song, Li, Q.: Multi-component graph convolutional collaborative filtering. In: AAAI, pp. 6267–6274 (2020)
13. Cen, Y., Zou, X., Zhang, J., Yang, H., Zhou, J., Tang, J.: Representation learning for attributed multiplex heterogeneous network. In: KDD, pp. 1358–1368 (2019)
14. Efraimidis, P., Spirakis, P.: Weighted random sampling with a reservoir. Inf. Process. Lett. **97**(5), 181–185 (2006)
15. Zhu, H., et al.: Bilinear graph neural network with neighbor interactions. In: IJCAI, pp. 1452–1458 (2020)
16. Koren, Y., Bell, R., Volinsky, C.: Matrix factorization techniques for recommender systems. Computer **42**(8), 30–37 (2009)
17. Sedhain, S., Menon, A., Sanner, S., Xie, L.: AutoRec: autoencoders meet collaborative filtering. In: ICWWW, pp. 111–112 (2015)

Spatial and Spatio-Temporal Databases

Velocity-Dependent Nearest Neighbor Query

Xue Miao[1], Xi Guo[1,2], Xiaochun Yang[3], Lijia Yang[1], Zhaoshun Wang[1(✉)], and Aziguli Wulamu[1,2(✉)]

[1] School of Computer and Communication Engineering,
University of Science and Technology Beijing, Beijing 100083, China
miaoxue@xs.ustb.edu.cn, xiguo@ustb.edu.cn, zhswang@sohu.com
[2] Beijing Key Laboratory of Knowledge Engineering for Materials Science,
University of Science and Technology Beijing, Beijing 100083, China
[3] School of Computer Science and Technology, Beijing Institute of Technology,
Beijing 100081, China

Abstract. Location-based services recommend points of interests (POIs) which are nearer to the user's position q. In practice, when the user is moving with a velocity $\overrightarrow{v}$, he may prefer the nearer POIs which match his moving direction. In this paper, we propose the *velocity-dependent nearest neighbor query* (VeloNN query), which selects the POIs that are nearer and best match the user's moving direction. In the VeloNN query, if the direction of a POI o highly matches the direction of $\overrightarrow{v}$, o is likely to be preferred. Since computing the directional preferences of all POIs is time-consuming, we propose rules to filter out the POIs with low directional preferences. We also divide the space into tiles, i.e., rectangular areas, and compute a candidate set for each tile in advance. The VeloNN candidates can be quickly prepared after finding the tile where the user is. We conduct experiments on both synthetic and real datasets and the results show the proposed algorithms can support VeloNN queries efficiently.

Keywords: Spatial database · Direction-aware · Nearest neighbor query · Von Mises distribution

1 Introduction

In spatial databases, the traditional nearest neighbor queries (NN queries) find the point of interest (POI) with the minimum distance to the user's position q. As Fig. 1(a) shows, the result of the NN query is o_i since it is the closest one to q. However, in real applications, users often issue queries when they are moving. They may prefer the POIs that are closer and more consistent with their moving directions. In this paper, we propose the *velocity-dependent nearest neighbor query* (*VeloNN query*), which finds nearer POIs which are in consistent with the user's moving direction. As Fig. 1(b) shows, the result of the VeloNN query is o_j which is nearer and also close to the user's moving direction.

© Springer Nature Switzerland AG 2021
L. H. U et al. (Eds.): APWeb-WAIM 2021, LNCS 12859, pp. 351–367, 2021.
https://doi.org/10.1007/978-3-030-85899-5_26

Our assumption is a user likes his moving direction better if he moves at a greater speed. To model a user's preference on directions, we consider both the speed and the direction of his velocity $\vec{v}$. An extreme case is he likes every direction equally if he stands still. We employ the Von Mises distribution [1] to quantify this assumption. The Von Mises distribution is a special normal distribution with the support $(-180°, 180°]$ and the mean value $0°$. We use the support to indicate all directions around the user, use the mean value to indicate the direction of $\vec{v}$, and use a more concentrated distribution if the speed is greater. According to this distribution, we can compute each POI's probability of being liked directionally. The VeloNN query aims at finding nearer POIs whose probabilities are higher than a preference threshold τ.

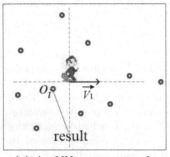

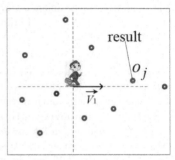

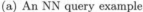

(a) An NN query example   (b) A VeloNN query example

Fig. 1. An NN query versus a VeloNN query

To answer a VeloNN query, a baseline algorithm is to compute POIs' probabilities one by one in the ascending order of their distances and return the ones who have satisfactory probabilities. However, this algorithm is slow due to the sorting. Since in spatial databases, POIs are often indexed by R-Tree, we propose an R-Tree-based algorithm, which runs faster than the baseline algorithm. Observing properties of the Von Mises distribution, we derive a pruning strategy to reduce the search space and also derive conditions to terminate earlier.

In addition, we find that the VeloNN query results change little if the query positions are limited to a small area. It means that we can pre-compute the candidates for small areas and identify the results among candidates. So we propose two tile-based algorithms which divide the whole space into many tiles and compute the candidates for each tile beforehand. When the user issues a query, we first find the tile where the user locates, and then identify the results from the candidates the tile holds. The tile-based algorithms can answer VeloNN queries faster than the R-Tree-based algorithm for the candidate set is quite small. One of the tile-based algorithms, i.e., the adaptive tile-based algorithm can guarantee that the number of candidates for each tile is at most K.

2   Velocity-Dependent Nearest Neighbors

We define velocity-dependent nearest neighbors in the two-dimensional Euclidean space $\mathbb{R}^2$. Let the user q and POIs $\mathcal{O} = \{o_1, o_2, \ldots, o_n\}$ be points in $\mathbb{R}^2$. The *velocity* $\overrightarrow{v}$ is a vector starting from q, which indicates both the user's speed $\|\overrightarrow{v}\|$ and his moving direction. Taking his moving direction as a reference direction, we define the *direction* of a POI o_i as the included angle ω_i between $\overrightarrow{qo_i}$ and $\overrightarrow{v}$. For example, in Fig. 2(a), The direction of o_3 is $\omega_3 = 112°$, while the direction of o_6 is $\omega_6 = -27°$.

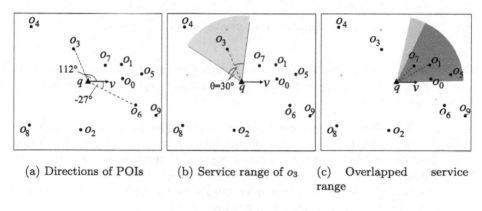

(a) Directions of POIs   (b) Service range of o_3 (c)   Overlapped   service range

Fig. 2. A toy example

According to the directions of POIs, we define the directional *service ranges* and *occupied ranges* of POIs.

Definition 1. Service Range. *The service range of a POI o_i is the angular range $serv_i = (\omega_i - \theta, \omega_i + \theta)$.*

The service range of o_3 is shown in Fig. 2(b) when $\theta = 30°$. In common sense, assuming the user prefers a direction ω^*, the user regards o_i is acceptable, if ω^* is in the service range of o_i. For instance, the user may roughly consider o_3 is directionally acceptable if he prefers a direction in o_3's service range. The service ranges of the POIs may overlap, for example, $serv_7$ and $serv_1$ overlap because $|\omega_7 - \omega_1| < 2\theta$. See the dark range in Fig. 2(c). Both o_7 and o_1 can serve this range. Comparing their distances to q, o_7 is better. Further, we define the *occupied range* of o_i.

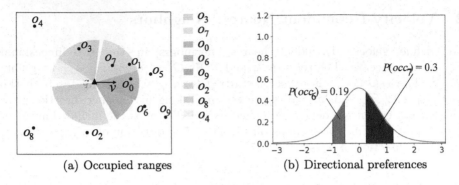

(a) Occupied ranges   (b) Directional preferences

Fig. 3. A toy example (Cont.)

Definition 2. *Occupied Range.* *The occupied range of o_i is an angular range $occ_i \in serv_i$. Comparing with the other POIs, whose service ranges include occ_i, o_i is the nearest one.*

Figure 3(a) shows the occupied ranges of the POIs in different colors. For example, the purple range indicates the occupied range occ_0 of o_0. It means that if the user prefers any direction in this range, o_0 is the nearest one. Specially, there are some vacant ranges because no POI can serve these directions. There are also some POIs who have no occupied ranges, for example, o_1 and o_5, because in their service ranges they are not the nearest ones.

Now we define the *directional preference* of the user, which is heavily dependent on the user's velocity $\vec{v}$. In common sense, the user may prefer the POIs that are in consistent with his moving direction. A larger moving speed $\|\vec{v}\|$ indicates the user likes this direction much. Specially, a zero speed indicates the user likes every direction in $[0°, 360°)$ equally. We model the distribution of the preference by using the Von Mises distribution [1]. The Von Mises distribution is similar to the normal distribution, except the support is $\omega \in (-180°, 180°]$. Its density function for ω is

$$f(\omega) = \frac{e^{\kappa \cos(\omega - \mu)}}{2\pi I_0(\kappa)}, \tag{1}$$

where μ is the mean value of the distribution, κ is the concentration parameter like σ in the normal distribution, and $I_0(\kappa)$ is the modified Bessel function with order zero. When κ is close to zero, the distribution is close to uniform. When κ is large, the distribution concentrates about μ. In this paper, μ is set to be $0°$ and κ is in proportion to $\|\vec{v}\|$ (i.e., $\kappa \propto \|\vec{v}\|$), since the larger the speed is, the more the user likes his moving direction.

Definition 3. *Directional Preference.* *The directional preference of o_i is the probability that the user prefers some direction in occ_i, i.e.,*

$$P(\omega \in [occ_i.s, occ_i.e]) = \int_{occ_i.s}^{occ_i.e} f(\omega)\, d\omega, \tag{2}$$

where $occ_i.s$ and $occ_i.e$ denote the starting and ending angle of occ_i.

In the following parts of this paper, $P(occ_i)$ is short for $P(\omega \in [occ_i.s, occ_i.e])$. Figure 3(b) shows the Von Mises distribution with $\kappa = 2$ and $\mu = 0°$, and the colored areas indicate the directional preference of o_6, i.e., $P(occ_6) = 0.19$, and the directional preference of o_7, i.e., $P(occ_7) = 0.3$, respectively. We select the POIs with high directional preferences, and we call such POIs *velocity-dependent nearest neighbors* (VeloNNs).

Definition 4. *VeloNN Given a threshold τ, if a POI o_i has a directional preference $P(occ_i)$ higher than τ, o_i is a VeloNN.*

For example, in Fig. 3(b), given $\tau = 0.2$, o_7 is a VeloNN, while o_6 is not a VeloNN. The *VeloNN query* aims at finding such VeloNNs.

Related Work. Traditional spatial queries only consider POIs' distances, such as kNN queries. However, the directions and distances are equally critical factors in location-based services. DESKS [2] retrieves POIs constrained by directions, distances and keywords. DCkNN query [3] recommends k POIs which are closest and constrained by directions, and it uses an index structure called MULTI to improve query efficiencies. Considering the distances and directions, RDBS query [4] searches a user who is seeing the POI as one of his direction-based surrounders [5]. Based on DESKS, [6] proposes optimization technology to deal with the situation where the results are lost because the user cannot fully describe the query. [7] uses a pie-shaped heat map to visualize the multiple views of the POIs set. The heat map can be widely used in decision-making applications where the tasks are directionally sensitive. Studies [8,9] search for POIs scattered around and close enough to the user. [10,11] study direction aware kNN queries in road network. Additionally, [12] proposes k-aggregate nearest neighbor query method of mobile objects in road network and designs a kANN query algorithm to answer the query. [13] presents a location privacy preserving nearest neighbor query in road network environment and proposes a local index mechanism to help solve the query. [14] studies the nearest neighbor query of line segment group in obstacle environment. Based on [14,15] studies the problem of group visible nearest surrounder query in obstacle space, and proposes the hybrid index structure to speed up the query. Our VeloNN query is the first work that considers the user's velocity to recommend POIs.

2.1   Baseline Algorithm

To answer a VeloNN query, we check o_i's in the ascending order of their distances, and identify the VeloNNs with $P(occ_i) > \tau$. The algorithm terminates when all POIs have been checked, or the union of occupied ranges of the present results can cover $(-180°, 180°]$.

Algorithm 1: Baseline Algorithm

---

    input : $\mathcal{O}, q, \theta, \tau, \overrightarrow{v}, \kappa$.
    output: The results R.
1 $\mathcal{O} \leftarrow \mathsf{SortPOI}(\mathcal{O}, q)$;
2 $Occ \leftarrow \emptyset$;
3 **for** $i \leftarrow 0$ **to** $n - 1$ **do**
4 $\omega_i \leftarrow \mathsf{GetDir}(o_i, \overrightarrow{v})$;
5 $serv_i \leftarrow (\omega_i - \theta, \omega_i + \theta)$;
6 $occ_i \leftarrow serv_i - Occ \cap serv_i$;
7   **if** $GetDirPref(occ_i, \overrightarrow{v}) > \tau$ **then**
8 $\big\lvert$ $R \leftarrow R \cup \{o_i\}$;
9 $Occ \leftarrow Occ \cup occ_i$;
10   **if** $Occ = (-180°, 180°]$ **then** **break** ;
11 **return** R;

As Algorithm 1 shows, first we sort all POIs (line 1) and initialize the total occupied range Occ as $\emptyset$ (line 2). Next, we use a **for** loop to check every o_i. In the loop, we compute o_i's direction (line 4), find its service range $serv_i$ (line 5), and further find its occupied range occ_i (line 6). Note that it cannot occupy the ranges which have been covered by the POIs nearer than it, i.e., the POIs that have been checked. Line 7 employs the Von Mises distribution to compute its directional preference. If the preference is larger than τ, it is a VeloNN (line 8). At last, we update Occ by adding occ_i (line 9). If Occ covers the whole range, the algorithm terminates (line 10), since farther POIs cannot have occupied ranges and they cannot be VeloNNs. The time complexity is $O(n \log n + mn)$ where n is the number of POIs and m is the number of VeloNNs found.

3   R-Tree Based Algorithm

In spatial databases, POIs are commonly organized by an R-Tree structure. To improve the baseline algorithm, we propose an R-Tree based algorithm. We check MBRs and POIs in the order of their distances. We maintain a priority queue to retrieve the R-Tree in the depth first order. In the priority queue, the distance of each element (a POI or an MBR) acts as the key. Each time we pop and check the top element with the minimum key. If it is a VeloNN, we add it into the result set and update the total occupied range Occ. If it is an MBR, we push its *useful* child mbr_i into the priority queue.

Here *useful* means (1) mbr_i contains VeloNN candidates or (2) mbr_i contains POIs that may influence the occupied ranges of the candidates, in spite of they are not VeloNNs in themselves. The algorithm terminates when all VeloNNs are found.

3.1   Useful MBRs

First, we discuss how to determine whether mbr_i contains no VeloNN. It means that in mbr_i no point has a directional preference which is larger than τ. Let

$[\omega_i^\perp, \omega_i^\top]$ denote the direction range of POIs in mbr_i. For example, in Fig. 4, the direction range of mbr_1 is $[\omega_1^\perp, \omega_1^\top]$. We have the following theorem.

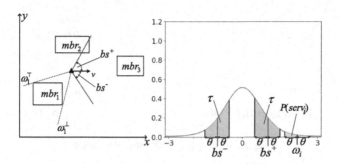

Fig. 4. An example to illustrate Theorem 1

Theorem 1. *The mbr_i must contain no VeloNN, if*

$$[\omega_i^\perp, \omega_i^\top] \cap (bs^-, bs^+) = \emptyset, \tag{3}$$

where bs^- and bs^+ are boundary directions satisfying

$$P(\omega \in (bs^{-(+)} - \theta, bs^{-(+)} + \theta)) = \tau. \tag{4}$$

As Fig. 4 shows, two blue areas illustrate the preferences $P(\omega \in (bs^- - \theta, bs^- + \theta))$ and $P(\omega \in (bs^+ - \theta, bs^+ + \theta))$, respectively. Both of them equal to τ. The yellow area illustrates $P(serv_i) < \tau$, which is the upper bound of the preference of o_i. We can see that if a POI's direction falls out of (bs^-, bs^+), the preference should be lower than τ. For simple, we use Φ_1 to denote (bs^-, bs^+). The POIs whose direction falls into Φ_1 are VeloNN candidates. According to the theorem, mbr_1 in the left of Fig. 4 contains no VeloNN, since its direction range does not overlap Φ_1. On the contrary, mbr_2 and mbr_3 overlap Φ_1 and they contain VeloNN candidates.

Next, we discuss how to determine whether mbr_i contains POIs that may influence the occupied ranges of VeloNN candidates. We call such POIs *influential POIs*. For example, in Fig. 5(a), mbr_1 falls outside of Φ_1, however, it contains o_m, which is nearer than the VeloNN candidate o_n and its service range having intersections with o_n's service range. Thus, o_n's occupied range should exclude these intersections. Here, o_m can influence the occupied range of a VeloNN candidate (i.e., o_n), it is an influential POI. We have the following theorem to identify the MBRs who may contain influential POIs.

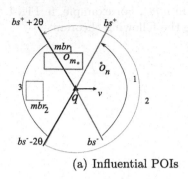
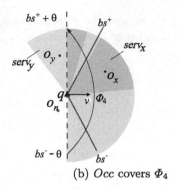

(a) Influential POIs   (b) *Occ* covers Φ_4

Fig. 5. Examples of Φ_1, Φ_2, Φ_3 and Φ_4

Theorem 2. *The mbr_i may contain influential POIs, if*

$$[\omega_i^\perp, \omega_i^\top] \cap (bs^- - 2\theta, bs^+ + 2\theta) \neq \emptyset. \tag{5}$$

For simple, we denote the angular range $(bs^- - 2\theta, bs^+ + 2\theta)$ as Φ_2 and denote $[-180°, 180°) - \Phi_2$ as Φ_3, as Fig. 5(a) shows. Further, we have the following theorem.

Theorem 3. *The mbr_i should be pruned, if*

$$[\omega_i^\perp, \omega_i^\top] \subseteq \Phi_3. \tag{6}$$

It means that an mbr_i satisfying

$$mbr_i \cap \Phi_2 \neq \emptyset \tag{7}$$

is useful and should be pushed into the priority queue.

   At last, we discuss when the algorithm terminates. All VeloNNs are found when either of the two conditions is met. The two conditions are (1) there is no element in the priority queue and (2) the total occupied range Occ has covered $\Phi_4 = (bs^- - \theta, bs^+ + \theta)$. As Fig. 5(b) shows, the current Occ covers Φ_4. On the one hand, assuming o_x's service range $serv_x \subseteq \Phi_4$, it is not a VeloNN for its occupied range is $\emptyset$. On the other hand, assuming o_y's service range is $serv_y \nsubseteq \Phi_4$, o_y is not a VeloNN for the preference $P(occ_y) < \tau$. Thus, we cannot find more VeloNNs in the future if condition (2) is satisfied.

3.2   Search Algorithm

We summarize the R-Tree based algorithm in Algorithm 2. First, we compute the bounds (bs^-, bs^+) (line 1), initialize the total occupied range Occ (line 2), and push the root node of R-Tree into the priority queue (line 3). Next, we pop and process the top element of the queue until the termination condition is satisfied (line 4). On the one hand, when the top element is a POI (line 6), we

---

Algorithm 2: R-TreeBasedAlgorithm

input : $tree$, q, θ, τ, $\overrightarrow{v}$, κ.
output: The result set R.

1   $(bs^-, bs^+) \leftarrow$ GetBounds$(\kappa, \tau, \theta, \overrightarrow{v})$;
2   $Occ \leftarrow \emptyset$;
3   Push $e(tree.root, 0)$ into the priority queue que;
4   **while** $que \neq \emptyset \wedge \Phi_4 \not\subseteq Occ$ **do**
5   Pop and get top of que;
6   **if** top is a POI **then**
7         $occ_{top} \leftarrow serv_{top} - Occ \cap serv_{top}$;
8   **if** GetDirPref$(occ_{top}, \overrightarrow{v}) > \tau$ **then**
9            $R \leftarrow R \cup \{top\}$;
10        $Occ \leftarrow Occ \cup occ_{top}$;
11   **else**
12   **foreach** $child$ c_t of top **do**
13   **if** $[\omega_t^\perp, \omega_t^\top] \cap \Phi_2 \neq \emptyset$ **then**
14   Push c_t into que;

15 **return** R;

---

compute its service range $serv_{top}$ and its occupied range occ_{top} (line 7). If the preference of top is larger than τ, we add it into the result set R (line 8 and line 9). Then we update the current Occ by adding occ_{top} (line 10). On the other hand, when the top element is a tree node, we check its child one by one (line 12). According to Theorem 3, we can determine whether the child is useful (line 13). If the child is useful, we push it into the queue (line 14). At last, we obtain all VeloNNs (line 15). This algorithm runs faster than the baseline algorithm, because (1) we can identify useless POIs in groups and prune them immediately (line 13) and (2) we can confirm all VeloNNs are found once the termination conditions are met (line 4).

4 Tile-Based Algorithms

Observing that VeloNNs change little when the user moves in a small area, we propose the following tile-based algorithms. In the preprocessing step, we cut the whole space into small rectangular areas, i.e., tiles. For each tile T_i, we find and store candidates $Candid_i$ from which we can further identify VeloNNs. To answer a VeloNN query, we find the tile T_q where the user q locates, then we identify the real results among $Candid_q$ considering the user's velocity $\overrightarrow{v}$. Such query runs faster than the R-Tree-based query, since we only search for results from a very small set $Candid_q$, at the expense of finding and storing the candidates beforehand.

    For a query point q, the candidates are the POIs that having occupied ranges. For a small area T_i, the candidates are the POIs that may have occupied ranges w.r.t. a point in T_i. Such candidates for T_i can be found by using the range-DNN algorithm in [9]. To save space, we will not introduce this algorithm. Next, we will introduce two ways of making tiles and the query algorithms based on the two kinds of tiles.

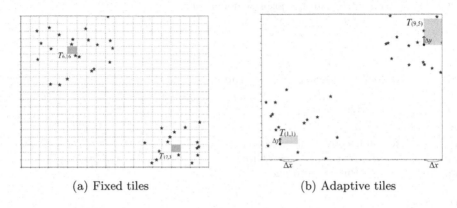

(a) Fixed tiles   (b) Adaptive tiles

Fig. 6. Two types of tiles

Queries on Fixed Tiles. A straightforward way of making tiles is to divide the whole plane $\mathbb{R}^2$ into a $M \times N$ grid. In the grid, each cell is a tile $T_{i,j}$ and we compute candidates for $T_{i,j}$. As Fig. 6(a) shows, we divide $\mathbb{R}^2$ into a 20×20 grid. For example, the blue stars around $T_{6,16}$ and $T_{17,3}$ are the candidates for them. We find and store the candidates for each tile beforehand. When a user issues a query, firstly we find the tile $T_{i,j}$ where the user is, secondly we select the real results from the candidates for $T_{i,j}$ using Algorithm 1. Since the tiles are fixed for different POI sets, we call this method *fixed tiles based algorithm*. The disadvantage of this method is we cannot control the number of candidates per tile. The query will be slow if users locate at "rich" tiles who own too many candidates.

4.1   Queries on Adaptive Tiles

To control the number of candidates per tile, we propose the adaptive tiles structure. The adaptive tiles are incrementally generated from seeds. As Fig. 6(b) shows, let $[X_{min}, Y_{min}, X_{max}, Y_{max}]$ denote the entire space $\mathbb{R}^2$. At the beginning, we randomly generate initial seed points $T^0_{(i,0)}(X_{min} + i * \Delta x, Y_{min})(i = 0, 1, \ldots, n - 1)$ where $\Delta x = (X_{max} - X_{min})/n$ and n is a specified positive integer. For each initial seed $T^0_{(i,0)}$, we gradually expand $T^0_{(i,0)}$ to larger rectangles $T^1_{(i,0)}$, $T^2_{(i,0)}$, $\ldots$, $T^j_{(i,0)}$ by enlarging height Δ_y. The superscript j denotes the times of enlargements. The enlargement terminates once the number of candidates exceeds K and $T^j_{(i,0)}$ becomes a tile. After generating $T^j_{(i,0)}$, we generate the next tile. We choose $T^0_{(i,1)}(X_{min} + i*\Delta x, Y_{min} + j*\Delta y)$ to be the next seed, and gradually enlarge $T^0_{(i,1)}$ until the number of candidates reaches K. Figure 6(b) shows an example of such tile and its candidates (i.e., the blue stars). In this way, we make tiles one by one until all tiles cover the whole space $\mathbb{R}^2$. To locate users fast when queries are issued, we organize the tiles by using an R-Tree.

Algorithm 3: Generate Adaptive Tiles

Input: K, $\mathcal{O}$, θ, $X_{min}, X_{max}, Y_{min}, Y_{max}, n$
Output: *rtree*

1   $\Delta x \leftarrow (X_{max} - X_{min})/n$;
2   $T_{(i,j)} \leftarrow (X_{min} + i*\Delta x, Y_{min})$;
3   **for** $i : 0 \rightarrow n-1$ **do**
4      $j \leftarrow 0$;
5   **while** $T_{(i,j)}.y \neq Y_{max}$ **do**
6         $T_{(i,j)}.candid \leftarrow$ **GetCandid**$(T_{(i,j)}, \Delta x, \theta, \mathcal{O})$;
7   **while** $|T_{(i,j)}.candid| < K$ **do**
8            $T_{(i,j)}.y+ = \Delta y$;
9            $T_{(i,j)}.candid \leftarrow$ **GetCandid**$(T_{(i,j)}, \Delta x, \theta, \mathcal{O})$;
10   Insert $T_{(i,j)}$ into *rtree*;
11       $j+ = 1$;
12       $T_{(i,j+1)} \leftarrow (X_{min} + i*\Delta x, T_{(i,j)}.y)$;

13 **return** *rtree*;

Algorithm 3 summarizes the procedure of generating tiles. Line 1 to line 2 calculate n initial seeds $T_{(i,j)}(X_{min} + i*\Delta x, Y_{min})(i = 0, 1, \ldots, n-1)$. For each initial seed $T_{(i,j)}$, we execute the **while** loop. When $T_{(i,j)}.y \neq Y_{max}$, we calculate its candidates using the algorithm in [9] (line 6). The inner **while** loop enlarges the current tile $T_{(i,j)}$ until the number of its candidates reaches K (line 7 to line 9). After the inner loop, the tile $T_{(i,j)}$ is ready and we insert it into the index *rtree* (line 10). Next, we obtain the next seed $T_{(i,j+1)}$ (line 12) and repeat the above process until the whole space is completely covered. This algorithm generates tiles which are adaptive to the distribution of POIs. The adaptive-tiles structure is better than the fixed-tiles structure because we can control the number of candidates per tile by using the parameter K.

To answer a VeloNN query, we find a tile T_q where the user q is by retrieving *rtree*, and then we identify the real results among the candidates of T_q by employing Algorithm 1. Using the adaptive-tiles R-Tree, we can answer the queries faster since the number of candidates is guaranteed to be at most K. The price is the storage space taken by the structure and the time consumed by generating and organizing the adaptive tiles.

5   Experiment

Experimental Environments. We implemented the proposed algorithms using Java and ran the programs on a PC with an Intel(R) Core(TM) i5-8300H CPU(2.30 GHz), 8 GB Memories and a Windows 10 operating system.

Datasets. We used three real datasets that contain 163031, 18549 and 9244 POIs of Shanghai, Kunshan and Changshu. We name them D_{sh}, D_{ks}, and D_{cs}, respectively. We also made three synthetic datasets that contain 10^3, 10^4, and 10^5 random points. We name them D_{1k}, D_{10k}, and D_{100k}, respectively.

We ran the baseline algorithm (named as baseline), the R-Tree-based algorithm (named as rtree), the fixed-tiles based algorithm (named as fixed), and the adaptive-tiles based algorithm (named as adaptive) on these real and synthetic datasets. Next, we will report the query performances of the four algorithms and the efficiencies of constructing tile-based structures.

5.1   Query Performances

Figure 7 shows the query time consumed by using baseline, rtree, fixed, and adaptive on both real and synthetic datasets. The baseline consumes much more time than the other three algorithms. Its query time has a dramatic increase when the dataset becomes large, because the time complexity of baseline is $O(n \log n + mn)$ where n is the dataset size. The rtree consumes less time than the baseline due to its pruning strategy and early termination conditions. However, the rtree consumes more time than fixed and adaptive, because the last two algorithms retrieve results from a candidate set which is far smaller than the full POI set. The adaptive is faster than fixed since it can guarantee a small candidate set.

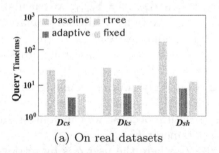
(a) On real datasets

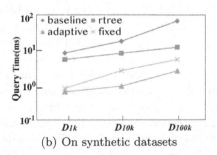
(b) On synthetic datasets

Fig. 7. Query time w.r.t. different datasets ($\kappa = 2, \theta = 25°, \tau = 0.25$)

Figure 8 shows the time consumed when the parameter θ is 15°, 25°, and 35°. Although θ varies, the baseline runs slowest, while fixed and adaptive run fastest. For baseline and rtree, when θ increases, the occupied ranges are easier to cover the angular range $(-180°, 180°]$, which makes the number of POIs checked less, so the query time will be less. Similarly, for fixed or adaptive, the larger the θ is, the fewer candidates each tile has, and the less time it takes to find the VeloNNs. Therefore, the four algorithms consume less time when θ becomes larger.

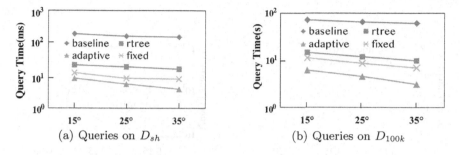

(a) Queries on D_{sh} (b) Queries on D_{100k}

Fig. 8. Query time w.r.t. different θ's ($\kappa = 2, \tau = 0.15$)

Figure 9 shows the time consumed when κ (i.e., the concentration parameter in Von Mises distribution) is 1, 2, and 8. When κ is bigger, the distribution concentrates more on $0°$. The adaptive and fixed run faster than baseline and rtree when κ varies. As the Algorithm 1 shows, when κ increases, the number of POIs satisfying the directional preference decreases, which makes the union of the occupied ranges have been found can not completely cover $(-180°, 180°]$, so it needs to check all POIs before the program stops, so the query time will be more. Therefore, in Fig. 9, when κ increases, the query time of baseline increases. However, the time of rtree decreases because bs^+ and bs^- will be closer to $0°$ and more tree nodes can be pruned. The time of fixed and the time of adaptive are not influenced by κ because they are tile-based methods which calculate candidates in advance.

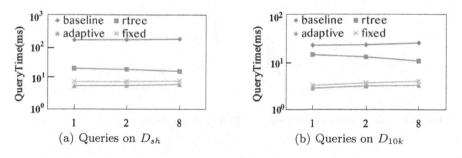

(a) Queries on D_{sh} (b) Queries on D_{10k}

Fig. 9. Query time w.r.t. different κ's ($\theta = 25°, \tau = 0.25$)

Figure 10 shows the time consumed when τ is 0.15, 0.25, and 0.35. When the preference threshold τ varies, the baseline still runs slowest, the rtree is in the medium, and the tile-based algorithms run fastest. When τ changes, the curve of baseline is smooth, because it is not affected by τ. The rtree takes less time because when τ becomes larger, bs^+ and bs^- go towards $0°$ and more nodes can be pruned. The tile-based algorithms, i.e., adaptive and fixed, are not influenced by τ.

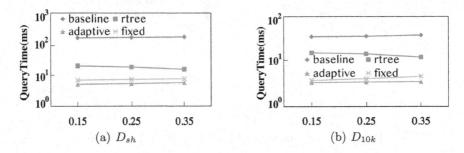

(a) D_{sh} (b) D_{10k}

Fig. 10. Query time w.r.t. different τ's ($\kappa = 2, \theta = 15°$)

5.2   Efficiencies of Tile-Based Structures

In this section, we evaluate the performances of the tile-based structures on both real and synthetic datasets, and we analyze the experimental results. In the experiments, fixed(len) means to set the side length of the tile to len in fixed-tile based algorithm and adaptive(K) means the candidates number of each tile does not exceed K in adaptive-tile based algorithm.

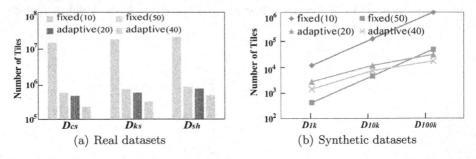

(a) Real datasets   (b) Synthetic datasets

Fig. 11. The number of tiles w.r.t. different datasets ($\kappa = 2, \theta = 30°, \tau = 0.35$)

Figure 11 shows the number of tiles generated by our two tile-based algorithms, i.e., fixed and adaptive, when the dataset changes. Figure 11 shows when the dataset increases, the number of the tiles generated by the two algorithms both increases. In fixed, a larger len means a smaller number of tiles, and in adaptive, a larger K means a smaller number of tiles too.

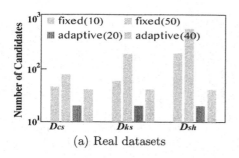
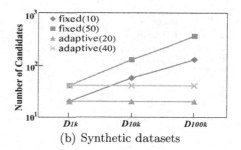

(a) Real datasets

(b) Synthetic datasets

Fig. 12. Average number of candidates per tile w.r.t. different datasets ($\kappa = 2, \theta = 30°, \tau = 0.35$)

Figure 12 shows the average number of candidates per tile when the dataset changes. In fixed, the average number is larger for bigger datasets, and it is also larger for bigger *len*. Because a larger *len* leads to a larger tile, which makes more candidates per tile. In adaptive, the average number is not influenced by the dataset size, and it is influenced by K. Therefore, the average number is stable in adaptive when dataset varies.

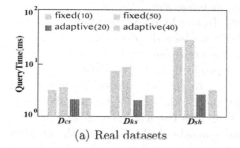
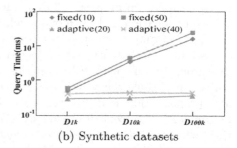

(a) Real datasets

(b) Synthetic datasets

Fig. 13. Query time w.r.t. different datasets ($\kappa = 2, \theta = 30°, \tau = 0.35$)

Figure 13 shows the time consumed by fixed when *len* is 10 and 50, and the time consumed by adaptive when K is 20 and 40. When the dataset changes, the time consumed by adaptive does not change significantly, because the efficiency of adaptive depends on K and does not depend on the dataset size. However, the efficiency of fixed is influenced by the dataset size, because a larger dataset size will lead to more candidates per tile.

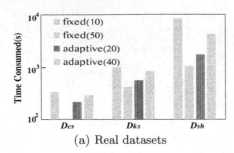
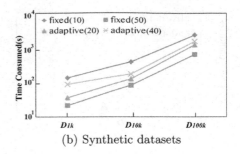

(a) Real datasets   (b) Synthetic datasets

Fig. 14. Performances of building tile-based structures ($\kappa = 2, \theta = 30°, \tau = 0.35$)

Figure 14 shows the time consumption of building the tile-based structures on different datasets. We have to spend more time on larger datasets. The fixed(10) spends more time than the fixed(50), because it should build more tiles. The adaptive(40) spends more time than the adaptive(20), because it takes more time to build per tile.

6   Conclusions

In this paper, we propose VeloNN query to recommend the POIs considering the user's location and his moving velocity. In the VeloNN query, we model the user's directional preferences by using the Von Mises distribution, where a POI o has a high probability to be selected if it is consistent with the user's moving direction. To answer VeloNN queries, we propose an R-Tree-based algorithm which can reduce the search space according to the boundaries directions. We also propose tile-based structures to store the candidates for rectangular areas beforehand. The fixed tile-based structure divides the whole space into $M \times N$ tiles, while the adaptive tile-based structure consists of tiles in which the number of candidates does not exceed K. We conduct experiments on real and synthetic datasets to evaluate the performances of these proposed algorithms.

Acknowledgments. This work is supported by the National Natural Science Foundation of China (No. 61602031), the Fundamental Research Funds for the Central Universities (No. FRF-BD-19-012A, No. FRF-IDRY-19-023), and the National Key Research and Development Program of China (No. 2017YFB0202303).

References

1. Jammalamadaka, S.R., SenGupta, A.: Circular Probability Distributions (chap. 2), pp. 44–45 (2001)
2. Guoliang, L., Jianhua, F., et al.: DESKS: direction-aware spatial keyword search. In: IEEE 28th International Conference on Data Engineering, pp. 474–485 (2012)
3. Min Joong, L., Dong Wan, C., et al.: The direction-constrained k nearest neighbor query. GeoInformatica **20**(3), 471–502 (2016). https://doi.org/10.1007/s10707-016-0245-2

4. Guo, X., Ishikawa, Y., Xie, Y., Wulamu, A.: Reverse direction-based surrounder queries for mobile recommendations. World Wide Web **20**(5), 885–913 (2016). https://doi.org/10.1007/s11280-016-0422-0
5. Xi, G., Zheng, B., Ishikawa, Y., et al.: Direction-based surrounder queries for mobile recommendations. VLDB J. **20**(4), 743–766 (2011). https://doi.org/10.1007/s00778-011-0241-y
6. Lei, C., Yafei, L., et al.: Towards why-not spatial keyword top-k queries: a direction-aware approach. IEEE Trans. Knowl. Data Eng. **30**(4), 796–809 (2018)
7. Guo, X., Yu, J.X., Li, R.-H., Miao, X.: Direction-based multiple views on data. World Wide Web **22**(1), 185–219 (2018). https://doi.org/10.1007/s11280-018-0557-2
8. Shen, B., Islam, M.S., Taniar, D., Wang, J.: Direction-based spatial skyline for retrieving surrounding objects. World Wide Web **23**(1), 207–239 (2019). https://doi.org/10.1007/s11280-019-00694-w
9. Xi, G., Xiaochun, Y.: Direction-aware nearest neighbor query. IEEE Access **7**, 30285–30301 (2019)
10. Tianyang, D., Lulu, Y., Qiang, C., Bin, C., Jing, F.: Direction-aware KNN queries for moving objects in a road network. World Wide Web **22**(4), 1765–1797 (2019). https://doi.org/10.1007/s11280-019-00657-1
11. Guozhu, D., Qingyun, Y., et al.: Direction-aware continuous moving K-nearest-neighbor query in road networks. Int. J. Geo-Inf. **8**(9), 379–400 (2019)
12. Wen, C.: K-aggregate nearest neighbor query method of moving objects in road networks. Int. J. Database Theory Appl. **9**(4), 151–160 (2016)
13. Weiwci, N., Lingqi, L., et al.: Voronoi-R*-based privacy-preserving k nearest neighbor query over road networks. J. Softw. **30**(12), 3782–3797 (2019)
14. Yingying, G., Liping, Z., et al.: Group nearest neighbor query method of line segment in obstacle space. Comput. Sci. **045**(006), 172–175 (2018)
15. Haoran, Z., Dongpu, S., et al.: Group visible nearest surrounder query in obstacle space. Access IEEE **8**, 50659–50673 (2020)

Finding Geo-Social Cohorts in Location-Based Social Networks

Muhammad Aamir Saleem[1(✉)], Toon Calders[2], Torben Bach Pedersen[1], and Panagiotis Karras[3]

[1] Aalborg University, Aalborg, Denmark
maas@cs.aau.dk
[2] University of Antwerp, Antwerp, Belgium
[3] Aarhus University, Aarhus, Denmark

Abstract. Given a record of geo-tagged activities, how can we suggest groups, or *cohorts* of likely companions? A brute-force approach is to perform a spatio-temporal join over past activity traces to find groups of users recorded as moving together; yet such an approach is inherently unscalable. In this paper, we propose that we can identify and predict such cohorts by leveraging information on social ties along with past geo-tagged activities, i.e., geo-social information. In particular, we find groups of users that (i) form cliques of friendships and (ii) maximize a function of common *pairwise* activities on record among their members. We show that finding such groups is an **NP**-hard problem, and propose a nontrivial algorithm, COVER, which works as if it were enumerating maximal social cliques, but guides its exploration by a pruning-intensive activity driven criterion in place of a clique maximality condition. Our experimental study with real world data demonstrates that COVER outperforms a brute-force baseline in terms of efficiency and surpasses an adaptation of previous work in terms of prediction accuracy regarding groups of companions, including groups that do not appear in the training set, thanks to its use of a social clique constraint.

1 Introduction

Advances in positioning and communication technologies enable sharing geo-tagged content, and hence location-based social networking services. Location-Based Social Networks (LBSNs) such as Weeplaces, Foursquare, Gowalla, GeoLife, and Twinkle are built around positioning capabilities, while Facebook and vKontakte provide a consensual *option* to check-in at visited locations.

Such online LBSNs can utilize user mobility in consensual recommendation services directed to *groups*, as opposed to individuals. For instance, a discount offer for a concert may be recommended to a group of friends that have habitually visited similar concerts and other events together; a car-pooling service may suggest group formations to its customers who may be unaware of their similar activities; or a travel agency may promote an offer for a group travel package to groups of users potentially interested in traveling together. Past research has

© Springer Nature Switzerland AG 2021
L. H. U et al. (Eds.): APWeb-WAIM 2021, LNCS 12859, pp. 368–383, 2021.
https://doi.org/10.1007/978-3-030-85899-5_27

proposed location-based recommendations of locations, routes, users, activities, and media [4]; while some works refer to individual predictions [15], others detect groups based on location histories and mobility profiles [10]. Yet these studies rely on clustering trajectories and co location traces [22] and Bayesian learning so as to predict co-location features [11], hence do not scale well. Further, there has been work on clustering *static locations* using geo-social information [18], and a long line of works on detecting communities of interest [6,7,13] Yet to our knowledge, no attempt has been made to suggest groups *of users* using *both social and mobility data*, i.e., geo-social information.

In this paper, we propose a method that suggests *cohorts* of social companions *without* clustering trajectories or traces; instead, it leverages *social* and *co-location* connections, which LBSNs record. We conjecture that recommendable groups of companions are prone to be directly or transitively connected in both the *social domain*—i.e., to form *cliques* in a graph of social ties—and the *activity domain*—i.e., to engage in *common geo-tagged activities* manifested as frequent pairwise location check-ins. Our rationale is that each person may have a large circle of friends and acquaintances, yet may engage in specific activities only with particular ones, with whom they share related interests. For instance, consider a socially linked group of people who have visited museums, at least in pairs; our method can detect such a cohort, so as to propose new interesting locations. We utilize location *categories* to tailor cohorts to particular interests, and test the power of our method to predict cohorts on real world data.

We build a graph G_A from geo-tagged activities, *distinct* from a graph of social ties, G, yet defined over the same vertex set; in G_A, a pair of nodes is connected by a weighted edge expressing the pairs' history of co-location in common activities. We reason that a group of tightly-connected users engaging in common activities frequently appear in G_A as a connected subgraph with high edge density, i.e., form a *quasi-clique* of high edge weight in G_A, and a *clique* in G. We formally define the problem as retrieving sets of nodes that induce subgraphs maximizing *edge density* in G_A and also induce *cliques* in G.

The rest of this paper is structured as follows. Section 2 discusses related work. In Sect. 3, we formulate the problem and study its hardness. Section 4 presents COVER, an efficient heuristic drawing from graph mining techniques to address the spatiotemporal cohort discovery challenge. Section 5 presents an extensive experimental study that showcases the effectiveness and predictive power of our technique. Section 6 concludes the paper.

2   Related Work

In our problem, groups are sought after and have no labels. That is different from *group recommendation*, in which we recommend items to a *given group* [1], and from *group discovery*, which retrieves labeled groups of users from collaborative rating data sets [19]. Our problem relates rather to the problems of finding *cliques*, dense subgraph discovery, and multi-layer community detection.

Tomita et al. [20] studied the worst-case complexity of enumerating maximal cliques on a graph. Such cliques can be used to define communities; for example, one may consider only maximal cliques of size above a threshold, and define communities as the disconnected components of the graph formed by the union of those cliques [8]. Alternatively, one may use cliques of fixed size, k; the *clique percolation* method [16] finds all such k-cliques in a network, and then finds clusters made out pairs of k-cliques sharing $k - 1$ nodes.

The *densest subgraph* problem asks for a vertex subset $S \subseteq V$ on graph $G(V, E)$ such that its induced subgraph achieves the maximum average degree; it is solvable in polynomial time with a maximum flow algorithm [9], while a greedy $\frac{1}{2}$-approximation scheme requires linear time [12]. Asahiro et al. [2] study the $k - f(k)$ dense subgraph problem, which calls for finding a k-vertex subgraph of a given graph G that has at least $f(k)$ edges, for different functions $f(k)$. When a restriction is imposed on the size of set S, the problem becomes **NP**-hard [12]. Recently, the problem has been studied in streaming and MapReduce models [3].

Boden et al. [5] mine *multi-layer coherent subgraphs*, i.e., subgraphs that contain vertices densely connected by edges with similar *labels* in a subset of layers in an edge-labeled multi-layer graph; this technique applies the same density criterion on multiple layers. We aim to apply *different density criteria* per layer: a clique constraint vs. quasi-clique optimality, a distinction consequential on predictive power—as we show, *if we relax the clique constraint, we lose predictive power*.

3   Problem Formulation

Let V be a set of LBSN users and $\mathcal{U}$ a universe of categories (i.e., types, based on function and audience) to which locations of interest are associated.

3.1   Preliminary Concepts

Definition 1. *A* point of interest *(POI) is a geographical location (e.g., the Metropolitan Museum of Art) represented by a quadruple (l, lat, lon, cat), where l is the identifier, lat and lon the latitude and longitude of the GPS coordinates of the center of the POI, and $cat \in \mathcal{U}$ a category that this location belongs to.*

Definition 2. *An* activity *refers to a visit of a user $u \in V$ at a location l at a discretized* time interval t, *represented as a triplet (u, l, t); when the user u is implied from context, we omit it and represent an activity by the pair (l, t).*

Definition 3. *The* activity set *of user u, $\mathcal{A}(u)$, is the set of activities user u has engaged in; likewise, the activity set for a category cat, $\mathcal{A}(cat)$, is the set of activities associated with category cat among users in V; last, $\mathcal{A}(u, cat)$ is the set of all activities by user u over POIs of category cat. We overload these notations to also denote ordered sequences of activities depending on context.*

Definition 4. *A* spatiotemporal join *operation among sets of activities S and T, $S \bowtie T$, returns the set of pairs of activities $\{(l, t) \in S, (l', t') \in T\}$, where locations and times match, i.e., $l = l'$ and $t = t'$. Furthermore, a* consecutive *spatiotemporal join is defined among two temporal sequences of activities $\mathcal{S}$ and $\mathcal{T}$, $\mathcal{S} \bowtie^c \mathcal{T}$, and returns the set of quadruples of activities $\{(l, t), (l_{suc}, t_{suc}) \in \mathcal{S}, (l', t'), (l'_{suc}, t'_{suc}) \in \mathcal{T}\}$, where (l_{suc}, t_{suc}) is the successor activity of (l, t) in sequence $\mathcal{S}$ and (l'_{suc}, t'_{suc}) the successor activity of (l', t') in sequence $\mathcal{T}$, such that locations and times match, i.e., $(l, t) = (l', t')$ and $(l_{suc}, t_{suc}) = (l'_{suc}, t'_{suc})$.*

The spatiotemporal join between $\mathcal{S}$ and $\mathcal{T}$ returns all pairs of activities occurring in $\mathcal{S}$ and $\mathcal{T}$, by the discretization we employ; a consecutive spatiotemporal join returns all *quadruples* of activities occurring, as two consecutive pairs, in sequences $\mathcal{S}$ and $\mathcal{T}$. We use these concepts to define weights in activity graph G_A.

3.2 Objective

Given a data set of users, their relationships, and records of activities, and a set of categories of interest, $\mathcal{L} \subset \mathcal{U}$, we are interested to identify any group of users $C \subset V$ that are likely to participate, as a group, in future activities related to $\mathcal{L}$.

We leverage (i) a *social graph* $G(V, E)$, where V is the set of users and E the set of friendship relationships; and (ii) an *activity graph* $G_A^{\mathcal{L}}(V, E')$, coterminous with (i.e., defined over the same set of vertices V as) G, built out of the log of user co-locations associated with $\mathcal{L}$; an edge $(u, v) \in E'$ between users $u, v \in V$ has a non-zero weight $w_{uv} \in (0, 1]$, representing the extent to which these two users participate in common activities associated with $\mathcal{L}$, by the following definition.

Definition 5. *The* edge weight *w_{uv} between the pair of users (u, v) in $G_A^{\mathcal{L}}$ is defined via the (consecutive) spatiotemporal join $\bigcup_{cat \in \mathcal{L}}\{\mathcal{A}(u, cat) \bowtie \mathcal{A}(v, cat)\}$, normalized by dividing by the highest value obtained among all pairs of users, as follows:*

$$w_{uv} = \frac{|\bigcup_{cat \in \mathcal{L}}\{\mathcal{A}(u, cat) \bowtie^{(c)} \mathcal{A}(v, cat)\}|}{max_{x,y \in V}|\bigcup_{cat \in \mathcal{L}}\{\mathcal{A}(x, cat) \bowtie^{(c)} \mathcal{A}(y, cat)\}|} \tag{1}$$

We aim to retrieve groups, or *cohorts*, of users that have a track record of pairwise common activities associated with $\mathcal{L}$, and also form a *clique* (i.e., are related to each other) in the social graph. Such cohorts are likely to act together, hence may be used for recommendation, prediction, and social analysis.

Problem 1. [COHORT RETRIEVAL] Given a set of LBSN users V, a set of categories $\mathcal{L}$, a social graph $G(V, E)$ among users in V, and an activity graph $G_A^{\mathcal{L}}(V, E')$ among users in V with edges in E' weighted according to activities in $\mathcal{L}$, and letting $\mathcal{C}$ denote the set of all *cliques* in the social graph G, where $\forall C \in \mathcal{C}, C \subseteq V$, find the top-k cliques in $\mathcal{C}$ in terms of an *activity density* function $f^{\mathcal{L}}$ calculated on the subgraphs they induce in $G_A^{\mathcal{L}}$, i.e., $arg\,max_{C \in \mathcal{C}}^k \{f^{\mathcal{L}}(C)\}$.

3.3 Maximizing Activity Density

Problem 1 requires an *activity density* function: (i) relying on *edge weights* of $G_A^{\mathcal{L}}$, and (ii) independent of subgraph (i.e., group) size, allowing for comparison among larger and smaller groups. A function that satisfies these properties is the *edge surplus* function f_α, maximized by an Optimal Quasi-Clique (OQC) [21]:

Definition 6. [OQC] *Given a graph* $G = (V, E)$ *and* $\alpha \in (0, 1)$, *an* optimal quasi-clique *of* G *is a subset of vertices* $S^* \subseteq V$ *such that:*

$$f_\alpha(S^*) = e[S^*] - \alpha\binom{|S^*|}{2} \geq f_\alpha(S), \text{ for all } S \subseteq V. \tag{2}$$

where $e[S]$ *is the number of edges in the subgraph of* G *induced by* S.

This *edge surplus* function provides a size-independent measure of edge density without favoring large subgraphs: a subgraph achieves a high value of edge surplus f_α *not merely* by means of a high average degree, as large subgraphs may have, but by coming close to completing a *clique* among its nodes. Besides, rather than imposing some arbitrary threshold on edge weights so as to obtain binary edges, it takes all weights in consideration, regardless of their values, and can be straightforwardly generalized to the weighted edges in an activity graph. We thus define our activity density function based on the edge surplus function:

Definition 7. *Given an activity graph* $G_A^{\mathcal{L}} = (V, E')$, *a vertex subset* $C \subseteq V$, *and a parameter* $\alpha \in (0, 1)$, *the* activity density *on* C *is:*

$$f_\alpha^{\mathcal{L}}(C) = w[C] - \alpha\binom{|C|}{2} \tag{3}$$

where $w[C]$ *is the sum of normalized edge weights for all edges in the subgraph induced by* C: $w[C] = \sum_{u,v \in C} w_{uv}$.

We aim to retrieve cohorts under the constraint of forming a clique in a social graph and the objective of maximizing edge surplus in the activity graph. To that end, it is useful to investigate the hardness of the problem of finding an OQC, which we henceforward name OQC. After all, in case our social graph is a complete graph, and all non-zero edge weights in the activity graph are equal to 1, then COHORT RETRIEVAL is reduced to OQC, hence it is at least as hard as OQC. Tsourakakis et al. [21] suspect OQC to be **NP**-hard, yet provide no formal proof of hardness. We provide such a proof in the following, starting out with some results regarding the nature of the OQC problem.

Lemma 1. *For* $\alpha \in (0, 1)$, *any clique in* $G = (V, E)$ *has positive edge surplus.*

Proof. By definition, the number of edges in a clique $S \subseteq V$ is $e[S] = \binom{|S|}{2}$. Then, the edge surplus of S is $f_\alpha(S) = e[S] - \alpha\binom{|S|}{2} = (1 - \alpha)\binom{|S|}{2} > 0$.

Lemma 2. *For any* $\alpha \in (0, 1)$, *a maximum clique of a graph* $G = (V, E)$ *has the maximum edge surplus among all cliques in* G.

Proof. By Lemma 1, the edge surplus of a clique $S \subseteq V$ is $f_\alpha(S) = (1-\alpha)\binom{|S|}{2} > 0$. A *maximum clique* achieves the maximum number of vertices $|S|$ among all cliques in G; therefore, it also has the maximum edge surplus.

Theorem 1. *Given a simple undirected graph* $G = (V, E)$, *for* $\alpha = 1 - \binom{|V|}{2}^{-1}$, *a subset of vertices* $S \subseteq V$ *has positive edge surplus if and only if it is a clique.*

Proof. The $\Leftarrow$ direction is provided by Lemma 1. We now prove the $\Rightarrow$ direction: The edge surplus of a subset of vertices $S \subseteq V$ is $f_\alpha(S) = e[S] - \alpha\binom{|S|}{2} = e[S] - (1 - \binom{n}{2}^{-1})\binom{|S|}{2} = e[S] - \binom{|S|}{2} + \frac{|S|(|S|-1)}{|V|(|V|-1)}$. If S has positive edge surplus, then $f_\alpha(S) > 0 \Leftrightarrow e[S] > \binom{|S|}{2} - \frac{|S|(|S|-1)}{|V|(|V|-1)}$. Since $S \subseteq V$, it follows that $\frac{|S|(|S|-1)}{|V|(|V|-1)} \leq 1$. Thus, $f_\alpha(S) > 0 \Rightarrow e[S] > \binom{|S|}{2} - 1$. Yet the only subgraph of $|S|$ vertices that has more than $\binom{|S|}{2} - 1$ edges is a clique.

Theorem 2. *Finding an OQC is* **NP***-hard.*

Proof. We construct our proof by reduction from the **NP**-hard CLIQUE problem, which calls for deciding whether a clique of certain size k exists in a simple undirected graph. Assume we are given a polynomial-time algorithm $\mathcal{A}(G, \alpha)$ that can find an OQC in any simple undirected graph $G(V, E)$ for any parameter $\alpha \in (0, 1)$. Then, given any instance of the CLIQUE problem on a simple undirected graph $G(V, E)$, we invoke $\mathcal{A}(G, \alpha)$ with $\alpha = 1 - \binom{|V|}{2}^{-1}$. We emphasize that an elaborate *reduction* is not necessary, as we use the *same graph* in both problems. By Theorem 1, if the returned optimal quasi-clique (OQC) has non-positive edge surplus, it follows that G has no cliques; otherwise, if the returned OQC has any positive edge surplus, it is a clique. Moreover, by definition, the returned OQC has the maximum edge surplus among all such cliques in G, hence, by Lemma 2, it *is a maximum clique* of G. In effect, an algorithm that finds an OQC in G in polynomial time would also effectively decide whether G contains a clique, and, if so, what the maximum clique size is; thus, it would solve any instance of CLIQUE, effectively deciding that a clique of size k exists if and only if k is no less than the maximum clique size. It follows that finding an OQC is at least as hard as any problem in **NP**.

Our proof resolves a question left open in [21]. Given this result, we should strive for non-optimal solutions to COHORT RETRIEVAL, which is at least as hard as the problem of finding an OQC.

4 COVER Algorithm

We present COVER, our algorithm for the cohort retrieval problem; COVER merges and builds upon techniques for maximal clique enumeration [20] and the OQC problem [21]. It searches for cliques on the social graph, yet, instead of striving to satisfy just a maximality condition upon them, it checks, for any possible clique candidate, the edge surplus of its induced subgraphs on the activity graph, pruning nodes that cannot lead to higher edge surplus than already found. Eventually, it outputs the top-k results by our problem definition.

A cohort should form a social clique and also achieve as high activity density as possible, as outlined in Sect. 3.3. COVER explores the social graph in order to find cliques, as an algorithm for maximal clique enumeration would do. Yet, for each clique it finds in the social graph G, it searches locally for its subgraphs of high activity density in the activity graph G_A, maintaining a queue of the top-k results, and, thereby, also a global queue of the top-k cohorts overall. In this process, when considering a new node v, it evaluates its strength, in terms of marginal activity density, that it may bring to any cohort under construction; node v is further considered only if its marginal activity density can bring an advantage compared to the top-k cohorts retrieved so far.

Algorithm 1: COVER: retrieving top-k geo-social cohorts

---

1   **Input:** $G(V, E)$, $G_{\mathcal{L}}(V, E)$, k, T_{Max}, α
2   **Output:** Set of k traveler groups : $\mathcal{CO}$
3   **begin**
4      $C = \emptyset$ /* a clique in G */
5      $cohG = \emptyset$ /* queue of top-k cohorts within C */
6      $\mathcal{CO} = \emptyset$ /* global queue of top-k cohorts */
7   searchCliques(V, V, C) /* recursive function */

Algorithm 2: searchCliques$(Sub, Cand, C)$

---

1   **begin**
2   /* Sub: seed set to be searched for cliques */
3   /* Cand: expansion set for building cliques */
4   /* $N_G(u)$: friends of u in G*/
5   **if** $Sub \neq \emptyset$ **then**
6         $u \leftarrow$ vertex $\in Sub$ maximizing $|Cand \cap N_G(u)|$
7   **foreach** $v \in Cand \backslash N_G(u)$ **do**
8            $Sub_v \leftarrow Sub \cap N_G(v)$
9            $Cand_v \leftarrow Cand \cap N_G(v)$
10           $cohG_M \leftarrow Cand_v \cup C \cup \{v\}$
11   /* $cohG_M$: largest possible clique on v */
12   **if** $\binom{|cohG_M|}{2}(1 - \alpha) > min_{S \in \mathcal{CO}} (f_\alpha(S))$ **then**
13   searchCliques$(Sub_v, Cand_v, C \cup \{v\})$
14           $Cand \leftarrow Cand \backslash \{v\}$
15   **else**
16         $cohG \leftarrow$ findCohorts(G_A, C, k)
17         $\mathcal{CO} \leftarrow \mathcal{CO} \cup cohG$

Algorithm 1 is the shell of COVER; it initializes variables and priority queues and finds top-k activity-based cohorts recursively on the back of social cliques. Algorithm 2 searches for promising cliques C in the social graph G. We start with the set of all users V, and recursively explore subgraphs having a clique property in depth-first-search manner. We maintain two set variables: Sub maintains the intersection of the neighbor sets of all nodes already entered in the clique C currently under construction. On the other hand, $Cand$ maintains the intersection of such neighbor sets *minus* any nodes that have already been checked, i.e., included, or considered for inclusion, in C. We use $Cand$ to generate new candidates for checking at each iteration (Line 7). Besides, to accelerate the search, at each iteration we pick up a high-degree *pivot* node $u \in Sub$ having many neighbors $N_G(u)$ in $Cand$ (Line 6). Then, we check candidate nodes $v \in Cand \backslash N_G(u)$ (Lines 7–14) for inclusion in C. We exclude those neighbors from the search (Line 7), since, if we have not already considered them, we consider them recursively later by virtue of them being neighbors of u. A critical check is performed in Line 12: if the largest possible clique that can be built by including v and its neighbors can yield a best-case activity density *among* the current top-k

values, then C is recursively expanded with v (Line 13); otherwise, we discard
the depth-first search path leading to v, as it cannot bring forth new results,
and *thereby we avoid redundant computations*. Lastly, when clique C cannot be
expanded further, we search for the top-k cohorts therein by calling Algorithm 3
and update the global priority queue $\mathcal{CO}$ accordingly (Lines 16–17).

Algorithm 3 finds top-k cohorts within G_A and social clique C by local search.
A candidate cohort S starts out as the node $u \in C$ of highest ratio of adjacent
triangles to degree and its neighbors (Line 3). We iteratively revise S, first by
adding nodes, as long as that can bring a benefit in activity density, choosing the
best such option (Lines 8–12); then by removing the best node whose removal
brings benefit (Lines 13–16); we repeat until we reach a local optimum or the
maximum iterations T_{max}. In each iteration, we insert the running S to the
priority queue $cohG$, and eventually merge the result in priority queue $\mathcal{CO}$.

Algorithm 3: findCohorts(G_A, C, k)

```
 1  begin
 2  │   u : vertex with max #triangles/degree ratio in G_A[C]
 3  │   S ← N(u) ∪ {u} /* u and G_A neighbors */
 4  │   cohG ← {S}
 5  │   b₁ ← True, t ← 1 /* local search begins */
 6  │   while b₁ and t ≤ T_max do
 7  │   │   b₂ ← True
 8  │   │   while b₂ do
 9  │   │   │   if ∃v ∈ C \ S such that f_α(S ∪ {v}) ≥ f_α(S) then
10  │   │   │   │   S ← S ∪ {v}; cohG ← cohG ∪ S
11  │   │   │   else
12  │   │   │   │   b₂ ← False /* growth of S stops */
13  │   │   if ∃x ∈ S such that f_α(S \ {x}) ≥ f_α(S) then
14  │   │   │   S ← S \ {x}; cohG ← cohG ∪ S
15  │   │   else
16  │   │   │   b₁ ← False /* local search stops */
17  │   │   t ← t + 1 /* iteration counter */
```

Given the worst-case complexity of clique enumeration [20], which forms the
backbone of COVER, the worst-case complexity of COVER is $O(3^{\frac{n}{3}} + cT_{max}m)$,
where n is the number of nodes, c the number of enumerated cliques that reach
Line 12 of Algorithm 2, m the number of activity graph edges, and T_{max} the
maximum number of iterations in Algorithm 3, which touches each edge at most
once per iteration [21]. We avoid this worst-case scenario by a *massive* discarding
of paths in Line 12 of Algorithm 2. Therefore the algorithm is efficient in practice.

5   Experimental Study

We present an extensive experimental evaluation of COVER, including its capacity to predict convoys of mobile companions, *regardless of whether they form a
social clique*. We ran all experiments on a 2.3 GHz, 4 AMD Opteron 6376 Linux
machine with 512 GB of RAM. All algorithms are implemented[1] in Scala.

---

[1] The code is available at http://bit.ly/2tUTEuu.

Datasets. We utilize three real-world datasets from Foursquare, Gowalla, and Weeplaces [14] (The Gowalla and Weeplaces data are available at https://www.yongliu.org/datasets/). Table 1 gathers information about the data. Each of the datasets consisted of three parts: the social friendship graph, an ordered list of check-ins, and a collection of Venues. A check-in record contains the user-id, check-in time, GPS coordinates, and a location-id. Venues provide the details of locations, i.e., city, country, and semantic categories of those locations.

Table 1. Dataset characteristics

	Users	Locations	Checkins	POIs	Friend pairs	Duration	Categories
FourSquare	4K	0.2M	0.47M	0.12M	32K	1322 days	35
Gowalla	77K	2.8M	18M	2M	4M	913 days	363
Wee	16K	0.9M	8M	0.76M	0.1M	2796 days	770

Data Preprocessing. The data required cleaning, as many locations were associated with multiple identifiers, each having slightly different GPS coordinates. We applied grid-based spatial clustering on GPS points, with a grid of size 10 m × 10 m, as in [17]. We assign a unique location Id to each resulting cluster and use these Ids as POIs in all experiments. All three datasets presented similar multiplicity problems, which we addressed in the same manner. Statistics regarding these new POI Ids are reported in Table 1.

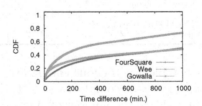

Fig. 1. CDF of time between consecutive activities

5.1   Brute-Force Convoy Retrieval

We first present a brute-force baseline that retrieves *groups of users moving together, i.e., convoys.* We divide all activities into a series of *time intervals*, or snapshots, using a time-stamp threshold t_s, recording *one* activity per interval: the last recorded activity. We can tune t_s so as to strike a fine balance in the tradeoff between time granularity and computation time. With larger t_s values, it becomes likelier to miss activities within a time snapshot. To set a suitable t_s value, we plot the cumulative distribution of time differences between consecutive user activities in Fig. 1. By this plot, we set $t_s = 1$ hour, which covers more than 90% of activities.

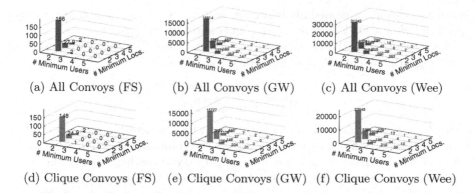

(a) All Convoys (FS)   (b) All Convoys (GW)   (c) All Convoys (Wee)

(d) Clique Convoys (FS)   (e) Clique Convoys (GW)   (f) Clique Convoys (Wee)

Fig. 2. Statistics on convoys: all convoys vs. convoys that also form social cliques

We detect convoys based on recorded activities. A convoy should: (i) contain *at least two users* moving together across locations; and (ii) involve *at least two* consecutively visited locations. We maintain a convoy list L and iterate over data snapshots in temporal order. In each snapshot, we group activities by location and check each group against L. If a group extends an existing convoy C, we update C accordingly; if a group forms a new convoy, we insert it in L. We store away items in L that are no longer expandable, and go on til the last snapshot. This approach is *more computationally demanding* than COVER's activity density estimation: it detects all groups in the training set, while COVER only considers pairs of users and at most pairs of consecutive activities, and social links. Figure 2 shows statistics on convoys so retrieved vs. those whose members *also* form social cliques. About 76% of all convoys form *social cliques*. This finding validates our conjecture that people are likely to *move in social cliques*, hence justifies our clique constraint.

5.2 Use Case: Convoy Prediction

We surmise that the cohorts COVER retrieves predict *convoys* of mobile companions; we design an experiment to assess that conjecture. We *do not test* an ability to predict *social cliques*; we claim that the clique constraint in our problem helps predict *convoys*. We use a *holdout approach*: we sort activities by timestamp and divide them into training (earlier) and test (later) sets, having an equal number of activities. A group retrieved from the training data that forms a convoy in the test data is a true positive. We apply two prediction regimes:

Without Input Categories: We find groups likely to form future convoys. COVER ranks groups by activity density; brute-force by appearances.

With Input Categories: In this case, we are given a set of categories of locations of interest $\mathcal{L}$. We find groups deemed likely to form future convoys, moving among locations of the given categories. To identify such groups, we filter the dataset so that we maintain only activities at locations of $\mathcal{L}$. Then, we retrieve groups as explained above; again the brute-force methods ranks convoys by count, while COVER ranks geo-social cohorts by surplus.

We measure a method's capacity to predict future convoys in the test data by averaging an accuracy measure, defined as follows:

$$Acc = \frac{|C \cap T|}{\min\{|C|, |T|\}} \tag{4}$$

where C is the returned set of top-k groups and T the set of convoys in the test data. We *sanitize* the measure, dividing by the minimum of $|C| = k$, and $|T|$. The rationale is that the denominator should exceed neither k, since the top-k results cannot be more than k, nor the number of existing convoys in the test data, which may be less than k, especially when we filter by input categories. In effect, this measure is the maximum of *precision* and *recall*; we think this is a reasonable measure given the sparsity of real-world LBSN data.

5.3   Revalidating the Social Clique Constraint

Before we proceed, we revalidate our social clique conjecture. To do so, we test COVER *without considering the social graph*. We extract top-k groups in terms of activity edge surplus in the training data, for $k = 1, 3, 5$. This way, we only get a positive prediction with the Wee dataset for $k = 3$, which is five times less accurate than what we achieved using the clique constraint. This result reconfirms the logic of that constraint: users who engage in common a activity but do not form a social clique are not likely to do so again. Further, we relaxed the clique constraint to find *quasi-cliques* in the social graph for several α values. Unfortunately, this way we could not predict *any* group of travel companions. We reiterate that the groups (convoys) we aim to *predict* are *not required* to form social cliques. We simply observe that groups of future travel companions *form social cliques, and we can well predict them using this constraint*.

5.4   Prediction Without Input Categories

We first present prediction results for the case *without* a restrictive set of given categories of interest $\mathcal{L}$.

Brute-Force Method. We run the brute-force method of Sect. 5.1 on the training data, retrieving the k most frequently observed convoys, and test its predictions on the test data. The last three columns in Table 2 show top-k convoy prediction accuracy for $k = 1, 3, 5$, reaching 100% in all but two cases.

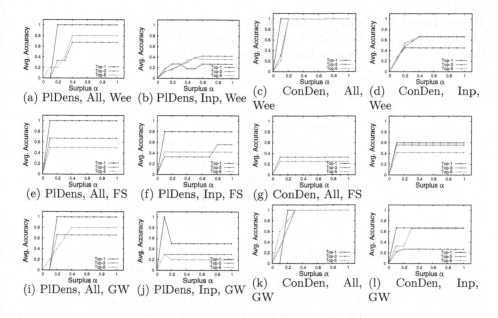

Fig. 3. Use Case: COVER's performance on convoy prediction with three datasets

COVER on Plain Activity Density. We test COVER on the same problem, setting weights in the activity graph without considering consecutive activities. Figures 3a, 3e, and 3i present results on top-k group prediction as a function of density surplus α. The top prediction becomes correct at $\alpha = 0.1$ and remains so for larger values of α; for top-3 and top-5 returned groups, the accuracy is lower. This is due to variations among training and test data; similar divergences appear in Table 2 even with the brute-force method. The fact that COVER does almost as well is remarkable, as it is up to 3 orders of magnitude faster, as we will see in Fig. 4b. In most cases, accuracy drops as k increases; it is easier to get a correct top group than the whole group of top 3 or 5.

COVER on Consecutive Activity Density. Next, we set density by consecutive spatiotemporal join. As Figs. 3c, 3g, and 3k show, smaller α achieve maximum accuracy. A large α forces the detection of small, tightly connected groups; the consecutivity requirement creates smaller cohorts on its own, rendering the impact of α less significant. COVER performs remarkably well.

5.5 Prediction with Input Categories

Now we examine the case *with* a restrictive set of categories of interest, $\mathcal{L}$. We construct 10 instances of $\mathcal{L}$, each consisting of 2–3 categories that appear together in real-world contexts, and report the *average* accuracy over all queries. For COVER, edge weights in activity graph $G_A^{\mathcal{L}}$ are based solely on locations in $\mathcal{L}$.

Brute-Force Method. The brute-force method achieves accuracy up to 66% (Table 2), as convoys specific to the input categories may not be met in the training data, but appear in the test data.

Table 2. Accuracy in brute-force convoy prediction

k	Input Cat			All Cat		
	FS	GW	Wee	FS	GW	Wee
1	0.60	0	0.50	1	1	1
3	0.66	0.17	0.60	1	1	1
5	0.64	0.20	0.70	0.30	0.80	1

COVER on Plain Activity Density. Figs. 3b, 3f, and 3j present the average top-k set prediction accuracy for COVER with plain activity density. While the problem is more challenging due to data sparsity, we still obtain high accuracy in most cases. Less accuracy variation with varying α appears on Foursquare, the smallest of our data sets, as fewer convoys arise in it. Accuracy still drops with increasing k, except for the case of the Wee data, where enlarging the set of results raises the chances they exist in the test data.

COVER on Consecutive Activity Density. Lastly, Figs. 3d, 3h, and 3l show the results for COVER with consecutive activity density. Remarkably, accuracy is either similar to or *significantly higher* than that in the non-consecutive case reaching 67% for the top-5 cohorts. This result vindicates the use of consecutive activity density. On Foursquare and Gowalla, accuracy increases sharply as α grows by virtue of smaller returned group sizes, then stabilizes above 60%.

5.6   Effect of Surplus Parameter α

Prediction accuracy grows with α, yet the size of retrieved geo-social cohorts decreases with α, as higher values demand stronger cohesion. To study this tradeoff, we measure the average retrieved cohort size vs. α on the top-5 cohorts with input categories and consecutive activity density. The results in Fig. 4a show that cohort size decreases with α up to 0.6, then stabilizes at 2; $\alpha = 0.4$ yields both large size and predictive power. We employ this value in Sect. 5.7.

5.7   Scalability and Prediction Quality

As there is no previous work on the problem we study, we juxtapose COVER with fixed $\alpha = 0.4$ vs. the following methods:

- **BF:** The Brute-Force convoy retrieval method of Sect. 5.1.

- **GroupFinder:** A method that finds groups of a given size k for a given user u and set categories [6]. We adapt this method to our problem so as to conduct a reasonable comparison: Given a set of categories, we apply GroupFinder to each user in the data set and then choose the best group of size k, where k is the most popular group size returned by COVER (in all cases, 2). We utilize both pairwise user-item relevance measures proposed in [6]: pairwise aggregated voting (PAV) and pairwise least misery (PLM).
- **OQC2:** A COVER variant that relaxes the clique constraint, finding groups of high edge surplus on both graphs, using two α values, one for each surplus component; we try out α values with step 0.1 and weights for the two components in $\{0, 0.25, 0.66, 1, 1.5, 4, \infty\}$, and present best results.

First, we assess all methods in terms of scalability, measuring runtime on 6.25%, 12.5% 25%, 50% and 100% of the Wee data. Figure 4b shows the results (Brute-Force as Naive, OQC2 with $\alpha = 0.6$). Despite an exponential worst-case complexity, the practical runtime of COVER is comparable to that of GroupFinder, and the most scalable of all examined algorithms, while Brute-Force (Naive) does not scale well. Other data produces similar trends.

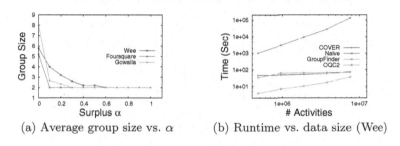

(a) Average group size vs. α (b) Runtime vs. data size (Wee)

Fig. 4. Effect of α and scalability in data size

Next, we evaluate the following measures of prediction quality on the Wee data, which has the highest number of observed convoys:

- *Accuracy*, the metric we have used in previous results;
- *Precision@K*, the ratio of the number of true top-k convoys *by frequency* returned, over k or the total number of true convoys, whichever is smaller;
- *Mean Average Precision* (MAP), the mean of Precision@K for all k values up to the examined one; and
- *Normalized Discounted Cumulative Gain* (NDCG), on the *ranking* of returned results vs. their frequency ranking in the test data.

Table 3 shows results on consecutive activity density, with input categories, for five values of k. Brute-Force sometimes outperforms COVER, yet COVER stands its ground in several measures, while avoiding an exhaustive calculation. GF-PAV, GFPLM and OQC perform poorly by all measures; their results are not in the top-20, resulting in 0 value for P@K and MAP. GroupFinder falters as it does not consider activities, but only interests; OQC performs poorly as it abolishes the social clique constraint; this finding *corroborates* that constraint.

Table 3. Comparative evaluation on Wee ($\alpha = 0.4$ for COVER, best OQC values)

K	Accuracy					P@K					MAP					NDCG				
	BF	GF PAV	GF PLM	OQC	COVER	BF	GF-PAV	GF-PLM	OQC	COVER	BF	GF-PAV	GF-PLM	OQC	COVER	BF	GF-PAV	GF-PLM	OQC	COVER
1	0.5	0.01	0.01	0.25	0.6	0	0	0	0	0	0	0	0	0	0	0.5	0.09	0.1	0.25	0.35
5	0.7	0.03	0.03	0.1	0.4	0.35	0	0	0	0.15	0.18	0	0	0	0.17	0.7	0.25	0.1	0.5	0.76
10	0.6	0.03	0.03	0.05	0.63	0.22	0	0	0	0.15	0.22	0	0	0	0.16	0.79	0.25	0.15	0.5	0.81
15	0.5	0.08	0.05	0.03	0.57	0.18	0	0	0	0.15	0.22	0	0	0	0.16	0.81	0.1	0.25	0.5	0.81
20	0.47	0.08	0.05	0.025	0.53	0.14	0	0	0.01	0.14	0.2	0	0	0	0.16	0.8	0.25	0.25	0.5	0.82

5.8   Analysis on Retrieved Groups

Figure 5 presents the cumulative density function of characteristics for all retrieved geo-social cohorts (5a) and those forming mobility convoys (5b), i.e., their size and number of activities performed by their members (i.e., individuals or pairs). Group size goes from 2 to 3 (green line), while we predict convoys correctly even when they have not performed any activities together on input categories. This capacity of COVER sets it apart from the brute-force baseline that can only predict convoys that appear in the training set.

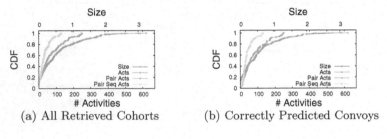

(a) All Retrieved Cohorts   (b) Correctly Predicted Convoys

Fig. 5. Analysis of Retrieved Groups (Wee) (Color figure online)

6   Conclusion

We proposed the problem of finding geo-social cohorts of frequent companions in LBSNs, defined in terms of (i) a *selective* clique constraint on a social graph, and (ii) a density objective on a coterminous graph (i.e., defined on the same set of nodes) capturing common (and *consecutive*) pairwise activities. We designed COVER, a nontrivial algorithm for that problem. Our experimental study with real-life data sets showed that COVER is effective, scalable, and efficient; moreover, it predicts future convoys (i.e., groups moving together), including convoys that do not appear in the training set, while neither an adaptation of previous work nor a brute-force approach based on user traces can deliver such a result.

   In the future, we intend to (i) expand our techniques so as to include different activity density functions, and (ii) study the robustness of our method, in terms of its predictive power, in the face of missing, incomplete, uncertain, noisy, and privacy-aware data.

References

1. Amer-Yahia, S., Roy, S.B., Chawla, A., Das, G., Yu, C.: Group recommendation: semantics and efficiency. PVLDB **2**(1), 754–765 (2009)
2. Asahiro, Y., Hassin, R., Iwama, K.: Complexity of finding dense subgraphs. Discrete Appl. Math. **121**(1–3), 15–26 (2002)
3. Bahmani, B., Kumar, R., Vassilvitskii, S.: Densest subgraph in streaming and mapreduce. PVLDB **5**(5), 454–465 (2012)
4. Bao, J., Zheng, Y., Wilkie, D., Mokbel, M.F.: Recommendations in location-based social networks: a survey. GeoInformatica **19**(3), 525–565 (2015)
5. Boden, B., Günnemann, S., Hoffmann, H., Seidl, T.: Mining coherent subgraphs in multi-layer graphs with edge labels. In: KDD (2012)
6. Brilhante, I., Macedo, J.A., Nardini, F.M., Perego, R., Renso, C.: Group finder: an item-driven group formation framework. In: MDM (2016)
7. Brown, C., Lathia, N., Mascolo, C., Noulas, A., Blondel, V.: Group colocation behavior in technological social networks. PLoS ONE **9**(8), 1–9 (2014)
8. Everett, M.G., Borgatti, S.P.: Analyzing clique overlap. Connections **21**(1), 49–61 (1998)
9. Goldberg, A.V.: Finding a Maximum Density Subgraph. Tech. Rep., UC Berkeley (1984)
10. Hung, C.C., Chang, C.W., Peng, W.C.: Mining trajectory profiles for discovering user communities. In: LBSN, pp. 1–8 (2009)
11. Jahromi, K.K., Zignani, M., Gaito, S., Rossi, G.P.: Predicting encounter and colocation events. Ad Hoc Netw. **62**, 11–21 (2017)
12. Khuller, S., Saha, B.: On finding dense subgraphs. In: ICALP (2009)
13. Liao, Y., Lam, W., Jameel, S., Schockaert, S., Xie, X.: Who wants to join me?: companion recommendation in location based social networks. In: ICTIR, pp. 271–280 (2016)
14. Liu, Y., Wei, W., Sun, A., Miao, C.: Exploiting geographical neighborhood characteristics for location recommendation. In: CIKM, pp. 739–748 (2014)
15. Noulas, A., Scellato, S., Lathia, N., Mascolo, C.: Mining user mobility features for next place prediction in location-based services. In: ICDM, pp. 1038–1043 (2012)
16. Palla, G., Derényi, I., Farkas, I., Vicsek, T.: Uncovering the overlapping community structure of complex networks in nature and society. Nature **435**(7043), 814–818 (2005)
17. Saleem, M.A., Kumar, R., Calders, T., Pedersen, T.B.: Effective and efficient location influence mining in location-based social networks. Knowl. Inf. Syst. **61**(1), 327–362 (2019)
18. Srivastava, S., Pande, S., Ranu, S.: Geo-social clustering of places from check-in data. In: ICDM, pp. 985–990 (2015)
19. Tehrani, B.O., Amer-Yahia, S., Dutot, P., Trystram, D.: Multi-objective group discovery on the social web. In: ECML PKDD, pp. 296–312 (2016)
20. Tomita, E., Tanaka, A., Takahashi, H.: The worst-case time complexity for generating all maximal cliques and computational experiments. Theor. Comput. Sci. **363**(1), 28–42 (2006)
21. Tsourakakis, C.E., Bonchi, F., Gionis, A., Gullo, F., Tsiarli, M.A.: Denser than the densest subgraph: extracting optimal quasi-cliques with quality guarantees. In: KDD, pp. 104–112 (2013)
22. Xiao, X., Zheng, Y., Luo, Q., Xie, X.: Inferring social ties between users with human location history. J. Amb. Intell. Humaniz. Comput. **5**(1), 3–19 (2014)

Modeling Dynamic Spatial Influence for Air Quality Prediction with Atmospheric Prior

Dan Lu[1], Le Wu[2], Rui Chen[1(✉)], Qilong Han[1], Yichen Wang[3], and Yong Ge[4]

[1] Harbin Engineering University, Harbin, Heilongjiang, China
{ludan,ruichen}@hrbeu.edu.cn
[2] Hefei University of Technology, Hefei, Anhui, China
[3] Hunan University, Changsha, Hunan, China
[4] The University of Arizona, Tucson, AZ 85721, USA
yongge@arizona.edu

Abstract. Air quality prediction is an important task benefiting both individual outdoor activities and urban emergency response. To account for complex temporal factors that influence long-term air quality, researchers have formulated this problem using an encoder-decoder framework that captures the non-linear temporal evolution. Besides, as air quality presents natural spatial correlation, researchers have proposed to learn the spatial relation with either a graph structure or an attention mechanism. As well supported by atmospheric dispersion theories, air quality correlation among different monitoring stations is dynamic and changes over time due to atmospheric dispersion, leading to the notion of dispersion-driven dynamic spatial correlation. However, most previous works treated spatial correlation as a static process, and nearly all models relied on only data-driven approaches in the modeling process. To this end, we propose to model dynamic spatial influence for air quality prediction with atmospheric prior. The key idea of our work is to build a dynamic spatial graph at each time step with physical atmospheric dispersion modeling. Then, we leverage the learned embeddings from this dynamic spatial graph in an encoder-decoder model to seamlessly fuse the dynamic spatial correlation with the temporal evolution, which is key to air quality prediction. Finally, extensive experiments on real-world benchmark data clearly show the effectiveness of the proposed model.

Keywords: Air quality prediction · Dynamic spatial correlation · Atmospheric dispersion

Supported by the National Key R&D Program of China under Grant No. 2020YF B1710200, the National Natural Science Foundation of China under Grant No. 61872105 and No. 62072136, the Fundamental Research Funds for the Central Universities under Grant No. 3072020CFT2402 and No. 3072020CFT0603, and the Opening Fund of Acoustics Science and Technology Laboratory under Grant No. SSKF2020003.

L. H. U et al. (Eds.): APWeb-WAIM 2021, LNCS 12859, pp. 384–398, 2021.
https://doi.org/10.1007/978-3-030-85899-5_28

1   Introduction

With the fast pace of urbanization and industrialization, air pollution has been an endemic threat to human health and the environment, especially in metropolitan cities. Air pollution generally refers to the release of pollutants into the air, which is detrimental to human health and the planet as a whole. To prevent human beings from long-term exposure of pollution and reduce air pollution, accurately predicting future air quality is essential. For example, policy makers can properly choose guides or policies, such as temporary traffic control or production ban for heavy-polluting factories, according to the future air quality trend in order to reduce the severity of local pollution levels.

Precisely predicting air quality, often in terms of the major pollutant PM2.5 value, is non-trivial. This is due to the fact that air quality depends on multiple complex factors, such as meteorology, road networks, and point of interests (POIs), and evolves over time. While previous works carefully designed sophisticated static features and temporal features for air quality prediction, recent studies have begun to use recurrent neural networks (RNNs) to capture the non-linear temporal evolution. In particular, researchers proposed to use an encoder-decoder framework, with the encoder fusing heterogeneous features and the decoder predicting long-term PM2.5 values [21].

Besides temporal correlation, PM2.5 values among different air quality monitoring stations naturally exhibit spatial autocorrelation, with nearby stations having similar PM2.5 values. Researchers have proposed to incorporate spatial correlation by including nearby stations' features in the input space [12,14] or by further considering the Pearson correlation of geo-context features between a target station and its neighboring stations [4,23]. Instead of having nearby stations defined by spatial distance contribute equally to a target station, attention mechanisms have been increasingly used to differentiate the weights of different monitoring stations, where the attentive weights are either static over time [5] or dynamic (i.e., having different weights at different time steps) [13]. Researchers have also proposed to leverage a graph structure to capture the higher-order spatial correlations among stations and to learn the graph structure to facilitate weather prediction [19]. These attempts have demonstrated that modeling spatial correlations among stations can boost air quality prediction performance.

In view of the importance of spatial correlation for air quality prediction, we argue that the current solutions for spatial modeling are still far from satisfactory. In fact, the well-established and widely-used atmospheric dispersion models [2,17] have pointed out that air quality correlation among different monitoring stations is inherently *dynamic* and changes over time. In particular, how air pollutants disperse from a station to another relies on not only their spatial distance and direction, but also other dynamic factors, such as wind direction and speed, leading to the notion of *dispersion-driven dynamic spatial correlation*. Atmospheric dispersion modeling provides a mathematical simulation of how air pollutants disperse in the ambient atmosphere, and is built on top of expert knowledge. For example, in the Gaussian plume model, the concentration of pollutant downwind from a source is treated as spreading outward from the centerline of the plume following a Gaussian statistical distribution in both vertical and horizontal directions [1]. These physical models provide us a solid theoretical foundation to guide air quality prediction. By far, atmospheric dispersion models are still the dominant models used in air quality policy making. However, most related works adopted only *static* spatial correlation modeling methods. What's worse, almost all of these works relied on a purely data-driven approach, which may introduce unnecessary noise and violate well-established dispersion theories due to the black box nature of deep learning models.

In this paper, we focus on modeling the dynamic spatial influence for air quality prediction with atmospheric prior. This is particularly challenging as it is still unknown how to leverage atmospheric prior to model dynamic spatial correlation among stations and integrate these well-established theories into a data-driven air quality prediction process. To tackle these challenges, we first build a dynamic spatial graph at each time step with the simple yet effective Gaussian plume model, which can well capture the dynamic higher-order spatial correlations among monitoring stations. Then, we incorporate the embeddings learned from dynamic spatial graphs using graph convolutional networks (GCNs) into an encoder-decoder model to seamlessly fuse the dynamic spatial correlation with the temporal evolution. The key technical contribution of this paper lies in combining knowledge-driven atmospheric dispersion models with data-driven deep learning techniques for air quality prediction in an elegant way. Finally, experimental results on real-world benchmark datasets clearly demonstrate the superiority of our proposed model over the state-of-the-art methods.

2   Related Work

Air quality prediction has been a long-standing research problem with practical importance. Existing methods roughly fall into two categories: classical physical models and data-driven models. Physical models have been widely used in the early stage of air quality prediction research. They explicitly simulate the actual physical dispersion process of air pollutants and feature a rigorous mathematical foundation. Gaussian plume models [2] and Street Canyon models [17] are most widely-used physical models that estimate future pollutants' concentration by considering a few important factors, such as meteorological conditions, source term, emissions or release parameters, and terrain elevations. While these physical models work well in relatively simple conditions, they lack the capability of learning from more complex urban big data involving a large number of external factors, and fall short of expectations in practice. In this paper, we propose a novel method to integrate such atmospheric prior into a data-driven approach, resulting in better performance.

With the availability of more urban big data that can be used for air quality prediction, data-driven models have gained increasing attention. Some early studies consider Gaussian processes as a nonparametric method to predict the average pollution level [6,10]. A semi-supervised method is used to make PM2.5 inference based on an PM2.5 affinity graph structure [7]. Another semi-supervised method focuses on the spatial correlation between a target area and its top-k nearest neighbors [4]. Multi-task learning based strategies are also used to incorporate spatio-temporal smoothness [22].

More recent research addresses the air quality prediction problem by deep learning techniques. Modeling the temporal and/or spatial correlation is key to air quality prediction because air pollutant dispersion is inherently a spatio-temporal process. A simple idea is to directly aggregate the air quality readings, spatial features (e.g., POIs, road networks) and meteorological data from neighboring stations to improve accuracy [23]. More advanced spatial partition and aggregation methods are also introduced to better model spatial correlation [20,24]. Attention mechanisms are another popular way of capturing spatial correlations. Cheng *et al.* [5] introduce an attention mechanism to learn the contributions of different monitoring stations to a target station's PM2.5 value. Liang *et al.* [13] further learn different attentive weights for different stations at different time steps while considering the geospatial similarities between stations. In a slightly different application, Wilson *et al.* [19] propose to capture the higher-order spatial correlations of monitoring stations by graph convolution operations. In contrast, our paper considers a novel type of dispersion-driven dynamic spatial correlation that betters prediction accuracy.

As to temporal correlation, RNNs have been a widely-used choice. For example, Li *et al.* [12] employ a stacked long short-term memory (LSTM) network to extract features from historical air quality data and other auxiliary data. To support long-term air quality prediction, encoder-decoder networks are used to model the non-linear temporal evolution [14,21].

There are also some very recent studies [8,16] that address the air quality prediction problem by considering social media information (e.g., tweets) as an auxiliary data source. Our contributions are orthogonal to them and can be used to further improve their performance.

3   Problem Formulation

Similar to previous studies [5,21], we consider the problem of air quality prediction based on multi-source heterogeneous data. We brief the data sources below.

Air Quality Data. It contains hourly readings of multiple pollutants (e.g., PM2.5, PM10, O_3, NO_2, CO, SO_2, etc.) from each air quality monitoring station $s_i \in \mathcal{S}$, where $\mathcal{S}$ is the entire set of stations under consideration. We denote all stations' air quality data by $\mathcal{M}$.

Weather Data. The weather data of a station s_i at time t is denoted by $\mathbf{w}_i^t$. It contains multiple weather attributes, such as temperature, humidity, wind speed and wind direction. We consider both historical weather data of all stations, denoted by $\mathcal{W}$, and forecast weather data, denoted by $\overline{\mathcal{W}}$.

Geospatial Topology Data. We consider the geospatial topology of all stations, which is denoted by $\mathcal{T}$. It contains the latitude and longitude of each station, and thus allows to calculate the distance and direction (i.e., bearing)

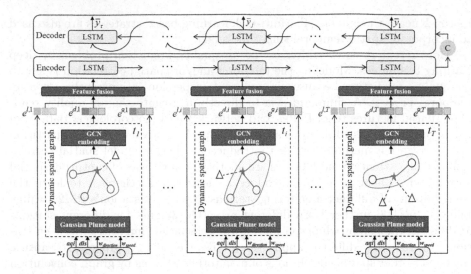

Fig. 1. Architecture overview of the proposed model

between two stations. The geospatial topology data itself is static, but we combine it with the above data sources to compute the stations' dynamic spatial correlation at each time step.

Geo-Context Data. The geo-context data $c_i \in \mathcal{C}$ of station s_i includes information about road networks and point of interests (POIs) extracted from s_i's affecting area (i.e., the area surrounding s_i). Note that this type of data does not change over time.

Now we are ready to present the problem definition.

Problem Definition. Consider a target station $s_i \in \mathcal{S}$, a historical time window T, and a forecast time window γ. Given all stations' air quality data $\mathcal{M} = \{\mathcal{M}^t\}_{t=1}^{T}$, historical weather data $\mathcal{W} = \{\mathcal{W}^t\}_{t=1}^{T}$, forecast weather data $\overline{\mathcal{W}} = \{\overline{\mathcal{W}}^t\}_{t=T+1}^{T+\gamma}$, geospatial topology data $\mathcal{T}$, and geo-context data $\mathcal{C}$, the goal is to predict the PM2.5 values of station s_i in the next γ hours, denoted by $\hat{\mathbf{y}} = (\hat{y}^{T+1}, \hat{y}^{T+2}, \cdots, \hat{y}^{T+\gamma})$. That is, we aim to learn a prediction function f such that

$$\hat{\mathbf{y}} = f(\mathcal{M}, \mathcal{W}, \overline{\mathcal{W}}, \mathcal{T}, \mathcal{C}, \Theta), \tag{1}$$

where Θ denotes the set of parameters of f to learn.

4   Proposed Method

In this section, we elaborate our proposed method that makes use of atmospheric dispersion theories to model the dynamic spatial correlations among monitoring stations in order to improve air quality prediction. The overall architecture of the proposed method is illustrated in Fig. 1.

4.1 Feature Representation

To predict the PM2.5 values of station s_i in the next γ hours, we construct three types of features as explained below.

Local Features. This set of features includes station s_i's air quality data, historical and forecast weather data, and geo-context data. Air quality data and weather data are observed or forecasted each hour, and naturally form time series. Thus, they lay the foundation for temporal correlation modeling.

Global Features. This set of features includes the local features of all nearby stations, defined by the Euclidean distance. While the air quality data and weather data of the neighboring stations change over time, global features fail to capture the dynamic spatial influence of neighboring stations on the target station s_i due to air dispersion, which is critical to achieve better prediction performance.

Dynamic Spatial Features. This is a set of novel features driven by atmospheric dispersion. Guided by atmospheric dispersion models, dynamic spatial features explicitly measure the spatial influence of neighboring stations by considering multiple external factors at each time step. We detail how to generate dynamic spatial features in the next section.

4.2 Dynamic Spatial Graph Construction

At time step t, we represent the dispersion-driven dynamic spatial influence of all other stations on a target station s_i by a weighted directed graph $\mathcal{G}_i^t = (\mathcal{S}, \mathcal{E}_i^t)$, where an edge $e_{ij} \in \mathcal{E}_i^t$ gives the dynamic spatial influence of station s_j on the target station s_i as per atmospheric dispersion modeling. Note that normally the dynamic spatial influence of station s_i on station s_j is different from that of s_j on s_i as shown in Fig. 2. In the following, we omit the superscript t as

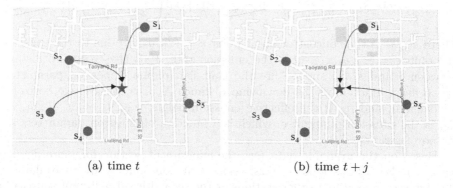

(a) time t (b) time $t + j$

Fig. 2. Illustration of the dynamic spatial influence. s_1, s_2 and s_3 are the associated stations of the star as the northwest wind in time t, and changed to s_1 and s_5 in time $t + j$ as the northeast wind

all discussions are for time t. Previous studies normally consider the geographic proximity between stations as the key factor to model their spatial correlations. For example, the top-k nearest neighbors' features are used to predict a target station's PM2.5 value. Wilson *et al.* [19] propose to use a graph structure to explicitly model the spatial correlations. All elements in the adjacency matrix of the spatial graph are model parameters that need to be learned from training data. However, the adjacency matrix is assumed to be *static*, that is, it is fixed at different time steps. This assumption directly violates the well-established dispersion models. In addition, considering all elements in the adjacency matrix as trainable parameters substantially increases the model complexity. Therefore, Wilson *et al.* [19] further assume that the adjacency matrix is either sparse or low rank to mitigate the number of parameters. However, this assumption is not backed up by any theoretical ground. To this end, we propose a novel domain knowledge driven method that not only allows to dynamically learn a different adjacency matrix at each time step, but also fully uses atmospheric dispersion theories to mitigate model complexity.

The first step is to select an appropriate atmospheric dispersion model that can be seamlessly integrated into a data-driven approach. Eulerian and Lagrangian models are used to predict air pollution in urban areas, which assume pollutants to be evenly distributed within the boundary [3]. Computational fluid dynamic (CFD) models are used to better understand fluid dispersion, but can also be used in urban air quality prediction [9]. The Gaussian plume model is one of the most widely-used models to assess the impacts of emission sources on local and urban air quality [2]. The dispersion of pollutants can be described in both horizontal and vertical directions by a Gaussian distribution, which well suits our setting. As such, we choose the Gaussian plume model as the domain model for modeling dispersion-driven dynamic spatial correlation. The spatial dynamics of pollutant dispersion in a Gaussian model can be described by the following equation [15]:

$$c(r,s) = \frac{Q}{2\pi\sigma_y\sigma_z\bar{u}} \exp\left(-\frac{1}{2}\left(\frac{Y}{\sigma_y}\right)^2\right) \exp\left(-\frac{1}{2}\left(\frac{h_e - z_r}{\sigma_z}\right)^2\right), \tag{2}$$

where $c(r,s)$ is the concentration at point $r = (x_r, y_r, z_r)$ due to the emissions at point $s = (x_s, y_s, z_s)$, Q is the emission rate, Y is the crosswind distance between r and s, σ_y and σ_z are the Gaussian plume dispersion parameters, which are a function of the downwind distance X, $\bar{u}$ is the average horizontal wind speed, and h_e is the effective emission height (i.e., $h_e = z_s + \Delta h$, and Δh is the emission plume rise, which is a function of emission parameters and meteorological conditions).

Based on the available data (see the experiment section for more details), we adapt Eq. (2) as follows. First, since emission sources are unavailable in the dataset, we consider other stations as the second-hand pollutant sources for the target station [20]. Second, since all stations in the data are *point sources* (i.e., without elevation information), we ignore all items related to height in Eq. (2). Third, we propose to use a data-driven method to learn a function $\phi(X)$

to determine σ_y. Then the dispersion-driven spatial influence of station s_j on target station s_i at time t can be formulated as:

$$c(s_i, s_j) = \frac{Q_j}{2\pi\phi(X)\bar{u}_j} \exp\left(-\frac{1}{2}\left(\frac{Y}{\phi(X)}\right)^2\right), \qquad (3)$$

where Q_j is the air quality of station s_j , $\bar{u}_j$ is the horizontal wind velocity at s_j, and X and Y are the downwind and crosswind distances between s_i and s_j, respectively. Here we model $\phi(\cdot)$ as a linear function, that is, $\phi(X) = \gamma X$, where γ is a learnable scalar. We can also model $\phi(\cdot)$ as a more complicated function that can be learned by a multi-layer perceptron (MLP). But our experiments indicate that a linear formulation already strikes a reasonable trade-off between performance and model complexity.

We further normalize the influence of station s_j on target station s_i among all other stations:

$$a_{ij} = \frac{c(s_i, s_j)}{\sum_{s_k \in (\mathcal{S}-s_i)} c(s_i, s_k)}. \qquad (4)$$

a_{ij} is the weight of the edge e_{ij}. All a_{ij} values form the adjacency matrix $\mathbf{A}_i$ of the dynamic spatial graph $\mathcal{G}_i$ for target station s_i.

It can be seen that with the help of atmospheric dispersion theories, we successfully reduce the number of learnable parameters of a dynamic spatial graph from $O(|\mathcal{S}|^2)$, where $|\mathcal{S}|$ is the number of stations, to $O(1)$. Note that the learnable parameter γ is shared among all time steps.

4.3   Dynamic Spatial Graph Embedding

After constructing the dynamic spatial graph $\mathcal{G}_i$ for target station s_i at time t, we need a way to convert $\mathcal{G}_i$ into a low dimensional space so that its spatial information can be effectively fused with the temporal correlation in an encoder-decoder network. We omit the subscript i when it is clear from the context. We consider graph convolutional networks (GCNs) [11] for this purpose due to its flexibility and good performance. For a K-layer graph convolutional network, the output of the l-th layer can be represented as $\mathbf{H}^l \in \mathbb{R}^{|\mathcal{S}| \times d^{(l)}}$. Each row in $\mathbf{H}^l$ represents the embedding of a station whose dimension is $d^{(l)}$. The embedding of a station after the $(l+1)$-th layer will be computed as the aggregation of its connected stations' embeddings from the l-th layer. This operation performed in a GCN layer can be formulated as:

$$\mathbf{H}^{(l+1)} = \sigma(\mathbf{A}\mathbf{H}^{(l)}\mathbf{W}^{(l)}), \qquad (5)$$

where $\sigma(\cdot)$ is a non-linear activation function, $\mathbf{A}$ is the adjacency matrix of the dynamic spatial graph $\mathcal{G}$, and $\mathbf{W}^{(l)} \in \mathbb{R}^{d^{(l)} \times d^{(l+1)}}$ is a layer-specific trainable transformation matrix for the l-th layer. The target station s_i's embedding in $\mathbf{H}^K$ is used as part of the input to encoder-decoder network.

4.4 Encoder-Decoder Based Spatio-Temporal Fusion

To support long-term air quality prediction, we use an encoder-decoder LSTM model [18] to fuse spatial and temporal information and infer future PM2.5 values. Let $\mathbf{e}_i^{l,t}$ and $\mathbf{e}_i^{g,t}$ denote station s_i's local feature embeddings and global feature embeddings at time t, where $\mathbf{e}_i^{g,t} = \sum_{s_j \in (\mathcal{S}-s_i)} \mathbf{e}_j^{l,t}$. Let $\mathbf{e}_i^{d,t}$ denote the embedding learned from the GCN over the dynamic spatial graph $\mathcal{G}_i^t$. We concatenate $\mathbf{e}_i^{l,t}$, $\mathbf{e}_i^{g,t}$ and $\mathbf{e}_i^{d,t}$, and feed it into the LSTM cell for time t in the encoder part. For ease of presentation, we drop all the subscripts. Then the hidden state h^t can be learned by

$$h^t = \mathrm{LSTM}(\mathbf{e}^{l,t} \parallel \mathbf{e}^{g,t} \parallel \mathbf{e}^{d,t}, h^{t-1}), \tag{6}$$

where $\parallel$ means the concatenation operation, and h^{t-1} is the hidden state at time $t-1$. The resultant hidden state h^t is regarded as the latent representation of the air quality status of s_i at time t.

The last hidden state h^T produced from the encoder part encapsulates the information of all historical data and serves as the initial hidden state of the decoder. The input to an LSTM cell for time t in the decoder consists of the forecast weather data at station s_i, denoted by $\bar{\mathbf{w}}^t$, and the predicted PM2.5 value of station s_i at time $t-1$, denoted by $\hat{y}^{t-1}$. Similarly, we concatenate $\bar{\mathbf{w}}^t$ and $\hat{y}^{t-1}$, and calculate the hidden state h^t at time t as

$$h^t = \mathrm{LSTM}(\bar{\mathbf{w}}^t \parallel \hat{y}^{t-1}, h^{t-1}). \tag{7}$$

4.5 Model Learning

Since we are tasked with a regression problem, we employ the mean squared error (MSE) as the objective function, which measures the average of squared distances between predicted PM2.5 values and the actual ones. We apply L_2 regularization to mitigate overfitting. Formally, the objective function $\mathcal{L}$ we optimize is:

$$\mathcal{L} = \frac{1}{M} \sum_{i=1}^{M} (y_i - f(\mathbf{x}_i, \Theta))^2 + \lambda \|\Theta\|_2, \tag{8}$$

where M is the number of training instances, $\mathbf{x}_i$ is a training instance, Θ is the set of trainable parameters in our proposed model, and λ is the regularization parameter. Early stopping is also used to reduce overfitting.

Recall that $\Theta = \{\Theta_1, \Theta_2\}$ consists of two subsets of parameters, where $\Theta_1 = \{\gamma, \{\mathbf{W}^{(l)}\}_{l=1}^K\}$ includes the parameters to learn the embeddings from a dynamic spatial graph, and Θ_2 includes the parameters of forget gates, input gates, and output gates in the encoder-decoder LSTM network.

5 Experiments

In this section, we conduct a comprehensive experimental study to demonstrate that our proposed method outperforms the state-of-the-art competitors. In addition, we provide a case study to intuitively show the benefits of dispersion-driven dynamic spatial modeling.

5.1   Datasets

We utilize the following real datasets in the experiments, which are commonly used in extensive literature.

Air Quality Data. We collect air quality data, including AQI, PM2.5, PM10, O_3, NO_2, CO, SO_2, from all 35 ground-based air quality monitoring stations in Beijing.[1] Since PM2.5 is the major pollutant widely used by government agencies for public communication, we predict the PM2.5 values in the experiments. We use linear interpolation to fill in missing values that occur within 3 h. Continuous missing data spanning over 3 h are discarded [21].

Meteorological Data. Following the previous study [21], we consider grid-based weather data obtained from the Global Data Assimilation System (GDAS).[2] The spatial resolution of the grid data is $0.25°$. We extract the region with latitudes between $39.5°$ and $40.75°$ and longitudes between $115.75°$ and $117.25°$, which covers all the monitoring stations in Beijing. We select five weather attributes: temperature, humidity, wind speed, and wind directions (including wind-u and wind-v in GDAS). As suggested in [21], we conduct a temporal linear interpolation to convert the 3-hourly raw data to hourly data.

POIs. POI types and density in a region directly affect its air quality. Similar to [23], we consider 12 types of POIs from Amap of Beijing,[3] and compute the number of POIs in each category within the affecting region of a station as a feature.

Road Networks. We download the road network data of Beijing from OpenStreetMap (OSM).[4] There are five types of roads, namely primary road, secondary road, tertiary road, residential road and footway road. Similarly, we calculate the number of each type of roads as a feature.

In addition, similar to the previous study [21], we extract 3 time features, including hour of day, day of week, and month, from the timestamp of each data point.

5.2   Experimental Settings

We process air quality data and meteorological data from January 1st, 2016 to January 31st, 2018, together with POI and road network data. The portions of training, validation, and test data are split by the ratio 8:1:1. In particular, training data and test data are split in temporal order in order to avoid data leakage. The historical time window T is set to 48, and we aim to predict the PM2.5 values in the next 24 h. We use 64 hidden units (i.e., the dimension of a hidden state) in an LSTM cell for feature representation, and optimize the objective function using the Adam

---

[1] http://beijingair.sinaapp.com.

[2] https://www.ncdc.noaa.gov/data-access/model-data/model-datasets/global-data-assimilation-system-gdas.

[3] https://lbs.amap.com/api/webservice/download.

[4] https://www.openstreetmap.org/.

Table 1. Performance comparisons of different models

	1–6 h		7–12 h		13–18 h		19–24 h	
	MAE	RMSE	MAE	RMSE	MAE	RMSE	MAE	RMSE
Naive approach	14.87	26.33	26.00	43.16	32.21	50.70	35.45	54.79
LSTM	14.17	20.91	25.88	33.83	32.67	40.23	37.03	44.08
Seq2seq	14.13	21.39	23.99	32.59	30.14	38.55	33.61	41.89
DeepAir [20]	19.18	25.15	23.13	29.64	25.20	31.88	28.43	35.37
GeoMAN [13]	14.03	19.10	19.42	25.06	22.95	29.31	24.23	32.14
WGC-LSTM [19]	12.78	18.24	18.05	23.59	18.92	28.00	25.42	29.74
MGED-Net [21]	13.44	17.35	18.05	22.83	20.95	26.01	21.91	26.88
Our method	**10.82**	**15.71**	**16.54**	**21.10**	**17.52**	**24.54**	**19.13**	**24.91**

Table 2. Performance comparison of different spatial correlation modeling methods

	1–6 h		7–12 h		13–18 h		19–24 h	
	MAE	RMSE	MAE	RMSE	MAE	RMSE	MAE	RMSE
Without dynamic spatial	15.52	23.53	20.02	25.81	21.13	30.71	24.80	32.66
Fixed **A**	15.30	19.99	19.63	24.71	22.03	29.97	25.07	32.12
Shared **A** [19]	12.78	18.24	18.05	23.59	18.92	28.00	25.42	29.74
Our method	**10.82**	**15.71**	**16.54**	**21.10**	**17.52**	**24.54**	**19.13**	**24.91**

optimizer with learning rate 0.001. To address overfitting, we use L_2 regularization with the regularization coefficient of 0.0001, and employ early stopping according to the validation error. Our code is implemented in PyTorch.

5.3   Compared Methods

We compare our proposed model with a wide range of representative approaches described below.

- **Naive approach** uses the PM2.5 value of the current time step as the predicted values for all future hours.
- **LSTM** uses a typical LSTM model to predict the 24 h' PM2.5 values.
- **Seq2seq** is an encoder-decoder network with stacked LSTMs in both encoder and decoder.
- **DeepAir** [20] is a distributed fusion network, which consists of 5 subnets powered by a FusionNet structure. Then, these subnets are merged to generate prediction results according to their weights.
- **GeoMAN** [13] is based on an encoder-decoder architecture with a multi-level attention mechanism. External factors are fused with the output of the encoder as the input to the decoder.
- **WGC-LSTM** [19] is a weighted graph convolutional LSTM network, which considers the adjacency matrix of the spatial graph as model parameters. The adjacency matrix is static and shared among all time steps.

- **MGED-Net** [21] is a multi-group encoder-decoder network with multiple encoders and a single decoder. All features are divided into different groups by correlation and merged by the encoder fusion strategy.

5.4   Experimental Results

Following the previous studies [13, 21], we use two widely-used evaluation metrics, *root mean squared error* (RMSE) and *mean absolute error* (MAE), to measure the performance of different prediction models. Similarly, we report the prediction results in four time intervals (1–6 h, 7–12 h, 13–18 h, and 19–24 h).

We report the main experimental results in Table 1. Among all models, our proposed model obtains the best results in all four time intervals on both metrics. Specifically, our method shows 12.6% to 19.4% improvement and 5.6% to 9.4% improvement over the state-of-the-art approach MGED-Net on MAE and RMSE, respectively. Compared to LSTM, encoder-decoder-based methods (i.e., Seq2seq, GeoMAN, MGED-Net and our model) achieve significant improvements in long-term predictions due to the decoder component. This justifies the adoption of an encoder-decoder architecture in our method to model the long-term temporal evolution. Moreover, it can be seen that our method's short-term prediction performance (e.g., 1–6 h and 7–12 h) is also much better than that of WGC-LSTM. We deem that it is due to the dispersion-driven dynamic spatial correlation modeling. In contrast, modeling the spatial influence by a static adjacency matrix in WGC-LSTM does not reflect the real air pollutant dispersion process well, and thus leads to less desirable prediction performance. In the following sections, we provide more experiments to study the effects of different spatial correlation modeling methods.

Benefits of Dynamic Spatial Graph. To demonstrate the benefits of modeling dynamic spatial influence with atmospheric prior, we conduct a set of experiments with different methods of modeling spatial correlation.

- **Without dynamic spatial** is a variant of our method that removes all dynamic spatial features. The rest is the same as the proposed method.
- **Fixed A** considers the geographic proximity (e.g., the Euclidean distance) between stations as edge weights of the spatial graph, which is set in advance before the training.
- **Shared A** is essentially the method in [19], where the elements in the adjacency matrix of the spatial graph are considered as learnable parameters. Note that the adjacency matrix here is shared among all time steps.

Table 2 shows the performance of different spatial correlation modeling methods. We can draw a few important observations. First, explicitly modeling the spatial correlations among monitoring stations, even only considering their Euclidean distance, is beneficial. Second, the spatial influence among different stations is indeed not simply determined by their geographic proximity. This explains why Fixed **A**'s performance is much worse than those of Shared **A** and

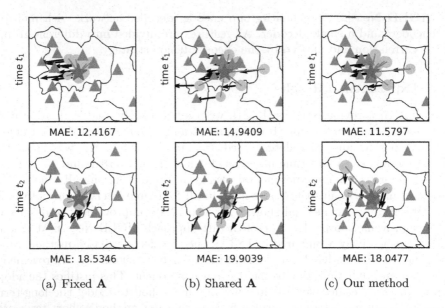

Fig. 3. Visualization of the spatial influence of different spatial correlation modeling methods on a target station

our method. Third, modeling dynamic spatial influence using well-established atmospheric prior is rewarding. It not only achieves much better performance, but also leads to a less complex model that is easier to train.

Dynamic Spatial Graph Visualization. Finally, to better understand how the dynamic spatial graph helps improve air quality prediction accuracy, we visualize the spatial influence of different stations on a target station (marked as a red star) at two representative time steps t_1 and t_2 in Fig. 3. The yellow dots represent the top-10 stations that have the most spatial influence on the target station. The size of a dot represents its pollution level. The larger a dot, the higher its PM2.5 value. The direction of an arrow indicates the wind direction at a station, and the length indicates the wind speed. The grey triangles denote other stations. Similarly, their sizes represent their air pollution level.

We have a few interesting observations. First, the most influential stations of our method at different time steps well align with the Gaussian plume model and one's intuition. The most influential stations at different time steps for a target station are also different, which are determined by multiple factors defined by the Gaussian plume model, such as the geographic distance, air quality, and meteorological conditions. This reflects the *dynamic* nature of the spatial correlation modeling in our method. Second, the most influential stations in both Fixed **A** and Shared **A** are fixed over time. For Fixed **A**, it is because the geographic proximity among stations does not change over time; for Shared **A**, it is due to the fact that the same adjacency matrix is shared among all time steps.

In particular, the most influential stations of Shared **A** are counter-intuitive. Third, while in general Shared **A** performs better than Fixed **A**, at time steps t_1 and t_2, its MAE values are worse than those of Fixed **A**. This is not difficult to understand—the adjacency matrix learned by minimizing the average error over all time steps cannot guarantee reasonable performance at every time step.

6   Conclusion and Future Work

In this paper, we took on a new perspective of air quality prediction, which models dynamic spatial influence among monitoring stations guided by atmospheric dispersion modeling. We proposed to construct a dynamic spatial graph based on the Gaussian plume model, generate graph embeddings by a GCN, and finally fuse spatial and temporal information seamlessly in an encoder-decoder LSTM network. Experiments on real-world benchmark datasets validate the superiority of the proposed model. In addition, we provided a case study to intuitively understand the benefits of dynamic spatial correlation modeling. In future work, we will investigate other possible factors to improve dynamic spatial correlation modeling, and explore more advanced prediction models to improve prediction accuracy (e.g., stacked LSTMs).

References

1. Abdel-Rahman, A.A.: On the dispersion models and atmospheric dispersion. Int. J. Glob. Warming **3**(4), 257–273 (2011)
2. Arystanbekova, N.K.: Application of gaussian plume models for air pollution simulation at instantaneous emissions. Math. Comput. Simul. **67**(4), 451–458 (2004)
3. Bergin, M.S., Noblet, G.S., Petrini, K., Dhieux, J.R., Milford, J.B., Harley, R.A.: Formal uncertainty analysis of a Lagrangian photochemical air pollution model. Environ. Sci. Technol. **33**(7), 1116–1126 (1999)
4. Chen, L., Cai, Y., Ding, Y., Lv, M., Yuan, C., Chen, G.: Spatially fine-grained urban air quality estimation using ensemble semi-supervised learning and pruning. In: Proceedings of the 2016 ACM International Joint Conference on Pervasive and Ubiquitous Computing (UbiComp), pp. 1076–1087 (2016)
5. Cheng, W., Shen, Y., Zhu, Y., Huang, L.: A neural attention model for urban air quality inference: learning the weights of monitoring stations. In: Proceedings of the 32th AAAI Conference on Artificial Intelligence (AAAI), pp. 2151–2158 (2018)
6. Guizilini, V., Ramos, F.: A nonparametric online model for air quality prediction. In: Proceedings of the 29th AAAI Conference on Artificial Intelligence (AAAI), pp. 651–657 (2015)
7. Hsieh, H., Lin, S., Zheng, Y.: Inferring air quality for station location recommendation based on urban big data. In: Proceedings of the 21th ACM SIGKDD International Conference on Knowledge Discovery and Data Mining (KDD), pp. 437–446 (2015)
8. Jiang, Y., Sun, X., Wang, W., Young, S.D.: Enhancing air quality prediction with social media and natural language processing. In: Proceedings of the 57th Conference of the Association for Computational Linguistics (ACL), pp. 2627–2632 (2019)

9. Jin, B.J., Bu, P.S., Jin, K.J.: Urban flow and dispersion simulation using a CFD model coupled to a mesoscale model. J. Appl. Meteorol. Climatol. **48**(8), 1667–1681 (2009)
10. Jutzeler, A., Li, J.J., Faltings, B.: A region-based model for estimating urban air pollution. In: Proceedings of the 28th AAAI Conference on Artificial Intelligence (AAAI), pp. 424–430 (2014)
11. Kipf, T.N., Welling, M.: Semi-supervised classification with graph convolutional networks. In: Proceedings of the 5th International Conference on Learning Representations (ICLR) (2017)
12. Li, X., et al.: Long short-term memory neural network for air pollutant concentration predictions: method development and evaluation. Environ. Pollut. **231**, 997–1004 (2017)
13. Liang, Y., Ke, S., Zhang, J., Yi, X., Zheng, Y.: GeoMAN: multi-level attention networks for geo-sensory time series prediction. In: Proceedings of the 27th International Joint Conference on Artificial Intelligence (IJCAI), pp. 3428–3434 (2018)
14. Luo, Z., Huang, J., Hu, K., Li, X., Zhang, P.: AccuAir: winning solution to air quality prediction for KDD cup 2018. In: Proceedings of the 25th ACM SIGKDD International Conference on Knowledge Discovery and Data Mining (KDD), pp. 1842–1850 (2019)
15. Paolo, Z.: Gaussian models. In: Air Pollution Modeling, pp. 141–183. Springer, Boston (1990). https://doi.org/10.1007/978-1-4757-4465-1_7
16. Pramanik, P., Mondal, T., Nandi, S., Saha, M.: AirCalypse: can Twitter help in urban air quality measurement and who are the influential users? In: Proceedings of the 29th International World Wide Web Conferences (WWW), pp. 540–545 (2020)
17. Rakowska, A., et al.: Impact of traffic volume and composition on the air quality and pedestrian exposure in urban street canyon. Atmos. Environ. **98**, 260–270 (2014)
18. Sutskever, I., Vinyals, O., Le, Q.V.: Sequence to sequence learning with neural networks. In: Proceedings of the 28th Conference on Neural Information Processing Systems (NIPS), pp. 3104–3112 (2014)
19. Wilson, T., Tan, P., Luo, L.: A low rank weighted graph convolutional approach to weather prediction. In: Proceeding of the 18th IEEE International Conference on Data Mining (ICDM), pp. 627–636 (2018)
20. Yi, X., Zhang, J., Wang, Z., Li, T., Zheng, Y.: Deep distributed fusion network for air quality prediction. In: Proceedings of the 24th ACM SIGKDD International Conference on Knowledge Discovery and Data Mining (KDD), pp. 965–973 (2018)
21. Zhang, Y., et al.: Multi-group encoder-decoder networks to fuse heterogeneous data for next-day air quality prediction. In: Proceedings of the 28th International Joint Conference on Artificial Intelligence (IJCAI), pp. 4341–4347 (2019)
22. Zhao, X., Xu, T., Fu, Y., Chen, E., Guo, H.: Incorporating spatio-temporal smoothness for air quality inference. In: Proceeding of the 17th IEEE International Conference on Data Mining (ICDM), pp. 1177–1182 (2017)
23. Zheng, Y., Liu, F., Hsieh, H.: U-air: when urban air quality inference meets big data. In: Proceedings of the 19th ACM SIGKDD International Conference on Knowledge Discovery and Data Mining (KDD), pp. 1436–1444 (2013)
24. Zheng, Y., et al.: Forecasting fine-grained air quality based on big data. In: Proceedings of the 21th ACM SIGKDD International Conference on Knowledge Discovery and Data Mining (KDD), pp. 2267–2276 (2015)

Learning Cooperative Max-Pressure Control by Leveraging Downstream Intersections Information for Traffic Signal Control

Yuquan Peng[1], Lin Li[1($\boxtimes$)], Qing Xie[1], and Xiaohui Tao[2]

[1] School of Computer Science and Technology, Wuhan University of Technology,
Wuhan 430070, China
{pengyuquan,cathylilin,felixxq}@whut.edu.cn
[2] School of Sciences, University of Southern Queensland, Toowoomba,
QLD 4350, Australia
Xiaohui.Tao@usq.edu.au

Abstract. Traffic signal control problems are critical in urban intersections. Recently, deep reinforcement learning demonstrates impressive performance in the control of traffic signals. The design of state and reward function is often heuristic, which leads to highly vulnerable performance. To solve this problem, some studies introduce transportation theory into deep reinforcement learning to support the design of reward function e.g., max-pressure control, which have yielded promising performance. We argue that the constant changes of intersections' pressure can be better represented with the consideration of downstream neighboring intersections. In this paper, we propose CMPLight, a deep reinforcement learning traffic signal control approach with a novel cooperative max-pressure-based reward function to leverage the vehicle queue information of neighborhoods. The approach employs cooperative max-pressure to guide the design of reward function in deep reinforcement learning. We theoretically prove that it is stabilizing when the average traffic demand is admissible and traffic flow is stable in road network. The state of deep reinforcement learning is enhanced by neighboring information, which helps to learn a detailed representation of traffic environment. Extensive experiments are conducted on synthetic and real-world datasets. The experimental results demonstrate that our approach outperforms traditional heuristic transportation control approaches and the state-of-the-arts learning-based approaches in terms of average travel time of all vehicles in road network.

Keywords: Deep reinforcement learning · Traffic signal control ·
Cooperative max-pressure · Downstream information

1 Introduction

With the population growth and the rapid development of cities, the problem of urban traffic congestion has become more and more serious, and optimizing

© Springer Nature Switzerland AG 2021
L. H. U et al. (Eds.): APWeb-WAIM 2021, LNCS 12859, pp. 399–413, 2021.
https://doi.org/10.1007/978-3-030-85899-5_29

traffic signal control is becoming increasingly important. Traditional traffic signal control approaches usually work with a fixed period, a fixed phase sequence,
manual intervention or expert knowledge. These approaches have difficulties in
adapting to the dynamic change of traffic flow, and their performance are not
satisfied in complex traffic situations [1–4]. Recently, researchers have begun
applying deep reinforcement learning techniques to traffic signal control problems, resulting better performance than traditional approaches [5–8]. One of
the main problems of current deep reinforcement learning based approaches is
that the design of the state and the reward function is mostly heuristic. The
reward function can be defined by queue length [6,7], vehicle delay [9,10] or the
combination of weighted traffic parameters [11,12]. Its selections usually rely on
arbitrary experience, leading to unstable performance.

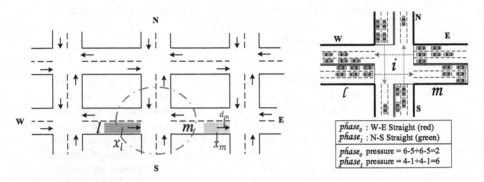

Fig. 1. The illustration of cooperative max-pressure by considering the information
of downstream neighboring intersections (left part); the calculation of phase pressure
based on max-pressure (right part).

Recent studies have pointed out that the design of reward function driven
by transportation theory can alleviate the above problems. The state-of-the-arts
max-pressure [3] in transportation literature has been applied to the control of
traffic lights [7,13]. The key idea of max-pressure is to minimize the "pressure" at
the intersection, which can be roughly defined as the difference in vehicle queue
length between an incoming lane and an outgoing lane. Through theoretical
analysis of max-pressure approach, we observe that traffic light phase control
is ineffective when the queue length on downstream segment of intersection is
greater than the queue length on upstream segment, or when two vehicle queues
are close. As the right part of Fig. 1 illustrates, for intersection i, its pressure
of $phase_0$(W-E straight) is 2 and that of $phase_1$(N-S straight) is 6 based on
max-pressure. Then $phase_1$ will be activated in the next time step for a larger
pressure, but accurately $phase_0$ needs to be prioritized because there are more
vehicles waiting to pass through the intersection. The same is applied to the W-E
and N-S left turn phases. The max-pressure approach considers the vehicle queue
information of an intersection, which leads to an inaccurate phase pressure. In
the left part of Fig. 1, the intersection i has a downstream intersection j, and the
pressure of $phase_0$ will increase when the phase p_j of downstream intersection j

is activated at the same time step t. The pressure of $phase_1$ will decrease likewise for the influence of neighboring intersections. It is obvious that the pressure of an intersection is easily affected by its neighboring intersections. Therefore, not only the queuing information of the intersection but also the information of downstream neighboring intersections need to be considered.

Inspired by the concept of traffic process ability [14] and cooperative max-pressure (CMP) control approach [15] in the transportation field, the phase pressure of an intersection can be learned by a cooperative way. As Fig. 1 illustrates, some vehicles leave the lane m, and the pressure on the lane l increases. In max-pressure control, the phase pressure can be loosely defined as $x_l - x_m$, while considering the leaving vehicles d_m in cooperative max-pressure, the phase pressure can be roughly defined as $x_l - (x_m - d_m)$. x_l and x_m are the number of the vehicle queue on the lane l and m respectively. d_m is the number of vehicles preparing to pass through the intersection. However, the traditional solution of cooperative max-pressure control approach is greedy and easily falls into local optimization for maximize throughput by minimizing intersection "pressure".

To address the above problem, we propose Cooperative Max-Pressure light control (CMPLight) based on deep reinforcement learning, theoretically driven by transportation theory. Most importantly, we apply neighboring information for traffic light control in two ways. Firstly, we leverage the vehicle queue length from downstream neighboring intersections to define cooperative max-pressure as the reward function. Not only the vehicle queue information at the intersection is considered, but also the information about its neighboring intersections is included. It accurately reflects the "pressure" conditions at the intersection. Secondly, we tranform the intersection states with lane-wise queue information from neighboring intersections as vectors into the deep reinforcement learning, which can help deep neural network extract effective state features and learn accurate states representation. The state transition of traffic flow in cooperative max-pressure is the same as the evolution equations of Markov chain in deep reinforcement learning. Deep Q-Network [16] is applied to control traffic signals by interacting with the environment for learning optimal policies in complex scenarios. In this paper, our main contributions are as follows:

1. The start-of-the-arts cooperative max-pressure theory in transportation literature is considered into the traffic signal control approaches as the reward function in deep reinforcement learning. It contributes to alleviating unstable performance of heuristics traffic signal control.
2. We prove that the design of reward function still maintains the stability of queuing traffic flow in road network by leveraging the information from downstream neighboring intersections.
3. A series of experiments are conducted on both synthetic and real-world datasets. Experimental results on different traffic flow and network structure scenarios show that our CMPLight outperforms the state-of-the-arts deep reinforcement learning based approaches and benefits from the transportation theoretical support.

2   Related Work

Traditional traffic signal control strategies such as Webster [1], Greenwave [2], Fixed-time [4] and Max-pressure [3] usually work with pre-designed fixed-cycle, fixed-phase sequences or expert knowledge, which are not well adapted to dynamic traffic flow environments. Reinforcement learning algorithm can learn from the environment and adapt to dynamic traffic flow well, and it demonstrates superior performance in traffic signal control [6,7,17,18].

The most commonly used value-based Q-learning [19] for reinforcement learning is applied in traffic signal control at single intersection. Q-learning has also been employed to solve multi-intersection traffic signal control problems in combination with the multi-agent model [11,17,18]. However, the key challenge comes from the dimensional curse for multi-intersection traffic control problems [16]. To effectively alleviate the above problems, Deep Q-Network is applied to traffic signal control with impressive performance [6,20], as well as to search problems [21] and car-sharing problems [22].

The design of reward function plays a major role in reinforcement learning based traffic signal control. The travel time of a vehicle is affected by multiple effects of traffic signals and traffic movements. If the travel time is used as reward directly, it would be delayed and ineffective in indicating the effect of traffic signals [7]. Therefore, the existing reinforcement learning based approaches have a tendency to apply more complex reward definition that can be effectively measured after an action. Some traffic parameters, such as queue length, vehicle delay, vehicle waiting time, etc. are used as reward function in traffic signal control [6,7,9–12]. However, different weight parameters may lead to different results in terms of average travel time, and the weight of each factor is tricky to set in the reward function. Some researchers explore the support from the transportation literature. The max-pressure is applied to deep reinforcement learning in traffic signal control and shows promising improvements [7]. Since then, researchers have proposed MPLight with max-pressure to address large-scale traffic signals control problems [13]. PDLight has redesigned the reward function, but lacks guideline from the transportation theory [23]. The max-pressure-based approach focuses on the phase pressure of a single intersection without considering the influence of the downstream neighboring intersections information. Inspired by the state-of-the-arts cooperative max-pressure approach [15] in transportation literature, we design the state and reward functions in deep reinforcement learning by leveraging the neighboring information. It can alleviate the risk of over-saturation in road network by balancing the queue lengths of neighboring intersections and minimize the pressure in each phase of intersection.

3   Preliminary

This paper focuses on multi-intersection traffic signal control scenarios. In Fig. 2(a), as an example, each intersection has four incoming approaches $l \in L_{in}$ and four outgoing approaches $m \in L_{out}$, and each road consists of three lanes.

Traffic movement (l, m) is the traffic flow that vehicles travel through the intersection from lane l to another lane m. There are eight traffic movements in each intersection. A phase p is a set of traffic movements that do not conflict with each other. Note that different intersection environments have different phase definitions, and we use the general representation here [7].

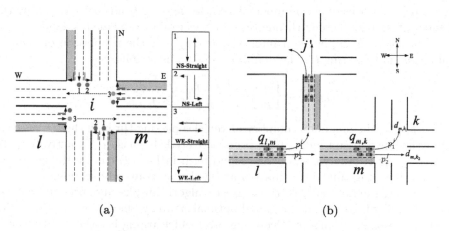

(a) (b)

Fig. 2. (a) The illustration of phases and traffic movements in traffic signal control of an intersection. (b) Cooperative max-pressure description. The pressure of straight phase is affected by downstream intersection j, likewise for left-turn phase is affected by downstream intersection j'. It should be noticed that the number of neighboring intersections is not only one. There are four neighboring intersections generally.

The max-pressure traffic signal controller is the properties of being scalable, distributed over intersections, and provable stability [3]. It have been used as the reward function in deep reinforcement learning with achieved impressive performance in recently studies [7,13]. However, the pressure of a phase is simply defined as the difference between the queue lengths of upstream and downstream of an intersection, which is easily affected by the neighboring intersections.

In this paper, the pressure of phase is defined by a cooperative way leveraging the information of downstream neighboring intersections. As illustrated in Fig. 2(b), there are vehicle queues in lane l and lane m. Some vehicles $(q_{l,m})$ pass through the intersection i from lane l to lane m when straight phase p_2^i is activated. For the intersection j, there is phase p_1^j and p_2^j, and $d_{m,k}$ denotes the number of vehicles departing from lane m to lane k. If the phase p_2^j is activated at the same time step, the number of vehicles on downstream lane will decrease and the phase pressure will increase. The same condition can also occur under the left turn phase p_1^i of intersection i. Therefore, the phase pressure at the intersection i is affected by the phase state and vehicle queues of the downstream intersections. By leveraging the neighboring information to correct the calculation of phase pressure in max-pressure control, an accurate phase pressure situation is obtained. Then the phase pressure is minimized to balance the distribution of all vehicles in road network and maximize throughput. Based on the above analysis, the calculation of phase pressure in cooperative max-pressure is as follows:

$$p_{l,m}(t) = q_{l,m}(t) - \sum_{p \in L_{out}} r_{m,k} \cdot (q_{m,k}(t) - d_{m,k}(t)), \tag{1}$$

where $d_{m,k}$ represents the number of vehicles leaving from m to k; $q_{l,m}$ is the number of vehicles passing through the intersection i from lane l to lane m; L_{out} is the set of outgoing lanes of intersection j; $r_{m,k}$ is the proportion of vehicles leaving m and entering k. The definition of $d_{m,k}$ is as follows:

$$d_{m,k}(t) = \begin{cases} p_n q_{m,k}(t) & q_{m,k}(t) < f_{\max} \\ p_n f_{\max} & q_{m,k}(t) \geq f_{\max} \end{cases}, \tag{2}$$

where $f_{\max}$ is the maximum number of vehicles passing through the intersection when the downstream light phase p_n is activated. If phase p_n is activated, the value of p_n is 1, otherwise, 0. The second term in Eq. (2) can be thought of as the overall average queuing situation at the downstream intersection.

However, the approach is also a greedy algorithm like max-pressure control and it is difficult to obtain the global optimal strategy among intersections with complex traffic environment. Deep reinforcement learning has the ability to find a better solution for traffic signal control. It is a challenge to combine them together. Whether cooperative max-pressure as the reward function can optimize traffic signal control and with the assurance of the stability of traffic flow in road network will be an challenging yet rewarding study.

4   Our Approach

4.1   Agent Design

The traffic light control problem is described as the Markov Decision Process (MDP) that is represented as a tuple $< S, A, R, P, \gamma >$. Traffic signal light at each intersection is controlled by an agent set for each intersection in road network. At each time step t, the agent receives state $s_t \in S$ and selects an action $a_t \in A$ based on its observation. After taking the action, the state of environment transitions to the next state $s_{t+1} \in S$. P is the state transition matrix which is the probability of moving among the environment states. Then the agent receives a reward r_t which is determined by the reward function $R_t = \sum_{k=0}^{\infty} \gamma^k r_{t+k+1}$.

- **State:** This paper follows the earlier work [7], the state includes the current phase p, the number of vehicles in each outgoing lane $q_m (m \in L_{out})$ and the number of vehicles in each incoming lane $q_l (l \in L_{in})$. In addition, the number of vehicles queue and the phase status of the downstream neighboring intersection are taken into the state definition, which helps the agent learn accurate environment state representation. There are many ways to introduce this information, such as convolutional neural network, and the simple concatenation is used to verify that it works.

- **Action**: Phase-based and step-based definitions are usually used as standard actions in traffic signal control. At each time step t, each agent chooses a phase p as its action a_t from action set A. Then the agent chooses whether to continue the current phase step or switch to the next phase as the learning progresses. As shown in Fig. 2(a), four phases of the traffic light are considered, i.e., W-E straight, N-S straight, W-E left, N-S left.
- **Reward**: The pressure of each intersection is defined by leveraging the information of downstream neighboring intersections in the cooperative max-pressure-based approach. It can be expressed as the difference between the number of vehicles in incoming lanes and the overall average queuing condition or average pressure of neighboring intersections. The reward definition based on the cooperative max-pressure is defined as:

$$R_i = -| \sum_{(l,m) \in M_i} p_{l,m}|, \tag{3}$$

where M_i is the set of all the traffic movements of an intersection i and $p_{l,m}$ is defined as the Eq. (1).

The action with the minimum intersection pressure calculated by the CMP-Light is selected as the action of the next time step. In contrast to the max-pressure-based approaches, the intersection pressure of CMPLight is effected by the downstream neighboring intersections conditions. As the exact way of calculating reward, it avoids conflicts caused by the number of passing vehicles over the maximum carrying capacity of neighborhoods.

4.2   Learning Process

In this paper, Deep Q-Network [16] is adapted to control traffic signal at each intersection. The pseudocode of CMPLight algorithm is shown in Algorithm 1. One of focuses in our approach is the redesigned reward function driven by transportation theory. It obtains the intersection pressure by leveraging information from downstream neighboring intersections. The other is that the neighboring information is considered into the input of the deep neural network to learn relevant and accurate state features. They are employed in Step 5 and 6 in Algorithm 1, respectively.

To stabilize the learning process, frozen target network is applied to provide temporal difference for updating the primary network, and the sample batches from replay memory are used to train the deep neural network. Step 6 shows that each agent observes the state of intersection environment at each time step t. Then the states are taken into the deep neural network to extract state features. The agent predicts the Q-value to choose actions, and the Q-function in Step 4 is updated by:

$$Q^\pi (s_t, a_t) \leftarrow Q^\pi (s_t, a_t) + \alpha (y_t - Q^\pi (s_t, a_t)), \tag{4}$$

where α is learning rate, and y_t is temporal difference. During the training process in Step 11 to 14, the main network parameter θ is updated after each action, and the target network parameter $\hat{\theta}$ is updated after a period of step. The goal of action selection is to maximize the reward R by choosing the action at each time step t with the highest Q-value as be shown in Step 4.

Algorithm 1. CMPLight

Input: replay buffer size M, batch size d, the number of episodes E, learning rate α, the number of simulation step T, discount factor γ, update frequency C

Initialize Main network Q with weights θ, Target network $\hat{Q}$ with weights $\hat{\theta}$, Replay memory with M

1: **for** $e = 1, \ldots, E$ **do**
2:     *Initialize* state s_1, and action a_1
3:     **for** $t = 1, \ldots, T$ **do**
4:         Take action $a_t = argmax_a Q^\pi(s_t, a; \theta)$ with probability $1 - \epsilon$ or a random action with probability ϵ
5:         Calculate cooperative max-pressure as the reward r_t by Equation.(1)
6:         Observe next state s_{t+1}
7:         Append (s_t, a_t, r_t, s_{t+1}) to replay memory
8:         **if** Replay buffer M is full **then**
9:             Delete the oldest memory
10:        **end if**
11:        Sample random d from memory
12:        $y_t = \begin{cases} r_t & \text{if } t = T \\ r_t + \gamma \max_a Q^\pi\left(s_{t+1}, a_{t+1}; \hat{\theta}_t\right), & \text{otherwise.} \end{cases}$
13:        Update θ by policy gradient
14:        Every C steps update Target network $\hat{\theta} = \theta$
15:    **end for**
16: **end for**

---

5   Stability Analysis

Stabilization on Traffic Movements with Our Proposed Reward Function. Some researchers have analyzed the stability and rationality of combining max-pressure and deep reinforcement learning as an optimization problem [3,7]. However, with the help of downstream neighboring intersections information to achieve cooperative max-pressure, it is necessary to prove that it is stable.

Definition: *Movement Process Stability.* Firstly, the traffic movement process stability is defined as follows: the vehicle queuing length process $X_t = \{q_{l,m}(t)\}$ is stable in the mean if for some $K < \infty$

$$\frac{1}{T} \sum_{t=1}^{T} \sum_{l,m} E[q_{l,m}(t)] < K, \quad \forall T, \tag{5}$$

where E denotes exception. The stability of the mean implies that the link is circular and has a unique stable probability distribution.

Theorem: The Cooperative Max-Pressure Control is Stabilizing. Considering the information of downstream neighboring intersections in deep reinforcement learning policy, the cooperative max-pressure control is stabilizing and still maintains the stability of traffic flow in road network, whenever the average demand is admissible.

Proof: Based on Theorem 1 in [3], the Lyapunov function still can be used to provide sufficient conditions for stability in traffic road network with vehicle queuing information of neighborhoods. Suppose $E\{X_i(t)\} < \infty$ for all $i \in \{1, 2, \ldots, N\}$, and there exist $B > 0$ and $\epsilon > 0$ satisfies

$$E\{L(X(t+1)) - L(X(t))|X(t)\} <= B - \epsilon \sum_{i=1}^{N} X_i(t), \tag{6}$$

then the network is stable, where the Lyapunov function is defined as

$$L(X) = \sum_{i=1}^{N} X_i^2. \tag{7}$$

The queue length $q_{l,m}$ of lane l waiting from lane l to m can be computed as follows:

$$q_{l,m}(t+1) = q_{l,m}(t) + q_{l,m}^{in}(P(t)) - q_{l,m}^{out}(P(t)), \tag{8}$$

where $q_{l,m}^{in}(P(t))$ and $q_{l,m}^{out}(P(t))$ denote the vehicles entering $q_{l,m}(t)$ and vehicles leaving from $q_{l,m}(t)$ under the current traffic light phase switching strategy $P(t)$ at each time step t, respectively.

According to the Lyapunov function and the properties of the traffic network:

$$L(X(t+1)) - L(X(t)) = \sum_{l,m} ((q_{l,m}^{in})^2 + (q_{l,m}^{out})^2)$$
$$- 2 \sum_{l,m} (q_{l,m}(t) - \sum_p r_{m,k}(q_{m,k}(t) - q_{m,k}^{out}))q_{l,m}^{out}. \tag{9}$$

Let B $= max(\sum_{l,m}((q_{l,m}^{in})^2 + (q_{l,m}^{out})^2))$, we have:

$$L(X(t+1)) - L(X(t)) \leq$$
$$B - 2 \sum_{l,m} (q_{l,m}(t) - \sum_p r_{m,k}(q_{m,k}(t) - q_{m,k}^{out}))q_{l,m}^{out}. \tag{10}$$

Since the queuing network model is similar to that in [3]:

$$\sum_{l,m} (q_{l,m}(t)[q_{l,m}^{in} - q_{l,m}^{out}] = \sum_{l,m} \sum_P \mu_{l,m}[q_{l,m}(t) - \sum_p r_{m,k} \cdot q_{m,k}]$$
$$\leq \sum_{l,m} \sum_P \mu_{l,m}[q_{l,m}(t) - \sum_p r_{m,k} \cdot (q_{m,k}(t) - d_{m,k}(t))]. \tag{11}$$

According to the above theorem, the traffic flow and road network controlled by the proposed cooperative max-pressure-based approach is stable under the admissible arrival rate in the capacity region. Then we have:

$$L(X(t+1)) - L(X(t)) \leq B - 2 \sum_{l,m} q_{l,m}(t)[q_{l,m}^{out} - q_{l,m}^{in}]. \tag{12}$$

Finally, we obtain:

$$E\{L(X(t+1)) - L(X(t))|X(t)\} <= B - 2\epsilon \sum_{l,m} q_{l,m}(t). \tag{13}$$

The modified cooperative max-pressure approach still satisfies the basic concept of max-pressure control and maintains the stability of traffic flow in road network. With the same traffic signal switching strategy, if the pressure of the downstream intersections can cooperative with the pressure of the upstream intersection, better throughput performance can be achieved. When the number of vehicles at the downstream intersection is zero, the cooperative max-pressure approach is degraded to the max-pressure approach.

6   Experiments

6.1   Datasets and Baselines

Datasets. In the experiments, we employ two kinds of synthetic and real-world datasets[1]. Each traffic dataset includes a road network data and traffic flow data. Traffic flow is defined as $(t, l_1, l_2, \cdots, l_n)$. t is the time when the vehicle enters the road network. l_1 is the rim edge lane of the vehicles entering the road network. l_n is the end lane of the vehicles leaving the road network.

- **Synthetic dataset**: The traffic flow datasets are extracted from the real traffic patterns of Jinan and Hangzhou with 6 intersections in arterial road network. Each intersection in the road network is a four-way intersection with each road being 300 m. There are two types of average vehicle arrival rates: 300 vehicles per hour/lane and 700 vehicles per hour/lane.
- **Real-world dataset**: The real-world datasets from New York City (NYC) are applied as benchmarks, which enable us to verify the performance of our approach in different real-world scenarios. The dataset contains a road network file of 16 intersections and four different traffic flows. There are 6,790, 4,513, 6,083 and 4,030 mean arrival rates (vehicles/hour) respectively.

Baseline. Our approach compares with the following baselines including conventional transportation control approaches and learning-based approaches.

---

[1] Open source, https://traffic-signal-control.github.io.

- **Fixed-time** [4]: This approach periodically cycles through the list of feasible phase configurations while not considering the traffic volume on the lanes of the road network. Each phase is under a fixed time of 15 s. There are four phases in traffic flow with turning vehicles.
- **GreenWave** [2]: It is the most classical approach in the transportation field to implement coordination, which aims to optimize the offset and reduce the number of stops for vehicles traveling at one certain direction. Each phase duration equals the ratio of the demand of an approach to total demand. The offset is the travel time of vehicles pass through the lane.
- **Max-Pressure** [3]: This approach favors control schedules that maximize the release of pressure on incoming and outgoing roads. The max-pressure controller tends to minimize the difference in the number of vehicles for the incoming and outgoing lanes.
- **GRL** [6]: GRL is a deep Q-learning approach for coordinated traffic signal control. Specifically, transfer planning and the max-plus coordination algorithm are employed for multi-intersection coordination.
- **LIT** [8]: LIT is a deep reinforcement learning approach that presents a simple but effective state and reward function to solve the traffic signal control problems. It uses the queue length as the reward function.
- **PressLight** [7]: It is a recently developed learning-based approach that incorporates pressure in the state and reward design for the deep reinforcement learning model. It has shown superior performance in multi-intersection control problems. And the baseline source code can be found in Github[2].

6.2 Experimental Settings

Experiments are conducted on Cityflow[3], an emerging open-source traffic simulator optimized for reinforcement learning. Our source code runs on the Intel(R) CPU Xeon(R) and NVIDIA GPU TITAN Xp. The average travel time as our evaluation measure is widely used in transportation field [7]. It is calculated as the average travel time of all vehicles spent in road network.

The state of each agent is represented by twelve-dimensional vectors. The queue information of intersection can be obtained through API in Cityflow, and there are sensors in the real world to obtain similar data. Each vehicle is set 5 m. In the synthetic dataset road network, each lane is 300 m. However, the length varys for the lanes in the real-world dataset. Generally, we use dynamic traffic flow to input into the road network. There are two different traffic flow modes: light and heavy. The speed of traffic flow on the road is set to 40 km per hour. Note that, the number of neighboring intersections relies on the structure of traffic road network with range two to four. After each phase switches, there is a 5 s yellow light to clear the vehicles in the intersection, which is in line with the setting of traffic lights in the real world. The right turn is not controlled by the signal light. The shortest green light time is set 10 s, that is, switch the

---

[2] https://github.com/wingsweihua/presslight.
[3] https://cityflow.readthedocs.io/en/latest/index.html.

phase in every 10 s. The length of each episode is 3,600 s. The training rounds are set to 600 and 700 for synthetic and real-world datasets respectively. Each experiment takes the last 50 rounds of results from the test round as the final verification data. In the deep Q-learning network, the discount factor γ is 0.8, the maximal sample size is 10,000, and the target network is updated every 10 steps. The source code of PressLight is provided by [7], and the experimental settings are retained.

6.3   Experimental Results

Performance Comparison. Table 1 shows the results of experiments on synthetic and real-world datasets in terms of average travel time (a.t.t.). Experimental results show that our approach outperforms traditional transportation control approaches and deep reinforcement learning approaches based on transportation theory. Our approach makes 31% and 30% performance improvement over state-of-the-arts deep reinforcement learning approaches on synthetic datasets and real-world datasets, respectively. Other interesting findings includes:

(1) The performance of traditional traffic signal control approaches [2–4] is unsatisfactory. Traditional approaches cannot adapt to the dynamical changing traffic flow since they overly rely on historical data and expert knowledge, and cannot handle complex scenarios.

(2) Our approach is superior to the other deep reinforcement learning approaches in about 30%. As the complexity of the traffic flow increases, it clearly outperforms the max-pressure-based approach PressLight [7]. We introduce downstream neighboring intersections information into the reward function and state features in deep reinforcement learning to help agents learn the pressure situation at the intersection and accurately estimate the Q-value better.

(3) Our CMPLight approach is comparable to the max-pressure-based approach in about 4% performance degradation when the traffic flow is relatively gentle and the number of vehicles is limited. In this case, downstream neighboring intersections have a negligible impact on the current intersection and our approach cannot obtain sufficient information from neighborhoods.

Table 1. Performance comparisons with all baselines in terms of a.t.t.

	Synthetic data (1 × 6 intersections)				Real-world data (1 × 16 intersections)			
	Light flat	Light peak	Heavy flat	Heavy peak	8th Ave. NYC	9th Ave. NYC	10th Ave. NYC	11th Ave. NYC
Fixed-time [4]	93.29	109.50	325.48	246.25	432.60	469.54	347.05	368.84
GreenWave [2]	98.39	124.09	263.36	286.85	451.98	502.30	317.02	314.08
Max-Pressure [3]	74.30	82.37	262.26	225.60	412.58	370.61	392.77	224.54
GRL [6]	123.02	115.85	525.64	757.73	704.98	669.69	676.19	676.19
LIT [8]	65.07	66.77	233.17	258.33	471.30	726.04	309.95	340.40
PressLight [7]	**59.96**	**61.34**	160.48	184.51	223.36	149.01	161.21	140.82
CMPLight(ours)	61.7	64.1	**119.37**	**116.4**	**147.51**	**106.82**	**110.50**	**104.00**

Performance in Different Network Scales. We compare the performance differences of our approach under different road network scales. Table 2 shows the results of different experimental settings. Our approach outperforms traditional traffic approaches and the max-pressure-based approach, achieving about 26% performance improvement on the grid road network (3×3 intersections). This is because intersections can take into account more downstream neighboring intersection information in grid road network. In the arterial network (1×6 intersections and 1×20 intersections), an intersection can consider up to two adjacent neighbors as downstream intersections. While in the grid road network, information about even four neighboring intersections can be included. However, in some small-scale scenarios (Light flat and Light peak in Table 1), leveraging downstream neighboring information to calculate intersection pressure well comparing with max-pressure-based reinforcement learning approaches. This is because in the case of small traffic flow situations, the pressure change at the intersection is not sensitive, and as a result, not easily affected by the intersections. In this case, the introduction of downstream neighboring information still has a comparable performance with about 4% degradation.

Table 2. Performance comparison under different traffic network scales.

	1×6 intersections		1×20 intersections		3×3 intersections	
	Heavy flat	Heavy peak	Heavy flat	Heavy peak	Heavy flat	Heavy peak
Max-pressure [3]	262.26	225.60	310.95	271.39	539.67	485.03
PressLight [7]	160.48	184.51	155.84	188.92	251.02	262.46
CMPLight(ours)	**119.37**	**116.4**	**113.68**	**109.68**	**164.13**	**218.72**

Visualising the Stability of Our Approach. Figure 3 shows the stable performance of our approach, which has been theoretically proven in stability analysis. At the beginning of the training, process max-pressure-based approach has a sharp peek, then it slowly reaches stability. In contrast to that, our approach reaches stability with smooth peak. Because the agent can learn more useful information in the road network with the help of queuing information from downstream neighboring intersections, our approach converges faster than state-of-the-arts approach of combining reinforcement learning and transportation theory. The queue information of neighboring intersections is considered in the pressure of target intersection as the reward function to provide accurate description of the effect of an action in road network.

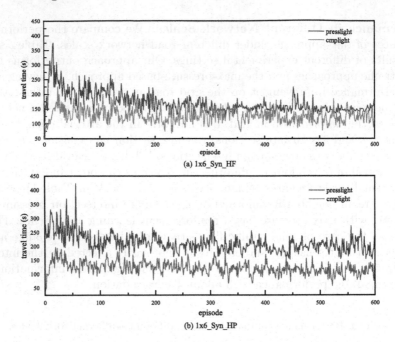

Fig. 3. The results of 1×6 intersections on synthetic datasets with heavy and peak traffic flow.

7   Conclusion and Future Work

In this paper, we introduce cooperative max-pressure in the transportation field as the reward function in deep reinforcement learning to control traffic signals. We prove that the reward function still maintains the stability of the network by theoretical analysis. In the future, we will try to introduce this reward function design in other deep reinforcement learning approaches. An open issue is how to deal with all the traffic flow planned for the network when there are more complex traffic network and more traffic flow.

References

1. Webster, F.: Traffic signals. Road research technical paper **56** (1966)
2. Roess, R.P., Prassas, E.S., McShane, W.R.: Traffic Engineering. Pearson/Prentice Hall (2004)
3. Varaiya, P.: Max pressure control of a network of signalized intersections. Transp. Res. Part C Emerging Technol. **36**, 177–195 (2013)
4. Miller, A.J.: Settings for fixed-cycle traffic signals. J. Oper. Res. Soc. **14**(4), 373–386 (1963)
5. Yau, K.L.A., Qadir, J., Khoo, H.L., et al.: A survey on reinforcement learning models and algorithms for traffic signal control. ACM Comput. Surv. **50**(3), 34:1–34:38 (2017)

6. Van der Pol, E., Oliehoek, F.A.: Coordinated deep reinforcement learners for traffic light control. In: Proceedings of Learning, Inference and Control of Multi-Agent Systems (at NIPS 2016) (2016)
7. Wei, H., Chen, C., Zheng, G., et al.: PressLight: learning max pressure control to coordinate traffic signals in arterial network. In: SIGKDD 2019, pp. 1290–1298 (2019)
8. Zheng, G., Zang, X., Xu, N., et al.: Diagnosing reinforcement learning for traffic signal control. arXiv preprint arXiv:1905.04716 (2019)
9. El-Tantawy, S., Abdulhai, B., Abdelgawad, H.: Multiagent reinforcement learning for integrated network of adaptive traffic signal controllers (MARLIN-ATSC): methodology and large-scale application on downtown Toronto. IEEE Trans. Intell. Transp. Syst. 14(3), 1140–1150 (2013)
10. Mousavi, S.S., Schukat, M., Howley, E.: Traffic light control using deep policy-gradient and value-function-based reinforcement learning. IET Intel. Transp. Syst. 11(7), 417–423 (2017)
11. Tan, T., Bao, F., Deng, Y., et al.: Cooperative deep reinforcement learning for large-scale traffic grid signal control. IEEE Trans. Cybern. 50(6), 2687–2700 (2020)
12. Chu, T., Wang, J., Codecà, L., Li, Z.: Multi-agent deep reinforcement learning for large-scale traffic signal control. IEEE Trans. Intell. Transp. Syst. 21(3), 1086–1095 (2020)
13. Chen, C., Wei, H., Xu, N., et al.: Toward a thousand lights: decentralized deep reinforcement learning for large-scale traffic signal control. In: AAAI 2020, pp. 3414–3421 (2020)
14. Wu, N., Li, D., Xi, Y.: Distributed weighted balanced control of traffic signals for urban traffic congestion. IEEE Trans. Intell. Transp. Syst. 20(10), 3710–3720 (2019)
15. Hao, S., Yang, L., Ding, L., et al.: Distributed cooperative backpressure-based traffic light control method. J. Adv. Transp. 2019, 1–13 (2019)
16. Mnih, V., Kavukcuoglu, K., Silver, D., et al.: Human-level control through deep reinforcement learning. Nat. 518(7540), 529–533 (2015)
17. Wiering, M.A.: Multi-agent reinforcement learning for traffic light control. In: ICML 2000, pp. 1151–1158 (2000)
18. Kuyer, L., Whiteson, S., Bakker, B., Vlassis, N.: Multiagent reinforcement learning for urban traffic control using coordination graphs. In: Daelemans, W., Goethals, B., Morik, K. (eds.) ECML PKDD 2008. LNCS (LNAI), vol. 5211, pp. 656–671. Springer, Heidelberg (2008). https://doi.org/10.1007/978-3-540-87479-9_61
19. Watkins, C.J., Dayan, P.: Q-learning. Mach. Learn. 8(3–4), 279–292 (1992)
20. Prashanth, L.A., Bhatnagar, S.: Reinforcement learning with function approximation for traffic signal control. IEEE Trans. Intell. Transp. Syst. 12(2), 412–421 (2011)
21. Zhou, N., Du, J., Yao, X., et al.: A content search method for security topics in microblog based on deep reinforcement learning. World Wide Web 23(1), 75–101 (2020)
22. Ren, C., An, L., Gu, Z., et al.: Rebalancing the car-sharing system with reinforcement learning. World Wide Web 23(4), 2491–2511 (2020)
23. Zhao, C., Hu, X., Wang, G.: PDLight: a deep reinforcement learning traffic light control algorithm with pressure and dynamic light duration. arXiv preprint arXiv:2009.13711 (2020)

Privacy-Preserving Healthcare Analytics of Trajectory Data

Carson K. Leung[✉] [iD], Anifat M. Olawoyin, and Qi Wen

University of Manitoba, Winnipeg, MB, Canada
kleung@cs.umanitoba.ca

Abstract. Technological advancements have led to generation and collection of big data from various data sources including mobile devices. For instance, to prevent, combat and detect COVID-19, citizens of many countries were encouraged to use contact tracing apps on their mobile devices. Collection of their trajectories can be analyzed and mined for social goods. At the same time, their privacy also needs to be preserved. In other words, the advent of COVID-19 has made releasing of patient records become imperative and yet privacy of individuals must be protected. Releasing spatio-temporal COVID-19 data plays a significant role in contact tracing and may help in reducing the spread of the disease due to likelihood of increasing adherence to social distancing and other health related guidelines by the people around the cluster of the released data. In this paper, we examine the problem of preserving privacy of spatio-temporal trajectory data and introduce a hierarchical temporal representative point (HTRP) differential privacy model. We evaluate our framework using a South Korean COVID-19 patient route dataset. Empirical results show a balance of utility and privacy provided by our framework with our HTRP for privacy-preserving healthcare data analytics.

Keywords: Big data · COVID-19 · Data analytics · Data mining · Privacy · Spatial and temporal data

1 Introduction and Related Works

Evolution and advancements in ubiquitous computing and communication technologies have led to pervasive and reliable computing solutions and communication services. For example, residents of many countries have used internet of things (IoT) like mobile devices for contact tracing, which helps identify people who may have come into contact with an infected person. Examples include contact tracing apps [1, 2] for monitoring the spread, and notifying the exposure, of the coronavirus disease 2019 (COVID-19). It broke out in 2019, became a pandemic in 2020 and is still prevailing in 2021.

We are witnessing huge volumes of patient data due to the outbreak of COVID-19. Data science [3, 4], data analytics [5–7], data mining [8–16] and machine learning [17–19] have become important tasks in understanding previously unknown symptoms, spreading patterns and other potentially useful data to prevent the spread of COVID-19. At the same time, preserving privacy [20–22] of individuals has become crucial to prevent

L. H. U et al. (Eds.): APWeb-WAIM 2021, LNCS 12859, pp. 414–420, 2021.
https://doi.org/10.1007/978-3-030-85899-5_30

stigmatization and societal bullying. For example, releasing detailed information such as school name, transportation route and classroom about a student who tested positive for COVID-19 may increase the risk of identifying the student and the spiral effects on the student's mental and psychological well-being could be enormous. Hence, it is desirable to have a privacy-preserving framework for healthcare analytics of COVID-19 data (e.g., trajectory of COVID-19 cases).

Privacy-preserving techniques have been applied to various tasks, such as privacy-preserving data mining (PPDM) [23], privacy-preserving keyword data search [24], and privacy-preserving data publishing (PPDP) [25–27]. Common techniques for preserving privacy include k-anonymity [28], l-diversity [29], t-closeness [30] and differential privacy [31]. For instance, Doka et al. [32] treated k-anonymization as a network problem with the objective to minimize information loss. They used mixed integer programming to obtain a minimal solution. In contrast, our framework is simpler but yet effective. We group data points with temporal hierarchy and adding noise (ε) to further protect the privacy of individual record. Kasiviswanathan and Smith [33] used (ε, δ)—which is a relaxed notion of privacy based on distance measure on probability distribution using Bayesian formulation—to define differential privacy. The additive error parameter δ depends largely on the size of the dataset. Conversely, we require only ε for our definition of differential privacy. Tschantz et al. [34] examined associations and cause views of differential privacy. However, they made independence assumption on the differential privacy association property. Instead, we relate data using temporal and spatial associations, i.e., individual data points are related in time and space. With or without the addition of noise (ε), temporal and spatial grouping limits the amount of inference an adversary can obtain from a dataset.

Our *key contributions* of this paper is our privacy-preserving framework for healthcare analytics of COVID-19 data. Specifically, our differential-privacy framework preserves privacy of spatio-temporal trajectory data by representing the corresponding information by hierarchical temporal representative points (HTRP). Evaluation of real-life South Korean COVID-19 patient route dataset show a balance of utility and privacy provided by our framework with our HTRP for privacy-preserving healthcare data analytics.

The remainder of our paper is organized as follows. The next section describes our framework for privacy-preserving healthcare analytics of trajectory data. Evaluation and conclusions are presented in Sects. 3 and 4, respectively.

2 Our Differential-Privacy Framework for Analytics of Spatio-Temporal Trajectory

In this section, we describe our differential-privacy framework for analytics of spatio-temporal trajectory. In particular, we present its key components—namely, spatio-temporal hierarchy, hierarchical temporal representative point (HTRP), and Laplace mechanism of differential privacy.

Spatio-temporal hierarchy is the aggregation of both spatial and temporal dimensions. More specifically, the *temporal hierarchy* aggregates time series data to a predefined periodic level. For instance, given a timestamp of a data point in the trajectory time series, our framework computes yearly information Y by aggregating four quarterly information Q_i, each of which is obtained by aggregating three monthly information M_j. Similarly, each monthly information is obtained by aggregating all d daily information D_k within a month (where $d = 28, 29, 30$ or 31 for the corresponding number of days in the month):

$$Y = \sum_{i=1}^{4} Q_i \text{ where } Q_i = \sum_{j=1}^{3} M_j \text{ where } M_j = \sum_{k=1}^{d} D_k \tag{1}$$

Along this direction, each daily information is obtained by aggregating 24 hourly information, and each hourly information is obtained by aggregating information of every minute within the hour.

Similarly, *spatial hierarchy* helps represent spatial geometric data at the appropriate level of hierarchy in the sense of revealing essential spatial geographic location information for healthcare analytics while preserving privacy of individuals. It generalizes specific named location (e.g., restaurant X, store Y, hospital Z) into a street, which is then generalized into a neighborhood. Along this direction, the neighborhood is generalized into a district, which is then generalized into a city. The city is generalized into a province. Our framework represents the resulting generalized location by a *hierarchical temporal representative point* (*HTRP*). The (x, y)-coordinates of this HTRP is computed as the average of (x_i, y_i)-coordinates of all data points in the time series trajectory during a hierarchical temporal unit (e.g., a day) and over N individuals within the same hierarchical spatial unit (e.g., a district within a city):

$$HTRP(x, y) = \left(\frac{\sum_i x_i}{N}, \frac{\sum_i y_i}{N} \right) \tag{2}$$

In the unlikely event that the (x, y)-coordinates of the HTRP happens to be the actual (x, y)-coordinates of a single point in the time series during a hierarchical temporal unit at a specific hierarchical spatial unit (e.g., the only diner in a restaurant at late night), our framework preserves privacy via *Laplace mechanism* by adding noise. By doing so, it guarantees that the both temporal and spatial information (e.g., actual timestamp, true location) is protected—via the spatio-temporal hierarchy and the HTRP differential-privacy mechanism. In general, at any temporal hierarchy level t, a randomized mechanism R satisfies ε-differential privacy on temporal representative point if, for any location output from a spatio-temporal dataset is not significantly different from its neighboring spatio-temporal dataset produced via addition or removal of a record:

$$\frac{\Pr(R(x_t = z_t))}{\Pr(R(x_t^* = z_t))} \leq e^{\varepsilon} \tag{3}$$

Then, the probability density function for the Laplace mechanism is given by:

$$f(x|\mu, \varepsilon) = \frac{1}{2\varepsilon} e^{-\left| \frac{x-\mu}{\varepsilon} \right|} \tag{4}$$

3 Evaluation

We evaluated our framework on a computer with 2.6 GHz Intel(R) core™ i7 64-bit operating system and 8 GB installed memory. The framework was programming in Python on Spyder scientific integrated development environment. Here, we used a real-life dataset[1] [35] capturing trajectory of some South Korean COVID-19 cases a few days prior to their positive test results. The dataset contains 5,321 trajectory points for 939 cases collected from the report materials of Korea Centers for Disease Control and Prevention (KCDC), which have now become Korea Disease Control and Prevention Agency (KDCA), and local governments in January–March 2020.

Table 1. 10 Sample trajectory data points collected for March 05–06, 2020.

ID	Date	District ("gu")	City ("si")	Province ("do")	Type	Lat	Long
89	Mar 06	Dongnam	Cheonan	Chungcheongnam	Hospital	36.8156	127.1136
92	Mar 06	Dongnam	Cheonan	Chungcheongnam	Hospital	36.7754	127.1800
98	Mar 06	Dongnam	Cheonan	Chungcheongnam	Hospital	36.8074	127.1512
142	Mar 05	Guro	Seoul		Restaurant	37.4954	126.8873
143	Mar 05	Guro	Seoul		Restaurant	37.4954	126.8873
154	Mar 05	Guro	Seoul		Restaurant	37.5065	126.8840
170	Mar 05	Gwanak	Seoul		Misc	37.4626	126.9383
177	Mar 05	Guro	Seoul		Restaurant	37.5031	126.8820
192	Mar 05	Gwanak	Seoul		Store	37.4679	126.9217
194	Mar 05	Gwanak	Seoul		Misc	37.4779	126.9343

Table 2. Privacy-preserving HTRP.

#ind. per grp	Date	District ("gu")	City ("si")	Province ("do")	Type	Lat.	Long.
3	Mar 06	Dongnam	Cheonan	Chungcheongnam	Hospital	36.7995	127.1483
4	Mar 05	Guro	Seoul		Restaurant	37.5017	126.8844
3	Mar 05	Gwanak	Seoul		Misc	37.4695	126.9314

As an illustrative example, let us consider Table 1 that shows trajectory data of 10 of these 939 cases who tested positive for COVID-19. Our framework first builds temporal hierarchy and generalizes temporal data into daily information. It then builds spatial hierarchy and generalizes spatial data to the district level. So, the three visits to the same

---

[1] https://www.kaggle.com/kimjihoo/coronavirusdataset.

hospital (by three individuals) in the district of Dongnam-gu (i.e., southeast district) in the city of Cheonan-si in the province of Chungcheongnam-do on March 06 are grouped and represented by a single HTRP with coordinate (36.7995N, 127.1483E). Similarly, the four dine-outs in the same restaurant in the district of Guro-gu in the special city of Seoul on March 05 are grouped and represented by a single HTRP with coordinate (37.5017N, 126.8844E). As for the two miscellaneous visits and one store visit (all in the district of Gwanak), each of these groups consists of fewer than the threshold number of individuals (say, three). They are grouped into a mega-group. See Table 2.

We varied the input parameter ε from 0.01 to 0.1, and found that $\varepsilon = 0.09$ gave the best protection in preserving privacy. When generalizing data into daily privacy-preserving HTRP within a district for the spatio-temporal hierarchy, our framework gave a spatial compression ratio of 34.7% (wrt the number of *unique* original coordinates) and a file compression ratio of 31.8% (wrt the number of original data points), which led to a small root mean square error (RMSE) of 0.355.

4   Conclusions

In this paper, we presented our privacy-preserving framework for healthcare analytics of trajectory data. To provide users with differential privacy, our framework first builds spatio-temporal hierarchy, and then groups and represents similar data points by hierarchical temporal representative points (HTRP). It adds Laplace noise if needed. Evaluation on real-life datasets capturing trajectory of South Korean COVID-19 cases shows a balance of utility and privacy provided by our framework. As ongoing and future work, we explore further enhancements to our framework, determine optimal levels of hierarchy, and transfer the learned knowledge to preserve privacy for other data analytics tasks.

Acknowledgement. This work is partially supported by NSERC (Canada) and U. Manitoba.

References

1. Akinbi, A., Forshaw, M., Blinkhorn, V.: Contact tracing apps for the COVID-19 pandemic: a systematic literature review of challenges and future directions for neo-liberal societies. Health Inf. Sci. Syst. **9**(1), 18:1–18:15 (2021)
2. Park, S., et al.: Privacy in the time of COVID-19: divergent paths for contact tracing and route-disclosure mechanisms in South Korea. IEEE Secur. Priv. **19**(3), 51–56 (2021)
3. Leung, C.K., et al.: Big data science on COVID-19 data. In: IEEE BigDataSE 2020, pp. 14–21 (2020)
4. Shang, S., et al.: Spatial data science of COVID-19 data. In: IEEE HPCC-SmartCity-DSS 2020, pp. 1370–1375 (2020)
5. Chen, Y., et al.: Temporal data analytics on COVID-19 data with ubiquitous computing. In: IEEE ISPA-BDCloud-SocialCom-SustainCom 2020, pp. 958–965 (2020)
6. Jiang, F., Leung, C.K.: A data analytic algorithm for managing, querying, and processing uncertain big data in cloud environments. Algorithms **8**(4), 1175–1194 (2015)

7. Tanbeer, S.K., Leung, C.K.-S.: Finding diverse friends in social networks. In: Ishikawa, Y., Li, J., Wang, W., Zhang, R., Zhang, W. (eds.) APWeb 2013. LNCS, vol. 7808, pp. 301–309. Springer, Heidelberg (2013). https://doi.org/10.1007/978-3-642-37401-2_31

8. Chanda, A.K., et al.: A new framework for mining weighted periodic patterns in time series databases. Expert Syst. Appl. **79**, 207–224 (2017)

9. Cuzzocrea, A., Jiang, F., Lee, W., Leung, C.K.: Efficient frequent itemset mining from dense data streams. In: Chen, L., Jia, Y., Sellis, T., Liu, G. (eds.) APWeb 2014. LNCS, vol. 8709, pp. 593–601. Springer, Cham (2014). https://doi.org/10.1007/978-3-319-11116-2_56

10. Fariha, A., Ahmed, C.F., Leung, C.K.-S., Abdullah, S.M., Cao, L.: Mining frequent patterns from human interactions in meetings using directed acyclic graphs. In: Pei, J., Tseng, V.S., Cao, L., Motoda, H., Xu, G. (eds.) PAKDD 2013, Part I. LNCS (LNAI), vol. 7818, pp. 38–49. Springer, Heidelberg (2013). https://doi.org/10.1007/978-3-642-37453-1_4

11. Gupta, P., Hoi, C.S.H., Leung, C.K., Yuan, Y., Zhang, X., Zhang, Z.: Vertical data mining from relational data and its application to COVID-19 data. In: Lee, W., Leung, C.K., Nasridinov, A. (eds.) BIGDAS 2018. AISC, vol. 899, pp. 106–116. Springer, Singapore (2021). https://doi.org/10.1007/978-981-15-8731-3_8

12. Jiang, F., Leung, C.K., Zhang, H.: B-mine: frequent pattern mining and its application to knowledge discovery from social networks. In: Li, F., Shim, K., Zheng, K., Liu, G. (eds.) APWeb 2016, Part I. LNCS, vol. 9931, pp. 316–328. Springer, Cham (2016). https://doi.org/10.1007/978-3-319-45814-4_26

13. Lee, W., Song, J.J.S., Leung, C.K.-S.: Categorical data skyline using classification tree. In: Du, X., Fan, W., Wang, J., Peng, Z., Sharaf, M.A. (eds.) APWeb 2011. LNCS, vol. 6612, pp. 181–187. Springer, Heidelberg (2011). https://doi.org/10.1007/978-3-642-20291-9_19

14. Leung, C.K., Carmichael, C.L.: FpVAT: a visual analytic tool for supporting frequent pattern mining. ACM SIGKDD Explor. **11**(2), 39–48 (2009)

15. Tong, W., Leung, C.K., Liu, D., Yu, J.: Probabilistic frequent pattern mining by PUH-Mine. In: Cheng, R., Cui, B., Zhang, Z., Cai, R., Xu, J. (eds.) APWeb 2015. LNCS, vol. 9313, pp. 768–780. Springer, Cham (2015). https://doi.org/10.1007/978-3-319-25255-1_63

16. Wei, W., Wang, J., Cheng, N., Chen, Y., Zhou, B., Xiao, J.: Epidemic Guard: a COVID-19 detection system for elderly people. In: Wang, X., Zhang, R., Lee, Y.-K., Sun, L., Moon, Y.-S. (eds.) APWeb-WAIM 2020, Part II. LNCS, vol. 12318, pp. 545–550. Springer, Cham (2020). https://doi.org/10.1007/978-3-030-60290-1_44

17. Gao, L., Pan, H., Liu, F., Xie, X., Zhang, Z., Han, J.: Brain disease diagnosis using deep learning features from longitudinal MR images. In: Cai, Y., Ishikawa, Y., Xu, J. (eds.) APWeb-WAIM 2018, Part I. LNCS, vol. 10987, pp. 327–339. Springer, Cham (2018). https://doi.org/10.1007/978-3-319-96890-2_27

18. Leung, C.K., et al.: Machine learning and OLAP on big COVID-19 data. In: IEEE BigData 2020, pp. 5118–5127 (2020)

19. Liu, Q., et al.: A two-dimensional sparse matrix profile DenseNet for COVID-19 diagnosis using chest CT images. IEEE Access **8**, 213718–213728 (2020)

20. Dai, H., et al.: On the vulnerability and generality of k-anonymity location privacy under continuous LBS requests. In: Wang, X., Zhang, R., Lee, Y.-K., Sun, L., Moon, Y.-S. (eds.) APWeb-WAIM 2020, Part II. LNCS, vol. 12318, pp. 351–359. Springer, Cham (2020). https://doi.org/10.1007/978-3-030-60290-1_28

21. Liu, S., et al.: Privacy-preserving collaborative web services QoS prediction via differential privacy. In: Chen, L., Jensen, C.S., Shahabi, C., Yang, X., Lian, X. (eds.) APWeb-WAIM 2017, Part I. LNCS, vol. 10366, pp. 200–214. Springer, Cham (2017). https://doi.org/10.1007/978-3-319-63579-8_16

22. Olawoyin, A.M., et al.: Preserving privacy of temporal big data. In: IEEE BigData 2020, pp. 4042–4051 (2020)

23. Leung, C.K., et al.: Privacy-preserving frequent pattern mining from big uncertain data. In: IEEE BigData 2018, pp. 5101–5110 (2018)
24. Wodi, B.H., et al.: Fast privacy-preserving keyword search on encrypted outsourced data. In: IEEE BigData 2019, pp. 6266–6275 (2019)
25. Eom, C.S., Lee, C.C., Lee, W., Leung, C.K.: Effective privacy preserving data publishing by vectorization. Inf. Sci. **527**, 311–328 (2020)
26. Fung, B.C.M., Wang, K., Chen, R., Yu, P.S.: Privacy-preserving data publishing: a survey of recent developments. ACM Comput. Surv. **42**(4), 1–53 (2010)
27. Olawoyin, A.M., Leung, C.K., Choudhury, R.: Privacy-preserving spatio-temporal patient data publishing. In: Hartmann, S., Küng, J., Kotsis, G., Tjoa, A.M., Khalil, I. (eds.) DEXA 2020, Part II. LNCS, vol. 12392, pp. 407–416. Springer, Cham (2020). https://doi.org/10.1007/978-3-030-59051-2_28
28. LeFevre, K., et al.: Incognito: efficient full-domain k-anonymity. In: ACM SIGMOD 2005, pp. 49–60 (2005)
29. Machanavajjhala, A., Kifer, D., Gehrke, J., Venkitasubramaniam, M.: L-diversity: privacy beyond k-anonymity. ACM Trans. Knowl. Discov. Data **1**(1), 3 (2007)
30. Li, N., et al.: t-closeness: privacy beyond k-anonymity and l-diversity. In: IEEE ICDE 2007, pp. 106–115 (2007)
31. Acs, G., Castelluccia, C.: A case study: privacy preserving release of spatio-temporal density in Paris. In: ACM KDD 2014, pp. 1679–1688 (2014)
32. Doka, K., et al.: k-anonymization by freeform generalization. In: ACM Asia CCS 2015, pp. 519–530 (2015)
33. Kasiviswanathan, S.P., Smith, A.: On the 'semantics' of differential privacy: a Bayesian formulation. J. Priv. Confident. **6**(1), 1–16 (2014)
34. Tschantz, M.C., et al.: SoK: differential privacy as a causal property. In: IEEE SP 2020, pp. 354–371 (2020)
35. Kim, J., et al.: DS4C patient policy province dataset: a comprehensive COVID-19 dataset for causal and epidemiological analysis. In: NeurIPS Workshop on CDML (2020)

Demo

PARROT: An Adaptive Online Shopping Guidance System

Da Ren[1], Yi Cai[2(✉)], Zhicheng Zhong[2], Zhiwei Wu[2], Zeting Li[2], Weizhao Li[2], and Qing Li[1]

[1] The Hong Kong Polytechnic University, Hong Kong, China
[2] South China University of Technology, Guangzhou, Guangdong, China
ycai@scut.edu.cn

Abstract. With the development of e-commerce, it is necessary to build an online shopping guidance system to help users to choose the products they desired. Task-oriented dialogue systems can be used as an online shopping guidance system in e-commerce websites. Current dialogue systems can only extract basic attributes which are the inherent attributes of products. These systems can not process users' requests containing high level attributes which describe products' functions and user experience. These requests, however, appear frequently in real scenarios. To solve this problem, we build PARROT, an adaptive online shopping guidance system. PARROT can extract both basic and high level attributes from dialogues and recommend suitable products to users. The novel features of PARROT are as follows: (1) We propose a new architecture of task-oriented dialogue systems which can extract both basic and high level products' attributes (functional attributes and experience attributes). (2) We construct knowledge base to map from high level attributes to basic level attributes or products. (3) We build a task oriented dialogue system which can finish the task of shopping guidance in websites. We test PARROT in three main scenarios and these tests demonstrate that PARROT can successfully recommend suitable products to users by extracting both basic and high level attributes.

Keywords: Online shopping guidance · Dialogue system · E-commerce

1 Introduction

With the development of the Internet, E-commerce gets remarkable development. More and more people buy products on e-commerce websites (e.g., Amazon). There are a large number of products on e-commerce websites. People can hardly find the products they desired quickly. Therefore, it is important for merchants to employ shopping guides for customers. Shopping guides can help customers to find their desired products quickly. It can not only improve the shopping experiences of customers but also increase the volumes of transactions.

However, employing shopping guides is not a proper way in the scenarios of online shopping. People may browse websites and ask questions at any time. It is difficult for shopping guides to finish such heavy works.

© Springer Nature Switzerland AG 2021
L. H. U et al. (Eds.): APWeb-WAIM 2021, LNCS 12859, pp. 423–428, 2021.
https://doi.org/10.1007/978-3-030-85899-5_31

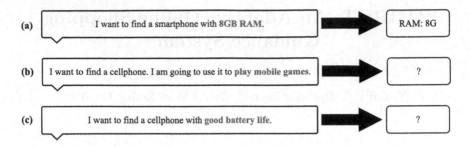

Fig. 1. Traditional task-oriented dialogue systems

One alternative way is to build a task-oriented dialogue systems [4,5,7], which can collect the demands of customers during the dialogues between customers, to be a shopping guidance system. Traditional task-oriented dialogue systems extract attributes from dialogues. There is an example in Fig. 1 (a). A user wants to buy a computer with "8G RAM". Dialogue systems will extract the attributes "RAM: 8G" from dialogues. Then systems may ask questions about products' attributes or recommend products to users according to the extracted attributes. We denote such inherent attributes of products as **basic attributes**.

However, traditional task-oriented dialogue systems can not extract other attributes which do not reflect the inherent attributes of products directly. We define this kind of attributes as **high level attributes**. In our system, we focus on two high level attributes: **functional attributes** and **experience attributes**. According to our observations, high level attributes are frequently used when customers are finding the product they want.

Functional attributes are the attributes related to products' functions. There is an example in Fig. 1 (b). A user wants to find a smartphone, and use it to "play mobile games". However, this user does not know the basic attributes of the products. In this case, traditional dialogue systems can not extract any information, since there are no basic attributes in dialogues. According to our observations, customers who do not have sufficient knowledge about professional products (e.g., computers, cameras and smartphones), always fail to describe the products directly and professionally. We consider that functional attributes should be related to basic attributes rather than certain products. Therefore, in PARROT, we construct knowledge base to bridge the gap between functional attributes and basic attributes.

Experience attributes are the attributes highly related to user experiences. People may concern about user experiences of products. However, user experiences can not be reflected from basic attributes directly. For example, people may want to buy a computer with "good battery life" (as shown in Fig. 1 (c)). It is difficult to judge the battery life according to the basic attributes. What's more, traditional dialogue systems can not extract experience attributes from dialogues. Different with functional attributes, these attributes should be related to certain products rather than basic attributes. The reason is that products with same basic attributes may have different user experiences. Thus, we construct knowledge base to build the connection between experience attributes and products.

PARROT is an adaptive dialogue system since the system can extract different kinds of attributes adaptively. Users can have a better experience based on this feature, since they can describe products in both basic attributes and high level attributes. Our contribution can be summarized as follows:

- We propose a new architecture of task-oriented dialogue systems which can extract both products' basic attributes and high level attributes (functional attributes and experience attributes).
- We construct knowledge base in PARROT. There are two kinds of knowledge base. One is the knowledge base which maps from functional attributes to basic attributes. The other is the knowledge base which connects the experience attributes and products.
- We build a task-oriented dialogue system which can finish the task of shopping guidance. People can communicate with this system in natural language. We use a website to build a friendly interface between humans and systems. Users can communicate with PARROT on smartphones or computers.

This paper is structured as follows. In Sect. 2, we introduce the structure of PARROT. In Sect. 3, we elaborate the scenarios of our systems. Finally, we draw a conclusion in Sect. 4.

2   System Implementation

As shown in Fig. 2. There are three main modules in PARROT: **Natural Language Understanding (NLU)**, **states tracking** and **Natural Language Generation (NLG)**. Different with traditional task-oriented dialogue systems, we adopt knowledge base in PARROT. The details of each modules are described in the following.

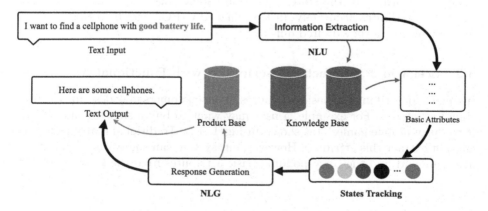

Fig. 2. General structure of PARROT

Natural Language Understanding. In this module, PARROT needs to extract both basic attributes and high level attributes. For the basic attributes, we train and adopt a Bi-LSTM [1] with CRF [3] model. It is a classical model in information extraction [2] and also gets satisfied performance in our scenarios. In PARROT, the high level attributes are stored in knowledge base. We manually extract high level attributes from products' comments and connect them with basic attributes and products. We use pattern matching to find high level attributes in dialogues.

States Tracking. We use a finite-state machine (FSM) in states tracking. It is a reliable way to use FSM in PARROT. What's more, it is convenient to update FSM in order to adapt to more complex scenarios.

Natural Language Generation. We consider that it is difficult to control the responses generated by generation models like Sequence-to-sequence models [6]. Therefore, we use predefined patterns to generate responses. In this way, PARROT can generate reliable responses.

3 Demo Scenarios

We choose the shopping guidance of smartphones as our scenarios. We crawl products' basic attributes and products' comments from websites. All our corpus are in Chinese. The demonstration video of PARROT is public online[1].

3.1 Scenario 1: Products' Descriptions with Basic Attributes

This scenario is the traditional scenario of task-oriented dialogue systems. Users describe the products with products' basic attributes. For example, a user may want to find a smartphone with "8G RAM" (as shown in Fig. 1 (a)). PARROT can extract a basic attribute "RAM: 8G". Then PARROT will continue the dialogue according to the states. There are some customers who can describe the basic attributes accurately. In this time, PARROT can help these users to find the products they desired quickly.

3.2 Scenario 2: Products' Descriptions with Functional Attributes

Instead of describing the basic attributes, some customers may describe the functional attributes. For example, a user may want to buy a smartphone, and use it to "play mobile games" (as shown in Fig. 1 (b)). Traditional dialogue systems can not extract this attribute. However, our system can successfully extract this attribute and find the corresponding basic attributes from the knowledge base.

---

[1] https://youtu.be/Ut71-8y1wgs.

3.3 Scenario 3: Products' Descriptions with Experience Attributes

A customer may use phrases like "good battery life", when this customer concerns about user experience of products (as shown in Fig. 1 (c)). Similarly, traditional dialogue systems can not find products according to these attributes. PARROT can extract the experience attributes from dialogues. Then, it will find suitable products from knowledge base and continue the dialogues with these products.

4 Conclusion

In this paper, we introduce PARROT. PARROT is an adaptive online shopping guidance system. Different with traditional task-oriented dialogue systems, PARROT can help users to choose products based on both basic and high level attributes. We implement PARROT with the data collected from the Internet and test PARROT in three main scenarios. Our test shows that PARROT can guide users to buy products in more scenarios and recommend products to customers more accurately.

Acknowledgement. This work was supported by National Natural Science Foundation of China (No. 62076100), National Key Research and Development Program of China (Standard knowledge graph for epidemic prevention and production recovering intelligent service platform and its applications), the Fundamental Research Funds for the Central Universities, SCUT (No. D2201300, D2210010), the Science and Technology Programs of Guangzhou (201902010046), the Science and Technology Planning Project of Guangdong Province (No. 2020B0101100002). The project has been supported by the Hong Kong Research Grants Council under the general research fund scheme (project number: PolyU 11204919).

References

1. Hochreiter, S., Schmidhuber, J.: Long short-term memory. Neural Comput. **9**(8), 1735–1780 (1997). https://doi.org/10.1162/neco.1997.9.8.1735
2. Kong, J., Cai, Y., Ren, D., Li, Z.: Deep multi-task learning with cross connected layer for slot filling. In: Tang, J., Kan, M.-Y., Zhao, D., Li, S., Zan, H. (eds.) NLPCC 2019, Part II. LNCS (LNAI), vol. 11839, pp. 308–317. Springer, Cham (2019). https://doi.org/10.1007/978-3-030-32236-6_27
3. Lafferty, J.D., McCallum, A., Pereira, F.C.N.: Conditional random fields: probabilistic models for segmenting and labeling sequence data. In: Proceedings of the Eighteenth International Conference on Machine Learning (ICML 2001), Williams College, Williamstown, MA, USA, 28 June–1 July 2001 [3]. pp. 282–289
4. Peng, B., Li, X., Gao, J., Liu, J., Wong, K.: Deep dyna-q: integrating planning for task-completion dialogue policy learning. In: Proceedings of the 56th Annual Meeting of the Association for Computational Linguistics, ACL 2018, Melbourne, Australia, 15–20 July 2018, Volume 1: Long Papers [4]. pp. 2182–2192

5. Peng, B., et al.: Composite task-completion dialogue policy learning via hierarchical deep reinforcement learning. In: Proceedings of the 2017 Conference on Empirical Methods in Natural Language Processing, EMNLP 2017, Copenhagen, Denmark, 9–11 September 2017 [5]. pp. 2231–2240
6. Sutskever, I., Vinyals, O., Le, Q.V.: Sequence to sequence learning with neural networks. In: Ghahramani, Z., Welling, M., Cortes, C., Lawrence, N.D., Weinberger, K.Q. (eds.) Advances in Neural Information Processing Systems, vol. 27, pp. 3104–3112. Curran Associates, Inc. (2014)
7. Xu, P., Hu, Q.: An end-to-end approach for handling unknown slot values in dialogue state tracking. In: Proceedings of the 56th Annual Meeting of the Association for Computational Linguistics, ACL 2018, Melbourne, Australia, 15–20 July 2018, Volume 1: Long Papers [7]. pp. 1448–1457

gStore-C: A Transactional RDF Store with Light-Weight Optimistic Lock

Zhe Zhang and Lei Zou$^{(\boxtimes)}$

Peking University, Beijing, China
{zhezhang97,zoulei}@pku.edu.cn

Abstract. RDF systems are widely applied in many areas such as knowledge base, semantic web, social network. Traditional RDF systems focus on speed up SPARQL queries on large RDF data but disregarding the performance of updates and transaction processing. In this demonstration, we propose a new transactional RDF system based on multi-version and MVCC. We introduce a lightweight optimistic lock upon atomic variables and operations that provides fine-grained locking and avoids scalability issues. The methods are fully implemented in an open-source RDF system gStore. And it outperforms other state-of-art RDF systems solutions on transactional workloads.

Keywords: Resource Description Framework (RDF) · Concurrency control · Optimistic lock · Online transaction processing

1 Introduction

Resource Description Framework (RDF) has been introduced for around two decades. This data model is designed for data of weak-schema or no-schema. Due to the flexibility of RDF, RDF data is blooming in recent years. The requirements of querying, indexing, storing over large RDF data have promoted many RDF systems. However, most RDF engines focus on speeding up SPARQL queries over large RDF data while disregarding updates and transaction processing. These highly read-optimized systems that employ aggressive indexing suffer serious downgrading and low throughput when run updates workload. Even so, there are still few transactional native RDF systems supporting transaction processing on RDF data, such as Apache Jena [2,9] and RDF-3X [4,5]. Both Jena and RDF-3X employ a lock-based method to achieve ACID compliance. RDF-3X uses a heuristic approach to gain proper lock granularity of predicate locks. Other RDF systems based on relational DBMS like Virtuoso [1] also can support transaction processing.

gStore [10] is a graph-based RDF system where a subject-predicate-object (SPO) triple can be viewed as two nodes (S and O) and an edge (P) in a labeled directed graph G (RDF graph). More details have been covered in past work [6,11]. Though gStore supports storage and fast query over billions of triples, it lacks efficient updates and transaction processing. We introduce a novel method

© Springer Nature Switzerland AG 2021
L. H. U et al. (Eds.): APWeb-WAIM 2021, LNCS 12859, pp. 429–433, 2021.
https://doi.org/10.1007/978-3-030-85899-5_32

to overcome the shortcomings and provide concurrent control. This method is fully implemented by extending the open-source system gStore. We refer to our extension as gStore-C; gStore-C is fully ACID-compliant with three isolation levels: read committed (RC), snapshot isolation (SI), serializable (SR).

In this demonstration, we design and implement a new transactional RDF system: gStore-C. A novel lightweight optimistic locking mechanism is the key to transaction processing in gStore-C. We build a web demo to illustrate online transaction processing (OLTP) with multiple isolation levels of gStore-C.

2   System Overview

gStore-C is constituted by two parts: offline part and online part. The offline part consists of an RDF parser and RDF graph builder for RDF data pre-processing; an encoding module to build a two-way mapping of literals and identifiers stored in a dictionary. The online part consists of a transaction manager for concurrency control, a SPARQL parser, and a SPARQL executor for queries and updates. As for the storage layer, a native multi-version key-value store for RDF graph storage is the key to MVCC in gStore-C. The architecture overview of gStore-C is illustrated in Fig. 1.

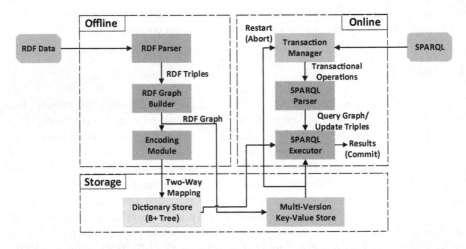

Fig. 1. gStore-C system architecture overview

Transaction Manager. Compared with gStore, gStore-C adds a transaction manager for concurrent transaction control. If a transaction issued by users aborts due to lock acquisition failure or rollback, the transaction manager will reclaim all locks held by the aborted transaction and restart it in a specified time. This "no-wait" policy we adopt can gain better performance and scalability in multi-core platforms.

Multi-version Key-Value Store. We extend the old key-value store to a multi-version implementation in gStore-C. Triples with the same subject or object are in an aggregation form, where a subject or object (vertex) is a key, pairs of predicate and another vertex (edge) constitute value. A large RDF graph contains billions of triples, so we should carefully choose the versioned object to minimize possible overheads. The appending-only versioning like Postgres [8] is not a practical method in our situation because the degree of nodes in an RDF graph follows some form of a power-law distribution. It suggests that a few nodes may have a large number of edges. We version value in a delta approach and only store the updated part of the value in a new delta version created when a transaction updates a key. This method can save up lots of space during transaction processing compared with other version approaches.

TimeStamp. Each version owns a pair of timestamps [begin_ts, end_ts] which depicts its complete lifespan. In gStore-C, we combine logical counter and UNIX timestamp as the timestamps of a version. The whole multi-version layout of value is illustrated in Fig. 2.

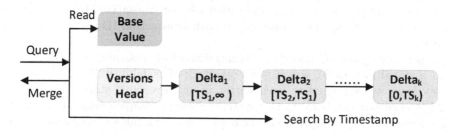

Fig. 2. Multi-version layout of value in key-value store

Concurrency Control. Multi-version concurrency control based on multi-version provides a data access method via timestamps. Select SPARQL queries can run on snapshots without any obstruction in gStore-C. Compared with gStore, gStore-C only adds an extra merge stage between master version and list of delta versions on the fly. The procedure of garbage collection keeps version lists at a proper length to avoid downgrading of the system. The write-write conflicts are resolved by a lightweight locking mechanism. We will discuss it further in Sect. 3.

3 Lightweight Optimistic Lock

Multi-version concurrency control (MVCC) guarantees that read operations never are blocked in snapshot isolation. However, two transactions will conflict if they try creating a new delta version of the value that belongs to the same key. To resolve write-write conflicts, We adopt the "first updater wins" [7] policy and use a read-write lock to decide which transaction creates a new version. We develop a lightweight read-write lock by using atomic variables and operations such as CAS instruction. In gStore-C, the locked object is vertex so that the attached lock can also be resident in memory. The read-write lock consists of two atomic integers, one integer stores 64-bits transaction identifier as an exclusive lock while the other stores 64-bits read counter that records the number of active transactions reading this key as a shared lock. Each transaction must acquire proper locks before it is allowed to perform reads or writes. For example, if a key's transaction ID is not zero, it suggests that a transaction is executing a write operation on it. So other transactions which try to write the same key will fail and abort. In SI or RC, read lock is unnecessary because a transaction always reads the latest committed versions or committed versions according to timestamp.

It is more complicated for a serializable transaction to perform a read operation. A transaction may find no proper version to read in a write-locked key then abort due to violating the principle of full serializability. Read-counter will increment by one if one transaction reads the latest committed version. So any transaction plan to perform a write operation have to abort after that. A transaction that performs a write operation will set transaction ID as its owned identifier and read counter as one only if both transaction ID and read counter are zero.

In practice, gStore-C adopts a decentralized lock management approach to avoid a global lock table, which is a bottleneck of scalability [3]. As mentioned before, locks are attached to each vertex in the key-value store. To eliminate possible occurred deadlock in the system, gStore-C implements an optimistic locking mechanism. Transactions have to abort and release all locks holding instead of waiting when conflicts happen. If all transactions run concurrently in the same no-wait manner, it is not difficult to prove that there will be no deadlock condition in our system. There are many advantages of the approach: 1) avoid a large global lock table. 2) simple deadlock avoidance. 3) better throughput in a low-contention situation. 4) better-grained and lightweight locking.

4   Demonstration

In this demo, we illustrate how to use gStore-C to perform the concurrent transaction processing. A simple web demo is built for online transaction processing (OLTP). As Fig. 3 shows, there is a "New Transaction" button to start a new transaction with a selected isolation level on the top. A user issues a transaction executing under RC then a transaction processing window is created below. The transaction information including transaction ID, isolation level, and the current state is showed in the left-up corner. On the other end, the user can perform four operations: executing SPARQL, commit, rollback, and delete this window. Under the information and control panel, the user can enter a SPARQL query in the box then the corresponding result is shown on the right. Users can run several transactions concurrently by creating several transaction processing windows and performing operations. Compared with other RDF engines, gStore-C

Fig. 3. A transaction processing window on web demo

maintains the fast query over massive RDF data and provides online transaction processing by adopting MVCC and a lightweight lock.

Acknowledgement. This work was supported by The National Key Research and Development Program of China under grant 2018YFB1003504.

References

1. Erling, O., Mikhailov, I.: RDF support in the virtuoso DBMS. In: Pellegrini, T., Auer, S., Tochtermann, K., Schaffert, S. (eds.) Networked Knowledge-Networked Media. Studies in Computational Intelligence, vol. 221, pp. 7–24. Springer, Heidelberg (2009). https://doi.org/10.1007/978-3-642-02184-8_2
2. Jena, A.: Semantic web framework for java (2007)
3. Jung, H., Han, H., Fekete, A., Heiser, G., Yeom, H.Y.: A scalable lock manager for multicores. ACM Trans. Database Syst. (TODS) **39**(4), 1–29 (2014)
4. Neumann, T., Weikum, G.: RDF-3X: a RISC-style engine for RDF. Proc. VLDB Endow. **1**(1), 647–659 (2008)
5. Neumann, T., Weikum, G.: x-RDF-3X: fast querying, high update rates, and consistency for RDF databases. Proc. VLDB Endow. **3**(1–2), 256–263 (2010)
6. Shen, X., et al.: A graph-based RDF triple store. In: 2015 IEEE 31st International Conference on Data Engineering, pp. 1508–1511. IEEE (2015)
7. Silberschatz, A., Korth, H.F., Sudarshan, S., et al.: Database System Concepts, vol. 4. Mcgraw-Hill, New York (1997)
8. Stonebraker, M.: The design of the POSTGRES storage system. California Univ Berkeley Electronics Research Lab, Technical report (1987)
9. Wilkinson, K., Sayers, C., Kuno, H.A., Reynolds, D., et al.: Efficient RDF storage and retrieval in Jena2. In: SWDB, vol. 3, pp. 131–150. Citeseer (2003)
10. Zou, L., Mo, J., Chen, L., Özsu, M.T., Zhao, D.: gStore: answering SPARQL queries via subgraph matching. Proc. VLDB Endow. **4**(8), 482–493 (2011)
11. Zou, L., Özsu, M.T., Chen, L., Shen, X., Huang, R., Zhao, D.: gStore: a graph-based SPARQL query engine. VLDB J. **23**(4), 565–590 (2014)

Deep-gAnswer: A Knowledge Based Question Answering System

Yinnian Lin, Minhao Zhang, Ruoyu Zhang, and Lei Zou$^{(\boxtimes)}$

Peking University, Beijing, China
{linyinnian,zhangminhao,ry_zhang,zoulei}@pku.edu.cn

Abstract. In this demonstration, we present Deep-gAnswer, a knowledge-based question answering system. gAnswer is based on semantic parsing and heuristic rules for entity recognition, relation recognition, and SPARQL generation. By making use of a pre-trained model, we implement new entity and relation recognition networks. Also, it is found that the traditional method works better when information of entity and relation is correctly given. Therefore, we combine entity and relation recognition networks with the previous SPARQL generation process to get Deep-gAnswer. Experimental results show that Deep-gAnswer outperforms the previous one, especially on Chinese dataset.

1 Introduction

Knowledge graph has been through rapid development and is applied in many fields. Knowledge-based question answering (KBQA) [9] is one of its most popular applications. Given a natural language question, KBQA systems are designed to extract the answers from a background knowledge base. A common solution in previous systems is transforming the question into a knowledge base query such as SPARQL [3] to return answers. gAnswer [4] is one of such systems with satisfying performance, which won the first place in QALD-9 [7].

However, gAnswer's performance severely relies on its two components: the dependency tree parser and paraphrase dictionary. gAnswer parses the question into a dependency tree for node and relation recognition that decides which parts of the question (usually called mentions) may refer to an entity, a relation, or a variable. Paraphrase dictionary aims to find the proper matching between relation mentions and predicates in the knowledge graph. However, most dependency tree parsers only work well on simple questions. When the number of relations in the question increases, errors often occur in the dependency parsing stage and are passed to the following stages, severely harming the overall performance. Meanwhile, the paraphrase dictionary requires a very large amount of data and time to construct. What's worse, the dictionary is closely related to the background knowledge graph. So, when we change to another knowledge graph, the former dictionary may become useless because the predicates in the new knowledge graph vary.

To overcome the problems above, we make use of the up-to-date pre-trained models. Such models like BERT [5] are trained on massive data and able to

L. H. U et al. (Eds.): APWeb-WAIM 2021, LNCS 12859, pp. 434–439, 2021.
https://doi.org/10.1007/978-3-030-85899-5_33

extract underlying features from natural language sentences. In other words, their generality is better than the old ways in gAnswer.

In this demo, we propose a novel KBQA framework based on gAnswer, named Deep-gAnswer. We take node recognition as a sequence labeling task while relation recognition as a ranking task, and train two models respectively. The recognition model is intended to improve mention detection and dependency tree parsing while the relation ranking model can replace paraphrase dictionary.

We conduct a comparative experiment between gAnwser and Deep-gAnswer and experimental results show that Deep-gAnswer prevails gAnswer in terms of F1 score, especially on Chinese questions and complex questions.

2   System Architecture

The Deep-gAnswer system consists of four parts: question understanding, query graph construction, SPARQL generation, and answer collection. The system architecture is depicted in Fig. 1.

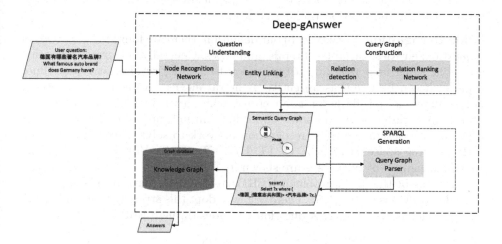

Fig. 1. The Deep-gAnswer architecture

Question Understanding. This is the first step for Deep-gAnswer to answer a question. The purpose of this procedure is to detect all the mentions of entities and variables via a node recognition network. Then, in entity linking module, every entity mention will be mapped to a set of exact entity names in the knowledge graph with a dictionary and string similarity. Notice that one mention may be linked to multiple entities as long as their similarity is high enough. In practice, the system will maintain a fixed number of linking results of a mention and generate a list of ranked SPARQL.

Query Graph Construction. In this step, the system first parses the question to find the relations among entity mentions and variable mentions. The system builds a dependency tree of the question to extract the relation between mentions. Then, the system enumerates every relation and feeds it to the relation ranking network to get its possible predicate. Having all entity, variable, and relation information, the system builds a semantic query graph in a depth-first search manner.

SPARQL Generation and Answer Collection. As mentioned before, most errors of gAnswer come from node and relation recognition and we have improved them with deep-learning-based models. Therefore, we simply follow the subgraph matching strategy from gAnswer for SPARQL generation and answer collection. The system generates a list of ranked SPARQLs and sends them as queries to a graph database to get the final answers.

3   Techniques

In this section, we mainly focus on the implementation of the new node recognition network and relation ranking network.

Node Recognition Network. In our definition, there are four kinds of nodes in a question: entities, variables, literals, and types. Generally, an entity represents a specific thing or person and a type refers to a category of entity. Sometimes type itself can be taken as an entity. A literal means a value or an attribute. For example, a specific actor is an entity, while his height and nickname are literals. A variable is an unknown node that can indicate an entity, a type, or a literal. We design the node recognition network to solve a sequence labeling task with tag space $\{O, Eb, Ei, Vb, Vi, VTb, VTi, Tb, Ti, VLb, VLi, Lb, Li\}$. The specific meanings of these tags are shown in Table 1.

In terms of the NER problem, BERT-based models have been proved successful in previous works [1,5]. Therefore, we adopt this strategy to use a BEAT-based model as an encoder. A question first goes through RoBERTa [6] encoder

Table 1. Tag meanings

Tag	Meaning
O	Not an entity nor variable
Eb, Ei	Mention to an entity
Vb, Vi	Mention to variable that refers to an entity
VTb, VTi	Mention to variable that refers to a type
Tb, Ti	Mention to a type
VLb, VLi	Mention to a variable that refers to a literal value
Lb, Li	Mention to literal value

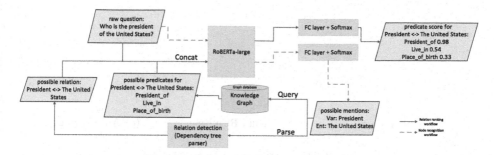

Fig. 2. Workflow of the node recognition network and the relation ranking network

and then to the output layer for the tag sequence. We choose RoBERTa because it outperforms other models in our experiments.

To train the model, we also developed a dataset by ourselves annotating node-to-mention mappings. We manually tagged natural language questions with the previously mentioned tag space. The questions come from the existing KBQA question sets. We mainly used LC-QUAD question set [8] for English questions and CCKS question set [2] for Chinese questions. Both question sets provide natural language questions and corresponding SPARQLs. Tagged questions serve as the input of our node recognition network and relations extracted from the given SPARQLs are feed to the relation ranking model.

Relation Ranking Network. The goal of relation recognition is to find all pairs of related nodes and their predicates. Due to the complexity of the natural language questions and lack of training data, an end-to-end model may not handle this task very well. However, we can first attain all related node pairs and use a ranking model to get the top k most likely predicates easily.

Our experiments show that with node mentions given, a dependency tree parser can reach a satisfying accuracy. Therefore, we can extract all related node pairs from the dependency tree. For each pair, we query the knowledge graph for candidate predicates. If one of the nodes is an exact entity set, we can simply search for its connected predicates. If both nodes are variables, we search the query graph to find an entity and get its k-hops-away predicates as candidates. For each candidate predicate, we concatenate the question, the mentions of the two related nodes, and the predicate itself to form an input sentence and sent it to RoBERTa encoder. We use a full connected layer as a decoder to output a score. The encoder is shared between both node recognition and relation ranking network to learn global information. In this way, we get a ranked predicate list for each relation. The workflow of the two models is in Fig. 2.

4 Demonstration

We build a website to demonstrate how Deep-gAnswer answers a natural language question, providing users with a friendly interface and straightforward

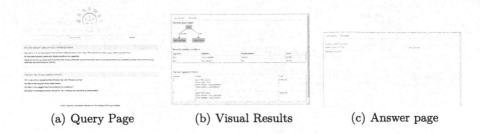

(a) Query Page   (b) Visual Results   (c) Answer page

Fig. 3. Demonstration of Deep-gAnswer

visual results of the translation from natural language questions to SPARQL. We use an English knowledge graph, DBpedia, to set up the background system.

Figure 3(a) is our query page. Users can input a question freely in the center text box and ask the system. Here we use a complex question, *In which films directed by Garry Marshall was Julia Roberts starring?* as an example.

Figure 3(b) shows the result demonstration page. At the top is the query graph. We can see *Gary Marshall, Julia Roberts* and *films* are recognized as mentions. In the middle, user can see the result of relation detection. With correct node mentions given, the dependency parser can successfully identify the relation and its corresponding mentions. The generated SPARQL list is at the bottom. Relation mentions become actual predicates with the help of the relation ranking model and the score of a SPARQL here is based on the score of each predicate. To check the final answer, users can jump to the answer page as shown in Fig. 3(c).

Acknowledgment. This work was supported by National Natural Science Foundation of China(NSFC) under grant 61932001. The corresponding author of this work is Lei Zou.

References

1. Akbik, A., Blythe, D., Vollgraf, R.: Contextual string embeddings for sequence labeling. In: Proceedings of the 27th International Conference on Computational Linguistics, pp. 1638–1649 (2018)
2. Han, X., et al.: Overview of the CCKS 2019 knowledge graph evaluation track: entity, relation, event and QA. arXiv preprint arXiv:2003.03875 (2020)
3. Hommeaux, E.P.: SparQL query language for RDF (2011)
4. Hu, S., Zou, L., Yu, J.X., Wang, H., Zhao, D.: Answering natural language questions by subgraph matching over knowledge graphs. IEEE Trans. Knowl. Data Eng. **30**(5), 824–837 (2017)
5. Kenton, J.D.M.W.C., Toutanova, L.K.: Bert: pre-training of deep bidirectional transformers for language understanding. In: Proceedings of NAACL-HLT, pp. 4171–4186 (2019)
6. Liu, Y., et al.: Roberta: a robustly optimized BERT pretraining approach. arXiv preprint arXiv:1907.11692 (2019)

7. Ngomo, N.: 9th challenge on question answering over linked data (QALD-9). Language 7(1) (2018)
8. Trivedi, P., Maheshwari, G., Dubey, M., Lehmann, J.: LC-QuAD: a corpus for complex question answering over knowledge graphs. In: d'Amato, C., et al. (eds.) ISWC 2017. LNCS, vol. 10588, pp. 210–218. Springer, Cham (2017). https://doi.org/10.1007/978-3-319-68204-4_22
9. Unger, C., Freitas, A., Cimiano, P.: An introduction to question answering over linked data. In: Reasoning Web International Summer School (2014)

ALMSS: Automatic Learned Index Model Selection System

Rui Zhu[1], Hongzhi Wang[1,2(✉)], Yafeng Tang[1], and Bo Xu[1]

[1] Harbin Institute of Technology, Harbin, China
[2] Peng Cheng Laboratory, Shenzhen, China
{20S003048,wangzh,1190201313,1190201620}@hit.edu.cn

Abstract. Index is an indispensable part of database. As we enter the era of big data, the traditional index structure is found not to support large-scale data well. Although many index structures such as learned indexes based on machine learning have been proposed to solve such problems of traditional indexes, it is a great challenge to select the most suitable learned indexes for the specific application. To solve this problem, we design ALMSS, an automatic learned index model selection system, which provides a user-friendly interface and can help users automatically select the learned index model. In this paper, we introduce the overall architecture and main technologies of ALMSS, and show the demonstration of this system.

Keywords: Learned index · Model selection · Machine learning

1 Introduction

Most of the existing database systems adopt traditional index structures, such as B+ trees. However, for big data, the traditional index structures have exposed some shortcomings. For example, B+ tree may cost too much space. At this time, the learned index was put forward. In 2018, Kraska et al. [1] first proposed the concept of combining machine learning with traditional index structures. Compared with traditional indexes, learned index can reduce the cost of index space and improve index query performance. In the following years, scientists have successively proposed many learned indexes to solve the problems of the initial version of learned index that cannot support insertion.

At present, most researches on one-dimensional learned indexes focus on data partition and data insertion strategy. For example, AIDEL [2] and ALEX [3] use the local insertion strategy, while PGM-index [4], XIndex [5] and FITing-Tree [6] use the remote insertion strategy. Local insertion strategy is to reserve a certain gap in the sorting array of leaf nodes. When some data needs to be inserted, we insert the data into gaps by using some policies. We update the model when gaps are reduced to a certain number. For example, ALEX predicts the location of data insertion through a model. If there is a gap in the predicted location, then the data can be inserted into the gap. On the contrary, if the location predicted

L. H. U et al. (Eds.): APWeb-WAIM 2021, LNCS 12859, pp. 440–445, 2021.
https://doi.org/10.1007/978-3-030-85899-5_34

by the model is not a gap, ALEX uses an exponential search method to search a gap and inserts the data into the gap. And the remote insertion strategy inserts the data into the buffer, and then formulates the strategy to merge the data in the buffer with the data corresponding to the original model. For example, XIndex sets a two-phase compacting strategy to support data merging. Their leaf node design strategy is relatively simple, mostly using linear regression model. However, in many cases, simple linear regression models cannot fit the data well. Therefore, how to choose the leaf node model has become an urgent problem to be solved.

In order to solve the above problems, we first designed an automatic learned index model selection system(ALMSS), which can automatically select the model according to the data set selected by users and provide a user-friendly interface. The main functions of the system are as follows:

- Automatic Index Selection: Our system implements the automatic index selection function, including not only the selection of traditional indexes such as B-tree, hash tree, etc., but also the selection of learned indexes for the automatic selection model that we design. Users can choose to use traditional indexes, such as hash, B-tree, or learning index according to their own needs. If the users choose learning index, the node model of learning index is automatically selected by our system. Users do not need to select the internal model of learning index.
- Friendly interface: ALMSS provides a graphical interface, and users can accomplish the automatic selection function of the index by simple operations such as selecting data sets and inputting SQL query statements. Users only need simple operations to achieve the required functions. At the same time, our ALMSS system will provide users with system information as much as possible, so that users can understand the internal implementation steps in our ALMSS more clearly.

Our paper is structured as follows. In Sect. 2, we will introduce the overall architecture of our ALMSS system in detail. Then in Sect. 3, based on the understanding of the overall architecture, we will introduce the key technologies of ALMSS system in more detail. Finally, in Sect. 4, we will show the demonstration scenarios of the system.

2 System Overview

Figure 1 shows the architecture of ALMSS. Users can select the appropriate dataset for the following operation, and then enter the SQL statement of the query. In the learned index module, according to the results of the automatic selection model, users can obtain accurate query location and model information involved in the query process. The learning index module includes traditional index models, such as b-tree, and machine learning models such as RMI. For example, in the upload dataset module, when the user selects the dataset from the existing dataset in the system, the corresponding dataset information will be displayed, including data set content, data distribution, etc. In SQL parsing module, users input SQL statements that need to be executed. ALMSS parses this statement regularly, and gives a large range of key location description of related fields according to uploading dataset. This description will be transmitted to the learning index module for further processing. This part provides some models or algorithms for users to reduce the scope of the key at the maximum speed. In addition, we show the training time and other information through visualization. The Automatic Selection module receives the results of the previous module, automatically selects the most suitable regression model to analyze and obtain accurate query location, and provides the selected model and its parameters to users (Fig. 1).

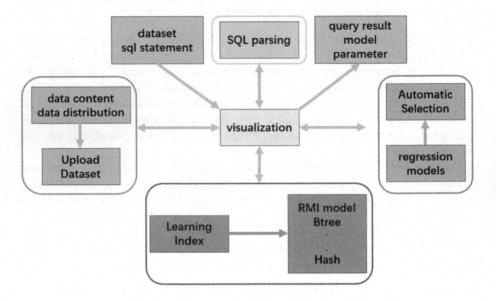

Fig. 1. System architecture

3   Key Technologies

In this section, we will introduce the key technologies of ALMSS from two parts. The core module of ALMSS is to select the best index suitable for the dataset for users. We divide the model selection part into two parts. One is the best distribution model fitting for the data set, called automatic model selection module. The other part is to combine the learned index with the automatic model selection module to generate the best index for users.

3.1   Automatic Model Selection Module

Considering the diversity of data stored in the database, it is difficult to ensure that the exact location is always queried at a faster speed and high accuracy if the same model has been used. Therefore, in ALMSS, we propose to use multiple regression models with diversity and accuracy guarantees such as linear regression, polynomial regression, elastic regression, etc. At the same time, we use the random forest as the classifier, so as to ensure that ALMSS has fast and accurate characteristics in the diversity of data for the whole database. The specific measures are as follows. Firstly, for the received key range input, training is carried out in the existing multiple regression models. We obtain the evaluation data of the regression effect of each model, such as R2-score, Median absolute error, RMSE, etc. Then we establish the evaluation function and use random forest classifier for classification training. Finally we optimize the model performance. The model trained in this way, in the face of new data test, also has the ability to select the data characteristics of the excellent model regression analysis. At the same time, we note that due to the establishment of an excellent evaluation function, the Median absolute error of the trained model is very low, which also indicates that our model has excellent regression performance.

3.2 Learned Index with Automatic Model Selection Module

The existing leaf nodes of learning index are fixed single models, such as linear regression. This is not suitable for all datasets. At the same time, when the data distribution is complex, the model of leaf node using artificial selection is inefficient and it is not easy to choose. Therefore, on the basis of learning index, we change the leaf nodes in the learning index from the fixed model to our automatic model selection module. First, the RMI module divides the dataset into smaller ones. Then, on a small-scale dataset, we can use the machine learning method to automatically fit the most suitable model for this dataset as the leaf node model. It is worth noting that over-fitting is allowed in the process of training the model of leaf node. Overfitting means that the model we choose fully fits the dataset corresponding to the model. This is allowed in the database. We also use the same strategy as the original learning index. We set an error threshold for leaf nodes in advance. If the actual error is greater than the threshold we set, the leaf node will degenerate into a traditional index such as B-tree. If the actual error is within the threshold range we set, we use the automatically generated model as the leaf node. This ensures the accuracy of the index and improves the efficiency of the index.

4   Demonstration Scenarios

We plan to demonstrate our ALMSS system in four steps:

- Upload Dataset. As in Fig. 2(a), we provide an operation button and information display interface. Users can browse the existing dataset and select the data set they need according to the content of the dataset, data distribution and other information. At the same time, users can choose which index structure to use. The currently available index structures are B-Tree, hash, and learning index.

- Sql Parsing. As in Fig. 2(b), users enter SQL statements that need to query, and then our system will be regular parsed. We associate SQL statements with corresponding fields and calculate a large range of key. At the same time below the page, we give the diagram of the whole process.
- Learned Index. As Fig. 2(c), ALMSS provides three schemes for rapidly reducing the range of key. We use the recursive learning index technology (RMI Model), and compare it with the traditional B-tree and hash index. Users can view the time and other information of the visual index establishment process of different schemes provided by us.
- Automatic Selection. As Fig. 2(d) presents, ALMSS automatically selects the appropriate regression model for training in the key range. Users can see some relevant information such as the selected optimal model, model-related parameters, training and evaluation results, and the precise location of the final query (Fig. 2).

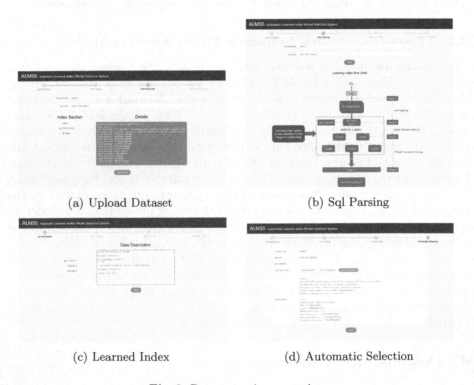

(a) Upload Dataset   (b) Sql Parsing

(c) Learned Index   (d) Automatic Selection

Fig. 2. Demonstration scenarios

References

1. Kraska, T., Beutel, A., Chi, E.H., Dean, J., Polyzotis, N.: The case for learned index structures. In: Proceedings of the International Conference on Management of Data, 489–504 (2018)

2. Li, P., Hua, Y., Zuo, P., Jia, J.: A scalable learned index scheme in storage systems. arXiv: Databases (2019)
3. Ding, J., Minhas, U.F., Yu, J., Wang, C., Do, J., Li, Y.: ALEX: an updatable adaptive learned index. In: International Conference on Management of Data, pp. 969–984 (2020)
4. Ferragina, P., Vinciguerra, G.: The PGM-index: a fully-dynamic compressed learned index with provable worst-case bounds. Proc. VLDB Endow. **13**(8), 1162–1175 (2020)
5. Tang, C., Wang, Y., Hu, G., Dong, Z., Wang, Z., Wang, M.: XIndex: a scalable learned index for multicore data storage. In: ACM (2020)
6. Galakatos, A., Markovitch, M., Binnig, C., Fonseca, R., Kraska, T.: FITing-tree: a data-aware index structure. In: International Conference on Management of Data, pp. 1189–1206 (2019)

GPKRS: A GPU-Enhanced Product Knowledge Retrieval System

Yuming Lin, Hao Song, Chuangxin Fang, and You Li$^{(\boxtimes)}$

Guangxi Key Laboratory of Trusted Software,
Guilin University of Electronic Technology, Guilin 541004, China
liyou@guet.edu.cn

Abstract. In this demonstration, we present a GPU-enhanced product knowledge retrieve system called GPKRS, which stores product knowledge based on the sparse matrix compression, and introduces a query transformation module to transform the query operation into the corresponding matrix operations. By this way, we can take advantage of the powerful parallel computing power of GPU to accelerate the processing of SPARQL query. Further, GPKRS adopts an optimized pipeline query strategy to speed up the query execution. The experiments show that the GPKRS achieves state-of-the-art query performances on the LUMB dataset and a synthetic product knowledge dataset.

Keywords: Knowledge graph · RDF data · Knowledge retrieval

1 Introduction

Knowledge graph has become the infrastructure of lots of intelligence systems. However, with a dramatic growth of the knowledge size, the effectiveness of query processing is turning into a bottleneck for providing users with high-quality knowledge service. Resource Description Framework (RDF) provides a unified specification for describing resources on the Web. A RDF triple is a statement representing data as the form of <subject, predicate, object>. Many works focus on engines for SPARQL query over various datasets with CPU. Among these works, two paradigms are dominant: the relational paradigm such as RDF-3X [1], SW-Store [2] and the graph-based paradigm such as gStore [3]. The former usually manage RDF data by establishing tables like triple tables, attribute tables and vertical tables, which results in additional storage pressure. The latter usually transforms query into subgraph matching. But such methods rely on the graph structure, which may effect the performance over large-scale RDF datasets. In recent years, some works try to take advantage of GPU to speed up the query processing of RDF data, such as [4–6]. On the other hand, product knowledge has the traits of massive volume, sparsity, heterogeneous and high scalability of query, which makes the query processing of product knowledge graph more challenging.

In this demonstration, we present a GPU-enhanced Product Knowledge Retrieve System (GPKRS), which adopts the sparse matrices to store large-scale

© Springer Nature Switzerland AG 2021
L. H. U et al. (Eds.): APWeb-WAIM 2021, LNCS 12859, pp. 446–451, 2021.
https://doi.org/10.1007/978-3-030-85899-5_35

RDF-based product knowledge. In order to give full play to the advantages of GPUs' parallel computing, we put forward a SPARQL query mode to transform the common database retrieval tasks into the corresponding matrix dot product operations. Furthermore, GPKRS utilizes a pipeline query strategy to decrease the unnecessary retrieval waiting time for improving the retrieval efficiency.

2   System Overview

In our work, the product knowledge graph includes the objective product taxonomy and the subjective user opinion, which consists of five layers: category layer, product layer, attribute layer, opinion layer and user layer The upper two layers, and the lower three layers are the subjective product knowledge. Figure 1 shows a fragment of the constructed product knowledge graph. For example, $s1$ is a subcategory of product category $c1$, product $p1$ has two attributes $a1$ and $a2$, user $u1$ holds the opinion $o1$ on product $p1$'s attribute $a1$.

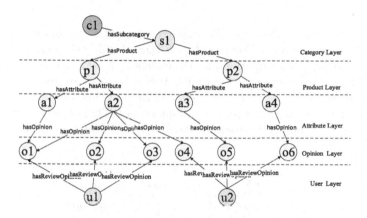

Fig. 1. The organization of product knowledge

GPRKS is composed of five components: RDF Parser, Matrix Builder, Mapping Dictionary, SPARQL Parser & Transformer, Dot Product & Join, as shown in Fig. 2.

RDF Parser. This module is responsible for decomposing RDF data into a large collection of triples and loading them into GPKRS.

Matrix Builder. Since a fact of product knowledge graph is a triple, such product knowledge corresponds to a cube in a three-dimensional space, as shown in Fig. 3(a). Based on this cube, we construct the matrices for each subject and each predicate. The Fig. 3(b) shows the process of generating P-O matrix for subject s_j. We slice the cube along the subject dimension to generate a P-O plane for each subject. In s_i's plane, the point (p_j, o_l) means the fact (s_i, p_j, o_l). Then, we can construct a matrix for each plane, in which the element is

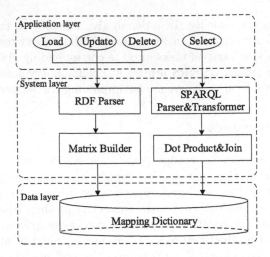

Fig. 2. The framework of GPKRS

1 or 0, and the matrix label is the corresponding IDS presented as the data format in the first module. Compared with IDS of different lengths, the sparse matrix can reduce the occupation and dependence on GPU memory as much as possible. The transmission speed of digital IDS is faster than text between CPU and GPU. In the end, we store the sparse matrix in this module, which is the real data we need during the execution of query, not IDS in the first module. We construct the S-O matrix for each predicate by the same operations, as shown in Fig. 3(c).

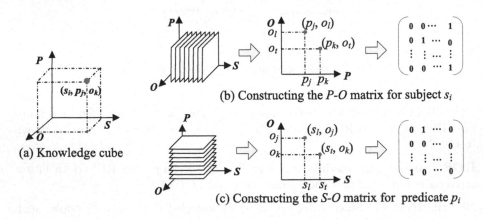

(a) Knowledge cube

(b) Constructing the *P-O* matrix for subject s_i

(c) Constructing the *S-O* matrix for predicate p_i

Fig. 3. The organization of product knowledge

SPARQL Parser and Transformer. This module firstly loads the SPARQL queries, and then filters the intermediate results according to the known variables. If the elements in both matrices are 1, then we set the corresponding elements in the result matrix to 1, otherwise 0. At last, the module outputs the final query matrix. For the simple query, such as the single condition query shown in Fig. 4(a), we can obtain the values of the object variable by projecting the column corresponding to the known subject in the predicate matrix.

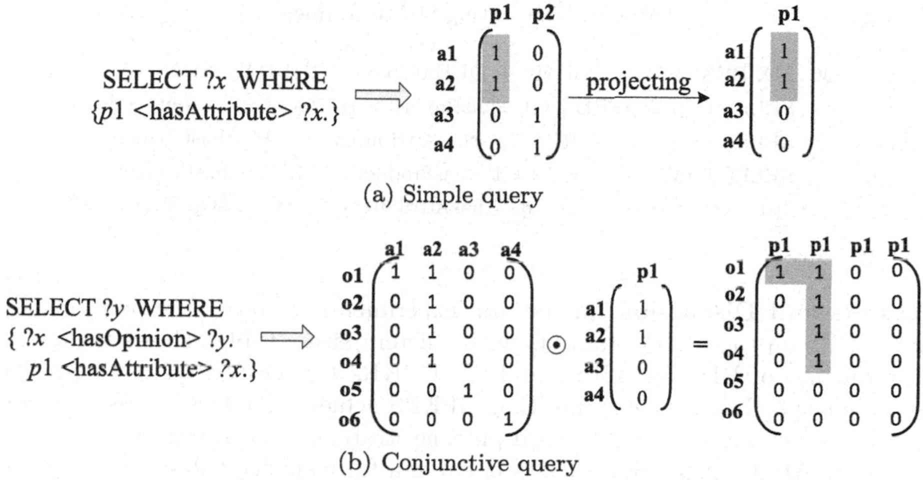

(a) Simple query

(b) Conjunctive query

Fig. 4. Transforming SPARQL queries into matrix operations

Dot Product and Join. For the complex query, such as the conjunctive query show in Fig. 4(b), we use the sparse query matrix and sparse data matrix for point multiplication and join operation during the execution of query. We filter out invalid intermediate results and connect the two sparse matrices according to the same matrix label. We also adopt the pipeline query strategy to speed up the execution of SPARQL. And it is unnecessary to execute the next subquery until all the intermediate results.

Mapping Dictionary. This module parses the output of Dot Product & Join according to the mapping dictionary and returns the result of query.

3   Demonstration

Experiment Settings. Two datasets are used in our experiments. The first one is standard LUBM datasets: LUBM1, LUBM8, LUBM32, which contains 11 thousand, 139 thousand and 1.2 million triples respectively. The second one is a synthetic product knowledge dataset, which contains 643 million triples conducted based on Amazon products. Nine queries are used in our experiments, which are shown in Table 1. Notably, Q7-Q9 are three queries frequently used by users in E-commerce. All of the experiments were conducted ten times, and the averages are shown as the experiment results. GPKRS is compared with two state-of-the-art RDF engines: RDF-3X and gStore.

The experimental workstation houses six 3.20 GHz Intel dual-core CPUs and 16 GB of RAM. An NVIDIA GeForce GTX 1060 graphics card is added to enable the use of CUDA, which contains 1280 SIMD processors and 6 GB of device memory. The version of CUDA is 9.0.

Table 1. The testing SPARQL queries

Q1 – Q6	SIX BENCHMARK SPARQL QUERIES of LUBM DATASETS
Q7	SELECT ?p WHERE { C1 <hasProduct> ?p. ?p <hasAttribute> A1. }
Q8	SELECT ?p ?o WHERE { ?p <hasAttribute> A1. A1 <hasOpinion> ?o. }
Q9	SELECT ?a ?o WHERE { C1 <hasProduct> ?p1. C1 <hasProduct> ?p2
	?p1 <hasAttribute> ?a. ?p2 <hasAttribute> ?a. ?a <hasOpinion> ?o. }

Results and Discussion. In the first experiment, we verify the performance of GPKRS on the LUBM datasets with different sizes. Table 2 shows the query performance of RDF-3x, gStore and our GPKRs for the $Q1$, $Q2$, $Q3$, $Q4$, $Q5$ and $Q6$ respectively. We can find that GPKRS achieves the best scores for most queries, which means the optimized pipeline strategy could speed up the execution of SPARQL query. Since RDF-3x stores a fully aligned subset of data, it is very effective for the simple query $Q1$. With the increase of the size of LUBM datasets, query performance improvement of GPKRS is more obvious than the other two. On the other hand, gStore achieves better query performance in the case of different amount of data.

Table 2. Query time (ms) on LUBM datasets. The best scores are highlighted in bold.

SPARQL	Datasets								
	LUBM1			LUBM8			LUBM32		
-	RDF-3X	gStore	GPKRS	RDF-3X	gStore	GPKRS	RDF-3X	gStore	GPKRS
Q1	**3**	23	12	**5**	34	19	**9**	45	32
Q2	76	**8**	16	417	**11**	22	53	**13**	29
Q3	11	5	**3**	15	8	**4**	17	9	**7**
Q4	6	**3**	8	8	**4**	11	14	**5**	16
Q5	5	3	**2**	9	5	**3**	12	6	**4**
Q6	141	21	**11**	183	27	**17**	296	37	**26**
Average	40.3	10.5	**8.7**	106.2	14.8	**12.7**	66.8	19.2	**19.0**

The $Q7$ is used to seek out those products with specific attributes under same category $C1$. The $Q8$ is used to query specific product with specific attribute and opinion. The $Q9$ is used to find out all attributes and opinions shared by product P1 and P2 under same category $C1$. In fact, the user's query problems used by users are mostly similar to such questions as $Q7$, $Q8$ and $Q9$. Our query system is inferior to RDF-3x and gStore as shown in Table 3. The simpler and more uncomplicated the query, the higher the efficiency of GPKRS, since GPKRS could take full advantage of the characteristics of GPU's multi-threading to realize maximized parallel to improve the retrieval efficiency.

Table 3. Query time (ms) on the synthetic product datasets. The best scores are highlighted in bold.

SPARQL	RDF-3X	gStore	GPKRS
Q7	796	543	**475**
Q8	1,758	891	**549**
Q9	4,324	3,517	**2,453**
Average	2,293	1,650	**1,159**

Acknowledgment. This work was supported by National Natural Science Foundation of China (62062027, U1711263), Guangxi Natural Science Foundations (2018GXNSFDA281049, 2020GXNSFAA159012, 2018GXNSFAA281326), Science and Technology Major Project of Guangxi Province (AA19046004), Innovation Project of GUET Graduate Education (2020YCXS046) and the project of Guangxi Key Laboratory of Trusted Software (kx202021).

References

1. Neumann, T., Weikum, G.: RDF-3X: a RISC-style engine for RDF. Proc. VLDB Endowment, 647–659 (2008)
2. Abadi, D.J., Marcus, A., Madden, S., et al.: SW-Store: a vertically partitioned DBMS for semantic web data management. VLDB J. **18**(2), 385–406 (2009)
3. Zou, L., Özsu, M.T., Chen, L., Shen, X., Huang, R., Zhao, D.: gStore: a graph-based SPARQL query engine. VLDB J. **23**(4), 565–590 (2013). https://doi.org/10.1007/s00778-013-0337-7
4. Atre, M., Chaoji, V., Zaki, M.J., Hendler, J.A.: Matrix "Bit" loaded: a scalable lightweight join query processor for RDF data. In: WWW 2010, pp. 41–50 (2010)
5. Zhang, X., Zhang, M., Peng, P., et al.: A scalable sparse matrix-based join for SPARQL query processing. In: DASFAA 2019, pp. 510–514 (2019)
6. Chantrapornchai, C., Choksuchat, C., Haidl, M., et al.: TripleID: a low-overhead representation and querying using GPU for large RDFs. In: BDAS 2015, pp. 400–415 (2015)

Standard-Oriented Standard Knowledge Graph Construction and Applications System

Haopeng Ren[1,2], Yi Cai[1,2(✉)], Mingying Zhang[3], Wenjian Hao[3], and Xin Wu[1,2]

[1] Key Laboratory of Big Data and Intelligent Robot (South China University of Technology), Ministry of Education, Guangzhou, China
[2] South China University of Technology, Guangzhou, China
ycai@scut.edu.cn
[3] China Electronics Standardization Institute, Beijing, China

Abstract. Standard is an important normative files in different industries, which can effectively guide the production process and ensure the quality of the products. However, the establishment and applications of the standards are time-consuming and human-intensive. Motivated by this, the technique of knowledge graph can effectively model the text data with the multiple triples. Considering the special characteristics of standard documents, we propose an architecture framework for the construction of standard knowledge graph and design two applications in our system.

Keywords: Standard · Knowledge graph · Recommendation · Conflict detection

1 Introduction

Standard is a kind of normative document which is designed to be used as a rule, guideline or definition in various industry domains. It effectively guides the design of industrial products, standardizes the production process and ensures the quality of product production. However, current standard documents are mainly organized in text format (i.e., natural language) and each industry has a large amount of standards. The establishment, understanding and usage of standard documents rely heavily on manual work, which are time-consuming and human-intensive. Currently, the technique of knowledge graphs (KGs) (e.g., DBpedia, Wikidata and Google KGs) can effectively model the text data by constructing graphs with multiple triples [5,7,8]. Each triple consists of two entities and the relation between them. KGs benefit a board range of intelligent applications such as question answering, personalized recommendations [6] and so on. Different from other domains, however, the standard domain has its own characteristics. For example, the description of a standard documents is often not the pure text (i.e., sentences) but a procedure which introduces the standard operation flow for testing the product and a set of semi-structured data (e.g., figure

ⓒ Springer Nature Switzerland AG 2021
L. H. U et al. (Eds.): APWeb-WAIM 2021, LNCS 12859, pp. 452–457, 2021.
https://doi.org/10.1007/978-3-030-85899-5_36

and table). Nevertheless, most of current information extraction techniques (e.g., named entity extraction [1,2,4] and relation extraction [3,9,10]) only focus on the text data and cannot effectively extract triples from unstructured data (e.g., procedure data). To solve these problems mentioned above, we propose an architecture framework for constructing the standard-oriented standard knowledge graph. What's more, two applications: standard template recommendation and standard conflict detection are also designed based on the standard knowledge graph in our system.

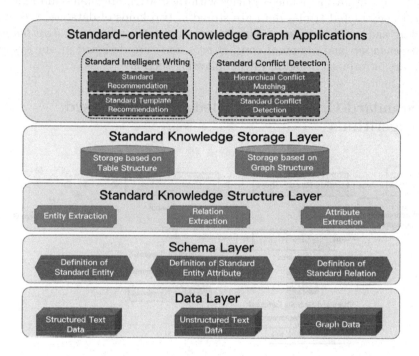

Fig. 1. Framework of the construction of standard knowledge graph

2 Architecture of Standard Knowledge Graph

The architecture framework of the standard-oriented standard knowledge graph mainly composes of five layers: *Data Layer, Schema Layer, Standard Knowledge Structure Layer, Standard Knowledge Storage Layer* and *Application Layers*, as shown in Fig. 1. According to the different characteristics of standard data, we can divide the data into three categories: structured data (e.g., table data), unstructured data (e.g., text description of standard requirement) and graph data (e.g., symbol standard data). Two kinds of special characteristics can be concluded for the standard document data. Firstly, the standard data is multimoddal, which contains text and picture data. Second, the procedure data, e.g., the specific testing operation steps, often emerge in the standard documents. Based on the data layer, the schema layer aims to construct the concept model. Specifically, it defines the schema of standard knowledge graph, including entities, entity attributes and relationships among entities. Our system deals with five types of entities (i.e., *Standard file, Standard object, Standard terminology, Standard requirement aspect* and *Standard process aspect*) and four relations (i.e., *Standard association, Terminology association, Technical requirement association* and *Standard process association*). Guiding by the concept model created in schema layer, three kinds of information extraction techniques (i.e., *Entity Extraction, Attribute Extraction* and *Relation Extraction*) are utilized to respectively obtain the defined entities with their attribute values and relations. Then, the extracted triples data are stored in two kinds of database (i.e., *table structure* and *graph structure*). Finally, two applications (i.e., *standard template recommendation* and *standard conflict detection*) are designed in our systems, which are introduced in detail in the following section.

3 Standard-Oriented Knowledge Graph Based Algorithms

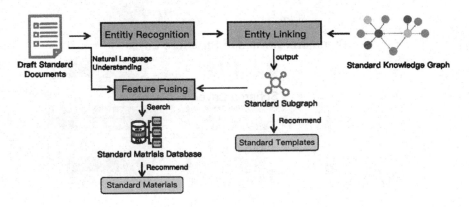

Fig. 2. The framework of standard recommendation algorithm

3.1 Standard Template Recommendation

With the continuous proposal and establishment of standards in various industries, the standards have the characteristics of standardization, diversity, and domain dependency. It is difficult for the standard writers to normatively-use standard terminologies, select standard materials and normalize the standard document format. Therefore, the application of standard template recommendation aims to assist the writers quickly and correctly obtain the standard writing materials and standard writing templates. The framework of this application is shown in Fig. 2. Specifically, given a draft version of standard documents, the entity recognition model [2] are applied to detect the key entities of the standard contents. Then the key entities are linked to the constructed standard knowledge graph and we can obtain the standard sub-graph. Finally, based on the semantic information of draft standard content and the graph feature of constructed sub-graph, we can search the top-k related standard materials and templates from the corresponding databases.

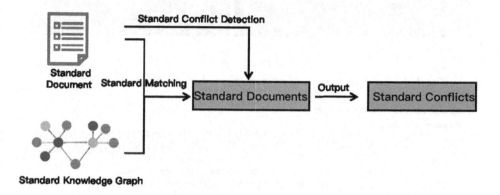

Fig. 3. The framework of conflict detection algorithm

3.2 Standard Conflict Detection

Standard conflict detection is an important step in the establishment and application of standards. However, standard conflicts detection heavily relies on the human work. The lack of a technique that quickly and automatically detect the standard conflicts makes it become time-consuming and human-intensive. Motivated by this, the algorithm of detecting conflicts between standards are designed based on the standard-oriented standard knowledge graph in our system. The framework of this application is shown in Fig. 3. Specifically, the similarity degree between the given sentences are calculated by the following equation.

$$similarity\_value = \frac{2 \times L}{L_1 + L_2} \tag{1}$$

where L denotes the matched char numbers between the given two sentences; L_1 and L_2 respectively denote the number of char numbers of the corresponding sentences.

4 Visualization and Case Study

As shown in Fig. 4, the standard-oriented standard knowledge graph is stored in the Neo4j database. In our system, around 10,000 standard knowledge triples are extracted to build the knowledge graph. Specifically, each standard document has one sub-graph, as shown in Figure 4(b). What's more, two cases for the

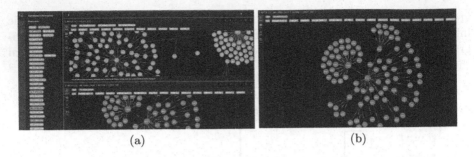

(a) (b)

Fig. 4. Visualization of the standard-oriented standard knowledge graph

Input Key Words: 口罩带 (Mask belt)

Recommend List:

Standard Name	Search Key Words	Content Recommendation
YY_T 0969-2013	口罩带 (Mask belt)	口罩带应戴取方便 (The mask strap should be easy to wear)
YY_T 0969-2013	口罩带 (Mask belt)	测试步骤：随机抽取3个样品进行测试．通过佩戴检查其调节情况，均应符合4.4.1的要求． (Test procedure: randomly select 3 samples for testing. Check its adjustment by wearing it, and all should meet the requirements of 4.4.1)
YY_T 0969-2013	口罩带 (Mask belt)	测试步骤：随机抽取3个样品进行测试．以10N的静拉力进行测量，持续5s，结果应符合4.4.2的要求． (Test procedure: randomly select 3 samples for testing. Measure with a static tension of 10N for 5s, and the result should meet the requirements of 4.4.2)

Fig. 5. A case for the content based Standard Template Recommendation

Detecting Standard File: GB_T 32610-2016

Standard Conflict List:

Conflict Standard	Standard tirple	Conflict Standard triple	Similarity (%)
GB 19083-2010	<过滤效率，英文名称, filtering efficiency>	<过滤效率，英文名称, filter efficiency>	91.89
GB 19083-2010	<过滤效率，术语修饰，在规定条件下，口罩对空气中的颗粒物滤除的>	<过滤效率，术语修饰，在规定条件下，口罩罩体滤除颗粒物的>	73.68

Fig. 6. A case for the Standard Conflict Detection

designed applications (i.e., Standard Template Recommendation and Standard Conflict Detection) are shown in Fig. 5 and 6. Specifically, Fig. 5 shows the case for the applications of standard template recommendation given the research key. Given the input key words (e.g., Mask belt), we can search the related standard file and the corresponding sentences. Meanwhile, the Fig. 6 describes the case of detecting the standard conflicts between the given two standards. Given the input standard file, our designed algorithm can effectively detect the specific conflict content. For example, the conflict between the two terms (i.e., "*filtering efficiency*" and "*filter efficiency*") can be effectively detected, as shown in Fig. 6.

Acknowledgement. This work was supported by National Natural Science Foundation of China (No. 62076100), National Key Research and Development Program of China (Standard knowledge graph for epidemic prevention and production recovering intelligent service platform and its applications), the Fundamental Research Funds for the Central Universities, SCUT (No. D2201300, D2210010), the Science and Technology Programs of Guangzhou(201902010046), the Science and Technology Planning Project of Guangdong Province(No. 2020B0101100002).

References

1. Cao, J., et al.: Incorporating boundary and category feature for nested named entity recognition. In: Nah, Y., Cui, B., Lee, S.-W., Yu, J.X., Moon, Y.-S., Whang, S.E. (eds.) DASFAA 2020. LNCS, vol. 12113, pp. 209–226. Springer, Cham (2020). https://doi.org/10.1007/978-3-030-59416-9_13
2. Jiang, D., Ren, H., Cai, Y., Xu, J., Liu, Y., Leung, H.F.: Candidate region aware nested named entity recognition. Neural Netw. (2021)
3. Ren, H., Cai, Y., Chen, X., Wang, G., Li, Q.: A two-phase prototypical network model for incremental few-shot relation classification. In: Proceedings of the 28th International Conference on Computational Linguistics, pp. 1618–1629 (2020)
4. Tang, Z., Wan, B., Yang, L.: Word-character graph convolution network for Chinese named entity recognition. IEEE/ACM Trans. Audio Speech Lang. Process. **28**, 1520–1532 (2020)
5. Tao, X., et al.: Mining health knowledge graph for health risk prediction. World Wide Web **23**(4), 2341–2362 (2020)
6. Wang, T., Shi, D., Wang, Z., Xu, S., Xu, H.: MRP2Rec: exploring multiple-step relation path semantics for knowledge graph-based recommendations. IEEE Access **8**, 134817–134825 (2020)
7. Wu, T., et al.: Knowledge graph construction from multiple online encyclopedias. World Wide Web **23**(5), 2671–2698 (2019). https://doi.org/10.1007/s11280-019-00719-4
8. Wu, X., Cai, Y., Li, Q., Xu, J., Leung, H.F.: Combining weighted category-aware contextual information in convolutional neural networks for text classification. World Wide Web **23**(5), 2815–2834 (2020)
9. Yu, Y., Wang, G., Ren, H., Cai, Y.: Incorporating bidirection-interactive information and semantic features for relational facts extraction (student abstract). In: Proceedings of the AAAI Conference on Artificial Intelligence, vol. 35, pp. 15947–15948 (2021)
10. Zeng, S., Xu, R., Chang, B., Li, L.: Double graph based reasoning for document-level relation extraction. In: Proceedings of the 2020 Conference on Empirical Methods in Natural Language Processing (EMNLP), pp. 1630–1640 (2020)

Author Index